# INTRODUCTION *to* BUSINESS

## *Fifth Edition*

# JEFF MADURA

### FLORIDA ATLANTIC UNIVERSITY

Paradigm PUBLISHING

St. Paul • Indianapolis

**Production Editor:** Amy McGuire, McGuire Book Services, Inc.
**Composition:** DPS Associates, Inc.
**Proofreader:** Pat Lewis
**Cover Image:** © Shutterstock/Dmitriy Shironosov

Care has been taken to verify the accuracy of information presented in this book. However, the authors, editors, and publisher cannot accept responsibility for Web, e-mail, newsgroup, or chat room subject matter or content, or for consequences from application of the information in this book, and make no warranty, expressed or implied, with respect to its content.

**Trademarks:** Some of the product names and company names included in this book have been used for identification purposes only and may be trademarks or registered trade names of their respective manufacturers and sellers. The authors, editors, and publisher disclaim any affiliation, association, or connection with, or sponsorship or endorsement by, such owners.

We have made every effort to trace the ownership of all copyrighted material and to secure permission from copyright holders. In the event of any question arising as to the use of any material, we will be pleased to make the necessary corrections in future printings.

ISBN 978-0-76383-620-7

Printed in the United States of America

18 17 16 15 14 13 12 11   2 3 4 5 6 7 8 9 10

To my mother,
Irene Madura,
and to the memory of my father,
Art Madura

# Brief Contents

**Part I** **Business Environment** **1**

Chapter 1     Functions of a Business   2
Chapter 2     Business Ethics and Social Responsibility   32
Chapter 3     Assessing Economic Conditions   64
Chapter 4     Assessing Global Conditions   96

**Part II** **Starting a New Business** **142**

Chapter 5     Selecting a Form of Business Ownership   144
Chapter 6     Entrepreneurship and Business Planning   172

**Part III** **Management** **214**

Chapter 7     Managing Effectively   216
Chapter 8     Organizational Structure   248
Chapter 9     Improving Productivity and Quality   280

**Part IV** **Managing Employees** **322**

Chapter 10     Motivating Employees   324
Chapter 11     Hiring, Training, and Evaluating Employees   354

**Part V** **Marketing** **400**

Chapter 12     Creating and Pricing Products   402
Chapter 13     Distributing Products   440
Chapter 14     Promoting Products   470

**Part VI** **Financial Management** **508**

Chapter 15     Accounting and Financial Analysis   510
Chapter 16     Financing   540
Chapter 17     Expanding the Business   580

# Contents

**Preface   xxv**

# Part I
# Business Environment   1

## Chapter 1   Functions of a Business   2

1. **Motives of a Business   4**
   1.1 How a Business Generates Profits   4
   1.2 Conditions That Affect Business Profits   4
   *Small Business Survey   5*
   1.3 Motives of Nonprofit Businesses   6

2. **Resources Used by Businesses   6**
   2.1 Natural Resources   6
   2.2 Human Resources   6
   2.3 Capital   7
   2.4 Entrepreneurship   9

3. **Key Stakeholders in a Business   10**
   3.1 Owners   10
   *Small Business Survey: Background of Owners   11*
   3.2 Creditors   13
   3.3 Employees   14
   3.4 Suppliers   15
   3.5 Customers   15
   3.6 Summary of Key Stakeholders   16

4. **The Business Environment   17**
   4.1 Social Environment   18
   *Responding to the Economy: Revising Business Decisions in Response to the Economy   17*
   4.2 Industry Environment   18
   *Small Business Survey: How Business Owners Use Their Time   19*
   4.3 Economic Environment   19
   4.4 Global Environment   19

5. **Key Types of Business Decisions   20**
   5.1 How Business Decisions Affect Performance   20
   5.2 How Business Decisions Rely on Information   21
   5.3 Applying the Key Types of Decisions to a Single Business   22

6. **Preview of This Text   23**
   COLLEGE HEALTH CLUB: BUSINESS DECISIONS AT COLLEGE HEALTH CLUB   24

**Summary of Learning Objectives   25**
**Self-Test of Key Concepts   26**
**Self-Test of Key Terms   28**
**Concept Review Questions   29**
**Class Communication Questions   29**
**Small Business Case: Key Decisions for Business Success   30**
**Web Insight: Business Functions at YouTube   30**
**Dell's Secret for Success   30**
**Video Exercise: Lessons in Starting a Business   31**
**Projects   31**

## Chapter 2  Business Ethics and Social Responsibility   32

1. **Responsibility to Customers   34**
   1.1  Responsible Production Practices   34
   1.2  Responsible Sales Practices   34
   1.3  How Firms Ensure Responsibility   35
   1.4  How the Government Ensures Responsibility   36
   *Small Business Survey: Illegal or Unethical Activities of Firms   37*

2. **Responsibility to Employees   38**
   2.1  Employee Safety   38
   2.2  Proper Treatment by Other Employees   39
   2.3  How Firms Ensure Responsibility Toward Employees   40
   *Global Business: Global Ethics   41*

3. **Responsibility to Stockholders   43**
   *Self-Scoring Exercises: Assessing the Ethical Standards of the Firm Where You Work   44*
   3.1  How Firms Ensure Responsibility   44
   *Self-Scoring Exercises: Assessing Whether Special Situations Are Ethical   45*
   3.2  How the Government Ensures Responsibility   47
   3.3  How Stockholders Ensure Responsibility   47

4. **Responsibility to Creditors   48**
   4.1  How Some Firms Violate Their Responsibility   48

5. **Responsibility to the Environment   48**
   5.1  Air Pollution   48
   5.2  Land Pollution   49
   5.3  Conflict with Environmental Responsibility   49

6. **Responsibility to the Community   50**
   6.1  Satisfying the Community Versus Stockholders   51
   *Responding to the Economy: Revising Business Responsibilities in Response to the Economy   52*
   *Small Business Survey: Ethical Behavior of Employees   52*

7. **Summary of Business Responsibilities   52**
   7.1  Business Responsibilities in an International Environment   53
   7.2  The Cost of Fulfilling Social Responsibilities   53
   *Cross-Functional Teamwork: Ethical Responsibilities Across Business Functions   54*
   COLLEGE HEALTH CLUB: SOCIAL RESPONSIBILITY DECISIONS AT CHC   55

**Summary of Learning Objectives   56**
**Self-Test of Key Concepts   58**
**Self-Test of Key Terms   60**
**Concept Review Questions   60**

Class Communication Questions **61**
Small Business Case: Responsibilities of a Business **61**
Web Insight: Social Responsibility at Starbucks **61**
Dell's Secret for Success **62**
Video Exercises: Lessons in Business Ethics **62**
Projects **62**

# Chapter 3 Assessing Economic Conditions 64

1. **Impact of Economic Growth on Business Performance** **66**
   1.1 Strong Economic Growth 66
   1.2 Weak Economic Growth 66
   1.3 Indicators of Economic Growth 68

2. **Impact of Inflation** **69**
   2.1 Types of Inflation 70

3. **Impact of Interest Rates** **72**
   3.1 Impact on a Firm's Expenses 72
   3.2 Impact on a Firm's Expansion 73
   3.3 Impact on a Firm's Revenue 73
   *Global Business: Capitalizing on Global Economic Conditions* *75*
   3.4 How Rising Interest Rates Affected the Housing Crisis 75

4. **How Market Prices Are Determined** **76**
   4.1 Demand Schedule for a Product 76
   4.2 Supply Schedule for a Product 76
   4.3 Interaction of Demand and Supply 77
   4.4 Effect of a Change in the Demand Schedule 78
   4.5 Effect of a Change in the Supply Schedule 79
   4.6 Effect of Demand and Supply on the General Price Level 81
   4.7 How Consumer Income Affects Market Prices 81
   4.8 Consumer Preferences 81
   4.9 Production Expenses 82

5. **Government Influence on Economic Conditions** **82**
   5.1 Monetary Policy 82
   5.2 Fiscal Policy 84
   5.3 Summary of Government Influence on Economic Factors 85
   5.4 Dilemma of the Federal Government 86
   *Cross-Functional Teamwork: Economic Effects Across Business Functions* *87*
   COLLEGE HEALTH CLUB: IMPACT OF ECONOMIC CONDITIONS ON CHC **87**
Summary of Learning Objectives **88**
Self-Test of Key Concepts **89**
Self-Test of Key Terms **91**
Concept Review Questions **92**
Class Communication Questions **92**
Small Business Case: Managing in Response to Economic Conditions **93**
Web Insight: Exposure of Harley-Davidson to Economic Conditions **93**
Dell's Secret for Success **93**
Video Exercise: Lesson in How Economic Conditions Affect Businesses **94**
Projects **94**

# Chapter 4 Assessing Global Conditions  96

1. **How International Business Can Enhance Performance  98**
   1.1 Attract Foreign Demand  98
   1.2 Capitalize on Technology  99
   1.3 Use Inexpensive Resources  99
   *Small Business Survey: International Business  100*
   *Small Business Survey  102*
   1.4 Diversify Internationally  102
   1.5 Combination of Motives  103

2. **How to Conduct International Business  103**
   2.1 Importing  104
   2.2 Exporting  104
   2.3 Direct Foreign Investment (DFI)  106
   2.4 Outsourcing  107
   2.5 Strategic Alliances  108

3. **Barriers to International Business  109**
   3.1 Reduction in Barriers  110
   3.2 Remaining Barriers  111
   3.3 Disagreements About Trade Barriers  111

4. **How Foreign Characteristics Influence International Business  112**
   4.1 Culture  112
   4.2 Economic System  113
   *Global Business: Nonverbal Communications in Different Cultures  114*
   4.3 Economic Conditions  117
   4.4 Exchange Rates  118
   4.5 Political Risk and Regulations  118
   *Cross-Functional Teamwork: Managing International Business Across Business Functions  119*

5. **How Exchange Rate Movements Can Affect Performance  121**
   5.1 Impact of a Weak Dollar on U.S. Importers  121
   5.2 Impact of a Strong Dollar on U.S. Importers  122
   5.3 Actual Effects of Exchange Rate Movements on U.S. Importers  122
   5.4 Impact of a Weak Dollar on U.S. Exporters  123
   5.5 Impact of a Strong Dollar on U.S. Exporters  124
   5.6 Hedging Against Exchange Rate Movements  124
   *Small Business Survey: Concern About Exchange Rate Movements  125*
   *Responding to the Economy: Capitalizing on International Business
      When the Local Economy Is Weak  125*
   5.7 How Exchange Rates Affect Foreign Competition  126
   COLLEGE HEALTH CLUB: CHC'S EXPOSURE TO GLOBAL CONDITIONS  127

**Summary of Learning Objectives  127**
**Self-Test of Key Concepts  128**
**Self-Test of Key Terms  130**
**Concept Review Questions  131**
**Class Communication Questions  132**
**Small Business Case: Managing in Response to Global Conditions  132**
**Web Insight: Nike's International Business  132**
**Dell's Secret for Success  133**
**Video Exercise: Lessons in How Global Conditions Affect a Business  133**
**Projects  133**

# Summary of Part I    134

**Summary    135**
**Video on Managing a Business: It Takes Money to Make Money    135**
**Self-Test for Part 1    136**
**Projects    138**
Project 1: Analyzing Your Favorite Business    138
Project 2: Building a Business Plan for Campus.com    139
Project 3: Running Your Own Business    140
Project 4: Planning Your Career    141
Project 5: Stock Market Contest    141

# Part II
# Starting a New Business    142

## Chapter 5  Selecting a Form of Business Ownership    144

1. **Sole Proprietorship    146**
   1.1 Characteristics of Successful Sole Proprietors    146
   1.2 Advantages of a Sole Proprietorship    146
   1.3 Disadvantages of a Sole Proprietorship    147

2. **Partnership    148**
   2.1 General Versus Limited Partnership    148
   2.2 Advantages of a Partnership    148
   2.3 Disadvantages of a Partnership    148
   2.4 S-Corporations    149
   2.5 Limited Liability Company (LLC)    149

3. **Corporation    149**
   3.1 Charter and Bylaws    150
   3.2 How Stockholders Earn a Return    151
   3.3 Private Versus Public Corporations    151
   3.4 Advantages of a Corporation    152
   3.5 Disadvantages of a Corporation    152
   3.6 Comparing Forms of Business Ownership    155
   3.7 How Business Ownership Can Change    156

4. **How Ownership Can Affect Return and Risk    157**
   4.1 Impact of Ownership on the Return on Investment    157
   4.2 Impact of Ownership on Risk    158
   *Cross-Functional Teamwork: Sources of Risk Across Business Functions    159*
   *Responding to the Economy: Revising Business Ownership Decisions*
      *in Response to the Economy    160*

5. **Obtaining Ownership of an Existing Business    160**
   5.1 Assuming Ownership of a Family Business    160
   5.2 Purchasing an Existing Business    161
   5.3 Franchising    161
   *Self-Scoring Exercises: Do You Have the Skills Necessary to Succeed in Business?    162*
   *Global Business: Ownership of Foreign Businesses    163*
   COLLEGE HEALTH CLUB: BUSINESS OWNERSHIP AT CHC    164

**Summary of Learning Objectives**  165
**Self-Test of Key Concepts**  166
**Self-Test of Key Terms**  168
**Concept Review Questions**  169
**Class Communication Questions**  169
**Small Business Case: Deciding the Type of Business Ownership**  170
**Web Insight: Franchising at Domino's Pizza**  170
**Dell's Secret for Success**  170
**Video Exercise: Lessons in Forms of Business Ownership**  171
**Projects**  171

## Chapter 6  Entrepreneurship and Business Planning    172

**1. Creating a New Business**  174
 1.1 Advantages of Being an Entrepreneur  175
 1.2 Disadvantages of Being an Entrepreneur  175
 1.3 Entrepreneurial Profile  175

**2. Assessing Market Conditions**  176
 2.1 Demand  176
 2.2 Competition  177
 *Small Business Survey: Competition  178*
 2.3 Labor Conditions  180
 *Global Business: Assessing a Market from a Global Perspective  180*
 *Small Business Survey: Impact of Regulations on Small Businesses  181*
 2.4 Regulatory Conditions  181
 2.5 Summary of Market Conditions  182

**3. Developing a Competitive Advantage**  182
 3.1 Common Strategies  183
 3.2 Using the Internet to Create a Competitive Advantage  183
 *Small Business Survey: Quality as a Competitive Advantage  184*
 3.3 Expenses of a Web-Based Business  185
 3.4 Using SWOT Analysis to Develop a Competitive Advantage  185
 *Small Business Survey: Technology as a Competitive Advantage  186*

**4. Developing the Business Plan**  186
 4.1 Assessment of the Business Environment  187
 4.2 Management Plan  188
 4.3 Marketing Plan  189
 4.4 Financial Plan  190
 4.5 Online Resources for Developing a Business Plan  192
 4.6 Summary of a Business Plan  193
 4.7 Assessing a Business Plan  193

**5. Risk Management by Entrepreneurs**  195
 *Cross-Functional Teamwork: Industry Effects Across Business Functions  196*
 *Small Business Survey: What Are the Major Concerns of Small Businesses?  197*
 5.1 Reliance on One Customer  198
 5.2 Reliance on One Supplier  198
 5.3 Reliance on a Key Employee  198
 *Small Business Survey: What Is the Cost of Employee Injuries?  199*
 *Responding to the Economy: Revising Entrepreneurial Plans in Response to the Economy  200*
 5.4 Exposure to E-risk  200
 COLLEGE HEALTH CLUB: DEVELOPING A BUSINESS PLAN  200

Summary of Learning Objectives    202
Self-Test of Key Concepts    203
Self-Test of Key Terms    205
Concept Review Questions    206
Class Communication Questions    206
Small Business Case: Creating a Business    206
Web Insight: Entrepreneurship at Amazon.com    207
Dell's Secret for Success    207
Video Exercise: Lessons in Entrepreneurship    207
Projects    207

**Summary of Part II   208**
Summary    209
Video on Managing a Business: Adjusting the Business Plan    209
Self-Test for Part II    210
Projects    212
    Project 1: Analyzing Your Favorite Business    212
    Project 2: Building a Business Plan for Campus.com    212
    Project 3: Running Your Own Business    212
    Project 4: Planning Your Career    213
    Project 5: Stock Market Contest    213

# Part III
# Management   214

## Chapter 7  Managing Effectively    216

1.  **Levels of Management    218**
    1.1 Top Management    218
    1.2 Middle Management    218
    1.3 Supervisory Management    218

2.  **Functions of Managers    218**
    2.1 Planning    218
    *Cross-Functional Teamwork: Interaction of Functions to Achieve the Strategic Plan    223*
    2.2 Organizing    225
    2.3 Leading    225
    *Global Business: Conflicts with the Goal of a Multinational Corporation    227*
    2.4 Controlling    228
    *Global Business: Leadership Styles for Global Business    229*
    2.5 Integration of Management Functions    231
    2.6 Use of Technology and Software to Improve Management Functions    231
    2.7 Software to Improve Management Functions    231
    *Responding to the Economy: Applying Management Functions
        in Response to the Economy    233*

3.  **Managerial Skills    234**
    3.1 Conceptual Skills    234
    3.2 Interpersonal Skills    234
    3.3 Technical Skills    235
    3.4 Decision-Making Skills    236
    3.5 Summary of Management Skills    237

**4. How Managers Manage Time    237**
   4.1 Set Proper Priorities    238
   4.2 Schedule Long Time Intervals for Large Tasks    238
   4.3 Minimize Interruptions    238
   4.4 Set Short-Term Goals    238
   *Small Business Survey: How Managers Run Meetings Efficiently    239*
   4.5 Delegate Some Tasks to Employees    239
   COLLEGE HEALTH CLUB: PLANNING AT CHC    240

**Summary of Learning Objectives    240**
**Self-Test of Key Concepts    241**
**Self-Test of Key Terms    244**
**Concept Review Questions    245**
**Class Communication Questions    245**
**Small Business Case: Using Management Skills    245**
**Web Insight: Managing at LA Fitness    246**
**Dell's Secret for Success    246**
**Video Exercise: Lessons in Leadership    346**
**Projects    247**

## Chapter 8  Organizational Structure    248

**1. Purpose and Types of Organizational Characteristics    250**
   1.1 Chain of Command    250
   1.2 How Organizational Structure Varies Among Firms    250
   1.3 Impact of Information Technology on Organizational Structure    252

**2. Accountability in an Organizational Structure    252**
   2.1 Role of the Board of Directors    254
   *Small Business Survey: Who Are the Board Members of Small Firms?    255*
   2.2 Oversight of the Internal Auditor    258
   2.3 Internal Control Process    259

**3. Distributing Authority Among the Job Positions    260**
   3.1 Centralization    260
   3.2 Decentralization    260
   *Self-Scoring Exercises: How Decentralized Is Your Company?    261*
   *Global Business: How Organizational Structure Affects the Control of Foreign Operations    262*

**4. Structures That Allow More Employee Input    264**
   4.1 Matrix Organization    264
   4.2 Intrapreneurship    266
   4.3 Informal Organizational Structure    266

**5. Methods of Departmentalizing Tasks    268**
   5.1 Departmentalize by Function    268
   5.2 Departmentalize by Product    268
   5.3 Departmentalize by Location    270
   *Global Business: Organizational Structure of a Multinational Corporation    270*
   *Responding to the Economy: Revising Organizational Structure in Response to the Economy    271*
   5.4 Departmentalize by Customer    271
   COLLEGE HEALTH CLUB: DEPARTMENTALIZING TASKS AT CHC    271
   *Cross-Functional Teamwork: Interaction Among Departments    272*

**Summary of Learning Objectives    272**
**Self-Test of Key Concepts    273**
**Self-Test of Key Terms    276**

**Concept Review   277**
**Class Communication Questions   277**
**Small Business Case: Organizational Structure Decisions   277**
**Web Insight:   Operational Structure at Schwinn   278**
**Dell's Secret for Success   278**
**Video Exercise: Lessons in Organizing an Effective Board of Directors   278**
**Projects   279**

## Chapter 9 Improving Productivity and Quality   280

1. **Resources Used for the Production Process   282**
   1.1 Human Resources   282
   1.2 Materials   282
   1.3 Other Resources   283
   1.4 Combining the Resources for Production   283

2. **Selecting a Site   284**
   2.1 Factors Affecting the Site Decision   284
   2.2 Evaluating Possible Sites   285
   *Small Business Survey: Location as a Competitive Advantage   285*
   *Global Business: Selecting a Foreign Production Site   286*

3. **Selecting the Design and Layout   286**
   3.1 Factors Affecting Design and Layout   287

4. **Production Control   288**
   4.1 Purchasing Materials   288
   *Small Business Survey: Why Do Firms Outsource Rather Than Produce
      Some Products Themselves?   289*
   4.2 Inventory Control   291
   4.3 Routing   292
   4.4 Scheduling   292
   *Responding to the Economy: Revised Production Decisions in Response to the Economy   295*
   4.5 Quality Control   296
   *Cross-Functional Teamwork: Interaction of Functions Involved in Total Quality Management   297*
   *Global Business: Global Quality Standards   299*
   *Small Business Survey: Exposure to Liability Lawsuits   300*

5. **Methods to Improve Production Efficiency   301**
   5.1 Technology   301
   5.2 Economies of Scale   302
   5.3 Restructuring   304
   5.4 Integration of the Production Tasks   305
   COLLEGE HEALTH CLUB: AVERAGE COST AT CHC   307

**Summary of Learning Objectives   307**
**Self-Test of Key Concepts   308**
**Self-Test of Key Terms   310**
**Concept Review Questions   311**
**Class Communication Questions   312**
**Small Business Case: Production Decisions   312**
**Web Insight: Production at the MTV Network   312**
**Dell's Secret for Success   313**
**Video Exercise: Lessons in Production Quality   313**
**Projects   313**

## Summary of Part III  314

Summary  315
Video on Managing a Business: Managing for Success  315
Self-Test for Part III  316
Projects  319
Project 1: Analyzing Your Favorite Business  319
Project 2: Building a Business Plan for Campus.com  319
Project 3: Running Your Own Business  320
Project 4: Planning Your Career  320
Project 5: Stock Market Contest  321

# Part IV
# Managing Employees  322

## Chapter 10  Motivating Employees  324

1. The Value of Motivation  326

2. Theories on Motivation  326
2.1 Hawthorne Studies  327
2.2 Maslow's Hierarchy of Needs  327
2.3 Herzberg's Job Satisfaction Study  328
2.4 McGregor's Theory X and Theory Y  330
2.5 Theory Z  330
2.6 Expectancy Theory  331
2.7 Equity Theory  331
2.8 Reinforcement Theory  332
Self-Scoring Exercise: The Frazzle Factor  333
2.9 Motivational Guidelines Offered by Theories  334

3. Motivating Disgruntled Employees  334

4. How Firms Can Enhance Job Satisfaction and Motivation  335
4.1 Adequate Compensation Program  335
Cross-Functional Teamwork: Spreading Motivation Across Business Functions  337
4.2 Job Security  338
4.3 Flexible Work Schedule  338
4.4 Employee Involvement Programs  339
Small Business Survey: Do Employees Want More Influence in Business Decisions?  342
Self-Scoring Exercise: Are You an Empowered Employee?  343
4.5 Comparison of Methods Used to Enhance Job Satisfaction  344
4.6 Firms That Achieve the Highest Job Satisfaction Level  344
Global Business: Motivating Employees Across Countries  345
COLLEGE HEALTH CLUB: MOTIVATING EMPLOYEES AT CHC  345
Responding to the Economy: Motivating Employees to Respond to the Economy  346

Summary of Learning Objectives  346
Self-Test of Key Concepts  347
Self-Test of Key Terms  350
Concept Review Questions  351
Class Communication Questions  351
Small Business Case: How Not to Motivate Employees  351
Web Insight: How Google Motivates Employees  352
Dell's Secret for Success  352

Video Exercise: Lessons in Employee Motivation    352
Projects    353

## Chapter 11  Hiring, Training, and Evaluating Employees    354

1. **Human Resource Planning**    356
   1.1 Forecasting Staffing Needs    356
   1.2 Job Analysis    356
   1.3 Recruiting    357
   *Small Business Survey: Recruiting*    360

2. **Providing Equal Opportunity**    362
   2.1 Federal Laws Related to Discrimination    362
   2.2 Diversity Incentives    363

3. **Compensation Packages That Firms Offer**    364
   3.1 Salary    365
   3.2 Stock Options    365
   *Small Business Survey: What Benefits Are Offered by Small Business*    367
   *Small Business Survey: Which Employee Benefits Are Most Important to Employees?*    367
   *Global Business: Compensating Employees Across Countries*    368
   3.3 Commissions    368
   3.4 Bonuses    368
   3.5 Profit Sharing    369
   3.6 Employee Benefits    369
   3.7 Perquisites    369
   3.8 Comparison Across Jobs    369

4. **Developing Skills of Employees**    369
   4.1 Technical Skills    370
   4.2 Decision-Making Skills    371
   *Responding to the Economy: Hiring Employees in Response to the Economy*    371
   *Small Business Survey: How Do CEOs Allocate Their Time When Managing Employees?*    372
   4.3 Customer Service Skills    372
   4.4 Safety Skills    372
   4.5 Human Relations Skills    373

5. **Evaluation of Employee Performance**    373
   5.1 Segmenting the Evaluation    374
   *Cross-Functional Teamwork: How Job Responsibilities Across Business Functions Can Complicate Performance Evaluations*    375
   5.2 Using a Performance Evaluation Form    375
   5.3 Assigning Weights to the Criteria    375
   5.4 Steps for Proper Performance Evaluation    377
   5.5 Action Due to Performance Evaluations    378
   5.6 Dealing with Lawsuits by Fired Employees    379
   5.7 Employee Evaluation of Supervisors    380
   COLLEGE HEALTH CLUB: DEVELOPING EMPLOYEE SKILLS AND EVALUATING PERFORMANCE AT CHC    380

Summary of Learning Objectives    381
Self-Test of Key Concepts    382
Self-Test of Key Terms    384
Concept Review Questions    385
Classroom Communication Questions    385
Small Business Case: Hiring, Compensation, and Performance Evaluation Decisions    386

**Web Insight: PepsiCo's Employee Diversity  386**
**Dell's Secret for Success  386**
**Video Exercises: Lessons in Hiring Employees  387**
**Projects  387**

# Appendix: Labor Unions  388

**A1.  Background on Unions  388**
    A1.1  History of Union Activities  388
    A1.2  Trends in Union Popularity  389

**A2.  Negotiations Between Unions and Management  389**
    A2.1  Salaries  389
    A2.2  Job Security  390
    A2.3  Management Rights  390
    A2.4  Grievance Procedures  390

**A3.  Conflicts Between Unions and Management  391**
    A3.1  Labor Strikes  391
    A3.2  Management's Response to Strikes  392
    A3.3  Management's Criticism of Unions  392
    A3.4  How Firms Reduce Employees' Desire for a Union  393

# Summary of Part IV  394

**Summary  395**
**Video on Managing a Business: Hiring the Best Employees  395**
**Self-Test for Part IV  396**
**Projects  398**
    Project 1: Analyzing Your Favorite Business  398
    Project 2: Building a Business Plan for Campus.com  398
    Project 3: Running Your Own Business  398
    Project 4: Planning Your Career  399
    Project 5: Stock Market Contest  399

# Part V
# Marketing  400

## Chapter 12  Creating and Pricing Products  402

**1.  Background on Products  404**
    1.1  Product Line  404
    1.2  Product Mix  404
    *Small Business Survey: Product Choices as a Competitive Advantage  405*
    1.3  Product Life Cycle  407

**2.  Identifying a Target Market  408**
    *Small Business Survey: Target Markets for Small Businesses  409*
    2.1  Factors That Affect the Size of a Target Market  409
    *Global Business: Targeting Foreign Countries  412*
    2.2  The Use of E-Marketing to Expand the Target Market  412

**3.  Creating New Products  413**
    3.1  Use of Marketing Research to Create New Products  414
    *Small Business Survey: New Products as a Competitive Advantage  414*

*Small Business Survey: What Are the Keys to Creating Successful Products?*  415
3.2  Use of Research and Development to Create Products  416
3.3  Steps Necessary to Create a New Product  417
*Cross-Functional Teamwork: Interaction Among Product Decisions and Other Business Decisions*  419

**4.  Product Differentiation  420**
4.1  Unique Product Design  420
4.2  Unique Packaging  421
4.3  Unique Branding  422
4.4  Summary of Methods Used to Differentiate Products  423

**5.  Pricing Strategies  424**
5.1  Pricing According to the Cost of Production  424
5.2  Pricing According to the Supply of Inventory  425
5.3  Pricing According to Competitors' Prices  425
5.4  Example of Setting a Product's Price  426
*Small Business Survey: Pricing as a Competitive Advantage*  427
5.5  Pricing Technology-Based Products  429

**6.  Additional Pricing Decisions  429**
6.1  Discounting  430
6.2  Sales Prices  430
6.3  Credit Terms  430
*Responding to the Economy: Revising Product Plans in Response to the Economy*  431
COLLEGE HEALTH CLUB: CHC'S PRODUCT DIFFERENTIATION, DISCOUNTING, AND CREDIT DECISIONS  431
**Summary of Learning Objectives  432**
**Self-Test of Key Concepts  433**
**Self-Test of Key Terms  435**
**Concept Review Questions  436**
**Class Communication Questions  437**
**Small Business Case: Product Decisions  437**
**Web Insight: Product Differentiation at Apple  437**
**Dell's Secret for Success  438**
**Video Exercise: Lessons in Creating New Products  438**
**Projects  438**

**Chapter 13  Distributing Products  440**

**1.  Channels of Distribution  442**
1.1  Direct Channel  442
1.2  One-Level Channel  444
1.3  Two-Level Channel  444
1.4  Comparison of Distribution Systems  445
1.5  Factors That Determine the Optimal Channel of Distribution  446

**2.  Selecting the Degree of Market Coverage  447**
2.1  Intensive Distribution  447
2.2  Selective Distribution  447
2.3  Exclusive Distribution  448
2.4  Selecting the Optimal Type of Market Coverage  448

**3.  Selecting the Transportation Used to Distribute Products  449**
3.1  Truck  449
3.2  Rail  449
3.3  Air  449

3.4 Water   450
3.5 Pipeline   450
3.6 Additional Transportation Decisions   450

4. **How to Accelerate the Distribution Process**   **450**
4.1 Streamline the Channels of Distribution   451
4.2 Use of the Internet for Distribution   451
4.3 Integrate the Production and Distribution Processes   452

5. **Characteristics of Retailers**   **454**
   *Cross-Functional Teamwork: Interaction Between Distribution Decisions and
   Other Business Decisions   455*
5.1 Number of Outlets   455
5.2 Quality of Service   455
5.3 Variety of Products Offered   456
5.4 Nonstore Retailers   457

6. **Services Offered by Wholesalers**   **457**
6.1 How Wholesalers Serve Manufacturers   457
6.2 How Wholesalers Serve Retailers   459
*Responding to the Economy: Revising Distribution Decisions in Response to the Economy   459*

7. **Vertical Channel Integration**   **460**
7.1 Vertical Channel Integration by Manufacturers   460
7.2 Vertical Channel Integration by Retailers   461
*Global Business: Global Distribution   461*
COLLEGE HEALTH CLUB: CHC'S DISTRIBUTION   461
**Summary of Learning Objectives**   **462**
**Self-Test of Key Concepts**   **463**
**Self-Test of Key Terms**   **466**
**Concept Review Questions**   **466**
**Class Communication Questions**   **467**
**Small Business Case: Distribution Decisions by Lada, Inc.**   **467**
**Web Insight: Urban Outfitters' Reliance on Producers**   **467**
**Dell's Secret for Success**   **468**
**Video Exercise: Lessons in Distributing Products**   **468**
**Projects**   **468**

## Chapter 14  Promoting Products   470

1. **Benefits of Promotion**   **472**
1.1 Promotion Mix   472

2. **Advertising**   **473**
2.1 Reasons for Advertising   473
2.2 Forms of Advertising   474
2.3 Summary of Forms of Advertising   477
*Small Business Survey: Small Businesses' Use of the Internet   478*

3. **Personal Selling**   **478**
3.1 Identify the Target Market   478
3.2 Contact Potential Customers   479
3.3 Make the Sales Presentation   479
*Small Business Survey: What Skills Are Needed to Be Successful in Sales?   480*
3.4 Answer Questions   480
3.5 Close the Sale   480
3.6 Follow Up   481
3.7 Managing Salespeople   481

4. **Sales Promotion  482**
   4.1 Rebates  482
   4.2 Coupons  482
   4.3 Sampling  483
   4.4 Displays  483
   4.5 Premiums  484
   4.6 Summary of Sales Promotion Strategies  484

5. **Public Relations  485**
   5.1 Special Events  485
   5.2 News Releases  485
   5.3 Press Conferences  485
   *Global Business: Promoting Products Across Countries  486*

6. **Determining the Optimal Promotion Mix  487**
   6.1 Target Market  487
   *Small Business Survey: Unique Marketing as a Competitive Advantage  489*
   6.2 Promotion Budget  489
   6.3 Evaluating and Revising a Firm's Promotions  490
   *Cross-Functional Teamwork: Interaction Between Promotion Decisions and
      Other Business Decisions  491*
   *Responding to the Economy: Revising Promotion Decisions in Response to the Economy  492*
   COLLEGE HEALTH CLUB: PROMOTION AT CHC  492

**Summary of Learning Objectives  493**
**Self-Test of Key Concepts  494**
**Self-Test of Key Terms  496**
**Concept Review Questions  497**
**Class Communication Questions  497**
**Small Business Case: Promotion Decisions  498**
**Web Insight: Coca-Cola's Web Promotions  498**
**Dell's Secret for Success  498**
**Video Exercise: Lessons in Promotion  499**
**Projects  499**

## Summary of Part V  500
**Summary  501**
**Video on Managing a Business: Marketing for Success  501**
**Self-Test for Part V  502**
**Projects  505**
   Project 1: Analyzing Your Favorite Business
   Project 2: Building a Business Plan for Campus.com  505
   Project 3: Running Your Own Business  505
   Project 4: Planning Your Career  506
   Project 5: Stock Market Contest  506

# Part VI
# Financial Management  508

### Chapter 15  Accounting and Financial Analysis  510

1. **How Firms Use Accounting  512**
   1.1 Reporting  512
   *Small Business Survey: Responsibility for Financial Reporting  513*

1.2 Decision Support   514
1.3 Control   515

## 2. Responsible Financial Reporting   515
2.1 The Role of Auditors in Ensuring Proper Reporting   515
2.2 The Role of Directors in Ensuring Proper Reporting   516
2.3 The Role of the Sarbanes-Oxley Act   517

## 3. Interpreting Financial Statements   518
3.1 Income Statement   518
3.2 Balance Sheet   520

## 4. Ratio Analysis   522
4.1 Measures of Liquidity   523
4.2 Measures of Efficiency   524
4.3 Measures of Financial Leverage   525
4.4 Measures of Profitability   526
4.5 Comparison of Ratios with Those of Other Firms   528
*Global Business: Effect of Exchange Rate Movements on Earnings*   *530*
4.6 Limitations of Ratio Analysis   531
4.7 Sources of Information for Ratio Analysis   532
Responding to the Economy: Financial Analysis in Responding to the Economy   532
COLLEGE HEALTH CLUB: FINANCIAL CONDITION OF CHC   533

**Summary of Learning Objectives   533**
**Self-Test of Key Concepts   534**
**Self-Test of Key Terms   536**
**Concept Review Questions   537**
**Class Communication Questions   538**
**Small Business Case: Use of Financial Reporting for Business Decisions   538**
**Web Insight: Financial Analysis at the Cheesecake Factory   538**
**Dell's Secret for Success   539**
**Video Exercise: Lessons in Financial Analysis   539**
**Projects   539**

# Chapter 16  Financing   540

## 1. Methods of Debt Financing   542
1.1 Borrowing from Financial Institutions   542
1.2 Issuing Bonds   546
1.3 Issuing Commercial Paper   548
1.4 Impact of the Debt Financing Level on Interest Expenses   548
1.5 Common Creditors That Provide Debt Financing   549

## 2. Methods of Equity Financing   549
2.1 Retaining Earnings   549
2.2 Issuing Stock   550
*Small Business Survey: Financing*   *553*
2.3 Comparison of Equity Financing with Debt Financing   553

## 3. How Firms Issue Securities   554
3.1 Origination   554
3.2 Underwriting   554
3.3 Distribution   554

## 4. Other Methods of Obtaining Funds   555
4.1 Financing from Suppliers   555
4.2 Leasing   556
*Small Business Survey: Leasing*   *557*

**5. Deciding the Capital Structure   558**
   5.1 Revising the Capital Structure   558
   5.2 How the Capital Structure Affects the Return on Equity   558
   *Small Business Survey: Financing Choices of Small Firms   560*
   *Global Business: Global Financing   561*
   *Cross-Functional Teamwork: Interaction Between Financing Decisions and*
      *Other Business Decisions   561*
   *Responding to the Economy: Financing Decisions in Response to the Economy   562*

**6. Remedies for Debt Problems   562**
   6.1 Extension   562
   6.2 Composition   563
   6.3 Private Liquidation   563
   6.4 Formal Remedies   563
     College Health Club: Financing at CHC   564
**Summary of Learning Objectives   565**
**Self-Test of Key Concepts   567**
**Self-Test of Key Terms   569**
**Concept Review Questions   570**
**Class Communication Questions   570**
**Small Business Case: Financing Decisions   571**
**Web Insight: Ebay's IPO   571**
**Dell's Secret for Success   572**
**Video Exercise: Lessons in Business Financing   572**
**Projects   572**

# Appendix: How Interest Rates Are Determined   573

**A1. How Interest Rates Change   573**
   A1.2 Demand for Loanable Funds   573
   A1.3 Supply of Loanable Funds   573
   A1.4 Combining Demand and Supply   574
   A1.5 Effect of a Change in the Demand Schedule   574
   A1.6 Effect of a Change in the Supply Schedule   575

**A2. Factors That Can Affect Interest Rates   576**
   A2.1 Monetary Policy   576
   A2.2 Economic Growth   577
   A2.3 Expected Inflation   577
   A2.4 Savings Behavior   578
   A2.5 Summary of Factors That Affect Interest Rates   578

## Chapter 17  Expanding the Business   580

**1. Investment Decisions   582**
   1.1 How Interest Rates Affect Investment Decisions   582
   1.2 Capital Budget   583
   1.3 Classification of Capital Expenditures   583
   *Small Business Survey: Allocation of Business Investment   584*

**2. Capital Budgeting Tasks   585**
   2.1 Proposing New Projects   585
   *Cross-Functional Teamwork: Cross-Functional Relationships Involved in*
      *Business Investment Decisions   585*
   2.2 Estimating Cash Flows of Projects   586
   2.3 Determining Whether Projects Are Feasible   586

2.4 Implementing Feasible Projects 587
2.5 Monitoring Projects That Were Implemented 587
*Small Business Survey: Time Allowed for Investments to Pay Off 587*
*Global Business: Global Investing 588*
2.6 Summary of Capital Budgeting Tasks 588

**3. Mergers 589**
3.1 Types of Mergers 589
3.2 Corporate Motives for Mergers 589
3.3 Merger Analysis 591
3.4 Merger Procedures 593
3.5 Target's Defense Against Takeover Attempts 594

**4. Short-Term Investment Decisions 595**
4.1 Liquidity Management 595
4.2 Accounts Receivable Management 596
*Small Business Survey: Investment Decisions by Small Businesses 597*
*Small Business Survey: Extending Credit 597*
4.3 Inventory Management 598
*Responding to the Economy: Business Investment Decisions in Response to the Economy 599*
COLLEGE HEALTH CLUB: ACCOUNTS RECEIVABLE MANAGEMENT AT CHC 599
**Summary of Learning Objectives 600**
**Self-Test of Key Concepts 601**
**Self-Test of Key Terms 603**
**Concept Review Questions 604**
**Class Communication Questions 605**
**Small Business Case: Deciding Whether to Acquire a Business 605**
**Web Insight: Business Expansion at Netflix 605**
**Dell's Secret for Success 606**
**Video Exercises: Lessons in Business Acquisitions 606**
**Projects 606**

**Appendix: Consolidating All Major Strategies in the Business Plan 607**

**Summary of Part VI 681**
**Summary 613**
**Video on Managing a Business: Financing for Success 613**
**Self-Test for Part VI 614**
**Projects 617**
Project 1: Analyzing Your Favorite Business 617
Project 2: Building a Business Plan for Campus.com 617
Project 3: Running Your Own Business 617
Project 4: Planning Your Career 618
Project 5: Stock Market Contest 619

**Appendix A Projects 621**

**Appendix B How to Invest in Stocks 633**

**Appendix C College and Career Guide 647**

**Appendix D  Lessons in Business as a Result of the Credit Crisis    665**

**Glossary    675**

**Company Index    685**

**Subject Index    687**

chapter, and a diagram that shows how those decisions affect the firm's value and performance.

**Small Business Surveys**   Surveys cover various topics that offer insight into the behavior of small business managers and other employees.

**Self-Scoring Exercises**   These exercises allow students to discover their own strengths and weaknesses when making business decisions.

**Responding to the Economy**   Each chapter contains a feature box that explains how key concepts within the chapter influence by prevailing economic growth, oil prices, or inflation in general.

**Global Business**   Most chapters have a feature box that explains one or more of the key chapter concepts from a global perspective.

**Cross-Functional Teamwork**   Most chapters have a feature box that explains how one or more of the key concepts covered in the chapter requires integrated decision making across the management, marketing, and finance functions in a business.

**College Health Club**   Just before the end of every chapter, some of the key concepts covered in the chapter are applied to a health club business that students follow as a continuing example throughout the textbook.

## Features at the End of Each Chapter

This text offers several features at the end of each chapter and several projects that allow students to build the learning skills that are endorsed by the American Association of Collegiate Schools of Business (AACSB) and by the Secretary's Commission on Achieving Necessary Skills (SCANS). In particular, this text emphasizes the development of decision making and planning, teamwork, and communication. Many end-of-chapter exercises can be adapted to allow for teamwork and communication.

## Summary of Learning Objectives

The learning objectives mentioned at the beginning of the chapter are repeated here, followed by a brief chapter summary related to that objective. In addition, key concepts presented within the chapter are summarized visually in an easy-to-understand diagram.

## Self Assessment

At the end of each chapter, there are two different self-assessments available for students:

**Self-Test of Key Concepts**   A large set of true-false and multiple-choice questions are provided, so that students can test their understanding of key concepts covered within the chapter. An answer key is provided here so that students can check their answers. They can re-test themselves on any questions in which their answers were incorrect. There is also a self-test at the end of each part on the key concepts covered within the chapters in that part.

**Self-Test of Key Terms**   Key terms are identified at the end of each chapter, followed by a self-test of key terms. Students fill in the key term that reflects each definition and can check their answers against the answer key that is provided at the end of the self-test. They can re-test themselves on any of their key-term answers that were incorrect.

## Exercises

At the end of each chapter, the following exercises are available to reinforce and apply key concepts.

**Concept Review Questions**   These questions encourage the students to review the key concepts and ensure that they understand the content of the chapter.

**Class Communication Questions**   These questions are focused on issues that are intended to encourage opinions and class discussion.

**Small Business Case**   A short case on a small business is provided in each chapter.

**Web Insight**   Students review the website of the well-known firm introduced in the chapter opener to learn how chapter concepts apply to that firm.

**Dell's Secret for Success**   Students are guided to review Dell's annual report or website in order to apply key concepts in each chapter to Dell's business.

**Video Exercise**   This exercise directs students to search for a video clip on a business that relates to each chapter, and to determine the main lesson from that clip. It allows students to watch video clips in which owners or employees of a real business discuss their challenges, strategies, and successes as related to each chapter.

## Features at the End of Each Part

**Video on Managing a Business**   This case directs a student to a video clip (at the website of the Small Business Administration) about a business that is related to each part of the text. The case helps students recognize how various concepts among the chapters within that part are related.

**Self-Test for Each Part**   Students can take the self-test containing multiple choice questions on various concepts covered in the chapters within that part.

**Projects**   This text offers five projects that enable students to make their own decisions, and improve their writing and communication skills. The portion of each project that relates to the chapters in each part is provided at the end of that part. The professor can also consider whether to require student presentations of their completed projects. The entire projects are also provided in Appendix A in the back of the text, and a Word file of the project is provided on the text website (www.emcp.net/business5e). The projects are:

+ **Analyzing Your Favorite Business**    Students select their own favorite publicly traded company, obtain an annual report for that company, and then are guided to learn how key concepts from each chapter are applied to that business.

+ **Building a Business Plan**    Students are put in the position of owners of a small business called Campus.com, which sells information about college campuses to prospective students over the Internet. They are asked to make decisions about how to apply business concepts covered within each part of the text. By the end of the semester, they will have completed a business plan for this small business. This project offers students the opportunity to work in teams and to develop their communication skills by sharing their ideas with their team or with the class.

+ **Running Your Own Business**    An alternative business plan project is the Running Your Own Business project. Students (individually or in teams) are allowed to create their own business idea. Students are guided step-by-step through issues and decisions they would face in running their own business. They develop a business plan as they go through the chapters of the text. At the end of the school term, students can convert their accumulated answers into a formal business plan.

+ **Planning Your Career**    This project challenges students to learn about various jobs, and select a career path that may fit their skills. Each student selects the career that he or she would like to pursue, and then is guided to review information on specific websites and answer specific questions that help them learn more about that type of career. Students are guided to investigate the career that they plan to pursue after they graduate or obtain more work experience. This project also allows students to learn about business indirectly as they investigate the tasks involved in the career they wish to pursue.

+ **Stock Market Contest**    This project puts students in the position of shareholders of a business. Each student selects a stock in which he or she would like to invest, and is guided on how to determine the gain on the investment over the school term. Students compare their results to determine who earned the highest return. They are also guided on how to determine why their stock performed well or poorly over the school term. This allows them to understand the types of factors that can affect the value of a business.

Students may be asked to present their results either individually or in teams. The team project allows all students on a particular team to combine their stock investments. Each student is still responsible for explaining the performance of the stock that he or she chose. However, the investment performance of the team is influenced by a portfolio of stocks, and this will allow students to see how a stock portfolio's performance is more stable over time than that of the individual stocks. This illustrates how investing in a portfolio of businesses is normally not as risky as investing all money in a single business.

# Common Course Competencies Covered by This Text

1. Consider how business decisions can affect the performance of a business.
2. Recognize the environment in which businesses operate.
3. Apply business ethics and social responsibilities to shape business decisions.
4. Analyze the economic and global conditions to which firms are exposed.
5. Compare alternative forms of business ownership.
6. Apply entrepreneurship concepts to develop business ideas and plans.
7. Recognize the key tasks and skills of managers.
8. Analyze the organizational structure within a business.
9. Analyze how managers motivate and manage employees.
10. Determine the factors that influence the pricing of products.
11. Compare alternative methods of distributing products.
12. Compare alternative methods for promoting products.
13. Analyze how to obtain financing to expand a business.
14. Analyze alternative methods for expanding a business.

# How This Textbook Develops Skills

While the self-assessment section of the text tests the student's general understanding about business, the exercises and projects in the text enable the student to think critically, make decisions, work with others, and communicate. For each of the exercises and projects listed below in the first column, the skills that can be developed are listed across the row. Those exercises that are especially valuable for teams of students and for class presentations are marked.

|  | Requires Critical Thinking | Requires Decision-Making | Allows for Teamwork | Develops Communication Skills |
|---|---|---|---|---|
| Concept Review Questions | X |  |  |  |
| Class Communication Questions | X | X | X | X |
| Small Business Case | X | X | X | X |
| Web Insight | X |  |  |  |
| Dell's Secret for Success | X | X |  |  |
| Video Exercise | X |  | X | X |
| End of Part Video on Managing a Business | X |  | X | X |
| **Projects** |  |  |  |  |
| 1. Analyzing your Favorite Business | X |  | X | X |
| 2. Building a Business Plan | X | X | X | X |
| 3. Running Your Own Business | X | X | X | X |
| 4. Planning Your Career | X | X | X | X |
| 5. Stock Market Contest | X | X | X | X |

In addition to these skills, students will have substantial practice at assessing their progress in order to improve, as a result of the self-tests at the end of every chapter and the comprehensive self-test at the end of every part.

## Course Website for Instructors and Students

The course website (www.emcp.net/business5e) provides rich resources for instructors and students. A major element of the Student Resources pages is a set of Projects, which are also included in the text Appendix A. Each project is provided as a Microsoft® Word file so that students can type in their answers over the course of the semester and save their work in a file. Chapter quizzes are provided as interactive Online Assessments that can be used in Practice or Reported mode (score is e-mailed to the instructor and the student). Additional reference information and study resources are also accessible at the course website.

### Instructor Resources

✦ List of Course Competencies
✦ How this Textbook Develops Skills
✦ Model Syllabus
✦ Instructor's Manual
✦ PowerPoint
✦ Learning Goals
✦ Test Bank
✦ Web links

### Student Resources

✦ Projects
  ✦ Analyzing your Favorite Business
  ✦ Building a Business Plan
  ✦ Running Your Own Business
  ✦ Planning Your Career
  ✦ Stock Market Contest
✦ Online Assessments

## Four Steps for Organizing Your Course

### Step 1: Create Your Course Schedule

Part I—focuses on the responsibilities of a business to its stakeholders and its potential exposure to the economic and global environment.

Part II—focuses on entrepreneurship and the business plan, which serves as an outline for the remaining parts of the text.

Parts III and IV—focus on business management.

Part V—explains marketing concepts and strategies.

Part VI—explains finance concepts and strategies.

The suggested course schedule is provided here, and additional downloadable course schedules for shorter school terms and syllabi are provided to professors on the course website (www.emcp.net/business5e).

**Suggested Course Schedule for a 16-Week Term**

| Week | Chapters Assigned | Topic |
|---|---|---|
| 1 | 1 | Functions of a Business |
| 2 | 2 | Business Ethics and Social Responsibility |
| 3 | 3 and 4 | Assessing Economic Conditions<br>Assessing Global Conditions |
| 4 | 5 | Selecting a Form of Business Ownership |
| 5 | 6 | Entrepreneurship and Business Planning<br>Exam 1 on Chapters 1-5 [Parts I and II] |
| 6 | 7 | Managing Effectively |
| 7 | 8 | Organizational Structure |
| 8 | 9 | Improving Productivity and Quality |
| 9 | 10 | Motivating Employees |
| 10 | 11 | Hiring, Training, and Evaluating Employees<br>Exam 2 on Chapters 6-11 [Parts III and IV] |
| 11 | 12 | Creating and Pricing Products |
| 12 | 13 | Distributing Products |
| 13 | 14 | Promoting Products |
| 14 | 15 | Accounting and Financial Analysis |
| 15 | 16 and 17 | Financing<br>Expanding the Business |
| 16 | Review | Final exam on Chapters 12–17 [Parts V and VI] |

Many professors may consider using a week for presentations or other types of class projects, and may remove one or more chapters from the schedule in order to make room for presentations. They may eliminate one or more chapters just to allow more time for the other chapters. Some professors rearrange the chapter order to teach marketing chapters before management chapters. The text is designed so that chapters are self-contained and can be reorganized to fit the professor's style.

## Step 2: Assign Exercises

The end-of-chapter exercises (listed earlier) are intended to reinforce the key concepts. Determine which of the exercises may be ideal for your class. Also, determine whether students should do any assignments on their own or should be required to submit their assignments. For example, the study guide provided at the end of each chapter is normally used by students to test their own knowledge of the chapter concepts and the answers are provided in the text so that they can assess their own work.

## Step 3: Assign Projects

The projects (listed earlier) involve students and allow them to learn by doing. The students are placed in positions where they must make decisions. The projects help them realize the tradeoffs involved in business decisions.

Determine which of the projects may be ideal for your class. You can adjust the instructions of any project to require presentations, or to have the projects completed by teams rather than individuals.

## Step 4: Create a Syllabus

A final step is to communicate your course schedule, assignments, and course rules to students. A sample syllabus is provided in the "Guide for Professors" section of the text website.

A second syllabus is provided for an online course, and it provides a suggested method of encouraging student participation online. This method can be adapted to fit the specific structure of your online course.

## Acknowledgments

I thank the following reviewers who offered valuable suggestions on the content or presentation of this text:

| | |
|---|---|
| Dina Adler | Moorpark College |
| Sally L. Andrews | Linn-Benton Community College |
| John Anstey | University of Nebraska – Omaha |
| Kenneth Armstrong | Anderson University |
| Jill Austin | Middle Tennessee State |
| Harold Babson | Columbus State Community College |
| Todd Baker | Salt Lake City Community College |
| Mary Jo Boehms | Jackson State Community College |
| John Bowdidge | Southwest Missouri State |
| Janet Caruso | Briarcliffe College |
| Ronald J. Cereola | James Madison University |
| Swee Chia | Baruch College – CUNY |
| Steven Christian | Jackson Community College |
| Charlie T. Cook | University of West Alabama |
| Ernest Cooke | Loyola College MD |
| Donna Cooke | Florida Atlantic University |
| Robert Costi | Concordia University |
| Robert Cox | Salt Lake City Community College |
| Sam Crowley | Devry University |
| Nancy D'Albergaria | University of Northern Colorado |
| Francis Dong | Devry University |
| Douglas Dorsey | Manchester Community College |
| H. Leroy Drew | Central Maine Technical College |
| Marianne Dunklin | Fresno City College |
| Jay Ebben | University of Wisconsin |
| Brenda Eichelberger | Portland State University |
| Bruce Erickson | University of Minnesota |
| Ken Fairweather | LaTourneau University |
| Jud Faurer | Metro State – Denver |
| Jan Feldbauer | Austin Community College |
| Dennis Foster | Northern Arizona University |
| Abhay Burjor Ghiara | Devry University |
| Debbie Gilliard | Metropolitan State College |
| Chris W. Grevesen | Devry University |
| Jacque Foust | University of Wisconsin – River Falls |

| | |
|---|---|
| Richard Grover | University of Southern Maine |
| Pola Gupta | University of Northern Iowa |
| Bruce E. Guttman | Katharine Gibbs School |
| Robert Hall | Adult Vocational Training Center – DOC Lakes |
| Bruce J. Hanson | Pepperdine University |
| Douglas Heeter | Ferris State University |
| Charlane Held | Onondaga Community College |
| Nathan Himelstein | Essex County College |
| Jennifer Howe | North Carolina State College |
| Craig Hollinshead | Marshall University |
| Raj Javalgi | Cleveland State University |
| Ralph Jagodka | Mt. San Antonio College |
| Annette Johnson | Johnson County Community College |
| Cheryl Johnson | Red Rocks Community College |
| Melinda Jones | Morehead State University |
| Carol Jones | Cuyahoga Community College |
| Daryl Kerr | University of North Carolina at Charlotte |
| David B. Klenosky | Purdue University |
| Mary Beth Klinger | Charles County Community College |
| John Knappenberger | Mesa State University |
| Kenneth Lacho | University of New Orleans |
| Thomas Lloyd | Westmoreland County Community College |
| Barbara Luck | Jackson Community College |
| Richard Magjuka | Indiana University |
| Trudi Manuel | Aims Community College |
| Rosalie Martin | El Paso Community College |
| John Mastriani | El Paso Community College |
| James McGowen | Southwestern Illinois College |
| Andrea McKeon | Florida Community College |
| Rodney D. Merkle | Indian Hills Community College |
| Jim Miles | Anoka Ramsey Community College |
| Rusty Mitchell | Inver Hills Community College |
| Bob Mitchum | Arkansas State at Beebe |
| Pete Moutsatson | Montcalm Community College |
| Susan Ockert | Charles County Community College |
| David Oliver | Edison College |
| Teresa Palmer | Illinois State University |
| Kathy Parkison | Indiana University Kokomo |
| Stephen Peters | Walla Walla Community College |
| Susan Peterson | Western International |
| Lana Podolak | Community College of Beaver County |
| John Porter | West Virginia University |
| Michael R. Potter | Devry University |
| Richard Randall | Nassau Community College |
| Jude Rathburn | University of Wisconsin, River Falls |
| Camille Reale | Sacred Heart University |
| Marvin Recht | Butler University |
| Fernando Rodriguez | Miami Dade Community College |
| Andy Saucedo | Dona Ana Community College |
| Robert Schramm | University of Wisconsin – Whitewater |
| Bernard Schmit | Florida Metropolitan University |
| Pat Setlik | William Rainey Harper College |
| Dennis Shannon | Southwestern Illinois College |
| Laurie Shapero | Miami Dade Community College |

| Peter Mark Shaw | Tidewater Community College |
|---|---|
| Dawn Sheffler | Central Michigan |
| Cindy Simerly | Lakeland Community College |
| Carolou Skeans | Miami University – Middletown |
| Dennis Smith | The Community College of Western Kentucky |
| Manny Stein | Queensborough Community College of CUNY |
| Louise Stephens | Volunteer State Community College |
| Charlene Terninko | Keiser College |
| Linda Tucker | Brooks College |
| Ted Valvoda | Lakeland Community College |
| Michael Vijuk | Harper College |
| Jeffrey Walls | Indiana Institute of Technology |
| John Warner | University of New Mexico |
| W.J. Waters | Central Piedmont Community College |
| Lewis Welshofer | Miami University |
| Randhi Wilson | Portland State University |
| Joel Wisner | University of Nevada – Las Vegas |
| Tim Wright | Lakeland Community College |
| Mary E. Zimmerer | Mesa State College |

I thank all the people in the business world who were willing to offer their insight on the business environment. In particular, I thank Dave Brooks, Bob Duever, Ed Everhart, Dan Hartnett, Victor Kalafa, Steve Kopetsky, Fernando Pereira, Randy Rudecki, Steve Spratt, Mike Suerth, and Tom Vogl.

I thank Bob Cassel of EMC Publishing for his insight and suggestions on the topic coverage. I thank Amy McGuire of McGuire Book Services for serving as Project Manager of this text, and for her excellent guidance and oversight. In addition, I thank Pat Lewis for her excellent proofreading and attention to detail.

## About the Author

Jeff Madura is the SunTrust Professor of Finance at Florida Atlantic University. Among his many publications are several other textbooks, including *International Financial Management*, *Financial Markets and Institutions*, and *Personal Finance*. His articles on business have appeared in numerous journals, including *Journal of Business Research*, *Journal of Business Strategies*, *Journal of Financial and Quantitative Analysis*, *Journal of Banking and Finance*, *Financial Review*, *Journal of Financial Research*, *Columbia Journal of World Business*, *Financial Management*, *Journal of International Money and Finance*, *Journal of High Technology Management*, and *Journal of Financial Education*. He has received awards for teaching and research and has served as a consultant for many businesses. He has served as Director for the Southern Finance Association and the Eastern Finance Association and has also served as President of the Southern Finance Association.

# Part I
# Business Environment

**1** Functions of a Business

**2** Business Ethics and Social Responsibility

**3** Assessing Economic Conditions

**4** Assessing Global Conditions

A business is created to provide products or services to customers. If it can conduct its operations effectively, its owners earn a reasonable return on their investment in the firm. In addition, it creates jobs for employees. Thus, businesses can be beneficial to society in various ways. The first step in understanding how businesses operate is to recognize their most important functions and the environment in which they operate. Part I, which contains Chapters 1 through 4, provides this background. A business must understand the environment in which it operates in order to be successful.

Chapter 1 describes the motives of people to create a business, identifies the stakeholders (participants) involved in a business, and explains the most important

functions of a business. Chapter 2 describes the responsibility of a business toward all of its stakeholders and to its social environment. It also explains how the firm can improve its performance by acting responsibly toward its stakeholders. Chapter 3 explains how a business is exposed to economic conditions and how it adapts its operations in response to these conditions. Chapter 4 explains how a business is exposed to global conditions and how it adapts its operations in response to these conditions. In general, businesses are exposed to the business environment. But some businesses are more successful than others because they make better decisions in response to changes in the business environment.

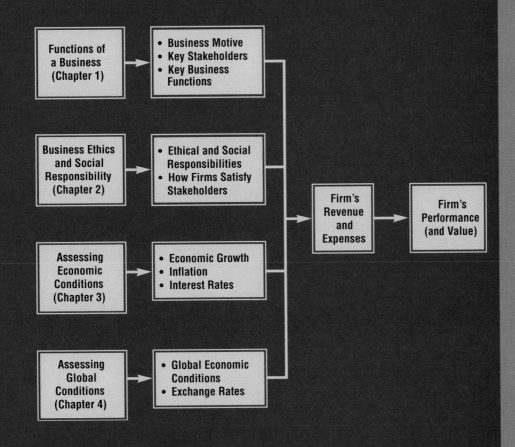

1

# Functions of a Business

## Chapter 1 Learning Objectives

**1** Explain the motives of a business.

**2** Identify the resources a business uses to produce a produce or service.

**3** Identify the key stakeholders who are involved in a business.

**4** Describe the business environment to which a firm is exposed.

**5** Describe the key types of business decisions.

# Chapter 1

## The Creation of YouTube

A business (or firm) is an enterprise that provides products or services desired by customers. People frequently create a business when they recognize a product or service that they can offer that would be desired by consumers. Consider the case of Steven Chen and Chad Hurley, who attended a dinner party in early 2005 where they used their video cameras. They wanted to share their video clips the next day, but recognized the difficulty in emailing long video clips. They believed that consumers would desire a service that could easily upload their videos to a website at no cost so that others could watch the videos. Steven Chen and Chad Hurley had motives to create this business, as they had the technical background necessary to create this type of service, and they might be able to earn a living by providing this service to consumers. They (along with Jawed Karim) established a website with the domain name YouTube.com in February 2005 and developed the website over time. In May 2005, the business YouTube was created, and this led to additional questions that would shape the business:

✦ What resources would the owners need for this business?

✦ Who would be the key stakeholders (customers, employees, lenders, etc.) of this business?

✦ How might the performance of this business be exposed to the business environment?

These questions should be addressed by any business as it is established, in order to clarify what the business is or wants to be. Even existing businesses attempt to address these questions, because the answers to the questions may change as the business evolves. This chapter explains how a business can address these basic questions to determine its identity, which will affect its future performance and value.

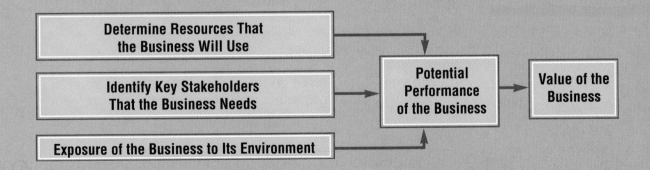

## 1. Motives of a Business

Businesses are established to sell products or services that satisfy the needs of customers. Businesses such as Dell, Gap, Ford Motor Company, and Motorola were created to provide products to customers. Businesses such as Southwest Airlines and Hilton Hotels were created to provide services to customers. Other service firms include dentists, travel agencies, insurance companies, tax services, and law firms. Some firms, such as AT&T, Microsoft, and IBM, provide both products and services to customers. Managing a service business can be just as challenging and rewarding as managing a business that produces products.

By offering products or services that have higher quality or a lower price, businesses increase the satisfaction level of consumers. As businesses are created and expand, they hire employees and therefore provide income to many people. Most businesses are established by owners who hope to make profits (also called *earnings*) in order to support their lifestyle. Profits are the reward to the business owner for providing products that satisfy customers.

### 1.1 How a Business Generates Profits

A business generates profits when the revenue it receives exceeds its expenses. It receives revenue when it sells its products or services. It incurs expenses from paying its employees and when it purchases machinery or facilities. The profits go to the owners of the business. Thus, owners who create a business have a strong incentive to ensure that it is successful, as they are directly rewarded for their efforts.

For example, assume that you have decided to offer to tutor other students in the basics of developing a website because you know that many students would be willing to pay for this service. During this year, you receive $5,000 from students for tutoring, and you pay a total of $1,000 in expenses to advertise your service in the college newspaper. Your profit is shown below:

|  |  |
|---|---|
| Revenue | $5,000 |
| − Expenses | − $1,000 |
| = Profit | = $4,000 |

*Profit = Revenue − Expenses*

Since you are the only owner of this business, all the profits go to you, although you may be taxed on the profits that you earn. You can increase your profits next year by either increasing your revenue or reducing your expenses.

### 1.2 Conditions That Affect Business Profits

The profits of a business are dependent on the following conditions. First, there needs to be a demand for the product or service offered by the business. If consumers have no interest in purchasing the product produced, the business will not generate revenue.

Second, the business must offer an advantage over its competition so that it attracts customers and generates revenue. The advantage may be that its products are higher quality or have a lower price, or that the business is more convenient to many customers.

## SMALL BUSINESS SURVEY

*Inc.* magazine recently surveyed chief executive officers of the 5,000 fastest growing private businesses in the United States about their motivation for starting a small business. The respondents to the survey could provide more than one reason. Here are some of the most commonly cited reasons:

| | |
|---|---|
| The challenge of building a business | 44% |
| Best way to achieve financial success | 30% |
| Desire to create a high-growth business | 24% |
| Desire to avoid working for someone else | 20% |

This survey also determined that 88 percent of the entrepreneurs who responded to this survey were millionaires.

③Third, the business needs to use an efficient system for producing its products or services so that it can limit its expenses. A business could fail even if it generates a large amount of revenue if its expenses consistently exceed its revenue.

**How the Profit Motive Is Influenced by the Government**   In the United States and most other countries, people are free to start businesses and profit from them. Countries such as the United States, in which people can create their own businesses to serve the preferences and needs of consumers, have a free-market economy. Governments of free-market economies recognize the advantages of allowing business ownership. Not only do businesses serve consumers, but by creating work for the business owners and employees, they also reduce the country's unemployment.

In socialistic countries such as the former Soviet Union, businesses were typically owned by the government and were not profit oriented. Without the prospect of earning a profit, most people could not afford to create a business and had to find some alternative form of work to earn an income. Furthermore, without a profit motive, businesses had no incentive to produce products that satisfy consumers' needs. Consequently,

Nonprofit firms (including nonprofit hospitals) must manage their resources properly so that they can continue to provide valuable services at a fair price to customers.

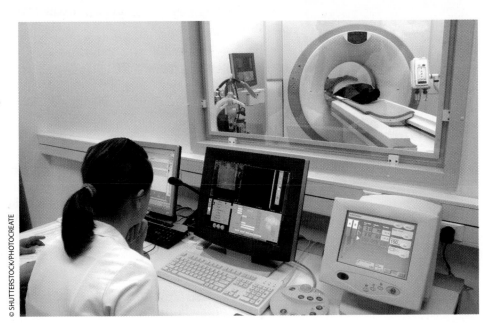

consumers were not able to obtain some products that they desired. In the last several years, many governments in these countries have sold the former government businesses to private owners and also are allowing people to start new businesses. In most countries, individuals are now allowed to own businesses, although some governments provide more incentives than others to encourage individuals to create new businesses.

## 1.3  Motives of Nonprofit Businesses

**nonprofit organization**
an organization that serves a specific cause and is not intended to make profits

Not all business are created to make a profit. A **nonprofit organization** is an organization that serves a specific cause and is not intended to make profits. For example, nonprofit hospitals may establish a goal of providing quality health care for residents in the local area. In the United States, a nonprofit organization is not taxed as long as it qualifies by meeting specific requirements established by the Internal Revenue Service. Common examples of nonprofit organizations include some hospitals, schools, charitable organizations, and churches.

A nonprofit hospital charges prices for its services just like a for-profit hospital. The hospital will still bill the patient's insurance for services rendered and bill the patient for any amounts not paid by the insurance company. If the hospital provided all of its services for free, it would quickly use up all the funds that were donated to finance it as well as any accumulated profits it had generated. Its employees earn salaries just like the employees of for-profit hospitals. If the hospital does not pay competitive salaries, its doctors, nurses, and other staff will seek employment elsewhere. Thus, it must provide its health-care services in an efficient manner, or it will not have adequate funding to stay in business and continue to serve the community. Like for-profit hospitals, if it wants to expand and needs more money than it has received from donations or accumulated over time, the hospital may even obtain financing from creditors. When its revenue exceeds its expenses, it reinvests the funds to support expansion or other business needs.

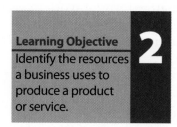

**Learning Objective**
Identify the resources a business uses to produce a product or service.

**2** 

# 2.  Resources Used by Businesses

To produce a product or service, firms rely on the following factors of production:

✦   Natural resources

✦   Human resources

✦   Capital

✦   Entrepreneurship

## 2.1  Natural Resources

**natural resources**
any resources that can be used in their natural form

**Natural resources** include any resources that can be used in their natural form. The most obvious natural resource that is commonly used by businesses to produce products or services is land. Agricultural businesses rely on land to grow crops. Other businesses rely on land to establish a site for their production.

## 2.2  Human Resources

**human resources**
people who are able to perform work for a business

**Human resources** are the people who are able to perform work for a business. They may contribute to production by using their physical abilities, such as working in a factory to construct a product. Alternatively, they may contribute by using their mental abilities, such as proposing a change in the existing production process or motivating other workers.

## 2.3  Capital *(amount that has to be invested in the business)*

**Capital** includes machinery, equipment, tools, and physical facilities. All of these types of capital are commonly used by human resources to produce products. Physical facilities are typically necessary to produce many services as well as products. Especially in recent years, technology has enabled businesses to use their capital more effectively.

**How Technology Has Helped Businesses Improve Their Capital**  Technology can be defined as knowledge or tools used to produce products or services. The Internet is an obvious example of technology. By using technology to improve their capital, many businesses are able to produce products and services more quickly and at a higher quality. Thus, they are better able to meet the needs of consumers.

An important subset of technology, **information technology**, involves the use of information to produce products and services. It includes the use of computers to transfer information among departments within a firm and the use of the Internet to provide customers with information. Information technology accounts for only about 8 percent of the total output produced in the United States, but it represents more than one-third of the growth in the U.S. output produced. A recent study by the U.S. Commerce Department estimates that about half of all U.S. workers will soon be employed in industries that produce information technology. It also found that information technology has reduced the cost of producing products and resulted in lower prices of products. Furthermore, workers in the technology industries earn about $53,000 per year on average versus $30,000 for workers in other industries.

A related type of technology is **electronic business (e-business),** also referred to as **electronic commerce (e-commerce),** which is the use of electronic communications to produce or sell products and services. E-business includes both business transactions, such as sales of products over the Internet, and interactions between a firm and its suppliers over the Internet. In fact, many people use the terms *information technology* and *e-commerce* interchangeably.

An example of a successful e-business idea is Amazon.com, which enables customers to purchase books and other products online. Amazon.com's creativity is not the product (books) but an alternative method of reaching customers. Its customers use the Internet to have their book orders delivered to them rather than having to go to a retail bookstore. Several other firms have applied the same idea to their own businesses. Computer firms now sell

---

**capital**
machinery, equipment, tools, and physical facilities used by a business

**technology**
knowledge or tools used to produce products and services

**information technology**
technology that enables information to be used to produce products and services

**electronic business (e-business) or electronic commerce (e-commerce)**
use of electronic communications, such as the Internet, to produce or sell products and services

Firms rely on technology such as that shown here to produce products. Advanced technology has improved the production process at many businesses and therefore allowed them to produce more efficiently and to improve the quality of their products.

© SHUTTERSTOCK/DEJAN LAZAREVIC

computers over the Internet, toy manufacturers sell toys over the Internet, and automobile manufacturers sell automobiles over the Internet. Hotels, airlines, and cruiselines allow customers to make reservations over the Internet.

Exhibit 1.1 describes some of the successful firms that have been created to capitalize on e-business. Notice that these businesses started out very small and were created to offer a product or service that was not being provided by other firms. Thus, these new businesses were created to accommodate the needs or preferences of customers. As these e-businesses were created, many existing firms recognized that they should develop their own e-business to satisfy their customers. Thus, the innovations of some e-businesses transformed the way that all firms conduct business.

**Exhibit 1.1**   Successful Internet Businesses

| Business Name | Business Description | How the Business Was Created |
|---|---|---|
| 1. Amazon.com | This online bookseller is frequently cited as an Internet success story. Customers can purchase books and music and participate in auctions at its website. Amazon's innovative bookselling idea allows the company to offer popular titles at deeply discounted prices due to low overhead costs. | Jeff Bezos founded the company in 1994. Bezos quit his job as vice president of a Wall Street firm, moved to Seattle, and started the business in his garage. When Amazon.com opened for business in July 1995, Bezos himself frequently dropped off the packages at the post office. |
| 2. Yahoo! | This Internet search engine is the most visited site on the Web. It has evolved to offer a wide variety of other products to attract users. Free e-mail, Web page hosting, and custom-designed start-up pages are just a few of the options available. Revenues are generated through advertising sales. | David Filo and Jerry Yang were Ph.D. students at Stanford who had put together an electronic directory of their favorite websites. It was essentially a list of their bookmarks that they titled Yahoo! The site was generating so much traffic that the students dropped out of school and launched their company in 1995. |
| 3. eBay | eBay is an online auction service that enables users to sell goods to each other. The person-to-person services attract a wide variety of goods, most of them used. Sellers develop a reputation, which creates some level of trust and excuses eBay from any responsibility. The company profits by charging fees based on the sale price. | Pierre Omidyar devised a website that allowed people to auction their products. By 1996, the volume of goods traded forced Omidyar to quit his job at General Magic and devote all his time to the company. |
| 4. Google | Google became very popular as a search engine because of its ability to effectively accommodate requests by users who wanted to search the Internet. This substantial reliance on Google meant that Google could sell advertising on its website or charge websites that want to have "sponsored links" displayed by Google in response to specific search terms. | In 1996, Sergey Brin and Larry Page were graduate students in Stanford's computer science department. They were interested in tracking the success of various websites. They then attempted to create a search engine that would account for the popularity of websites when identifying websites that fit search terms. The value in this search engine is that it screened out websites that were less likely to satisfy the search. This led to the creation of Google. On August 18, 2004, Google went public. At that time, Brin and Page still retained ownership of some shares, making their net worth more than $3 billion each. |
| 5. YouTube | In 2005, the YouTube website became popular as a way for people to easily upload and share videos for free. The videos were tagged so that viewers could easily find videos that they wanted to watch. In October 2006, Google acquired YouTube for $1.65 billion. The YouTube website now uses selective advertising in order to generate revenue and attracts millions of viewers every day. | Steven Chen and Chad Hurley met while they were employees at PayPal, the online payment site owned by eBay. In 2005, they went to a dinner party and took some digital videos of the event. They wanted to share the videos with each other the next day, but emailing these videos would have taken too long. They decided to create their YouTube website as a means of allowing people to easily upload and share their own videos in May 2005. |

Many firms applied e-business to facilitate their existing operations. The Internet allows for easier communication from the firm to the consumer, from the firm to another firm, and from the consumer to the firm. Information flows freely between firms and consumers, avoiding the delays and disrupted business transactions that used to occur when the two parties were not available at the same time to communicate. Firms are also using e-business to complement rather than replace their traditional operations. Consumers who want to use traditional channels to place orders can still do so, while other consumers can communicate their orders electronically. Thus, even if a firm is not classified as an Internet company, it can still use e-business to enhance its value.

Although the use of the Internet to serve consumers has attracted considerable attention, the Internet is also having an important impact on the way businesses serve other businesses (referred to as "business-to-business e-commerce" or "B2B e-commerce"). Business-to-business e-commerce might be used, for example, when a firm needs construction work to repair its facilities, wants an outside firm to conduct seminars to improve relationships among employees, or requires specific supplies for its production process. The firm can request bids online from several businesses that may meet its needs and then select the firm that submits the best bid. This process is much easier and faster than calling various firms and waiting for return phone calls. Furthermore, having to send a message online forces the bidders to specify their bids in writing.

Business-to-business e-commerce has already reduced the expenses associated with transactions between firms and is expected to reduce them even further once all firms take full advantage of the technology. In particular, firms that rely on other businesses for supplies, transportation services, or delivery services can reduce their expenses substantially by using business-to-business e-commerce.

## 2.4  Entrepreneurship

**entrepreneurship**
the creation of business ideas and the willingness to take risk; the act of creating, organizing, and managing a business

**entrepreneurs**
people who organize, manage, and assume the risk of starting a business

**Entrepreneurship** involves the creation of business ideas and the willingness to accept risk. **Entrepreneurs** attempt to identify business opportunities. When they find one, they invest some of their own money to create a business with the expectation that they will earn adequate profits as a reward for their efforts. However, they face the risk that the profits of the business may not be as high as expected. In fact, if expenses exceed revenue, the profits may be negative and the business could fail. In a free-market economy, many businesses may be created within the same industry, which results in intense competition. In this situation, a firm that charges too high a price for its product may fail because customers will switch to its competitors. Similarly, a firm that is not well managed may fail because its expenses are too high. This risk of failure can reduce the motive to create a business.

Entrepreneurs realize that if they overestimate the potential profitability of a business or manage the business poorly, they will lose the money that they invested. Thus, they will incur a direct penalty if they make a bad decision. To limit their risk, entrepreneurs should be cautious and realistic before deciding to invest their money to create a new business. However, those entrepreneurs who develop good business ideas that serve consumer needs and who manage their business efficiently may be rewarded with large profits.

**stakeholders**

people who have an interest in a business; the business's owners, creditors, employees, suppliers, and customers

# 3.  Key Stakeholders in a Business

Every business involves transactions with people. Those people are affected by the business and therefore have a stake in it. They are referred to as **stakeholders**, or people who have an interest (or stake) in the business. Five types of stakeholders are involved in a business:

✦  Owners

✦  Creditors

✦  Employees

✦  Suppliers

✦  Customers

Each type of stakeholder plays a critical role for firms, as explained next.

## 3.1  Owners

Every business begins as a result of ideas about a product or service by one or more entrepreneurs. As explained earlier, entrepreneurship is the act of creating, organizing, and managing a business. Today, more than 8 million people in the United States are entrepreneurs. Entrepreneurs are critical to the development of new business because they create new products (or improve existing products) desired by consumers.

People will be willing to create a business only if they expect to be rewarded for their efforts. The rewards of owning a business come in various forms. Some people are motivated by the chance to earn a large income. Others desire to be their own boss rather than work for someone else. Many people enjoy the challenge or the prestige associated with owning a business. Most business owners would agree that *all* of these characteristics motivated them to start their own business.

A recent survey by the Center for Entrepreneurial Leadership found that 69 percent of high school students were interested in starting their own business. Yet, about 86 percent of the students rated their business knowledge as very poor to fair. People need to learn how a business operates before they set out to create a business.

Out of Business

## SMALL BUSINESS SURVEY

### Background of Owners

In a recent National Small Business poll conducted for the NFIB Research Foundation, small business owners were asked how many years they worked for another firm before they began their own business. Their responses are shown here:

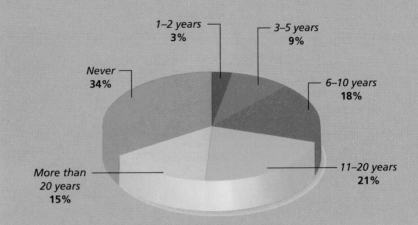

Notice the large proportion of owners who never worked for any other business before starting their own business.

Those business owners who previously worked for another business were asked what type of firm they worked for before starting their own business. Their responses are shown here:

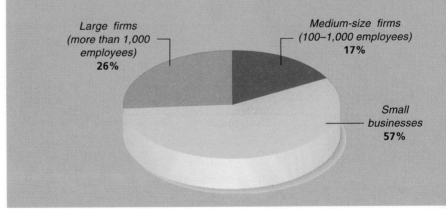

**How Ownership Spreads** An entrepreneur who creates a business initially serves as the sole owner. Yet, in order to expand, the business may need more funding than the entrepreneur can provide. Consequently, the entrepreneur may allow other people to invest in the firm and become co-owners.

When the ownership of the firm is shared, the proportion of the firm owned by the existing owners is reduced. Consider a bakery that two people created with a $100,000 investment each. Each person owns one-half of the firm. They can obtain more funds by allowing a third person to invest in the firm. If the third person invests $100,000, each of the three people will own one-third of the firm. Any profits (or earnings) of the firm

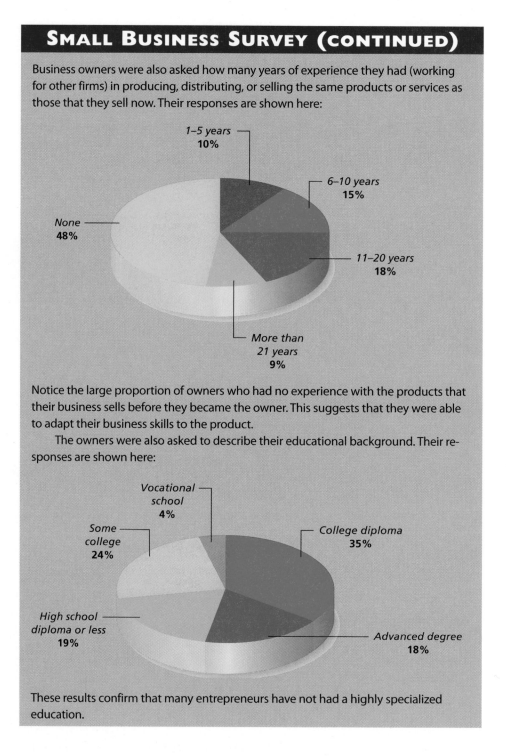

## SMALL BUSINESS SURVEY (CONTINUED)

Business owners were also asked how many years of experience they had (working for other firms) in producing, distributing, or selling the same products or services as those that they sell now. Their responses are shown here:

- 1–5 years 10%
- 6–10 years 15%
- None 48%
- 11–20 years 18%
- More than 21 years 9%

Notice the large proportion of owners who had no experience with the products that their business sells before they became the owner. This suggests that they were able to adapt their business skills to the product.

The owners were also asked to describe their educational background. Their responses are shown here:

- Vocational school 4%
- Some college 24%
- College diploma 35%
- High school diploma or less 19%
- Advanced degree 18%

These results confirm that many entrepreneurs have not had a highly specialized education.

that are distributed to the owners will be shared among three owners. By accepting investment from more owners, however, the firm may be able to expand its business so that the original owners benefit despite their decreased share of ownership.

Many firms have grown by issuing stock to other investors; that is, they essentially sell a portion of the ownership to these investors. The **stock** received by investors is a certificate representing ownership of the specific business. The investors who purchase stock are called **stockholders** (or **shareholders**) of those firms. The funds received by a firm that issues stock can be used to expand the business. Large firms such as Cisco Systems,

**stock**
certificates of ownership of a business

**stockholders (shareholders)**
investors who become partial owners of firms by purchasing the firm's stock

IBM, and General Motors now have millions of stockholders, but when they were created, they were small businesses.

When a firm's performance improves, its value may increase as well, as reflected in a higher stock price for those who own the stock. Stockholders can sell their stock to other investors whenever they want. They benefit when a firm performs well because they will be able to sell the stock at a higher price than they paid for it if the firm's value rises. As an extreme example, stockholders of Dell, Inc., have doubled their investment in some years because Dell performed so well. At the other extreme, stockholders who owned the stock of firms such as Enron and Global Crossing at the time these firms went bankrupt lost their entire investment.

A firm has a responsibility to the stockholders who have invested funds. It is expected to invest those funds in a manner that will increase its performance and value. Consequently, it should be able to provide the stockholders with a decent return on their investment. Some firms perform much better than others, however, so investors must carefully assess a firm's potential performance before investing in its stock.

## 3.2  Creditors

Firms typically require financial support beyond that provided by their owners. When a firm is initially created, it incurs expenses before it sells a single product or service. For example, it may have to buy machinery, rent a facility, and hire employees before it has any revenue. In the first several months, its expenses may exceed its revenue even if it is well managed. Therefore, the firm cannot rely on cash from sales to cover its expenses. The owners of a new business may initially have to rely on friends or family members for credit because their business does not have a history that proves it is likely to be successful and therefore able to pay off its credit in a timely manner.

Even firms that have existed for a long time, such as Little Caesars Pizza, Disney, and Nike, need financial support as they attempt to expand.

When a business builds a factory (like this one), it typically requires a loan from a financial institution. A portion of the revenue generated from selling the products produced by the factory is used to pay off the loan over time.

© SHUTTERSTOCK/BRIAN GOODMAN

A fast-growing business such as Little Caesars Pizza would not generate sufficient earnings to cover new investment in equipment or buildings.

**creditors**
financial institutions or individuals who provide loans

Many firms that need funds borrow from financial institutions or individuals called **creditors**, who provide loans. Bank of America, SunTrust Bank, and thousands of other commercial banks commonly serve as creditors for firms. Firms that borrow from creditors pay interest on their loans. The amount borrowed represents the debt of the firm, which must be paid back to the creditors along with interest payments over time. Large firms such as General Motors and DuPont have billions of dollars in debt.

Creditors will lend funds to a firm only if they believe the firm will perform well enough to pay the interest on the loans and the principal (amount borrowed) in the future. The firm must convince the creditors that it will be sufficiently profitable to make the interest and principal payments.

## 3.3 Employees

Firms hire employees to conduct their business operations. Some firms have only a few employees; others, such as General Motors and IBM, have more than 200,000 employees. Many firms attribute their success to their employees. Consider the following statements that firms made about their employees in recent annual reports:

*"Sara Lee is determined to be an employer of choice for highly talented people, retaining and attracting world-class individuals who have a passion to excel, strong ethical values and a driving entrepreneurial character."*

—Sara Lee

*"We continually invest in our people—the source of our innovation and competitiveness—who strive each day to find new products and technologies that will significantly improve everyday living."*

—The Dow Chemical Company

The performance of a business is highly influenced by the employees it hires. For this reason, firms devote much attention to the hiring and training of employees.

© SHUTTERSTOCK/MONKEY BUSINESS IMAGES

Those employees who are responsible for managing job assignments of other employees and making key business decisions are called **managers**. The performance of a firm is highly dependent on the decisions of its managers. Although managers' good decisions can help a firm succeed, their bad decisions may cause a firm to fail.

**Goals of Managers**   The goal of a firm's managers is to maximize the firm's value and, therefore, to maximize the value of the firm's stock. Maximizing firm value is an obvious goal for many small businesses since the owner and manager are often the same. In contrast, most stockholders of a publicly traded firm do not work for the firm. They rely on the firm's managers to maximize the value of the stock held by stockholders. The following statements from recent annual reports illustrate the emphasis firms place on maximizing shareholder value:

*"We are not promising miracles, just hard work with a total focus on why we're in business: to enhance stockholder value."*

—Zenith Electronics

*"We believe that a fundamental measure of our success will be the shareholder value we create over the long term."*

—Amazon.com

*"Everything we do is designed to build shareholder value over the long haul."*

—Wal-Mart

*"We create value for our share owners, and that remains our true bottom line."*

—The Coca-Cola Company

Maximizing the firm's value encourages prospective investors to become shareholders of the firm.

To illustrate how managers can enhance a firm's value, consider the case of Dell, Inc., which created an efficient system for producing computers. This resulted in low costs and allowed Dell to provide high-quality computers at low prices. Over time, Dell's sales increased substantially, as did its profits. The ability of Dell's managers to control costs and sell computers at low prices satisfied not only its customers but also its owners (shareholders).

## 3.4 Suppliers

Firms commonly use materials to produce their products. For example, automobile manufacturers use steel to make automobiles, while home builders need cement, wood siding, and many other materials. Firms cannot complete the production process if they cannot obtain the materials. Therefore, their performance is partially dependent on the ability of their suppliers to deliver the materials on schedule.

## 3.5 Customers

Firms cannot survive without customers. To attract customers, a firm must provide a desired product or service at a reasonable price. It must also ensure that the products or services produced are of adequate quality so that

Many businesses rely on suppliers to provide them with supplies and materials (like those shown here) that are used to produce their products.

customers are satisfied. If a firm cannot provide a product or service at the quality and price that customers desire, customers will switch to the firm's competitors. Motorola and Saturn (a division of General Motors) attribute some of their recent success to recognizing the types of products that consumers want. These firms also are committed to quality and to pricing their products in a manner that is acceptable to customers.

## 3.6 Summary of Key Stakeholders

Firms rely on entrepreneurs (owners) to create business ideas and possibly to provide some financial support. They rely on other owners and creditors to provide additional financial support. They rely on employees (including managers) to produce and sell their products or services. They rely on suppliers to provide the materials needed for production. They rely on customers to purchase the products or services they produce. The president of Goodyear Tire and Rubber Company summarized the relationship between a firm and its stakeholders in a recent annual report: "Last year I reaffirmed our values—protecting our good name, focusing on customers, respecting and developing our people [employees], and rewarding investors."

To illustrate the roles of stakeholders, consider the example of a DVD rental business. The owner who created the business makes decisions about its location, the types of DVDs to offer for rent, whether to sell other products (such as video games), and the prices to charge for DVD rentals and other products. The business needs creditors to support it with funding so that it has sufficient funds to cover its expenses. It needs employees to receive deliveries of new DVDs, organize them, and serve customers. It needs suppliers to supply the DVDs. Finally, the business needs customers to generate revenue.

**Interaction Among Stakeholders** The interaction among a firm's owners, employees, customers, suppliers, and creditors is illustrated in Exhibit 1.2. Managers decide how the funds obtained from owners, creditors, or sales to customers should be utilized. They use funds to pay for the resources (including employees, supplies, and machinery) needed to produce and

Interaction Among Owners, Employees, Customers, Suppliers, and Creditors

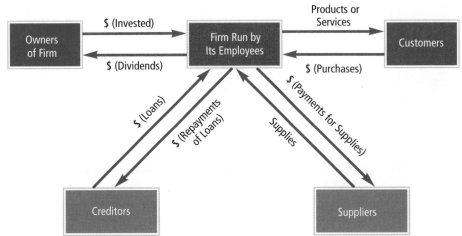

promote their products. They also use funds to repay creditors. The money left over is profit. Some of the profit (or earnings) is retained and reinvested by the firm. Any remaining profit is distributed as **dividends**, or income that the firm provides to its owners.

**dividends**
income that the firm provides to its owners

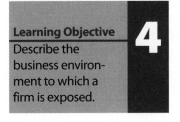

**Learning Objective**
Describe the business environment to which a firm is exposed.

**4**

# 4.  The Business Environment

The success of a business is generally dependent on the business environment. Even after a business is created, its entrepreneurs and managers must continually monitor the environment so that they can anticipate how the demand for its products or its cost of producing products may change. The business environment can be segmented into the following parts:

✦  Social environment

✦  Industry environment

✦  Economic environment

✦  Global environment

## 4.1  Social Environment

The social environment, which includes demographics and consumer preferences, represents the social tendencies to which a business is exposed. The **demographics**, or characteristics of the population, change over time. As the proportions of children, teenagers, middle-aged consumers, and senior citizens in a population change, so does the demand for a firm's products. Thus, the demand for the products produced by a specific business may increase or decrease in response to a change in demographics. For example, an increase in the elderly population has led to an increased demand for many prescription drugs.

Changes in consumer preferences over time can also affect the demand for the products produced. Tastes are highly influenced by technology. For example, the availability of pay-per-view television channels may cause some consumers to stop renting DVDs. The ability of consumers to download music may cause them to discontinue their purchases of CDs in retail stores. As technology develops, demand for some products increases, while demand for other products decreases. Many businesses

**demographics**
characteristics of the human population or specific segments of the population

## Responding to the Economy

### Revising Business Decisions in Response to the Economy

The creation of a new product is based on an assessment of what consumers want, and consumer needs adjust in response to economic conditions. When oil prices increase, transportation costs increase, which reduces demand for some products (such as the larger gas guzzling sports utility vehicles) and services (such as airline flights). Conversely, the demand for products such as bicycles and fuel-efficient cars increases.

As consumer demand changes, firms can revise their offering of products in their attempt to satisfy changes in demand. Consequently, firms revise the management of their business by reallocating their resources to produce products in anticipation of the changes in consumer demand. Firms change their marketing decisions in line with their new production plans. That is, they reduce the marketing of the products that have become less popular in response to new economic conditions and focus their marketing on their products that will now be more popular. If their planned production has been reduced because of expectations of a reduced consumer demand, they will need less funding to support their production. Therefore, their financing decisions are also affected in response to these economic conditions. These adjustments in the business are not necessarily permanent. If oil prices decline or the economic growth changes, firms will attempt to anticipate how those changes will affect consumer demand, and will revise their production, marketing, and financing plans accordingly.

closely monitor changes in consumer preferences so that they can accommodate the changing needs of consumers and increase their profitability as a result.

## 4.2 Industry Environment

The industry environment represents the conditions within the firm's industry to which the firm is exposed. The conditions in each industry vary according to the demand and the competition. Firms benefit from being in

A business attempts to closely monitor various industry, economic, and global indicators in order to assess how demand for its product will change in the future. An entrepreneurial decision to create a new business is influenced by the environment.

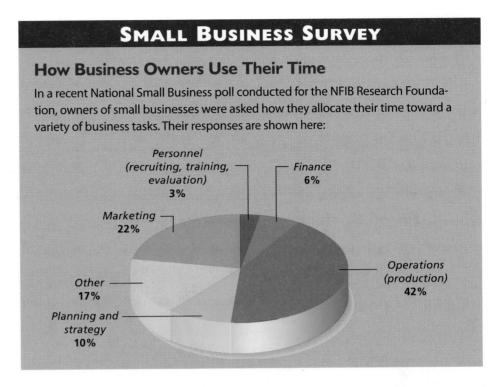

## SMALL BUSINESS SURVEY

### How Business Owners Use Their Time

In a recent National Small Business poll conducted for the NFIB Research Foundation, owners of small businesses were asked how they allocate their time toward a variety of business tasks. Their responses are shown here:

Personnel (recruiting, training, evaluation) 3%

Finance 6%

Marketing 22%

Operations (production) 42%

Other 17%

Planning and strategy 10%

an industry that experiences a high consumer demand for its products. For example, the demand for cell phones is very high. However, industries that have a high demand for their products also tend to have substantial competition because many firms enter the industry. Intense competition is good for consumers because it forces firms to keep their prices relatively low in order to compete. For firms, however, competition may result in lower revenue and, therefore, lower profits.

## 4.3  Economic Environment  Macro

Economic conditions have a strong impact on the performance of each business. When the economy is strong, employment is high, and compensation paid to employees is also high. Since people have relatively good income under these conditions, they purchase a large amount of products. The firms that produce these products benefit from the large demand. They hire many employees to ensure that they can produce a sufficient amount of products to satisfy the demand. They can also afford to pay high wages to their employees.

When the economy is weak, firms tend to lay off some of their employees and cannot afford to pay high wages. Since people have relatively low income under these conditions, they purchase a relatively small amount of products. The firms that produce these products are adversely affected because they can not sell all the products that they produce. Consequently, they may need to lay off some employees. Under these circumstances, some firms fail, and all of their employees lose their jobs. The unemployment rate rises as a result. The economic environment is more fully described in Chapter 3.

## 4.4  Global Environment

The global environment may affect all firms directly or indirectly. Some firms rely on foreign countries for some of their supplies or sell their

**Exhibit 1.3**

Common Business Decisions

**Management Decisions**

1.  What equipment is needed to produce the product?

2.  How many employees should be hired to produce the product?

3.  How can employees be motivated to perform well?

**Marketing Decisions**

1.  What price should be charged for the product?

2.  Should the product be changed to be more appealing to customers?

3.  Should the firm use advertising or some other strategy to promote its product?

**Finance Decisions**

1.  Should financial support come from the sale of stock or from borrowing money? Or a combination of both?

2.  Should the firm attempt to obtain borrowed funds for a short-term period (such as one year) or a long-term period?

3.  Should the firm invest funds in a new business project that has recently been proposed (such as expansion of its existing business or development of a new product), or should it use these funds to repay debt?

products in various countries. They may even establish subsidiaries in foreign countries where they can produce products and sell them. Even if a firm is not planning to sell its products in foreign countries, it must be aware of the global environment because it may face foreign competition when it sells its products locally.

Furthermore, global economic conditions can affect local economic conditions. If economic conditions weaken in foreign countries, the foreign demand for U.S. products will decrease. Consequently, sales by U.S. firms will decrease, and this may result in some layoffs. The general income level in the United States will decline, and U.S. consumers will have less money to spend. The demand for all products will decline, even those that are sold only in the United States. Thus, even firms that have no international business can be affected by the global environment. The global environment is described more fully in Chapter 4.

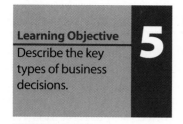

**Learning Objective**

Describe the key types of business decisions.

**5**

**management**

means by which employees and other resources (such as machinery) are used by the firm

**marketing**

means by which products (or services) are developed, priced, distributed, and promoted to customers

**finance**

means by which firms obtain and use funds for their business operations

# 5.  Key Types of Business Decisions

The key types of decisions involved in running a business can be classified as management, marketing, and finance decisions. **Management** is the means by which employees and other resources (such as machinery) are used by the firm. **Marketing** is the means by which products (or services) are developed, priced, distributed, and promoted to customers. **Finance** is the means by which firms obtain and use funds for their business operations.

Examples of management, marketing, and finance decisions are provided in Exhibit 1.3. Notice from this exhibit that management decisions focus on the use of resources, marketing decisions focus on the products, and finance decisions focus on obtaining or using funds.

## 5.1  How Business Decisions Affect Performance

As mentioned earlier, a firm's performance is commonly measured by its earnings (or profits). The effect that each type of business decision has on a firm's earnings is illustrated in Exhibit 1.4. Since management decisions focus on the utilization of employees and other resources, they affect the

**How Business Decisions Affect a Firm's Earnings**

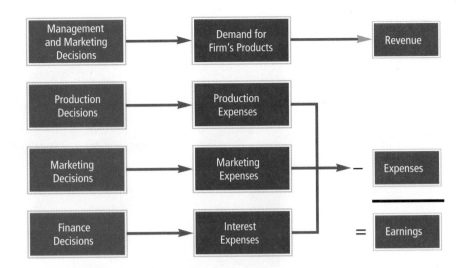

amount of production expenses incurred. Since marketing decisions focus on strategies that will make the product appealing to customers, they affect the firm's revenue. Marketing decisions also influence the amount of expenses incurred in distributing and promoting products. Since finance decisions focus on how funds are obtained (borrowing money versus issuing stock), they influence the amount of interest expense incurred. As the management, marketing, and finance decisions affect either a firm's revenue or expenses, they affect the earnings and therefore the performance of the firm.

Although some decisions focus on only one function, many decisions require interaction among management, marketing, and finance. For example, production managers of a cell phone manufacturer receive sales projections from the marketing managers to determine how much of the product to produce. The finance managers must receive the planned production volume from the production managers to determine how much funding is needed.

## 5.2  How Business Decisions Rely on Information

Proper business decisions rely on accounting and information systems.

**Accounting**   A firm's decisions are commonly based on data and information which are provided by its accounting and information systems. **Accounting** is the summary and analysis of the firm's financial condition and is used to make various business decisions. Managers of firms use accounting to monitor their operations and to report their financial condition to their owners or employees. They can also assess the performance of previous production, marketing, and finance decisions. They may even rely on accounting to detect inefficient uses of business resources that can be eliminated. Consequently, a firm's accounting function can be used to eliminate waste, thereby generating higher earnings.

**accounting**
summary and analysis of the firm's financial condition

**information systems**
represent information technology, people, and procedures that work together to provide appropriate information to the firm's employees so they can make business decisions

**Information Systems**   **Information systems** represent information technology, people, and procedures that provide appropriate information so that the firm's employees can make business decisions. Firms use information systems to continually update and analyze information about their operations. This information can be used by the firm's managers to make business decisions. In addition, the information can be used by any employee within the firm who has access to a personal computer. For

Many business decisions involve several employees within a department or from various departments. These types of business decisions require interaction among the employees.

example, FedEx uses information on its computer system to track deliveries and determine when packages will arrive at their destination.

## 5.3   Applying the Key Types of Decisions to a Single Business

To illustrate the key types of business decisions, consider an example of a DVD rental business. The management decisions of this business determine how its employees and other resources should be used. The typical management decisions of this firm are:

✦   How many employees should it hire?

✦   What salary should it pay each employee?

✦   What should be the job description of each employee?

✦   To whom should each employee report within the business?

✦   How should the business motivate its employees to perform well?

✦   How should it use the space in its store?

✦   Should it charge a late fee?

The marketing decisions of the DVD rental business determine how the DVD rentals should be priced, distributed, and promoted. The typical marketing decisions of this firm are:

✦   What is the profile of the typical customer who will rent its DVDs?

✦   Should it charge a membership fee to rent DVDs?

✦   What price should it charge per rental?

✦   Should it allow a discount for frequent customers?

✦   Should it consider distributing DVD rentals by delivery or through the Internet?

✦   Should it advertise its business? If so, where should it advertise?

The finance decisions of the DVD rental business determine how it obtains funds and uses the funds it obtains. The typical finance decisions of this firm are:

◆ How much money should it borrow?

◆ Where should it apply to obtain a loan?

◆ Should it use some of the borrowed funds to expand?

◆ How can it expand its business so that its value will increase?

The DVD rental business relies on accounting and information systems to report its financial condition on a periodic basis. This information would be used to help make some of the decisions described above. For example, by monitoring how its revenue changes in response to a change in the membership fee, the business can decide what fee is most appropriate. Its decision about how much money to borrow is based on how much money it has (as reported by the accounting function) versus what it needs to meet its business objectives.

## 6.   Preview of This Text

The focus of this text is on decision making by a business, and the chapters are organized with this focus in mind. A broad overview of the text is provided in Exhibit 1.5. A firm needs to understand its environment before it can make business decisions. Accordingly, Part I contains chapters on business ethics, the firm's social responsibility to its environment (Chapter 2), the economic environment (Chapter 3), and the global environment (Chapter 4).

Part II is focused on creating a business. It contains chapters on selecting a form of business organization (Chapter 5) and entrepreneurship (Chapter 6). These chapters explain how a business is created and discuss the initial planning decisions that are necessary to guide the business toward profitability.

Part III describes how to manage business operations, with chapters on effective management (Chapter 7), the organizational structure of a business (Chapter 8), and improving productivity and quality (Chapter 9). These chapters explain the organization of jobs within the firm, the sequence of production tasks, and the methods of improving quality.

**Exhibit 1.5**

Overview of the Text

| Part I Business Environment | → | Part II Starting a New Business | → | Part III Management |
| | | | | Part IV Managing Employees |
| | | | | Part V Marketing |
| | | | | Part VI Financial Management |

Part IV describes how to manage employees, with chapters on motivating employees (Chapter 10) and hiring, training, and performance evaluation (Chapter 11). A firm is only as strong as its employees, and these chapters discuss how a firm's treatment of its employees can improve its performance.

Part V is focused on marketing, with chapters on creating and pricing products (Chapter 12), distributing products (Chapter 13), and promoting products (Chapter 14). These chapters cover all the major decisions that are intended to make products and services attractive and accessible to customers.

Part VI is focused on financial management, with chapters on accounting (Chapter 15), financing (Chapter 16), and expanding the business, (Chapter 17). These chapters explain how a firm's financial condition is reported, how firms obtain funds, and how firms decide to use funds.

## COLLEGE HEALTH CLUB: BUSINESS DECISIONS AT COLLEGE HEALTH CLUB

Some of the key concepts in each chapter are applied to one small business (a health club) in a feature that appears near the end of each chapter. The applications demonstrate how business decisions are made. They also show that even the smallest business must make decisions about all types of business functions.

Here is a background of the small business. Sue Kramer recently graduated with a degree in business from Texas College in Dallas, Texas. She has always wanted to own and manage a business. Throughout her college years, she belonged to Energy Health Club, a 20-minute drive from the college campus. She noticed that many other students from Texas College were members of this club. She also knew other students who wanted to join a health club, but lived on campus and did not have a car. There was a health club called Magnum Club in the shopping mall just across the street from the college, but it was very expensive and focused on personal training. Magnum Club recently closed those facilities and moved to a downtown location far from Texas College.

Sue considered opening a health club next to the Texas College campus that would cater to students. Shortly after graduation, Sue distributed a survey to hundreds of students at the college to determine whether they would be interested in joining a health club and what types of facilities and equipment they would desire. Now that Magnum Club has moved, there are no health clubs very close to campus. The shopping center where Magnum Club was located is a perfect location for a health club catering to students because students frequently go to stores in that center.

Sue is motivated to start the health club business because she believes that she satisfies all three conditions necessary to make the business successful. First, there is a demand for the service. Second, her business could attract customers because there is not much competition nearby. Third, she has the business skills that would allow her to run the business efficiently and keep expenses low.

Near the end of each chapter, the key concepts of the chapter will be applied to develop the health club business. As a preview, Sue will establish ethical guidelines for her business (Chapter 2) and consider the economic (Chapter 3) and global environment (Chapter 4) surrounding her business. Next, she will select a form of business organization (Chapter 5) and use her entrepreneurial skills to develop goals and a broad plan for her business (Chapter 6). Then she will make decisions about the management of the firm's operations (Chapters 7–9), managing employees (Chapters 10–11), marketing (Chapters 12–14), and financial management (Chapters 15–17). By the end of the text, Sue will have covered all the major decisions regarding how to run her health club.

# Summary of Learning Objectives

**1** Businesses are established to serve the needs of consumers. Entrepreneurs are encouraged to start a business because they can earn income (profits) if their business is successful. They are motivated to make decisions that will increase business revenue and keep expenses low so that they can earn high profits. The creation of successful businesses can be beneficial to the entrepreneurs and other owners who earn profits, the employees who are paid income, and the consumers whose needs are satisfied.

**2** Businesses use factors of production such as:

- land (a natural resource) to establish a location for producing or selling products,
- human resources to perform production tasks and make other business decisions,
- capital (such as machinery and equipment) to produce their products, and
- entrepreneurship for guidance at the time they are created and as they evolve.

**3** The key stakeholders in a business are:

- owners, who invest funds in the firm,
- creditors, who lend money to the firm,
- employees, who are hired to conduct the firm's operations efficiently in order to satisfy the owners,
- suppliers, who provide the materials that the firm needs to produce the product, and
- customers, who purchase the products produced.

**4** The performance of a business is exposed to the environment. Consequently, businesses monitor the:

- social environment to anticipate changes in the demand for their products in response to changing demographics and changing preferences of consumers,
- industry environment to assess the level of competition, and
- economic and global environments to anticipate how the local and global economies may affect the demand for their products.

**5** The key types of business decisions are:

- management decisions, which determine how the firm's resources are allocated,
- marketing decisions, which determine the product to be sold, along with the pricing
- distribution, and promotion of that product, and
- finance decisions, which determine how the firm obtains and invests funds.

Business decisions are improved as a result of:

- accounting, which is used to monitor performance and detect inefficient uses of resources in order to improve business decisions, and
- information systems, which provide the firm's employees with information that enables them to improve business decisions.

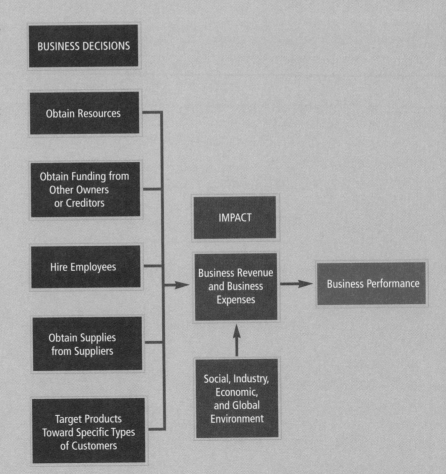

# Self-Test of Key Concepts

The following self-assessment allows you to test your understanding of the key concepts covered in this chapter. Answers are provided at the end of this exercise so that you can assess your understanding of the key concepts. If you answer any question incorrectly, mark that answer and attempt to answer that question again on the following day.

## True or False

1. Suppliers organize, manage, and assume the risks of the business.

2. The goal of a firm's management is to maximize the firm's value, which is in the best interests of the firm's owners.

3. A firm must satisfy its customers by providing the products or services that customers desire at a reasonable price.

4. Firms typically repay loans with their stock.

5. A firm's earnings (or profits) are equal to its revenue plus its expenses.

6. Firms use information systems primarily to determine how to finance their businesses.

7. Managers use accounting to monitor and assess the performance of a business.

8. Capital includes machinery and facilities.

9. Assessing the business environment includes information from industry, economic, and global environments.

10. A business must have poor performance in order to be classified to as a nonprofit business.

## Multiple Choice

11. An enterprise that provides products or services that customers desire is a(n):
    a) institution.
    b) philanthropy.
    c) market.
    d) agency.
    e) business.

12. The _____ of a business are typically responsible for creating the business idea.
    a) owners
    b) creditors
    c) couriers
    d) employees
    e) customers

13. Most business owners would agree that the following characteristics motivated them to start their own business except:
    a) potential for earning large incomes.
    b) being their own boss.
    c) the challenge.
    d) prestige associated with owning a business.
    e) risk.

14. The stakeholders of a firm include all of the following except:
    a) owners.
    b) creditors.
    c) employees.
    d) suppliers.
    e) government officials.

15. When investors invest in the business, they become:
    a) creditors.
    b) brokers.
    c) employees.
    d) sponsors.
    e) stockholders.

16. A certificate of ownership of a business is a:
    a) bond.
    b) stock.
    c) mutual fund.
    d) co-article.
    e) contract.

17. Many firms that need funds borrow from financial institutions or individuals called:
    a) debtors.
    b) creditors.
    c) collateral.
    d) joint ventures.
    e) investors.

18. Employees responsible for making key business decisions are:
    a) stockholders.
    b) owners.
    c) managers.
    d) business agents.
    e) creditors.

19. A nonprofit organization is one that:
    a) has a profit motive.
    b) does not have stakeholders.
    c) invests only in technology products.
    d) serves a specific cause.
    e) is not run like a business.

20. Business decisions regarding which products are created, priced, distributed, and promoted to customers are _____ decisions.
    a) finance
    b) information systems
    c) accounting
    d) management
    e) marketing

21. The expenses associated with transactions between firms have been reduced by:
    a) accounting transaction systems.
    b) systems engineering.
    c) environmental assessments.
    d) business-to-business e-commerce.
    e) feasibility studies.

22. Business decisions involving the efficient use of employees and other resources (such as machinery) are _____ decisions.
    a) finance
    b) accounting
    c) management
    d) information systems
    e) marketing

23. Business decisions that focus on strategies to make the product more appealing to customers and improve the firm's revenue are _____ decisions.
    a) production
    b) marketing
    c) manufacturing
    d) personnel
    e) finance

24. _____ gather(s) information about a firm and then provide(s) that information to management for use in decision making.
    a) Management
    b) Information systems
    c) Economics
    d) Finance
    e) Marketing

25. _____ summarize(s) the firm's financial condition for use in making various business decisions.
    a) Accounting
    b) Information systems
    c) Production
    d) Marketing
    e) Management

26. Business decisions involving how to obtain the necessary funds to be used by the firm are _____ decisions.
    a) finance
    b) marketing
    c) accounting
    d) information systems
    e) management

27. Managers rely on _____ to detect the inefficient use of resources.
    a) owners
    b) creditors
    c) marketing research
    d) marketing mix studies
    e) accounting data

28. The purpose of an industry environment assessment is to determine the:
    a) degree of competition.
    b) inflation rate.
    c) unemployment rate.
    d) population growth.
    e) economic growth.

29. The _____ environment includes changes in consumer preferences over time.
    a) industry
    b) social
    c) economic
    d) global
    e) retail

30. The profit motive is influenced by the government because:
   a) governments of free-market economies encourage the profit motive.
   b) businesses are owned by the government.
   c) governments of free-market economies discourage the profit motive.
   d) governments are shareholders of the firm.
   e) governments buy most businesses from individuals.

| True/False | | Multiple Choice | | |
|---|---|---|---|---|
| 1. False | 9. True | 11. e | 19. d | 27. e |
| 2. True | 10. False | 12. a | 20. e | 28. a |
| 3. True | | 13. e | 21. d | 29. b |
| 4. False | | 14. e | 22. c | 30. a |
| 5. False | | 15. e | 23. b | |
| 6. False | | 16. b | 24. b | |
| 7. True | | 17. b | 25. a | |
| 8. True | | 18. c | 26. a | |

# Self-Test of Key Terms

accounting 21
capital 7
creditors 14
demographics 17
dividends 17
electronic business (e-business) 7
electronic commerce (e-commerce) 7

entrepreneurs 9
entrepreneurship 9
finance 20
human resources 6
information systems 21
information technology 7
management 20
managers 15
marketing 20

natural resources 6
nonprofit organization 6
stakeholders 10
stock 12
stockholders (shareholders) 12
technology 7

Fill in each blank with the proper key term. To assess your understanding of the key terms, answers are provided at the end of this self-test.

1. _____ is the means by which firms obtain and use funds for their business operations.

2. _____ is the difference between the revenue and expenses of a business.

3. _____ refer to characteristics of the population.

4. Institutions that provide loans to a business are called _____.

5. _____ is the means by which products are developed, priced, distributed, and promoted.

6. _____ are the people who are able to perform work for a business.

7. _____ is the means by which employees and other resources are used by the firm.

8. _____ is the use of electronic communications to produce or sell products and services.

9. Owners of a firm who received stock from a business are called _____.

10. _____ involves the creation of a business idea and the willingness to accept risk.

**Answers:**

| | | |
|---|---|---|
| 1. Finance | 5. Marketing | 9. stockholders |
| 2. Profit | 6. Human resources | 10. Entrepreneurship |
| 3. Demographics | 7. Management | |
| 4. creditors | 8. E-business | |

# Concept Review Questions

1. **Motive.** What is a motive for creating a business? What is the risk of creating a business?

2. **Profits and Business Value.** How does a business generate a profit? How can profits be measured? Why do higher profits result in a higher business value?

3. **Competition.** Explain how the profit motive for businesses ensures that many businesses are created to satisfy all preferences by customers. How can the profit motive ensure that there will be sufficient competition among businesses? Why is this beneficial to customers?

4. **Stakeholders.** Describe the roles of the five key stakeholders in a business.

5. **Reliance on Resources.** Explain the resources that you would need if you started a small business.

6. **Financing.** Describe the role of financing for a business as it expands.

7. **Creditors.** Why do you think it is difficult for some small businesses to obtain funding from creditors?

8. **Business Decisions.** Describe the key types of decisions involved in running a business. Explain how you would apply these decisions if you owned a business that produces bicycles.

9. **Business Environment.** Explain the various ways in which the performance of a business is affected by the environment.

10. **Business Functions.** Describe how management, marketing, and financing would be necessary if you started your own pizza delivery service.

# Class Communication Questions

1. **Being a Manager Versus Owner.** You have a choice of being the primary manager (without any ownership) or the owner of a very small business. Would you have more to gain if you were the manager or the owner? Would you have more to lose if you were the manager or the owner?

2. **Obtaining Funds from Creditor Versus Owner.** You own a small business and need some financing. You could either borrow $20,000 or allow an investor to invest $20,000 in your business and become part-owner. You expect that your business will be very profitable this year. Would you prefer to finance the business by borrowing or by allowing someone to become part-owner of your business?

3. **Importance of Management Versus Marketing.** Assuming that you own a small clothing store at the mall, consider the key management and marketing functions for this store. Do you think the store's management or marketing function would have a bigger influence on the performance of the business?

## Small Business Case

### Key Decisions for Business Success

Emma Murray created a business called 4-Eyes DVD Rental because she recognized that customers desired a product that she could provide. To start this business, she borrowed some money from her sister and received an investment from her parents, who are co-owners of the business. In order to have a successful business, Emma needed to offer products desired by customers and keep her expenses low so that she could price her DVD rentals low and still make a profit. She believed she could offer a wider selection of DVDs and at a lower price than the only other DVD rental outlet in town. She also can keep her rent expenses low by renting store space in an area of midpriced stores rather than in the exclusive shopping mall where the competitor DVD rental shop is located.

1. **How the Product Affects Success.** Explain how the decision by Emma to offer DVD rentals rather than other types of products will influence the success of her new business.

2. **How the Pricing Affects Success.** Explain how the decision by Emma to offer DVD rentals at a relatively low price will influence the success of the business.

3. **How Factors of Production Affect Success.** What is the danger of this business hiring too many employees?

4. **How Stakeholders Benefit from Business Success.** How does the performance of this business affect the co-owners (Emma's parents) or the creditor (Emma's sister) who provided funding to start the business?

## Web Insight

### Business Functions at YouTube

The business YouTube was introduced at the beginning of this chapter. Review its website (www.youtube.com) as you answer these questions.

1. What resources are needed to run YouTube?

2. Describe the key stakeholders of YouTube.

3. In October 2006, Google acquired YouTube for $1.65 billion. Why do you think YouTube is valued so high? That is, how can YouTube generate large profits that will make Google's investment worthwhile?

## Dell's Secret for Success

Go to Dell's website (www.dell.com) and click on the link "About Dell" near the bottom of the Web page. You can also review a recent annual report of Dell for more information.

1. **Unique Business Idea.** When Michael Dell started the business in 1984, he focused on building relationships directly with customers, as explained on Dell's website. Explain how this business idea differed from those of other computer manufacturers.

2. **Goals.** How does Dell describe its goals in its annual report as they relate to its customers? To its employees? To its shareholders? Are these goals related? Explain.

3. **Appeal to Stakeholders.** How do Dell's stockholders gain from the attention that Dell gives to its customers and its employees?

# Video Exercise

### Lessons in Starting a Business

Many free business videos are available on websites such as YouTube (www.youtube.com), and more are added every day. Search for a recent video clip about an existing business that offers lessons on "starting your own business" in YouTube or any other website that provides video clips.

1. **Main Lesson.** What is the name of the business in the video clip? Does the video focus on the owners, creditors, employees, suppliers, or customers? What is the main lesson of the video clip that you watched?

2. **Bad Business Decisions.** Some related videos suggest that many businesses fail becuase they made poor decisions about their product. Other videos say that many business fail because they made poor decisions about hiring employees. Yet, some other videos suggest that businesses fail because they did not ensure adequate financing. Which of these lessons do you think is most important?

3. **Power Struggle.** Business videos commonly suggest that an entrepreneur has trouble giving up power, which restricts the ability to grow. Yet, there are also cases in which the entrepreneur gave too much responsibility to enployees. Describe the tradeoff.

# Projects

To encourage further comprehension of concepts covered in Chapter 1, the following five projects are available:

1. Analyzing Your Favorite Business

2. Building a Business Plan for Campus.com

3. Running Your Own Business

4. Planning Your Career

5. Stock Market Contest

All of these projects are provided in Appendix A at the end of the text. In addition, projects are available by part division at the end of each part.

A Word file for each project is also available at the textbook website (www.emcp.net/business5e) so that you may maintain one ongoing file for each project.

# Business Ethics and Social Responsibility

## Chapter 2 Learning Objectives

**1** Describe the responsibilities of firms to their customers.

**2** Describe the responsibilities of firms to their employees.

**3** Describe the responsibilities of firms to their stockholders.

**4** Describe the responsibilities of firms to their creditors.

**5** Describe the responsibilities of firms to the environment.

**6** Describe the responsibilities of firms to their communities.

## Social Responsibility at Starbucks

A firm's employees should practice business ethics, which involves following a set of principles when conducting business. Each firm has a social responsibility, which reflects the firm's responsibility to its community and to the environment. However, social responsibility may also be interpreted more broadly to include the firm's responsibility to its customers, employees, stockholders, and creditors.

Starbucks Coffee Company has established many programs that are intended to give back to its communities. For example, it established programs that allow college students to help preschoolers develop their skills. It created a program that uses poetry and soccer to promote literacy. It donates money to libraries and to children's programs. Recently, it expanded its community reach by establishing programs to improve literacy in China. Starbucks' goals to improve literacy and education are respected by its customers. In fact, many of its customers are well educated and frequently read books. Thus, they can relate to Starbucks' efforts to help its communities. However, Starbucks has a social responsibility that extends beyond its communities. It must decide:

✦ What is its responsibility to its customers?

✦ What is its responsibility to its employees?

✦ What is its responsibility to its investors?

✦ What is its responsibility to its creditors?

✦ What is its responsibility to its environment?

While Starbucks incurs costs from meeting its responsibilities, it is also rewarded. Its favorable treatment of its customers can increase the volume of customers, and therefore increase its revenue. Its favorable treatment of its employees can increase employee efforts to please customers, and therefore increase its revenue. This chapter explains how decisions by Starbucks or any business to meet its social responsibility can be made in a manner that maximizes its value.

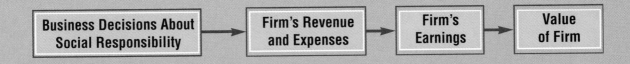

Out of
Business

OUR CUSTOMERS ARE NOT SATISFIED WITH OUR PRODUCTS.
OUR INVESTORS ARE NOT SATISFIED WITH OUR PERFORMACE.
SO THERE IS ONLY ONE SOLUTION... GO FIND NEW CUSTOMERS
AND INVESTORS WHO DO NOT KNOW US VERY WELL

SOCIAL RESPONSIBILITY MEETING IN PROGRESS

**Learning Objective**

**1**

Describe the
responsibilities
of firms to their
customers.

**social responsibility**
a firm's recognition of how its
business decisions can affect
society

**consumerism**
the collective demand by
consumers that businesses satisfy
their needs

# 1. Responsibility to Customers

A firm's responsibility to customers goes beyond the provision of products or services. Firms have a **social responsibility** when producing and selling their products, which ensures customer safety and proper disclosure of information.

Specific groups of consumers are also calling for firms to fulfill their responsibilities toward customers. **Consumerism** is the collective demand by consumers that businesses satisfy their needs. Consumer groups became popular in the 1960s and have become increasingly effective as they have grown.

## 1.1 Responsible Production Practices

Firms should produce products in a way that ensures customer safety. Products should carry proper warning labels to prevent accidents that could result from misuse. For some products, information on possible side effects should be provided. For example, Tylenol gelcaps, Nyquil cough syrup, and Coors beer all have warning labels about possible adverse effects.

## 1.2 Responsible Sales Practices

Consider the following sales practices that are commonly used. An employee of a car dealership tries to sell a car at the sticker price to any customers who are not aware that the usual selling price is at least $2,000 below the sticker price. The employee earns a higher commission from selling the car at a higher price. A salesperson at a health food store sells supplements, claiming that they will build muscle, even though he knows that they could have dangerous side effects. A phone company salesperson sells a customer a specific plan that appears cheap, but will typically result in very high fees because of some requirements that are not disclosed during the sale.

When employees may benefit from commissions, they may be tempted to hide the truth in order to sell products or services. Therefore, firms need guidelines that discourage employees from using overly aggressive sales strategies or deceptive advertising. They may also use customer satisfaction surveys to ensure that customers were treated properly by salespeople. The surveys should be conducted after customers make a purchase to determine whether the product worked as the salesperson said that it would.

Drug companies need to ensure that customers are aware of any possible side effects when taking their drugs. They provide warnings in writing right on the drug containers to ensure that customers are aware of instructions on dosage and any possible side effects.

© SHUTTERSTOCK/WELLFORD TILLER

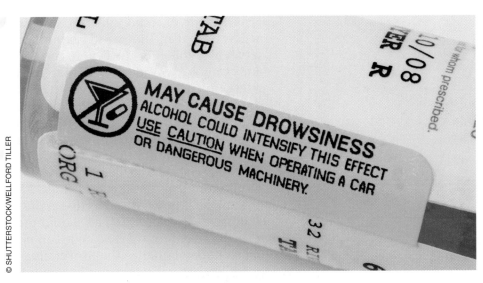

## 1.3  How Firms Ensure Their Responsibility

A firm can ensure responsibility toward its customers by following these steps:

**business responsibilities**
a set of obligations and duties regarding product quality and treatment of customers, employees, and owners that a firm should fulfill when conducting business

a. **Establish a Code of Responsibilities.** Firms can establish a code of **business responsibilities** that sets guidelines for product quality, as well as guidelines for how employees, customers, and owners should be treated. The pledge (from an annual report) by Bristol-Myers Squibb Company in Exhibit 2.1 is an example of a code of ethics and responsibilities. Many firms distribute a booklet on ethics and responsibilities to all their employees.

| Exhibit 2.1 | Excerpts from a Pledge of Ethics and Responsibility by Bristol-Myers Squibb Company |

**The Bristol-Myers Squibb Pledge**

TO THOSE WHO USE OUR PRODUCTS . . .
We affirm Bristol-Myers Squibb's commitment to the highest standards of excellence, safety and reliability in everything we make. We pledge to offer products of the highest quality and to work diligently to keep improving them.

TO OUR EMPLOYEES AND THOSE WHO MAY JOIN US . . .
We pledge personal respect, fair competition and equal treatment. We acknowledge our obligation to provide able and humane leadership throughout the organization, within a clean and safe working environment. To all who qualify for advancement, we will make every effort to provide opportunity.

TO OUR SUPPLIERS AND CUSTOMERS. . .
We pledge an open door, courteous, efficient and ethical dealing, and appreciation of their right to a fair profit.

TO OUR SHAREHOLDERS . . .
We pledge a companywide dedication to continued profitable growth, sustained by strong finances, a high level of research and development, and facilities second to none.

TO THE COMMUNITIES WHERE WE HAVE PLANTS AND OFFICES . . .
We pledge conscientious citizenship, a helping hand for worthwhile causes, and constructive action in support of civic and environmental progress.

TO THE COUNTRIES WHERE WE DO BUSINESS . . .
We pledge ourselves to be a good citizen and to show full consideration for the rights of others while reserving the right to stand up for our own.

ABOVE ALL, TO THE WORLD WE LIVE IN . . .
We pledge Bristol-Myers Squibb to policies and practices which fully embody the responsibility, integrity and decency required of free enterprise if it is to merit and maintain the confidence of our society.

The code of responsibilities is not intended to cover every possible action by a firm that would be unfair to customers. Nevertheless, it serves as a guide for the firm to consider when expanding its business. For example, consider a firm that implements a code that emphasizes safety for customers. Whatever the firm may produce in the future, it should always ensure that the products are not harmful. Thus, this code does not force the firm to produce any particular product but simply ensures that any product will be tested to ensure that it is safe for customers. If another provision of the code is honest communication with customers, then the advertising of all of the firm's products should conform to these guidelines. Although some government laws prohibit blatantly false advertising, this type of provision within a code of ethics and responsibilities would prevent advertising that is deceptive. To the extent that the code can enhance a firm's image and credibility, it may enhance the firm's value.

b. **Monitor Complaints.** Firms should make sure that customers have a phone number that they can call if they have any complaints about the quality of the product or about how they were treated by employees. The firm can attempt to determine the source of the complaint and ensure that the problem does not occur again. Many firms have a department that receives complaints and attempts to resolve them. This step may involve assessing different parts of the production process to ensure that the product is produced properly. Or it may require an assessment of particular employees who may be violating the firm's code of responsibilities to its customers.

c. **Obtain and Utilize Customer Feedback.** Firms can ask customers for feedback on the products or services they recently purchased, even if the customers do not call to complain. This process may detect some other problems with the product's quality or with the way customers were treated. For example, automobile dealers such as Saturn send a questionnaire to customers to determine how they were treated by salespeople. Customers may also be asked whether they have any complaints about the automobile they recently purchased. Once the firm is informed of problems with either production defects or customer treatment, it should take action to correct these problems.

## 1.4  How the Government Ensures Responsibility

In addition to the codes of responsibility established by firms and the wave of consumerism, the government attempts to ensure that firms fulfill their responsibility to customers through various laws on product safety, advertising, and industry competition.

**Government Regulation of Product Safety**  The government protects consumers by regulating the quality of some products produced by firms. For example, the Food and Drug Administration (FDA) is responsible for testing food products to determine whether they meet specific requirements. The FDA also examines new drugs that firms have recently developed. Because potential side effects may not be known immediately, the FDA tests some drugs continually over several years.

**Government Regulation of Advertising**  The federal government has also established laws against deceptive advertising. Nevertheless, it may not be able to prevent all unethical business practices. Numerous examples

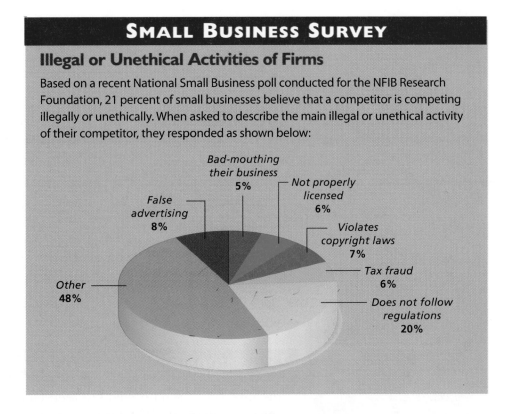

## SMALL BUSINESS SURVEY

### Illegal or Unethical Activities of Firms

Based on a recent National Small Business poll conducted for the NFIB Research Foundation, 21 percent of small businesses believe that a competitor is competing illegally or unethically. When asked to describe the main illegal or unethical activity of their competitor, they responded as shown below:

- Bad-mouthing their business 5%
- Not properly licensed 6%
- Violates copyright laws 7%
- Tax fraud 6%
- Does not follow regulations 20%
- False advertising 8%
- Other 48%

of advertising could be called deceptive. It is difficult to know if a product is "new and improved." In addition, a term such as *lowest price* may have different meanings or interpretations.

**Government Regulation of Industry Competition**   Another way the government ensures that consumers are treated properly is to promote competition in most industries. Competition between firms is beneficial to consumers, because firms that charge excessive prices or produce goods of unacceptable quality will not survive in a competitive environment. Because of competition, consumers can avoid a firm that is using deceptive sales tactics.

A firm has a **monopoly** if it is the sole provider of goods or services. It can set prices without concern about competition. However, the government regulates firms that have a monopoly. For example, it regulates utility firms that have monopolies in specific locations and can control the pricing policies of these firms.

In some industries, firms negotiated various agreements to set prices and avoid competing with each other. The federal government has attempted to prevent such activity by enforcing antitrust laws. Some of the more well-known antitrust acts are summarized in Exhibit 2.2. All of these acts share the objective of promoting competition, with each act focusing on particular aspects that can influence the degree of competition within an industry.

The trucking, railroad, airline, and telecommunications industries have been deregulated, allowing more firms to enter each industry. In addition, banks and other financial institutions have been deregulated since 1980 and now have more flexibility on the types of deposits and interest rates they can offer. They also have more freedom to expand across state lines. In general, deregulation results in lower prices for consumers.

**monopoly**
a firm that is the sole provider of goods or services

+ **Sherman Antitrust Act (1890)** Encouraged competition and prevented monopolies.

+ **Clayton Act (1914)** Reinforced the rules of the Sherman Antitrust Act and specifically prohibited the following activities because they reduced competition:

   + *Tying agreements* Forced firms to purchase additional products as a condition of purchasing the desired products.

   + *Binding contracts* Prevented firms from purchasing products from a supplier's competitors.

   + *Interlocking directorates* The situation in which the same person serves on the board of directors of two competing firms.

+ **Federal Trade Commission Act (1914)** Prohibited unfair methods of competition; also provided for the establishment of the Federal Trade Commission (FTC) to enforce antitrust laws.

+ **Robinson-Patman Act (1936)** Prohibited price policies or promotional allowances that reduce competition within an industry.

+ **Celler-Kefauver Act (1950)** Prohibited mergers between firms that reduce competition within an industry.

**Learning Objective**

Describe the responsibilities of firms to their employees.

**2**

## 2. Responsibility to Employees

Firms also have a responsibility to their employees to ensure their safety, proper treatment by other employees, and equal opportunity.

### 2.1 Employee Safety

Firms ensure that the workplace is safe for employees by closely monitoring the production process. Some obvious safety precautions are to check machinery and equipment for proper working conditions, require safety glasses or any other equipment that can prevent injury, and emphasize any special safety precautions in training seminars.

Firms need to ensure that their employees use proper safety equipment for their jobs. Some types of jobs (such as welding shown here) are more exposed to possible injuries and therefore require equipment.

© SHUTTERSTOCK/NANOSTOCK

Firms that create a safe working environment prevent injuries and improve the morale of their employees. Many firms now identify workplace safety as one of their main goals. Dow Chemical Company has adopted a pledge of no accidents and no injuries to its employees. Levi Strauss & Co. imposes safety guidelines not only on its U.S. facilities but also on the Asian factories where some of its clothes are made. Starbucks Coffee Company has developed a code of conduct in an attempt to improve the quality of life of its employees in coffee-producing countries.

Owners of a firm recognize that the firm will incur costs in meeting responsibilities such as employee safety. The firm's efforts to provide a safe working environment represent a necessary cost of doing business.

## 2.2  Proper Treatment by Other Employees

Firms are responsible for ensuring that employees are treated properly by other employees. Two key issues concerning the treatment of employees are diversity and the prevention of sexual harassment, which are discussed next.

**Diversity**   In recent years, the workforce has become much more diverse. More women have entered the job market, and more minorities now have the necessary skills and education to qualify for high-level jobs. Exhibit 2.3 shows the proportions of various job categories held by women, African Americans, and Hispanics.

Diversity issues are not restricted to gender and race. Employees may come from completely different backgrounds and have different beliefs, which could lead to conflict in the workplace. For example, some employees may have strong political beliefs, which could cause friction with others who do not share those beliefs, even if their work assignments are unrelated to politics. In addition, some employees may be much older than others, which may lead to opposing views about issues in or outside the workplace. Many firms attempt to integrate employees with various backgrounds so that they learn to work with each other toward common goals of the firm even if they have differing views on issues outside the workplace.

Many firms have responded to the increased diversity among employees by offering diversity seminars, which inform employees about cultural diversity. Such information can help employees recognize that certain statements or behavior may be offensive to other employees.

Based on a recent survey by the Society for Human Resource Management, 73 percent of firms integrate diversity initiatives into key business practices for employees in substantially different groups. In addition, 85 percent of all firms integrate diversity initiatives into key business practices for employees of various racial backgrounds.

**Exhibit 2.3**

Proportion of Women and Minorities in Various Occupations

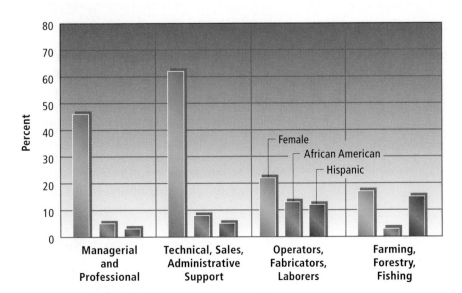

Firms benefit from a diverse workplace. Diversity among employees (shown here) has increased substantially at many firms in recent years.

© SHUTTERSTOCK/STEPHEN COBURN

**Examples of Diversity Effects**    The following statement from a recent annual report of General Motors reflects the efforts that have been made by many firms to encourage diversity:

*"Internally, we are working to create an environment where diversity thrives. We are trying to remove barriers that separate people and find new ways to engage teams to maximize productivity and profitability. This is being done through communication, teamwork, mutual support, and pulling together to achieve common objectives. Our challenge is to seek a diverse population in leadership roles with a wide range of backgrounds, views, and expeiences to ensure we capture diverse perspectives to meet and exceed customer expectations."*

Johnson & Johnson, The Coca-Cola Company, IBM, Sara Lee Corporation, and many other firms have made major efforts to promote diversity. Xerox has improved its workplace diversity in recent years.

**sexual harassment**
unwelcome comments or actions of a sexual nature

**Prevention of Sexual Harassment**    Another workplace issue is **sexual harassment**, which involves unwelcome comments or actions of a sexual nature. For example, one employee might make unwelcome sexual advances toward another and use personal power within the firm to threaten the other employee's job status. Firms attempt to prevent sexual harassment by offering seminars on the subject. Like diversity seminars, these seminars can help employees recognize that some statements or behavior may be offensive to other employees. These seminars are not only an act of responsibility to employees but also can improve a firm's productivity by helping employees get along.

## 2.3  How Firms Ensure Responsibility Toward Employees

Firms can ensure that their responsibility toward employees will be fulfilled by taking the following steps.

## Global Business

### Global Ethics

U.S. firms typically have a code of ethics that provides guidelines for their employees. However, these guidelines may be much more restrictive than those generally used in some foreign countries. Consider a U.S. firm that sells supplies to foreign manufacturers. Both its code of ethics and the U.S. Foreign Corrupt Practices Act prevent the firm from offering payoffs ("kickbacks") to any employees of the manufacturing companies that order its supplies. Competitors based in other countries, however, may offer payoffs to employees of the manufacturing companies. In some countries, this type of behavior is acceptable. Thus, the U.S. supplier is at a disadvantage because its employees are required to follow a stricter code of ethics. This is a common ethical dilemma that U.S. firms face in a global environment. The employees of U.S. firms must either ignore their ethical guidelines or be at a disadvantage in certain foreign countries.

Another ethical dilemma that U.S. firms may face involves their relationship with certain foreign governments. Firms that conduct business in foreign countries are subject to numerous rules imposed by the local government. Officials of some foreign governments commonly accept bribes from firms that need approval for various business activities. For example, a firm may need to have its products approved for safety purposes, or its local manufacturing plant may need to be approved for environmental purposes. The process of approving even minor activities could take months and prevent the firm from conducting business. Those firms that pay off government officials may receive prompt attention from the local governments.

Many U.S. firms attempt to follow a worldwide code of ethics that is consistent across countries. This type of policy reduces the confusion that could result from using different ethical standards in different countries. Although a worldwide code of ethics may place a U.S. firm at a disadvantage in some countries, it may also enhance the firm's credibility.

**Code of Responsibility**  A firm's responsibility toward its employees should be disclosed in its code of responsibilities. As with the responsibilities toward customers, the code will not attempt to spell out the recommended behavior in every situation, but it can offer some guidance for the decisions made by the firm. For example, the code may state that hiring decisions should be made without any form of bias. The firm should establish a hiring procedure that satisfies this provision. The procedure may specify that an ad describing the main duties of the job position be placed in the local newspaper for two weeks before anyone is hired. Doing this will help to ensure that the most qualified person is hired for the job. Thus, the procedure is implemented in a manner that is consistent with the firm's responsibility of hiring without any form of bias.

**Grievance Policy**  To ensure that employees receive proper treatment, many firms establish a grievance policy for employees who believe they are not being given equal opportunity. A specific person or department is normally assigned to resolve such complaints. This procedure is similar to that used to address customer complaints. By recognizing the complaints, the firm attempts both to resolve them and to revise its procedures to prevent further complaints.

A good example of a firm that has made an effort to resolve employee complaints is Marriott, which has implemented three strategies. First, it has set up a mediation process, in which a neutral person outside the firm (called a *mediator*) assesses the employee complaint and suggests a solution. The mediator does not have the power to enforce a final judgment but may help the employee and the firm resolve the conflict.

Second, Marriott offers a toll-free number for employees to call if they believe they were subjected to discrimination, harassment, or improper firing. Marriott begins to investigate the complaint within three days of the call. Third, Marriott allows the employee to voice complaints in front of a panel of other employees who determine whether the employee's complaints are valid, based on Marriott's existing guidelines.

Marriott's procedure for resolving employee complaints has improved employee satisfaction. However, the cost of attempting to listen to every employee complaint can be substantial. Firms must attempt to distinguish between complaints that are valid and those that are not and then focus on resolving the valid complaints.

**Job Satisfaction Initiatives**   Some firms go beyond the responsibility of ensuring safety, proper treatment, and equal opportunity. These firms have taken initiatives to ensure that employees enjoy their jobs. This can increase the job satisfaction level of employees and reduce employee turnover. These firms realize that satisfied employees will do a better job for customers and that the customers, in turn, will be more satisfied. Here are some examples of initiatives by firms that were recently rated as the best for employees.

✦ Wegmans Food Market (in New York) has provided college scholarships for more than 17,000 of its full-time and part-time employees over the last 20 years. It also provides extensive training to ensure that its employees have the knowledge they need to perform their specific jobs. Its employee turnover is substantially lower than that of other grocery stores.

✦ Station Casinos (in Nevada) offers full-service on-site dentistry and 24-hour child care for employees.

✦ General Mills (in Minnesota) reimburses tuition up to $6,000 per year for its new employees.

✦ CarMax (in Virginia) holds frequent meetings with employees to ask their opinions about what the company should change.

✦ Publix Super Markets (in Florida) provides health benefits for some part-time employees and an annual bonus of up to a week's salary plus an extra week of vacation time.

✦ J.M. Smucker (in Ohio) offers complimentary bagels and muffins to its employees every day.

✦ SAS Institute (in North Carolina) has a gym, a pool, ping-pong tables, and tennis courts for its employees.

Many businesses have created an exercise room like the one shown here so that employees can work out during the lunch break and can enjoy their jobs to a greater degree.

© SHUTTERSTOCK/BENIS ARAPOVIC

**Conflict with Employee Layoffs** Some business decisions are controversial because although they improve the firm's performance, they may adversely affect employees and the local community. Consider the following example, which reflects a common dilemma that many firms face. As your firm's business grew, you hired more employees. Unfortunately, demand for your product has declined recently, and you no longer need 20 of the employees that you hired over the last two years. If you lay off 20 employees, you will reduce your expenses substantially and satisfy your stockholders. However, you may be criticized for not serving employees' interests. This situation is unpleasant because the layoffs may be necessary (to cut expenses) for your firm to survive. If your firm fails, all your other employees will be out of work as well. This dilemma has no perfect solution. Many firms may do what's best for the business, while attempting to reduce the adverse effects on their employees. For example, they may help laid-off employees find employment elsewhere or may even attempt to retrain them for other jobs within the firm.

**Equal Employment Opportunity** Employees who apply for a position at a firm should not be subjected to discrimination because of their national origin, race, gender, or religion. The Civil Rights Act of 1964 prohibits such forms of discrimination. The act is enforced by a federal agency known as the Equal Employment Opportunity Commission (EEOC). Beyond the federal guidelines, many firms attempt to ensure equal treatment among applicants for a position by assigning someone to monitor the hiring process. The concept of equal treatment applies not only to the initial hiring of an employee but also to annual raises and promotions within the firm. Many firms and government agencies implement **affirmative action** programs, which represent a set of activities intended to increase opportunities for minorities and women. The government implemented the Civil Rights Act of 1991, which protects against discrimination in the hiring process, and protects against sexual harassment in the workplace.

**affirmative action**
a set of activities intended to increase opportunities for minorities and women

---

**Learning Objective**
Describe the responsibilities of firms to their stockholders.

**3**

## 3. Responsibility to Stockholders

Firms are responsible for satisfying their owners (or stockholders). Employees may be tempted to make decisions that satisfy their own interests rather than those of the owners. For example, some employees may use the firm's money to purchase computers for their personal use rather than for the firm.

# Self-Scoring Exercises

## Assessing the Ethical Standards of the Firm Where You Work

Think about the organization you currently work for or one you know something about and complete the following Ethical Climate Questionnaire. Use the scale below and write the number that best represents your answer in the space next to each item.

To what extent are the following statements true about your company?

| Completely false | Mostly false | Somewhat false | Somewhat true | Mostly true | Completely true |
|---|---|---|---|---|---|
| 0 | 1 | 2 | 3 | 4 | 5 |

_____ 1. In this company, people are expected to follow their own personal and moral beliefs.

_____ 2. People are expected to do anything to further the company's interests.

_____ 3. In this company, people look out for each other's good.

_____ 4. It is very important to follow the company's rules and procedures strictly.

_____ 5. In this company, people protect their own interests above other considerations.

_____ 6. The first consideration is whether a decision violates any law.

_____ 7. Everyone is expected to stick by the company rules and procedures.

_____ 8. The most efficient way is always the right way in this company.

_____ 9. Our major consideration is what is best for everyone in the company.

_____ 10. In this company, the law or ethical code of the profession is the major consideration.

_____ 11. It is expected at this company that employees will always do what is right for the consumer and the public.

To score the questionnaire, first add up your responses to questions 1, 3, 6, 9, 10, and 11. This is subtotal number 1. Next, reverse the scores on questions 2, 4, 5, 7, and 8 (5 = 0, 4 = 1, 3 = 2, 2 = 3, 1 = 4, 0 = 5). Add the reverse scores to form subtotal number 2. Add subtotal 1 to subtotal 2 for an overall score.

Subtotal 1 _____ + Subtotal 2 _____ = Overall Score _____.

Overall scores can range from 0 to 55. The higher the score, the more the organization's culture encourages ethical behavior.

## 3.1 How Firms Ensure Responsibility

Managers of a firm monitor employee decisions to ensure that they are made in the best interests of the owners. Employee compensation may be directly tied to the firm's performance. For example, a firm may provide its top managers with some of the firm's stock as partial compensation. If the managers make decisions that lead to a high level of performance, the value of the firm's stock should increase, and therefore

# Self-Scoring Exercises

## Assessing Whether Specific Situations Are Ethical

The purpose of this exercise is to explore your opinions about ethical issues faced in organizations. The class should be divided into 12 groups. Each group will randomly be assigned one of the following issues:

1. Is it ethical to take office supplies from work for home use? Make personal long-distance calls from the office? Use company time for personal business? Or do these behaviors constitute stealing?
2. If you exaggerate your credentials in an interview, is it lying? Is lying to protect a co-worker acceptable?
3. If you pretend to be more successful than you are to impress your boss, are you being deceitful?
4. How do you differentiate between a bribe and a gift?
5. If there are slight defects in a product you are selling, are you obligated to tell the buyer? If an advertised "sale" price is really the everyday price, should you divulge the information to the customer?
6. Suppose you have a friend who works at the ticket office for the convention center where Shania Twain will be appearing. Is it cheating if you ask the friend to get you tickets so that you won't have to fight the crowd to get them? Is buying merchandise for your family at your company's cost cheating?
7. Is it immoral to do less than your best in work performance? Is it immoral to accept workers' compensation when you are fully capable of working?
8. What behaviors constitute emotional abuse at work? What would you consider an abuse of one's position of power?
9. Are high-stress jobs a breach of ethics? What about transfers that break up families?
10. Are all rule violations equally important? Do employees have an ethical obligation to follow company rules?
11. To what extent are you responsible for the ethical behavior of your co-workers? If you witness unethical behavior and don't report it, are you an accessory?
12. Is it ethical to help one work group at the expense of another group? For instance, suppose one group has excellent performance and you want to reward its members with an afternoon off. The other work group will have to pick up the slack and work harder if you do this. Is this ethical?

Once your group has been assigned its issue, you have two tasks:

1. First, formulate your group's answer to the ethical dilemmas.
2. After you have formulated your group's position, discuss the individual differences that may have contributed to your position. You will want to discuss the individual differences presented in this chapter as well as any others that you believe affected your position on the ethical dilemma.

Your instructor will lead the class in a discussion of how individual differences may have influenced your positions on these ethical dilemmas.

the value of the stock held by the managers should increase. In this way, employees benefit directly when they make decisions that maximize the value of the firm.

**Conflicts in the Efforts to Ensure Responsibility**   The compensation of chief executive officers (CEOs) has increased substantially over recent decades. Some customers and stockholders may argue that firms that pay executives such high salaries are not meeting their social responsibilities. These firms may be serving the interests of the executives and not the stockholders who own the firm. Although it may be possible to justify very high compensation for CEOs who have been successful, it is difficult to justify such compensation for CEOs whose companies have performed poorly. In some recent years, the compensation of many CEOs increased even though the earnings or stock price of their firm declined. CEOs of larger firms tend to earn higher salaries, even when their firm performs poorly. In 1980, the average compensation of CEOs was about 42 times the average compensation of employees. In 1990, it was about 85 times the average salary of employees. In 2007. the average CEO compensation was about $11 million, or 364 times the average salary of employees.

**Temptations to Distort Performance**   Even if firms use a proper method to align executive compensation with firm performance, another problem may arise. Some top managers who have received stock have later reported an artificially high performance level for the firm in a period when they wanted to sell their stock holdings. This allowed them to sell their stock at a relatively high price. Rather than improving the firm's performance, these managers manipulated the financial reporting to exaggerate the firm's performance. When investors decide whether to buy stock, they commonly rely on information disclosed by the firm to determine whether its stock would be a good investment.

There are many cases of firms misleading existing and prospective investors by neglecting to mention relevant information that would have made their stock less desirable. In addition, there are many cases of firms issuing exaggerated estimates of their revenue or earnings. When a firm misleads investors by creating an overly optimistic view of its potential performance, it can cause investors to pay too much for its stock. The stock's price will likely decline once the firm's true financial condition becomes apparent.

**Enron Example**   One of the most blatant examples of a firm's managers misleading its existing and prospective stockholders is the case of Enron, Inc. Enron was one of the fastest-growing firms in the 1990s. Nevertheless, it created misleading financial statements, which led investors to believe that it was performing better than it really was. Consequently, some investors were fooled into paying much more for the stock than they should have during the 1999–2000 period. While Enron was creating such an optimistic view of its financial condition, some of its top managers were selling their holdings of Enron stock. Thus, they were dumping their shares while the price was high—before investors recognized that Enron's financial condition was much weaker than reported. While Enron's top managers earned large gains on their stock holdings, the investors who purchased Enron stock at this time lost most or all of their investment. In November 2001, Enron filed for bankruptcy, and the stock essentially became worthless. Thus, the top managers of Enron who were able to sell their stock at a high price (before the bad news was disclosed) benefited at the expense of other stockholders.

## 3.2  How the Government Ensures Responsibility

In 2002, Congress passed the Public Company Accounting Reform and Investor Protection Act, also known as the Sarbanes-Oxley Act after the politicians who created it. This law was intended to encourage publicly traded firms to behave more responsibly toward their stockholders. First, the law attempts to ensure that publicly traded firms clarify the information that they provide to stockholders. Second, firms are required to establish methods to ensure that they can detect errors in their financial reporting systems. Third, top executives and board members are held more accountable for errors in financial reporting. Despite these measures, the act does not necessarily prevent managers from serving their own interests rather than stockholders' interests. For example, an executive could still hire family members or friends or make bad decisions about investing in projects. Thus, the act does not correct bad performance, but only attempts to ensure that firms accurately report their performance and document the processes and information that they use to make decisions.

## 3.3  How Stockholders Ensure Responsibility

**shareholder activism**
active efforts by stockholders to influence a firm's management policies

**institutional investors**
financial institutions that purchase large amounts of stock

In recent years, there has been much **shareholder activism**, or active efforts by stockholders to influence a firm's management policies. Stockholders have been especially active when they are dissatisfied with the firm's executive salaries or other policies.

The stockholders who have been most active are **institutional investors**, or financial institutions that purchase large amounts of stock. For example, insurance companies invest a large portion of the insurance premiums that they receive in stocks. If institutional investors invest a large amount of money in a particular stock, the return on their investment is highly dependent on how that firm performs. Since many institutional investors commonly invest $10 million or more in a single firm's stock, they pay close attention to the performance of any firm in which they invest.

If an institutional investor believes the firm is poorly managed, it may attempt to meet with the firm's executives and express its dissatisfaction. It

Business executives are commonly required to meet with representatives of financial institutions that provided funding to the business. They are frequently asked to explain why their business performance was weaker than expected.

may even attempt to team up with other institutional investors who also own a large proportion of the firm's stock. This gives them more negotiating power because the firm's executives are more likely to listen to institutional investors who collectively hold a large proportion of the firm's stock. The institutional investors do not attempt to dictate how the firm should be managed. Instead, they attempt to ensure that the firm's managers make decisions that are in the best interests of all stockholders.

**Learning Objective**
Describe the responsibilities of firms to their creditors.

**4**

# 4. Responsibility to Creditors

Firms are responsible for meeting their financial obligations to their creditors. If a firm is experiencing financial problems and is unable to meet its obligations, it should inform its creditors. Sometimes creditors are willing to extend payment deadlines and may even offer advice on how the firm can improve its financial condition. A firm has a strong incentive to satisfy its responsibility to creditors. If the firm does not pay what it owes to creditors, it may be forced into bankruptcy.

## 4.1 How Some Firms Violate Their Responsibility

Some firms violate their responsibility to creditors by providing misleading financial information that exaggerates their financial condition. For example, Enron's financial reporting misled its creditors as well as its stockholders. Enron received some loans from creditors that it would not have received if the creditors had known of its weaknesses. Specifically, Enron did not disclose some of its debt. Creditors would have been concerned about extending more credit if they had fully understood how much debt Enron already had. By hiding some debt, Enron was able to more easily borrow funds. Ultimately, however, it went bankrupt because it could not cover the payments on all of its debt. Many creditors lost hundreds of millions of dollars because of the large amount of credit they provided to Enron that would never be paid back. Although creditors recognize the possible risk that a business will fail and be unable to repay its loans, they were angry that Enron used unethical financial reporting methods to obtain loans. While some firms have received bad publicity for distorting their financial condition, others have taken the initiative to give creditors more detailed and clear financial information.

**Learning Objective**
Describe the responsibilities of firms to the environment.

**5**

# 5. Responsibility to the Environment

The production processes that firms use, as well as the products they produce, can be harmful to the environment. The most common abuses to the environment are discussed next, along with recent actions that firms have taken to improve the environment.

## 5.1 Air Pollution

Some production processes cause air pollution, which is harmful to society because it inhibits breathing. For example, the production of fuel and steel, as well as automobile use, increases the amount of carbon dioxide in the air.

**How Firms Prevent Air Pollution**    Automobile and steel firms have reduced air pollution by changing their production processes so that less carbon dioxide escapes into the air. For example, firms such as Honeywell and Inland Steel spend substantial funds to reduce pollution. Ford Motor Company has formulated an environmental pledge, which states that it is dedicated to developing environmental solutions and intends to preserve the environment in the future.

**How the Government Prevents Air Pollution**   The federal government has also become involved by enforcing specific guidelines that call for firms to limit the amount of carbon dioxide caused by the production process. In 1970, the Environmental Protection Agency (EPA) was created to develop and enforce pollution standards. In recent years, pollution control laws have become more stringent.

## 5.2 Land Pollution

Land has been polluted by toxic waste resulting from some production processes. A related form of land pollution is solid waste, which does not deteriorate over time. As a result of waste, land not only looks less attractive but also may no longer be useful for other purposes, such as farming.

**How Firms Prevent Land Pollution**   Firms have revised their production and packaging processes to reduce the amount of waste. They now store toxic waste and deliver it to specified toxic waste storage sites. They also recycle plastic and limit their use of materials that would ultimately become solid waste. Many firms have environmental programs that are designed to reduce damage to the environment. For example, Homestake Mining Company recognizes that its mining operations disturb the land, so it spends money to minimize any effect on the environment. PPG Industries restructured its production processes to generate about 6,000 fewer tons of waste in a single year. Kodak recycles more than a half-billion pounds of material a year and also supports a World Wildlife Fund environmental education program. IBM typically spends more than $30 million a year for environmental assessments and cleanup. ChevronTexaco and DuPont spend hundreds of millions of dollars every year to comply with environmental regulations.

## 5.3 Conflict with Environmental Responsibility

Although most firms agree that a clean environment is desirable, they may disagree on how much responsibility they have for improving the

Firms like the paper factory shown here are supposed to meet various emission standards so that they do not cause air pollution. They need to be monitored by the Environmental Protection Agency to ensure that they meet the standards.

© SHUTTERSTOCK/GONCALO VELOSO DE FIGUEIREDO

environment. Consider two firms called Firm A and Firm B, which have similar revenue and expenses. Firm A, however, makes a much greater effort to clean up the environment; it spends $10 million, while Firm B spends $2 million. The profit of each firm is shown in Exhibit 2.4. Firm A has an annual profit of zero, while Firm B has an annual profit of $8 million. If you could invest in the stock of either Firm A or Firm B, where would you invest your money? Most investors desire to earn a high return on their money. Although they recognize that a firm may have some environmental cleanup expenses, they do not want those expenses to be excessive. Therefore, most investors would prefer to invest in Firm B rather than Firm A.

Firm A could attempt to recapture its high environmental cleanup expenses by charging a higher price for its product. In this way, it may be able to spend heavily on the environment, while still generating a reasonable return for its stockholders. This strategy makes the customers pay for its extra environmental cleanup. A problem, however, is that if Firm A charges a higher price than Firm B, many customers will switch to Firm B so that they can pay the lower price.

As this example illustrates, there is a limit to how much firms can spend on improving the environment. Firms have a responsibility to avoid damaging the environment, but if they spend excessively on environmental improvement, they will not satisfy most of their customers or owners.

## 6. Responsibility to the Community

**Learning Objective**
Describe the responsibilities of firms to their communities.

**6**

When firms establish a base in a community, they become part of that community and rely on it for customers and employees. Firms demonstrate their concern for the community by sponsoring local events or donating to local charities. For example, SunTrust Bank, IBM, and many other firms have donated funds to universities. Bank of America has provided loans to low-income neighborhoods and minority communities. The Cheesecake Factory, a famous restaurant chain, established a foundation that not only raises funds for charities but also demonstrates the company's concern for its customers and community. In 2003, total cash donations by 500 large U.S. firms amounted to $3.26 billion. Wal-Mart was the top donor, with donations of $176 million. Ford Motor Company donated $120 million, while Johnson & Johnson donated $99 million and Exxon-Mobil donated $97 million.

For a multinational corporation, the community is its international environment. Many of the firms that engage in substantial international business have increased their international donations. Nike's donations to foreign countries now represent 39 percent of its total donations, while

**Exhibit 2.4**

Effect of Environmental Expenses on Business Performance

| | Firm A | Firm B |
|---|---|---|
| Revenue | $90,000,000 | $90,000,000 |
| Total operating expenses | −80,000,000 | −80,000,000 |
| Environmental cleanup expenses | −10,000,000 | −2,000,000 |
| Profit | 0 | $8,000,000 |

IBM's foreign donations represent about 30 percent of its total. When the tsunami disaster struck Indonesia and other Southeast Asian nations in December 2004, many U.S. firms quickly responded with contributions. FedEx made some of its planes available to help move 230 tons of medical supplies to the devastated areas. Coca-Cola, Dow Chemical, ExxonMobil, Microsoft, and Wal-Mart each contributed millions of dollars. Coca-Cola also delivered 500,000 bottles of water.

## 6.1  Satisfying the Community Versus Stockholders

The decisions of a firm's managers that maximize social responsibility could conflict with maximizing firm value. The costs involved in achieving such a goal will have to be passed on to consumers. Thus, the attempt to maximize responsibility to the community may reduce the firm's ability to provide products at a reasonable price to consumers.

Many companies support charitable organizations that promote nutrition, education, performing and visual arts, or amateur athletics. Even though this social support requires a considerable financial commitment, the firm can gain from an enhanced image in the eyes of the consumers to whom it sells its products. In a sense, the charitable support not only can help society but also can be a valuable marketing tool to improve the firm's image. People expect firms to give something back to society. In a recent Corporate Citizenship Study, 78 percent of all respondents said that firms have a responsibility to support causes, while 84 percent said that they want the firms serving their communities to be committed to social issues. Consequently, both society and stockholders can benefit from the charitable donations. If a company identifies a charitable cause that is closely related to its business, it may be able to simultaneously contribute to society and maximize the firm's value. For example, a running shoe manufacturer may sponsor a race, or a tennis racket manufacturer may sponsor a tennis tournament.

**Examples**  Apple and IBM invest substantial funds in local education programs. Not only is this investment helpful to the communities, but it also results in computer sales to schools. Home Depot donates to community programs that use much of the money for housing projects. Many Checkers restaurants have been located in inner-city areas. They not only provide jobs to many minorities but also have been profitable.

One of the best examples of a firm that has demonstrated its social responsibility in a manner that has also enhanced its performance is The Coca-Cola Company. It initiated a 10-year, $60 million sponsorship of Boys & Girls Clubs of America—the largest donation of funds by a firm to a specific cause. The sponsorship involves several events, such as basketball and golf tournaments and after-school reading sessions. Coca-Cola's name will be promoted at the events, which can help attract new young customers to its products.

Dow Chemical Company has created a Community Advisory Panel, which identifies community needs and ensures that Dow gives to its communities. Its recent community acts include funding education programs in South America where it conducts some of its business, supporting a Habitat for Humanity homebuilding project in Korea, and funding a new art center in West Virginia.

# Responding to the Economy

## Revising Business Responsibilities in Response to the Economy

As economic conditions change, the responsibility of firms to customers, employees, stockholders, creditors, and the environment may change. For example, as gasoline prices increased, some firms searched for ways to reduce the impact of gas prices on customers. Some car manufacturers offered special deals on new cars, such as a year of free gasoline. Other firms revised their delivery services so that customers could order products by phone or online and did not need to drive to pick up products that they purchased. These adjustments can ultimately benefit the firms, as customers may develop an allegiance to the firms that reduced the adverse impact of the high gas prices.

Many firms adjusted their policies for their employees in response to the high gasoline prices. One of the most common adjustments was to allow employees to work at home rather than drive to work. This not only reduced gas expenses for employees, but it also may have increased their job satisfaction.

In periods when the economy weakens, firms face a difficult challenge in simultaneously serving their employees, stockholders, and creditors. As the economy weakens and consumer demand declines, firms reduce their production and may need to temporarily lay off some employees. While this can reduce morale of employees, it may be necessary so that the firms can continue to make their debt payments to creditors.

## SMALL BUSINESS SURVEY

### Ethical Behavior of Employees

A recent survey of employees at large and small businesses by the Ethics Resource Center found that:

✦ 56 percent of employees had witnessed misconduct by other employees that violated the firm's ethics standards or policies, or the law.

✦ 54 percent of the employees who had witnessed misconduct believed that reporting the misconduct would not lead to corrective action.

✦ 42 percent of the employees who had witnessed misconduct reported it. The percentage rose to 61 percent for employees whose employers have a well-implemented ethics and compliance program.

✦ 36 percent of employees who had witnessed misconduct but did not report it cited fear of retaliation as their reason for not reporting it.

## 7. Summary of Business Responsibilities

Firms have many responsibilities to employees, stockholders, creditors, the environment, and the community that must be recognized when doing business. The following quotations from recent annual reports illustrate firms' general concern about ethics and social responsibility:

*"We will continue to . . . strengthen our competitiveness and enhance Disney's long-term value."*

—Walt Disney Co.

*"We are determined to . . . deliver long-term value to our shareholders."*

—National Instruments

*"The company's business model is built to . . . providing long-term value to shareholders."*

—IBM

*"We . . . believe that to create long term value for shareholders, we must also create value in our relationships with customers, employees, suppliers and the communities in which we operate."*

—Briggs & Stratton

Most firms have procedures in place to ensure that their social responsibilities are satisfied. They also enforce codes that specify their responsibilities.

## 7.1  Business Responsibilities in an International Environment

When firms compete in an international environment, they must be aware of cultural differences. Firms from some countries do not necessarily view certain business practices such as payoffs to large customers or to suppliers as unethical. This makes it difficult for other firms to compete for international business. Nevertheless, firms typically attempt to apply their ethical guidelines and corporate responsibilities in an international setting. By doing so, they establish a global reputation for running their business in an ethical manner.

Gap, Inc., took a major step toward social responsibility in the international environment that may serve as a model for other firms in the future. It conducted a major assessment of the 3,000 factories in Africa, China, India, South America, and other locations that produce the clothing it sells. The workers in these factories are not employees of Gap, but since Gap relies on these factories for its clothing, it felt responsible for ensuring that the workers have reasonable working conditions. It reported that many of these factories do not follow reasonable labor standards. This was a bold move by Gap, because it acknowledged that it was unaware that some workers who produce its clothing did not have adequate working conditions. As a result of its assessment, Gap stopped using some factories where conditions were inadequate. This is Gap's way of protesting against bad working conditions and indicating that it does not want to do business with any factory that does not treat its employees properly. Other U.S. firms that rely on factories in less developed countries have taken similar actions.

## 7.2  The Cost of Fulfilling Social Responsibilities

A summary of possible expenses incurred as a result of social responsibilities is provided in Exhibit 2.5. Some firms incur large expenses in all areas of social responsibility. For example, automobile manufacturers such as Ford Motor Company and General Motors must ensure that their

**Exhibit 2.5**

Possible Expenses Incurred as a Result of Social Responsibilities

| Responsibility to: | Expenses Incurred as a Result: |
| --- | --- |
| Customers | Establishing program to receive and resolve complaints<br>Conducting surveys to assess customer satisfaction<br>Lawsuits by customers (product liability) |
| Employees | Establishing program to receive and resolve complaints<br>Conducting surveys to assess employee satisfaction<br>Lawsuits by employees based on allegations of discrimination |
| Stockholders | Disclosing financial information periodically<br>Lawsuits by stockholders based on allegations that the firm's managers are not fulfilling their obligations to stockholders |
| Environment | Complying with governmental regulations on environment<br>Complying with self-imposed environmental guidelines |
| Community | Sponsoring community activities |

production of automobiles does not harm the environment. Second, they must ensure that all employees in their massive workforces are treated properly. Third, they must ensure that they deliver a safe and reliable product to their customers.

In recent years, many new government regulations have been imposed to create a cleaner environment and ensure that firms do not neglect other social responsibilities. Normally, all the firms in an industry will raise their prices to cover the expenses associated with following new government regulations. For example, restrictions on cutting down trees resulted in higher expenses for paper companies. These companies raised their prices to cover these higher expenses. Maintaining social responsibilities is necessary but costly, and customers indirectly pay the expenses incurred.

## Cross-Functional Teamwork

### Ethical Responsibilities Across Business Functions

The perception of a firm's ethical standards is dependent on its team of managers. The ethical responsibilities of a firm's managers vary with their specific job assignments. Production managers are responsible for producing a product that is safe. They should also ensure that the production process satisfies environmental standards.

Marketing managers are responsible for marketing a product in a manner that neither misrepresents the product's characteristics nor misleads consumers or investors. Marketing managers must communicate with production managers to ensure that product marketing is consistent with the production. Any promotion efforts by marketing managers that make statements about product quality should be assessed by production managers to ensure accuracy.

Financial managers are responsible for providing accurate financial reports to creditors or investors who may provide financial support to the firm. They rely on information from production and marketing managers when preparing their financial reports.

A firm earns a reputation for being ethical by ensuring that ethical standards are maintained in all business functions. If some members of its team of managers are unethical, the entire firm will be viewed as unethical.

**Cost of Complaints**   When ensuring responsibility toward customers or employees, firms incur the cost of hiring people to resolve the complaints. They must also consider the cost of defending against possible lawsuits by customers and employees. Customers suing firms for product defects or deceptive advertising and employees suing their firms for discrimination are common practices today.

A number of expenses can be associated with a lawsuit. First, the court may fine a firm that is found guilty. Some court-imposed fines have amounted to several million dollars. Second, some lawsuits are settled out of court, but the settlement may require the firm to make some payment to customers or employees. Third, a firm may incur substantial expenses when hiring an attorney. Many lawsuits continue for several years, and the expenses of the attorney (or a law firm) for a single case may exceed $1 million. Fourth, an indirect cost of a lawsuit is the decline in demand for a firm's product because of bad publicity associated with the lawsuit. This results in less revenue to the firm.

The high cost of customer complaints is a reason by itself for firms to be ethical and socially responsible. Yet, even when firms establish and enforce a comprehensive code of social responsibility, they do not necessarily avoid complaints and lawsuits. They must recognize this when estimating the expenses involved in ensuring social responsibility.

## COLLEGE HEALTH CLUB: SOCIAL RESPONSIBILITY DECISIONS AT COLLEGE HEALTH CLUB

As a college student, Sue Kramer always had an interest in the social responsibility of businesses. Now that she is establishing the College Health Club (CHC), she can apply her beliefs about social responsibility to her own business. Sue recognizes that being socially responsible may reduce her firm's earnings or result in higher prices to her customers because attending to many social responsibilities can increase expenses. Sue's goal is to develop strategies for satisfying CHC's social responsibilities in a manner that can still maximize the firm's value.

Sue identifies the following specific responsibilities of CHC to her customers, employees, environment, and community:

✦ **Responsibility to Customers**   Sue plans to spend some of her time talking with customers at the health club to determine whether the customers (members) are satisfied with the facilities that CHC offers. She also plans to send out a survey to all the members to obtain more feedback. Furthermore, she offers a money-back guarantee if the customers are not satisfied after a two-week trial period.

Sue's efforts are intended not only to fulfill a moral responsibility but also to increase the firm's memberships over time. In the health club business, the firm's reputation for satisfying the customer is important. Many customers choose a health club because of referrals by other customers. Therefore, Sue hopes that her efforts will identify ways in which she can make CHC more appealing to potential members. She also wants to show her interest in satisfying the existing members.

✦ **Responsibility to Employees**   Sue started the business with herself as the only full-time employee. However, she has one part-time employee (Lisa Lane) and expects to hire more employees over time as the number of memberships increases. Sue plans to pay employee wages that are consistent with those of other health clubs in the area. She also plans to have employees who are diverse in gender and race. Her goal is not just to demonstrate her willingness to seek diversity but also to attract diversity among customers as well.

✦ **Responsibility to the Environment**  Since the health club is a service, no production process is involved that could damage the environment. Sue purchases towels that are made from 100 percent chemically untreated cotton, since conventional cotton production uses pesticides and is bad for the environment.

✦ **Responsibility to the Community**  Sue feels a special allegiance to Texas College, which she has attended over the last four years. She has volunteered to offer a free seminar on health issues for the college students. She believes that this service will not only fulfill her moral responsibility but also allow her to promote her new health club located next to the college campus. Therefore, her community service could ultimately enhance the value of CHC.

✦ **Summary of CHC's Social Responsibilities**  In general, Sue is developing strategies that will not only satisfy social responsibilities but also retain existing customers and attract new customers. She has created the following pledge, which she will use as a guideline when making various business decisions:

### Pledge of Social Responsibilities at CHC

CHC intends to offer its customers excellent service at reasonable prices. It will consider feedback from customers and attempt to continually improve its services to satisfy customers. It will offer its employees a safe working environment and equal opportunities without bias. CHC recognizes its responsibility to make timely payments on debt owed to creditors.

# Summary of Learning Objectives

**1** The behavior of firms is molded by their business ethics, or set of moral values. Firms have a responsibility to produce safe products and to sell their products without misleading the customers. They ensure social responsibility toward customers by establishing a code of ethics, monitoring customer complaints, and asking customers for feedback on products that they recently purchased.

**2** Firms can fulfill their responsibility to employees by providing:
✦ safe working conditions, treatment,
✦ equal opportunity for employees, and

✦ establishing a grievance procedure that allows employees to report any complaints.

**3** Firms have a responsibility to satisfy the owners (or stockholders) who provided funds. They attempt to ensure that managers make decisions that are in the best interests of stockholders.

**4** Firms have a responsibility to meet their financial obligations to their creditors. This responsibility includes:
✦ paying their debts, and
✦ not providing creditors with misleading information about their financial condition.

**5** Firms have a responsibility to maintain a clean environment when operating their businesses. However, they incur expenses when attempting to fulfill their environmental responsibility.

**6** Firms have a social responsibility to the local communities where they attract customers and employees. They provide donations and other benefits to these communities.

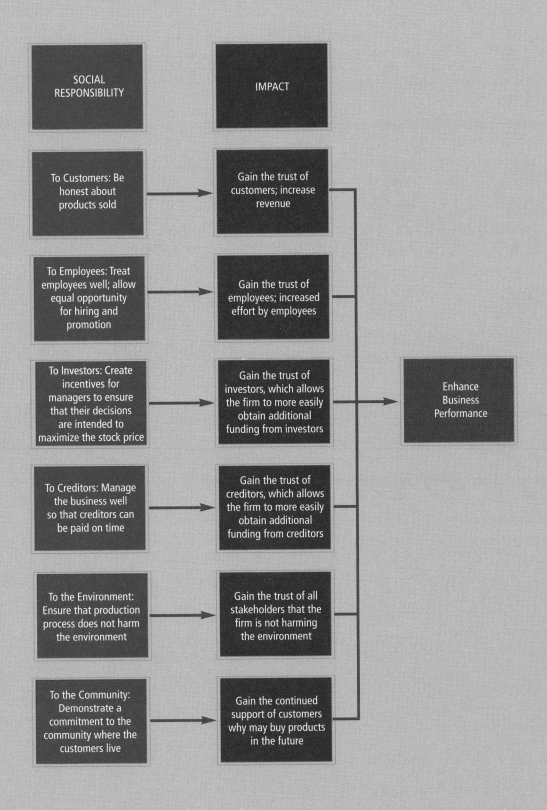

## Self-Test of Key Concepts

The following self-assessment allows you to test your understanding of the key concepts covered in this chapter. Answers are provided at the end of this exercise.

### True or False

1. The responsibility of firms toward customers can be encouraged by specific groups of consumers.

2. The government protects consumers by regulating the quality of some products that firms produce.

3. Deregulation results in lower prices for consumers.

4. The Clayton Act is intended to restrict competition.

5. U.S. firms that conduct business in foreign countries are not subject to the rules enforced by the local government.

6. In recent years, stockholders have been active in trying to influence a firm's management practices.

7. An attempt by a firm to maximize social responsibility to the community may reduce the firm's ability to provide products at a reasonable price to consumers.

8. In recent years, pollution laws have become less stringent.

9. Employees commonly sue firms for product defects or deceptive advertising.

10. Marketing managers are primarily responsible for providing accurate financial information to creditors and investors.

### Multiple Choice

11. The recognition of how a firm's business decisions can affect society is its:
    a) moral code.
    b) social responsibility.
    c) conservation policies.
    d) recycling program.
    e) consumer bill of rights.

12. A firm's _____ is measured by its stock price, which can be negatively affected by unethical business practices:
    a) value
    b) revenue
    c) bond rating
    d) risk
    e) return on equity

13. Many U.S. firms provide guidelines of behavior to employees through a code of:
    a) reciprocity.
    b) cartel arrangements.
    c) kickback arrangements.
    d) technical production manuals.
    e) responsibilities and ethics.

14. Firms can ensure responsibility to customers by:
    a) safe manufacturing techniques.
    b) proper disposal of toxic waste.
    c) employee diversity programs.
    d) soliciting feedback about products.
    e) full financial disclosure.

15. _____ represents the collective consumer demand that businesses satisfy their needs.
    a) Conservationism
    b) Consumerism
    c) Social responsibility
    d) Business ethics
    e) Recycling

16. The act that prohibits unfair methods of competition is the:
    a) Humphrey Act.
    b) Civil Rights Act of 1964.
    c) Federal Trade Commission Act.
    d) Garn Act.
    e) Reagan Antitrust Act.

17. Tying agreements, binding contracts, and interlocking directorates are prohibited by the:
    a) Clayton Act.
    b) Sherman Antitrust Act.
    c) Robinson-Patman Act.
    d) Celler-Kefauver Act.
    e) Federal Trade Commission Act.

18. The act that prohibits mergers between firms that reduce competition within an industry is the:
    a) Robinson-Patman Act.
    b) Celler-Kefauver Act.
    c) Federal Trade Commission Act.
    d) Clayton Act.
    e) Sherman Antitrust Act.

19. Which of the following represents legislation passed to prevent firms from entering into agreements to set prices and avoid competition?
    a) affirmative action laws
    b) deregulation codes
    c) antitrust laws
    d) consumerism laws
    e) Food and Drug Administration Act

20. If a firm is the sole provider of a good or service, it is a(n):
    a) unsuccessful organization.
    b) sole proprietorship.
    c) deregulated firm.
    d) institutional investor.
    e) monopoly.

21. The following industries have been deregulated, allowing more firms to enter the industry, except for:
    a) trucking.
    b) railroads.
    c) airlines.
    d) boating.
    e) telecommunications.

22. The act that prohibits price differences on promotional allowances that reduce competition within an industry is the:
    a) Celler-Kefauver Act.
    b) Robinson-Patman Act.
    c) Clayton Act.
    d) Sherman Antitrust Act.
    e) Federal Trade Commission Act.

23. The act that encourages competition and prevents monopolies is the:
    a) Deregulation Act.
    b) Federal Trade Commission Act.
    c) Robinson-Patman Act.
    d) Celler-Kefauver Act.
    e) Sherman Antitrust Act.

24. Unwelcome comments or actions of a sexual nature are examples of:
    a) business as usual.
    b) sexual harassment.
    c) equal employment opportunities.
    d) workplace diversity.
    e) deregulation.

25. Which of the following terms describes a set of activities intended to increase opportunities for minorities and women?
    a) affirmative action
    b) Americans with Disabilities Act
    c) minimum wage law
    d) antitrust action
    e) consumerism

26. The act that prohibits discrimination due to national origin, race, gender, or religion is the:
    a) Clayton Act.
    b) Sherman Antitrust Act.
    c) Federal Trade Commission Act.
    d) Civil Rights Act of 1964.
    e) Robinson-Patman Act.

27. One example of a firm's attempt to ensure the proper and equal treatment of all employees is the establishment of a:
    a) labor contract.
    b) strike.
    c) grievance procedure.
    d) walkout.
    e) lockout.

28. An active role by stockholders in influencing a firm's management policies is called:
    a) empowerment.
    b) reengineering.
    c) self-managed teams.
    d) quality circles.
    e) shareholder activism.

29. Shareholder activism is most commonly practiced by:
    a) customers.
    b) chief executive officers.
    c) institutional investors.
    d) managers.
    e) the government.

30. If a firm fails to meet its responsibilities to _____, it may be forced into bankruptcy.
    a) its employees
    b) the environment
    c) the government
    d) its creditors
    e) its owners

# Self-Test of Key Terms

affirmative action  43
business responsibilities  35
consumerism  34

institutional investors  47
monopoly  37
sexual harassment  40

shareholder activism  47
social responsibility  34

Fill in each blank with the proper key term. To assess your understanding of the key terms, answers are provided at the end of this self-test.

1. _____ represents active efforts by stockholders to influence a firm's management policies.

2. _____ represents unwelcome comments or actions of a sexual nature.

3. _____ represent financial institutions that purchase large amounts of stock.

4. A firm has a(n) _____ if it is the sole provider of a particular good or service.

5. A code of _____ sets guidelines for product quality, as well as guidelines for how employees, customers, and owners should be treated.

6. _____ programs are a set of activities intended to increase opportunities for minorities and women.

7. _____ is a firm's recognition of how its business decisions can affect society.

8. _____ represents the collective demand by consumers that businesses satisfy their needs.

**Answers:**

1. Shareholder activism
2. Sexual harassment
3. Institutional investors
4. monopoly
5. business responsibilities
6. Affirmative action
7. Social responsibility
8. Consumerism

# Concept Review Questions

1. **Responsibility to Stakeholders.** Explain how a firm's responsibility to its stakeholders can affect its performance and value.

2. **Responsibility to Customers and Employees.** Explain how businesses have a responsibility to employees.

3. **Motivating Employees.** How can firms motivate managers to maximize the value of the firm by tying employee compensation to a firm's performance? Explain why this strategy is not always effective.

4. **Satisfying Employees Versus Owners.** Consider a firm that is suffering losses and has more employees than it needs. Explain the dilemma for managers who try to satisfy the owners of the firm and also try to satisfy the employees.

5. **Responsibility to Owners.** Explain how businesses have a responsibility to their owners.

6. **Responsibility to Creditors.** Explain how businesses have a responsibility to their creditors.

7. **Responsibility to the Environment.** Explain how businesses have a responsibility to the environment.

8. **Government Laws.** How does the government attempt to ensure that firms are socially responsible to customers?

9. **Responsibility to Community.** Describe the firm's responsibility toward its community.

10. **Impact of Lawsuits.** Explain why potential lawsuits against firms should motivate firms to be socially responsible.

# Class Communication Questions

1. **Ethics of a Pricing Policy.** Many car dealerships set the price of a car at a higher level than they are willing to sell the car. Customers who do not understand the car dealership's pricing process will pay more than other customers. Is this pricing policy ethical?

2. **Ethics of a Hiring Decision.** You are a manager of a business. Is it fair for you to hire your friends instead of other applicants? Discuss.

3. **Ethics of a Loan Application.** You need funds to start your business. You will need to show a creditor your business plan when you apply for a loan. You will only receive the loan if you convince creditors that you will be able to repay the loan. Should you exaggerate your expectations of your business performance in order to ensure that you receive a loan?

# Small Business Case

## Responsibilities of a Business

Cool Jewel Company sells costume jewelry. Its sales people receive a commission based on the amount of products that they sell. The business attempts to meet social responsibilities in the following ways. It warns the sales people that they must tell customers that the jewelry is not real gold. It has established guidelines to ensure fair treatment toward employees. It provides safety training to employees who make the jewelry. It also has a policy stating that sexual harassment will not be tolerated. It relies on creditors for

funding. It plans to do some community service in order to increase its visibility. It considered giving cash awards for accomplishments by people in the community. Alternatively, it considered providing jewelry that has its name inscribed on it to these people.

1. **Responsibility to Customers.** How can honest sales practices result in higher sales over time?

2. **Responsibility to Employees.** Why might Cool Jewel's policies for employees reduce employee turnover and expenses?

3. **Responsibility to Creditors.** Cool Jewel has borrowed some funds from creditors in the past. Why would the owner fulfill the company's obligations to creditors before granting himself a bonus?

4. **Responsibility to the Community.** If Cool Jewel wants to increase its visibility, should it give cash awards for accomplishments by people in the community, or should it provide free jewelry that has its name inscribed to these people?

# Web Insight

## Social Responsibilities at Starbucks

At the opening of the chapter, Starbucks was introduced. Review its

website (www.starbucks.com) and the link to the year in review (or the link to its most recent annual report). Summarize comments made

about Starbucks' social responsibilities to its customers, employees, or environment.

## Dell's Secret for Success

Go to Dell's website (www.dell.com) and click on the link "About Dell," near the bottom of the web page. Review the section called "Values." You can also review a recent annual report of Dell for more information.

1. **Goals.** Describe Dell's goals with respect to the communities where it works.

2. **Environment.** Briefly summarize Dell's efforts to improve the environment.

3. **Code of Conduct.** Summarize Dell's corporate responsibilities to its employees and customers.

## Video Exercise

### Lessons in Business Ethics

Many free business videos are available on websites such as YouTube (www.youtube.com), and more are added every day. Search for a recent video clip about an existing business that offers lessons on "business ethics" in YouTube or any other website that provides video clips.

1. **Main Lesson.** What is the name of the business in the video clip? Is the video clip focused on the firm's responsibility to its customers, employees, stockholders, creditors, or the environment? What is the main lesson of the video clip that you watched?

2. **Improper Treatment.** Why do you think some firms do not offer proper treatment to their customers or their employees or to the environment?

3. **Benefits of Business Ethics.** A common lesson in related videos is that good business ethics pays off. Explain how firms can enhance their performance when they make the effort to treat their customers and employees well.

## Projects

To encourage further comprehension of concepts covered in Chapter 2, the following five projects are available:

1. Analyzing Your Favorite Business

2. Building a Business Plan for Campus.com

3. Running Your Own Business

4. Planning Your Career

5. Stock Market Contest

All of these projects are provided in Appendix A at the end of the text. In addition, projects are available by part division at the end of each part.

A Word file for each project is also available at the textbook website (www.emcp.net/business5e) so that you may maintain one ongoing file for each project.

# Assessing Economic Conditions

© SHUTTERSTOCK/YAKOBCHUK VASYL

## Chapter 3 Learning Objectives

**1** Explain how economic growth affects business performance.

**2** Explain how inflation affects business performance.

**3** Explain how interest rates affect business performance.

**4** Explain how market prices are determined.

**5** Explain how the government influences economic conditions.

### Harley-Davidson's Assessment of Economic Conditions

Economic conditions reflect the level of production and consumption for a particular country, area, or industry. Macroeconomic conditions reflect the overall U.S. economy; microeconomic conditions are more focused on the business or industry of concern. This chapter focuses on U.S. macroeconomic conditions, and the following chapter focuses on how global conditions affect business decisions made by a firm.

Economic conditions can affect the revenue or expenses of a business and therefore can affect the value of that business. Consider the case of Harley-Davidson, which produces motorcycles. The performance of Harley-Davidson is influenced by the economic conditions. When the economy is strong, the income level of consumers is relatively high, and the demand for Harleys should be high. Conversely, a weak economy can cause income levels to be lower, which results in lower consumer spending. High inflation can affect the performance because it may result in higher expenses from producing Harleys. Interest rates can also affect the demand for Harleys, because consumers may be more willing to borrow funds and buy Harleys if interest rates are lower. Given its exposure to economic conditions, Harley-Davidson commonly attempts to address the following questions:

✦ How much will the economy grow this year, and how will that growth affect the demand for Harleys?
✦ How much inflation will there be this year, and how will that inflation affect its expenses?
✦ How will interest rates change this year, and will that affect the demand for Harleys?
✦ How will U.S. government policies affect economic conditions this year, and how will those policies affect the demand for Harleys?

The forecasts of economic conditions are conducted by most businesses, along with an assessment of how the expected change in economic conditions will affect the firm's demand (and therefore revenue), expenses, and performance. This chapter explains how Harley-Davidson or any other firm can assess the economic environment to determine how its performance and value may be affected.

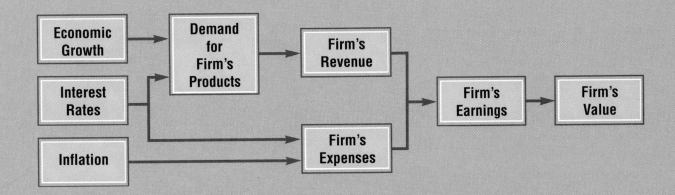

# 1. Impact of Economic Growth on Business Performance

**Economic growth** represents the change in the general level of economic activity. Sometimes economic growth is strong, and other times it is relatively weak.

## 1.1 Strong Economic Growth

**economic growth**
the change in the general level of economic activity

When U.S. economic growth is stronger than normal, the total income level of all U.S. workers is relatively high, so there is a higher volume of spending on products and services. Since the demand for products and services is high, firms that sell products and services should generate higher revenue.

**How the Impact of a Strong Economy Spreads Across Firms**   The impact of a stronger economy can spread quickly across all businesses. Once consumers begin to increase their spending, firms experience a stronger demand for their products and may begin to hire more employees to accommodate that increased demand. They may also need to expand their operations, which results in increased demand for supplies, construction services, and materials. Then, the construction firms may have to hire more workers to accommodate the increased demand for construction. As more jobs are created, the general income level of consumers rises, allowing them to spend more money. In addition, investors who invested in businesses tend to earn a higher return on their investment when the economy is strong, and they may spend much or all of that return on products and services. Thus, the extra income causes a favorable ripple effect throughout the economy.

## 1.2 Weak Economic Growth

Whereas strong economic growth enhances a firm's revenue, slow economic growth results in low demand for products and services, which can reduce a firm's revenue. Even firms that provide basic products or services

When economic growth increases, consumer demand for products increases. Businesses increase their production to accommodate the stronger demand, and commonly need to hire more people for this purpose. Consequently, the income levels of some consumers increase, which helps to stimulate the economy and create more jobs.

are adversely affected by a weak economy because customers tend to reduce their demand. For example, the demand for coffee at Starbucks is affected by general economic conditions. Since specialty coffee is not really a necessity, demand for it is stronger when consumers are earning a relatively high income and can afford it. The demand for soft drinks and bottled water is also affected, as some people rely more on tap water under weak economic conditions. The potential impact of slower economic growth is reflected in the following statements:

> *"Our caution stems largely from the macroeconomic environment, in which some forecasts are for slower growth."*
>
> —Hewlett-Packard

> *"[The company] expects to experience significant fluctuations in future [performance] due to . . . general economic conditions."*
>
> —Amazon.com

**recession**
two consecutive quarters of negative economic growth

When economic growth is negative for two consecutive quarters, the period is referred to as a **recession**.

When the U.S. economy is weak, some U.S. workers are laid off by firms and therefore have less money that they can use to buy products or services. Other U.S. workers fear that they may be laid off and try to save more of their income in case they lose their jobs in the future. They only spend money on necessities. Thus, the demand for many products and services is reduced. This results in reduced revenue (and profits) for many firms. Since the firms are not able to sell all the products or services they can produce, they may attempt to reduce their expenses by laying off even more workers. Because a recession causes a reduction in income and demand, it has a major adverse impact on the performance of firms.

**Example**  In the 2007–2008 period, the economy weakened substantially. The aggregate demand for products and services by consumers declined, which resulted in a decrease in the revenue received by firms. Job opportunities were limited, and some firms laid off employees because of the low level of spending by consumers. Many consumers were concerned that they might lose their jobs, and they reduced their spending because of concerns about their future income. In general, there is a high correlation between the income earned by consumers and the income earned by businesses. When the income received by consumers is stagnant or declines, this results in less spending by consumers, which reduces the revenue and income (earnings) generated by businesses.

**How the Impact of a Weak Economy Spreads Across Firms**  The impact of weak economic conditions can spread quickly across all businesses. For example, the demand for new cars sold by automakers such as Ford Motor Company and General Motors declines, leaving them with more cars produced than they can sell. They may respond by closing production plants and laying off workers. Those workers have less income, so they reduce their demand for various products. Then, the firms that produce those products experience a decline in sales because of the reduced demand. Because they cannot sell all the products that they produce, they may need to reduce production and lay off workers. So the effect ripples through the economy. In addition, when the automakers reduce their production, their need for materials such as steel declines. Thus, the firms that produce steel may experience a decline in demand and may need to lay off workers.

Even when firms are not laying off workers, they tend to cut back on any plans for expansion during a weak economy. Thus, their demand for construction services and materials declines. Even if people are not laid off, they recognize that the economy is weak and are less willing to spend money because they could be laid off in the future. This also results in a reduction in the demand for products.

When conditions are weak, some businesses are affected more than others. Nevertheless, most businesses are adversely affected by economic conditions because the demand for products in almost all industries declines.

## 1.3   Indicators of Economic Growth

Three common measures of economic growth are the level of total production of products and services in the economy, the total amount of expenditures (also called **aggregate expenditures**), and the unemployment level.

**aggregate expenditures**
the total amount of expenditures in the economy

**Aggregate Expenditures**   The aggregate expenditures represent the total amount of spending by consumers. The greater the degree of spending, the greater is the level of revenue earned by businesses. When spending is high, businesses tend to employ more people.

**gross domestic product (GDP)**
the total market value of all final products and services produced in the United States

**Total Production Level**   The total production level is dependent on the total demand for products and services. Businesses can monitor the U.S. total production level by keeping track of the **gross domestic product (GDP)**, which is the total market value of all final products and services produced in the United States. The GDP is reported quarterly in the United States. In general, the annual GDP has risen gradually over time, as shown in Exhibit 3.1. The bars within the graph show recessions, reflecting a decline in GDP. Improved technology is one reason for the increase in GDP over time. However, another reason is that prices of products rise over time due to inflation, so the value of products produced rises as prices increase. The portion of the rise in GDP over time that is due to higher prices does not really reflect an increase in productivity. If the annual GDP increased 5 percent over a year, but prices of products and services increased by 4 percent in that year, the actual increase in productivity is 1 percent. Some

---

**Exhibit 3.1**   Trend of Gross Domestic Product (GDP)

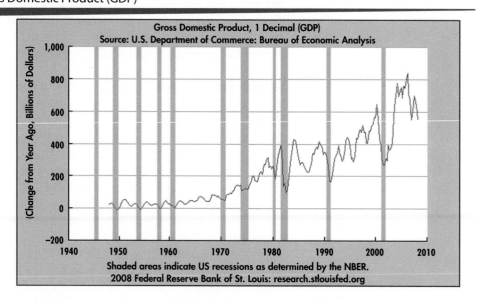

Gross Domestic Product, 1 Decimal (GDP)
Source: U.S. Department of Commerce: Bureau of Economic Analysis

Shaded areas indicate US recessions as determined by the NBER.
2008 Federal Reserve Bank of St. Louis: research.stlouisfed.org

people monitor the inflation-adjusted GDP as explained here so that they can monitor the increase in productivity.

Businesses may monitor various unemployment indicators because they can indicate whether economic conditions are improving. The four different types of unemployment are as follows:

**frictional unemployment**
people who are between jobs

✦ **Frictional unemployment** (also referred to as *natural unemployment*) represents people who are between jobs. That is, their unemployment status is temporary, as they are likely to find employment soon. For example, a person with marketable job skills might quit her job before finding a new one because she believes she will find a new job before long.

**seasonal unemployment**
people whose services are not needed during some seasons

✦ **Seasonal unemployment** represents people whose services are not needed during some seasons. For example, ski instructors may be unemployed in the summer.

**cyclical unemployment**
people who are unemployed because of poor economic conditions

✦ **Cyclical unemployment** represents people who are unemployed because of poor economic conditions. When the level of economic activity declines, the demand for products and services declines, which reduces the need for workers. For example, a firm may lay off factory workers if the demand for its product declines.

**structural unemployment**
people who are unemployed because they do not have adequate skills

✦ **Structural unemployment** represents people who are unemployed because they do not have adequate skills. For example, people who have limited education may be structurally unemployed.

Of the four types of unemployment, the cyclical unemployment level is probably the best indicator of economic conditions. When economic growth improves, businesses hire more people and the unemployment rate declines. Unfortunately, determining how much of the unemployment level is cyclical can be difficult. Some people assume that when the unemployment rate changes, the change is primarily due to economic cycles. A lower unemployment rate may be interpreted as an indicator of increased economic growth. Conversely, a higher unemployment rate is commonly interpreted as a sign of reduced economic growth.

Many other indicators of economic growth, such as the industrial production index, new housing starts, and the personal income level, are compiled by divisions of the federal government and reported in business magazines and newspapers.

**Variation in the Sensitivity to Economic Growth**   Some firms are more sensitive than others to economic conditions because the demand for their product is more sensitive to such conditions. For example, the demand for the product (food) provided by McDonald's is not very sensitive to economic conditions because people still purchase McDonald's food even when the economy is weak. In contrast, the demand for new automobiles is more sensitive to economic conditions. When the economy is weak, the demand for new automobiles declines. Therefore, the performance of car manufacturers is very sensitive to economic conditions.

**Learning Objective**
Explain how inflation affects business performance.

**2**

# 2. Impact of Inflation

**Inflation** is the increase in the general level of prices of products and services over a specified period of time. The inflation rate can be estimated by measuring the percentage change in the consumer price index, which indicates the prices on a wide variety of consumer products such as grocery

**inflation**
the increase in the general level of prices of products and services over a specified period of time

products, housing, gasoline, medical services, and electricity. The annual U.S. inflation rate is shown in Exhibit 3.2. The inflation rate was generally higher in the 1970s than it has been in more recent years, which was partially attributed to an abrupt increase in oil prices then.

Inflation can affect a firm's operating expenses from producing products by increasing the cost of supplies and materials. Wages can also be affected by inflation. A higher level of inflation will cause a larger increase in a firm's operating expenses. A firm's revenue may also be high during periods of high inflation because many firms charge higher prices to compensate for their higher expenses.

## 2.1 Types of Inflation

Inflation is commonly categorized as either "cost-push" or "demand-pull," as explained next. Inflation may result from a particular event that increases the costs of production. When the price of aluminum rises, for example, firms such as PepsiCo and Coca-Cola incur higher costs and may increase the prices of their soft drinks. If the cost of steel increases, firms such as General Motors and Ford Motor Company that use steel to produce vehicles may increase the prices of their vehicles. When firms charge higher prices due to higher costs, **cost-push inflation** occurs. To illustrate the potential impact of cost-push inflation, consider how all the manufacturers of products must deliver their products to stores across the country. The transportation cost includes the price of gasoline. When oil prices increase, the cost of producing gasoline increases as well. Suppliers of gasoline tend to pass the high cost on by raising their gasoline prices. Consequently, the manufacturers of products incur higher costs for transporting their products. If they do not increase the prices of their products to reflect the higher costs, their profits will decline.

**cost-push inflation**
the situation when higher prices charged by firms are caused by higher costs

Sometimes firms increase the prices of their products to reflect their higher costs. In this case, the consumers pay higher prices for products because of the higher price of oil. Also, consider that the higher gasoline prices increase airlines' cost of providing travel services. If airlines increase airfares to reflect the higher costs, all the businesses that rely on air travel incur higher costs. In addition, consumers using airlines will be forced to pay higher prices.

**Exhibit 3.2** U.S. Inflation Rates over Time

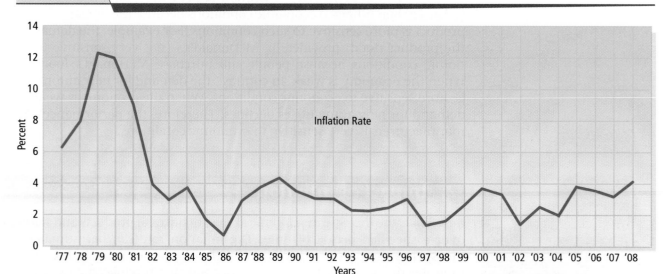

The business expense of transporting products increases when gasoline prices rise. Businesses commonly pass the increased transportation expenses on to consumers.

© SHUTTERSTOCK/HEATHER A. CRAIG

When consumers pay higher prices for products as a result of inflation, they have less money available to buy other products. They struggle to stay within their spending budget and may need to borrow money. Alternatively, they may be forced to reduce their spending on other products, which causes the demand for those products to decline. Consequently, firms will experience a lower level of revenue.

Inflation can also be caused by strong consumer demand. Consider a situation in which consumers increase their demand for most products and services. Some firms may respond by increasing their prices. When prices of products and services are pulled up because of strong consumer demand, **demand-pull inflation** occurs. In periods of strong economic growth, strong consumer demand can cause shortages in the production of some products. Firms that anticipate shortages may raise prices because they are confident they can sell the products anyway.

Strong economic growth may place pressure on wages as well as prices. Strong economic growth may mean fewer unemployed people, so workers may negotiate for higher wages. Firms may be more willing to pay higher wages to retain their workers when no other qualified workers are available. As firms pay higher wages, production costs rise, and firms may attempt to increase their prices to recover the higher expenses.

**demand-pull inflation**

the situation when prices of products and services are pulled up because of strong consumer demand

**Impact of Inflation Across Products**    Products and services commonly experience much different rates of inflation. For example, in 2008, when oil prices increased, the inflation was especially high for products and services whose costs of production required the use of oil. Airlines increased the fares on flights to account for their higher cost of fuel. Taxi cab and limousine services increased their rates to account for higher gas prices. Moving companies that transport household products when people move to different homes increased their rates to account for higher gas prices. The prices of some products sold by retail stores were increased because the cost of delivery from the manufacturer to the retail store increased as a result of higher gas prices. The prices of some other products and services are less exposed to high oil prices. For example, services provided by a dentist or hairstylist are not directly affected when oil prices increase.

Some firms are much more exposed to inflation than others because of the types of expenses they incur in their production process. For example, delivery service firms such as FedEx and UPS are very exposed to the cost of oil because they need to purchase so much gasoline for their delivery trucks every day. Travel agencies are also very exposed because people may travel less when the cost of driving or flying is high due to high gasoline prices. Conversely, service firms (such as a dental or doctor's office) may not be affected by the increased cost of oil.

**Learning Objective**

**3**

Explain how interest rates affect business performance.

# 3. Impact of Interest Rates

Interest rates determine the cost of borrowing money. They can affect a firm's performance by having an impact on its expenses or on its revenue, as explained next.

## 3.1 Impact on a Firm's Expenses

Firms closely monitor interest rates because they determine the amount of expense a business will incur if it borrows money. If a business borrows $100,000 for one year at an interest rate of 8 percent, the interest expense is $8,000 (computed as .08 × $100,000). At an interest rate of 15 percent, however, the interest expense would be $15,000 (computed as .15 × $100,000). Imagine how the interest rate level can affect some large firms that have borrowed more than $1 billion. An interest rate increase of just 1 percent on $1 billion of borrowed funds results in an extra annual interest expense of $10 million.

Changes in market interest rates can influence a firm's interest expense because the loan rates that commercial banks and other creditors charge on loans to firms are based on market interest rates. Even when a firm obtains a loan from a commercial bank over several years, the loan rate is typically adjusted periodically (every six months or year) based on the prevailing market interest rate at that time.

Exhibit 3.3 illustrates the annual interest expense for a reputable U.S. firm that borrows $1 million from a bank each year and earns $100,000 in annual profits before paying its interest expense. The interest expenses are adjusted each year according to the market interest rates prevailing in the United States during that year. As this exhibit shows, interest rates can significantly influence a firm's profit. Firms incurred much higher interest expenses in the early 1980s because interest rates were so high then.

In 2007, an excessive number of homes were built. But when the standards to qualify for a mortgage were increased in 2008, the supply of new homes far exceeded the demand. Consequently, home prices dropped abruptly, and many homes under construction (like those shown here) were abandoned because home builders could not sell them.

© SHUTTERSTOCK/RACHEAL GRAZIAS

## 3.2  Impact on a Firm's Expansion

Since interest rates affect the cost of financing, some possible projects considered by the firm that would be feasible during periods of low interest rates may not be feasible during periods of high interest rates. That is, the project may not generate an adequate return to cover financing costs. Consequently, firms tend to reduce their degree of expansion when interest rates are high.

## 3.3  Impact on a Firm's Revenue

Some products that are sold by firms are commonly purchased with credit. When consumers buy new cars, they may make just a small down

| **Exhibit 3.3** | Effect of Interest Rates on Interest Expenses and Profits |
| --- | --- |

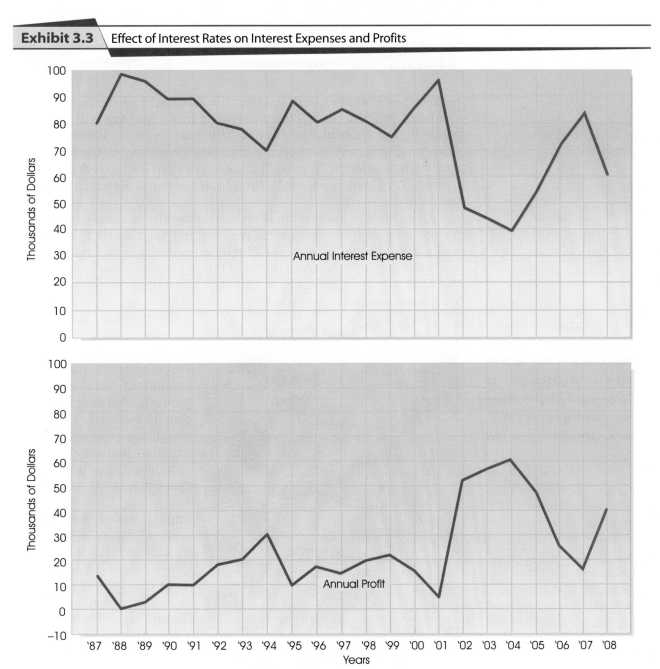

Note: Assume that the firm earns $100,000 in annual profits before paying its interest expense.

Out of
Business

payment and obtain a loan to cover the remainder of the purchase price. If interest rates increase, consumers who buy a new car will be forced to make higher monthly payments. This may prevent some consumers from buying a new car because they are unwilling or unable to make such high payments. Thus, high interest rates can lead to reduced demand for new cars, which results in lower sales at car dealerships and for the car manufacturers.

An increase in interest rates can also reduce the demand for new homes for the same reason. Consumers typically rely on a small down payment and a loan to cover most of the purchase price of a home. If interest rates are high when they consider buying a home, they may not be able to afford the high monthly payments on the loan. Therefore, the demand for new homes typically declines, and firms that build homes experience a decline in business. Firms such as Caterpillar and Weyerhaeuser that produce equipment and construction products also experience a decline in business. This explains why firms involved in the construction industry are highly influenced by interest rate movements.

**Impact Varies Among Firms**
Some firms are more sensitive to changes in interest rates than others. For example, firms that sell products or services that are paid for with cash should not experience major shifts in the demand for their products when interest rates change.

When interest rates are high, financing a new car (like those shown here) is expensive because of high monthly interest charged on the loan. Consequently, higher interest rates can reduce the consumer demand for new cars.

© SHUTTERSTOCK/MONKEY BUSINESS IMAGES

# Global Business

## Capitalizing on Global Economic Conditions

The demand for a firm's products is dependent on the economic growth where the products are sold. Given the mature economy of the United States, its potential for economic growth is limited. Less-developed countries, however, have much greater potential for economic growth because they have not yet taken full advantage of existing technology. Furthermore, the governments of many less-developed countries are trying to accelerate their economic growth by encouraging more business development by entrepreneurs. Many of these governments have also allowed U.S. firms to enter their markets. These U.S. firms are attempting to capitalize on the changing economic and political conditions in less-developed countries by selling their products there.

The Coca-Cola Company is among many U.S. firms that have targeted countries with high potential for economic growth. Its sales have increased substantially in Brazil, Chile, Eastern Europe, North Africa, and China. The Coca-Cola Company's increased sales in these countries can be attributed in part to economic growth, which increases the amount of consumer spending. It can also be attributed to reductions in government restrictions imposed on U.S. firms that desire to conduct business in these countries.

Other U.S. firms are planning major expansion in less-developed countries to capitalize on the changes in economic and political conditions. General Motors plans to expand in various Asian markets, including China, India, and Indonesia, where the potential for economic growth is strong.

U.S. firms that attempt to capitalize on economic growth in foreign countries can be adversely affected if these countries experience a recession. If a U.S. firm diversifies its business among several different countries, however, a recession in any single foreign country should not have a major effect on the firm's worldwide sales.

## 3.4  How Rising Interest Rates Affected the Housing Crisis

In the 2003–2004 period, interest rates were very low, which allowed home buyers to finance the purchases of homes at a low interest rate. Some mortgage lenders had more funds to lend than the amount of funds needed by qualified home buyers. So the lenders loosened their guidelines in order to attract additional customers who wanted to buy homes. With the looser guidelines, more people were able to obtain mortgage loans to buy homes. Consequently, there was a strong demand for homes, and by 2005 the prices of homes increased substantially.

Many mortgages had variable interest rates that were adjusted periodically in line with existing market interest rates. As market interest rates increased in the 2004–2007 period, so did mortgage rates, which made it more difficult for homeowners to make their mortgage payments. Consequently, many homeowners attempted to sell their homes, which resulted in many more homes for sale than potential buyers of homes and a substantial decline in home prices. Thus, many homeowners sold homes in the 2007–2008 period at prices that were about 30 percent less than what they paid for the homes in the 2004–2005 period. Many homeowners defaulted on their mortgages because the proceeds from selling the home were not sufficient to repay the mortgage loans.

**Impact on the Economy**   The housing crisis weakened the economy. Because of the excess supply of existing homes that were for sale, there was no need for new homes to be built. Many home builders stopped building new homes, laid off some of their employees, and stopped hiring various firms to do other work (electrical, plumbing, etc.). Firms that sold new home products experienced major declines in sales. Mortgage companies laid off employees since the demand for new mortgages declined substantially. All of these effects resulted in less income for some people, which resulted in a lower amount of spending throughout the economy.

---

## 4.  How Market Prices Are Determined

**Learning Objective**
Explain how market prices are determined.

**4**

The performance of firms is affected by changes in the prices they charge for products (which influence their revenue) and the prices they pay for supplies and materials (which influence their operating expenses). The prices of products and supplies are influenced by demand and supply conditions.

The following framework uses demand and supply conditions to explain how prices of products change over time. The market price of a product is influenced by the total demand for that product by all customers. It is also affected by the supply of that product produced by firms. The interaction between demand and supply determines the price, as explained in detail next.

### 4.1  Demand Schedule for a Product

**demand schedule**
a schedule that indicates the quantity of a product that would be demanded at each possible price

The demand for a product can be shown with a **demand schedule**, or a schedule that indicates the quantity of the product that would be demanded at each possible price. Consider personal computers as an example. Assume that the demand schedule for a particular type of personal computer is as shown in the first and second columns in Exhibit 3.4 for a given point in time. If the price is relatively high, the quantity demanded by consumers is relatively low. For example, if the price is $3,000, only 8,000 of these computers will be demanded (purchased) by consumers. At the other extreme, if the price is $1,000, a total of 25,000 of these computers will be demanded by customers. The quantity of personal computers demanded is higher when the price is lower.

**Graphic Example**   The graph in Exhibit 3.4, which is based on the table, shows the relationship between the price of a computer and the quantity of computers demanded by consumers. The demand curve (labeled $D_1$) shows that as the price decreases, the quantity demanded increases.

### 4.2  Supply Schedule for a Product

**supply schedule**
a schedule that indicates the quantity of a product that would be supplied (produced) by firms at each possible price

The supply of a product can be shown with a **supply schedule**, or a schedule that indicates the quantity of the product that would be supplied (produced) by firms at each possible price. Assume that the supply schedule for the type of personal computer already discussed is as shown in the first and third columns of Exhibit 3.4 for a given point in time. When the price at which the personal computer can be sold is relatively high, firms will produce a large supply of this computer. For example, if the price is $3,000, 30,000 of these computers will be produced. Firms are willing to produce

| | If the Price of a Particular Computer Is: | The Quantity of These Computers Demanded by Consumers Will Be: | The Quantity of These Computers Supplied (Produced) by Firms Will Be: |
|---|---|---|---|
| | $3,000 | 8,000 | 30,000 |
| | 2,500 | 14,000 | 24,000 |
| | 2,000 | 18,000 | 18,000 |
| | 1,500 | 22,000 | 16,000 |
| | 1,000 | 25,000 | 10,000 |

**Exhibit 3.4**

How the Equilibrium Price Is Determined by Demand and Supply

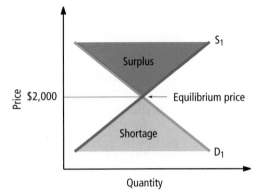

the computers at this price because they will earn a high profit if they can sell the computers at such a high price.

At the other extreme, if the price of computers is only $1,000, only 10,000 of these computers will be produced. The quantity supplied is much smaller at a low price because some firms will be unwilling to produce the computers if they can sell them for only $1,000. If some firms' actual cost of producing the computers is above this price of $1,000, these firms will be unwilling to produce the computers.

**Graphic Example**    The graph accompanying Exhibit 3.4, which is based on the table, shows the relationship between the price of a computer and the quantity of computers supplied (produced) by firms. The supply curve (labeled $S_1$) shows that as price increases, the quantity of computers supplied increases.

## 4.3  Interaction of Demand and Supply

The interaction of the demand schedule and supply schedule determines the price.

**Surplus**    Notice from Exhibit 3.4 that at relatively high prices of computers (such as $3,000), the quantity supplied by firms exceeds the quantity demanded by customers, resulting in a so-called **surplus** of computers. For example, at the price of $3,000 the quantity supplied is 30,000 units and the quantity demanded is 8,000 units, resulting in a surplus of 22,000 units. This surplus occurs because consumers are unwilling to purchase computers when the price is excessive.

**surplus**
the situation when the quantity supplied by firms exceeds the quantity demanded by customers

**shortage**
the situation when the quantity supplied by firms is less than the quantity demanded by customers

**equilibrium price**
the price at which the quantity of a product supplied by firms equals the quantity of the product demanded by customers

**Shortage**    When the price of a computer is relatively low, the quantity supplied by firms will be less than the quantity demanded by customers, resulting in a so-called **shortage** of computers. For example, at a price of $1,000, the quantity demanded by customers is 25,000 units, while the quantity supplied by firms is only 10,000 units, causing a shortage of 15,000 units.

**Equilibrium**    Notice from Exhibit 3.4 that at a price of $2,000, the quantity of computers supplied by firms is 18,000 units, and the quantity demanded by customers is also 18,000 units. At this price, there is no surplus and no shortage. The price at which the quantity of a product supplied by firms equals the quantity of the product demanded by customers is called the **equilibrium price**. This is the price at which firms normally attempt to sell their products.

At any price above the equilibrium price, the firms will be unable to sell all the computers they produce, resulting in a surplus. Therefore, they would need to reduce their prices to eliminate the surplus. At any price below the equilibrium price, the firms will not produce a sufficient quantity of computers to satisfy all the customers willing to pay that price (resulting in a shortage). The firms could raise their price to correct the shortage.

The demand and supply concepts just applied to a particular type of computer can also be applied to every product or service that firms produce. Each product or service has its own demand schedule and supply schedule, which will determine its own equilibrium price.

## 4.4  Effect of a Change in the Demand Schedule

As time passes, changing conditions can cause a demand schedule or a supply schedule for a specific product to change. Consequently, the equilibrium price of that product will also change.

**Graphic Example**    Reconsider the previous example and assume that computers become more desirable to potential consumers. Assume that the demand schedule for the computer changes as shown at the top of Exhibit 3.5. At any given price, the quantity demanded is now 10,000 units higher

The price charged for concert tickets is dependent on the demand. For a very popular band like the one shown here, the demand for tickets is high and will likely exceed the supply of tickets available, which results in a high ticket price.

**Exhibit 3.5**

How the Equilibrium Price
Is Affected by a Change
in Demand

| If the Price of a Particular Computer Is: | The Quantity of These Computers Demanded by Consumers Was: | But the Quantity of These Computers Demanded by Consumers Will Now Be: |
|---|---|---|
| $3,000 | 8,000 | 18,000 |
| 2,500 | 14,000 | 24,000 |
| 2,000 | 18,000 | 28,000 |
| 1,500 | 22,000 | 32,000 |
| 1,000 | 25,000 | 35,000 |

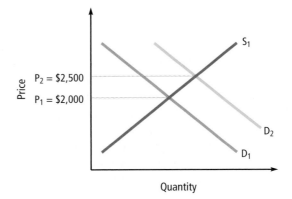

than it was before the computer became more popular. The graph accompanying Exhibit 3.5 shows how the demand curve shifts outward from $D_1$ to $D_2$.

**Impact on Price**   Now consider the effect of this change in the demand schedule on the equilibrium price of computers. Assuming that the supply schedule remains unchanged, the effect of the change in the demand schedule on the equilibrium price is shown in Exhibit 3.5. At the original equilibrium price of $2,000, the quantity of computers demanded is now 28,000, while the quantity of computers supplied is still 18,000. A shortage of computers occurs at that price. At a price of $2,500, however, the quantity of computers supplied by firms equals the quantity of computers demanded by customers. Therefore, the new equilibrium price is $2,500. The graph at the bottom of Exhibit 3.5 confirms that the shift in the demand schedule from $D_1$ to $D_2$ causes the new equilibrium price of computers to be $2,500.

The graph illustrating the effect of a shift in the demand schedule on the equilibrium price of a product can be supplemented with simple logic. When a product becomes more popular, consumers' demand for that product increases, resulting in a shortage. Under these conditions, firms recognize that they can sell whatever amount they produce at a higher price. Once the price is raised to the level at which the quantity supplied is equal to the quantity demanded, the shortage is corrected.

## 4.5   Effect of a Change in the Supply Schedule

Just as the demand for a product may change, so may the supply. A change in the supply can also affect the equilibrium price of the product.

The price of flat screen LCD televisions (like the one shown here) declined substantially over time as producers learned how to produce them more efficiently, and the supply of televisions produced exceeded the demand.

© SHUTTERSTOCK/STUDIO ARAMINTA

**Graphic Example**    Reconsider the original example in which the equilibrium price of computers was $2,000. Now assume that improved technology allows firms to produce the computer at a lower cost. In this case, firms will be willing to produce a larger supply of computers at any given price, which reflects a change in the supply schedule.

Assume that as a result of the improved technology (lower production costs), the supply schedule changes as shown in Exhibit 3.6. At any given price, the quantity supplied is now 6,000 units higher than it was before the improved technology. The graph accompanying Exhibit 3.6 shows how the supply schedule shifts outward from $S_1$ to $S_2$.

**Impact on Price**    Now consider the effect of this change in the supply schedule on the equilibrium price of computers. Assuming that the demand schedule remains unchanged, the effect of the change in the supply schedule on the equilibrium price is shown in Exhibit 3.6. At the original

**Exhibit 3.6**

How the Equilibrium Price Is Affected by a Change in Supply

| If the Price of a Particular Computer Is: | The Quantity of These Computers Supplied by Firms Was: | But the Quantity of These Computers Supplied by Firms Will Now Be: |
|---|---|---|
| $3,000 | 30,000 | 36,000 |
| 2,500 | 24,000 | 30,000 |
| 2,000 | 18,000 | 24,000 |
| 1,500 | 16,000 | 22,000 |
| 1,000 | 10,000 | 16,000 |

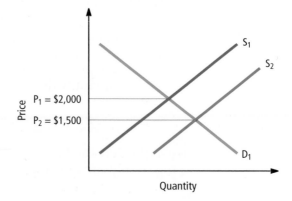

equilibrium price of $2,000, the quantity of computers demanded is 18,000, while the quantity of computers supplied (produced) is now 24,000. A surplus of computers occurs at that price. At a price of $1,500, however, the quantity of computers supplied by firms equals the quantity of computers demanded by consumers. Therefore, the new equilibrium price is $1,500. The graph at the bottom of Exhibit 3.6 confirms that the shift in the supply schedule from $S_1$ to $S_2$ causes the new equilibrium price of computers to be $1,500.

The graph illustrating the effect of a shift in the supply schedule on the equilibrium price of a product can be supplemented with simple logic. When improved technology allows firms to produce a product at a lower cost, more firms will be willing to produce the product. This results in a larger supply produced, which causes a surplus. Firms recognize that the only way they will be able to sell all that is supplied (produced) is to lower the price of the product. Once the price is lowered to the level at which the quantity supplied is once again equal to the quantity demanded, the surplus is eliminated.

## 4.6 Effect of Demand and Supply on the General Price Level

So far the discussion of demand and supply has focused on one product to show how the equilibrium price of that product might change. Now consider how the general price level for all products might change. The general price level is an average of prices of all existing products and services. If the total (aggregate) demand by consumers for all or most products suddenly increases (perhaps because of an increase in the income level of most consumers), the general level of prices could rise. The general price level may also be affected by shifts in the supply schedules for all goods and services. If the supply schedule of all or most products suddenly decreases (perhaps because of increasing expenses when producing the products), the general level of prices should rise.

## 4.7 How Consumer Income Affects Market Prices

Consumer income determines the amount of products and services that individuals can purchase. A high level of economic growth results in more income for consumers. When consumers' income rises, they may demand a larger quantity of specific products and services. That is, the demand schedules for various products and services may shift out in response to higher income, which could result in higher prices.

Conversely, when consumers' income level declines, they may demand a smaller quantity of specific products. For example, in 2008, weak economic conditions resulted in a lower demand for new homes, causing a surplus of new homes. The firms that were building new homes were forced to lower their prices because of the surplus.

## 4.8 Consumer Preferences

As consumer preferences (or tastes) for a particular product change, the quantity of that product demanded by consumers may change. There are numerous examples of products whose prices rose in response to increased demand. For example, the price of a scalped ticket at a sold-out event such as a concert, the World Series, or the Super Bowl may easily exceed $500.

When a product becomes less popular, the demand for the product declines. The resulting surplus may force firms to lower their prices to sell what they produce. For example, when specific clothes become unpopular, clothing manufacturers sell these clothes at discounted prices just to eliminate the surplus.

## 4.9 Production Expenses

Another factor that can affect equilibrium prices is a change in production expenses. When firms experience lower expenses, they are willing to supply (produce) more at any given price (as explained earlier). This results in a surplus of the product, forcing firms to lower their price to sell all that they have produced. Improved technology allows firms to produce products at a lower cost, and firms may be more willing to supply products at a given price.

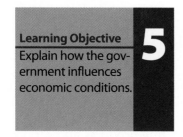

**Learning Objective**
Explain how the government influences economic conditions.

**money supply**
demand deposits (checking accounts), currency held by the public, and traveler's checks

**Federal Reserve System**
the central bank of the United States

**monetary policy**
decisions on the money supply level in the United States

## 5. Government Influence on Economic Conditions

The federal government can influence the performance of businesses by imposing regulations, such as the environmental regulations discussed in the preceding chapter, or by enacting policies that affect economic conditions. To influence economic conditions, the federal government implements monetary and fiscal policies, which are discussed next.

## 5.1 Monetary Policy

In the United States, the term **money supply** normally refers to demand deposits (checking accounts), currency held by the public, and traveler's checks. This is a narrow definition, as there are broader measures of the money supply that count other types of deposits as well. Regardless of the precise definition, any measure of money represents funds that financial institutions can lend to borrowers.

The U.S. money supply is controlled by the **Federal Reserve System** ("the Fed"), which is the central bank of the United States. The Fed sets the **monetary policy**, which represents decisions on the money supply level in the United States. The Fed can easily adjust the U.S. money supply by billions of dollars in a single day. Because the Fed's monetary policy affects the money supply level, it affects interest rates. When the Fed affects interest rates with its monetary policy, it directly affects a firm's interest expenses. Second, it can affect the demand for the firm's products if those products are commonly purchased with borrowed funds.

**A Typical FOMC Meeting** The Fed's monetary policy is decided by the Federal Open Market Committee (FOMC), which has 12 voting members. This committee meets about every six weeks to determine whether interest rates should be adjusted. Each FOMC meeting begins with an assessment of several measures of aggregate production levels, inventory levels, and price levels in the United States. The objective of this assessment is to predict U.S. economic growth and inflation, assuming that the Fed does not adjust its monetary policy. The minutes of the meetings show that the committee members carefully consider any economic indicators that can be used to anticipate future economic growth or inflation. For example, a

The Federal Reserve (shown here) is located in Washington, D.C. It is at this building where the members of the Federal Open Market Committee periodically meet to make monetary policy decisions.

© SHUTTERSTOCK/JONATHAN LARSEN

recent reduction in business inventories may suggest that economic growth is increasing and that firms will need to boost production to replenish their inventories. Conversely, an increase in inventories may indicate that firms will have to lower production and possibly reduce their workforces.

The committee also pays close attention to any factors that can affect inflation. Oil prices are closely monitored because they affect the cost of producing and transporting many products. A reduction in business inventories when production is near full capacity may indicate an excessive demand for products that will pull prices up. The Fed becomes concerned when several indicators suggest that higher inflation is likely.

**How the Fed Can Reduce Interest Rates**   The Fed maintains some funds outside the banking system, which are not loanable funds. These funds are not available to firms or individuals who need to borrow. The Fed can use these funds to purchase Treasury securities held by individuals and firms. These purchases provide individuals and firms with new funds, which they deposit in their commercial banks. Consequently, the money supply increases because the commercial banks and other financial institutions can loan out these funds. In other words, the Fed's action increases the supply of loanable funds. Assuming that the demand for loanable funds remains unchanged, the increase in the supply of loanable funds should cause interest rates to decrease. The impact of the supply of loanable funds on interest rates is discussed in more detail in the Chapter 16 appendix. By reducing interest rates, the Fed may be able to stimulate economic growth. The lower borrowing rates may entice some consumers and firms to borrow more funds and spend more money, which can result in higher revenue and earnings for businesses.

**How the Fed Can Increase Interest Rates**   When the Fed reduces the U.S. money supply, it pulls funds out of commercial banks and other financial institutions. This reduces the supply of funds that these financial institutions can lend to borrowers. Assuming that the demand for loanable funds remains unchanged, the decline in the supply of loanable funds should cause interest rates to rise. The higher interest rates increase the cost of borrowing and thus tend to discourage consumers and firms from borrowing. The Fed raises interest rates when it wants to reduce the degree of spending in the United States. The Fed might do this because an excessive amount of spending can cause a higher degree of inflation. Therefore, when the Fed raises interest rates in an effort to reduce spending, it is actually trying to reduce the level of inflation.

Though the Fed may succeed in reducing inflation by increasing interest rates, the higher interest rates can adversely affect the performance of businesses in the short term. As already mentioned, higher interest rates increase the cost of borrowing and may reduce total spending in the United States. Higher interest rates force firms to incur higher interest expenses when they borrow, which can reduce their profits. In addition, when there is less total spending in the United States, the total demand for products and services is reduced, and the demand for each firm's products or services may be reduced. This results in less revenue and therefore lower profits for firms.

**Common Fed Dilemma**   The Fed experienced a dilemma in 2008, when there was a weak economy. Normally, the Fed would attempt to correct a weak economy by lowering interest rates. However, oil prices increased substantially during 2008, which resulted in higher gas prices and costs of transportation. Thus, the Fed had to deal with a slow economy and relatively high inflation (for some products and services) simultaneously. It did not have much power to reduce the inflation, since the higher prices were caused mostly by high oil prices. Even if the Fed reduced inflation by slowing economic growth, this action would have prevented the Fed from stimulating the economy. Since the Fed does not have direct control over oil prices, it decided to focus more on controlling economic growth. It reduced interest rates, hoping to stimulate the economy. However, it did not reduce interest rates as much as it would have preferred, because of fears that stimulating the economy too much might cause inflation to rise even higher.

## 5.2 Fiscal Policy

**fiscal policy**
decisions on how the federal government should set tax rates and spend money

**Fiscal policy** involves decisions on how the federal government should set tax rates and spend money. These decisions are relevant to businesses because they affect economic growth and therefore can affect the demand for a firm's products or services.

**Revision of Personal Income Tax Rates**   Consider a fiscal policy that reduces personal income taxes. With this policy, people would have higher after-tax incomes, which might encourage them to spend more money. Such behavior reflects an increase in the aggregate demand for products and services produced by businesses, which would improve the performance of businesses.

**Revision of Corporate Taxes**   Fiscal policy can also affect a firm's after-tax earnings directly. For example, assume the corporate tax rate is reduced from 30 percent to 25 percent. If a specific corporation's before-tax earnings are $10 million, its taxes would have been $3 million (computed as 30% × $10,000,000) at the old tax rate. Now, however, at a corporate tax rate of 25 percent, its taxes are $2.5 million (computed as 25% × $10,000,000). Therefore, the corporation's after-tax earnings are now $500,000 higher, simply because the corporate taxes are $500,000 lower.

**excise taxes**
taxes imposed by the federal government on particular products

**Revision in Excise Taxes**   **Excise taxes** are taxes imposed by the federal government on particular products. These taxes raise the cost of producing these goods. Consequently, manufacturers tend to incorporate the tax into the price they charge for the products. Thus, consumers indirectly incur the tax. The tax may also discourage consumption of these goods by indirectly affecting the price. Excise taxes are imposed on various products, including alcohol and tobacco.

**Revision in the Budget Deficit**   The fiscal policy set by the federal government dictates the amount of tax revenue generated by the federal government and the amount of federal spending. If federal government spending exceeds the amount of federal taxes, a **federal budget deficit** results.

**federal budget deficit**
the situation when the amount of federal government spending exceeds the amount of federal taxes and other revenue received by the federal government

When the federal government receives less revenue than it spends, it must borrow the difference. For example, if the federal government plans to spend $900 billion but receives only $700 billion in taxes (or other revenue), it has $200 billion less than it desires to spend. It must borrow $200 billion to have sufficient funds for making its expenditures (as shown in Exhibit 3.7). If the federal government needs to borrow additional funds, it creates a high demand for loanable funds, which may result in higher interest rates (for reasons explained earlier).

In the 1998–2000 period, the federal government spent less funds than it received, which resulted in a small surplus. Under these conditions, the government's budget policy does not place upward pressure on interest rates. In 2001, the tax revenue received by the U.S. government declined because income levels declined as the economy weakened. In addition, the U.S. government spent more money in 2001 due to expenses associated with the September 11 tragedy and the subsequent war. The U.S. government has experienced a large budget deficit each year since 2001.

## 5.3 Summary of Government Influence on Economic Factors

Exhibit 3.8 provides a summary of how the federal government can affect the performance of firms. Fiscal policy can affect personal tax rates and therefore influence consumer spending behavior. It can also affect corporate tax rates, which influence the earnings of firms. Monetary policy can affect interest rates, which may influence the demand for a firm's product (if the purchases are sometimes paid for with borrowed funds). By influencing interest rates, monetary policy also affects the interest expenses that firms incur.

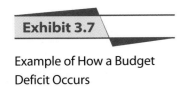

**Exhibit 3.7**

Example of How a Budget Deficit Occurs

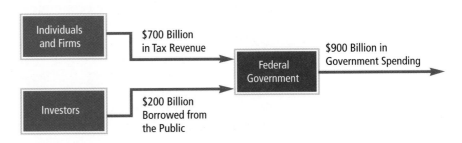

**Exhibit 3.8**

How Government Policies
Affect Business Performance

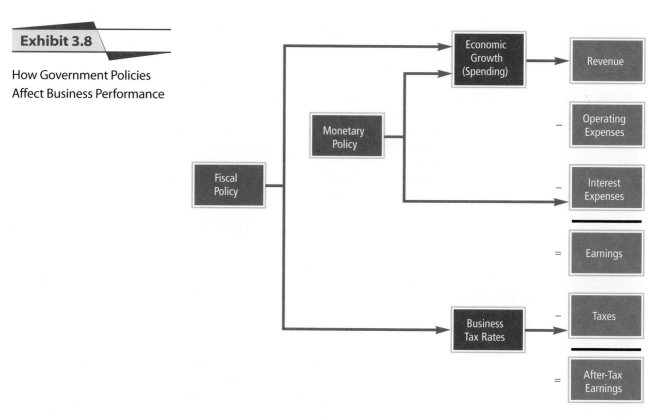

## 5.4 Dilemma of the Federal Government

The federal government faces a dilemma when attempting to influence economic growth. If it can maintain a low rate of economic growth, it can prevent inflationary pressure caused by an excessive demand for products. A restrictive monetary or fiscal policy may be used for this purpose. A restrictive monetary policy leads to low growth in the money supply over time, which tends to place upward pressure on interest rates. This discourages borrowing and therefore can reduce total spending in the economy. A restrictive fiscal policy results in high taxes and low government spending.

Although restrictive monetary and fiscal policies may keep inflation low, a critical tradeoff is involved. The unemployment rate may be higher when the economy is stagnant. The federal government can use a more stimulative policy (such as low tax rates or a monetary policy designed to reduce interest rates) to boost economic growth. Although these policies increase economic growth, they may also cause higher inflation.

Rarely is a consensus reached on whether the government should use a stimulative or restrictive policy at a given point in time. During the late 1990s, the federal government used stimulative monetary policies because inflation was very low and was not expected to be a serious problem. This monetary policy helped to increase economic growth during that period. As the economy weakened in 2008, stimulative monetary policies were used in an effort to increase economic growth.

# Cross-Functional Teamwork

## Economic Effects Across Business Functions

Since managers of a firm have different responsibilities, they assess different aspects of the economic environment. Managers who focus on production monitor the changes in economic conditions that could affect the firm's production costs. They tend to monitor inflationary trends, or changes in the price levels of specific supplies or equipment that they purchase.

Marketing managers attempt to forecast sales of their products and assess economic conditions that affect the demand for the products, such as economic growth. They may also monitor interest rates if the products are commonly purchased with borrowed funds because the demand for these products may increase in response to a reduction in interest rates. Since the firm's production volume is dependent on the forecasted demand for the product, it is influenced by economic conditions.

The firm's financial managers monitor the economic conditions that affect the cost of financing. They tend to focus on interest rates because the firm's financing expenses are directly affected by changes in interest rates.

When different types of managers forecast economic conditions so that they can make business decisions, they should work as a team. Otherwise, some forecasts of some economic conditions may vary across managers, which may cause their business decisions to be different. For example, if the marketing managers of an automobile manufacturer forecast low interest rates, they will expect a high sales volume, which will require a large production of automobiles. However, if the production managers forecast high interest rates, they will expect a lower level of sales and will be concerned that a large production volume could cause excessive inventories.

Some firms assign one person or department to develop the forecasts of all economic conditions, which the managers use in all business functions. In this way, all managers make decisions according to the same forecasts of economic conditions.

## COLLEGE HEALTH CLUB: IMPACT OF GLOBAL CONDITIONS ON CHC

As Sue Kramer develops her business plan for College Health Club (CHC), she needs to recognize the exposure of her business to economic conditions. Based on expected economic conditions, she anticipates that she will have 300 memberships over the first year. If economic conditions weaken, however, some students will probably lose their part-time jobs in the local community and will not be able to afford a health club membership. If the economy weakens, Sue expects that there will be only 260 memberships. Conversely, if the economy strengthens, she expects that there will be 340 memberships in the first year. Thus, CHC's revenue will be lower when economic conditions are weaker. Since most of CHC's expenses (such as rent) are fixed, any change in revenue has a direct effect on earnings. Thus, if a weaker economy causes CHC's revenue to be lower, CHC's earnings will also be lower. A weaker economy could even force Sue to lower the membership price, which could also reduce revenue.

# Summary of Learning Objectives

**1** Economic growth affects a firm's performance because it can affect the income levels of consumers and therefore affect the demand for a firm's products. When the economy is strong, the demand for a firm's products is strong, and its profits are relatively high. When the economy is weak, the demand for a firm's products is low, and its profits are relatively low.

**2** When inflation is high, firms incur higher costs of production. If they pass on the higher cost to consumers by raising prices, the consumers may reduce their demand for the products, and revenue (and profits) will decline. If the firms do not pass on the higher cost, their revenue may not be affected. However, since their expenses are higher, their profits will decline.

**3** When interest rates increase, the firm's cost of borrowing increases. Therefore, its expenses increase, and its profits may decline. In addition, high interest rates can discourage consumers from buying particular products (such as new cars or homes) that they normally purchase with credit, because the loan payments would be too high. The firms that offer these products experience a decline in demand and therefore a decline in revenue when interest rates are high. Therefore, they tend to experience lower profits under these conditions.

**4** Market prices are determined by demand and supply conditions. The demand for a product is influenced by consumer income and preferences. Higher consumer income generally results in a higher demand for products. The amount of a product produced is influenced by production expenses. Firms will supply products to the market only if the market price is high enough to more than cover expenses.

**5** The federal government influences macroeconomic conditions by enacting monetary or fiscal policies. Its monetary policy affects the amount of funds available at commercial banks and other financial institutions and therefore affects interest rates. Its fiscal policy affects the taxes imposed on consumers, which can influence the amount of spending by consumers and therefore affect the performance of firms. Fiscal policy is also used to tax the earnings of firms.

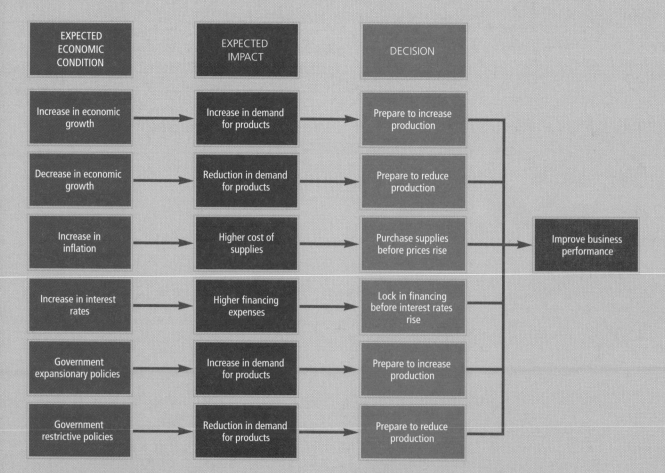

## Self-Test of Key Concepts

The following self-assessment allows you to test your understanding of the key concepts covered in this chapter. Answers are provided at the end of this exercise.

**True or False**

1. Macroeconomics is focused on a specific business or industry of concern.

2. When U.S. economic growth is lower than normal, the total income level of all U.S. workers is relatively high.

3. Economic growth represents the change in the general level of economic activity.

4. The total amount of expenditures in the economy is known as aggregate expenditures.

5. Structural unemployment refers to workers who lose their jobs due to a decline in economic conditions.

6. A higher level of inflation will cause a larger decrease in a firm's operating expenses.

7. Inflation is usually measured as the percentage change in gross domestic product.

8. The demand for a product can be shown with a demand schedule, which indicates the quantity of the product that would be demanded at each possible price.

9. The Federal Reserve System sets the monetary policy that determines the money supply in the United States.

10. The Fed affects interest rates by changing the supply of funds banks can loan.

**Multiple Choice**

11. _____ conditions reflect the overall performance of the nation's economy.
    a) Microeconomic
    b) Multi-economic
    c) Macroeconomic
    d) Proto-economic
    e) Supraeconomic

12. All of the following are examples of macroeconomic concerns except:
    a) a drop in the nation's gross domestic product.
    b) an increase in the rate of inflation.
    c) a strike by workers at a local bakery.
    d) an increase in the amount of cyclical unemployment.
    e) an increase in the rate of interest charged on bank loans.

13. The total market value of all final goods and services produced in the United States is known as:
    a) gross domestic product.
    b) aggregate expenditures.
    c) fiscal output.
    d) the production quota.
    e) aggregate supply.

14. Jan is currently between jobs, but she has marketable job skills and is confident she will find work in the near future. Jan's current situation would be an example of _____ unemployment.
    a) seasonal
    b) structural
    c) functional
    d) frictional
    e) cyclical

15. The type of unemployment that represents people who are unemployed because of poor economic conditions is:
    a) functional unemployment.
    b) cyclical unemployment.
    c) seasonal unemployment.
    d) structural unemployment.
    e) general unemployment.

16. The type of inflation that requires firms to increase their prices to cover increased costs is referred to as:
    a) demand-pull inflation.
    b) stagflation.
    c) cost-push inflation.
    d) disequilibrium.
    e) unemployment.

17. The prices firms pay for supplies or materials directly influence their:
    a) operating expenses.
    b) operating revenue.
    c) dividends.
    d) stockholders' equity.
    e) economic assets.

18. An increase in the general level of prices of products and services over a specified period of time is called:
    a) inflation.
    b) stagflation.
    c) unemployment.
    d) disinflation.
    e) equilibrium.

19. A typical demand schedule shows that:
    a) as price decreases, quantity demanded will also decrease.
    b) as price decreases, quantity demanded will increase.
    c) quantity supplied can never be less than quantity demanded.
    d) the total quantity of goods consumers want to buy will fall during periods of inflation.
    e) a firm can always increase its revenue by increasing the prices it charges for its products.

20. At the equilibrium price for a product, the:
    a) firms in the market are maximizing their total revenue.
    b) consumers in the market have spent all of their income.
    c) firms in the market are maximizing their total output.
    d) firms in the market are just breaking even.
    e) quantity demanded by consumers equals the quantity supplied by firms.

21. If the market price of a good is above the equilibrium price:
    a) a surplus will exist, which will put downward pressure on prices.
    b) the supply curve will shift to the right as firms rush to take advantage of the high price.
    c) the demand curve will shift to the left as consumers decrease the quantity they buy.
    d) the government will intervene to force the price downward.
    e) a shortage will exist, which will force the price even higher.

22. An increase in the demand for a product is likely to cause:
    a) a matching decrease in supply.
    b) an increase in the equilibrium price.
    c) the supply curve to shift to the right.
    d) a decrease in the equilibrium price.
    e) the government to attempt to increase production quotas.

23. If consumer incomes increase, the effect on consumer decisions about how much they want to buy can be shown by:
    a) shifting the demand curve outward (to the right).
    b) shifting the supply curve outward.
    c) shifting the demand curve inward (to the left).
    d) moving downward to the right along the demand curve.
    e) shifting the supply curve inward.

24. The _____ of the United States is defined as the total amount of demand deposits, currency held by the public, and traveler's checks.
    a) financial wealth
    b) financial reserves
    c) money supply
    d) total banking assets
    e) gross domestic product

25. The central bank of the United States, where the money supply is controlled and regulated, is the:
    a) Federal Reserve System.
    b) Senate.
    c) Department of Congress.
    d) Council of Economic Advisers.
    e) Board of Directors.

26. Which of the following is the best example of the federal government's use of fiscal policy?
    a) The Federal Reserve places new regulations on the nation's banks that require them to make more loans to minorities and women.
    b) The U.S. Treasury announces that it has redesigned the nation's paper money to make the bills more difficult to counterfeit.
    c) The government cuts taxes during an economic downturn.
    d) The president appoints a new commission to look into concerns about how pollution is damaging the environment.
    e) The Federal Reserve gives banks more funds to enable them to make more loans.

27. Taxes that the federal government imposes on particular products are called:
    a) excise taxes.
    b) import taxes.
    c) export taxes.
    d) quotas.
    e) embargoes.

28. When the amount of federal government spending exceeds the amount of federal taxes, the result is called a:
    a) trade deficit.
    b) federal budget deficit.
    c) balance of payments.
    d) price equilibrium.
    e) opportunity cost.

29. Restrictive monetary and fiscal policies may keep inflation low, but the critical tradeoff is that they may also cause:
    a) disinflation.
    b) environmental problems.
    c) massive crime.
    d) unemployment.
    e) higher inflation.

30. The government can prevent inflationary pressure caused by an excessive demand for products by maintaining a low rate of:
    a) fiscal policies.
    b) economic growth.
    c) monetary policies.
    d) unemployment.
    e) savings.

**True/False**

| | |
|---|---|
| 1. False | 9. True |
| 2. False | 10. True |
| 3. True | |
| 4. True | |
| 5. False | |
| 6. False | |
| 7. False | |
| 8. True | |

**Multiple Choice**

| | | |
|---|---|---|
| 11. c | 18. a | 25. a |
| 12. c | 19. b | 26. c |
| 13. a | 20. e | 27. a |
| 14. d | 21. a | 28. b |
| 15. b | 22. b | 29. d |
| 16. c | 23. a | 30. b |
| 17. a | 24. c | |

# Self-Test of Key Terms

aggregate expenditures  68
cost-push inflation  70
cyclical unemployment  69
demand schedule  76
demand-pull inflation  71
economic growth  66
equilibrium price  78
excise taxes  85

federal budget deficit  85
Federal Reserve System  82
fiscal policy  84
frictional unemployment  69
gross domestic product (GDP)  68
inflation  70
monetary policy  82
money supply  82

recession  67
seasonal unemployment  69
shortage  78
structural unemployment  69
supply schedule  76
surplus  77

Fill in each blank with the proper key term. To assess your understanding of the key terms, answers are provided at the end of this self-test.

1. _____ occurs when firms incur higher production costs and increase their prices.

2. The _____ controls the monetary policy of the United States.

3. _____ represents the total production level in the United States.

4. _____ are imposed by the federal government on particular products.

5. If federal government spending exceeds the amount of federal taxes in a particular period, the result is a _____ during that period.

6. _____ represents people who are unemployed because economic conditions are weak.

7. _____ represents people who are unemployed because they are in between jobs.

8. When the demand for a product at a specific price is less than the quantity supplied at that price, this results in a _____.

9. _____ represents the increase in the general level of prices of products and services over a specified period of time.

10. _____ occurs when the demand for products is very strong, which enables firms to increase their prices and still sell their products.

11. When the demand for a product at a specific price exceeds the quantity supplied at that price, this results in a _____.

12. _____ represents the change in the general level of economic activity.

13. The price at which the quantity of a product is equal to the quantity demanded is called the _____.

14. _____ is used to make decisions about the size of the money supply, which affects interest rates and the economy.

15. _____ is used to make decisions about tax rates and federal spending, which affect the economy.

16. _____ represents people who are unemployed because they do not have adequate skills.

**Answers:**
1. Cost-push inflation
2. Federal Reserve System
3. Gross domestic product
4. Excise taxes
5. federal budget deficit
6. Cyclical unemployment
7. Frictional unemployment
8. surplus

9. Inflation
10. Demand-pull inflation
11. shortage
12. Economic growth
13. equilibrium price
14. Monetary policy
15. Fiscal policy
16. Structural unemployment

# Concept Review Questions

1. **Impact of Economy on Business Value.** Explain why the value of a business is affected by economic conditions.

2. **Impact of Inflation.** Explain why the value of a business is influenced by inflation.

3. **Unemployment.** Describe the four different types of unemployment. Which type is the best indicator of a possible weak economy?

4. **Inflation.** Explain the difference between cost-push inflation and demand-pull inflation.

5. **Inflation.** Why are businesses affected by inflation?

6. **Interest Rates.** Explain how interest rate movements affect the performance of a business.

7. **Product Shortage.** Explain how demand and supply conditions can cause a shortage to occur. What happens to the price in response to a shortage?

8. **Price Level.** Explain the effect of demand and supply on the general price level in the economy.

9. **Monetary Policy.** Explain how monetary policy can affect the performance of businesses.

10. **Monetary and Fiscal Policies.** Explain the difference between monetary policy and fiscal policy.

# Class Communication Questions

1. **Impact of Demand-Pull Versus Cost-Push Inflation on Your Business.** As a business owner, would you prefer a situation in which there is demand-pull inflation or cost-push inflation?

2. **Impact of the Fed on Businesses.** Assume that the U.S. economy is currently weak, and the Fed wants to enact a monetary policy that will lower interest rates in order to stimulate the economy. However, this policy could cause higher inflation. Alternatively, the Fed could leave interest rates at their present level and avoid the danger of higher inflation. Do you think businesses would be better off in this case if the Fed lowered interest rates?

3. **Budget Deficit Dilemma.** Assume that the U.S. unemployment rate is high. The U.S. government could use a fiscal policy to stimulate the economy, in which it reduces personal tax rates. This policy would be beneficial because it would provide

consumers with more money to spend. However, the federal government would receive less tax revenue and would therefore experience a larger federal budget deficit. Is it appropriate for the government to go into more debt every time that it wants to stimulate the economy?

## Small Business Case

### Managing in Response to Economic Conditions

Prestige Tile Company specializes in the production of fancy tile that it installs in the lobbies of hotels, banks, restaurants, and other companies. The economy has been strong, so the businesses that it serves have been experiencing high profits and have been able to afford the services of Prestige Tile. However, the production plant that it rents is currently at full capacity.

1. **Responding to Economic Growth.** As a result of recent economic growth, Prestige Tile is considering the purchase of a very large production plant and hiring more full-time employees so that it can produce a larger volume of tile. What is the risk of investing substantial funds to expand the plant and hiring new employees?

2. **Impact of Inflation on Business Expenses.** Prestige Tile Company incurs expenses in the form of purchases of materials, rent payments for its production plant, utility expenses to run the production, and salaries paid to employees. Explain why an increase in inflation could affect its expenses and profits.

3. **Impact of Interest Rates on Business Expenses.** Prestige Tile Company relies on short-term loans to support some of its operations. Explain how its expenses and profits may be affected by an increase in interest rates.

4. **Impact of Monetary Policy on Business Expenses.** The Federal Reserve is planning to increase interest rates in order to slow economic growth because it believes the economy is too strong and will cause higher inflation if it continues to grow so fast. Explain how the Fed's policy might affect the expenses and profits of Prestige Tile Company.

## Web Insight

### Exposure of Harley-Davidson to Economic Conditions

At the opening of the chapter, Harley-Davidson was introduced. Go to its website (www.harley-davidson .com) and go to the section called "Investor Relations." Summarize Harley-Davidson's stock price performance during the last quarter or year. Does it appear that its performance has been influenced by economic conditions during the last quarter or year? [You can also learn about its recent performance by reviewing the Letter to Shareholders, which is near the beginning of its annual report.]

## Dell's Secret for Success

Go to Dell's website (www.dell.com) and click on the link "About Dell," near the bottom of the web page. Review the information about Dell's recent performance. You can also review a recent annual report of Dell for more information.

1. **Exposure to Economy.** Describe Dell's recent business performance. Do you think that Dell's business performance was sensitive to the economy? Explain.

2. **Comparison of Product Exposure.** During a weak economy, the demand for some of Dell's products may decline. Which products would likely experience a decline in demand?

3. **Impact of Interest Rates.** If interest rates increase, why might the demand for Dell's products be affected?

## Video Exercise

### Lessons in How Economic Conditions Affect Businesses

Many free business videos are available on websites such as YouTube (www.youtube.com), and more are added every day. Search for a recent video clip about an existing business that offers lessons on "U.S. economy" in YouTube or any other website that provides video clips.

1. **Main Lesson.** Is the video clip focused on interest rates, economic growth, unemployment, inflation, or some other aspect of the economy? What is the main lesson of the video clip that you watched?

2. **Adapting to Changes.** Many related videos suggest that a key lesson for entrepreneurs is to be ready to adapt to changes in the business environment. How do you think a business can stay more "flexible" in order to adapt to changing economic conditions?

3. **Impact of Interest Rate Movements.** An important lesson is how a change in the interest rate affects the amount of interest expenses incurred by the business and its ability to repay its loans. Explain why some businesses experience problems when interest rates rise.

## Projects

To encourage further comprehension of concepts covered in Chapter 3, the following five projects are available:

1. Analyzing Your Favorite Business

2. Building a Business Plan for Campus.com

3. Running Your Own Business

4. Planning Your Career

5. Stock Market Contest

All of these projects are provided in Appendix A at the end of the text. In addition, projects are available by part division at the end of each part.

A Word file for each project is also available at the textbook website (www.emcp.net/business5e) so that you may maintain one ongoing file for each project.

# Assessing Global Conditions

## Chapter 4 Learning Objectives

**1** Explain the motives for U.S. firms to engage in international business.

**2** Describe how firms conduct international business.

**3** Explain how barriers to international business have been reduced and describe the barriers that remain.

**4** Explain how foreign characteristics can influence a firm's international business.

**5** Explain how exchange rate movements can affect a firm's performance.

# Chapter 4

## Nike's Assessment of Global Conditions

Many U.S. firms have capitalized on opportunities in foreign countries by engaging in international business. Even small U.S. firms are now engaging in international business by purchasing foreign supplies or by selling their products in foreign countries.

International economic conditions affect a firm's revenue and expenses and therefore affect its value. To illustrate how the international environment can affect the value of a business, consider the case of Nike, Inc., which is the world's biggest producer of athletic shoes, apparel, and sports equipment. It has more than 30,000 employees worldwide. It sells its products in many different countries. In addition, it produces its products in many foreign countries, such as China, India, Indonesia, Thailand, Vietnam, and Malaysia. By producing its products in countries where labor is cheap, it is able to maintain low expenses. As a result of expanding its sales of its products across numerous countries, it generates revenue of more than $16 billion per year.

As Nike considers possible expansion opportunities, it must address the following questions:

✦ Which countries would offer the best opportunities for expansion?
✦ In what way should it expand in particular countries?
✦ Are there any international barriers that could prevent its expansion?
✦ What characteristics of the countries where it plans to expand would affect its performance?
✦ How will exchange rate movements affect its performance?

Even small businesses periodically address these questions to consider whether and how they should pursue international business. This chapter explains how the assessment of the global environment by Nike or any other firm can be conducted in a manner that maximizes the firm's performance and value.

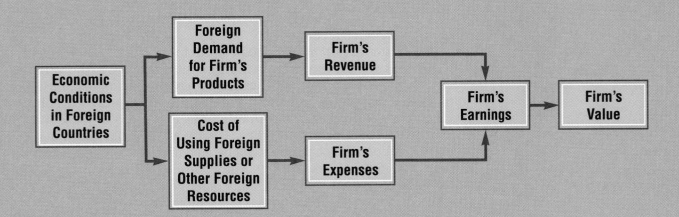

97

# 1. How International Business Can Enhance Performance

International business can enhance a firm's performance by increasing its revenue or reducing its expenses. Either result leads to higher profits for the firm. There are various motives for international business, and each of them allows the firm to benefit in a manner that can enhance its performance. Some of the more common motives to conduct international business are:

✦ Attract foreign demand

✦ Capitalize on technology

✦ Use inexpensive resources

✦ Diversify internationally

Firms that engage in international business are commonly referred to as multinational corporations. Some multinational corporations such as Amazon.com, The Gap, IBM, and Starbucks are large well-known firms, but many small U.S. firms also conduct international business so that they can enhance their performance.

## 1.1 Attract Foreign Demand

Some firms are unable to increase their market share in the United States because of intense competition within their industry. Alternatively, the U.S. demand for the firm's product may decrease because of changes in consumer tastes. Under either of these conditions, a firm might consider foreign markets where potential demand may exist. Many firms, including DuPont, IBM, and PepsiCo, have successfully entered new foreign markets to attract new sources of demand. Wal-Mart Stores has recently opened stores in numerous countries, including Mexico and Hong Kong. Boeing (a U.S. producer of aircraft) recently received orders for jets from China Xinjiang Airlines and Kenya Airways.

**Examples**   Avon Products has opened branches in many countries, including Brazil, China, and Poland. McDonald's is now in more than 80 different countries and generates more than half of its total revenue from foreign countries. Hertz has expanded its agencies in Europe and in other foreign markets. Amazon.com has expanded its business by offering its services in many foreign countries.

Blockbuster has more than 3,000 stores located in 27 markets outside the United States. It is focusing its efforts for future growth in those markets because it already has business there and therefore has some name recognition. General Electric's philosophy is that economic growth will be uneven across countries, so it must position its businesses in those markets where demand will increase. It believes that as globalization continues, only the most competitive companies will be able to effectively serve their employees and stockholders. In 1999, Autozone established its first retail store for auto parts in Mexico because many older vehicles are still in use in that country, so demand for auto parts is high. Today, Autozone has 49 stores in Mexico. eBay has provided some foreign markets with a service that was not previously available in those areas. It has served hundreds of millions of requests to buy or sell products from consumers in more than 150 countries.

Wed — Part 1,2 of business plan
— Test 1-4

stock market Project — 5 companys on NYSE

The Coca-Cola Company's business has also expanded globally over time. Now the company has a significant presence in almost every country. It expanded throughout Latin America, western Europe, Australia, and most of Africa before 1984. Since then, it has expanded into eastern Europe and most of Asia.

The motivation of firms to attract foreign demand is summarized in a recent annual report of Procter & Gamble (P&G):

*"More than 80 percent of P&G's sales come from the top 10 markets. We need to keep driving P&G growth in these countries, which are some of the biggest and strongest economies in the world. P&G's business in the top 10 countries taken together is growing at a rate of 11% per year. P&G is a leader in these markets. . . . Yet, despite this strength in P&G's 10 largest countries, we still have significant opportunities to grow."*

— Procter & Gamble

## 1.2 Capitalize on Technology

Many U.S. firms have established new businesses in the so-called developing countries (such as those in Latin America), which have relatively low levels of technology. AT&T and other firms have established new telecommunications systems in developing countries. Other U.S. firms that create power generation, road systems, and other forms of infrastructure have extensive business in these countries. Ford Motor Company and General Motors have attempted to capitalize on their technological advantages by establishing plants in developing countries throughout Asia, Latin America, and eastern Europe. IBM is doing business with the Chinese government to capitalize on its technology. Amazon.com can capitalize on its technology advantage by expanding in foreign countries where technology is not as advanced.

## 1.3 Use Inexpensive Resources

Labor and land costs can vary significantly among countries. Firms often attempt to set up production at a location where land and labor are

The economy of China (shown here) has grown substantially because of its ability to produce products at very low cost. Many firms in the United States and other countries have their products produced in China.

© SHUTTERSTOCK/MAYSKYPHOTO

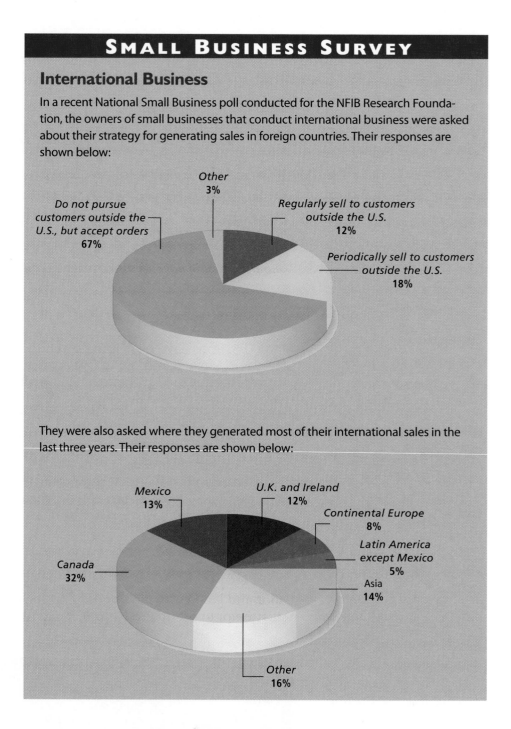

## SMALL BUSINESS SURVEY

### International Business

In a recent National Small Business poll conducted for the NFIB Research Foundation, the owners of small businesses that conduct international business were asked about their strategy for generating sales in foreign countries. Their responses are shown below:

*Other*
*3%*

*Do not pursue customers outside the U.S., but accept orders*
*67%*

*Regularly sell to customers outside the U.S.*
*12%*

*Periodically sell to customers outside the U.S.*
*18%*

They were also asked where they generated most of their international sales in the last three years. Their responses are shown below:

*Mexico*
*13%*

*U.K. and Ireland*
*12%*

*Continental Europe*
*8%*

*Latin America except Mexico*
*5%*

*Canada*
*32%*

*Asia*
*14%*

*Other*
*16%*

inexpensive. Exhibit 4.1 illustrates how hourly compensation (labor) costs can vary among countries. The costs are much higher in the developed countries (such as the United States and Germany) than in other countries (such as Mexico and Taiwan). Numerous U.S. firms have established subsidiaries in countries where labor costs are low. For example, Converse has shoes manufactured in Mexico. Dell, Inc., has disk drives and monitors produced in Asia. General Electric, Motorola, Texas Instruments, Dow Chemical, and Corning have established production plants in Singapore and Taiwan to take advantage of lower labor costs. Many firms from the United States and western Europe have also established plants in Hungary, Poland, and other eastern Europe countries, where labor costs are lower. General Motors pays its assembly-line workers in Mexico about $12 per

Exhibit 4.1

Approximate Hourly
Compensation Costs for
Manufacturing Across
Countries

Japan $22

Taiwan $8

South Korea $9

Hong Kong $7

Germany $24

Italy $16

France $21

Netherlands $22

United Kingdom $20

Canada $18

United States $20

Mexico $6

## SMALL BUSINESS SURVEY

When asked about the profitability of their sales to customers outside the United States as compared to their profitability of their sales to U.S. customers, they responded as shown below:

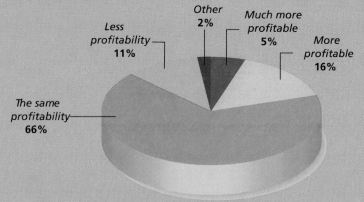

The small business owners were also asked whether the majority of their orders from outside the United States were placed on their website. Their responses here are classified according to the size of the business:

|  | Businesses with 1 to 9 Employees | Businesses with 10 to 19 Employees | Businesses with 20 to 249 Employees |
|---|---|---|---|
| Yes | 29% | 20% | 10% |
| No | 65% | 77% | 89% |
| Not applicable | 6% | 3% | 1% |

Notice that the website was most important for the smallest businesses and less important for the larger small businesses, which may have employees who can contact foreign customers directly.

These small business owners were also asked whether barriers imposed by foreign governments limit their ability to increase sales outside the United States. Their responses are shown here for various types of government barriers:

|  | Tariffs | Excessive Red Tape and Regulations |
|---|---|---|
| Severely limits | 10% | 18% |
| Somewhat limits | 27% | 22% |
| Does not limit | 59% | 58% |
| Other | 4% | 2% |

day (including benefits) versus about $250 per day for its assembly-line workers in the United States.

## 1.4  Diversify Internationally

When all the assets of a firm are designed to generate sales of a specific product in one country, the profits of the firm are normally unstable. This instability is due to the firm's exposure to changes within its industry or within the economy. The firm's performance is dependent on the demand for this one product and on the conditions of the one economy in which it conducts business. The firm can reduce such risk by selling its product in various countries.

U.S. firms commonly rely on foreign companies to produce products for them, and then the firms sell the products in the United States. The U.S. firms have a social responsibility to ensure adequate working conditions and treatment of employees at the factories where these products are produced.

© SHUTTERSTOCK/TAOLLMOR

Because economic conditions can vary among countries, U.S. firms that conduct international business are affected less by U.S. economic conditions. A U.S. firm's overall performance may be more stable if it sells its product in various countries so that its business is not influenced solely by the economic conditions in a single country. For example, the demand for PepsiCo's products in Mexico might decline if the Mexican economy is weak, but at the same time economic growth in Brazil, the Netherlands, and Spain might result in a higher overall demand for PepsiCo's products.

## 1.5  Combination of Motives

Many U.S. firms engage in international business because of a combination of the motives just described. For example, when 3M Company engages in international business, it attracts new demand from customers in foreign countries. Second, it is able to capitalize on its technology, which is often more advanced than the technology available to local firms in these countries. Third, it is able to use low-cost land and labor in some countries. Finally, it is able to diversify its business among countries. It has also reduced its exposure to U.S. economic conditions by increasing its international business over time.

General Electric is another example of a major firm that has expanded internationally in recent years. It has substantial business in Europe. Its sales have also increased in Latin America and the Pacific Basin. Wal-Mart is another firm that has been motivated by the reasons just described to expand into foreign countries.

**Learning Objective**

Describe how firms conduct international business.

**2**

# 2. How Firms Conduct International Business

A firm may use various methods to conduct international business. The more common methods of conducting international business that a firm should consider are:

+ Importing
+ Exporting
+ Direct foreign investment (DFI)
+ Outsourcing
+ Strategic alliances

## 2.1 Importing

**importing**
the purchase of foreign products or services

**Importing** involves the purchase of foreign products or services. For example, some U.S. consumers purchase foreign automobiles, clothing, cameras, and other products from firms in foreign countries. Many U.S. firms import materials or supplies that are used to produce products. Even if these firms sell the products locally, they can benefit from international business. They import foreign supplies that are less expensive or of a higher quality than alternative U.S. supplies.

**Factors That Influence the Degree of Importing**   The degree to which a firm imports supplies is influenced by government trade barriers. Governments may impose a **tariff** (or tax) on imported products. The tax is normally paid directly by the importer, who typically passes the tax on to consumers by charging a higher price for the product. Thus, the product may be overpriced compared with products produced by firms based in that country. When governments impose tariffs, the ability of foreign firms to compete in those countries is restricted.

**tariff**
a tax on imported products

Governments can also impose a **quota** on imported products, thereby limiting the amounts of specific products that can be imported. This type of trade barrier may be even more restrictive than a tariff because it places an explicit limit on the amount of a specific product that can be imported.

**quota**
a limit on the amounts of specific products that can be imported

In general, trade barriers tend to both discourage trade and protect specific industries from foreign competition. However, many trade barriers have been removed in Europe and in many Asian countries. In addition, since 1993 when the North American Free Trade Agreement (NAFTA) removed many restrictions on trade among Canada, Mexico, and the United States, U.S. firms have had more opportunities to expand their businesses in Canada and Mexico. At the same time, however, they are also more exposed to competition from foreign firms within the United States.

Imports arriving by sea are typically packaged in large containers, as shown here. The imported products within these containers commonly represent supplies to be delivered to manufacturers or finished products to be delivered to retail stores.

© SHUTTERSTOCK/DIEGO CERVO

## 2.2 Exporting

**exporting**
the sale of products or services (called exports) to purchasers residing in other countries

**Exporting** is the sale of products or services (called exports) to purchasers residing in other countries. Many firms, such as DuPont, Intel, and Zenith, use exporting as a means of selling products in foreign markets. Many smaller firms in the United States also export to foreign countries.

**Exhibit 4.2**

Trend of U.S. Exports
and Imports

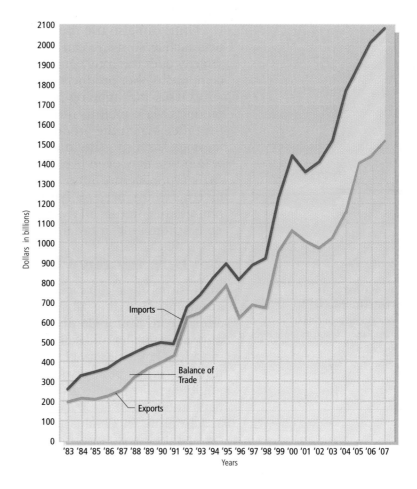

**Trend of U.S. Exports and Imports**   The trend of U.S. exports and imports is shown in Exhibit 4.2. Notice that the amount of both U.S. exports and imports increased by more than seven times between 1983 and 2007, reflecting the increased importance of international trade.

**balance of trade**
the level of exports minus the level of imports

**trade deficit**
the amount by which imports exceed exports

The U.S. **balance of trade**, which is also shown in Exhibit 4.2, is equal to the level of U.S. exports minus the level of U.S. imports. A negative balance of trade is referred to as a **trade deficit** and means that the United States is importing (purchasing) more products and services from foreign countries than it is selling to foreign countries. The United States has consistently had a trade deficit since 1980, and it has become even more negative (larger deficit) in recent years.

When a country has a trade deficit, its consumers may be benefiting from imported products that are less expensive than locally produced products. At the same time, however, the purchase of imported products implies less reliance on domestic production in favor of foreign production. Thus, it may be argued that a large trade deficit causes a transfer of jobs to some foreign countries.

**How the Internet Facilitates Exporting**   Many firms use their websites to identify the products that they sell, along with the price for each product. This allows them to easily advertise their products to potential importers anywhere in the world without mailing brochures to various countries. In addition, they can add to their product line and change prices by simply revising the website. Thus, importers can keep abreast of an exporter's product information by monitoring the exporter's website.

Firms can also use their websites to accept orders online. Some products such as software can be delivered from the exporter to the importer directly over the Internet in the form of a file that lands in the importer's computer. Other products must be shipped, but the Internet makes it easier to track the shipping process. The importer can transmit its order for products via e-mail to the exporter. The exporter's warehouse then fills the order. When the products are shipped from the warehouse, an e-mail message is sent to the importer and to the exporter's headquarters. The warehouse may even use technology to monitor its inventory of products so that suppliers are automatically notified to send more supplies when the inventory is reduced to a specific level. If the exporter uses multiple warehouses, the Internet allows them to work as a network so that if one warehouse cannot fill an order, another warehouse will.

## 2.3 Direct Foreign Investment (DFI)

**direct foreign investment (DFI)**

a means of acquiring or building subsidiaries in one or more foreign countries

Many firms engage in **direct foreign investment (DFI)**, which is a means of acquiring or building subsidiaries in one or more foreign countries. For example, Ford Motor Company has facilities in various countries that produce automobiles and sell them in those locations. Blockbuster has stores in various countries that rent DVDs to customers in those countries. A U.S. firm may either build a subsidiary in a foreign country or acquire an existing foreign firm and convert that into its subsidiary. Many U.S. firms expand internationally by acquiring foreign firms. They most commonly acquire firms in Canada and the United Kingdom but have recently increased their acquisitions in countries such as Brazil, the Czech Republic, and Hungary. Direct foreign investment is feasible in a variety of situations, including the following:

1. ***Reducing Transportation Costs.*** A firm that has successfully exported to a foreign country desires to reduce its transportation costs. It establishes a subsidiary in the foreign country to manufacture the product and sell it in that country. Kellogg Company uses this strategy and has production plants in 19 different countries, including China and India. Nike initially subcontracted with factories

Hong Kong (shown here) is one of many markets that have grown substantially in recent years and attracted substantial direct foreign investment from the United States.

in Taiwan and Korea to produce athletic shoes to be sold in Asian countries. It then expanded its production facilities in foreign countries so that they could produce shoes to be sold in Europe and South America.

2. **Circumventing Trade Barriers.** A firm that has been exporting products is informed that the foreign government will impose trade barriers. Therefore, the firm establishes a subsidiary that can manufacture  and sell products in that country. In this way, it avoids the trade barriers.

3. **Host Government Incentives.** A foreign country is desperately in need of advanced technology and offers a U.S. firm incentives, such as free use of land, to establish a subsidiary in that country. The foreign country also expects that the firm will employ some local workers.

4. **Reducing Labor Costs.** A U.S. firm believes that it can substantially reduce its labor costs by shifting its production facilities to a developing country where labor and land are less expensive.

Although DFI can often be feasible, firms should conduct a thorough analysis of the costs and benefits before investing. Once funds are spent on DFI, the decision cannot easily be reversed because the foreign facilities would have to be sold at a loss in most cases.

**Foreign Expansion in the United States**    Just as U.S. firms have expanded into foreign countries, foreign firms have expanded into the United States. In some industries, such as the automobile, camera, and clothing industries, many foreign firms offer their products in the United States. Some foreign firms have established new subsidiaries in the United States, such as Toyota (expanded its Kentucky plant), Mitsubishi Materials (built a silicon plant in Oregon), and Honda (expanded its Ohio plant). Other foreign firms such as Sony have acquired firms in the United States. Many foreign firms have spent hundreds of millions of dollars to develop or expand their U.S. businesses. Since foreign firms have expanded into the United States, even those U.S. firms that only sell their products domestically are subject to foreign competition.

## 2.4  Outsourcing

Firms commonly outsource some of their services to foreign countries as a means of using cheaper labor. For example, a U.S. manufacturing firm may outsource its technology support staff to Bulgaria, China, or another country where labor costs are low. A U.S. computer company may outsource its computer help desk to India. Some U.S. firms use outsourcing as a means of reducing their expenses.

When a U.S. firm outsources, the employees whose jobs are transferred from the United States to other countries, and especially those people who lose their jobs due to the outsourcing, are highly critical of the firm. However, the firm might counter that it needs to outsource in order to compete with other firms that also rely on cheaper foreign labor in some manner. In addition, it may suggest that its use of outsourcing is no different than the actions of other U.S. firms that import supplies or engage in direct foreign investment in low-wage countries. All of these actions are motivated by the desire to benefit from the use of cheap foreign labor.

Out of Business

AND SO Mr. JOHNSON, UPON YOUR ADVICE THAT OUTSOURCING SHOULD BE USED FOR ALL BASIC JOB POSITIONS THAT CAN BE DONE CHEAPER IN OTHER COUNTRIES, WE HAVE DECIDED TO OUTSOURCE YOUR CEO POSITION.

BOARD MEMBERS

## 2.5 Strategic Alliances

**strategic alliance**
a business agreement between firms whereby resources are shared to pursue mutual interests

U.S. and foreign firms commonly engage in **strategic alliances**, which are business agreements that are in the best interests of the firms involved. Various types of international alliances between U.S. firms and foreign firms can be made.

**joint venture**
an agreement between two firms about a specific project

**Joint Venture**   One type is a **joint venture**, which involves an agreement between two firms about a specific project. Joint ventures between U.S. and non-U.S. firms are common. The U.S. firm may produce a product and send it to a non-U.S. firm, which sells the product in that country. The non-U.S. firm is involved because it knows the culture of that country and is more capable of selling the product there.

In another type of joint venture, two firms participate in the production of a product. This type of joint venture is common in the automobile industry. The automakers in the United States are involved in a variety of ventures with foreign manufacturers. General Motors dealerships and Ford Motor Company dealerships sell cars manufactured by firms in France, Japan, and South Korea. Kraft Foods has engaged in joint ventures with some food producers in some of the former Soviet republics. This gives Kraft access to local production facilities and skilled workers. These joint ventures reflect the improved commercial relations with the former Soviet republics that have led to a major change in attitude by U.S. companies about doing business in those areas.

**international licensing agreement**
a type of alliance in which a firm allows a foreign company (called the "licensee") to produce its products according to specific instructions

**International Licensing Agreement**   Another type of alliance is an **international licensing agreement**, in which a firm allows a foreign company (called the "licensee") to produce its products according to specific instructions. Many U.S. beer producers engage in licensing agreements with foreign firms. The foreign firm is given the technology to produce the products. As the foreign firm sells the products, it channels a portion of revenue to the licensing firm. The advantage of licensing is that the firm is able to sell its product in foreign markets without the costs involved in exporting or direct foreign investment. One disadvantage, however, is that the foreign firm shares the profits from products sold in the foreign country.

U.S. firms commonly engage in strategic alliances with manufacturers where labor costs are very low, such as Africa (shown here) and Asia.

© SHUTTERSTOCK/LUCIAN COMAN

**How the Internet Facilitates Licensing**   Some firms with international reputations use their brand name to advertise products over the Internet. They then license manufacturers in foreign countries to produce some of their products subject to their specifications. For example, Mesa Company set up a licensing agreement with a manufacturer in Indonesia to produce its product, which Mesa advertises over the Internet. When Mesa receives orders for its product from customers in Asia, it relies on this manufacturer to produce and deliver the products ordered. This expedites the delivery process and may even enable Mesa to have the products manufactured at a lower cost than if it produced them itself.

**Learning Objective**

**3**

Explain how barriers to international business have been reduced and describe the barriers that remain.

## 3.  Barriers to International Business

Barriers to international trade may be imposed for various reasons. Some governments impose barriers in order to protect their local firms or to punish certain countries for their actions.

1. **Barriers Used to Protect Local Firms.** Any government may be tempted to impose barriers to protect its own firms. For example, the U.S. government may impose trade barriers such as tariffs on imported steel, even though such barriers are in conflict with previous trade agreements with other countries. The government may argue that such action is appropriate because the foreign steel firms receive subsidies from their government that enable them to be more competitive and therefore can afford to sell their steel at a price that is lower than their expenses (referred to as **dumping**). The foreign government, in turn, may claim that it does not provide subsidies, and the dispute may take years to resolve. Meanwhile, the foreign government may retaliate by imposing tariffs on products that its consumers import from the United States, such as chemicals. Any such intervention by a government to protect its local firms disrupts the spirit of global competition between firms.

**dumping**

selling products in a foreign country at a price below the cost of producing those products

2. **Barriers Used to Punish Countries.** Trade barriers are sometimes used to punish countries for various actions. For example, trade restrictions may be imposed on countries that do not enforce environmental laws or child labor laws, or initiate war against another country, or are unwilling to participate in a war against an unlawful dictator of another country.

In recent years, however, there has been a trend toward trade barriers in many parts of the world.

## 3.1  Reduction in Barriers

The barriers to international business have been reduced over time through various free trade agreements and the formation of free trade zones such as the European Union. The following are some examples of how barriers have been reduced.

**NAFTA**   As a result of the North American Free Trade Agreement (NAFTA) of 1993, trade barriers between the United States, Mexico, and Canada were eliminated. Consequently, firms in the United States now have more freedom to export their products to the other countries, while firms in Mexico have more freedom to export their products to the United States.

**GATT**   Following NAFTA, the General Agreement on Tariffs and Trade (GATT) called for the reduction or elimination of trade restrictions on specified imported products across 117 countries. It also led to the creation of the World Trade Organization (WTO), which now has more than 150 member countries. This accord has enabled firms to more easily export their products to other countries.

**Latin America**   In June 2003, the United States and Chile signed a free trade agreement to remove tariffs on more than 90 percent of the products that are sent between the two countries. Many other trade agreements are in the process of being negotiated between the United States and Latin American countries.

**European Union**   During the 1980s and 1990s, the countries in the European Union agreed to eliminate many trade barriers. By 2002, most of these countries had also adopted the euro as their currency. This has made it easier for firms in one European country to export their products to firms in other European countries because the importers and exporters now use the same currency and thus no longer face the costs and risks associated with exchanging currencies.

In 2004, the European Union accepted the following new members, most of which are in eastern Europe: Cyprus, the Czech Republic, Estonia, Hungary, Latvia, Lithuania, Malta, Poland, Slovakia, and Slovenia. In 2007, two more eastern European countries, Bulgaria and Romania, joined the European Union. Consequently, the restrictions on the new members' trade with western Europe were reduced. Since these countries have substantially lower wages than those in western Europe, firms from the United States and elsewhere can establish manufacturing plants in these countries to produce products and export them to western Europe.

**Reduced Barriers on Direct Foreign Investment**   In recent years, many Asian, European, and Latin American countries have reduced their barriers on direct foreign investment. Consequently, firms now have more freedom to establish subsidiaries or to acquire existing companies there. In some countries, the governments have even offered firms incentives to encourage them to establish facilities there. These governments recognize that foreign ownership of local facilities could benefit the economy by creating jobs.

## 3.2  Remaining Barriers

Firms should recognize, however, that even though barriers to international business have been reduced, some governments continue to impose barriers in order to protect their local firms or to punish certain countries for their actions. These barriers may prevent a firm from pursuing international business in a specific country. Alternatively, they may increase the cost of pursuing international business. In some cases, the potential advantages of pursuing international business are outweighed by the costs of circumventing the barriers. Common barriers include trade barriers such as the tariffs and quotas described earlier, as well as barriers aimed at preventing a firm from establishing a subsidiary (direct foreign investment) in another country.

## 3.3  Disagreements About Trade Barriers

Disagreements on international trade barriers will always exist. People whose job prospects are affected either positively or negatively by international trade tend to have very strong opinions about international trade policy. Most people agree that free trade can encourage more intense competition among firms, which can be beneficial because it gives consumers the opportunity to obtain products where the quality is highest and the prices are low. Free trade should cause production to move to those countries where it can be done most efficiently. Each country's government wants to increase its exports because a rise in exports results in a higher level of production and income and may create jobs. A job created in one country, however, may be lost in another. Therefore, any workers who might lose their jobs because of free trade will likely argue against free trade policies and call for the imposition of trade barriers.

People also disagree on the type of strategies a government should be allowed to use to increase its respective country's share of the global market. They may agree that a tariff or quota on imported goods prevents free trade and gives local firms an unfair advantage in their own market. At the same time, however, they may disagree on whether governments should be allowed to use other more subtle trade restrictions against foreign firms or provide incentives that give their local firms an advantage. Consider the following situations that commonly occur:

✦ **Different Environmental Restrictions.** Firms based in one country are not subject to environmental restrictions and therefore can produce at a lower cost than firms in other countries.

✦ **Different Labor Laws.** Firms based in one country are not subject to labor laws and are able to produce products at a lower cost than firms in other countries by relying mostly on children to produce the products.

✦ **Different Laws Regarding Bribes.** Firms based in one country are allowed by their government to offer bribes to large customers when pursuing business deals in a particular industry. These firms have a competitive advantage over firms in other countries that are not allowed to offer bribes.

✦ **Different Tax Brackets.** Firms in one country receive tax breaks if they are in specific industries. Such breaks are not necessarily subsidies, but they are still a form of government financial support.

**Meetings to Resolve Trade Agreements**   In each of these situations described above, firms in one country may have an advantage over firms in other countries. Every government uses some strategies that may give its local firms an advantage. This leads to international trade meetings that are intended to resolve the conflicts among countries.

Every meeting held to discuss international trade attracts a large number of protesters. These protesters tend to have their own agendas, which are not always closely related to each other. International trade may not even be the focus of each protest, but it is often regarded as the ultimate cause of the problem (at least in the mind of that protester). Although the protesters are generally dissatisfied with existing trade policies, they do not agree on how trade policies should be changed. These disagreements are similar to those that occur between government representatives when they are negotiating international trade policy.

A firm is not responsible for resolving the conflicts over international trade policy. Nevertheless, it should recognize how international trade policy affects its competitive position in the industry and how changes in policy could affect its position in the future.

**Learning Objective**

Explain how foreign characteristics can influence a firm's international business.

**4**

# 4. How Foreign Characteristics Influence International Business

When a firm engages in international business, it must consider the following characteristics of foreign countries:

✦ Culture

✦ Economic system

✦ Economic conditions

✦ Exchange rates

✦ Political risk and regulations

## 4.1 Culture

Because cultures vary, a firm must learn a foreign country's culture before engaging in business there. Poor decisions can result from an improper assessment of a country's tastes, habits, and customs. Many U.S. firms know that cultures vary and adjust their products to fit the culture. For example, McDonald's sells vegetable burgers instead of beef hamburgers in India. PepsiCo (owner of Frito Lay snack foods) sells Cheetos without cheese in China because Chinese consumers dislike cheese, and it has developed a shrimp-chip to satisfy consumers in Korea. Beer producers sell nonalcoholic beer in Saudi Arabia, where alcohol is not allowed.

Firms that pursue international business must first learn the culture of the country where they wish to do business. The culture influences consumer behavior, which determines the types of products that consumers wish to demand.

© SHUTTERSTOCK/ICEO

Wal-Mart is still learning from its experience in many countries. When it established stores in Argentina, it initially used the same store layout as in the United States, but it quickly learned that the local people preferred a different layout. In addition, it conducted meetings with suppliers in English, even though the primary language of the suppliers was Spanish. Wal-Mart's expansion into Mexico was more effective because it acquired a large Mexican retail firm and was able to rely on it for information about the local culture.

## 4.2   Economic System

A firm must recognize the type of economic system used in any country where it considers doing business. A country's economic system reflects the degree of government ownership of businesses and intervention in business. A U.S. firm will normally prefer countries that do not have excessive government intervention.

Although each country's government has its own unique policy on the ownership of businesses, most policies can be classified as capitalism, communism, or socialism.

**capitalism**
an economic system that allows for private ownership of businesses

**Capitalism**   Capitalism allows for private ownership of businesses. Entrepreneurs have the freedom to create businesses that they believe will serve the people's needs. The United States is perceived as a capitalist society because entrepreneurs are allowed to create businesses and compete against each other. In a capitalist society, entrepreneurs' desire to earn profits motivates them to produce products and services that satisfy customers. Competition allows efficient firms to increase their share of the market and forces inefficient firms out of the market.

U.S. firms can normally enter capitalist countries without any excessive restrictions by the governments. Typically, though, the level of competition in those countries is high.

## Global Business

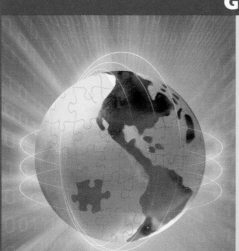

### Nonverbal Communications in Different Cultures

Nonverbal behavior can only be interpreted within a specific cultural context. Here are five common nonverbal behaviors and how they are interpreted in different countries or geographic areas. Caution is always the better part of valor in using nonverbal behaviors outside your native land.

◆ *Withholding eye contact:*
  ◆ In the United States, it indicates shyness or deception.
  ◆ In Libya, it is a compliment to a woman.
  ◆ In Japan, it is done in deference to authority.

◆ *Crossing legs when seated:*
  ◆ In the United States, it is done for comfort.
  ◆ In Arab countries, it is an insult to show the soles of the feet.

◆ *Displaying the palm of the hand:*
  ◆ In the United States, it is a form of greeting, such as a wave or handshake.
  ◆ In Greece, it is an insult.

◆ *Joining the index finger and thumb to make an O:*
  ◆ In the United States, it means "okay."
  ◆ In Mediterranean countries, it means "zero" or "the pits."
  ◆ In Japan, it means money.
  ◆ In Tunisia, it means "I'll kill you."
  ◆ In Latin America, it is an obscene gesture.

◆ *Standing close to a person while talking:*
  ◆ In the United States, it is an intrusion, and the speaker is viewed as pushy.
  ◆ In Latin America and southern Europe, it is the normal spatial distance for conversations.

---

**communism**

an economic system that involves public ownership of businesses

**Communism**  Communism is an economic system that involves public ownership of businesses. In a purely communist system, entrepreneurs are restricted from capitalizing on the perceived needs of the people. The government decides what products will be produced and in what quantity. It may even assign jobs to people, regardless of their interests, and sets the wages to be paid to each worker. Wages may be somewhat similar, regardless of individual abilities or effort. Thus, workers do not have much incentive to excel because they will not be rewarded for abnormally high performance.

In a communist society, the government serves as a central planner. It may decide to produce more of some type of agricultural product if it observes a shortage. Since the government is not concerned about earning profits, it does not focus on satisfying consumers (determining what they want to purchase). Consequently, people are unable to obtain many types of products even if they can afford to buy them. In addition, most people do not have much money to spend because the government pays low wages.

Countries in eastern Europe, such as Bulgaria, Poland, and Romania, had communist systems before 1990. During the 1990s, however, government intervention in these countries declined. Prior to the 1990s, communist countries restricted most U.S. firms from entering, but as they began to allow more private ownership of firms, they also allowed foreign firms to enter.

**socialism**

an economic system that contains some features of both capitalism and communism

**Socialism**   **Socialism** is an economic system that contains some features of both capitalism and communism. For example, governments in some so-called socialist countries allow people to own businesses and property and to select their own jobs. However, these governments are highly involved in the provision of various services. Health-care services are run by many governments and are provided at a low cost. Also, the governments of socialist countries tend to offer high levels of benefits to unemployed people. Such services are indirectly paid for by the businesses and the workers who earn income. Socialist governments impose high tax rates on income so that they have sufficient funds to provide all their services.

Socialist countries face a tradeoff when setting their tax policies, though. To provide a high level of services to the poor and unemployed, the government must impose high tax rates. Many businesses and workers in socialist countries, however, would argue that the tax rates are excessive. They claim that entrepreneurs may be discouraged from establishing businesses when the government taxes most of the income to be earned by the business. Entrepreneurs thus have incentive to establish businesses in other countries where taxes are lower. But if the government lowers the tax rate, it may not generate enough tax revenue to provide the services.

A socialist society may discourage not only the establishment of new businesses but also the desire to work. If the compensation provided by the government to unemployed workers is almost as high as the wages earned by employed workers, unemployed people have little incentive to look for work. The high tax rates typically imposed on employed people in socialist countries also discourage people from looking for work.

**Comparison of Socialism and Capitalism**   In socialist countries, the government has more influence because it imposes higher taxes and can spend that tax revenue as it chooses. In capitalist countries, the government has less influence because it imposes lower taxes and therefore has less funds to spend on the people. Businesses and highly skilled workers generally prefer capitalist countries because there is less government interference.

Even if a capitalist country is preferred, people may disagree on how much influence the government should have. For example, some people in the United States believe that the government should provide fewer services to the unemployed and the poor, which would allow for lower taxes. Other people believe that taxes should be increased so that the government can allocate more services to the poor.

Many countries exhibit some combination of capitalism and socialism. For example, the governments of many developed countries in Europe (such as Sweden and Switzerland) allow firms to be privately owned but provide various services (such as health care) for the people. Germany's government provides child-care allowances, health care, and retirement pensions. The French government commonly intervenes when firms experience financial problems.

Like many countries, Russia has been transformed into a market-oriented economy for many products. The new business center in Moscow, Russia, is shown here.

European countries have recently attempted to reduce their budget deficits as part of a treaty supporting closer European relations. This may result in less government control because the governments will not be able to spend as much money.

**Conversion Toward Capitalism**   Historically, the governments of many countries in eastern Europe, Latin America, and the Soviet Bloc owned most businesses, but in recent years they have allowed for private business ownership. Many government-owned businesses have been sold to private investors. As a result of this so-called **privatization**, many governments are reducing their influence and allowing firms to compete in each industry. Privatization allows firms to focus on providing the products and services that people desire and forces the firms to be more efficient to ensure their survival. Thousands of businesses in the former Soviet Bloc have been privatized. Some U.S. firms have acquired businesses sold by the governments of the former Soviet republics and other countries. Privatization has provided an easy way for U.S. firms to acquire businesses in many foreign countries.

Privatization in many countries, such as Brazil, Hungary, and the countries of the former Soviet Bloc, is an abrupt shift from tradition. Most people in these countries have not had experience in owning and managing a business. Even those people who managed government-owned businesses are not used to competition because the government typically controlled each industry. Therefore, many people who want to own their own businesses have been given some training by business professors and professionals from capitalist countries such as the United States. In particular, the MBA Enterprise Corps, headquartered at the University of North Carolina, has sent thousands of business students to less-developed countries.

Even the industrialized countries have initiated privatization programs for some businesses that were previously owned by the government. The telephone company in Germany has been privatized, as have numerous large government-owned businesses in France.

**privatization**
the sale of government-owned businesses to private investors

## 4.3  Economic Conditions

To predict demand for its product in a foreign country, a firm must attempt to forecast the economic conditions in that country. The firm's overall performance is dependent on the foreign country's economic growth and on the firm's sensitivity to conditions in that country, as explained next.

**Economic Growth**    Many U.S. firms have recently expanded into smaller foreign markets because they expect that economic growth in these countries will be strong, resulting in a strong demand for their products. For example, Heinz has expanded its business throughout Asia. General Motors, Procter & Gamble, AT&T, Ford Motor Company, and General Electric plan new direct foreign investment in Brazil. The Coca-Cola Company has expanded in China, India, and eastern Europe.

The primary factor influencing the decision by many firms to expand in a particular foreign country is the country's expected economic growth, which affects the potential demand for their products. If firms overestimate the country's economic growth, they will normally overestimate the demand for their products in that country. Consequently, their revenue may not be sufficient to cover the expenses associated with the expansion.

In addition, foreign countries may experience weak economies in some periods, which can adversely affect firms that serve those countries. When Asian economies are weak, U.S. firms with business in Asia, such as Nike and Hewlett-Packard, typically experience a decline in the demand for their products. In some periods, most countries around the world can experience weak economic conditions. Thus, even firms with business diversified across different countries are not insulated from the weak economic conditions because these conditions exist in most countries. To illustrate the impact of global economic conditions, consider the comments made by Dell, Inc., in a recent annual report:

*"During the year 2002, worldwide economic conditions negatively affected demand for the Company's products and resulted in declining revenue and earnings. . . . The Company believes that worldwide economic conditions will improve. However, if economic conditions continue to worsen, or if economic conditions do not improve as rapidly as expected, the Company's revenue and earnings could be negatively affected."*

**Sensitivity to Foreign Economic Conditions**    A U.S. firm's exposure to a foreign country's economy is dependent on the proportion of the firm's business conducted in that country. To illustrate, compare the influence of Canada's economy on two U.S. firms (Firm X and Firm Y), as shown in Exhibit 4.3. Assume that Firm X typically generates 20 percent of its total revenue from selling its products in Canada and 80 percent of its total revenue from the United States. Firm Y typically generates 60 percent of its total

| Exhibit 4.3 | Comparing the Influence of the Canadian Economy on Two U.S. Firms |

| U.S. Firm | Total Annual Revenue | Proportion of Canadian Business | Proportion of U.S. Business | Annual Revenue from Canadian Business | Annual Revenue from U.S. Business |
|---|---|---|---|---|---|
| Firm X | $100,000,000 | 20% | 80% | $20,000,000 | $80,000,000 |
| Firm Y | 10,000,000 | 60% | 40% | 6,000,000 | 4,000,000 |

revenue from Canada and 40 percent of its total revenue from the United States. A weak economy in Canada will likely have a more negative effect on Firm Y because it relies more on its Canadian business.

Some U.S. firms, such as The Coca-Cola Company, Dow Chemical, and ExxonMobil, generate more than half of their total revenue from foreign countries. Nevertheless, they are not heavily influenced by any single foreign country's economy because their international business is scattered across many countries. The Coca-Cola Company, for example, conducts business in more than 200 foreign countries. The demand for Coca-Cola's soft drink products may decline in some countries where the weather is cooler than normal, but this unfavorable effect can be offset by a higher demand for the company's products in other countries where the weather is warmer than normal.

## 4.4  Exchange Rates

Countries generally have their own currency. The United States uses dollars ($), the United Kingdom uses British pounds (£), Canada uses Canadian dollars (C$), and Japan uses Japanese yen (¥). As mentioned earlier, a number of European countries recently adopted the euro (€) as their currency. Exchange rates between the U.S. dollar and any currency fluctuate over time. Consequently, the number of dollars a U.S. firm needs to purchase foreign supplies may change even if the actual price charged for the supplies by the foreign producer does not. When the dollar weakens, foreign currencies strengthen; thus, U.S. firms need more dollars to purchase a given amount of foreign supplies. Exchange rate fluctuations can also affect the foreign demand for a U.S. firm's product because they affect the actual price paid by the foreign customers (even if the price in dollars remains unchanged).

## 4.5  Political Risk and Regulations

**political risk**

the risk that a country's political actions can adversely affect a business

A firm must also consider the political risk and regulatory climate of a country before deciding to do business there. **Political risk** is the risk that a country's political actions may adversely affect a business. Political crises have occurred in many countries throughout eastern Europe, Latin

The euro (shown here) is the currency used by many European countries today. Its value against the U.S. dollar changes over time. As the value changes, it affects the amount of dollars needed to purchase European products (denominated in euros) and the amount of euros needed to purchase U.S. products (denominated in dollars).

© SHUTTERSTOCK/c.

# Cross-Functional Teamwork

## Managing International Business Across Business Functions

When a firm plans to conduct business in a foreign country, it should request input from its managers across various departments. The production managers may assess a country according to the expenses associated with production and therefore may focus on the following questions:

1. What is the cost of hiring the necessary labor?
2. What is the cost of developing a new facility?
3. What is the cost of purchasing an existing facility?
4. Does the country have access to the necessary materials and technology?

The marketing managers may assess a country according to the potential revenue to be earned from selling a product in that country and therefore may focus on the following questions:

1. What is the foreign demand for the firm's product?
2. What changes need to be made in the product to satisfy local consumers?
3. What types of marketing strategies would be effective in that country?
4. What is the cost of marketing the product in that country?

The financial managers may assess a country according to the costs of financing any business conducted in that country and therefore may focus on the following questions:

1. Is it possible to obtain a local loan in that country?
2. What is the interest rate charged on local loans?
3. Should the firm use some of its retained earnings from its domestic business to support any foreign business?
4. How would the firm's earnings increase as a result of doing business in the foreign country?

The production department cannot properly estimate the production costs in a specific country until the marketing department determines whether the product must be revised to satisfy the local consumers. Also, the financial managers cannot estimate the earnings from this business until they receive estimates of revenue (from the marketing department), production expenses (from the production department), and marketing expenses (from the marketing department).

America, and the Middle East. U.S. firms are subject to policies imposed by the governments of the foreign countries where they do business. Firms are also vulnerable to the possibility that political problems between two governments may cause consumers to react negatively against the firms because of their country of origin. During the war in Iraq in 2003, anti-American protests against the war in the Middle East and other countries forced some U.S.-based multinational corporations to temporarily shut down their operations in some countries. In addition, the protests led to a decline in the demand for the products of some U.S.-based firms.

As an extreme form of political risk, a foreign government may take over a U.S. firm's foreign subsidiary without compensating the U.S. firm in any way. A more common form of political risk is that the foreign government imposes higher corporate tax rates on foreign subsidiaries. Some governments impose a tax on funds sent by a subsidiary to the parent firm (headquarters) in the home country. They may even prevent the funds from being sent for a certain period of time. The exposure of multinational companies to political risks is clearly emphasized in a recent annual report of Dell, Inc.:

*"The Company's future growth rates and success are dependent on continued growth and success in international markets. . . . The success and profitability of the Company's international operations are subject to numerous risks and uncertainties, including local economic and labor conditions, political instability, unexpected changes in the regulatory environment, trade protection measures, tax laws, and foreign currency exchange rates."*

**Corruption**   Corruption is a form of political risk that can have a major impact on firms attempting to do business in a country. For example, a firm that wants to establish a business in a specific country may obtain a quick approval only if it provides payoffs to some government officials. Thus, corruption increases the cost of doing business. It may also be viewed as illegal. Firms may therefore be discouraged from doing business in those countries that have more corruption. Transparency International (see www.transparency.org) calculates a corruption index for most countries. The ratings for selected countries are shown in Exhibit 4.4. Countries with relatively high ratings have less corruption.

**Regulatory Climate**   Government regulations such as environmental laws vary among countries. By increasing costs, these laws can affect the feasibility of establishing a subsidiary in a foreign country. Stringent

**Exhibit 4.4**

Corruption Index Ratings for Selected Countries (Maximum rating = 10. High ratings represent low corruption.)

| Country | Index Rating | Country | Index Rating |
|---|---|---|---|
| Denmark | 9.4 | Belgium | 7.1 |
| Finland | 9.4 | Chile | 7.0 |
| New Zealand | 9.4 | Spain | 6.7 |
| Singapore | 9.3 | Taiwan | 5.7 |
| Sweden | 9.3 | Uruguay | 5.5 |
| Netherlands | 9.0 | Italy | 5.2 |
| Switzerland | 9.0 | Malaysia | 5.1 |
| Canada | 8.7 | Hungary | 4.8 |
| United Kingdom | 8.4 | Greece | 4.6 |
| Hong Kong | 8.1 | Brazil | 3.9 |
| Austria | 8.0 | Czech Republic | 3.9 |
| Germany | 7.8 | Mexico | 3.6 |
| Ireland | 7.5 | China | 3.5 |
| France | 7.3 | India | 3.5 |
| United States | 7.2 | Russia | 2.3 |

Source: Transparency International, 2008.

building codes, restrictions on the disposal of production waste materials, and pollution controls are examples of regulations that may force subsidiaries to incur additional costs. Many European countries have recently imposed tougher anti-pollution laws as a result of severe pollution problems.

Another type of regulatory problem occurs when countries do not enforce their laws. Some countries do not enforce regulations that protect copyrights laws. Thus, a firm that produces products such as books or music CDs may not benefit from establishing a business in these countries because the product may be easily copied by local firms without any penalty for violating copyright laws.

Some countries also do not enforce bribery laws. As a result of the Foreign Corrupt Practices Act, U.S. firms are not allowed to offer bribes to government officials or political candidates. Some U.S. firms argue that they are at a disadvantage because they are unable to offer bribes to government officials in a foreign country, when some other firms can.

Countries also differ in the penalties they may impose on businesses for producing defective products or discriminating against employees. The U.S. court system has a worldwide reputation for imposing excessive penalties on businesses. In numerous cases, a person who was injured because of poor judgment blamed the injury on the product and won a lawsuit against a business in a U.S. court. Even if a business can prove that it was not at fault, defending against a lawsuit can be very expensive. Non-U.S. firms may be discouraged from establishing businesses in the United States for this reason.

Given the major differences in regulations among countries, a firm must understand the rules of any country where it is considering conducting business. Firms should pursue only those international business opportunities where the potential benefits are not offset by costs associated with regulations.

**Learning Objective**

Explain how exchange rate movements can affect a firm's performance.

**5**

# 5. How Exchange Rate Movements Can Affect Performance

International trade transactions typically require the exchange of one currency for another. For example, if a U.S. firm periodically purchases supplies from a British supplier, it will need to exchange U.S. dollars for the British currency (pounds) to make the purchase. This process is shown in Exhibit 4.5.

Generally, the exchange rate between a given currency and the U.S. dollar fluctuates daily. When the exchange rate changes, U.S. firms involved in international trade are affected. The impact of exchange rate movements on a U.S. firm can be favorable or unfavorable, depending on the characteristics of the firm, as illustrated by the following examples.

## 5.1 Impact of a Weak Dollar on U.S. Importers

Assume that the value of the pound (£), the British currency, at a given point in time is $2.00. That is, each dollar is worth one-half of a British pound. If a U.S. firm needs £1,000,000 to purchase supplies from a British supplier, it will need $2,000,000 to obtain those pounds, as shown:

**Exhibit 4.5**

Example of Importing
by a U.S. Firm

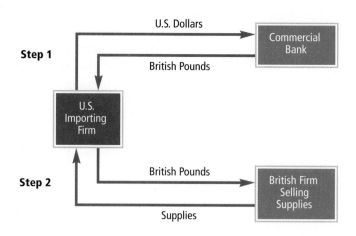

$$
\begin{aligned}
\text{Amount of \$ Needed} &= (\text{Amount of £ Needed} \times \text{Value of £}) \\
&= £1{,}000{,}000 \times \$2.00 \\
&= \$2{,}000{,}000
\end{aligned}
$$

**appreciates**
strengthens in value

Now assume that the pound **appreciates** (or strengthens in value) against the dollar. This also means that the dollar weakens (is worth less) against the pound. For example, assume the pound is now equal to $2.02 instead of $2.00. Now the U.S. firm needs $20,000 more to obtain the pounds than it needed before the pound appreciated. Thus, the cost of the supplies has increased for the U.S. firm as a result of the appreciation in the British pound (a weaker dollar). This illustrates why a weak dollar adversely affects U.S. firms that frequently import supplies.

## 5.2 Impact of a Strong Dollar on U.S. Importers

**depreciates**
weakens in value

Now consider a situation in which the pound **depreciates**, or weakens in value against the dollar. This also means that the dollar strengthens against the pound. For example, assume the pound's value was $2.00 but has declined to $1.90 over the last month. If the U.S. firm needs to obtain £1,000,000, it will be able to purchase the pounds for $100,000 less than was needed before the pound depreciated. The firm's payment has declined by 5 percent because the pound's value has declined by 5 percent.

This example shows how the depreciation of a foreign currency against the dollar (a stronger dollar) reduces the expenses of a U.S. firm that is purchasing foreign supplies. This explains why a strong dollar favorably affects U.S. firms that frequently import supplies.

## 5.3 Actual Effects of Exchange Rate Movements on U.S. Importers

To illustrate the impact of a change in a currency's value on U.S. importers, consider how many dollars you would pay for a pair of jeans that are sold in the United Kingdom at two different points in time. Assume that the jeans are priced at 50 British pounds. In Year 1, the value of a British pound (£) was about $1.43, so you would have paid:

$$
\begin{aligned}
\text{Payment in Dollars} &= (\text{Payment in £}) \times (\text{Exchange Rate}) \\
&= £50 \times \$1.42 \\
&= \$71.00
\end{aligned}
$$

In Year 2, the value of a British pound was about $1.76, so you would have paid:

$$\text{Payment in Dollars} = (\text{Payment in £}) \times (\text{Exchange Rate})$$
$$= £50 \times \$1.76$$
$$= \$88.00$$

Your cost increased by $17, or by about 24 percent, because the value of pound increased by about 24 percent over this period.

Now consider the impact on U.S. firms that import a large amount of products from the United Kingdom. If the U.K. exporter charges the same price in Year 2 as in Year 1, the cost to the importers would rise by 24 percent over this period because of the change in the exchange rate. The pound has depreciated substantially in some periods, such as 1981–1984, 1991–1993, and 2001. In other periods, such as 2006–2007, the pound has appreciated. When the pound appreciated, the amount of dollars needed to buy British imports increased. Conversely, when the pound depreciated, the amount of dollars needed to buy British imports declined. The expenses of a U.S. importing firm are highly sensitive to changes in the value of the pound.

The exchange rates of currencies of less-developed countries fluctuate more than those of developed countries. For example, some currencies have depreciated by more than 20 percent in a single month. Consequently, U.S. firms that do business in less-developed countries are exposed to wide swings in exchange rates.

## 5.4 Impact of a Weak Dollar on U.S. Exporters

Just as exchange rate movements can affect U.S. importing firms, they can also affect U.S. firms that export products to other countries. The effect of a weak dollar will be examined first, followed by the effect of a strong dollar.

Consider how a U.S. firm that exports equipment to a British firm is affected by a weak dollar. The exporting process is shown in Exhibit 4.6. If the U.S. exporter wants to receive U.S. dollars for its equipment, the British firm must first exchange its currency (pounds) into dollars at a commercial bank (Step 1 in Exhibit 4.6). Then the British firm uses these dollars to purchase the equipment of the U.S. exporting firm (Step 2).

**Exhibit 4.6**

Example of Exporting by a U.S. Firm

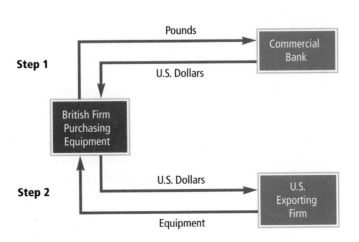

If the dollar weakens, the British firm can obtain the dollars it needs with fewer pounds. Therefore, it may be willing to purchase more equipment from the U.S. exporting firm. The U.S. firm's revenue will rise in response to a higher demand for the equipment it produces. Therefore, its profits should increase as well.

As this example shows, a weak dollar can result in higher revenue and profits for U.S. firms that frequently export their products. U.S. exporting firms tend to benefit from a weak dollar because their prices are perceived as inexpensive by foreign customers who must convert their currencies into dollars. A weak dollar favorably affects U.S. firms that export heavily because foreign demand for the products they export increases substantially when the dollar is weak.

## 5.5 Impact of a Strong Dollar on U.S. Exporters

Now consider a situation in which the value of the pound depreciates against the dollar. As the pound's value declines, the British firm must exchange more British pounds to obtain the same amount of dollars as before. That is, it needs more pounds to purchase equipment from the U.S. firm. Consequently, it may reduce its purchases from the U.S. firm and perhaps will search for a British producer of the equipment to avoid having to obtain dollars.

As this example shows, a strong dollar can result in lower revenue for U.S. firms that frequently export their products. A strong dollar adversely affects U.S. exporting firms because the prices of their exports appear expensive to foreign customers who must convert their currencies into dollars. When the dollar strengthens, U.S. exporting firms such as Procter & Gamble and Boeing are adversely affected.

## 5.6 Hedging Against Exchange Rate Movements

**hedge**
action taken to protect a firm against exchange rate movements

U.S. firms commonly attempt to **hedge**, or protect against exchange rate movements. They can hedge most effectively when they know how much of a specific foreign currency they will need or will receive on a specific date in the future.

**Hedging Future Payments in Foreign Currencies** Consider a firm that plans to purchase British supplies and will need £1,000,000 in 90 days to pay for those supplies. It can call a large commercial bank that exchanges foreign currencies and request a so-called **forward contract**, which provides that an exchange of currencies will occur for a specified exchange rate at a future point in time. In this case, the forward contract will specify an exchange of dollars for £1,000,000 in 90 days. In other words, the firm wants to purchase pounds 90 days forward.

**forward contract**
provides that an exchange of currencies will occur at a specified exchange rate at a future point in time

**forward rate**
the exchange rate that a bank will be willing to offer at a future point in time

**spot exchange rate**
the exchange rate quoted for immediate transactions

The bank will quote the **forward rate**, or the exchange rate that the bank will be willing to offer at a future point in time. The forward rate is normally close to the **spot exchange rate**, which is the exchange rate quoted for immediate transactions. Assume that the bank quotes a 90-day forward rate of $1.80 for the British pound. If the firm agrees to this quote, it has agreed to a forward contract. It will lock in the purchase of £1,000,000 in 90 days for $1.80 per pound, or $1,800,000 for the £1,000,000. Once the firm hedges its position, it has locked in the rate at which it will exchange currencies on that future date, regardless of the actual spot exchange rate that occurs on that date. In this way, the U.S. firm hedges against the possibility that the pound will appreciate over that period.

## SMALL BUSINESS SURVEY

### Concern About Exchange Rate Movements

In a recent National Small Business poll conducted for the NFIB Research Foundation, small businesses that conduct international business were asked whether exchange rate movements limit their willingness to pursue international business. Their responses are shown below:

Other
5%

Severely
limit
16%

Do not limit
57%

Somewhat
limit
22%

**Hedging Future Receivables in Foreign Currencies**   U.S. firms can also hedge when they expect to receive a foreign currency in the future. For example, consider a U.S. firm that knows it will receive £1,000,000 in 90 days. It can call a commercial bank and negotiate a forward contract in which it will provide the £1,000,000 to the bank in exchange for dollars. Assuming that the 90-day forward rate is $1.80 (as in the previous example), the firm will receive $1,800,000 in 90 days (computed as $1.80 × £1,000,000). By using a forward contract, this firm locks in the rate at which it can exchange its pounds for dollars, regardless of the spot ex-

## Responding to the Economy

### Capitalizing on International Business When the Local Economy Is Weak

As the U.S. economy weakened in 2007 and 2008, many U.S. firms relied more on selling products to foreign countries. During that period, the value of the U.S. dollar weakened against other currencies. For example, the euro was worth about $1.58 in July 2008, versus about $1.10 in 2003. In other words, 1,000 euros could be exchanged for $1,580 in July 2008, versus $1,100 in 2003. The weak dollar resulted in a stronger European demand for products produced by U.S. firms.

Some U.S. firms that previously had no international business suddenly began to pursue business in Europe for this reason. These firms not only benefited from a weak dollar, but also from the European economy, which was stronger than the U.S. economy. Consequently, European consumers were willing to spend more money at the time. The strategy by U.S. firms to increase their international business during this period helped to offset the decline in their sales within the United States. As economic conditions change across countries, firms need to be flexible so that they can capitalize on opportunities wherever they may be.

change rate that occurs on that date. In this way, the U.S. firm hedges against the possibility that the pound will depreciate over the period of concern.

**Limitations of Hedging**  A major limitation of hedging is that it prevents favorable exchange rate effects as well as unfavorable effects. For example, reconsider the initial example in which the firm locks in the purchase of pounds 90 days ahead at a forward rate of $1.80. If the actual spot exchange rate in 90 days is $1.70, the firm would have been better off without the hedge. Nevertheless, it is obligated to fulfill its forward contract by exchanging dollars for pounds at the forward exchange rate of $1.80. This example illustrates why many U.S. firms hedge only when they expect that their future international business transactions will be adversely affected by exchange rate movements.

## 5.7  How Exchange Rates Affect Foreign Competition

Many U.S. firms compete with foreign firms in the U.S. market. Exhibit 4.7 shows a common situation in the United States. RCA is a U.S. firm that sells televisions in the U.S. market. It competes with many foreign competitors that export televisions to the United States. Retail stores purchase televisions from RCA as well as other firms.

Assume that the stores mark up the price of each television by 20 percent. When these stores purchase Japanese televisions, they convert dollars

**Exhibit 4.7**

How Exchange Rates Affect the Degree of Foreign Competition

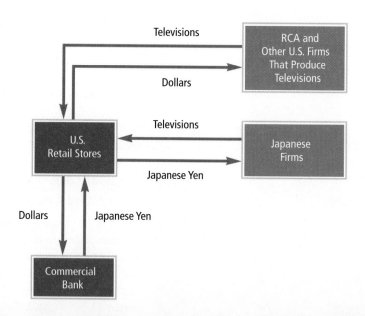

| Scenario | Result |
|---|---|
| 1. Japanese yen depreciates against the dollar. | U.S. retail stores can purchase Japanese televisions with fewer dollars, so the demand for Japanese televisions increases (and therefore the demand for U.S. televisions decreases). |
| 2. Japanese yen appreciates against the dollar. | U.S. retail stores must pay more dollars to purchase Japanese televisions, so the demand for Japanese televisions decreases (and therefore the demand for U.S. televisions increases). |

to Japanese yen (the Japanese currency). If the value of the yen depreciates against the dollar, the store needs fewer dollars to purchase the Japanese televisions. If it applies the same markup, it can reduce its price on the Japanese televisions. Therefore, increased foreign competition (due to depreciation of one or more foreign currencies) may cause RCA to lose some U.S. business.

If the foreign currency appreciates against the dollar, the foreign competitors may be unable to compete in the United States because the prices of imported products will rise. Using our example, if the Japanese yen appreciates, the retail store will need more dollars to purchase the Japanese televisions. When applying its markup, it will need to increase its price on the Japanese televisions. Therefore, U.S. firms such as RCA may gain more U.S. business.

## COLLEGE HEALTH CLUB: CHC's EXPOSURE TO GLOBAL CONDITIONS

College Health Club (CHC) sells its services locally, and its competitors are local. Therefore, global conditions do not have a direct effect on its business. However, Sue Kramer (owner of CHC) recognizes that even her small health club business could be affected by foreign competition. A British health club chain called Maximum Shape has established some health clubs in other parts of Texas. When the value of the British pound (the British currency) is high (strong) against the dollar, this health club expands into the United States because an investment of 100,000 British pounds can be converted to a large amount of dollars. If this health club expands into Dallas in the future, it could become a competitor of CHC.

## Summary of Learning Objectives

**1** The main reasons U.S. firms engage in international business are to

♦ attract foreign demand,

♦ capitalize on technology,

♦ use inexpensive resources, or

♦ diversify internationally.

The first two reasons reflect higher revenue, while the third reason reflects lower expenses. The fourth reason reflects less risk by reducing exposure to a single economy.

**2** The primary ways in which firms conduct international business are:

♦ importing,

♦ exporting,

♦ direct foreign investment,

♦ outsourcing, and

♦ strategic alliances.

Many U.S. firms have used all of these strategies.

**3** Even though barriers to international business have been reduced over time, some barriers to international business still exist. Some governments continue to impose barriers in order to protect their local firms or to punish countries for their actions. Barriers can either prevent firms from entering foreign markets or make it more expensive for them to do so. The status of barriers can change over time. Firms need to recognize the existing barriers so that they can decide whether entering

a specific foreign market is worthwhile.

**4** When firms sell their products in international markets, they must assess the cultures, economic systems and conditions, exchange rate risk, and political risk and regulations in those markets. The larger the proportion of the firm's total sales generated in a specific foreign country, the more sensitive is the firm's revenue to that country's economic conditions.

**5** U.S. importers benefit from a strong dollar. U.S. exporters benefit from a weak dollar but are adversely affected by a strong dollar.

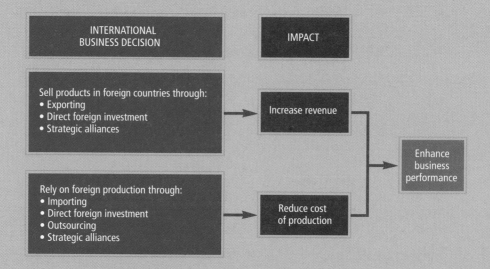

# Self-Test of Key Concepts

The following self-assessment allows you to test your understanding of the key concepts covered in this chapter. Answers are provided at the end of this exercise.

## True or False

1. An important reason U.S. firms establish new businesses in less-developed countries is to capitalize on technological advantages.

2. The best way for a firm to stabilize its profits over time is to focus its efforts on producing and selling one specific product in one specific country.

3. Land and labor costs can vary significantly among countries.

4. U.S. firms that provide services are more likely to face strong foreign competition than firms that produce manufactured goods.

5. A tax placed on imported goods is called a tariff.

6. Competition among firms is usually more intense in communist economies than it is in capitalist economies.

7. A key advantage of socialist economies is the emphasis on keeping tax rates as low as possible.

8. A firm's performance in a foreign country is dependent on that country's economic growth.

9. If firms overestimate the economic growth in a particular country, they will normally overestimate the demand for their products in that country.

10. The values of most currencies are not allowed to change relative to the dollar.

## Multiple Choice

11. A country that has relatively low technology is termed a(n):
    a) least-favored nation.
    b) post-communist country.
    c) pre-industrial nation.
    d) backward nation.
    e) developing country.

12. All of the following are important reasons why U.S. firms engage in international business except to:
    a) attract foreign demand.
    b) capitalize on technology.
    c) take advantage of lower taxes in socialist economies.
    d) use inexpensive labor and natural resources available in less-developed countries.
    e) diversify internationally.

13. A major reason U.S. firms want to achieve international diversification is that it:
    a) exposes them to cultural diversity.
    b) enables them to take big tax write-offs.
    c) helps them stabilize profits, thus reducing their risk.
    d) allows them to acquire more advanced technology.
    e) allows them to offer stock to foreign investors, thus increasing their financial base.

14. With the implementation of NAFTA in 1993:
    a) most trade restrictions between the United States, Canada, and Mexico were removed.
    b) European nations began using a common currency.
    c) U.S. firms were encouraged to invest in the less-developed nations of Asia, Central America, and Africa.
    d) the World Bank was given the authority to set interest rates on international business loans.
    e) countries were no longer allowed to have trade deficits continue for more than three years.

15. A number of European nations recently agreed to share a common currency known as the:
    a) gifspen.
    b) francmarc.
    c) European pound.
    d) euro.
    e) NAFTA.

16. The purchase of foreign supplies by IBM is an example of:
    a) direct foreign investment.
    b) exporting.
    c) importing.
    d) international licensing.
    e) a joint venture.

17. The U.S. government just imposed a numerical limit on the amount of widgets that may be imported, which is called a:
    a) quota.
    b) tariff.
    c) call rate.
    d) exchange factor.
    e) limit order.

18. A negative balance of trade is referred to as a:
    a) trade deficit.
    b) trade surplus.
    c) favorable balance of payments.
    d) direct investment.
    e) hedge.

19. The sale of film produced by Kodak in the United States to Chinese firms is an example of:
    a) direct foreign investment.
    b) exporting.
    c) importing.
    d) international licensing.
    e) a joint venture.

20. When a firm in one country acquires or builds a subsidiary in another country, it is engaging in:
    a) arbitrage.
    b) a joint venture.
    c) foreign aid.
    d) a forward contract.
    e) direct foreign investment.

21. A(n) _____ is a strategic alliance in which a firm allows a foreign company to produce its products according to specific instructions.
    a) international cartel
    b) international licensing agreement
    c) joint venture
    d) international limited partnership
    e) limited liability contract

22. Under _____ the government owns most businesses and decides what products to produce and in what quantity.
    a) socialism
    b) capitalism
    c) communism
    d) dualism
    e) pluralism

23. In a _____ economy, businesses are privately owned and profit-seeking entrepreneurs are free to start businesses they believe will serve the people's needs.
    a) capitalist
    b) communist
    c) feudalist
    d) mercantilist
    e) pluralist

24. _____ is an economic system that allows some private ownership of businesses and property but also has an active government sector and high tax rates to support the government's programs.
   a) Socialism
   b) Capitalism
   c) Feudalism
   d) Mercantilism
   e) Dualism

25. In recent years, governments of many nations have sold government-owned and -operated businesses to private investors. This process is known as:
   a) public disinvestment.
   b) privatization.
   c) repatriation.
   d) democratization.
   e) public capitalization.

26. The dollar weakens against the British pound if the value of the pound:
   a) depreciates.
   b) sells off.
   c) softens.
   d) appreciates.
   e) declines.

27. If the dollar depreciates relative to the Japanese yen:
   a) Japanese goods will seem cheaper to American importers.
   b) gold will flow from the United States to Japan.
   c) American goods will seem less expensive to Japanese consumers.
   d) the dollar must appreciate relative to some other Asian currency.
   e) the U.S. government will have to intervene to increase the value of the dollar.

28. A _____ states an exchange of currencies that will occur at a specified exchange rate at some future point in time.
   a) reserve clause
   b) forward contract
   c) limit order
   d) market order
   e) fixed time exchange contract

29. When businesses take action to lock in a specific exchange rate for a future international transaction in order to reduce risk, their strategy is referred to as:
   a) rate fixing.
   b) trading on reserve.
   c) selling short.
   d) hedging.
   e) trading on margin.

30. If you plan to convert dollars to obtain Japanese yen today, you would pay the:
   a) spot rate.
   b) open market rate.
   c) discount rate.
   d) hedge rate.
   e) forward rate.

**True/False**

| | |
|---|---|
| 1. True | 9. True |
| 2. False | 10. False |
| 3. True | |
| 4. False | |
| 5. True | |
| 6. False | |
| 7. False | |
| 8. True | |

**Multiple Choice**

| | | |
|---|---|---|
| 11. e | 18. a | 25. b |
| 12. c | 19. b | 26. d |
| 13. c | 20. e | 27. c |
| 14. a | 21. b | 28. b |
| 15. d | 22. c | 29. d |
| 16. c | 23. a | 30. a |
| 17. a | 24. a | |

## Self-Test of Key Terms

appreciates 122
balance of trade 105
capitalism 113
communism 114
depreciates 122
direct foreign investment (DFI) 106
dumping 109
exporting 104

forward contract 124
forward rate 124
hedge 124
importing 104
international licensing agreement 108
joint venture 108
political risk 118

privatization 116
quota 104
socialism 115
spot exchanger rate 124
strategic alliance 108
tariff 104
trade deficit 105

Fill in each blank with the proper key term. To assess your understanding of the key terms, answers are provided at the end of this self-test.

1. _____ allows for the private ownership of businesses, and entrepreneurs have the freedom to create businesses that serve the people's needs.

2. If the euro _____ against the dollar, this means that the euro's value has declined.

3. The _____ reflects the exchange rate at which a firm can obtain a particular currency for immediate delivery.

4. U.S. firms commonly attempt to hedge against exchange rate movements by using a _____ contract.

5. A _____ involves an agreement between two firms about a specific project.

6. In a(n) _____ agreement, a firm allows a foreign company to produce its products according to specific instructions.

7. A(n) _____ is a tax imposed by the government on imported goods.

8. _____ represents acquiring foreign firms or building foreign subsidiaries.

9. _____ is the risk that a country's political actions will adversely affect a business.

10. A(n) _____ sets the limit on the quantity of a specific product that can be imported by a country.

11. If the Japanese yen increases in value against the U.S. dollar, this means that the yen _____.

12. The U.S. _____ is equal to the level of U.S. exports minus the level of U.S. imports.

13. _____ refers to the sale of government-owned businesses to private investors.

**Answers:**
1. Capitalism
2. depreciates
3. spot exchange rate
4. forward
5. joint venture
6. international licensing
7. tariff
8. Direct foreign investment
9. Political risk
10. quota
11. appreciates
12. balance of trade
13. Privatization

# Concept Review Questions

1. **International Business Motives.** Explain why a U.S. firm is motivated to pursue international business.

2. **Trade Barriers.** Explain the difference between a tariff and a quota. Explain why these international trade barriers protect a local firm's business from foreign competition.

3. **Exporting Versus Importing.** What is the difference between exporting and importing?

4. **International Business Methods.** Describe common methods used to conduct international business.

5. **China's Advantage.** What is the major reason why U.S. consumers desire products that are produced in China and other Asian countries?

6. **Direct Foreign Investment.** Explain why U.S. firms may pursue direct foreign investment (DFI).

7. **Strategic Alliance.** Why might a firm pursue a strategic alliance rather than direct foreign investment?

8. **Economic Systems.** Explain the different types of economic systems that may be found among countries.

9. **Foreign Economic Conditions.** Explain why a firm's sales to customers in a foreign country may be highly influenced by the foreign country's economic conditions.

10. **Weak Dollar Effect.** Explain how a weak dollar affects the performance of U.S. firms that attempt to export their products.

## Class Communication Questions

1. **Imposing Barriers on Imports from China.** U.S. imports from China exceed U.S. exports to China by more than $150 billion each year. Many U.S. businesses want the U.S. government to place barriers on imports from China because they believe that China has an unfair advantage (they allege that China uses children in factories). However, if the U.S. government places barriers on the imports, U.S. consumers would have to pay a higher price for many products. Should the U.S. government impose barriers on China?

2. **Outsource Decision.** You want to start a business in the United States, but you would outsource some of the work to Mexico because you can achieve low labor costs, and this would be necessary for your business to survive. Some critics may suggest that in order to reduce the U.S. unemployment rate, you should hire people in the United States rather than outsource. What is your opinion?

3. **Foreign Competition.** Do you think foreign competitors have an unfair advantage over U.S. firms?

## Small Business Case

### Managing in Response to Global Conditions

Victory Company produces computer games and sells them in the United States. Its major concern is the high cost of producing the computer chips that it uses for the computer games. It contacts a supplier of chips in China and describes the types of chips that it needs. The supplier offers to produce the chips and sell them to Victory Company for a price that is 30 percent lower than its cost of production and is much lower than U.S. chip manufacturers charge. By relying on chips made in China, Victory can reduce its expenses and charge a lower price for its computer games. This will likely result in a much higher demand for its games, and its revenue and profits should increase.

1. **Reason for Reliance on Foreign Materials.** Why do you think that China is able to produce chips at a lower cost than the U.S. firms?

2. **Impact of Reliance on Foreign Materials.** When Victory Company relies on a foreign manufacturer to produce the chips rather than producing the chips itself, what do you think will happen to its employees who produced the chips in the past?

3. **Impact of a Tariff on Businesses.** If Victory Company decides to import computer chips, and the U.S. government imposes a tariff on imports from China, how would this affect the overall expenses incurred by Victory?

4. **Impact of Exchange Rate Movements.** If Victory Company decides to import computer chips, and the price is denominated in Chinese currency (called the yuan), how will the cost of the imports to Victory Company change if the yuan appreciates over time against the dollar?

## Web Insight

### Nike's International Business

At the opening of the chapter, Nike, Inc. was introduced. Go to the Nike website (www.nikebiz.com/company_overview). Summarize the comments made about Nike's international business. Discuss how Nike has expanded its exporting business and its direct foreign investment.

# Dell's Secret for Success

Go to Dell's website (www.dell.com) and click on the link "About Dell," near the bottom of the web page. Review the section that describes Dell's international business. You can also review a recent annual report of Dell for more information.

1. **International Business.** Describe Dell's business in international markets.

2. **Direct Foreign Investment.** What do you think motivated Dell to pursue direct foreign investment in international markets?

3. **Expansion in Asia.** Why do you think some Asian countries could appeal to Dell even if the demand for computers in those countries is low?

# Video Exercise

### Lessons in How Global Conditions Affect a Business

Many free business videos are available on websites such as YouTube (www.youtube.com), and more are added every day. Search for a recent video clip about an existing business that offers lessons on "company international business" in YouTube or any other website that provides video clips.

1. **Main Lesson.** Is the video clip focused on the potential impact of different cultures in the international environment, different regulations, exchange rate effects, or some other global factor that affects a business? What is the main lesson of the video clip that you watched?

2. **Adapting to a Culture.** A common lesson in many business video clips is that a business must adjust its products or services to fit the culture of the host country. Explain how a firm's international business performance may be dependent on whether it adjusts its products or services to fit the culture of the host country.

3. **Impact of Changing Exchange Rates.** U.S. businesses commonly explain in video clips how they experience a reduction in international business when foreign currencies weaken against the dollar. Furthermore, exchange rate movements are difficult to forecast accurately. What is the lesson here for a U.S. business entrepreneur who is planning expansion in another country and is attempting to forecast its revenue from sales in that country?

# Projects

To encourage further comprehension of concepts covered in Chapter 4, the following five projects are available:

1. Analyzing Your Favorite Business

2. Building a Business Plan for Campus.com

3. Running Your Own Business

4. Planning Your Career

5. Stock Market Contest

All of these projects are provided in Appendix A at the end of the text. In addition, projects are available by part division at the end of each part.

A Word file for each project is also available at the textbook website (www.emcp.net/business5e) so that you may maintain one ongoing file for each project.

# Summary/Part I

# Business Environment

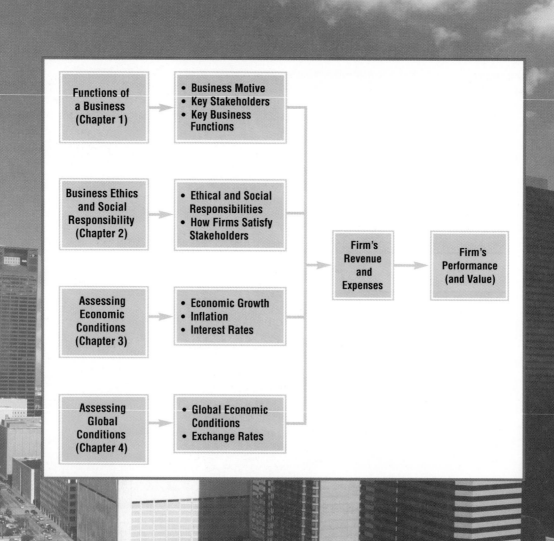

## Summary

The first two chapters in Part I set the foundation for a business. The motives to establish a business and the functions of a business are described in Chapter 1, while the social responsibilities of a business are described in Chapter 2. Chapters 3 and 4 explain how business decisions are influenced by the economic environment. Chapter 3 focuses on the domestic economic environment, while Chapter 4 focuses on the international economic environment to which a business is exposed. An assessment of the economic environment is necessary in order to complete the business planning of a new or existing business.

## Video on Managing a Business

### It Takes Money to Make Money

The Small Business Administration plays a very important role in helping many small businesses. Its website, which offers a wide range of services and information for small businesses, has a section called Delivering Success (www.sba.gov/tools/audiovideo/deliveringsuccess/index.html) that provides video clips of small business success stories. Go to this website, and watch the video called "Getting Started" (total time of clip is 3 minutes, 45 seconds).

In this video clip, two entrepreneurs explain their success. One of the key points is that it takes money to make money. Entrepreneurs commonly need funding in order to achieve their business plans. The Small Business Administration (SBA) helps many entrepreneurs obtain financing by providing a guarantee to commercial banks that the loan will be repaid. That is, if the small business does not repay the loan, the SBA will cover the loan. Since the bank does not have to worry about the risk of loan default, it is more willing to provide loans to small businesses.

1. **Interaction Between Financing and Corporate Responsibilities.** As entrepreneurs obtain financing, their priority is to cover their financing and other expenses so that they can continue their business. Does this mean that their focus on maximizing their value (Chapter 1) requires them to ignore corporate responsibilities (Chapter 2)?

2. **Interaction Between Financing and Economic Exposure.** Explain how the financing decision (amount of debt financing versus equity financing) of a small business (Chapter 1) affects its exposure to economic conditions (Chapter 3). That is, would a firm that obtains mostly debt financing from a bank or equity financing from other investors be more likely to fail if a recession occurred? Why?

3. **Interaction Between Financing and International Business.** Explain how the financing decision (amount of debt financing versus equity financing) of a small business (Chapter 1) affects its ability to pursue international business (Chapter 4). That is, would a firm that obtains mostly debt financing from a bank or equity financing from other investors be more likely to expand into a foreign country? Why?

# Self-Test for Part I

**Chapters 1–4.** Answers are provided at the end of the self-test.

1. The _____ are typically responsible for creating the business idea.
   a) owners
   b) creditors
   c) couriers
   d) employees
   e) customers

2. The stakeholders of a firm include all of the following except:
   a) owners.
   b) creditors.
   c) employees.
   d) suppliers.
   e) government officials.

3. A certificate of ownership of a business is a:
   a) bond.
   b) stock.
   c) mutual fund.
   d) co-article.
   e) contract.

4. Business decisions regarding which products are created, priced, distributed, and promoted to customers are _____ decisions.
   a) finance
   b) information systems
   c) accounting
   d) management
   e) marketing

5. Business decisions that focus on strategies to make the product more appealing to customers and improve the firm's revenue are _____ decisions.
   a) production
   b) marketing
   c) manufacturing
   d) personnel
   e) finance

6. Managers rely on _____ to detect the inefficient use of resources.
   a) owners
   b) creditors
   c) marketing research
   d) marketing mix studies
   e) accounting data

7. The profit motive is influenced by the government because:
   a) governments of free-market economies encourage the profit motive.
   b) businesses are owned by the government.
   c) governments of free-market economies discourage the profit motive.
   d) governments are shareholders of the firm.
   e) governments buy most businesses from individuals.

8. The recognition of how a firm's business decisions can affect society is its:
   a) moral code.
   b) social responsibility.
   c) conservation policies.
   d) recycling program.
   e) consumer bill of rights.

9. Firms can ensure responsibility to customers by:
   a) safe manufacturing techniques.
   b) proper disposal of toxic waste.
   c) employee diversity programs.
   d) soliciting feedback about products.
   e) full financial disclosure.

10. The act that prohibits mergers between firms that reduce competition within an industry is the:
    a) Robinson-Patman Act.
    b) Celler-Kefauver Act.
    c) Federal Trade Commission Act.
    d) Clayton Act.
    e) Sherman Antitrust Act.

11. If a firm is the sole provider of a good or service, it is a(n):
    a) unsuccessful organization.
    b) sole proprietorship.
    c) deregulated firm.
    d) institutional investor.
    e) monopoly.

12. Unwelcome comments or actions of a sexual nature are examples of:
    a) business as usual.
    b) sexual harassment.
    c) equal employment opportunities.
    d) workplace diversity.
    e) deregulation.

13. An active role by stockholders in influencing a firm's management policies is called:
    a) empowerment.
    b) reengineering.
    c) self-managed teams.
    d) quality circles.
    e) shareholder activism.

14. If a firm fails to meet its responsibilities to _____, it may be forced into bankruptcy.
    a) its employees
    b) the environment
    c) the government
    d) its creditors
    e) its owners

15. All of the following are examples of macroeconomic concerns except:
    a) a drop in the nation's gross domestic product.
    b) an increase in the rate of inflation.
    c) a strike by workers at a local bakery.
    d) an increase in the amount of cyclical unemployment.
    e) an increase in the rate of interest charged on bank loans.

16. The type of inflation that requires firms to increase their prices to cover increased costs is referred to as:
    a) demand-pull inflation.
    b) stagflation.
    c) cost-push inflation.
    d) disequilibrium.
    e) unemployment.

17. A typical demand schedule shows that:
    a) as price decreases, quantity demanded will also decrease.
    b) as price decreases, quantity demanded will increase.
    c) quantity supplied can never be less than quantity demanded.
    d) the total quantity of goods consumers want to buy will fall during periods of inflation.
    e) a firm can always increase its revenue by increasing the prices it charges for its products.

18. If the market price of a good is above the equilibrium price:
    a) a surplus will exist, which will put downward pressure on prices.
    b) the supply curve will shift to the right as firms rush to take advantage of the high price.
    c) the demand curve will shift to the left as consumers decrease the quantity they buy.
    d) the government will intervene to force the price downward.
    e) a shortage will exist, which will force the price even higher.

19. The central bank of the United States, where the money supply is controlled and regulated, is the:
    a) Federal Reserve System.
    b) Senate.
    c) Department of Congress.
    d) Council of Economic Advisers.
    e) Board of Directors.

20. Which of the following is the best example of the federal government's use of fiscal policy?
    a) The Federal Reserve places new regulations on the nation's banks that require them to make more loans to minorities and women.
    b) The U.S. Treasury announces that it has redesigned the nation's paper money to make the bills more difficult to counterfeit.
    c) The government cuts taxes during an economic downturn.
    d) The president appoints a new commission to look into concerns about how pollution is damaging the environment.
    e) The Federal Reserve gives banks more funds to enable them to make more loans.

21. When the amount of federal government spending exceeds the amount of federal taxes, the result is called a(n):
    a) trade deficit.
    b) federal budget deficit.
    c) balance of payments.
    d) price equilibrium.
    e) opportunity cost.

22. The government can prevent inflationary pressure caused by an excessive demand for products by maintaining a low rate of:
    a) fiscal policies.
    b) economic growth.
    c) monetary policies.
    d) unemployment.
    e) savings.

23. A country that has relatively low technology is termed a(n):
    a) least-favored nation.
    b) post-communist country.
    c) pre-industrial nation.
    d) backward nation.
    e) developing country.

24. Many European nations recently agreed to share a common currency known as the:
    a) franc.
    b) mark.
    c) European pound.
    d) euro.
    e) peso.

25. A negative balance of trade is referred to as a:
    a) trade deficit.
    b) trade surplus.
    c) favorable balance of payments.
    d) direct investment.
    e) hedge.

26. A(n) _____ is a strategic alliance in which a firm allows a foreign company to produce its products according to specific instructions.
    a) international cartel
    b) international licensing agreement
    c) joint venture
    d) international limited partnership
    e) limited liability contract

27. In a _____ economy, businesses are privately owned and profit-seeking entrepreneurs are free to start businesses they believe will serve the people's needs.
    a) capitalist
    b) communist
    c) feudalist
    d) mercantilist
    e) pluralist

28. The dollar weakens against the British pound if the value of the pound:
    a) depreciates.
    b) sells off.
    c) softens.
    d) appreciates.
    e) declines.

29. If the dollar depreciates relative to the Japanese yen:
    a) Japanese goods will seem cheaper to American importers.
    b) gold will flow from the United States to Japan.
    c) American goods will seem less expensive to Japanese consumers.
    d) the dollar must appreciate relative to some other Asian currency.
    e) the U.S. government will have to intervene to increase the value of the dollar.

30. A _____ states an exchange of currencies that will occur at a specified exchange rate at some future point in time.
    a) reserve clause
    b) forward contract
    c) limit order
    d) market order
    e) fixed time exchange contract

**Answers:**

| | | | |
|---|---|---|---|
| 1. a | 9. d | 17. b | 25. a |
| 2. e | 10. b | 18. a | 26. b |
| 3. b | 11. e | 19. a | 27. a |
| 4. e | 12. b | 20. c | 28. d |
| 5. b | 13. e | 21. b | 29. c |
| 6. e | 14. d | 22. b | 30. b |
| 7. a | 15. c | 23. e | |
| 8. b | 16. c | 24. d | |

# Projects

## PROJECT 1: ANALYZING YOUR FAVORITE BUSINESS

The following exercise allows you to apply the key concepts covered in each chapter to your favorite business. Select a publicly traded business in which you have a strong interest, perhaps a business in which you would like to work someday. By the end of the school term, you will have a complete report about this firm. This project will not only help you learn more about your favorite business, but it will reinforce the key concepts covered in this text.

**Obtain the Annual Report.** You will need access to the firm's annual report, which can often be found on the firm's website. You can do an Internet search to access the most recent annual report (use the name of the firm as your search term along with "annual report"). Or you may be able to access the annual report from Yahoo's financial website.

**Answering the Questions.** This entire project is provided in Appendix A. You can retrieve the Word file of this project from the textbook website (www.emcp .net/business5e), and insert your answer just below each question. The portion of the project that is

related to the chapters in this part is provided here.

Using the annual report of the firm you selected, answer the following questions:

**Business Description (related to Chapter 1).** Describe the business of the firm that you selected. What products does it produce?

**Ethics Policy (related to Chapter 2).** Many firms disclose their policies on ethics and social responsibilities within their annual reports. Briefly summarize the firm's policy.

**Exposure to Economic Conditions (related to Chapter 3).**

Firms commonly summarize how their recent performance was affected by economic conditions. How was the firm affected by economic conditions last year?

**Firm's International Business (related to Chapter 4).** Does the firm export products? Does it import products? Does it have any subsidiaries in foreign countries?

**Firm's Exposure to International Conditions (related to Chapter 4).** Was the firm affected by international economic conditions last year? If so, how?

## PROJECT 2: BUILDING A BUSINESS PLAN FOR CAMPUS.COM

### Instructions

Create a business plan for Campus .com by filling in the blank sections below. Your instructor will provide you with additional guidelines, such as whether you work on this individually or in teams, and the deadline for completing your business plan.

**Completing the Information.** You can complete the information on the Word file of this project from the textbook website (www.emcp .net/business5e). This allows you to insert all of your information on one file for this project by the end of the school term. The portion of the project that is related to the chapters in this part is provided here.

### Business Idea

Campus.com will provide an information service for high school students who are assessing different colleges to which they may apply. It will provide information on the lifestyles of any college that they select. High school students might find this service useful for several reasons. First, many books compare academic requirements at colleges, but provide very limited information on student lifestyles. Second, some high school students do not rely on the lifestyle information in these books because they question

whether the authors really understand students. Third, students do not necessarily want to purchase an entire volume on all colleges across the country just to obtain information on the few colleges to which they may apply. Fourth, students recognize that the material in these books can become outdated.

Campus.com will show a directory of all colleges. Customers (high school students) will then click on those colleges for which they want information. They must submit a credit card number and will be charged $1 for each college that they select. They will receive immediate information on their computer about the campus lifestyles of each college selected.

The main expenses for Campus .com are (a) the creation of the website and (b) gathering information about every college campus from reliable sources. Initially, this information will be gathered by ordering back issues of campus newspapers for the last year and then summarizing the campus activities for each college. In addition, the plan is to send a brief survey to about thirty students at each school (offering $20 to each respondent who fills out the survey), asking them to answer general questions about their opinions of the activities and to rate the

campus in terms of its sports activities, entertainment on campus, and nightlife. You hope to receive responses from at least twenty students before you summarize the information for each college. The information will be updated every three months by paying some of the same students who filled out the first survey to fill out an updated survey. Thus, the information that you provide to customers is frequently updated, which is an advantage over any books they could buy in stores.

### Business Environment

**Main Sources of Revenue and Expenses (related to Chapter 1).** The main source of Campus.com's revenue will be:

_____

_____

_____

_____

_____

_____

_____

_____

_____

The main source of Campus.com's expenses will be:

_____

_____

_____

How the earnings of the firm will be used (to pay owners? to be reinvested?):

_____

_____

_____

**Ethics and Social Responsibilities (related to Chapter 2).** What is the mission of Campus.com? Include statements on how the

business will fulfill its responsibilities to its customers, its employees, and its owners:

_____

_____

_____

**Economic Conditions (related to Chapter 3).** Campus.com's performance will be affected in the following ways if economic conditions change:

_____

_____

_____

**Global Conditions (related to Chapter 4).** Campus.com may expand outside the United States by:

_____

_____

_____

_____

A logical choice of a foreign country to target would be:

_____

_____

_____

## PROJECT 3: RUNNING YOUR OWN BUSINESS

### Instructions

Create a business plan for your own business by filling in the blank sections below. You may want to fill in each section after completing each chapter or part of the text, while the information is fresh on your mind. Your instructor will provide you with additional guidelines, such as whether you work on this individually or in teams, and the deadline for completing your business plan.

### Completing the Information.

You can complete the information on the Word file of this project from the textbook website (www.emcp .net/business5e). This allows you to insert all of your information on one file for this project by the end of the school term. The portion of the project that is related to the chapters in this part is provided here.

### Your Business Environment

**Business Idea (related to Chapter 1).** The main idea of your business is:

_____

_____

_____

**Main Sources of Revenue and Expenses (related to Chapter 1).** Your main source of revenue will be:

_____

_____

_____

Your main sources of expenses resulting from your business will be:

_____

_____

_____

How will the earnings of the business be used?  (to pay yourself? to be reinvested?)

_____

_____

_____

**Establishing Ethics and Social Responsibilities (related to Chapter 2).** How will your business fulfill responsibilities to your

customers, your employees, and other owners (if any)?

_____

_____

_____

**Assessing Economic Conditions (related to Chapter 3).** How will the performance of your business be affected if economic conditions change?

_____

_____

_____

_____

**Assessing Global Conditions (related to Chapter 4).** Will your business expand outside the United States? If so, what foreign country will you target?

_____

_____

_____

## PROJECT 4: PLANNING YOUR CAREER

This entire project is provided in Appendix A at the end of the text, and you can access a Word file of this project from the textbook website (www.emcp.net/business5e), and insert your answer just below each question.

If you are very interested in the topics covered in this section, you may want to consider a major in economics. Some of the more common courses taken by economics majors are summarized here.

### Common Courses for Economics Majors

• **Principles of Macroeconomics** Focuses on the economy as a whole, inflation, and the impact of government policies on economic conditions.

• **Principles of Microeconomics** Focuses on how firms set prices and determine how much to produce.

• **Intermediate Macroeconomics** Analyzes the tradeoffs resulting from government policies.

• **Intermediate Microeconomics** Focuses on profits, wages, and the market structure.

• **International Economics** Focuses on the comparison of different economies, international trade and capital flows, and the development of emerging economies.

• **Labor Economics** Focuses on the relationships between firms and their employees, including the role of labor unions.

• **Mathematical Economics** Explains how mathematics can be used to solve economics problems.

• **Econometrics** Applies statistical models to assess economic relationships.

• **Urban Economics** Emphasizes economic development and the environment within urban areas.

• **Managerial Economics** Examines how economic theories can be used in making managerial decisions related to production and pricing.

• **Money and Banking** Focuses on money, the banking system, and credit, as well as the impact of monetary policy on economic conditions.

• **Industrial Economics** Focuses on economic concepts related to industry, including pricing, competition, and market share.

### Careers in Economics

The following websites provide information about common job positions, salaries, and careers for students who major in economics:

**http://jobsearch.monster.com** Information on jobs in Finance, Economics, Government, or Policy.

**http://careers.yahoo.com** Information on jobs in Banking, Mortgage Loans, or Government.

**http://collegejournal.com/salary data** Information on jobs in Banking or Financial Services.

Some of the job positions described in these websites may require work experience or a graduate degree.

## PROJECT 5: STOCK MARKET CONTEST

This entire project is provided in Appendix A at the end of the text, and you can access a Word file of the project from the textbook website (www.emcp.net/business5e). Your instructor may ask you to assess the performance of your investment up to this point, and whether the performance of your stock is attributed to any of the business concepts that were described in the chapters contained in this part.

# Part II

# Starting a New Business

Part II explains the general functions involved in organizing a business. Chapter 5 describes the alternative forms of business ownership that entrepreneurs can select when they create a new business. Since no single type of ownership is perfect for all firms, the advantages and disadvantages of each form are considered. Entrepreneurs must consider the characteristics of their new business when deciding which form of ownership would be most appropriate. Chapter 6 explains how entrepreneurship can be used to create or improve a business. A successful business requires not only a good business idea, but also effective planning to ensure that the idea is properly implemented. Chapter 6 also explains the key components of a business plan.

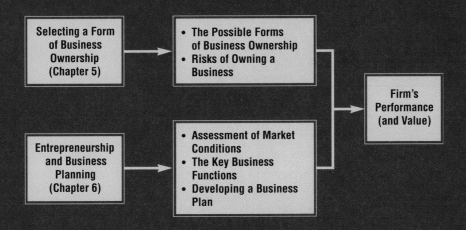

| Selecting a Form of Business Ownership (Chapter 5) | → | • The Possible Forms of Business Ownership<br>• Risks of Owning a Business | → | Firm's Performance (and Value) |
| Entrepreneurship and Business Planning (Chapter 6) | → | • Assessment of Market Conditions<br>• The Key Business Functions<br>• Developing a Business Plan | | |

# Selecting a Form of Business Ownership

© SHUTTERSTOCK/JELENA POPIC

## Chapter 5 Learning Objectives

**1** Describe the advantages and disadvantages of a sole proprietorship.

**2** Describe the advantages and disadvantages of a partnership.

**3** Describe the advantages and disadvantages of a corporation.

**4** Explain how the potential return and risk of a business are affected by its form of ownership.

**5** Describe methods of owning existing businesses.

## Domino's Form of Ownership Decision

When entrepreneurs establish a business, they must decide on the form of business ownership. There are three basic forms of business ownership: sole proprietorship, partnership, and corporation. The form that is chosen can affect the profitability, risk, and value of the firm.

Tom Monaghan purchased a pizza parlor in Michigan in 1960. As Tom expanded by creating additional pizza parlors (which he called Domino's Pizza), he converted the firm into a partnership so that he could obtain funding from investors who were willing to invest funds in the firm. The partnership form of business allowed for expansion, but the funding was limited. In July 2004, Domino's Pizza converted from a partnership to a public corporation so that it could raise a much larger amount of funds from investors. As a public corporation, it engaged in an initial public offering (IPO) of stock and raised about $131 million.

Like Tom Monaghan, every entrepreneur who creates a business periodically attempts to determine the optimal form of ownership for the business by addressing these questions:

✦ What would be the advantages and disadvantages of a sole proprietorship, a partnership, and a corporation?

✦ How will the form of business ownership affect the risk of the business?

✦ What methods can be used to obtain ownership of existing businesses?

The business ownership decision determines how the earnings of a business are distributed among the owners of the business, the degree of liability of each owner, the degree of control that each owner has in running the business, the potential return of the business, and the risk of the business. These types of decisions are necessary for all businesses. This chapter explains how entrepreneurs determine the proper form of business ownership.

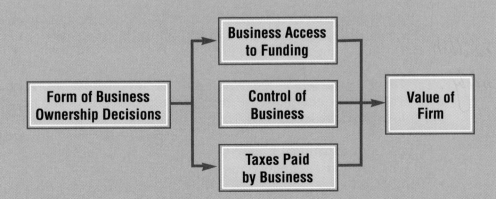

```
Form of Business          Business Access
Ownership Decisions   →     to Funding
                                              ↘
                      →    Control of          →   Value of
                           Business                 Firm
                                              ↗
                      →    Taxes Paid
                           by Business
```

**sole proprietorship**
a business owned by a single owner

**sole proprietor**
the owner of a sole proprietorship

# 1. Sole Proprietorship

A business owned by a single owner is referred to as a **sole proprietorship**. The owner of a sole proprietorship is called a **sole proprietor**. A sole proprietor may obtain loans from creditors to help finance the firm's operations, but these loans do not represent ownership. The sole proprietor is obligated to cover any payments resulting from the loans but does not need to share the business profits with creditors.

Typical examples of sole proprietorships include a local restaurant, a local construction firm, a barber shop, a laundry service, and a local clothing store. About 70 percent of all firms in the United States are sole proprietorships. But because these firms are relatively small, they generate less than 10 percent of all business revenue. The earnings generated by a sole proprietorship are considered to be personal income received by the proprietor and are subject to personal income taxes collected by the Internal Revenue Service (IRS).

## 1.1 Characteristics of Successful Sole Proprietors

Sole proprietors must be willing to accept full responsibility for the firm's performance. The pressure of this responsibility can be much greater than any employee's responsibility. Sole proprietors must also be willing to work flexible hours. They are on call at all times and may even have to substitute for a sick employee. Their responsibility for the success of the business encourages them to continually monitor business operations. They must exhibit strong leadership skills, be well organized, and communicate well with employees.

Many successful sole proprietors had previous work experience in the market in which they are competing, perhaps as an employee in a competitor's firm. For example, restaurant managers commonly establish their own restaurants. Experience is critical to understanding the competition and the behavior of customers in a particular market.

## 1.2 Advantages of a Sole Proprietorship

The sole proprietor form of ownership has several advantages over other forms of business ownership.

**All Earnings Go to the Sole Proprietor**   The sole proprietor (owner) does not have to share the firm's earnings with other owners. Thus, the rewards of establishing a successful firm come back to the owner.

**Easy Organization**   Establishing a sole proprietorship is relatively easy. The legal requirements are minimal. A sole proprietorship need not establish a separate legal entity. The owner must register the firm with the state, which can normally be done by mail. The owner may also need to apply for an occupational license to conduct a particular type of business. The specific license requirements vary with the state and even the city where the business is located.

**Complete Control**   Having only one owner with complete control of the firm eliminates the chance of conflicts during the decision-making process. For example, an owner of a restaurant can decide on the menu, the prices, and the salaries paid to employees.

Sole proprietorships like the one shown here make up about 70 percent of all businesses. However, in aggregate they generate only about 10 percent of all business revenue.

**Lower Taxes**    Because the earnings in a proprietorship are considered to be personal income, they may be subject to lower taxes than those imposed on some other forms of business ownership, as will be explained later in this chapter.

## 1.3  Disadvantages of a Sole Proprietorship

Along with its advantages, the sole proprietorship has a number of disadvantages.

**The Sole Proprietor Incurs All Losses**    Just as sole proprietors do not have to share the profits, they are unable to share any losses that the firm incurs. For example, assume you invest $10,000 of your funds in a lawn service and borrow an additional $8,000 that you invest in the business. Unfortunately, the revenue is barely sufficient to pay salaries to your employees, and you terminate the firm. You have not only lost all of your $10,000 investment in the firm but also are liable for the$8,000 that you borrowed. Since you are the sole proprietor, no other owners are available to help cover the losses.

**unlimited liability**
no limit on the debts for which the owner is liable

**Unlimited Liability**    A sole proprietor is subject to **unlimited liability**, which means there is no limit on the debts for which the owner is liable. If a sole proprietorship is sued, the sole proprietor is personally liable for any judgment against that firm.

**Limited Funds**    A sole proprietor may have limited funds available to invest in the firm. Thus, sole proprietors have difficulty engaging in airplane manufacturing, shipbuilding, computer manufacturing, and other businesses that require substantial funds. Sole proprietors have limited funds to support the firm's expansion or to absorb temporary losses. A poorly performing firm may improve if given sufficient time. But if this firm cannot obtain additional funds to make up for its losses, it may not be able to continue in business long enough to recover.

**Limited Skills**   A sole proprietor has limited skills and may be unable to control all parts of the business. For example, a sole proprietor may have difficulty running a large medical practice because different types of expertise may be needed.

**Learning Objective**

Describe the advantages and disadvantages of a partnership.

**2**

## 2. Partnership

A business that is co-owned by two or more people is referred to as a **partnership**. The co-owners of the business are called **partners**. The co-owners must register the partnership with the state and may need to apply for an occupational license. About 10 percent of all firms are partnerships.

### 2.1  General Versus Limited Partnership

In a **general partnership**, all partners have unlimited liability. That is, the partners are personally liable for all obligations of the firm. Conversely, in a **limited partnership**, the firm has some **limited partners**, or partners whose liability is limited to the cash or property they contributed to the partnership. Limited partners are only investors in the partnership and do not participate in its management, but because they have invested in the business, they share its profits or losses. A limited partnership has one or more **general partners**, or partners who manage the business, receive a salary, share the profits or losses of the business, and have unlimited liability. The earnings distributed to each partner represent personal income and are subject to personal income taxes collected by the IRS.

### 2.2  Advantages of a Partnership

The partnership form of ownership has three main advantages.

**Additional Funding**   An obvious advantage of a partnership over a sole proprietorship is the additional funding that the partner or partners can provide. Therefore, more money may be available to finance the business operations. Some partnerships have thousands of partners, who are all required to invest some of their own money in the business. This type of partnership has much potential for growth because of its access to substantial funds.

**Losses Are Shared**   Any business losses that the partnership incurs are spread across all of the partners. Thus, a single person does not have to absorb the entire loss. Each owner will absorb only a portion of the loss.

**More Specialization**   With a partnership, partners can focus on their respective specializations and serve a wide variety of customers. For example, an accounting firm may have one accountant who specializes in personal taxes for individuals and another who specializes in business taxes for firms. A medical practice partnership may have doctors with various types of expertise.

### 2.3  Disadvantages of a Partnership

Along with its advantages, the partnership has several disadvantages.

**partnership**
a business that is co-owned by two or more people

**partners**
co-owners of a business

**general partnership**
a partnership in which all partners have unlimited liability

**limited partnership**
a firm that has some limited partners

**limited partners**
partners whose liability is limited to the cash or property they contributed to the partnership

**general partners**
partners who manage the business, receive a salary, share the profits or losses of the business, and have unlimited liability

**Control Is Shared** The decision making in a partnership must be shared. If the partners disagree about how the business should be run, business and personal relationships may be destroyed. Some owners of firms do not have the skills to manage a business.

**Unlimited Liability** General partners in a partnership are subject to unlimited liability, just like sole proprietors.

**Profits Are Shared** Any profits that the partnership generates must be shared among all partners. The more partners there are, the smaller the amount of a given level of profits that will be distributed to any individual partner.

## 2.4 S-Corporations

**S-corporation**
a firm that has 100 or fewer owners and satisfies other criteria. The earnings are distributed to the owners and taxed at the respective personal income tax rate of each owner.

A firm that has 100 or fewer owners and satisfies other criteria may choose to be a so-called **S-corporation**. The owners of an S-corporation have limited liability (like owners of corporations), but they are taxed as if the firm were a partnership. Thus, the earnings are distributed to the owners and taxed at the respective personal income tax rate of each owner. Some state governments also impose a corporate tax on S-corporations. Many accounting firms and small businesses select the S-corporation as a form of ownership.

## 2.5 Limited Liability Company (LLC)

**limited liability company (LLC)**
a firm that has all the favorable features of a typical general partnership but also offers limited liability for the partners

A type of general partnership called a **limited liability company (LLC)** has become popular in recent years. An LLC has all the favorable features of a typical general partnership but also offers limited liability for the partners. It typically protects a partner's personal assets from the negligence of other partners in the firm. This type of protection is highly desirable for partners, given the high frequency of liability lawsuits. The assets of the company (such as the property or machinery owned by the company) are not protected. Although S-corporations may also provide liability protection, various rules may restrict the limited liability of some owners of S-corporations. An LLC is not subject to such stringent rules.

An LLC must be created according to the laws of the state where the business is located. The precise rules on liability protection vary among the states. Numerous general partnerships (including many accounting firms) have converted to LLCs to capitalize on the advantages of a partnership, while limiting liability for their owners.

**Learning Objective 3**
Describe the advantages and disadvantages of a corporation.

## 3. Corporation

**corporation**
a state-chartered entity that pays taxes and is legally distinct from its owners

A third form of business is a **corporation**, which is a state-chartered entity that pays taxes and is legally distinct from its owners. Since the shareholders of the corporation are legally separated from the entity, they have limited liability, meaning that they are not held personally responsible for the firm's actions. The most that the stockholders of a corporation can lose is the amount of money they invested.

Although only about 20 percent of all firms are corporations, corporations generate almost 90 percent of all business revenue. Exhibit 5.1 compares the relative contributions to business revenue made by sole proprietorships, partnerships, and corporations.

**Exhibit 5.1**

**Exhibit 5.1**

Relative Contributions to Business Revenue of Sole Proprietorships, Partnerships, and Corporations

**Proportion of Existing Businesses Under Each Form of Ownership**

Sole Proprietorships
70%

Partnerships
10%

Corporations
20%

**Proportion of Business Revenue Generated by Each Form of Ownership**

Corporations
90%

Sole Proprietorships
6%

Partnerships
4%

## 3.1 Charter and Bylaws

**charter**

a document used to incorporate a business. The charter describes important aspects of the corporation.

**bylaws**

general guidelines for managing a firm

To form a corporation, an individual or group must adopt a corporate **charter**, or a document used to incorporate a business, and file it with the state government. The charter describes important aspects of the corporation, such as the name of the firm, the stock issued, and the firm's operations. The people who organize the corporation must also establish **bylaws**, which are general guidelines for managing the firm.

**Board of Directors**    The stockholders of a corporation elect the members of the board of directors, who are responsible for establishing the general policies of the firm. One of the board's responsibilities is to elect the president and other key officers (such as vice-presidents), who are then given the responsibility of running the business on a day-to-day basis.

If the board of directors becomes displeased with the performance of the key officers, the board has the power to replace them. Similarly, if the stockholders become displeased with the performance of members of the board, the stockholders can replace the directors in the next scheduled election. In some corporations, one or a few individuals may serve as a stockholder, as a member of the board of directors, and as a key officer of the firm. The chief executive officer of a business commonly serves as the chair of the board.

Out of Business

I THINK WE ARE READY TO BECOME A CORPORATION, AS WE HAVE ALREADY WASTED ALL THE MONEY INVESTED BY THE PARTNERS.

## 3.2  How Stockholders Earn a Return

Stockholders can earn a return on their investment in a firm in two different ways. First, they may receive dividends from the firm, which are a portion of the firm's recent earnings over the last three months that are distributed to stockholders. Second, the stock they hold may increase in value. When the firm becomes more profitable, the value of its stock tends to rise, meaning that the value of stock held by owners has increased. Thus, they can benefit by selling that stock for a much higher price than they paid for it.

In the late 1990s, stock prices of many firms more than doubled. When stockholders invest in a stock, however, they also face the risk that the stock price may decline. During weak economic periods (such as 2002 and 2008), stock prices of many firms declined by more than 50 percent. Some firms failed, causing investors in the firms' stock to lose 100 percent of their investment.

## 3.3  Private Versus Public Corporations

**privately held**
ownership is restricted to a small group of investors

**publicly held**
shares can be easily purchased or sold by investors

People become owners of a corporation by purchasing shares of stock. Many small corporations are **privately held**, meaning that ownership is restricted to a small group of investors. Some well-known privately held firms include L. L. Bean, Enterprise Rent-A-Car, and Rand McNally & Co. Most large corporations are **publicly held**, meaning that shares can be easily purchased or sold by investors.

Stockholders of publicly held corporations can sell their shares of stock when they need money, are disappointed with the performance of the corporation, or simply expect that the stock price will not rise in the future. Their stock can be sold (with the help of a stockbroker) to some other investor who wants to invest in that corporation.

**going public**
the act of initially issuing stock to the public

Although virtually all firms (even Ford Motor Company) were privately held when they were created, some of these firms became publicly held when they needed funds to support large expansion. The act of initially issuing stock to the public is called **going public**. Recently, well-known firms such as Barnesandnoble.com, United Parcel Service (UPS), and Google have gone public to raise funds.

When privately held firms need to substantially expand their production space and machinery in order to carry out their plans, they may consider going public. The proceeds of the stock offering can finance their investment in their plant and machinery.

© SHUTTERSTOCK/MEHMET DILSIZ

Stock certificates like those shown here represent partial ownership of a corporation. Firms issue shares of stock when they wish to expand by allowing many more investors to invest in their business. However, this reduces the proportional ownership of the existing owners.

© SHUTTERSTOCK/MAREK SLUSARCZYK

Publicly held corporations can obtain additional funds by issuing new common stock. This means that either their existing stockholders can purchase more stock, or other investors can become stockholders by purchasing the corporation's stock. By issuing new stock, corporations may obtain whatever funds are needed to support any business expansion. Corporations that wish to issue new stock must be able to convince investors that the funds will be utilized properly, resulting in a reasonable return for the investors.

## 3.4  Advantages of a Corporation

The corporate form of ownership offers several advantages.

**Limited Liability**   Owners of a corporation have limited liability (as explained earlier), whereas sole proprietors and general partners typically have unlimited liability.

**Access to Funds**   A corporation can easily obtain funds by issuing new stock (as explained earlier). This allows corporations the flexibility to grow and to engage in new business ventures. Sole proprietorships and partnerships have less access to funding when they wish to finance expansion. To obtain more funds, they may have to rely on their existing owners or on loans from creditors.

**Transfer of Ownership**   Investors in large, publicly traded companies can normally sell their stock in minutes by calling their stockbrokers or by selling it online over the Internet. Conversely, owners of sole proprietorships or partnerships may have some difficulty in selling their share of ownership in the business.

## 3.5  Disadvantages of a Corporation

Along with its advantages, the corporate form of ownership has a number of disadvantages.

**High Organizational Expense**   Organizing a corporation is normally more expensive than creating the other forms of business because of the necessity to create a corporate charter and file it with the state. Some expense may also be incurred in establishing bylaws. Issuing stock to investors also entails substantial expenses.

**Financial Disclosure**   When the stock of a corporation is traded publicly, the investing public has the right to inspect the company's financial data, within certain limits. As a result, firms may be obligated to publicly disclose more about their business operations and employee salaries than they would like. Privately held firms are not forced to disclose financial information to the public.

**Agency Problems**    Publicly held corporations are normally run by managers who are responsible for making decisions for the business that will serve the interests of the owners. Managers may not always act in the best interests of stockholders, however. For example, managers may attempt to take expensive business trips that are not necessary to manage the business. Such actions may increase the expenses of running a business, reduce business profits, and therefore reduce the returns to stockholders. When managers do not act as responsible agents for the shareholders who own the business, a so-called **agency problem** results. There are many examples of high-level managers who made decisions that were in their best interests, at the expense of shareholders. One of the most blatant examples occurred at Enron, Inc., which went bankrupt in 2001. Agency problems are less likely in proprietorships because the sole owner may also serve as the sole manager and make most or all business decisions.

**agency problem**
when managers do not act as responsible agents for the shareholders who own the business

**High Taxes**    Since the corporation is a separate entity, it is taxed separately from its owners. The annual taxes paid by a corporation are determined by applying the corporate tax rate to the firm's annual earnings. The corporate tax rate is different from the personal tax rate. Consider a corporation that earns $10 million this year. Assume that the corporate tax rate applied to earnings of corporations is 30 percent this year(the corporate tax rates can be changed by law over time). Thus, the taxes and after-tax earnings of the corporation are as follows:

Earnings Before Tax = $10,000,000
Corporate Tax =    3,000,000 (computed as 30% × $10,000,000)
Earnings After Tax =    $7,000,000

If any of the after-tax earnings are paid to the owners as dividends, the dividends represent personal income to the stockholders. Thus, the stockholders will pay personal income taxes on the dividends. Continuing with our example, assume that all of the $7 million in after-tax earnings is distributed to the stockholders as dividends. Assume that the dividend tax rate is 10 percent for all owners who will receive dividends. The actual dividend income received by the stockholders after paying income taxes is as follows:

Dividends Received = $7,000,000
Taxes Paid on Dividends =    $700,000 (computed as 10% × $7,000,000)
Income After Tax = $6,300,000

Since the corporate tax was $3,000,000 and the personal tax was $700,000, the total tax paid as a result of the corporation's profits was $3,700,000, which represents 37 percent of the $10,000,000 profit that the corporation earned.

As this example shows, owners of corporations are subject to double taxation. First, the corporation's entire profits from their investment are subject to corporate taxes. Then, any profits distributed as dividends to individual owners are subject to personal income taxes. Exhibit 5.2 shows the flow of funds between owners and the corporation to illustrate how owners are subject to double taxation.

**Exhibit 5.2**

Illustration of Double Taxation

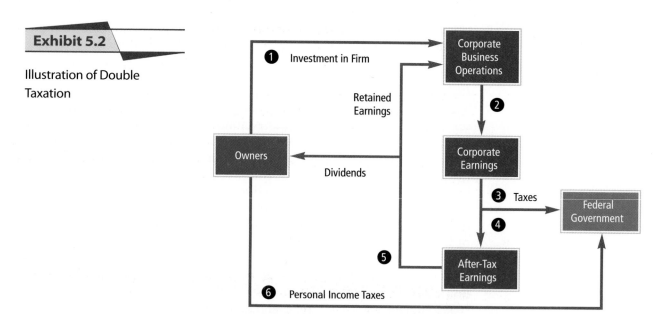

To recognize the disadvantage of double taxation, consider what the taxes would have been for this business if it were a sole proprietorship or partnership rather than a corporation. The $10,000,000 profit would have been personal income to a sole proprietor or to partners and would have been subject to personal taxes. Assuming a personal tax rate of 20 percent, the total tax would be $2,000,000 (computed as 20 percent × $10,000,000), which is less than the total amount that a corporation that earned the same profit and its stockholders together would pay. Even if the personal income tax rate of a sole proprietor or a partner was higher than 20 percent, the taxes paid by a corporation and its stockholders would probably still be higher. A comparison of the tax effects on corporations and sole proprietorships is provided in Exhibit 5.3.

One way that a corporation may reduce the taxes paid by its owners is to reinvest its earnings (called "retained earnings") rather than pay the

**Exhibit 5.3** Comparison of Tax Effects on Corporations and Sole Proprietorships

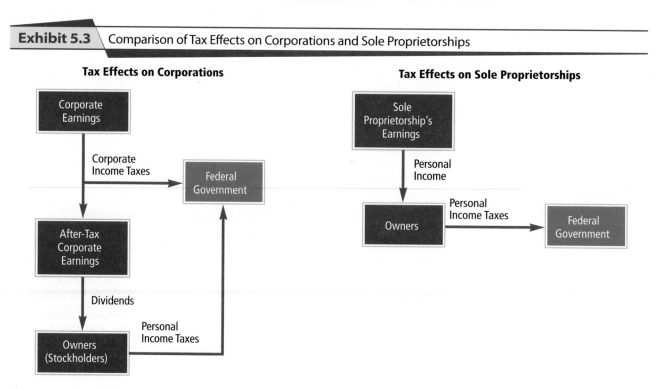

earnings out as dividends. If owners do not receive dividends from a corporation, they will not be subject to taxes on the earnings of the corporation. This strategy makes sense only if the corporation can put the retained earnings to good use.

When stockholders of a corporation sell their shares of stock for more than they paid for them, they earn a **capital gain**, which is equal to the amount of dollars received from the sale of stock minus the amount of dollars they paid for the stock. The stockholders must pay a capital gains tax on the capital gain, however. Thus, whether stockholders receive income from selling the stock at a gain or from receiving dividend payments, they are subject to taxes.

**capital gain**
the price received from the sale of stock minus the price paid for the stock

### 3.6  Comparing Forms of Business Ownership

No single form of business ownership is ideal for all business owners. An individual setting up a small business may choose a sole proprietorship. Some people who decide to co-own a small business may choose a partnership. If they wish to limit their liability, however, they may decide to establish a privately held corporation. If this corporation grows substantially over time and needs millions of dollars to support additional business expansion, it may convert to a publicly held corporation so that it can obtain funds from stockholders.

**Using the Internet to Compare Forms of Business Ownership** Many excellent sources of information on forms of business ownership are available on the Internet. A one starting point is the Small Business Administration (SBA). Among the resources offered at the SBA's home page (www.sbaonline.sba.gov) are the following:

✦ Information on local SBA offices.

✦ Access to the Service Corps of Retired Executives (SCORE), consisting of thousands of retired business people who have volunteered to help small businesses for free.

✦ SBA publications. The range of topics covered by the publications is enormous, and each can be copied directly to the entrepreneur's computer at no charge.

Once a firm goes public, its stock price changes over time in response to demand for that stock by investors. The price is publicly displayed by the stock exchange (as shown here). It can also be found on financial news websites and in some newspapers.

© SHUTTERSTOCK/MDD

Dentists and health care professionals commonly establish a sole proprietorship when they start their business. However, they often convert to partnerships over time in order to expand their business and include other dentists with different specializations.

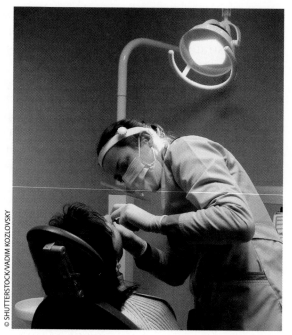

© SHUTTERSTOCK/VADIM KOZLOVSKY

In addition to government agencies, many private organizations provide information and services to small businesses that are just being formed. Many of these organizations, such as The Company Corporation, allow corporations and other forms of businesses to be set up entirely over the Internet. A particularly attractive feature of these services is their low cost. Nevertheless, some entrepreneurs may still prefer to hire an attorney to form the business, especially if their ownership situation is complicated.

## 3.7   How Business Ownership Can Change

As an example of how the optimal form of ownership for a specific business can change over time, consider the history of PC Repair Company, which specializes in repairing personal computers. The owner, Ed Everhart, started his business in Columbus, Ohio. He initially used his garage as work space to fix customers' computers. Since he was the sole owner at that time, his business was a proprietorship. Over the next six years, the business grew, and Ed wanted to open a computer repair shop downtown. He needed more funds to purchase a shop and hire employees. He asked a friend, Maria Rosas, if she wanted to become a partner by investing funds in the firm and working for the business. She agreed, so the business was converted from a proprietorship to a partnership. From Ed's point of view, the main benefit was that Maria could invest money that would help the business grow. In addition, she had good computer repair skills. The main disadvantage was that he was no longer the sole decision maker, but he and Maria usually agreed on how to run the business.

During the next several years, the business grew even more. Ed and Maria wanted to establish three more computer repair shops in Columbus, so they obtained funds from eight friends who served as limited partners. These limited partners invested in the business because they expected that it would flourish and provide them with a good return on their investment. After experiencing success with their new computer repair shops in Columbus, Ed and Maria wanted to expand their business throughout Ohio, but they needed a substantial amount of funds to do so. They decided to issue stock to the public, with the help of a financial institution. Their stock offering raised $20 million, although about $1.5 million of the proceeds went to pay expenses associated with the stock offering. At this time, the ownership of the business was converted from a partnership to a corporation. The corporate form of ownership allowed the business to expand. With the establishment of several repair shops throughout Ohio, the firm now had the potential to generate large earnings. The organization was also much more complex than when the business was a proprietorship. Ed and Maria still made the business decisions, but they were now accountable to hundreds of other investors who were part-owners of the business.

## 4.  How Ownership Can Affect Return and Risk

When business owners assess a possible investment in any business, they consider both the potential return and the risk from that type of investment. The potential return and the risk from investing in a business are influenced by its form of ownership. Thus, entrepreneurs should consider how the form of ownership affects the potential return and the risk when deciding on the optimal form of ownership for their business.

### 4.1  Impact of Ownership on the Return on Investment

The return on investment in a firm is derived from the firm's profits (also called "earnings" or "income"). As described earlier, when a firm generates earnings, it pays a portion to the IRS as income taxes. The remaining (after-tax) earnings represent the return (in dollars) to the business owners. However, the dollar value of a firm's after-tax earnings is not necessarily a useful measure of the firm's performance unless it is adjusted for the amount of the firm's **equity**, which is the total investment by the firm's stockholders. For this reason, business owners prefer to measure a firm's profitability by computing its **return on equity (ROE)**, which is the earnings as a proportion of the equity:

**equity**
the total investment by the firm's stockholders

**return on equity (ROE)**
earnings as a proportion of the firm's equity

$$ROE = \frac{\text{Earnings After Tax}}{\text{Equity}}$$

For example, if the stockholders invested $1 million in a firm and its after-tax earnings last year were $150,000, its return on equity last year was:

$$ROE = \frac{\$150,000}{\$1,000,000}$$
$$= .15, \text{ or } 15\%$$

Thus, the firm generated a return equal to 15 percent of the owners' investment in the firm.

The return on equity for Zemax Company is shown in Exhibit 5.4. Notice that Zemax generated earnings before taxes of $100 million. Of this amount, $30 million (30 percent) was used to pay corporate taxes. The remaining $70 million represents after-tax earnings. Given the total investment (equity) in Zemax Company of about $350 million, the after-tax earnings represent a return of 20 percent (computed as $70 million divided by $350 million).

The large amount of equity that Zemax Company obtained as a result of choosing the corporate form of ownership has enabled it to grow and generate a large amount of sales and earnings. If Zemax had chosen the partnership form of ownership, its growth would have been limited.

However, access to a large amount of equity is beneficial only if the firm can put the equity to good use. If a firm has more equity than it can use, its performance will be weak. Consider the situations of Firms A and B. Firm A is a partnership and Firm B is a corporation.

|                              | Firm A (Partnership) | Firm B (Corporation) |
|------------------------------|:--------------------:|:--------------------:|
| Earnings after taxes last year | $15 million        | $15 million          |
| Owners' equity               | $100 million         | $300 million         |
| Return on equity             | 15%                  | 5%                   |

Notice that the firms had the same dollar value of earnings after taxes. However, the corporation has three times the equity investment of the partnership. The return on equity is much higher for the partnership than for the corporation because the partnership achieved the same level of earnings with a smaller equity investment.

## 4.2 Impact of Ownership on Risk

**risk**
the degree of uncertainty about a firm's future earnings

The **risk** of a firm represents the degree of uncertainty about the firm's future earnings, which causes uncertainty about the return to the owners. A firm's future earnings are dependent on its future revenue and its expenses. Firms can experience losses if the revenue is less than expected or

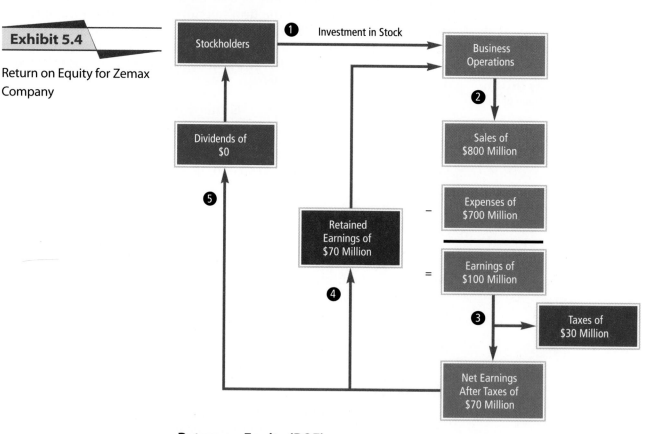

**Exhibit 5.4**

Return on Equity for Zemax Company

**Return on Equity (ROE)**
Given that the equity of Zemax was about $350 million, its ROE was:

$$ROE = \frac{\text{Earnings After Taxes}}{\text{Equity}}$$

$$ROE = \frac{\$70 \text{ million}}{\$350 \text{ million}}$$

$$= 20\%$$

# Cross-Functional Teamwork

## Sources of Risk Across Business Functions

Poor performance can normally be attributed to poor management of resources, poor marketing, or poor financing, as explained next.

The following are typical mistakes that can cause excessive production expenses.

✦ Hiring more employees than necessary, which results in high operating expenses.

✦ Hiring fewer employees than necessary, which prevents the firm from achieving the desired volume or quality of products.

✦ Hiring employees who lack proper skills or training.

✦ Investing in more equipment or machinery than necessary, which results in high operating expenses.

✦ Investing in less equipment or machinery than necessary, which prevents the firm from achieving the desired volume or quality of products.

The following are typical marketing mistakes that can cause poor performance.

✦ Excessive spending on marketing programs.

✦ Ineffective marketing programs, which do not enhance the firm's revenue.

The following are typical finance mistakes that can cause poor performance:

✦ Borrowing too much money, which results in a high level of interest expenses incurred per year.

✦ Not borrowing enough money, which prevents the firm from investing the necessary amount of funds to be successful.

Since business decisions are related, a poor decision in one department can affect other departments. For example, a computer manufacturer's production volume is based on the forecasted demand for computers by the marketing department. When the marketing department underestimates the demand, the manufacturer experiences shortages.

---

if the expenses are more than expected. Some firms that experience severe losses ultimately fail. In these cases, the owners may lose most or all of the funds they invested in the firms.

Since sole proprietorships tend to be small businesses with very limited funds, they are generally riskier than larger businesses such as partnerships and corporations. Consider a sole proprietorship that has revenue of $200,000 and expenses of $300,000 this year. It needs $100,000 of equity to cover its loss. If it has only $60,000, it cannot cover the loss. If the business had another owner, it would have more equity and might be able to cover its loss.

The limited funding of sole proprietorships also means that they are not able to diversify their business. If their single line of business experiences problems, they are highly susceptible to failure. An event such as a workers' strike in a supplier firm or reduced demand for the type of products they produce can result in failure. In contrast, a larger firm that sells a diversified product line may not be severely affected by events that adversely affect only one of its products. The death or retirement of a key manager can also have a great impact on a sole proprietorship. Larger businesses typically have several employees in high-level positions who can make key decisions, so no one person is irreplaceable.

# Responding to the Economy

## Revising Business Ownership Decisions in Response to the Economy

As economic conditions change, a firm may rethink its form of business ownership. During the 2007–2008 period, oil prices increased substantially, which increased transportation (delivery) costs of many U.S. firms. In addition, the U.S. economy was weak during this period. Some firms cut back on their plans for business expansion, which reduced their need for funding. Under these conditions, sole proprietors may prefer to retain their full ownership of businesses rather than invite partners to invest in their businesses. In addition, existing partnerships that had considered going public may prefer to defer that decision until they really need additional funding for expansion.

Conversely, some firms may consider expanding their business ownership during a weak economy in order to reduce their risk. For example, some sole proprietors may want to invite partners to invest in the firm even if they are not expanding the business. By using some of the proceeds to pay off their debt, they will be less exposed to the possibility of going bankrupt. Thus, they can more easily survive during a weak economy.

When deciding on ownership, the following tradeoff should be obvious. The greater the number of owners, the larger the amount of funds that can be accessed, but the larger the number of people who share in the performance of the business. Thus, a sole proprietorship can reduce its risk by converting to a partnership so that it can access more funds. A partnership can reduce its risk by converting to a corporation so that it can access more funds.

**Learning Objective 5**
Describe methods of owning existing businesses.

# 5. Obtaining Ownership of an Existing Business

Some people become the sole owners without starting the business. The following are common methods by which people become owners of existing businesses:

✦ Assuming ownership of a family business

✦ Purchasing an existing business

✦ Franchising

## 5.1 Assuming Ownership of a Family Business

Many people work in a family business and after a period of time assume the ownership of it. This can be an ideal way to own a business because its performance may be somewhat predictable as long as the key employees continue to work there. Major decisions regarding the production process and other operations of the firm have been predetermined. If the business has historically been successful, a new owner's main function may be to ensure that the existing operations continue to run efficiently. Alternatively, if the business is experiencing poor performance, the new owner may have to revise management, marketing, and financing policies.

## 5.2  Purchasing an Existing Business

Businesses are for sale on any given day in any city. They are often advertised in the classified ads section of local newspapers. Businesses are sold for various reasons, including financial difficulties and the death or retirement of an owner.

People considering the purchase of an existing business must determine whether they have the expertise to run the business or at least properly monitor the managers. Then they must compare the expected benefits of the business with the initial outlay required to purchase it. The seller of the business may provide historical sales volume, which can be used to estimate the future sales volume. However, the prospective buyer must be cautious when using these figures. In some businesses such as dentistry and hairstyling, personal relationships between the owner and customers are critical. Many customers may switch to competitors if the ownership changes. For these types of businesses, the historical sales volume may substantially overestimate future sales. For other, less personalized businesses such as grocery stores, a change of ownership is not likely to have a significant effect on customer preferences (and therefore on sales volume).

## 5.3  Franchising

**franchise**
an arrangement whereby a business owner allows others to use its trademark, trade name, or copyright, under specific conditions

**franchisor**
a firm that allows others to use its trade name or copyright, under specified conditions

**franchisee**
a firm that is allowed to use the trade name or copyright of a franchise

**distributorship**
a type of franchise in which a dealer is allowed to sell a product produced by a manufacturer

A **franchise** is an arrangement whereby a business owner (called a **franchisor**) allows another (the **franchisee**) to use its trademark, trade name, or copyright, under specified conditions. Each individual franchise operates as an independent business and is typically owned by a sole proprietor. Thus, a new business is created using the trademark and name of the existing franchisor.

Restaurants (like the one shown here) are commonly established as franchises. One of the most important benefits of a franchise restaurant is name recognition, which attracts more customers.

© SHUTTERSTOCK/JAMES STEIDL

Franchises in the United States number over 500,000, and they generate more than $800 billion in annual revenue. Some well-known franchises include McDonald's, Thrifty Rent-a-Car System, Dairy Queen, Super 8 Motels, Inc., TGI Fridays, Pearle Vision, Inc., and Baskin-Robbins. The costs of purchasing a franchise can vary significantly, depending on the specific trademarks, technology, and services provided to the franchisees.

**Types of Franchises**  Most franchises can be classified as a distributorship, a chain-style business, or a manufacturing arrangement.

In a **distributorship**, a dealer is allowed to sell a product produced by a manufacturer. For example, Chrysler and Ford dealers are distributorships.

# Self-Scoring Exercises

## Do You Have the Skills Necessary to Succeed in Business?

According to the U.S. Department of Labor, achieving success in the workplace, now and in the future, will require that a person possess three enabling skills as a foundation for the five functional skills required in the business environment. Answer each of these three basic questions:

1. Do you believe you possess the basic reading, speaking, listening, and mathematics skills required for future learning?
2. Do you believe you possess the intellectual skills for effective decision making and problem solving?
3. Do you believe you possess the skills required for you to cooperate with others and achieve effective sociability?

If you answered yes to each question, you have the basic skills needed to enable you to master five functional skills in the business environment. How do you rate yourself in each of these five functional skill areas? In the blank before each skill, place the number from 1 (very good) to 5 (needs improvement) that reflects your self-rating.

_____ 1. Resource management skills, such as human resource management, time management, and financial resources management.
_____ 2. Information management skills, such as identifying and interpreting information.
_____ 3. Personal interaction skills, such as teamwork, negotiation, and working with customers.
_____ 4. Systems behavior and performance skills, such as anticipating consequences of behavior and cause-and-effect relationships.
_____ 5. Technology utilization skills, such as selecting, using, maintaining, and/or troubleshooting technology.

If you rated yourself a 4 or 5 on any of the five functional skills, you may want to talk with your instructor or the university's career and counseling office about specific opportunities that will enable you to strengthen those skills.

**chain-style business**
a type of franchise in which a firm is allowed to use the trade name of a company and follows guidelines related to the pricing and sale of the product

**manufacturing arrangement**
a type of franchise in which a firm is allowed to manufacture a product using the formula provided by another company

In a **chain-style business**, a firm is allowed to use the trade name of a company and follows guidelines related to the pricing and sale of the product. Some examples are McDonald's, CD Warehouse, Holiday Inn, Subway, and Pizza Hut.

In a **manufacturing arrangement**, a firm is allowed to manufacture a product using the formula provided by another company. For example, Microsoft might allow a foreign company to produce its software, as long as the software is sold only in that country. Microsoft would receive a portion of the revenue generated by that firm.

**Advantages of a Franchise** The typical advantages of a franchise are as follows:

✦ **Proven Management Style.** Franchisees look to the franchisors for guidance in production and management. McDonald's provides extensive training to its franchisees. The management style of a

# Global Business

## Ownership of Foreign Businesses

Opportunities in foreign countries have encouraged many entrepreneurs in the United States to establish foreign businesses in recent years. A common way for an entrepreneur to establish a foreign business is to purchase a franchise created by a U.S. firm in a foreign country. For example, McDonald's, Pizza Hut, and KFC have franchises in numerous foreign countries. The potential return on these franchises may be higher than in the United States if there is less competition.

Given the uncertainties faced by new businesses in these foreign countries, some entrepreneurs made agreements with existing foreign firms rather than establishing their own business. For example, suppose that an entrepreneur recognizes that various household products will be popular in some Latin American countries but prefers not to establish a firm there because of uncertainty about tax rates and other government policies. The entrepreneur may make an agreement with an existing firm that distributes related products to retail stores throughout Latin America. This firm will earn a fee for selling the household products produced by the entrepreneur. This example is just one of many possible arrangements that allow U.S. entrepreneurs to capitalize on opportunities in a foreign country without owning a business there.

franchise is already a proven success. A franchise's main goal is to duplicate a proven business in a particular location. Thus, the franchise is a less risky venture than a new type of business, as verified by a much higher failure rate for new businesses.

✦ **Name Recognition.** Many franchises are nationally known because of advertising by the franchisor. This provides the franchisee with name recognition, which can significantly increase the demand for the product. Therefore, owners of Holiday Inn, Pizza Hut, and other franchises may not need to spend money on advertising because the franchises are already popular with consumers.

✦ **Financial Support.** Some franchisees receive some financial support from the franchisor, which can ensure sufficient start-up funds for the franchisee. For example, some McDonald's franchisees receive funding from McDonald's. Alternatively, franchisees can purchase materials and supplies from the franchisor on credit, which represents a form of short-term financing.

**Disadvantages of a Franchise**    Two common disadvantages of franchising are as follows:

✦ **Sharing Profits.** In return for services provided by the franchisor, the franchisee must share profits with the franchisor. Annual fees paid by the franchisee may be 8 percent or more of the annual revenue generated by the franchise.

✦ **Less Control.** The franchisee must abide by guidelines regarding product production and pricing, and possibly other guidelines as well. Consequently, the franchisee's performance is dependent on these guidelines. Owners are not allowed to revise some of the guidelines.

Though decision making is limited, owners of a franchise still make some critical decisions. They must decide whether a particular franchise can be successful in a particular location. In addition, even though the production and marketing policies are somewhat predetermined, the owners are responsible for managing their employees. They must provide leadership and motivation to maximize production efficiency. Thus, a franchise's performance is partially dependent on its owners and managers.

**The Popularity of Business-to-Business Franchises**   Franchises that serve other businesses (called business-to-business or B2B franchises) have grown substantially in the last few years. In particular, many franchises focus on providing hiring services, consulting services, and training services for firms. These types of franchises are popular because they normally require a smaller initial investment than many other franchises such as hotels and restaurants. Many B2B franchises can be operated by computer from a home office and therefore can be started with an investment of between $30,000 and $100,000. In contrast, restaurant franchises may require an investment of $150,000 or more. In addition, a B2B franchise can use computer technology instead of employees to do some of the work, such as sorting résumés and offering training with animated computer files. Furthermore, since a B2B franchise interacts with other businesses, less weekend work may be required than with restaurant franchises, which commonly operate seven days a week.

## COLLEGE HEALTH CLUB: BUSINESS OWNERSHIP AT CHC

One of the decisions that Sue Kramer needs to make as part of her business plan is the appropriate form of business ownership for College Health Club (CHC). Diane Burke, a relative of Sue's, has offered a loan of $40,000 if she believes that the business plan is feasible. Diane is willing to provide the funds as a 10-year loan and will charge an interest rate of 10 percent. If Sue accepts the funds as a loan, then she will be the sole owner of CHC. However, she will have to pay Diane interest of $4,000 at the end of each year (computed as $40,000 × 10%).

Alternatively, Diane is willing to provide the funds as an equity investment. This would make her an owner of the firm. In this case, Diane's investment would be two-thirds of the total investment in the firm, and she would receive two-thirds of the proceeds when the business is sold, perhaps several years from now.

Sue realizes that CHC's earnings would be $4,000 higher each year if she accepts the funds as an equity investment rather than a loan, because she would avoid the interest expense. This is the advantage of the partnership form of ownership. In addition, any losses incurred by CHC would be shared if she allows Diane to be a partner.

If Sue uses the partnership form, however, she would receive only one-third of the proceeds when the business is sold, and Diane would receive the remainder. In addition, Sue would have to share the decision making with Diane. With the proprietorship form of ownership, Sue would receive the entire proceeds if she sells the business someday. Furthermore, she would have complete control. She believes that she can run CHC better by herself than if other partners are involved in the business decisions.

After weighing the advantages and disadvantages of a sole proprietorship versus a partnership, Sue decides that the proprietorship is the more desirable form of ownership. She risks losing more of her own money as the sole proprietor, but she is willing to take that risk because she is confident that her business will be successful.

Sue does not even consider the corporation form of ownership at this point because she is just starting a very small business. If she ever decides to expand the business by allowing for additional owners, the partnership form would be more appropriate than the corporation form. She would consider forming a corporation only if she plans to expand her health clubs throughout Texas.

# Summary of Learning Objectives

**1** A sole proprietorship is owned by a single person who often manages the firm as well. Its advantages are that

✦ all earnings go to the sole owner,

✦ it is easy to organize,

✦ the owner has complete control, and

✦ taxes may be lower.

Its disadvantages are that the sole owner

✦ incurs all losses (if there are any),

✦ has unlimited liability,

✦ has limited funds, and

✦ may have limited skills and thus be unable to run the entire business.

**2** A partnership has two or more co-owners who may manage the firm as well. It can allow for more financial support by owners than a sole proprietorship, but it also requires that control and profits of the firm be shared among owners. In addition, its owners have unlimited liability.

**3** A corporation is an entity that is viewed as separate from its owners. Owners of a corporation have limited liability, while owners of sole proprietorships and partnerships have unlimited liability.

**4** The return and the risk from investing in a business are dependent on the form of business ownership. The return on equity is higher if a business can use a limited amount of equity. Sole proprietorships have the potential to generate a high return to the owners because there is only one owner. However, they are generally more risky because of their limited funding, among other reasons. A business can reduce its risk by allowing additional owners, but the tradeoff is that its profitability is spread among all the owners.

**5** The common methods by which people can obtain ownership of existing businesses are as follows:

✦ Assuming ownership of a family business

✦ Purchasing an existing business

✦ Franchising

Assuming the ownership of a family business is desirable because a person can normally learn much about that business before assuming ownership. Many people are not in a position to assume a family business, however. Before purchasing an existing business, one must estimate future sales and expenses to determine whether making the investment is feasible. Franchising may be desirable for people who will need some guidance in running the firm. However, the franchisee must pay annual fees to the franchisor.

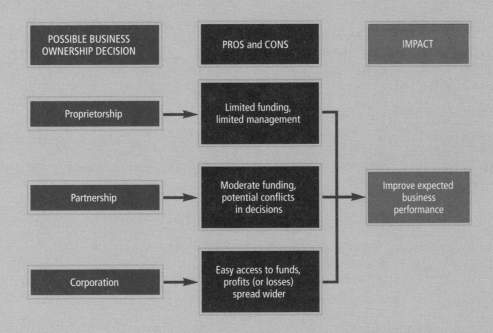

# Self-Test of Key Concepts

The following self-assessment allows you to test your understanding of the key concepts covered in this chapter. Answers are provided at the end of this exercise.

**True or False**

1. The legal requirements for establishing a sole proprietorship are very difficult.

2. One advantage of sole proprietorships is that this form of ownership provides easy access to additional funds.

3. Limited partners are investors in the partnership and participate in the management of the business.

4. The limited liability feature is an advantage of owning a sole proprietorship.

5. When a corporation distributes some of its recent earnings to stockholders, the payments are referred to as capital gains.

6. If the board of directors becomes displeased with the performance of the key officers, the board has the power to replace them.

7. Publicly held corporations can obtain additional funds by issuing new common stock.

8. Publicly held corporations are required to disclose financial information to the investing public.

9. To incorporate a business, one must adopt a corporate charter and file it with the state government where the business is to be located.

10. The form of ownership of a firm should not be changed unless there are major tax advantages.

11. Distributorships, chain-style businesses, and manufacturing arrangements are all common types of franchises.

**Multiple Choice**

12. When entrepreneurs establish a business, they must first decide on the form of:
    a) divestiture.
    b) global expansion.
    c) joint venture.
    d) ownership.

13. The following are possible forms of business ownership except for a:
    a) sole proprietorship.
    b) partnership.
    c) bureaucracy.
    d) corporation.

14. Joe wants to form his own business. He wants to get started as quickly and inexpensively as possible and has a strong desire to control the business himself. He is confident he will be successful and wants to keep all the profits himself. Joe's goals indicate he would probably choose to operate his business as a(n):
    a) limited partnership.
    b) limited liability company.
    c) S-corporation.
    d) franchise.
    e) sole proprietorship.

15. A business owned by a single owner is referred to as a:
    a) partnership.
    b) sole proprietorship.
    c) limited partnership.
    d) corporation.
    e) subchapter S-corporation.

16. A disadvantage of a sole proprietorship is that:
    a) sole proprietors have very little control over the operations of the business.
    b) sole proprietors have unlimited liability.
    c) it is more difficult and expensive to establish than other forms of business.
    d) its earnings are subject to higher tax rates than other forms of business.
    e) sole proprietors are required to share the firm's profits with employees.

17. Partners have unlimited liability in a:
    a) general partnership.
    b) corporation.
    c) limited partnership.
    d) cooperative.

18. In a limited partnership:
    a) all partners have limited liability.
    b) the partnership exists only for a limited time period, or until a specific task is accomplished.
    c) the limited partners do not participate in management of the company.
    d) the partners agree to operate in a limited geographic area.
    e) no more than 100 partners may invest in the company at any one time.

19. When two or more people, having complementary skills, agree to co-own a business, this agreement is referred to as a:
    a) partnership.
    b) sole proprietorship.
    c) cooperative.
    d) corporation.
    e) joint venture.

20. A firm that has 100 owners or less and also meets other criteria may choose to be a so-called:
    a) cooperative.
    b) proprietorship.
    c) joint venture.
    d) S-corporation.
    e) bureaucracy.

21. A general partnership that protects a partner's personal assets from the negligence of other partners is called a:
    a) limited liability company.
    b) cooperative.
    c) private corporation.
    d) master limited partnership.
    e) protected partnership.

22. Important aspects of a corporation, such as the name of the firm, information about the stock issued, and a description of the firm's operations, are contained in a:
    a) mission.
    b) policy.
    c) charter.
    d) plan.
    e) venture.

23. The members of the board of directors of a corporation are chosen by the corporation's:
    a) president and chief executive officer.
    b) creditors.
    c) general partners.
    d) stockholders.
    e) charter members.

24. When a corporation's shares can be easily purchased or sold by investors, it is:
    a) publicly held.
    b) privately held.
    c) institutionalized.
    d) monopolized.
    e) franchised.

25. People become owners of a corporation by purchasing:
    a) shares of stock.
    b) corporate bonds.
    c) retained earnings.
    d) inventory.
    e) accounts receivable.

26. When stockholders of a corporation sell shares of stock for more than they paid for the shares, they receive a:
    a) dividend.
    b) premium.
    c) capital gain.
    d) discount.
    e) stock option.

27. The total amount invested in a company by its owners is called:
    a) the corporate margin.
    b) equity.
    c) working capital.
    d) the stock premium.
    e) treasury stock.

28. The degree of uncertainty about future earnings, which reflects an uncertain return to the owners, is known as:
    a) certainty.
    b) profits.
    c) risk.
    d) equity.
    e) dividends.

29. All of the following are common types of franchise arrangements except:
    a) business agencies.
    b) chain-style businesses.
    c) manufacturing arrangements.
    d) distributorships.

30. Sharing profits and less control of the business ownership are two common disadvantages of:
    a) sole proprietorships.
    b) downsizing.
    c) divestiture.
    d) franchising.

| True/False | | Multiple Choice | | |
|---|---|---|---|---|
| 1. False | 7. True | 12. d | 19. a | 26. c |
| 2. False | 8. True | 13. c | 20. d | 27. b |
| 3. False | 9. True | 14. e | 21. a | 28. c |
| 4. False | 10. False | 15. b | 22. c | 29. a |
| 5. False | 11. True | 16. b | 23. d | 30. d |
| 6. True | | 17. a | 24. a | |
| | | 18. c | 25. a | |

## Self-Test of Key Terms

agency problem 153
bylaws 150
capital gain 155
chain-style business 162
charter 150
corporation 149
distributorship 161
equity 157
franchise 161
franchisee 161

franchisor 161
general partners 148
general partnership 148
going public 151
limited liability company (LLC) 149
limited partners 148
limited partnership 148
manufacturing arrangement 162
partners 148
partnership 148

privately held 151
publicly held 151
return on equity (ROE) 157
risk 158
S-corporation 149
sole proprietor 146
sole proprietorship 146
unlimited liability 147

Fill in each blank with the proper key term. To assess your understanding of the key terms, answers are provided at the end of this self-test.

1. The total investment by the firm's stockholders represents the firm's _____.

2. In a(n) _____ firm, ownership is restricted to a small group of investors.

3. A(n) _____ is a business that is co-owned by two or more people.

4. In a(n) _____, a firm is allowed to use the trade name of a company and follows guidelines related to pricing and sale of the product.

5. _____ who are partial owners of a partnership have limited liability.

6. In a(n) _____, each partner's personal assets are protected from the negligence of other partners in the firm.

7. A(n) _____ is a document that is used to incorporate a business and is filed with the state government.

8. A firm's _____ can be measured as annual earnings (income) after taxes divided by the firm's equity.

9. A(n) _____ results from managers of a corporation making decisions that are not in the best interests of the shareholders who own the business.

10. When investors sell their stock for a higher price than the price they paid for it, they earn a(n) _____.

11. The term "_____" means there is no limit on the debts for which the owner is liable.

12. In a(n) _____, a dealer is allowed to sell a product produced by a manufacturer.

13. A business owned by a single owner is referred to as a(n) _____.

14. The _____ of a firm represents the degree of uncertainty about the firm's future earnings.

15. A(n) _____ is an arrangement in which a business allows another business to use its trademark, trade name, or copyright under specified conditions.

16. In a(n) _____, a firm is allowed to manufacture a product using a formula provided by another company.

**Answers:**
1. equity
2. privately held
3. partnership
4. chain-style business
5. Limited partners
6. limited liability company
7. charter
8. return on equity
9. agency problem
10. capital gain
11. unlimited liability
12. distributorship
13. sole proprietorship
14. risk
15. franchise
16. manufacturing arrangement

## Concept Review Questions

1. **Forms of Business Ownership.** Compare and contrast a sole proprietorship, a partnership, and a corporation.

2. **Advantages of a Sole Proprietorship.** Why is the sole proprietorship such a popular form of business?

3. **Advantage of a Limited Partnership.** Explain why owners may establish a limited partnership instead of a general partnership.

4. **Advantage of an LLC.** What is a limited liability company (LLC), and why is it so popular?

5. **Return to Stockholders.** How can stockholders earn a return on their investment?

6. **Private Versus Public Firms.** Distinguish between privately held and publicly held corporations.

7. **Motive for Going Public.** Why might a business want to become a publicly held corporation?

8. **Concern About Going Public.** Why would a partnership worry about the possible mismanagement of its business if it converted to a publicly held corporation?

9. **Advantages of a Franchise.** Describe a franchise and explain why an entrepreneur may prefer to obtain ownership of a business through franchising.

10. **Types of Franchises.** Identify the common types of franchises and explain each type.

## Class Communication Questions

1. **Proprietorship Versus Partnership.** You own a proprietorship that is successful. You would like to expand your business but are constrained because you cannot obtain more loans. You have a very good friend who would provide your business with funding if he is allowed to be a part-owner. However, he does not understand your business and would not be helpful in running your business. Should you allow him to be a part-owner in order to obtain more funding?

2. **Franchise Decision.** You have an opportunity to buy a small restaurant franchise, which is part of a popular chain in your city. Alternatively, you could start your own restaurant business and would have more control regarding how to run the restaurant. Which investment would be less risky?

3. **Ownership of a Corporation.** You are aware of a company that is going public by selling 10 million shares of stock. You consider purchasing 300 shares of the stock. The company suggests that as a shareholder, you can influence its business decisions. Do you agree?

## Small Business Case

### Deciding the Type of Business Ownership

Dave Books and Kevin Warden have decided to start a partnership in which they create a golf instruction video. Dave has $30,000 to invest. He plans to run the business on his own but needs additional funding. Kevin has agreed to invest $30,000 in this business. Dave will produce the video and attempt to sell it directly to customers through a website. Dave will manage the business, while Kevin's main role will be to invest funds to support the business. The business is expected to earn net income of about $10,000 in the first year. If Dave expands the business over time, he will allow other investors to invest funds, but he will manage the business on his own.

1. **Business Ownership.** What form of business ownership would you recommend for this business?

2. **Liability.** Would Dave's liability be different from Kevin's?

3. **Return on Investment.** Explain how the expected return on equity of this business would be affected if the business could achieve the same net income in the first year with only $40,000 of equity instead of $60,000.

4. **Business Risk.** Describe the risk of this business.

## Web Insight

### Franchising at Domino's Pizza

At the opening of the chapter, Domino's Pizza was introduced. Go to Domino's website (www.franchise .org/Dominos_Pizza_franchise.aspx) or select another related website by using the search terms "Domino's" and "franchising." Summarize the comments made about qualifications and training for a Domino's Pizza franchise.

## Dell's Secret for Success

Go to Dell's website (www.dell.com) and click on the link "About Dell," near the bottom of the web page. Review the section called "Investors." You can also review a recent annual report of Dell for more information.

1. **Form of Ownership.** Could Dell have achieved its existing level of business if it had been organized as a partnership instead of a corporation? Explain.

2. **Change in Form of Ownership.** When Michael Dell created the company in 1984, do you think Dell was a corporation?

3. **Advantage of a Corporation.** What do you think caused Dell to become a corporation?

# Video Exercise

## Lessons in Forms of Business Ownership

Many free business videos are available on websites such as YouTube (www.youtube.com), and more are added every day. Search for a recent video clip about an existing business that offers lessons on "business ownership" in YouTube or any other website that provides video clips.

1. **Main Lesson.** What is the name of the business in the video clip?

Is the video clip focused on a proprietorship, a partnership, or a corporation? What is the main lesson of the video clip that you watched?

2. **Shift in Business Ownership.** Some related video clips explain the evolution of a business from proprietor to partnership to corporation. What do you think is the main reason for the shift in business ownership?

3. **Adjustment for the Entrepreneur.** Some related videos illustrate how the shift to the corporate form of ownership is a difficult adjustment for the entrepreneur. Why? How does the business decision-making process change in a manner that affects the entrepreneur?

# Projects

To encourage further comprehension of concepts covered in Chapter 5, the following five projects are available:

1. Analyzing Your Favorite Business
2. Building a Business Plan for Campus.com
3. Running Your Own Business
4. Planning Your Career
5. Stock Market Contest

All of these projects are provided in Appendix A at the end of the text. In addition, projects are available by part division at the end of each part.

A Word file for each project is also available at the textbook website (www.emcp.net/business5e) so that you may maintain one ongoing file for each project.

# Entrepreneurship and Business Planning

## Chapter 6 Learning Objectives

**1** Identify the advantages and disadvantages of being an entrepreneur and creating a business.

**2** Identify the market conditions that should be assessed before entering a market.

**3** Explain how a new business can develop a competitive advantage.

**4** Explain how to develop a business plan.

**5** Identify the risks to which a business is exposed, and explain how they can be managed.

# Chapter 6

## The Creation of Amazon.com

Entrepreneurs seek to create a business that will generate profits for themselves. They search for opportunities where they may be able to offer consumers a product or service that is either priced lower or of better quality than what is offered by existing firms. In this way, they may be able to satisfy customers and generate revenue. They also hope to produce the product at a relatively low cost so that their revenue exceeds their cost, resulting in profits.

Consider the case of Jeff Bezos, who moved from New York to Seattle to start an online book store in 1994. Bezos recognized that many consumers would be willing to purchase books by ordering them online and having them delivered. Furthermore, he made the website very user-friendly so that consumers could quickly find the books that they were interested in. Bezos named his business Amazon.com in 1995. In response to the popularity of the online book business, Bezos realized that consumers might purchase other products online as well. Amazon.com now offers many different products online, including movies, music, games, electronics, toys, apparel, and even industrial tools.

When considering the creation of a business, Jeff Bezos needed to address the following questions:

✦ Were the market conditions favorable for the creation of a new business?

✦ Could he create a comparative advantage for his business?

✦ What would be the business plan to execute his idea?

✦ What were the risks of his business, and how could he limit those risks?

All entrepreneurs have to address these types of questions when they consider starting a new business. This chapter explains how entrepreneurs can assess these questions in order to decide whether to establish a new business and how they attempt to capitalize on their ideas. Even after a business is created, it periodically reassesses these questions because it may revise its strategy as market conditions change.

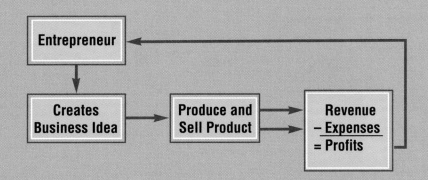

**Learning Objective**

Identify the advantages and disadvantages of being an entrepreneur and creating a business.

**1**

# 1. Creating a New Business

Each year, hundreds of thousands of small businesses are created. Though the largest businesses receive the most publicity, small businesses are vital to the economy. More than 99 percent of all firms have fewer than 500 employees. Small businesses are created by entrepreneurs who have a business idea and are willing to invest their own money to back the idea. Many new businesses are created with a very small amount of money, which limits the amount of funds that the entrepreneur might lose. Here is a brief summary of how three successful small businesses were created:

✦ **Domino's Pizza.** A classic example of a business that started with little funding is Domino's Pizza. It was established when Tom Monaghan (a college dropout) and his brother bought a bankrupt pizza parlor in 1960. Tom had to borrow the $500 that he needed to invest in the firm. Later, he bought his brother's interest in the business. Domino's Pizza now generates sales of about $1 billion per year.

✦ **Glow Dog, Inc.** Beth Marcus created Glow Dog, Inc., which sells light-reflective clothing for pets. Marcus thought of this business idea when she was walking her dog at night and realized that the dog was not visible to passing motorists. After just two years in business, her firm averaged annual sales of more than $1 million.

✦ **YouTube.** In May 2005, Steven Chen and Chad Hurley created a business called YouTube, which allowed people to easily upload their videos to a website at no cost so that others could watch the videos. The videos were tagged so that viewers could easily find videos that they wanted to watch. In addition, viewers were allowed to rate the videos, and the ratings became a useful guide for other viewers. In October 2006, Google acquired YouTube for $1.65 billion.

The point of these examples is that business ideas are not restricted to unusual inventions, as many simple ideas have led to successful businesses.

This single photo displays hundreds of entrepreneurial ideas. Products are created by entrepreneurs in order to satisfy customers. Entrepreneurs who are successful in satisfying customers typically generate enough sales to have a successful business.

Many business ideas are revisions of previous business ideas that failed. For example, many restaurant businesses have failed in one location, but succeeded when they were moved to a different location.

## 1.1  Advantages of Being an Entrepreneur

People are not born entrepreneurs. They choose to be entrepreneurs, rather than working as employees for a business. Being an entrepreneur offers several important advantages.

**Profits**   As an entrepreneur, you may possibly earn large profits from your business and therefore have a much higher income than if you worked for another business.

**Be Your Own Boss**   You can be your own boss and run the business the way that you want. Because you are in control, you do not need to fear being mistreated by a boss or being fired.

*Direct Rewards*

**Satisfaction**   You have the satisfaction of working in a business that you created, and you will likely be more willing to work hard because you are directly rewarded for your work in the form of higher business profits.

## 1.2  Disadvantages of Being an Entrepreneur

Being an entrepreneur also has some disadvantages that should be considered.

**Risk**   You may possibly incur large losses and could even lose your entire investment in the business. You could lose your source of income if the business fails.

*Failure Possibility*

**Responsibility**   While you may be in control of the business, you have to ensure that the business functions properly. Being in control does not necessarily mean that you can skip work whenever you desire; the income you earn is tied to how well the business is managed on a daily basis.

## 1.3  Entrepreneurial Profile

Entrepreneurs tend to have specific characteristics that distinguish them from other people. While entrepreneurs may have numerous characteristics, most fit the following profile. Consider whether you fit the entrepreneurial profile.

+ **Risk Tolerance.** Entrepreneurs must be willing to accept the risk of losing their business investment.

+ **Creativity.** Entrepreneurs recognize ways to increase customer satisfaction. They may detect a need by customers for a product or service that does not exist, and then attempt to satisfy that need. Or they may recognize that an existing product or service has deficiencies and attempt to improve on it.

+ **Initiative.** Entrepreneurs must be willing to take the initiative to make their ideas happen. They are able to recognize challenges and deal with them directly. To take the initiative, entrepreneurs need to have ambition and be persistent.

All of these characteristics are needed. Risk tolerance is necessary to invest in a new business. Creativity is needed not just to create a business idea, but to make the idea work. It may be used to detect customers' preferences for a new product, to design a new product that will satisfy customers, to ensure efficient production of that product, and to advertise the product. The business idea is just a part of the overall process necessary to have a successful business, however. Creativity is also required to expand the business's product line and to compete against other firms that produce related products. Initiative and ambition are necessary to obtain information before making decisions about where to produce, how much to produce, how to advertise, and how to obtain financing.

There are creative people who do not have the initiative, ambition, or risk tolerance to capitalize on their creativity. They may believe that a specific new product would be popular, but they lack the initiative, risk tolerance, or ambition to pursue the business idea. Conversely, there are people who have initiative, but lack creativity. They may not be able to recognize the need for a new product or an improved product.

Starting a small business can be a difficult process. Yahoo!'s Small Business site (http://smallbusiness.yahoo.com) is a good place to find links to more specific information. American Express (http://americanexpress.com /smallbusiness) provides information about building a business. The Small Business Administration (SBA) (www.sbaonline.sba.gov) offers information about government programs and other relevant information for small businesses.

Obtaining financing is crucial to beginning any business, and there are websites to facilitate this process, too. Quicken Small Business (www .quicken.com/small_business) matches entrepreneurs with lenders. Once a questionnaire has been completed, the site offers advice on the most appropriate financing. It also provides a list of interested banks and the appropriate applications. Garage.com (www.garage.com) targets startup companies in the high-tech sector and matches the companies with investors.

Some of the more useful websites on starting a small business are:

✦ Yahoo!'s Small Business (http://smallbusiness .yahoo.com)

✦ American Express (http://americanexpress .com/smallbusiness)

✦ Small Business Administration (www .sbaonline.sba.gov)

✦ Quicken Small Business (www.quicken.com/ small_business)

✦ Garage.com (www.garage.com)

---

**Learning Objective 2**

Identify the market conditions that should be assessed before entering a market.

## 2. Assessing Market Conditions

Before creating a new business for a particular market, the following conditions in that market should be considered:

✦ Demand

✦ Competition

✦ Labor conditions

✦ Regulatory conditions

*Microeconomic conditions*
*— conditions of the industry that the business operates in.*

### 2.1 Demand

*Economic conditions*
*Demographics*
*Consumer preferences*

Every product has its own market, where there are consumers who purchase the product and businesses that sell the product. In the market for personal computers (PCs), there is demand by millions of people for PCs, and there are many businesses (such as Dell and Hewlett-Packard) that produce PCs to accommodate that demand. There is also a market for services such as those provided by hairstylists, dentists, and mechanics. Since these services cannot be shipped, the demand for services within an area is accommodated by firms within that area. For example, the entire demand for auto mechanic services in a specific small town may be accommodated by a total of three auto mechanic businesses. Thus, there are many markets for a single service, with each market representing a specific area.

Over a given time period, firms in a specific market can perform much better than others because the total demand for the products in that market is high. The demand for most products is generally influenced by general economic conditions because consumers tend to buy more products and services when the economy is strong and they have a good income. The demand is also influenced by conditions within the specific market of concern. The demand for baby clothes is highly dependent on the number of children that are born. The demand for hotels in Florida during the winter is partially dependent on the weather in the northern states. In cold winters, more tourists travel to Florida.

**Change in Demand over Time**   The demand within a particular market changes over time. When it increases, the businesses within that market tend to benefit because their sales increase. Entrepreneurs tend to develop new businesses in markets where there is a strong demand so that they can benefit from that demand.

Just as an increase in demand is beneficial to firms in that market, a decline in demand has adverse effects. Consider the case of Bell Sports Corporation, which was once the largest producer of motorcycle helmets. It experienced a decline in business because the demand for these helmets leveled off. As the demand for bicycles increased, Bell switched its production process to make bicycle helmets instead. It also began to produce other bicycle accessories, such as child seats, safety lights, and car racks. In this way, it diversified its product line so that it was not completely reliant on its bicycle helmet business.

## 2.2  Competition

**market share**
a firm's sales as a proportion of the total market

Each business has a **market share**, which represents its sales volume as a percentage of the total sales in a specific market. If the total sales in the market for a particular product are $10 million this year, a firm that experienced sales of $2 million has a market share of 20 percent (computed as

New business ideas are commonly created in response to shifts in consumer preferences. When gas prices increased substantially, consumers shifted their demand away from gas guzzlers and toward fuel-efficient cars. Manufacturers of fuel-efficient hybrid cars (shown here) capitalized on anticipating the shift in consumer demand.

© SHUTTERSTOCK/MICHAEL SHAKE

*(handwritten)* (1) firm's market share
(2) level of competition
(3) Development of competitive advantage

# SMALL BUSINESS SURVEY

## Competition

Based on a recent National Small Business poll conducted for the NFIB Research Foundation, small businesses see their main competition as shown below:

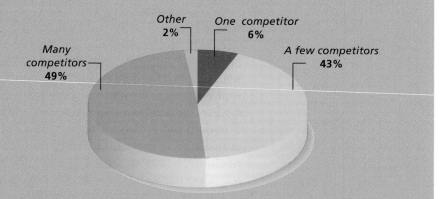

In general, most small businesses are concerned about more than one competitor. When asked how the number of competitors has changed in the last three years, the small businesses responded as follows:

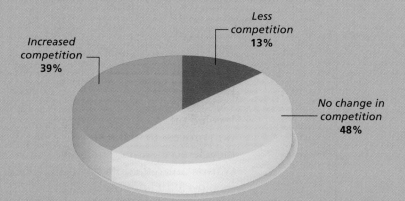

When asked where their main competition is located, the small businesses responded as follows:

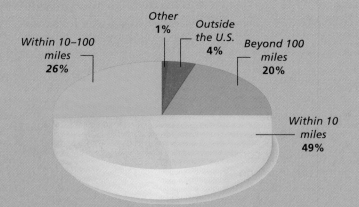

When asked about exposure to competition from Internet and mail-order companies, 9 percent of small businesses stated that they faced significant competition from this type of company, while 16 percent stated that they faced marginal competition from this type of company.

$2 million divided by $10 million). That is, the firm has 20 percent of the market.

If the competition within a particular market is limited, firms can more easily increase their market share and therefore increase their revenue. In addition, they may also be able to increase their price without losing their customers. Therefore, entrepreneurs prefer to pursue markets where competition is limited.

Firms that compete within a market for a particular product or service typically want to increase their market share. However, all firms cannot increase their share simultaneously. One firm's increase in market share occurs at the expense of another firm's decline in market share. For example, suppose that in a particular market (such as a small town), there will be a total of 6,000 visits to dentists this year. That is, the total demand for dentistry services in one year is 6,000. At this time, there are two dentists in the market. If a new dentistry business enters the market, any customers that it attracts will represent a reduction in business for the other two dentists. As a new business penetrates (enters) a market, it takes a portion of the market from other firms. Thus, it gains market share, while other firms may lose market share. Since its competitors prefer not to give up any of their market share, they may use various business strategies to counter the entrance of a new business into the market. It is difficult for a new business to continually increase its market share, especially when additional new businesses enter the market.

**Change in Competition over Time**   When competition in a particular market increases, it can reduce each firm's market share, thereby reducing the quantity of units sold by each firm in the market. Second, a high degree of competition may force each firm in the market to lower its price to prevent competitors from taking away its business. Consider the intense competition recently in the market for long-distance phone services.

**segments**
subsets of a market that reflect a specific type of business and the perceived quality

**Competition Within Segments**   Each market has **segments**, or subsets that reflect a specific type of business and the perceived quality. Thus, a market can be narrowly defined by type of business and quality. Segmenting the market in this way allows a firm to identify its main competitors so that they can be assessed.

A market can be segmented by specific types of customers. For example, in the car rental market, some firms (such as Hertz) focus heavily on business customers, while others (such as Dollar and Payless) focus more on individuals who are on vacation. Thus, an entrepreneur who plans to create a new car rental business must decide which segment to enter. This decision will affect the types of customers that it targets for its business.

A market may also be segmented by quality. Exhibit 6.1 shows different quality segments (based on customer perceptions) in the market for small cars. Each type of car in this market is represented by a point. Some cars, such as the BMW and the Corvette, are perceived to have high quality (measured according to engine size and other features that customers desire) and a relatively high price. Other cars have a moderate quality level and a lower price, such as the Toyota Camry. The Ford Focus and the Chevy Cobalt represent cars in a lower quality and price segment. Because each consumer focuses only on one particular market segment, the key competitors are within that same segment. For example, the Focus and Cobalt are competitors within the low-priced segment. The Focus is not

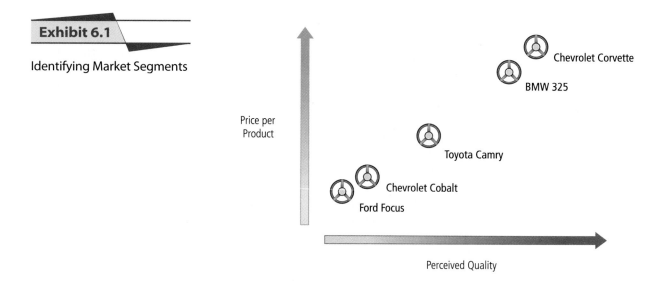

viewed as a competitor to the higher-priced cars. If a car company wants to produce a new small car, it assesses the competition according to the segment that it plans to target.

## 2.3  Labor Conditions

Some markets have specific labor characteristics. The cost of labor is much higher in industries such as health care that require specialized skills. Unions may also affect the cost of labor. Some manufacturing industries, particularly those in the northern states, have labor unions, and labor costs in these industries are relatively high. Industries that have labor unions may also experience labor strikes. Understanding the labor environment within an industry can help an entrepreneur estimate labor expenses and decide whether a new business could produce products at lower costs than existing firms.

1. Cost of labor
2. Skills needed
3. Unions

# Global Business

## Assessing a Market from a Global Perspective

When U.S. firms engage in international business, they must consider the segments within the foreign countries of concern. A specific product that is classified in a specific segment in the United States may be classified in a different segment in other countries. A product that is perceived as an inexpensive necessity in the United States may be perceived as an expensive luxury product in less-developed countries. U.S. firms may revise the quality and price of their products to satisfy a particular market segment. For example, household products that U.S. consumers view as basic necessities may not be affordable to consumers in some less-developed countries, so entrepreneurs considering producing such products would need to revise their strategies for competing in those markets. They may need to price their products low enough in those countries to attract demand.

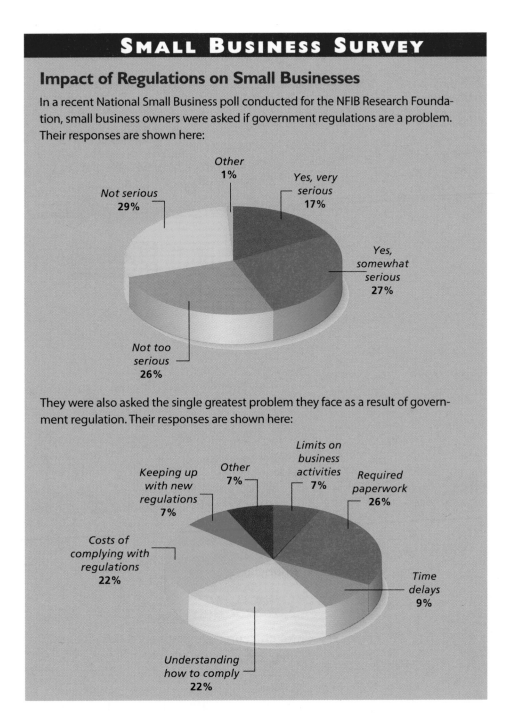

## SMALL BUSINESS SURVEY

### Impact of Regulations on Small Businesses

In a recent National Small Business poll conducted for the NFIB Research Foundation, small business owners were asked if government regulations are a problem. Their responses are shown here:

*Other* 1%
*Yes, very serious* 17%
*Not serious* 29%
*Yes, somewhat serious* 27%
*Not too serious* 26%

They were also asked the single greatest problem they face as a result of government regulation. Their responses are shown here:

*Keeping up with new regulations* 7%
*Other* 7%
*Limits on business activities* 7%
*Required paperwork* 26%
*Costs of complying with regulations* 22%
*Time delays* 9%
*Understanding how to comply* 22%

## 2.4  Regulatory Conditions

*1. Government Regulation*
*2. Industry Regulation*

The federal government may enforce environmental rules or may prevent a firm from operating in particular locations or from engaging in particular types of business. For example, Blockbuster is affected by state and federal regulations regarding advertising, consumer protection, provision of credit, franchising, zoning, land use, health and safety, and working conditions.

Although all industries are subject to some form of government regulation, some industries face especially restrictive regulations. Automobile and oil firms have been subject to increased environmental regulations. Firms in the banking, insurance, and utility industries have been subject to

**Exhibit 6.2**

Effects of Market Conditions on a Firm's Performance

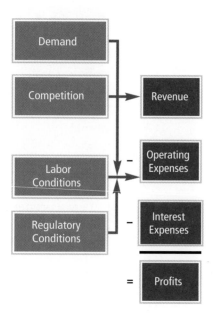

regulations on the types of services they can provide. Companies such as Amazon.com that rely heavily on the Internet for their business are exposed to some additional regulations governing the Internet and e-commerce. For example, they could be affected by laws regarding the protection of consumer data. If more regulations are implemented to ensure greater protection, the costs to Amazon.com of running its business could increase. Entrepreneurs who wish to enter any industry must recognize all the regulations that are imposed on that industry.

Firms that are already operating in an industry must also monitor industry regulations because they may change over time. For example, recent regulations in the banking industry have been imposed because banks were taking excessive risk when extending loans to individuals and businesses. The regulations are intended to enhance the safety of the financial system.

## 2.5  Summary of Market Conditions

An entrepreneur must consider all of the market conditions identified here before deciding to create a new business. The means by which these conditions affect the potential performance of the business are shown in Exhibit 6.2. Demand and competition affect the demand for a firm's products and therefore affect its revenue. Since these conditions also influence the quantity of products that a new business would produce, they also affect operating costs, such as manufacturing and administrative expenses. Any changes in the labor and regulatory environments typically affect the expenses of a new business.

**Learning Objective**

Explain how a new business can develop a competitive advantage.

**3**

## 3.  Developing a Competitive Advantage

Once entrepreneurs have identified and assessed their key competitors, they can search for ways to increase or at least maintain their market share. They must assess their specific market segment to determine whether they have a competitive advantage.

## 3.1  Common Strategies

While businesses use numerous strategies to develop a competitive advantage, most strategies are intended to produce products more efficiently or to produce a higher quality.

**Produce Products Efficiently**    If a new business can produce a product of similar quality at a lower cost, it can price the product lower than its competitors. This should enable the new firm to take away some of its competitors' market share. The low production cost may result from efficient management of the firm's employees (human resources) and its production process.

Some entrepreneurs attempt to achieve a price advantage even when they do not have a cost advantage. For example, an entrepreneur may notice that the only gas station in a populated area is charging high prices for its gasoline. The entrepreneur may consider establishing a new gas station in the area, with lower prices as its competitive advantage. However, the existing gas station may lower its prices in response to the new competitor. In this example, the entrepreneur's competitive advantage may be eliminated unless it has a cost advantage.

New airlines commonly attempt to achieve a price advantage over their competitors by advertising special fares on various routes over a particular period. The objective is to attract a higher demand by pulling customers away from other airlines. In many cases, the other airlines respond by lowering their airfares by the same amount. If some of the airlines are less efficient, however, they may not be able to continue the low fares for a long period of time (because their costs may exceed the fares charged). Thus, the new firms may drive the inefficient competitors out of the industry.

**Produce Higher-Quality Products**    If a new business can produce a product of higher quality without incurring excessive costs, it has a competitive advantage over other competitors in the same price range. Various characteristics may cause a product to be of better quality. It may be easier to use, last longer, or provide better service. The specific characteristics that determine perceived quality vary among products. For soft drinks, quality may be measured by taste. For outdoor furniture, quality may be measured by durability. For computers, quality may be measured by ease of use, the service provided, and processing speed. By achieving higher quality, a firm can satisfy customers to a greater degree.

## 3.2  Using the Internet to Create a Competitive Advantage

Many firms rely on the Internet to create a competitive advantage. They establish a website, where they advertise their products. Web-based businesses can accept credit card payments online for their products and then ship the products to customers. Some Web-based businesses rely completely on their website for all of their business, while other Web-based businesses rely on their website to complement their existing operations.

**Reduce Expenses**    One of the most important advantages of a website is that it may be able to replace a store and therefore may avoid the cost of renting a store. Amazon.com's website serves as a great example of how

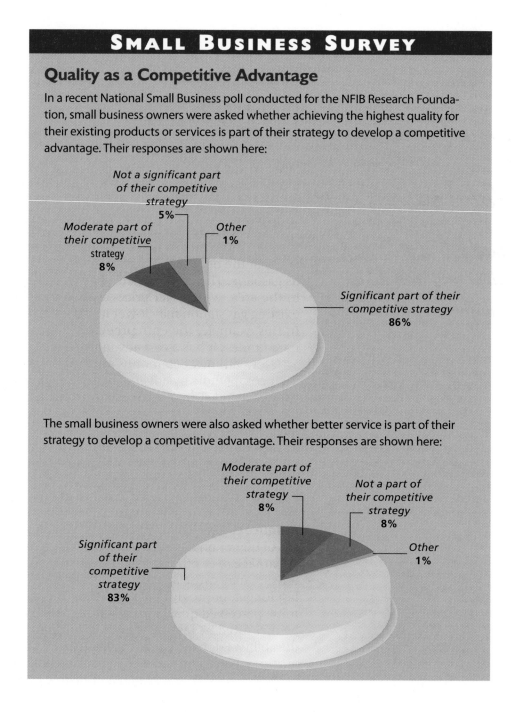

## SMALL BUSINESS SURVEY

### Quality as a Competitive Advantage

In a recent National Small Business poll conducted for the NFIB Research Foundation, small business owners were asked whether achieving the highest quality for their existing products or services is part of their strategy to develop a competitive advantage. Their responses are shown here:

Not a significant part of their competitive strategy
5%

Moderate part of their competitive strategy
8%

Other
1%

Significant part of their competitive strategy
86%

The small business owners were also asked whether better service is part of their strategy to develop a competitive advantage. Their responses are shown here:

Moderate part of their competitive strategy
8%

Not a part of their competitive strategy
8%

Other
1%

Significant part of their competitive strategy
83%

a website can provide personalized service to customers. The site allows customers to use a search term to browse existing books for sale and to access information and opinions by previous purchasers about any book. The site can also inform customers about other books that are related to the book they are viewing. It can even remind them about other books that they have purchased recently. In many ways, the site provides personalized service beyond what you would normally expect to receive in a bookstore.

A business website can reduce expenses when it provides services in the form of information. Many travel services such as flights, hotel rooms, and car rentals can be easily booked online. Some travel agencies do all of their work through their website, while others use the website to complement their existing shops. Hotels, airlines, and car rental agencies rely on some travel agencies to book reservations. In addition, they have established their own websites so that customers can make reservations there.

**Reach Additional Customers**   Another benefit of a Web-based business is that it can reach additional customers and therefore increase the revenue that the business generates. Some websites focus on providing information about what the business sells. Car dealers offer information about their latest models. Restaurants provide updates on their menus. Many retail stores do not view the Internet as a perfect substitute for the store, however, because some shoppers still prefer to shop at a store. Nevertheless, by establishing a website, stores can appeal to other shoppers who have no interest in going to a store. Furthermore, they can advertise their products and attract more customers to the store.

### 3.3  Expenses of a Web-Based Business

Along with the competitive advantages, some expenses are associated with a Web-based business.

**Website Development**   First, there is the cost of developing a website and installing a shopping cart system on the site to accept orders. A Web design firm may charge as little as $500 to develop a basic website for a business, but a very comprehensive website can cost more than $20,000.

**Credit Card Process**   A firm is needed to screen the credit card payments and ensure that the customers are using legitimate credit cards. This firm will accept payment and deposit the funds received into a bank account established by the business. It will charge a monthly fee for its services. In addition, the business will have to pay fees to credit card sponsors (MasterCard, Visa, etc.), such as 3 percent of the payments.

**Website Hosting**   A business commonly pays a website firm a small monthly fee to host the site and ensure that the site is constantly accessible to potential clients.

**Increase Visibility**   A business may need to pay marketing expenses to increase its visibility to customers. A business may rely on search engines (such as Google or Yahoo!) to direct customers to its site, but many other competitive websites may offer similar products. Furthermore, many websites that are not trying to sell products may receive higher priority from search engines. Consequently, a search online by a customer for a particular product may result in a list of more than 1,000 websites. Few customers are likely to search beyond the first 10 sites on the list. Thus, a business may need to hire a Web marketing firm to help it receive higher priority on search engines. Consider how many more customers would visit a website if it is the very first site, rather than the fiftieth site, shown by a search engine in response to a specific search term.

### 3.4  Using SWOT Analysis to Develop a Competitive Advantage

**SWOT**
method by which entrepreneurs develop a competitive advantage for their business

Entrepreneurs commonly use *SWOT analysis* to develop a competitive advantage. The acronym **SWOT** stands for *s*trengths, *w*eaknesses, *o*pportunities, and *t*hreats. Thus, a new business can use SWOT analysis to assess its

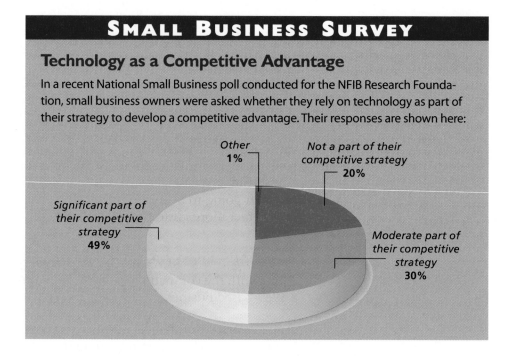

## SMALL BUSINESS SURVEY

### Technology as a Competitive Advantage

In a recent National Small Business poll conducted for the NFIB Research Foundation, small business owners were asked whether they rely on technology as part of their strategy to develop a competitive advantage. Their responses are shown here:

Other
1%

Not a part of their
competitive strategy
20%

Significant part of
their competitive
strategy
49%

Moderate part of
their competitive
strategy
30%

own strengths (such as a lower price or higher quality) and weaknesses, as well as the external opportunities and threats it faces.

For example, when Amazon.com was created, its strengths included the creativity of its employees and its ability to apply technology. A possible weakness was the lack of traditional retail outlets to sell books (although that is also its strength because Amazon.com can avoid intermediaries). Its opportunities were the potential markets for other related products online and the potential growth in the demand for online services in foreign countries. Its threats included competitors that could create similar online book businesses to provide the same type of services for consumers.

SWOT analysis is useful for existing businesses as well as for new businesses. It can help direct a firm's future business by using the firm's strengths to capitalize on opportunities, while reducing its exposure to threats.

**Learning Objective**

**4**

Explain how to develop a business plan

**business plan**

a detailed description of the proposed business, including a description of the product or service, the types of customers it would attract, the competition, and the facilities needed for production

## 4. Developing the Business Plan

After entrepreneurs assess markets and consider their competitive advantages, they may decide to create a particular business. They will need to develop a **business plan**, which is a detailed description of the proposed business, including a description of the product or service, the resources needed for production, the marketing needed to sell the product or service, and the financing required.

The business plan forces the entrepreneurs to think through the details of how they would run the business. Thus, it serves as a checklist to ensure that they have considered all the key functions of the business. Second, the entrepreneurs can provide the business plan to investors who may be willing to serve as partial owners or to various creditors (such as commercial banks or other financial institutions) that may be willing to provide business loans. Thus, the business plan should be clear and must convince others that the business will be profitable. If investors do not believe in the business plan, they will be unwilling to invest funds in the business. If

Out of Business

creditors do not believe in the plan, they will not supply any loans. In that case, the entrepreneurs will have to rely only on their own funds, which may not be sufficient to support the business.

The business plan's usefulness is not limited to helping the entrepreneurs raise funds to support the opening of the business. The plan will be used as a guide for making business decisions throughout the life of the business. It provides a sense of direction for the business's future development. The success or failure of any firm is partially dependent on its business plan. Many business planning packages and software are available and can be used to develop the business plan. However, the key contents of the business plan require the vision and insight of the entrepreneur. A complete business plan normally includes an assessment of the business environment, a management plan, a marketing plan, and a financial plan, as explained in detail next.

## 4.1  Assessment of the Business Environment

The business environment surrounding the business includes the economic environment, the industry environment, and the global environment.

**Economic Environment**   The economic environment is assessed to determine how demand for the product may change in response to future economic conditions. The demand for a product can be highly sensitive to the strength of the economy. Therefore, the feasibility of a new business may be influenced by the economic environment.

**Industry Environment**   The industry environment is assessed to determine the degree of competition. If a market for a specific product is served by only one or a few firms, a new firm may be able to capture a significant portion of the market. One must also ask whether a similar product could be produced and sold at a lower price, while still providing reasonable earnings. A related question is whether the new business would be able to produce a higher-quality product than its competitors. A new business idea is more likely to be successful if it has either a price or a quality advantage over its competitors.

**Global Environment**   The global environment is assessed to determine how the demand for the product may change in response to future global conditions. The global demand for a product can be highly sensitive to changes in foreign economies, the number of foreign competitors, exchange rates, and international trade regulations.

## 4.2 Management Plan

A management plan, which includes an operations plan, focuses on the firm's proposed organizational structure, production, and human resources.

**Organizational Structure**   An organizational structure identifies the roles and responsibilities of the employees hired by the firm. The organizational structure of a new factory is more complicated than that of a pizza delivery shop. If the owner plans to manage most of the operations, the organizational structure is simple. Some businesses begin with the owner assuming most responsibilities, but growth requires the hiring of managers. Even if the owners initially run the business, they should develop plans for the future organizational structure. A job description for each employee should be included, along with the estimated salary to be paid to each employee.

**Production**   Various decisions must be made about the production process, such as the site (location) of the production facilities and the design and layout of the facilities. The location decision can have a major effect on a firm's performance because it influences both the cost of renting space in a building and the revenue generated by the business. The proposed design and layout of the facilities should maximize the efficiency of the space available. This proposal should include cost estimates for any machinery or equipment to be purchased. The cost estimates for factories are normally more complicated than those for retail stores.

The business plan should also include the owners' plans for the business's future growth. As a business grows, it needs more space to allow for more production or to accommodate more customers. Its size will need to be sufficient to allow it to meet its production goals or accommodate all of its customers. It could easily meet these goals by selecting a site with extra space. The more space it obtains, however, the higher will be the cost of leasing the space. The entrepreneurs do not want to pay for space that they will not use. The business's future production is based on demand for its product, which is uncertain. Since the entrepreneurs do not know how much production will be necessary, they face a tradeoff. If they select a site with too much space, the business will not use all of its space. Alternatively, if they select a site that is too small, the business may not be able to produce a sufficient volume to accommodate demand.

Those businesses that require a large investment in facilities to produce their product can survive only if they attract substantial demand for their product. For example, a book publisher needs a printing press. If it prints and sells just a few copies of a book, it will not generate enough revenue to pay for producing the book. Therefore, it needs to sell a large number of the books that it produces so that it can recover the cost of its printing press. In this type of business, there are **economies of scale**, which means that the average cost per unit produced declines as the firm produces more units. Firms that have expensive machinery can benefit from economies of

**economies of scale**
as the quantity produced increases, the cost per unit decreases

scale. However, they must be able to sell a large volume of their product in order to benefit from economies of scale.

Many firms that provide services also have economies of scale. A dental office may spend $30,000 or more on X-ray machines and drills. If the dentist uses the drills only a few times, the cost for each use will be very high. However, if the dentist uses the drills frequently, the cost for each use will be low. To use the drills frequently, the dentist needs many customers. In this way, the dental office can generate enough revenue to recover the cost of the drills.

**Human Resources**   Many businesses begin with just a single owner who works without any employees. The owner is focused on making the business successful because the owner has invested his or her own funds in the business and is entitled to the profits of the business. As a business grows, it tends to hire more employees. In general, employees are not as concerned about a business as its owners because they have not invested their own money in the firm. Thus, they may not be motivated to ensure that the business is successful.

Managers of a business are supposed to ensure that employees are doing their job. However, if managers have to oversee a large number of employees, they may not be able to adequately monitor the employees. A firm could become inefficient if it has many employees and their job descriptions are not clear. In addition, some managers may decide to hire additional employees to make their own job easier, but these extra employees may not be necessary.

A business must set up a work environment that will motivate the employees. It must also have a plan for monitoring and evaluating employees. By monitoring and compensating employees properly, the business can ensure that the employees are striving to maximize its performance.

## 4.3  Marketing Plan

A marketing plan focuses on the target market, product characteristics, pricing, distribution, and promotion.

**Target Market**   A new business needs to decide on its target market, which reflects the specific traits (such as age) of customers who would purchase its products. The business can then consider methods to ensure that the target market is aware of its product. If the business believes its product is better than other products, it will need to prove that its product is better. Customers are not necessarily going to switch to a new product, especially if they are satisfied with existing products with which they are familiar. New businesses rely on various marketing strategies to attract customers, such as advertising their product, offering a special discount, or even providing free samples to the customers.

Once a new business establishes a base of initial customers, it may benefit from repeat business or referrals. Many new small businesses generate much of their revenue from repeat customers. Businesses that produce services such as hairstyling, maid service, and dentistry can benefit from repeat customers because the service is needed frequently. If the first customers are satisfied, they may not only be repeat customers, but may refer the business to their family members or friends. Then those referrals may purchase the product or service, and if satisfied, they may refer the business to others. The customer base of the business can expand as the referrals continue to spread.

In many cases, a firm will find that it cannot rely only on referrals to achieve the volume of business it desires. It will likely need to spend money on advertising or on other marketing strategies to increase its customer base.

**Product Characteristics**    The business plan should describe the characteristics of the product, with an emphasis on what makes the product more desirable than similar products offered by competitors. A product may be desirable because it is easier to use, is more effective, or lasts longer. Any competitive advantage of this product over similar products should be identified.

**Pricing**    The proposed price of the product should be included. Prices of similar products sold by competitors should also be mentioned. The price will influence the demand for the product.

**Distribution**    The business plan should describe the means by which the product will be distributed to the customers. Some products are sold to customers directly, while others are distributed through retail outlets.

**Promotion**    The business plan should also describe the means by which the product will be promoted. The promotion strategy should be consistent with the customer profile. For example, products that appeal to college students may be advertised in student newspapers.

## 4.4 Financial Plan

The financial plan determines the means by which the business is financed. It also attempts to demonstrate that the creation of the business is feasible.

**Financing**    The creation of a business requires funds to purchase machinery and materials, rent space, hire employees, and conduct marketing. Most firms rely heavily on funding from the entrepreneurs who established them.

Creditors typically prefer that a business demonstrate that it is capable of covering its loan payments before they will provide a loan. Because a new business does not have a history, creditors may be willing to provide a loan only if it is backed by collateral, such as a building or computers owned by the owner. The creditors will claim the collateral if their loan is

When developing a plan for a new business or the restructuring of an existing business, an entrepreneur commonly asks for input from employees or other business associates.

© SHUTTERSTOCK/MORGAN LANE PHOTOGRAPHY

not repaid. They may limit the size of the loan to the market value of the owner's collateral.

In addition, creditors will want to look closely at the financial condition of the owners. In some cases, they may require personal financial information that the owners may prefer not to disclose. Creditors may also require that the owners back the loan with their own assets (such as a home). Given the restrictions imposed by many creditors, entrepreneurs may initially attempt to borrow funds from family members or friends who are more willing to provide loans.

Even after a business is established, it may need financing as it grows. The funds may be used to invest in a larger production site or to hire more employees. As time passes, the business's growth should result in higher revenue, and part of that revenue can be used to cover the interest expenses on a loan or to pay off the loan.

Once a business grows and establishes a track record of good performance, it may be able to borrow funds from financial institutions. To obtain a loan from a financial institution (such as a commercial bank), the firm will need to present a detailed business plan. The lending institution assesses the business plan to determine whether the business is likely to be successful and therefore deserves a loan. A business might consider issuing stock only after demonstrating adequate performance for several years.

**Funding by the SBA**   As mentioned earlier, the Small Business Administration (SBA) has been a key source of funding for new businesses. It is a federal agency that was created in 1953 to assist and protect the interests of small businesses. The SBA relies on financial institutions (such as banks) to provide loans to applicants who qualify, but it sets the financial requirements for obtaining the loans. It backs the loans by guaranteeing a portion of each loan. The lenders are more willing to provide the loans because the SBA promises partial repayment of the loans. Since 1964, the SBA has had a program under which it backs loans to small business owners below the poverty level who do not meet the standard credit and collateral requirements but have promising business ideas. Over time, the SBA has added numerous programs, including one that provides management assistance for small businesses owned by women, minorities, and armed forces veterans.

The SBA also offers the SBA Express program, which is tailored to start-up retail firms that have revenue of $6 million or less and manufacturing firms with less than 500 employees.

Once a business plan is created, the entrepreneur may present the idea to investors who may be willing to invest equity in the business. Alternatively, the entrepreneurs may present the business plan to commercial banks in an attempt to obtain business loans to finance the business.

© SHUTTERSTOCK/DOREEN SALCHER

This program provides a fast response to requests for loans by entrepreneurs. In 2003, about 37,000 loans—about half of all SBA loans—were provided through the SBA Express program. Recently, the volume of micro-business loans (less than $100,000) to small businesses has increased substantially.

**Feasibility**   Another benefit of developing a business plan is that it forces entrepreneurs to assess the feasibility of their potential business before they invest their money and time in creating it. As briefly described in an earlier chapter, a business's feasibility can be measured by calculating its expected earnings (profits). Earnings are measured as revenue minus expenses, as shown in Exhibit 6.3. The expected revenue to be generated by the business is based on the sales volume (number of units sold) times the price per unit. A firm's revenue is influenced by its marketing. Expenses can be categorized as operating expenses or interest expenses. Operating expenses can be broadly defined as the expenses associated with business operations, such as production and marketing expenses. Therefore, operating expenses are dependent on the firm's production and marketing. Interest expenses are the interest payments made to creditors from which funds were borrowed. The interest expenses are dependent on how much money the firm borrows.

When revenue exceeds total expenses, earnings are positive. Entrepreneurs will seriously consider establishing a business only if it is expected to generate positive earnings over time, as those earnings will provide the return on their investment. Entrepreneurs should also consider the risk of a business, which can be measured as the uncertainty of the future earnings. The less uncertainty surrounding the future earnings, the more desirable is the business.

## 4.5  Online Resources for Developing a Business Plan

In the past, putting a business plan together was both time-consuming and expensive. Today, business plan software can make the process much easier. Most of the software packages contain a collection of options, which can be used to create a thorough business plan. The best packages incorporate a number of capabilities.

**Exhibit 6.3**

How a Firm's Earnings Are Measured

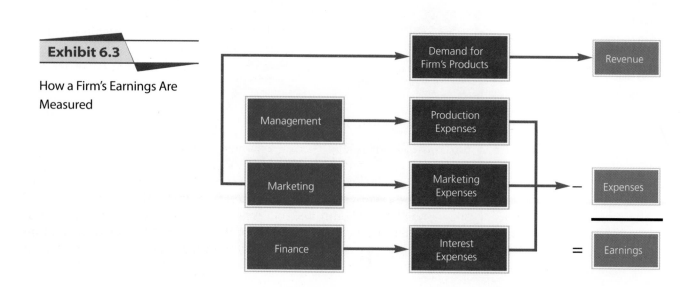

**Business Plan Outlines**   Packages normally offer one or more outlines of business plans that can be altered to fit most businesses. Some packages take entrepreneurs through a series of questions in order to create a tailor-made plan.

**Text Generation**   Much of the information that goes into a business plan is standardized. Business plan software can insert such text directly into the plan, making the appropriate substitutions for company names and products. Once in place, the text can be edited as needed.

**Forecasting**   Any business plan software packages should include the ability to create consistent projections. The software package should be able to predict sales and costs in various ways (for example, using percentage growth models, market share models, or values that are individually specified by the planner) and should ensure that interrelated data are consistent. For example, when the planner changes values in a table of projected market shares, forecasted sales in other parts of the document should automatically be updated.

**Supplementary Documents**   A number of business plan packages offer supplementary documents, such as disclosure agreements, which are often used in conjunction with business plans, although not necessarily as part of the document.

## 4.6  Summary of a Business Plan

The key parts of a business plan are summarized in Exhibit 6.4. Exhibit 6.5 shows the typical sequence of business decisions that are made in developing a business plan. Many decisions can be made only after the entrepreneur has decided on the type of product or service that will be produced and sold. The management and marketing decisions can be made after identifying the product (or product line). Once all management and marketing decisions are made, the amount of funds needed to support the business can be determined. The financing decision of how to finance the firm is dependent on how much funding is needed. All of these key business decisions must be reassessed periodically as the firm's business grows and its product line expands.

The remaining chapters in this text are organized so that each part of the text represents a part of the business plan. The management plan is discussed in Part III, and managing employees is described in Part IV. The marketing plan is discussed in Part V. The financial plan is covered in Part VI. Thus, the key concepts discussed in each part of the text can be applied to develop a specific part of the business plan.

## 4.7  Assessing a Business Plan

Many business ideas that seem reasonable at first may not be undertaken because the entrepreneur has various concerns after developing the business plan. For example, the plan may reveal that the revenue will not be sufficient or the expenses will be too high to make the business worthwhile. Under these conditions, the business idea should be completely discarded. Perhaps one or more aspects of the proposed business need to be changed, and then a new assessment of the revenue and expenses should

1. Potential revenue
2. Demand for product
3. Expense of production
4. Overall potential for profitability

**Exhibit 6.4**

Contents of a Typical
Business Plan

I. DESCRIPTION AND OWNERSHIP OF PROPOSED BUSINESS

◆ Describe the product (or service) provided by the proposed business.

II. ASSESSMENT OF THE BUSINESS ENVIRONMENT

◆ *Economic Environment:* Describe the prevailing economic conditions and the exposure of the firm to those conditions.

◆ *Industry Environment:* Describe the competition in the industry and the general demand for the product in the industry.

◆ *Global Environment:* Describe the prevailing global conditions that relate to the business, such as foreign markets where the business may sell products in the future or obtain supplies.

III. MANAGEMENT PLAN

◆ *Organizational Structure:* Describe the organizational structure and show the relationships among the employee positions. This structure should also identify the responsibilities of each position in overseeing other positions and describe the specific tasks and salaries of managers and other employees.

◆ *Production Process:* Describe the production process, including the site, design, and layout of the facilities needed to produce a product. Also, describe the planned amount of production per month or year.

IV. MANAGING EMPLOYEES

◆ Describe the work environment used to motivate employees and the plans for training, evaluating, and compensating employees.

V. MARKETING PLAN

◆ *Target Market:* Describe the profile (such as the typical age and income level) of the customers who will purchase the product and therefore make up the target market. (Who will buy the product?)

◆ *Product Characteristics:* Explain desirable features of the product. (Why will customers buy the product?)

◆ *Pricing:* Describe how the product will be priced relative to competitors' products. (How much will customers pay for the product?)

◆ *Distribution:* Describe how the product will be distributed to customers. (How will customers have access to the product?)

◆ *Promotion:* Describe how the product will be promoted to potential customers. (How will customers be informed about the product?)

VI. FINANCIAL PLAN

◆ *Funds Needed:* Estimate the amount of funds needed to establish the business and to support operations over a five-year period.

◆ *Feasibility:* Estimate the revenue, expenses, and earnings of the proposed business over the next five years. Consider how the estimates of revenue, expenses, and earnings of the proposed business may change under various possible economic or industry conditions.

be conducted to determine whether the business is feasible. Even after a business is created, it must have long-term plans for its production, management of employees, marketing, and financing. Therefore, business planning is not confined to the creation of the business, but must be continued as the business evolves.

**Exhibit 6.5**

Common Sequence of
Business Decisions Made in
Developing a Business Plan

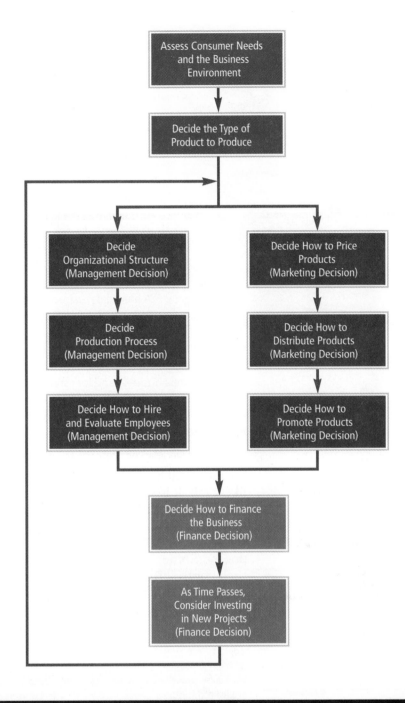

Exhibit 6.5 Common Sequence of Business Decisions Made in Developing a Business Plan

Assess Consumer Needs and the Business Environment → Decide the Type of Product to Produce →

Decide Organizational Structure (Management Decision) → Decide Production Process (Management Decision) → Decide How to Hire and Evaluate Employees (Management Decision)

Decide How to Price Products (Marketing Decision) → Decide How to Distribute Products (Marketing Decision) → Decide How to Promote Products (Marketing Decision)

→ Decide How to Finance the Business (Finance Decision) → As Time Passes, Consider Investing in New Projects (Finance Decision)

**Learning Objective 5**

Identify the risks to which a business is exposed, and explain how they can be managed.

**business risk**

the possibility that a firm's performance will be lower than expected because of its exposure to specific conditions

# 5. Risk Management by Entrepreneurs

As entrepreneurs plan their new business, they recognize that they are exposed to **business risk**, or the uncertainty of the future performance of a business. The future profits of a business are uncertain because of uncertainty surrounding the expected revenue and expected expenses. Some businesses have much more risk than others. For example, a business of tutoring on a college campus has business risk, but the investment of funds to create the business is minimal, so the potential losses are limited. Conversely, consider a business that wants to produce a drug that will cure a particular disease. It must invest substantial funds in laboratories and highly skilled employees to try to develop the drug. This business will perform very well if a cure is found. But if its drug is not effective, the

## Cross-Functional Teamwork

### Industry Effects Across Business Functions

When a new business is considered, the assessment of a market will vary with the perspective. Entrepreneurs must consider different perspectives. For the purpose of managing production, the focus is on labor costs in the industry of concern. Production costs will also be influenced by the level of technology and regulatory changes in the industry that could require revisions to the production process.

A marketing perspective assesses the competitors in the industry to become aware of the features of competing products. This information is used when developing strategies to make a new product superior to those sold by competitors. The marketing perspective must consider the insight from the production perspective on the expenses that would result from making the product superior.

A financial perspective focuses on determining the amount of funding that will be needed to support the new business, and the possible ways to obtain the funds. It relies on the production perspective for estimates on the amount of funds needed to support the production process. It relies on the marketing perspective for estimates on the amount of revenue that will be generated by the new business and for estimates on the expenses associated with advertising the business. Overall, the entrepreneurs must consolidate the production, marketing, and finance perspectives before they can decide whether it is worthwhile to create a new business.

*Protecting against risk:*

*\* Eliminate the risk*

*\* Shift the risk*
  *(purchasing insurance)*

*\* Assume the risk*

business will have no revenue, will have incurred large expenses, and will likely fail. It is subject to a very high degree of business risk because there is much uncertainty about its future performance.

As part of the business planning process, entrepreneurs must consider the sources of business risk that could cause their business to perform poorly. Some sources of risk such as economic conditions are beyond their control. But many other sources of risk are within their control. Such sources of risk are said to result from firm-specific characteristics. Exhibit 6.6 lists some of the more common firm-specific sources of business risk. Several of these are discussed here, along with strategies that

---

**Exhibit 6.6**

Exposure to Firm-Specific Characteristics

| Characteristic | How Firm Is Exposed |
| --- | --- |
| Limited funding | Limited ability to cover expenses. |
| Reliance on one product | Revenue will be reduced substantially if there is a large decline in the demand for a single product. |
| Reliance on one customer | Revenue will decline substantially if the customer no longer purchases the firm's product. |
| Reliance on one supplier | Potential shortages of supplies if supplier experiences problems. |
| Reliance on a key employee | Performance will decline if the employee dies, becomes ill, or leaves the firm. |
| Property losses | Expenses incurred from covering damage to property. |
| Liability losses | Expenses incurred from covering liability for damage to others or their property. |
| Employee compensation claims | Expenses incurred from covering compensation claims. |

# SMALL BUSINESS SURVEY

## What Are the Major Concerns of Small Businesses?

A survey of small businesses was conducted to determine their major concerns. The businesses were segmented into two groups: those with annual sales of less than $3 million and those with annual sales of more than $3 million. The following table shows the percentage of firms in each group that identified various problems as a serious concern:

| Problem | Firms with Less Than $3 Million in Sales | Firms with More Than $3 Million in Sales |
| --- | --- | --- |
| Inadequate planning | 58% | 33% |
| Inadequate financing | 48% | 21% |
| Inadequate managerial skills of some employees in key positions | 46% | 23% |
| Not prepared for economic downturns | 37% | 26% |
| Inability to respond to market changes | 30% | 31% |
| Environmental regulations | 29% | 38% |
| Nonenvironmental regulations | 18% | 22% |
| Litigation (such as defending against lawsuits) | 15% | 21% |
| Employee theft or fraud | 13% | 11% |
| Foreign competition | 11% | 24% |

Many of the major concerns detected by this survey have already been discussed in this text; others will be discussed in later chapters. Some of the concerns reflect exposure to economic conditions (economic downturns), industry conditions (regulations), and global conditions (foreign competition). Other concerns focus on the firm's management (planning), marketing (response to market changes), and financing.

One of the most common entrepreneurial ideas is a retail clothing store (as shown here) that sells clothes produced by other entrepreneurs. While many clothing stores have become very successful, others have failed. Perhaps the primary reasons for failure are poor planning and unrealistic expectations.

© SHUTTERSTOCK/LOSEVSKY PAVEL

entrepreneurs can use to reduce their exposure. One way that entrepreneurs may reduce their risk exposure is by purchasing insurance; Exhibit 6.7 lists some types of insurance that a firm might purchase.

It may seem that entrepreneurs are being pessimistic if they anticipate conditions that could adversely affect their business. However, any entrepreneurs who ignore possible adverse conditions when planning their business are not being realistic. Proper business planning includes preparing for the possibility of adverse conditions so that the business can survive even if such conditions occur.

## 5.1  Reliance on One Customer

Firms that rely on a single customer for most of their business have a high degree of business risk because their performance will decline substantially if the customer switches to a competitor. For example, a firm may rely on selling some of the products it produces to the federal government. If the federal government reduces its spending, it will order fewer products from the firm. Firms can reduce their reliance on a single customer by attempting to spread the sales of their products across various customers.

## 5.2  Reliance on One Supplier

Firms that rely on a single supplier for most of their supplies may be severely affected if that supplier does not fulfill its obligations. If that supplier suddenly goes out of business, the firm may experience a major shortage of supplies. Firms that use several suppliers are less exposed to the possibility of a single supplier going out of business, because they will still receive their supply orders from the other suppliers.

## 5.3  Reliance on a Key Employee

When a firm relies on a key employee for its business decisions, the death or resignation of that employee could have a severe impact on the firm's performance. Consider a computer repair business that has only one employee who can perform the repairs. If the employee dies or leaves the

---

**Exhibit 6.7**

Some Types of Insurance a Firm Might Purchase

| Type of Insurance | Coverage Provided |
| --- | --- |
| Business interruption insurance | Covers against losses due to a temporary closing of the business. |
| Credit line insurance | Covers debt payments owed to a creditor if a borrower dies. |
| Fidelity bond | Covers against losses due to dishonesty by employees. |
| Marine insurance | Covers against losses due to damage during transport. |
| Malpractice insurance | Covers professionals from losses due to lawsuits by dissatisfied customers. |
| Surety bond | Covers losses due to a contract not being fulfilled. |
| Umbrella liability insurance | Provides additional coverage beyond that provided by other existing insurance policies. |
| Employment liability insurance | Covers claims against wrongful termination and sexual harassment. |

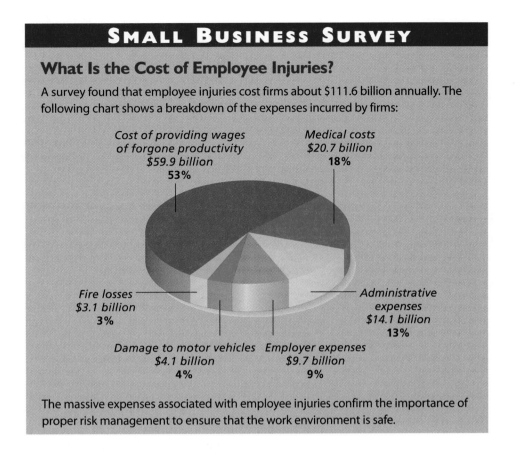

# SMALL BUSINESS SURVEY

## What Is the Cost of Employee Injuries?

A survey found that employee injuries cost firms about $111.6 billion annually. The following chart shows a breakdown of the expenses incurred by firms:

*Cost of providing wages of forgone productivity*
**$59.9 billion**
**53%**

*Medical costs*
**$20.7 billion**
**18%**

*Fire losses*
**$3.1 billion**
**3%**

*Administrative expenses*
**$14.1 billion**
**13%**

*Damage to motor vehicles*
**$4.1 billion**
**4%**

*Employer expenses*
**$9.7 billion**
**9%**

The massive expenses associated with employee injuries confirm the importance of proper risk management to ensure that the work environment is safe.

firm, other employees may not be able to perform this job. Until the employee can be replaced, business performance may decline. Since a business cannot be managed as well following the loss of a key employee, it may be less capable of covering its expenses.

**Hedging Against Losses Resulting from a Key Employee's Death**    Firms can hedge against losses resulting from a key employee's death by purchasing life insurance for their key employees. The policy identifies the firm as the beneficiary in the event that a key employee dies. Thus, when a key employee dies, this type of insurance provides the firm with compensation, which the firm can use to offset the possible losses or reduced performance. The firm is cushioned from the loss of a key employee and may be able to survive while it attempts to hire a person to fulfill the key employee's responsibilities. Consider an individual who runs a small business and applies for a business loan at a local bank. If the individual is killed in an accident, the business may deteriorate and the loan would not be paid off. A life insurance policy could designate creditors (such as a bank) as the beneficiaries to protect them against such a risk. Using this strategy, the business is more likely to be approved for a loan.

**Hedging Against the Illness or Loss of a Key Employee**    The illness or resignation of a key employee may also adversely affect the performance of a firm. To try to prevent employees from becoming ill, many firms offer a program that enables their employees to obtain health insurance from health insurance companies. The insurance is generally cheaper when purchased through the firm. Even if a firm provides a health insurance plan for its employees, it may still be affected by the temporary absence of

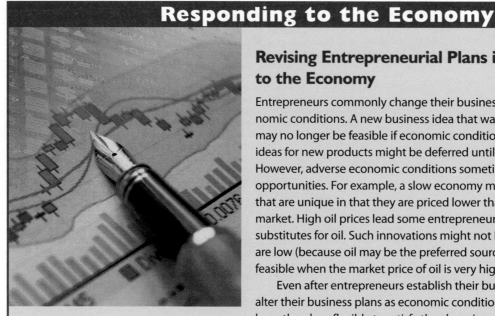

# Responding to the Economy

## Revising Entrepreneurial Plans in Response to the Economy

Entrepreneurs commonly change their business plans in response to economic conditions. A new business idea that was planned for the future may no longer be feasible if economic conditions weaken. In this case, ideas for new products might be deferred until the economy improves. However, adverse economic conditions sometimes lead to new business opportunities. For example, a slow economy may lead to new products that are unique in that they are priced lower than existing products in the market. High oil prices lead some entrepreneurs to consider innovative substitutes for oil. Such innovations might not be feasible when oil prices are low (because oil may be the preferred source of energy), but become feasible when the market price of oil is very high.

Even after entrepreneurs establish their businesses, they periodically alter their business plans as economic conditions change. Ideally, they keep the plans flexible to satisfy the changing needs of consumers.

an employee. Firms can reduce the potential adverse effect of an employee's illness by ensuring that more than one employee can perform each task. To attempt to prevent key employee from resigning, firms can offer good compensation and benefits.

## 5.4   Exposure to E-risk

Information technology has created new risks and increased the complexity of risk management. For example, there is the risk that electronic data may be stolen and used in a manner that adversely affects the business. Online banking and securities trading have created large exposures to risk. These services are vulnerable to potential losses from security breaches through network hacking, viruses, and electronic thefts. New businesses can hire firms to establish a computer system that is protected from this exposure. Alternatively, a business may attempt to purchase insurance to cover against loss of business income, damage to reputation, loss of intellectual property, interruption of service liability, and liabilities incurred as a result of electronically published information.

## COLLEGE HEALTH CLUB: DEVELOPING A BUSINESS PLAN

Now that Sue Kramer has assessed the environment (from Chapters 1–4) and selected the proprietorship form of business organization (Chapter 5), she needs to develop a business plan for College Health Club (CHC). She can lease space where Magnum Club was located (across the street from the college campus) before it relocated to downtown. Since Magnum purchased new equipment when it moved, it is willing to lease the equipment and weight machines that are still in its previous location for $600 per month or $7,200 per year.

Sue has accumulated savings of $20,000 over the years. Her husband's income will cover their normal household expenses, so she can use the $20,000 to invest in her business. She develops her business plan, which is summarized next.

## Business Idea

The business is a health club called College Health Club (CHC) that will be located in a shopping mall just across from the Texas College campus. It will sell memberships on an annual basis. The health club should appeal to the students because it is convenient and would be affordable to them.

## Management Plan

+ **Production Process**  The business will provide its members with health club services, such as access to exercise machines, weight machines, and aerobics classes. It will rent the exercise and weight machines that were previously owned by Magnum Club for $7,200 per year. It will rent the space in the shopping mall across from the Texas College where Magnum Club was located. The rent expense for the facilities will be $5,000 per month, or $60,000 per year. Utility expenses are estimated to be $700 per month, or $8,400 for the first year.

+ **Organizational Structure**  Sue Kramer will be the president of CHC and will also manage CHC. She will not require a salary as manager of the business, as she wants to limit the salary expenses in the first few years.

## Managing Employees

Sue will hire some part-time employees who are majoring in exercise science at Texas College. Typically, one or two employees will be working whenever the health club is open. Sue will train the employees. The total salary expense of CHC is estimated to be $4,000 per month, or $48,000 during the first year.

## Marketing Plan

+ **Target Market**  CHC will primarily target students at Texas College, but will also attempt to attract nonstudents who live nearby. The main competitor is Energy Club, but it is a 20-minute drive from the campus. Based on her survey of students about their interest in joining a health club, Sue is very confident that a minimum of 200 students will become members in CHC's first year of business. Her best guess is that 300 students will become members in CHC's first year. She expects that the membership will grow each year.

+ **Pricing**  The price for an annual membership will be $500, which is less than the prices of most health clubs in the area.

+ **Promotion**  CHC will advertise in the Texas College newspaper and use other promotion methods such as posters throughout the campus. Sue estimates that the cost of promoting CHC will be $300 per month, or $3,600 for the first year.

## Financial Plan

+ **Funding**  Sue will invest $20,000 in the business. She expects that she will need an additional $40,000 to run the business. Diane Burke, a relative of Sue's, has offered to lend the business $40,000 if she believes that the business plan is feasible. She will charge an interest rate of 10 percent on the loan. If Sue accepts the funds as a loan, she will have to pay Diane interest of $4,000 at the end of each year (computed as $40,000 × 10%).

+ **Revenue**  CHC's main source of revenue will be the annual membership fees. Sue estimates that there will be 300 paid memberships over the first year. Since the membership fee is $500, CHC should receive a total of $150,000 in revenue (estimated as $500 × 300 members). The revenue is expected to increase yearly as the number of members increases.

+ **Expenses**  The monthly expenses expected to be incurred by CHC are summarized in Exhibit 6.8. The expenses are segmented into operating expenses, which result from operating the business, and interest expenses, which are incurred as a result of financing the business. CHC's main operating expenses will be the cost of renting the facilities, salaries, utility expenses, the cost of renting the exercise and weight machines, marketing expenses, and the cost of insuring the business. The total expenses in the first year are expected to be $142,000. The annual expenses are expected to be stable over time.

✦ **Earnings** CHC's earnings (before taxes) in the first year are derived by subtracting the annual expenses from the annual revenue, as shown in Exhibit 6.9. Since the total revenue should increase over time (due to an increase in memberships) while the expenses remain stable, the earnings should increase over time. The earnings generated by CHC will be reinvested to support future expansion of the existing club or the possible establishment of an additional health club near a different college campus.

**Exhibit 6.8**

Expected Monthly
Expenses at CHC

| | Monthly Expenses | Total Expenses in First Year |
|---|---|---|
| **Operating Expenses** | | |
| Rent facilities | $5,000 | $60,000 |
| Salaries | 4,000 | 48,000 |
| Utilities | 700 | 8,400 |
| Rent exercise and weight machines | 600 | 7,200 |
| Marketing expenses | 300 | 3,600 |
| Liability insurance | 800 | 9,600 |
| Miscellaneous | 100 | 1,200 |
| **Total Operating Expenses** | | **$138,000** |
| Interest expenses | | 4,000 |
| **Total Expenses** | | **$142,000** |

**Exhibit 6.9**

Expected Performance
of CHC in the First Year

| | |
|---|---|
| **Revenue** | **$150,000** |
| Total operating expenses | −138,000 |
| Interest expenses | −4,000 |
| **Earnings Before Taxes** | **$8,000** |

# Summary of Learning Objectives

**1** The advantages of starting your own business include being directly rewarded if the business performs well and being your own boss. Being an entrepreneur also has some disadvantages that should be considered; these include the possible loss of your investment in the new business and the heavy responsibility of ensuring that the business functions properly on a daily basis.

To be an entrepreneur, you must

✦ be willing to accept the risk of losing your investment in a new business,

✦ be creative so that you can develop a good business idea, and

✦ be willing to take the initiative to make your business ideas happen.

**2** The main market characteristics that an entrepreneur should assess before entering the market are

✦ total demand in the market, which affects the potential demand for a firm's products,

✦ competition, which affects the potential demand for a firm's products,

✦ labor conditions, which affect the firm's potential expenses from producing the product, and

✦ regulatory conditions, which affect the firm's potential expenses from producing products.

**3** A new business can develop a competitive advantage within its market segment through efficient production (which allows it to charge a lower price) or by offering a product of better quality.

**4** A business plan forces an owner of a proposed business to specify all the key plans for the business. The business plan normally consists of

✦ an assessment of the business environment;

✦ a management plan that explains how the firm's resources are to be used;

✦ a marketing plan that explains the product pricing, distribution, and promotion plans; and

✦ a financial plan that demonstrates the feasibility of the business and explains how the business will be financed.

Even after the business is established, the business plan is continually revised in response to changes in market conditions, competition, and economic conditions.

**5** An entrepreneur who creates a business must consider its exposure to various forms of risk, along with methods to protect against those forms of risk. Some of the common forms of risk include heavy reliance of the business on one customer, or one supplier, or one employee.

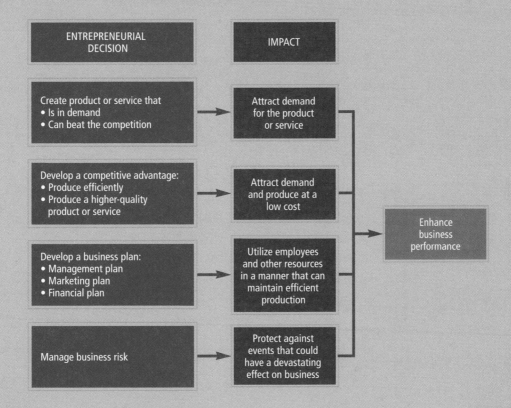

# Self-Test of Key Concepts

The following self-assessment allows you to test your understanding of the key concepts covered in this chapter. Answers are provided at the end of this exercise.

**True or False**

1. A firm can safely conclude that it will perform well over the next year if there are favorable economic conditions in the United States.

2. Total revenue is dependent on the quantity of units sold and the expenses of producing those units.

3. A firm that faces a high degree of competition can sell a low-quality product at a high price and thereby generate a high level of profit.

4. The cost of labor is high in industries that require specialized skills.

5. All industries are subject to some form of government regulation.

6. Market share refers to an individual firm's sales expressed as a proportion of the total market sales.

7. All firms in an industry commonly increase their market share at the same time.

8. The risk to business owners with a firm is limited, because they are guaranteed to receive their initial investment back.

9. Diversification can reduce a firm's exposure to poor performance in a particular market.

10. Improved product quality can create a competitive advantage for a firm.

11. A business plan is intended to provide information for potential investors or creditors of a proposed business.

12. A marketing plan focuses on various decisions that must be made about the production process, such as site location and design and layout of the facilities.

## Multiple Choice

13. As market demand changes, so does the _____ of firms in the industry.
    a) performance
    b) business ethics
    c) consumerism
    d) conservationism
    e) regulatory environment

14. Total revenue is the result of multiplying the selling price of the product times the:
    a) quantity of units sold.
    b) quantity of units produced.
    c) quantity of labor hours used.
    d) quality demanded by consumers.
    e) quantity of government regulations.

15. A firm can charge a higher price without losing its customers if it does not have much:
    a) production.
    b) competition.
    c) marketing.
    d) advertising.
    e) industry demand.

16. Labor costs are often higher in industries that have:
    a) labor unions.
    b) unemployment.
    c) savings.
    d) demand schedules.
    e) interest expense.

17. According to the text, industry regulations have recently been increased in the:
    a) automobile industry.
    b) chemical industry.
    c) oil industry.
    d) banking industry.
    e) steel industry.

18. Managers will monitor changes in labor costs in order to control:
    a) marketing costs.
    b) macroeconomics.
    c) production costs.
    d) social responsibility.
    e) industry demand.

19. The performance of a firm can be highly dependent on the following market conditions except for:
    a) regulatory conditions.
    b) labor conditions.
    c) competition.
    d) demand.
    e) taxes.

20. Changes in demand and competition affect both the demand for a firm's products and the firm's:
    a) location.
    b) customer service.
    c) revenue.
    d) recycling.
    e) segmentation.

21. A firm's share of total sales in the market is called its:
    a) market demand.
    b) regulatory environment.
    c) market share.
    d) economic segment.
    e) competitive advantage.

22. Another name for subsets in a market that reflect a specific type of business and the perceived quality is:
    a) demographics.
    b) marketing.
    c) sales.
    d) segments.
    e) economics.

23. After a firm identifies a specific market, it can segment that market by:
    a) level of employees.
    b) scrap reworked.
    c) labor environment.
    d) conservationism.
    e) quality segments.

24. Once a firm has identified and assessed its key competitors, it must search for ways to increase or at least maintain its:
    a) labor environment.
    b) regulatory environment.
    c) market share.
    d) competition.
    e) social costs.

25. Even if a firm does not have a cost advantage, it may still create a(n):
    a) inflation advantage.
    b) condition advantage.
    c) monopoly advantage.
    d) price advantage.
    e) ethics advantage.

26. Firms commonly use a _____ analysis to develop a competitive advantage.
    a) SWOT
    b) SPUR
    c) SNAP
    d) STEP
    e) SPOT

27. The aspect of a management plan that identifies the roles and responsibilities of the employees hired by the firm is the:
    a) unity of command.
    b) division of work.
    c) degree of specialization.
    d) organizational structure.
    e) standardization concept.

28. A marketing plan focuses on all the following except:
    a) financing the business.
    b) a profile of typical customers.

c) product characteristics.
d) pricing of the product.
e) distribution of the product.

29. A plan that demonstrates why the business is feasible and proposes how the business should be financed is the:
    a) production report.
    b) marketing plan.
    c) financial plan.
    d) human resource plan.
    e) bottom-up plan.

30. A business plan is a detailed description of the proposed business that includes all of the following except:
    a) description of the business.
    b) types of customers it would attract.
    c) competition.
    d) facilities needed for production.
    e) monetary and fiscal policy.

| True/False | | Multiple Choice | | |
|---|---|---|---|---|
| 1. False | 7. False | 13. a | 19. e | 25. d |
| 2. False | 8. False | 14. a | 20. c | 26. a |
| 3. False | 9. True | 15. b | 21. c | 27. d |
| 4. True | 10. True | 16. a | 22. d | 28. a |
| 5. True | 11. True | 17. d | 23. e | 29. c |
| 6. True | 12. False | 18. c | 24. c | 30. e |

# Self-Test of Key Terms

business plan  186
business risk  195

economies of scale  188
market share  177

segments  179
SWOT  185

Fill in each blank with the proper key term. To assess your understanding of the key terms, answers are provided at the end of this self-test.

1. The uncertainty of a company's performance is referred to as _____.

2. Market _____ are identified according to a specific type of business and a perceived quality.

3. Entrepreneurs use a(n) _____ analysis to determine their strengths, weaknesses, opportunities, and threats.

4. A _____ is a detailed description of a proposed business, including a description of the

product or service, the resources needed for production, the marketing needed to sell the product or service, and the financing.

5. _____ represent the reduction in average cost per unit in response to an increase in the quantity produced.

6. _____ represents the sales of a company as a proportion of the total market sales.

**Answers:**
1. business risk
2. segments
3. SWOT
4. business plan
5. Economies of scale
6. Market share

# Concept Review Questions

1. **Business Planning and Value.** Why does a firm's business plan affect its performance and value?

2. **Entrepreneur Advantages.** What are the advantages of being an entrepreneur?

3. **Entrepreneur Disadvantages.** What are disadvantages of being an entrepreneur?

4. **Assessing Market Conditions.** Suppose that you have an idea for a new business. Identify the market conditions that you would assess to determine whether to create the business.

5. **Competitive Advantage.** Explain how a firm's production and pricing decisions could help it achieve a competitive advantage.

6. **Categories of a Business Plan.** Explain the four key parts of a business plan, and briefly describe each part.

7. **Management Plan.** The management plan is a component of the business plan. What does it contain?

8. **Marketing Plan.** The marketing plan is a component of the business plan. What does it contain?

9. **Revised Business Plan.** A business plan is periodically revised even after the firm is created and evolves. Why do you think a business plan is revised?

10. **Business Plan.** What are some common characteristics of a business that could make it very risky?

# Class Communication Questions

1. **Profile of an Entrepreneur.** Are people born as entrepreneurs, or can they develop the skills to become an entrepreneur?

2. **Purchasing a Business.** Weigh the tradeoffs of starting a new business versus purchasing a very successful business that is currently for sale. Why might you decide to start your own business instead of purchasing a successful business?

3. **Why Businesses Fail.** Entrepreneurs must recognize the key factors that make a business risky so that they can reduce their exposure to the risk. What do you think is the key reason why some businesses fail? [Is it because the business idea is weak, or because of bad management decisions, bad marketing decisions, or bad finance decisions?]

# Small Business Case

## Creating a Business

Alys Navarro used to tutor her friends in math for free. She realized that she was very effective at tutoring and has decided to create a math tutoring business. She will not just try to explain the concepts, but will create a set of questions that can help students determine whether they really understand the concepts. She views this strategy as a competitive advantage over other students who already provide math tutorial services. Alys established this business with very little funding because she does not need an office

to provide the service. She will rely on cheap advertising in the school newspaper and will post messages on bulletin boards for students who may need to hire a tutor. She also hopes to receive referrals from previous customers.

1. **Impact of Competition on Demand.** Why might the demand for the math tutorial services offered by Alys change over time in response to the competition?

2. **Establishing a Competitive Advantage.** How do you think

customers who rely on Alys for the tutorial service will judge whether her service was worthwhile?

3. **Risk of Business Expansion.** If Alys expands her business by hiring new employees, why might she possibly lose her competitive advantage over time?

4. **Risk of a Business Dominated by One Person.** Explain why the math tutorial business is risky as a result of heavy reliance on one owner.

# Web Insight

## Entrepreneurship at Amazon.com

At the opening of the chapter, Amazon.com was introduced. Amazon.com is a great example of entrepreneurship, not only because of the business it created, but because it continues to rely on entrepreneurship for its expansion plans. Go to the website (www.amazon.com) and click on Investor Relations at the bottom of the website and then go to the annual reports section (or you could do a web search using "Amazon.com" and "Annual Report" as search terms). Review the Letter to Share- holders. Summarize the comments made about Amazon.com's future business opportunities.

Amazon.com has grown sub- stantially, but it still has potential for more growth. In recent years, it has expanded its business internationally.

# Dell's Secret for Success

Go to Dell's website (www.dell.com) and click on the link "About Dell," near the bottom of the web page. Review information about Dell's business of serving customers directly. You can also review a recent annual report of Dell for more information.

1. **Competitive Advantage.** What is Dell's competitive ad- vantage over its competitors?

2. **Distribution Plan.** Explain how Dell benefits from selling products directly to customers rather than relying on retail stores for much of its sales.

3. **Reputation Effect.** Explain how Dell's reputation can create a competitive advantage.

# Video Exercise

## Lessons in Entrepreneurship

Many free business videos are avail- able on websites such as YouTube (www.youtube.com), and more are added every day. Search for a recent video clip about an existing business that offers lessons on "entrepreneur- ship" in YouTube or any other web- site that provides video clips.

1. **Main Lesson.** What is the name of the business in the video clip?

Is the video clip focused on the creation of a business idea, the development of a business plan, or some other aspect of entre- preneurship? What is the main lesson of the video clip that you watched?

2. **Impact of Timing.** Some video clips on entrepreneurship sug- gest that timing is critical. Ex- plain how timing would affect the performance of the business in your video clip. For example, how might a change in market conditions affect this business?

3. **Competitive Advantage.** Does the business in your video clip have a competitive advantage? If so, what is it? That is, what makes this business successful?

# Projects

To encourage further comprehen- sion of concepts covered in Chapter 6, the following five proj- ects are available:

1. Analyzing Your Favorite Business

2. Building a Business Plan for Campus.com

3. Running Your Own Business

4. Planning Your Career

5. Stock Market Contest

All of these projects are provided in Appendix A at the end of the text. In addition, projects are available by part division at the end of each part.

A Word file for each project is also available at the textbook website (www.emcp.com.net/business5e) so that you may maintain one ongoing file for each project.

# Summary/Part II

# Starting a New Business

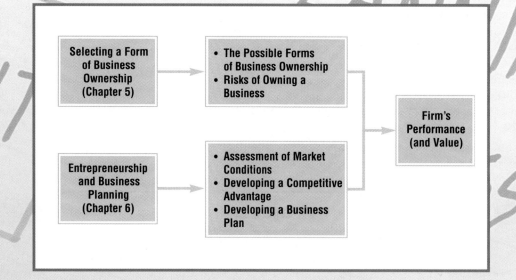

Selecting a Form of Business Ownership (Chapter 5) → • The Possible Forms of Business Ownership • Risks of Owning a Business

Entrepreneurship and Business Planning (Chapter 6) → • Assessment of Market Conditions • Developing a Competitive Advantage • Developing a Business Plan

→ Firm's Performance (and Value)

# Summary

Entrepreneurs determine a form of ownership that is based on their size, their need for funding, and other factors. Next, they can determine the strategies that can allow a competitive advantage. These strategies are articulated within the business plan. The strategies to develop a competitive advantage and other aspects of the business plan (Chapter 6) are influenced by the form of ownership selected for the business (Chapter 5).

# Video on Managing a Business

## Adjusting the Business Plan

The Small Business Administration plays a very important role in helping many small businesses. Its website, which offers a wide range of services and information for small businesses, has a section called Delivering Success (www.sba.gov /tools/audiovideo/deliveringsuccess /index.html) that provides video clips of small business success stories. Go to this website, and watch the video called "Business Reality Check" (total time of clip is 8 minutes, 50 seconds).

In this video clip, the success stories of two small businesses are described. Each business had a specific business plan that was altered as a result of the business environment. One business adjusted its plans as it recognized that it could achieve more efficiency by revising its target customers. The other business (based in New Orleans) had to change its business plan when hurricane Katrina hit, and many local residents were evacuated. While the two businesses are not related, they both enjoyed success as a result of having the flexibility to adjust their business in response to abrupt changes in their business environment. While they could not fully prepare for the unexpected, they quickly responded to the events that altered their business environment.

1. **Impact of Form of Business on Business Planning.** Explain how the business plan (Chapter 6) is highly dependent on the form of business ownership that is planned (Chapter 5).

2. **How a Change in Form of Business Alters the Business Plan.** Explain how a change in the form of business ownership (Chapter 5) affects the business plan (Chapter 6).

3. **Impact of Business Planning on Form of Ownership.** How might the form of business ownership (Chapter 5) be affected by the business plan (Chapter 6)?

# Self-Test for Part II

**Chapters 5–6.** Answers are provided at the end of the self-test.

1. When entrepreneurs establish a business, they must first decide on the form of:
   a) divestiture.
   b) global expansion.
   c) joint venture.
   d) ownership.

2. Joe wants to form his own business. He wants to get started as quickly and inexpensively as possible and has a strong desire to control the business himself. He is confident he will be successful and wants to keep all the profits himself. Joe's goals indicate he would probably choose to operate his business as a(n):
   a) limited partnership.
   b) limited liability company.
   c) S-corporation.
   d) franchise.
   e) sole proprietorship.

3. A disadvantage of a sole proprietorship is that:
   a) sole proprietors have very little control over the operations of the business.
   b) sole proprietors have unlimited liability.
   c) it is more difficult and expensive to establish than other forms of business.
   d) its earnings are subject to higher tax rates than other forms of business.
   e) sole proprietors are required to share the firm's profits with employees.

4. In a limited partnership:
   a) all partners have limited liability.
   b) the partnership exists only for a limited time period, or until a specific task is accomplished.
   c) the limited partners do not participate in management of the company.
   d) the partners agree to operate in a limited geographic area.
   e) no more than 100 partners may invest in the company at any one time.

5. A firm that has 100 owners or less and also meets other criteria may choose to be a so-called:
   a) cooperative.
   b) proprietorship.
   c) joint venture.
   d) S-corporation.
   e) bureaucracy.

6. Important aspects of a corporation, such as the name of the firm, information about the stock issued, and a description of the firm's operations, are contained in a:
   a) mission.
   b) policy.
   c) charter.
   d) plan.
   e) venture.

7. When a corporation's shares can be easily purchased or sold by investors, it is:
   a) publicly held.
   b) privately held.
   c) institutionalized.
   d) monopolized.
   e) franchised.

8. When stockholders of a corporation sell shares of stock for more than they paid for them, they receive a:
   a) dividend.
   b) premium.
   c) capital gain.
   d) discount.
   e) stock option.

9. The degree of uncertainty about future earnings, which reflects an uncertain return to the owners, is known as:
   a) certainty.
   b) profits.
   c) risk.
   d) equity.
   e) dividends.

10. Sharing profits and less control of the business ownership are two common disadvantages of:
    a) sole proprietorships.
    b) downsizing.
    c) divestiture.
    d) franchising.

11. As market demand changes, so does the _____ of firms in the industry
    a) performance
    b) business ethics
    c) consumerism
    d) conservationism
    e) regulatory environment

12. A firm can charge a higher price without losing its customers if it does not have much:
    a) production.
    b) competition.
    c) marketing.
    d) advertising.
    e) industry demand.

13. According to the text, industry regulations have recently been reduced in the:
    a) automobile industry.
    b) chemical industry.
    c) oil industry.
    d) banking industry.
    e) steel industry.

14. Managers will monitor changes in labor costs in order to control:
    a) marketing costs.
    b) macroeconomics.
    c) production costs
    d) social responsibility.
    e) industry demand.

15. A firm's share of total sales in the market is called its:
    a) market demand.
    b) regulatory environment.
    c) market share.
    d) economic segment.
    e) competitive advantage.

16. After a firm identifies a specific market, it can segment that market by:
    a) level of employees.
    b) scrap reworked.
    c) labor environment.
    d) conservationism.
    e) quality segments.

17. Even if a firm does not have a cost advantage, it may still create a(n):
    a) inflation advantage.
    b) condition advantage.
    c) monopoly advantage.
    d) price advantage.
    e) ethics advantage.

18. The aspect of a management plan that identifies the roles and responsibilities of the employees hired by the firm is the:
    a) unity of command.
    b) division of work.
    c) degree of specialization.
    d) organizational structure.
    e) standardization concept.

19. A plan that demonstrates why the business is feasible and proposes how the business should be financed is the:
    a) production report.
    b) marketing plan.
    c) financial plan.
    d) human resource plan.
    e) bottom-up plan.

20. A business plan is a detailed description of the proposed business that includes all of the following except:
    a) description of the business.
    b) types of customers it would attract.
    c) competition.
    d) facilities needed for production.
    e) monetary and fiscal policy.

**Answers:**

| | | | |
|---|---|---|---|
| 1. d | 6. c | 11. a | 16. e |
| 2. e | 7. a | 12. b | 17. d |
| 3. b | 8. c | 13. d | 18. d |
| 4. c | 9. c | 14. c | 19. c |
| 5. d | 10. d | 15. c | 20. e |

# Projects

## PROJECT 1:  ANALYZING YOUR FAVORITE BUSINESS

**Answering the Questions.** This entire project is provided in Appendix A. You can retrieve the Word file of this project from the textbook website (www.emcp .net/business5e), and insert your answer just below each question. The portion of the project that is related to the chapters in this part is provided here.

Using the annual report of the firm you selected, answer the following questions:

**Firm's Competition (related to Chapter 6).** Briefly summarize any industry conditions (such as competition) that affected the firm's performance last year.

**Competitive Advantage (related to Chapter 6).** Does the firm have a competitive advantage?

## PROJECT 2:  BUILDING A BUSINESS PLAN FOR CAMPUS.COM

**Completing the Information.** You can complete the information on the Word file of this project from the textbook website (www.emcp .net/business5e). This allows you to insert all of your information on one file for this project by the end of the school term. The portion of the project that is related to the chapters in this part is provided here.

**Form of Business Ownership (related to Chapter 5).** The optimal form of ownership for Campus.com is:

_____
_____
_____
_____
_____

Reasons for choosing that type of ownership:

_____
_____
_____
_____

**Entrepreneurship (related to Chapter 6).** Campus.com's existing competition is:

_____
_____
_____
_____
_____
_____
_____
_____

## PROJECT 3:  RUNNING YOUR OWN BUSINESS

**Completing the Information.** This entire project is provided in Appendix A. You can retrieve the Word file of this project from the textbook website (www.emcp.net/ business5e), and insert your answer just below each question. The portion of the project that is related to the chapters in this part is provided here.

**Selecting a Form of Business Ownership (related to Chapter 5).** The optimal form of ownership for your business is:

_____
_____
_____

Reasons for choosing that type of ownership:

_____
_____
_____
_____

**Entrepreneurship (related to Chapter 6).** Your business will target these industry segments:

_____
_____
_____

Describe the existing competition that your business must face:

_____
_____
_____
_____
_____
_____
_____
_____
_____

## PROJECT 4:  PLANNING YOUR CAREER

This entire project is provided in Appendix A at the end of the text, and you can access a Word file of this project from the textbook website (www.emcp.net/business5e), and insert your answer just below each question.

If you are interested in the topics covered in this section, you may want to consider a major in entrepreneurship. Some of the more common courses taken by entrepreneurship majors are summarized here.

### Common Courses for Entrepreneurship Majors

• **Financial Management** Explains the different types of business or-ganizations, along with the advantages and disadvantages of each, financing decisions by firms, and investment decisions by firms.

• **Management** Explains the basics of a business organization, the skills necessary to be a manager, and the resources needed by a business.

• **Marketing** Focuses on how to price a product, advertise a product, and distribute a product to the market.

• **Financing for Small Businesses** Explores how small businesses can finance their growth, the types of institutions that may facilitate the financing, and the phases of financing that may ultimately lead to an initial public offering of stock once the firm has grown substantially.

• **Entrepreneurship** Focuses on developing product ideas, testing the product, surveying the market, and using creativity to expand the product line.

## PROJECT 5:  STOCK MARKET CONTEST

This entire project is provided in Appendix A at the end of the text, and you can access a Word file of the project from the textbook website (www.emcp.net/business5e).

Your instructor may ask you to assess the performance of your investment up to this point, and determine whether the performance of your stock is attributed to any of the business concepts that were described in the chapters contained in this part.

# Part III
# Management

Capacity planning

Branches

Time

Long – term strategy

**7** Managing
Effectively

**8** Organizational
Structure

**9** Improving
Productivity
and Quality

The chapters in Part III describe some of the key components of effective management. These components are (1) recognition of the skills necessary to be effective managers (Chapter 7), (2) proper assignments of job responsibilities (Chapter 8), (3) efficient allocation of resources for production (Chapter 9), and (4) proper monitoring and improvement of product quality (Chapter 9).

Effective management requires that job responsibilities be properly assigned within the organizational structure. Ideally, the organizational structure allows some control over each job assignment so that all types of tasks can be monitored. The organizational structure may also attempt to ensure employee input on various tasks by assigning extra responsibilities to employees.

Effective management also requires an efficient production process, which involves the selection of a plant site and the design and layout of the production facilities.

Effective management also requires an effort to continuously improve the quality of each product that is produced. Quality management forces employees to specify the desired quality level, to consider how the production process can be revised to achieve that quality level, and to continuously monitor the quality level by using various quality control methods.

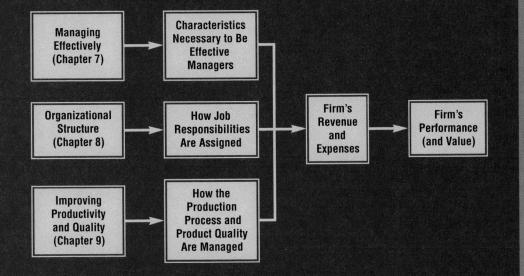

# Managing Effectively

## Chapter 7 Learning Objectives

**1** Identify the levels of management.

**2** Identify the key functions of managers.

**3** Describe the skills that managers need.

**4** Describe methods that managers can use to utilize their time effectively.

## Managing at LA Fitness

Management involves the utilization of human and other resources (such as machinery) in a manner that best achieves the firm's plans and objectives. According to a survey by Shareholder Surveys, shareholders rank good management and long-term vision as the two most important characteristics of a firm. Consider the situation of LA Fitness, which established a mission to help as many people as possible achieve the benefits of a healthy lifestyle. To fulfill this mission, it developed a plan to create sports clubs in which it offers members a wide range of services at an affordable price. To achieve its plan, it relies heavily on its managers to make proper decisions regarding the types of services to offer, the locations to establish new clubs, strategies for promoting its business, and ways to finance its expansion. LA Fitness must determine the following questions about its management:

✦ What levels of management does it need to manage its business?

✦ What functions are required of its managers?

✦ What skills do its managers need?

Ideally, LA Fitness would like to ensure that its managers run the business efficiently (keep expenses low). In addition, proper management can result in more favorable customer service, which attracts more members to the clubs and generates more revenue. This chapter explains how decisions by LA Fitness or any business regarding the characteristics of its management can be made in a manner that maximizes its value.

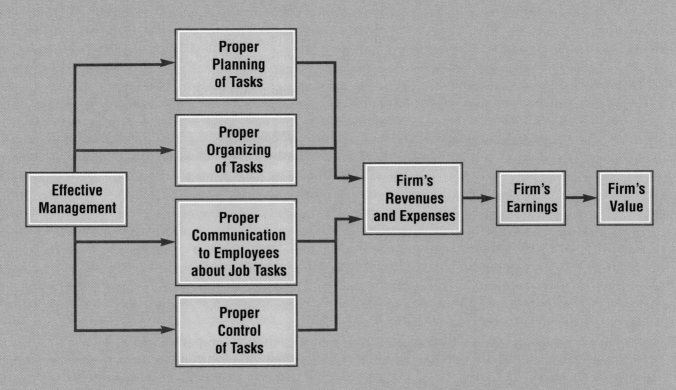

**top (high-level) management**
managers in positions such as president, chief executive officer, chief financial officer, and vice-president who make decisions regarding the firm's long-run objectives

**middle management**
managers who are often responsible for the firm's short-term decisions

**supervisory (first-line) management**
managers who are usually highly involved with the employees who engage in the day-to-day production process

# 1. Levels of Management

Employees who are responsible for managing other employees or other resources serve as managers, even if their official title is different. The functions of managers vary with their respective levels within the firm.

## 1.1 Top Management

The **top (high-level) management** includes positions such as president, chief executive officer (who commonly also serves as president), chief financial officer, and vice-president. These managers make decisions regarding the firm's long-run objectives (such as three to five years ahead).

## 1.2 Middle Management

The **middle management** is often responsible for the firm's short-term decisions, as these managers are closer to the production process. Middle managers resolve problems and devise new methods to improve performance. Middle management includes positions such as regional manager and plant manager.

## 1.3 Supervisory Management

The **supervisory (first-line) management** is usually highly involved with the employees who engage in the day-to-day production process. Supervisors deal with problems such as worker absenteeism and customer complaints. Supervisory management includes positions such as account manager and office manager. The types of functions that each level of management conducts are summarized in Exhibit 7.1.

**Comparison of Management Levels** The relationships among top, middle, and supervisory managers can be more fully understood by considering a simple example. Exhibit 7.2 shows the responsibilities of all managers in light of a firm's new plans to expand production and increase sales. The middle and top managers must make production, marketing, and finance decisions that will achieve the new plans. The supervisory managers provide specific instructions to the new employees who are hired to achieve the higher production level.

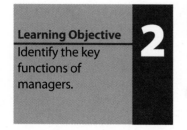

# 2. Functions of Managers

Most managerial functions can be classified into one of the following categories:
+ Planning
+ Organizing
+ Leading
+ Controlling

## 2.1 Planning

**planning**
the preparation of a firm for future business conditions

The **planning** function represents the preparation of a firm for future business conditions. As the first step in the planning process, the firm

**Exhibit 7.1**

Comparison of Different
Levels of Management

| Title | Types of Decisions |
|---|---|
| **Top Management** | |
| President | 1) Should we create new products?<br>2) Should we expand?<br>3) How can we expand? Through acquisitions? |
| Chief Financial Officer | 1) Should more funds be borrowed?<br>2) Should we invest available funds in proposed projects? |
| Vice-President of Marketing | 1) Should an existing product be revised?<br>2) Should our pricing policies be changed?<br>3) Should our advertising strategies be changed? |
| **Middle Management** | |
| Regional Sales Manager | 1) How can we boost sales in a particular city?<br>2) How can complaints from one of our largest customers be resolved?<br>3) Should an additional salesperson be hired? |
| Plant Manager | 1) Should the structure of the assembly line be revised?<br>2) Should new equipment be installed throughout the plant? |
| **Supervisory Management** | |
| Account Manager | 1) How can workers who process payments from various accounts be motivated?<br>2) How can conflicts between two workers be resolved? |
| Supervisor | 1) How can the quality of work by assembly-line workers be assessed?<br>2) How can assembly-line tasks be assigned across workers?<br>3) How can customer complaints be handled? |

**Exhibit 7.2**

Comparison of
Responsibilities
Among Managers

**Top Management**
1. Set new plan to expand production and increase sales.
2. Communicate those plans to all managers.

↓

**Middle and Top Managers**
1. Determine how many new employees to hire.
2. Determine how to charge lower prices to increase sales.
3. Determine how to increase advertising to increase sales.
4. Determine how to obtain funds to finance the expansion.

↓

**Supervisory Managers**
1. Provide job assignments to the new employees who are hired.
2. Set time schedules for new employees who are hired.

Supervisory managers (like the one shown here) closely monitor the production process and interact with employees who are involved in the production.

© SHUTTERSTOCK/JOE GOUGH

**mission statement**
a description of a firm's primary goal

establishes its **mission statement**, which describes its primary goal. For example, here is the mission statement of Bristol-Myers Squibb:

*"The mission of Bristol-Myers Squibb is to extend and enhance human life by providing the highest quality health and personal care products."*

Most mission statements are general, like that of Bristol-Myers Squibb. The mission of many large companies in the automobile industry is to be the world's leader in producing automotive products and services.

**strategic plan**
identifies a firm's main business focus over a long-term period, perhaps three to five years

**Strategic Plan**   The **strategic plan** identifies the firm's main business focus over a long-term period. The strategic plan is more detailed than the mission statement and describes in general terms how the firm's mission is to be achieved. For example, if a firm's mission is to produce quality computer products, its strategic plan might specify the particular computer products to be produced and the manner in which they will be sold (retail outlets, Internet, etc.).

The strategic plan typically includes goals and strategies that can be used to satisfy the firm's mission. For example, a recent annual report of Bristol-Myers Squibb listed the following among its main goals and strategies:

## Goals:
*"Leadership in each product category and in each geographic market in which we compete. We aim to achieve number one or number two position with increasing market shares."*

*"Superior customer satisfaction by providing the highest quality products and services to our customers. We will strive to be rated number one or two with continuous improvement as rated by our customers."*

*"Superior steady shareholder returns, as measured by a number one or two competitive position in economic performance within our industry."*

## Out of Business

*"An organization which is committed to winning through teamwork, empowerment, customer focus, and open communications."*

### Strategies:

*"Our mission and goals will be achieved by adhering to the following core strategies:*

✦ *Achieve unit growth fueled internally by new products, geographic expansion, and marketing innovation, and externally through acquisition, joint venture and licensing agreements.*

✦ *Dedicate ourselves to being recognized as the best in research and development across our businesses . . .*

✦ *Achieve continuous improvement in our cost structure . . .*

✦ *Attract, develop, motivate, and retain people of the highest caliber. The company's reporting, reward and recognition systems will be built around attainment of the goals identified above."*

Once a firm specifies its mission, it can develop plans to achieve that mission.

A firm's mission can change over time. When eBay was created, its mission was to create an online auction system that would allow buyers and sellers to interact to purchase and sell products. As eBay became increasingly popular, it expanded its system to include several foreign countries, and it established a more ambitious mission—to serve buyers and sellers anywhere who wish to buy or sell practically anything.

**tactical planning**
smaller-scale plans (over one or two years) that are consistent with the firm's strategic (long-term) plan

**Tactical Planning**   High-level and middle managers also engage in **tactical planning**, or smaller-scale plans (over one or two years) that are consistent with the firm's strategic (long-term) plan. Tactical planning normally focuses on a short-term period, such as the next year or so. To develop their tactical plan, managers of AT&T and other firms assess economic conditions, the general demand for various products, the level of competition among firms producing those products, and changes in technology. They use their vision to capitalize on opportunities in which they have some advantages over other firms in the industry. If a firm's strategic plan is to

Employees commonly attempt to establish tactical plans that are consistent with the strategic plan, as shown here. They also develop plans that are intended to satisfy the tactical plans.

© SHUTTERSTOCK/ZSOLT NYULASZI

increase its market share by 20 percent, its tactical plans may focus on increasing sales in specific regions that have less competition. As time passes, additional tactical planning will be conducted in accordance with the strategic plan.

**Operational Planning**   Another form of planning, called **operational planning**, establishes the methods to be used in the near future (such as the next year) to achieve the tactical plans. Continuing our example of a firm whose tactical plan is to increase sales, the operational plan may specify the means by which the firm can increase sales. That is, the operational plan may specify an increase in the amount of funds allocated to advertising and the hiring of additional salespeople.

The goals of operational planning are somewhat dependent on the firm's long-term goals. For example, a firm's top managers may establish a goal of 12 percent annual growth in sales over the next several years. The firm's salespeople may be asked to strive for a 1 percent increase in total sales per month during the upcoming year. Their month-to-month goals are structured from the long-term goals established by top management.

When firms engage in operational planning, they must abide by their **policies**, or guidelines for how tasks should be completed. For example, a policy on the hiring of employees may require that a specific process be followed. Policies enforced by firms ensure that all employees conduct specific tasks in a similar manner. The policies are intended to prevent employees from conducting tasks in a manner that is inefficient, dangerous, or illegal.

Most policies contain **procedures**, or steps necessary to implement a policy. For example, a policy for hiring may specify that an ad is to be placed in the local newspaper for so many days and that the criteria for the job must be disclosed in the ad. These procedures are intended to prevent abuses, such as a manager hiring a friend or relative who is not really qualified for the job. Without procedures, managers could make decisions that conflict with the company's goals.

**operational planning**
establishes the methods to be used in the near future (such as the next year) to achieve the tactical plans

**policies**
guidelines for how tasks should be completed

**procedures**
steps necessary to implement a policy

# Cross-Functional Teamwork

## Interaction of Functions to Achieve the Strategic Plan

The development of a strategic plan requires interaction among the firm's managers who are responsible for different business functions. The firm's strategies to achieve those goals include the creation of new products, continuous improvement in cost structure (high production efficiency), and retaining good employees.

The management function can help achieve the firm's goals by assessing the needs of consumers so that the firm can create new products. It can also attempt to assess customers' satisfaction with existing products and use marketing strategies to increase the market share of these products. The financing function can help achieve the firm's goals by determining the level of borrowing that will be sufficient to support the firm's operations.

Since the business functions are related, a strategic plan can be implemented only when the interaction among business functions is recognized. A strategic plan that focuses on increased sales will likely require more production and financing.

As another example, a firm may implement procedures for air travel to ensure that employees use airlines that have relatively low prices. These procedures are intended to prevent managers from incurring excessive travel expenses.

**contingency planning**
alternative plans developed for various possible business conditions

**Contingency Planning**   Some of a firm's plans may not be finalized until specific business conditions are known. For this reason, firms use **contingency planning**; that is, they develop alternative plans for various possible business conditions. The plan to be implemented is contingent on the business conditions that occur. For example, a firm that produces sports equipment may plan to boost its production of rollerblades in response to recent demand. At the same time, however, it may develop an alternative plan for using its resources to produce other equipment instead of rollerblades if demand declines. It may also develop a plan for increasing its production if the demand for its rollerblades is much higher than expected.

Some contingency planning is conducted to prepare for possible crises that may occur. For example, airlines may establish contingency plans in the event that various problems arise, as illustrated in Exhibit 7.3.

The September 11 crisis prompted many firms to develop a contingency plan in the event of a future crisis. Some firms established backup production plans in case their normal facilities are not functioning properly. Other firms have identified backup office space that can be used if their normal offices are destroyed or otherwise are unusable. Many firms have also attempted to back up their information files and store them at an alternative location.

**Relationships Among Planning Functions**   The relationships among the planning functions are shown in Exhibit 7.4. Notice how the tactical plan is dependent on the strategic plan and the operational plan is based on the tactical plan. The contingency plan offers alternatives to consider instead

**Exhibit 7.3**

Illustration of Contingency Planning

| Situation | Contingency Plan |
|---|---|
| Overbooked reservations | To reduce the number of customers who need that flight, offer customers who are willing to be bumped (wait for next flight) a free round-trip ticket to the destination of their choice in the future. |
| Minor airplane repair needed | Have airline mechanics available at each major airport in the event that a minor repair is needed. |
| Major airplane repair needed | If the airplane is not suitable for flying, attempt to reroute the passengers who were supposed to be on that plane by reserving seats for them on other flights. |

of the operational plan in specific situations (such as higher or lower demand for the product than anticipated).

To fully understand how these plans fit together, assume that your firm produces men's shirts and that your strategic plan specifies goals of expanding into related products. In this case, your tactical plan may focus on producing one other product along with men's shirts, such as women's shirts. The operational plan will specify the changes in the firm's operations that are necessary to produce and sell women's shirts. Specifically, the plan will determine how much more fabric must be purchased each month, how the women's shirts will be priced, and where they will be sold. A contingency plan can also be prepared in the event that excessive competition develops in the market for women's shirts. If this occurs, the contingency plan may be to expand into different products, such as men's pants.

**Exhibit 7.4**

How Planning Functions Are Related

Example

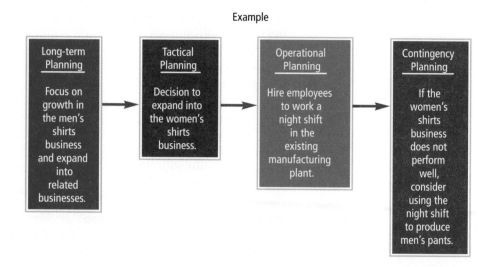

## 2.2  Organizing

**organizing**
the organization of employees and other resources in a manner that is consistent with the firm's goals

The **organizing** function involves the organization of employees and other resources in a manner that is consistent with the firm's goals. Once a firm's goals are established (from the planning function), resources are obtained and organized to achieve those goals. For example, employees of Toyota are organized among assembly lines to produce cars or trucks in a manner consistent with the company's goals.

The organizing function occurs continuously throughout the life of the firm. This function is especially important for firms that frequently restructure their operations. Organizational changes such as the creation of a new position or the promotion of an employee occur frequently. These changes may even necessitate revisions of job assignments of employees whose job positions have not changed.

To illustrate the importance of the organizing function, consider a construction company that builds homes. The general contractor assigns tasks to the employees. From the laying of the foundation to painting, most tasks must be completed in a particular order. Since all tasks cannot be completed simultaneously, the contractor has workers working on different homes. In this way, employees can apply their respective specialties (such as painting, electrical, and so on) to whatever homes are at the proper stage of construction. The organizational structure of a business is discussed in more detail in the following chapter.

## 2.3  Leading

**leading**
the process of influencing the habits of others to achieve a common goal

The **leading** function is the process of influencing the habits of others to achieve a common goal. It may include the communication of job assignments to employees and possibly the methods of completing those assignments. It may also include serving as a role model for employees. The leading should be conducted in a manner that is consistent with the firm's strategic plan.

The leading function involves not only instructions on how to complete a task but also incentives to complete it correctly and quickly. Some forms of leading may help motivate employees. One method is to delegate authority by assigning employees more responsibility. Increased responsibility can encourage employees to take more pride in their jobs and raise their self-esteem. If employees are more actively involved in the production process and allowed to express their concerns, problems can be resolved more easily. Managers who allow much employee feedback may prevent conflicts between management and employees, or even conflicts among employees. To the extent that the leading function can enhance the performance of employees, it will enhance the performance of the firm.

**initiative**
the willingness to take action

For managers to be effective leaders, they need to have **initiative,** which is the willingness to take action. Managers who have all other skills but lack initiative may not be very effective. Some managers who recognize the need to make changes are unwilling to take action because making changes takes more effort than leaving the situation as is, and change may upset some employees. For example, consider a manager who recognizes that the firm's expenses could be reduced, without any adverse effect on the firm, by eliminating a particular department. Nevertheless, this manager may refrain from suggesting any action because it might upset some employees. Managers are more likely to initiate change if they are directly rewarded for suggesting any changes that enhance the firm's value.

Managers can lead their employees by showing them how to do their assignments (as shown here) or by serving as a role model for them.

**autocratic**
a leadership style in which the leader retains full authority for decision making

© SHUTTERSTOCK/MARCIN BALCERZAK

**Autocratic Leadership Style**
Although all managers have their own leadership styles, styles can be classified generally as autocratic, free-rein, or participative, as discussed next. Managers who use an **autocratic** leadership style retain full authority for decision making; employees have little or no input. For example, if managers believe that one of their manufacturing plants will continue to incur losses, they may decide to close the plant without asking for input from the plant's workers. Autocratic managers may believe that employees cannot offer input that would contribute to a given decision. Employees are instructed to carry out tasks as ordered by autocratic leaders and are discouraged from being creative. In general, employees who desire responsibility are likely to become dissatisfied with such a management style.

**free-rein**
a leadership style in which the leader delegates much authority to employees

**Free-Rein Leadership Style**   Managers who use a **free-rein** (also called "laissez-faire") management style delegate much authority to employees. This style is the opposite extreme from the autocratic style. Free-rein managers communicate goals to employees but allow the employees to choose how to complete the objectives. For example, managers may inform workers in a manufacturing plant that the plant's performance must be improved and then allow the workers to implement an improvement strategy. Employees working under a free-rein management style are expected to manage and motivate themselves daily.

**participative**
a leadership style in which the leaders accept some employee input but usually use their authority to make decisions

**Participative Leadership Style**   In the **participative** (also called democratic) leadership style, the leaders accept some employee input but usually use their authority to make decisions. This style requires frequent communication between managers and employees. Managers who use a participative management style allow employees to express their opinions but do not pressure employees to make major decisions. For example, managers of an automobile plant may consider the ideas of assembly-line workers on how to improve the plant's performance, but the managers will make the final decisions.

**Comparison of Leadership Styles**   A comparison of leadership styles is provided in Exhibit 7.5. The optimal leadership style varies with the situation and with employees' experience and personalities. The free-rein style may be appropriate if employees are highly independent, creative, and motivated. An autocratic style may be most effective for managing employees with low skill levels or high turnover rates. Participative management is

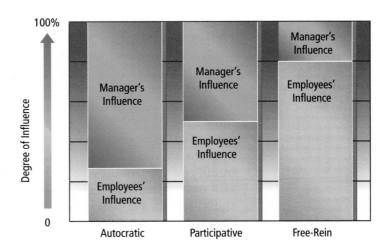

**Exhibit 7.5**

How Leadership Style
Affects Employee Influence
on Management Decisions

effective when employees can offer a different perspective because of their closer attention to daily tasks.

**Using All Leadership Styles**   Within a given firm, all three leadership styles may be used. For example, the top management of an automobile producer may use autocratic leadership to determine the types of automobiles (large versus small cars, luxury versus economy cars, and so on) to design in the future. These plans are made without much employee input because the top managers can rely on recent surveys of consumer

# Global Business

## Conflicts with the Goal of a Multinational Corporation

The costs of ensuring that managers maximize shareholder wealth (referred to as *agency costs*) are normally larger for multinational corporations than for purely domestic firms, for several reasons. First, monitoring managers of distant subsidiaries is more difficult. Second, managers of foreign subsidiaries who have been raised in different cultures may not follow uniform goals. Third, the sheer size of the larger multinational corporations can also create large agency problems.

If the U.S. managers of the parent company conduct their function of leading properly, they will communicate the goals that the subsidiary managers should follow. The U.S. managers should ensure that the subsidiary managers understand that a decision that maximizes the value of a subsidiary may be detrimental to the firm overall. Thus, in making decisions, the managers of a subsidiary should always consider the potential impact on other subsidiaries and on the parent.

When a U.S. firm has foreign subsidiaries in several different countries, its choice of a leadership style may vary with the characteristics of the foreign country. For example, it may allow a participative style in industrialized countries where managers are experienced in making business decisions aimed at maximizing the firm's value. The same firm may impose an autocratic style in a country where most business managers are not accustomed to making business decisions in this manner. Furthermore, the proper leadership style for any particular country may change over time in response to changes in the country's conditions.

preferences along with their own vision of what types of cars will be in demand in the future.

Once top management identifies the types of automobiles to produce, a participative leadership style may be used to design each type of car. That is, top management may establish general design guidelines for a particular type of car to be produced (such as specifying a small economy car) and ask employees for their suggestions on developing this type of car. These employees have experience on specific assembly-line operations and can offer useful input based on various production or quality problems they experienced with other cars. The top managers will make the final decisions after receiving the engineers' proposed designs, which are based on input from numerous employees. This example reflects a participative style because managers use their authority to decide on the particular type of product to be produced but solicit input from many employees.

After the design of a specific car is completed, managers use a free-rein style for some parts of the production process. For example, a group of employees may be assigned to a set of assembly-line tasks. They may be allowed to assign the specific tasks among themselves. They may also be allowed to rotate their specific jobs to avoid boredom. This example reflects the free-rein style because the employees are allowed to choose how to achieve the firm's objectives.

## 2.4 Controlling

**controlling**
the monitoring and evaluation of tasks

The **controlling** function involves the monitoring and evaluation of tasks. To evaluate tasks, managers should measure performance in comparison with the standards and expectations they set. That is, the controlling function assesses whether the plans set within the planning function are achieved. Standards can be applied to production volume and cost, sales volume, profits, and several other variables used to measure a firm's performance. The controlling function allows for continual evaluation so that the firm can ensure that it is following the course intended to achieve its strategic plan.

The strategic plan of Bristol-Myers Squibb (presented earlier) states that its reward systems will be based on standards set by the goals identified within that plan. An example of how the controlling function can be used to assess a firm's operations is shown in Exhibit 7.6.

**Control Used to Correct Deficiencies**    The main reason for setting standards is to detect and correct deficiencies. When deficiencies are detected, managers must take corrective action. For example, if labor and equipment repair expenses are too high, the firm will attempt to identify the reason

---

**Exhibit 7.6**

Example of the Controlling Function

|  | Actual Level Last Week | Standards (Expected Level) | Assessment |
|---|---|---|---|
| Sales volume | 300 units | 280 units | OK |
| Production volume | 350 units | 350 units | OK |
| Labor expenses | $10,000 | $9,000 | Too high |
| Administrative expenses | $14,500 | $15,000 | OK |
| Equipment repair | $3,000 | $1,000 | Too high |

# Global Business

## Leadership Styles for Global Business

When U.S. firms establish subsidiaries in foreign countries, they must determine the type of leadership style to use in those subsidiaries. The firms do not automatically apply the style they use in the United States because conditions in foreign countries may be different. In some countries that have only recently encouraged private ownership of businesses (such as Hungary, Ukraine, and China), people are not accustomed to making decisions that will maximize the value of the business. Many people have had experience only in managing government-owned businesses. In those businesses, management decisions tended to focus on satisfying government goals rather than on maximizing the value of the business. Furthermore, the businesses had little or no competition, so managers could make decisions without concern about losing market share. Now, when U.S. firms establish subsidiaries in such countries, the firms may use a more autocratic leadership style for their subsidiaries. Instructions come from the U.S. headquarters, and the managers of the foreign subsidiaries are responsible for carrying out those instructions. When the managers have problems, they contact U.S. headquarters for advice.

Although many U.S. firms have recently adopted free-rein and participative styles in the United States, they may nevertheless be reluctant to give too much power to managers of some of their foreign subsidiaries. As the managers of the subsidiaries gain experience working for the firm and in a competitive environment, they may be given more power to make decisions.

for the high costs so that it can prevent them in the future. If a firm finds that its sales volume is below standards, its managers will determine whether to revise the existing marketing strategies or penalize those employees who are responsible for the deficiency. Deficiencies that are detected early may be more easily corrected. By identifying deficiencies that must be corrected, the controlling function can help to improve a firm's performance.

**Control Used to Correct Standards**  In some cases, the standards rather than the strategies need to be corrected. For example, a particular advertising strategy to boost automobile sales may fail when interest rates are high because consumers are unwilling to borrow money to purchase automobiles at those interest rates. The failure to reach a specified sales level may be due to the high interest rates rather than a poor advertising strategy.

**Control of Management Process**  Corporate governance involves the oversight or governance of corporate management. High-level managers are indirectly controlled by the corporate governance process. Investors of publicly traded firms try to ensure that the managers make effective decisions that will maximize the firm's performance and value. Investors have some influence over management because they can complain to the board of directors or to executives if the managers are making poor decisions. The board and executives are especially concerned about satisfying institutional investors that hold large amounts of the firm's shares because if those investors sell all their holdings of the firm's shares, a pronounced decline in the stock's price could occur.

Managers organize employees and resources in order to achieve the firm's goals. When the performance of the firm is weaker than expected, managers may attempt to detect deficiencies in the existing process and communicate them to employees.

In some cases, the institutional investors form a group so that they will have greater influence on the firm's management. Institutional Shareholder Services (ISS), Inc., is a firm that organizes institutional shareholders to push for a common cause. When ISS receives feedback from institutional investors about a particular firm, it organizes a conference call with high-ranking executives of the firm and allows investors to listen in on the call. Unlike earnings conference calls, which are controlled by the firm, the conference call is run by ISS, which asks questions that focus on the institutional shareholders' concerns about the firm's management. Typical questions asked by ISS include:

✦ Why is your chief executive officer (CEO) also the chairman of the board?

✦ Why is your executive compensation much higher than the industry norm?

✦ What is your process for nominating new board members?

Transcripts of the conference call are available within 48 hours after the call.

**Control of Reporting** Another objective of the controlling process is to ensure accurate reporting. Investors of publicly traded firms attempt to have some control over a firm's management by reviewing the financial statements that the firm releases on a quarterly basis. In recent years, some publicly traded firms used reporting procedures that intentionally exaggerated the firm's revenue or profit over a particular time period. Such inaccurate reporting may mislead investors who are trying to monitor a firm's management by causing the management to look better than it actually is. Consequently, investors may overestimate the value of the firm and therefore pay too much for its stock. In addition, executives who hold the firm's stock may be able to sell it for a high price to investors who were misinformed about the firm's profits.

The Sarbanes-Oxley Act (SOX) was enacted in 2002 in an effort to prevent such reporting abuses. It requires firms to implement a system that allows their level of productivity and profitability to easily be monitored. The system must be designed to detect reporting discrepancies so that a firm's reported financial performance can easily be checked on a periodic basis. In general, the financial performance is based on the firm's revenue and expenses. Most firms use software programs that can verify their information about revenue and expenses and determine whether the financial reporting is consistent with the information provided by various departments within the firm.

## 2.5   Integration of Management Functions

To illustrate how the four different functions of management are integrated, consider a firm that makes children's toys and decides to restructure its operations. Because of low sales, the top managers create a new strategic plan to discontinue production of plastic toys and to begin producing computer games. This planning function will require the use of the other management functions, as shown in Exhibit 7.7. The organizing function is needed to reorganize the firm's production process so that it can produce computer games. The leading function is needed to provide employees with instructions on how to produce the computer games. The controlling function is needed to determine whether the production process established to produce computer games is efficient and whether the sales of computer games are as high as forecasted.

In a small business, the owner may frequently perform all the management functions. For example, an owner of a small business may revise the strategic plan (planning function), reorganize the firm's production facility (organizing function), assign new tasks to the employees (leading function), and then assess whether all these revisions lead to acceptable results (controlling function).

## 2.6   Use of Technology to Improve Management Functions

Technology facilitates the integration of management functions. The planning function may easily involve input from various managers through an online network. Once specific plans are set, they can be immediately communicated to managers at all offices or plants. Next, the managers decide how to achieve the plans that have been established. Then they perform the leading function by offering instructions to their employees. They may provide some general instructions online and other instructions on a more personal level. Finally, an online network can be used to conduct the controlling function. As employees perform their duties, their managers are informed of the amount of output produced, and they relay the information to the top managers who initially established the plans. If the operations are not working according to the plan, this will be detected within the controlling function. Under these circumstances, either the operations or the plan can be modified.

## 2.7   Software to Improve Management Functions

Although it is unlikely that software will ever substitute for managerial experience, managers are increasingly using software to supplement their own management techniques. Various computer software packages have been developed to help managers conduct their functions more effectively. This software supports a wide range of activities, including the following activities.

**Exhibit 7.7**

Integration of Management
Functions

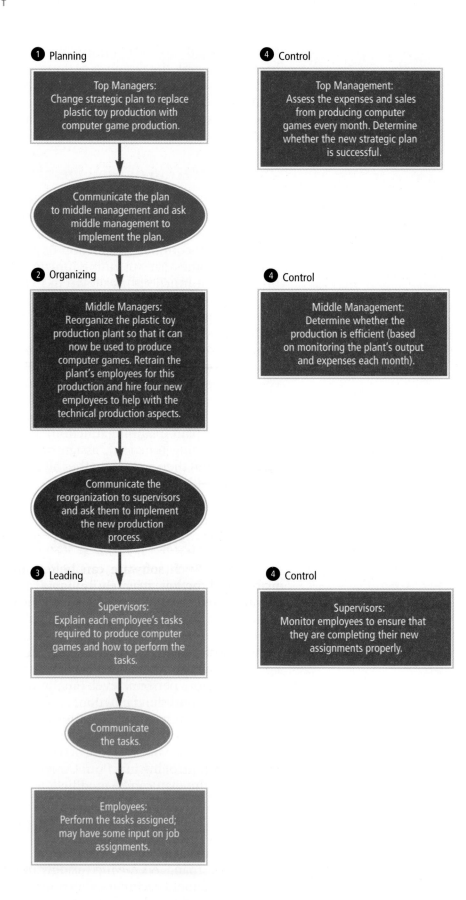

**1 Planning**

Top Managers:
Change strategic plan to replace plastic toy production with computer game production.

Communicate the plan to middle management and ask middle management to implement the plan.

**2 Organizing**

Middle Managers:
Reorganize the plastic toy production plant so that it can now be used to produce computer games. Retrain the plant's employees for this production and hire four new employees to help with the technical production aspects.

Communicate the reorganization to supervisors and ask them to implement the new production process.

**3 Leading**

Supervisors:
Explain each employee's tasks required to produce computer games and how to perform the tasks.

Communicate the tasks.

Employees:
Perform the tasks assigned; may have some input on job assignments.

**4 Control**

Top Management:
Assess the expenses and sales from producing computer games every month. Determine whether the new strategic plan is successful.

**4 Control**

Middle Management:
Determine whether the production is efficient (based on monitoring the plant's output and expenses each month).

**4 Control**

Supervisors:
Monitor employees to ensure that they are completing their new assignments properly.

# Responding to the Economy

## Applying Management Functions in Response to the Economy

When economic conditions change, a firm may change its business plans even if its mission statement remains the same. Managers use their planning, organizing, leading, and controlling functions when adapting to changing economic conditions. For example, they may use the planning function to revise planned product offerings so that they can more effectively satisfy changing consumer needs as economic conditions change. They use the organizing function to reorganize the resources needed for production in response to the new plans. They use the leadership function to revise the job assignments of employees and communicate the new assignments to employees. They use the controlling function to monitor and evaluate the new tasks that are assigned, in order to ensure that the tasks are being completed in a manner that is consistent with the revised plans. As economic conditions continue to change, so may the plans, and the management functions will continually be applied to ensure that the revised plans are achieved.

**Personnel Hiring**   Software for screening job applicants, based upon psychological principles, can be used to assess attitudes and potential fit with the company.

**Personnel Evaluation**   Software is available that helps managers in constructing and writing reviews, as well as recording employee progress toward goals. Such software can help managers get through the review process and can be extremely valuable in documenting poor performance leading to an employee termination. Such documentation can be extremely valuable if the terminated employee sues his or her former employer.

**General Management**   A wide range of software is available to assist managers in day-to-day management activities. Calendar and scheduling software can be used for appointments and for time management. Personnel software can form the basis of a personnel system, keeping track of assorted information such as vacation usage, medical benefits, pension contributions, and so forth.

**Negotiating**   A number of software packages have been developed that employ psychological models to help managers devise negotiating strategies for various situations. The software design is based on the principle that different negotiating styles should be employed when dealing with different types of individuals.

**Decision Making**   A growing number of software packages are designed to help managers make decisions more rationally. Using tested decision-making techniques, they force managers to identify and prioritize alternatives in such a way that they can be ranked in an internally consistent fashion.

**Creativity** Some software is designed to stimulate managerial creativity. Such packages employ techniques drawn from brainstorming research and may also employ question-and-answer sessions designed to inspire managers with new ideas.

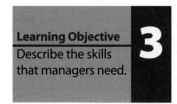

**Learning Objective 3**
Describe the skills that managers need.

# 3. Managerial Skills

To perform well, managers rely on four types of skills:

- ✦ Conceptual skills
- ✦ Interpersonal skills
- ✦ Technical skills
- ✦ Decision-making skills

## 3.1 Conceptual Skills

**conceptual skills**
the ability to understand the relationships among the various tasks of a firm

Managers with **conceptual skills** (also referred to as analytical skills) have the ability to understand the relationships among the various tasks of a firm. They see how all the pieces fit together. For example, top managers of Motorola understand how the production process is related to the marketing and finance functions. Their emphasis is not so much on the precise method of accomplishing any specific task as on having a general understanding of the firm's operations. This enables them to anticipate the potential problems that could arise if, for example, a particular production plant experiences shortages. Managers need conceptual skills to make adjustments when problems like this occur. Managers with good conceptual skills have backup strategies when problems in the production process occur. Such strategies allow the firm to continue using its resources effectively.

Conceptual skills are commonly used by the top-level and middle-level managers who are not directly involved in the production assembly process. These skills are necessary to optimally utilize employees and other resources in a manner that can achieve the firm's goals. Managers with good conceptual skills tend to be creative and are willing to consider various methods of achieving goals.

## 3.2 Interpersonal Skills

**interpersonal skills**
the skills necessary to communicate with customers and employees

Virtually all managers perform tasks that require good **interpersonal skills** (also referred to as communication skills), which are the skills necessary to communicate with customers and employees, as discussed next.

**Communication with Customers** Many managers must communicate with customers to ensure satisfaction. They listen to customer complaints and attempt to respond in an acceptable manner. They may also bring other complaints to the attention of top management. Managers lacking good interpersonal skills may ignore customer complaints. Consequently, problems go unnoticed until a large number of dissatisfied customers stop buying the firm's products. By that time, it may be too late for the firm to regain customers' trust.

One of the most important interpersonal skills is the ability to ask good questions. Without this, the real story behind customer or employee dissatisfaction may not be uncovered.

Managers rely on inter-personal skills when communicating assignments to employees and when showing employees how they can improve their performance.

© SHUTTERSTOCK/STEPHEN COBURN

**Communication with Employees**  Managers need good interpersonal skills when communicating with employees. They must be able to clearly communicate assignments to employees and must communicate with employees who have made mistakes on the job so that they can be corrected. In addition, managers must listen to complaints from employees and attempt to resolve their problems.

Middle- and top-level managers who use good interpersonal skills in communicating with lower management will be better informed about problems within the firm. Interpersonal skills are often used by top and middle managers when they must make decisions based on information provided by other managers. For example, financial managers who develop next year's budget rely on projections of sales volume and prices provided by the marketing department. They also rely on production cost projections provided by the production department. All these managers must communicate with each other because their projections are interrelated.

Some companies have initiated an e-mail newsletter from the CEO or other executives to all of their employees. The employees are allowed to use e-mail to reply to the executives. This has encouraged more communication between high-level management and other employees.

## 3.3  Technical Skills

**technical skills**
skills used to perform specific day-to-day tasks

Managers need **technical skills** to understand the types of tasks that they manage. Managers who are closer to the actual production process use their technical skills more frequently than high-level managers. For example, first-line managers of an assembly line of a computer manufacturer must be aware of how computer components are assembled. A technical understanding is important for all managers who evaluate new product ideas or are involved in solving problems.

Many firms are using technology to help managers improve their technical skills. They provide information online that can be accessed by the

Managerial decision making requires effective communication with employees in both directions, as shown here. Managers should obtain input from the employees before they implement decisions that will affect those employees. Once they make decisions, they should communicate the decisions to their employees.

managers from any location. Some firms have established networks so that managers can collaborate to improve and develop their skills. Such a network reduces training and travel budgets because their managers no longer have to travel to conferences for training.

## 3.4 Decision-Making Skills

**decision-making skills**

skills for using existing information to determine how the firm's resources should be allocated

Managers need **decision-making skills** so that they can use existing information to determine how the firm's resources should be allocated. The types of decisions made by managers vary with the position. The following are some typical decisions regarding the utilization of the firm's resources:

✦ Should more employees be hired?

✦ Should more machinery be purchased?

✦ Should a new facility be built?

✦ Should the assembly-line operation be revised?

✦ Should more supplies be ordered?

✦ Should salaries be adjusted?

These decisions affect either the revenue or the operating expenses of the firm and therefore affect its earnings. Managers who make proper decisions can improve the firm's earnings and thereby increase its value.

**Steps for Decision Making**   The decision-making process involves several specific stages. First, any possible decisions that are consistent with the firm's strategic plan are identified. Then, information relevant to each possible decision is compiled. Using this information, the costs and benefits of each possible decision are estimated. From these estimates, one or more managers can make and implement the best decision. As time passes, this decision should be evaluated to determine if any changes are necessary. The stages of the decision-making process are summarized in Exhibit 7.8.

**Exhibit 7.8**

Stages Involved in Making
a Decision

| Identify the possible decisions. | → | Gather information on all possible decisions. | → | Estimate costs and benefits of each possible decision. | → | Make a decision and implement it. | → | Periodically evaluate the previous decision to determine whether it should be changed. |

As an example, consider the task of accommodating increased demand for products at IBM. Managers first think of alternative means of achieving this goal, such as hiring more workers or allowing more overtime for existing workers. Compiling the relevant information, including the cost of adding more workers or allowing more overtime, enables the managers to estimate the costs and benefits of each alternative. Once managers have this information, they can conduct a cost-benefit analysis and select the better alternative. As time passes, the cost of each alternative may change, and the managers may reconsider their decisions.

### 3.5 Summary of Management Skills

The various management skills that have been described are summarized in Exhibit 7.9. All of these skills are necessary for managers to be successful. Managers who have good skills are more capable of ensuring a high level of productivity from the employees and facilities that they manage. They are also able to make business decisions that will improve the performance of the firm.

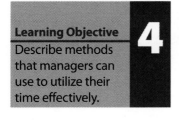

**Learning Objective**

Describe methods that managers can use to utilize their time effectively.

**4.** **How Managers Manage Time**

Managers have a limited amount of time to spend managing their responsibilities. Therefore, they use **time management**, which refers to the way managers allocate their time when managing tasks. Although there is no single perfect formula for using time efficiently, the following guidelines should be followed:

**Exhibit 7.9**

Summary of Key Managerial
Skills

| Skill | Example of How the Skill Can Be Used by a Firm |
|---|---|
| Conceptual | Used to understand how the production level must be large enough to satisfy demand and how demand is influenced by the firm's marketing decisions. |
| Interpersonal | Used to inform employees about the goals of the firm and about specific policies that they must follow; also used to hear complaints from employees or customers and to resolve any conflicts among people. |
| Technical | Used to understand how components must be assembled to produce a product; also used to understand how machines and equipment should be used. |
| Decision making | Used to determine whether the firm should expand, change its pricing policy, hire more employees, or obtain more financing; proper decision making requires an assessment of the costs and benefits of various possible decisions that could be implemented. |

**time management**

the way managers allocate their time when managing tasks

- ✦ Set proper priorities.
- ✦ Schedule long time intervals for large tasks.
- ✦ Minimize interruptions.
- ✦ Set short-term goals.
- ✦ Delegate some tasks to employees.

Each of these guidelines is discussed in turn.

## 4.1 Set Proper Priorities

One of the main reasons for time management problems is that managers lose sight of their role. Consider a regional sales manager who has two responsibilities: (1) resolving any problems with existing sales orders and (2) entertaining new clients. The sales manager may allocate much more time to entertaining because it is more enjoyable. Consequently, problems with sales orders may accumulate. Time management is a matter of priorities. Managers who set priorities according to what is best for the firm, rather than what they enjoy the most, are more successful.

## 4.2 Schedule Long Time Intervals for Large Tasks

Managers may be able to complete large tasks efficiently by scheduling large intervals (blocks) of time to focus on those tasks. Within each block, managers can focus all of their attention on the large task. In general, more work on a large project can be accomplished within one three-hour interval than in three separate one-hour intervals spread throughout a day or a week. When using short time intervals, managers waste time refreshing their memories on the issue of concern and the potential solutions. They would be more efficient if they could focus on the issue for a longer interval.

The best strategy for a task that requires less than one day of work may be to focus completely on that task until it is done. Short appointments that must be kept during a given day and are unrelated to the large task should be consolidated so that they do not continually break up the time allocated to the large task.

## 4.3 Minimize Interruptions

Virtually all managers are interrupted during the normal working day. Some problems may require immediate attention, but others can be put off until later. Managers should stay focused on the task at hand and avoid unscheduled interruptions (except for emergencies).

Some managers have a natural tendency to create their own interruptions. For example, they may stop in offices of other employees to socialize. Although socializing during work hours may help reduce stress or boredom, managers should attempt to complete a certain amount of work before taking a social break. In this way, the break is a reward for accomplishing some work, not simply a means of putting off work.

## 4.4 Set Short-Term Goals

A common problem for managers is meeting deadlines, especially on large tasks. Managers should set short-term goals so that they can chip away at large tasks. For example, consider a manager who is assigned the task of

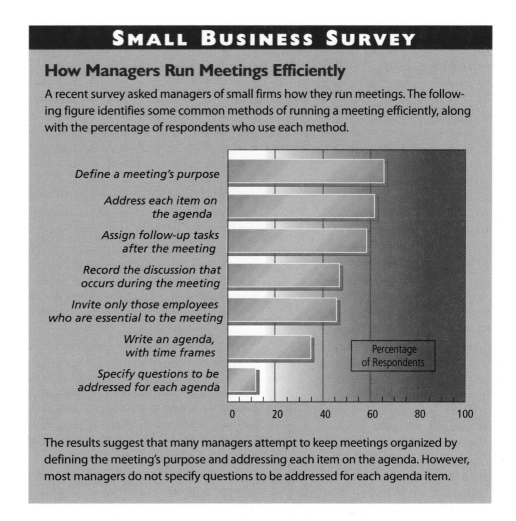

## SMALL BUSINESS SURVEY

### How Managers Run Meetings Efficiently

A recent survey asked managers of small firms how they run meetings. The following figure identifies some common methods of running a meeting efficiently, along with the percentage of respondents who use each method.

*Define a meeting's purpose*

*Address each item on the agenda*

*Assign follow-up tasks after the meeting*

*Record the discussion that occurs during the meeting*

*Invite only those employees who are essential to the meeting*

*Write an agenda, with time frames*

*Specify questions to be addressed for each agenda*

Percentage of Respondents

0   20   40   60   80   100

The results suggest that many managers attempt to keep meetings organized by defining the meeting's purpose and addressing each item on the agenda. However, most managers do not specify questions to be addressed for each agenda item.

purchasing a new computer system for the firm. The manager should break down the assignment into smaller tasks, such as (1) obtaining all the relevant information from other employees on the features that the computer system should have (Task A), (2) calling firms that sell computer systems to obtain price quotes (Task B), and (3) visiting firms where similar computer systems are in place to determine how well they work (Task C). Task C cannot be done until Task B is completed, and Task B cannot be done until Task A is completed.

If the assignment must be done in 10 weeks, the manager may set a goal of completing Task A during the first three weeks, Task B during the fourth and fifth weeks, and Task C during the sixth and seventh weeks. This schedule allows a few extra weeks before the deadline in case unexpected problems cause a task to take more time than was planned.

## 4.5  Delegate Some Tasks to Employees

Managers have only so much time to complete the tasks they are assigned. If they can delegate some authority to their employees, they will have more time to be creative. By delegating, managers may even increase the job satisfaction of employees who prefer extra responsibility. However, managers should delegate only those tasks that employees can handle.

## COLLEGE HEALTH CLUB: PLANNING AT CHC

Sue Kramer realizes that the success of College Health Club (CHC) is highly dependent on proper planning. She establishes the following plans:

✦ **Strategic Plan**  The main objective of the business is to provide quality health club services, which should attract more members over time. The success of the health club is dependent on the number of memberships. In the long run, a goal is to apply the CHC business idea elsewhere by establishing health clubs near other colleges and universities. This will involve identifying other colleges and universities that do not have a convenient health club for the students nearby. Consider establishing health clubs near those campuses that would focus on serving the students. The membership fee should be affordable to students.

✦ **Tactical Plan**  To achieve the strategic plan of establishing new health clubs near other colleges, the following tactical plan will be implemented. Conduct an informal survey of friends who are currently attending other colleges or universities nearby to determine whether they have convenient access to a health club next to the campus. The initial focus should be on colleges and universities that are within 50 miles because overseeing the establishment of a new health club will be easier if it is not far away.

✦ **Operational Plan**  For any college or university whose students are not being served by a local health club or by facilities on campus, determine the potential benefits and costs of starting a new health club. The potential benefits are dependent on the number of students who might join a new health club. Determine the number of students who live on campus, and conduct an informal survey to estimate how many might be interested in joining a new health club if one is established. The costs of establishing a new health club are dependent on the cost of rental space near that college campus. Use the local newspaper to determine the cost of rental space at shopping centers near the campus. If a new health club appears to be feasible, consider the possible sources of financing that would be needed.

# Summary of Learning Objectives

**1**  The levels of management are

✦ top (high-level) management, which concentrates on the firm's long-run objectives;

✦ middle management, which is responsible for intermediate and short-term decisions; and

✦ supervisory management, which is highly involved with employees who engage in the day-to-day production process.

**2**  The key functions of management are

✦ planning for the future (objectives);

✦ organizing resources to achieve objectives;

✦ leading employees by providing them with instructions on how they should complete their tasks; and

✦ controlling, which involves monitoring and evaluating employee tasks.

**3**  The most important managerial skills needed are

✦ conceptual skills, which are used to understand relationships among various tasks;

✦ interpersonal skills, which are used to communicate with other employees and with customers;

✦ technical skills, which are used to perform specific day-to-day tasks, such as accounting skills to develop financial statements or electrical skills to understand how the wiring of a product is arranged; and

✦ decision-making skills, which are used to assess alternative choices on the allocation of the firm's resources.

**4** Some of the key guidelines for effective time management are to

✦ set proper priorities in order to focus on the most important job responsibilities;

✦ schedule long time intervals for large tasks in order to focus on those tasks until the work is done;

✦ minimize interruptions in order to complete assignments;

✦ set short-term goals in order to chip away at long-term projects; and

✦ delegate tasks that employees can complete on their own.

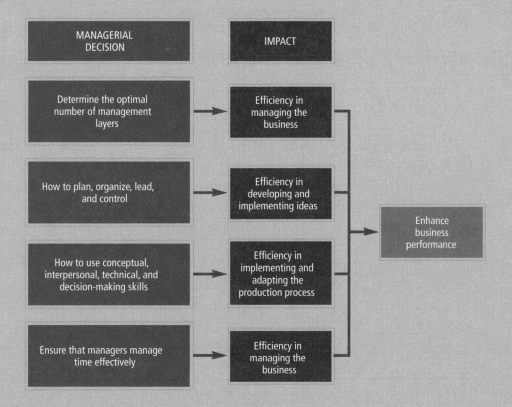

## Self-Test of Key Concepts

The following self-assessment allows you to test your understanding of the key concepts covered in this chapter. Answers are provided at the end of this exercise.

**True or False**

1. Top management is usually highly involved with employees who are engaged in the day-to-day production process.

2. Planning is the managerial function that influences the habits of others to achieve a common goal.

3. A firm's mission statement will identify the goals of the firm.

4. Contingency planning identifies the firm's main business focus over a long-term period.

5. Leading is the management function that provides employees with the instructions they need to complete a task, as well as incentives to encourage the employees to do the job correctly and quickly.

6. A U.S. firm with several foreign subsidiaries should vary its leadership style in the different countries, depending upon the characteristics of the foreign country.

7. The free-rein leadership style is more appropriate than the autocratic style if employees are highly independent, creative, and motivated.

8. The controlling function of management involves organizing employees and other resources in order to achieve the firm's goals.

9. In a small business, the owner may frequently perform all the management functions.

10. Conceptual skills are commonly required by assembly-line employees who are directly involved in the production assembly process.

## Multiple Choice

11. The position of chief financial officer is considered to be a:
    a) supervisory position.
    b) top-management position.
    c) first-line management position.
    d) bottom-line position.
    e) middle-management position.

12. Which of the following describes the primary goal of a firm?
    a) tactical plan
    b) mission statement
    c) operating plan
    d) bottom-up plan
    e) contingency plan

13. Middle- and high-level managers engage in short-term, small-scale plans that are consistent with the firm's strategic plan. These short-term, smaller-scale plans are known as:
    a) tactical plans.
    b) mission statements.
    c) leadership plans.
    d) bottom-up plans.
    e) contingency plans.

14. The type of planning that identifies the methods used to achieve a firm's tactical plans is called:
    a) operational planning.
    b) mission planning.
    c) strategic planning.
    d) contingency planning.
    e) procedure planning.

15. All of the following are typical goals that the management function can help to achieve except:
    a) high production efficiency.
    b) high production quality.
    c) limited competition.
    d) customer satisfaction.
    e) employee satisfaction.

16. The management of a firm would benefit from having _____ in order to effectively handle various possible unexpected business conditions.
    a) interpersonal plans
    b) various leadership styles
    c) strategic plans
    d) tactical management
    e) contingency plans

17. Business firms develop and enforce _____ to prevent employees from conducting tasks in an inefficient, dangerous, or illegal manner.
    a) kickbacks
    b) reciprocity
    c) policies
    d) time management
    e) prioritizing tasks

18. The steps necessary to implement a policy are known as:
    a) contingency plans.
    b) operational goals.
    c) initiative statements.
    d) production standards.
    e) procedures.

19. The leading function of management should be conducted in a manner that is consistent with the firm's:
    a) competition.
    b) strategic plan.
    c) customers.
    d) industry demands.
    e) labor union.

20. When employees have little or no input in decision making, managers use a(n):
    a) free-rein style.
    b) interpersonal communication style.
    c) autocratic leadership style.
    d) participative style.
    e) employee-centered style.

21. The style of leadership that is the opposite extreme of the autocratic style is:
    a) free-rein.
    b) authoritative.
    c) manipulative.
    d) boss-centered.
    e) commanding.

22. The type of leadership style that allows employees to express their opinions to their managers is the _____ style.
    a) autocratic
    b) command-oriented
    c) contingency
    d) authoritative
    e) participative

23. The function of management that evaluates employee performance in comparison with established standards is:
    a) planning.
    b) controlling.
    c) organizing.
    d) leading.
    e) time management.

24. The four functions of management:
    a) must be enacted in the proper sequence.
    b) must be integrated.
    c) are stand-alone, independent functions.
    d) cannot be performed by one individual.
    e) are human functions not compatible with technology.

25. The skills managers use to understand the relationships among the various tasks of the firm are:
    a) interpersonal skills.
    b) technical skills.
    c) decision-making skills.
    d) conceptual skills.
    e) problem-solving skills.

26. The skills that managers need to communicate with customers and employees are:
    a) organizing skills.
    b) control skills.
    c) motivating skills.
    d) conceptual skills.
    e) interpersonal skills.

27. Since they are closer to the production process, first-line managers use their _____ skills more frequently than do high-level managers.
    a) conceptual
    b) interpersonal
    c) decision-making
    d) management
    e) technical

28. Using existing information, managers need _____ to determine how the firm's resources should be allocated.
    a) micro-skills
    b) interpersonal skills
    c) technical skills
    d) decision-making skills
    e) autocratic management skills

29. All of the following guidelines should be followed when using time management except:
    a) setting proper priorities.
    b) centralizing responsibility.
    c) scheduling long intervals of time for large tasks.
    d) minimizing interruptions.
    e) delegating some tasks to employees.

30. A manager faced with a large task that will take more than one day to complete should:
    a) demand help from other employees.
    b) take frequent breaks to refresh his/her concentration.
    c) retain sole responsibility for the project.
    d) set short-term goals.
    e) automatically assign the project top priority.

| True/False | | Multiple Choice | | |
| --- | --- | --- | --- | --- |
| 1. False | 7. True | 11. b | 18. e | 25. d |
| 2. False | 8. False | 12. b | 19. b | 26. e |
| 3. True | 9. True | 13. a | 20. c | 27. e |
| 4. False | 10. False | 14. a | 21. a | 28. d |
| 5. True | | 15. c | 22. e | 29. b |
| 6. True | | 16. e | 23. b | 30. d |
| | | 17. c | 24. b | |

# Self-Test of Key Terms

autocratic 226
conceptual skills 234
contingency planning 223
controlling 228
decision-making skills 236
free-rein 226
initiative 225
interpersonal skills 234

leading 225
middle management 218
mission statement 220
operational planning 222
organizing 225
participative 226
planning 218
policies 222

procedures 222
strategic plan 220
supervisory (first-line)
    management 218
tactical planning 221
technical skills 235
time management 237
top (high-level) management 218

Fill in each blank with the proper key term. To assess your understanding of the key terms, answers are provided at the end of this self-test.

1. The _____ function involves the monitoring and evaluation of tasks.

2. _____ is usually highly involved with employees who engage in the day-to-day production process.

3. _____ refers to the way managers allocate their time when managing tasks.

4. Managers need _____ skills to understand the types of tasks that they manage.

5. The _____ describes the firm's primary goal.

6. The _____ identifies the firm's main business focus over a long-term period.

7. _____ establishes the methods to be used in the near future (such as the next year) to achieve the tactical plans.

8. The _____ makes decisions regarding the firm's long-term objectives.

9. _____ skills are used to obtain feedback from customers on the products or services provided by employees.

10. _____ are guidelines for how tasks should be completed.

11. _____ are steps necessary to implement a policy.

12. Managers who use the _____ leadership style retain full authority for decision making.

13. Managers who use the _____ leadership style delegate much authority to employees.

14. _____ establishes alternative plans for various possible business conditions.

15. Managers who use the _____ leadership style allow some employee input, but usually use their authority to make decisions.

16. The _____ function represents the preparation of a firm for future business conditions.

17. The _____ function is the process of influencing the habits of others to achieve a common goal.

**Answers:**
1. controlling
2. Supervisory (first-line management)
3. Time management
4. technical
5. mission statement
6. strategic plan
7. Operational planning
8. top management
9. Interpersonal
10. Policies
11. Procedures
12. autocratic
13. free-rein
14. Contingency planning
15. participative
16. planning
17. leading

# Concept Review Questions

1. **Strategic Planning and Value.** Explain why a firm's strategic plan affects its value.

2. **Levels of Management.** Explain the responsibilities of each of the three levels of management.

3. **Mission Statement.** Why does a firm create a mission statement?

4. **Strategic Planning.** What is a strategic plan, and how is it related to the firm's mission statement?

5. **Tactical Planning.** What is tactical planning, and how is it related to the firm's strategic plan? What is operational planning, and how is it related to tactical planning?

6. **Organizing.** Describe the organizing function and explain how it is used to achieve the firm's goals.

7. **Leadership Styles.** Explain the common leadership styles used by managers. Explain why the attitudes and abilities of employees may affect the most appro-

priate leadership style to be applied.

8. **Manager Skills.** Describe the different types of skills that managers need.

9. **Time Management.** Describe how time management could be used to efficiently complete a long-term project.

10. **Controlling Function.** Explain why the controlling function would be important when monitoring the development of a long-term project such as building a production plant.

# Class Communication Questions

1. **Challenge for High-Level Management.** In a large corporation, high-level managers make key decisions about the type of product to produce, the location of the production plant, the size of the business (number of employees), the size and

layout of the production plant, the marketing of the product, and financing. What do you think is the most challenging task for high-level management?

2. **Management Functions.** If you were a manager of a retail store, which management

function would be most important to your success? Why?

3. **Management Skills.** If you were a manager of a retail store, which management skill would be necessary for your success? Why?

# Small Business Case

### Using Management Skills

Tom Lancer is the owner of Zycles Company, which produces and sells motorcycles. Tom requires much interaction among the managers who manage the company. The supervisory managers interact with the assembly-line workers on a daily basis. The middle managers are heavily involved with selling the motorcycles to various dealerships. They determine what types of motorcycles the dealerships want to buy, and they also respond to

complaints from dealerships about previous orders. The middle managers interact with the supervisory managers when problems occur with the assembly-line production. The high-level managers determine the future design of the motorcycles, how to finance future operations, and how to advertise the company's products. They consider information provided by the middle managers before making key decisions.

1. **Impact of Feedback from Managers on Decisions.** Why

should high-level managers consider feedback from middle managers?

2. **Impact of Interpersonal Skills.** If Zycles Company wants to create a better design for its motorcycles to improve customer satisfaction, why is it important that its managers have good interpersonal skills?

3. **Impact of Conceptual Skills.** The high-level managers of Zycles Company are aware that many of its customers are under

30 years of age. They want to consider how to change their image so they can also appeal to customers who are older than 30. Why are conceptual skills needed to achieve this goal?

4. **Time Management.** Zycles Company's managers will soon provide the engineers with input and ask them to redesign some motorcycles for next year. They request that the engineers focus only on this task for a two-week period rather than allocating an hour a day over a period of three months. What is the benefit of concentrating the effort?

# Web Insight

### Managing at LA Fitness

At the opening of the chapter, LA Fitness was introduced. Go to the website (www.lafitness.com) and review the information about the company. Based on the club's operations, what key functions are required of LA Fitness managers? What skills do its managers need?

The managers of LA Fitness need interpersonal skills to ensure that its employees are motivated to satisfy customers. The managers may also need to listen to customer input regarding preferences (specific workout facilities) that LA Fitness can provide.

# Dell's Secret for Success

Go to Dell's website (www.dell.com) and click on the link "About Dell," near the bottom of the web page. You can also review a recent annual report of Dell for more information.

1. **Mission.** What is Dell's mission or objectives?

2. **Strategic Planning.** What strategic plans does Dell use to achieve its mission?

3. **Benefits of Planning.** Explain why the planning process and the organizing function of managers are critical for a growing company like Dell.

# Video Exercise

### Lessons in Leadership

Many free business videos are available on websites such as YouTube (www.youtube.com), and more are added every day. Search for a recent video clip about an existing business that offers lessons on "leadership" in YouTube or any other website that provides video clips.

1. **Main Lesson.** What is the name of the business in the video clip?

Is the video clip focused on how to develop leadership skills, how to convert employees into leaders, or some other aspect of entrepreneurship? What is the main lesson of the video clip that you watched?

2. **Leadership.** In what ways can a leader improve a firm's performance? If examples are provided in the video you watched, mention them here.

3. **Leader's Environment.** Some videos suggest that a leader needs the right type of business workplace environment in order to lead properly. Offer an example of a situation in which a manager with good leadership skills is ineffective because of conditions in the workplace.

# Projects

To encourage further comprehension of concepts covered in Chapter 7, the following five projects are available:

1. Analyzing Your Favorite Business

2. Building a Business Plan for Campus.com

3. Running Your Own Business

4. Planning Your Career

5. Stock Market Contest

All of these projects are provided in Appendix A at the end of the text. In addition, projects are available by part division at the end of each part.

A Word file for each project is also available at the textbook website (www.emcp.net/business5e) so that you may maintain one ongoing file for each project.

# Organizational Structure

© SHUTTERSTOCK/DASILVA

## Chapter 8 Learning Objectives

**1** Explain the purpose of an organizational structure and how organizational structure varies among firms.

**2** Explain how accountability can be achieved in an organizational structure.

**3** Describe how centralized and decentralized organizational structures differ.

**4** Discuss methods firms can use to obtain employee input.

**5** Identify methods that can be used to departmentalize tasks.

## Organizational Structure at Schwinn

Each firm should have a strategic plan that identifies the future direction of its business. The responsibilities of its managers should be organized to achieve the strategic plan. Each firm establishes an organizational structure that identifies responsibilities for each job position and the relationships among those positions. The organizational structure also indicates how all the job responsibilities fit together.

Consider the case of Schwinn, which has been in the business of creating bicycles for more than 100 years. While it was successful for many decades, it struggled to compete with foreign firms that entered the U.S. market. It went bankrupt in 2001 and has changed ownership since then. Schwinn had to rethink its operational structure. It expanded its business of fitness equipment and motor scooters. When Schwinn's top managers consider the ideal organizational structure, they must address the following questions:

◆ What type of organizational structure would ensure that each job position is fully accountable?

◆ Should Schwinn use a centralized or a decentralized management structure in order to ensure that its operations run efficiently?

◆ How can Schwinn ensure that its managers receive much input from their employees?

◆ Should Schwinn departmentalize tasks by product (have separate departments for bicycles, fitness equipment, and motor scooters)?

The organizational structure decision determines how many different layers of management the firm will have. Schwinn can reduce expenses by having fewer layers of management, but it also wants to ensure that it has enough employees to cover all necessary tasks. The way it decides to departmentalize will affect the number of employees needed to complete all tasks and therefore will also affect its expenses. Since these decisions affect the level of Schwinn's expenses, they also affect the level of its earnings and therefore influence its value.

All businesses must make the types of decisions described above. This chapter explains how Schwinn or any other firm can establish an organizational structure and departmentalize in a manner that maximizes the firm's value.

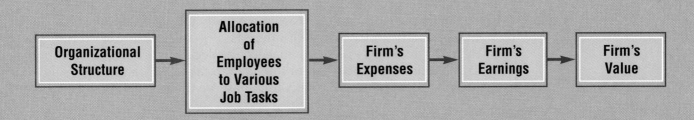

**Learning Objective**

**1**

Explain the purpose of an organizational structure and how organizational structure varies among firms.

# 1. Purpose and Types of Organizational Characteristics

An **organizational structure** identifies responsibilities for each job position and the relationships among those positions. In general, a firm wants to establish an organizational structure that ensures that all employees are in positions where they can be properly guided and monitored by someone above them to ensure that they do their jobs efficiently. If some job positions are not under the supervision of any other position, those positions may not contribute much to production because the employees will lack the guidance that they need. Alternatively, if job positions report to two or more higher-level positions, they may not contribute much to production because the employees may receive conflicting guidance from multiple bosses. Thus, a proper organizational structure can allow the firm to utilize its employees efficiently, which will enable it to produce its product or service at a relatively low cost.

**organizational structure**

identifies responsibilities for each job position and the relationships among those positions

## 1.1 Chain of Command

A firm's organizational structure can be illustrated with an organization chart, which shows the interaction among job positions. This chart indicates the **chain of command**, which identifies the job positions to which all types of employees must report. The chain of command also indicates who is responsible for various activities. Since employees often encounter problems that require communication with other divisions, it helps to know who is responsible for each type of task.

**chain of command**

identifies the job position to which each type of employee must report

The president (who also typically holds the position of chief executive officer, or CEO) has the ultimate responsibility for the firm's success. The president normally attempts to coordinate all divisions and provide direction for the firm's business. In most firms, many managerial duties are delegated to other managers. Vice-presidents normally oversee specific divisions or broad functions of the firm and report to the president.

The chain of command can be used to ensure that managers make decisions that maximize the firm's value rather than serve their own interests. For example, some managers may be tempted to hire friends for specific job positions. To the extent that their actions are monitored within the chain of command, they are more likely to make decisions that serve the firm rather than their self-interests. If managers at each level report their key decisions to other managers, the decisions are subject to scrutiny. This monitoring process is not intended to take away a manager's power, but to ensure that the power is used to serve the goals of the firm.

## 1.2 How Organizational Structure Varies Among Firms

Different firms use different organizational structures. The specific organizational structure used by a firm may be influenced by the specific characteristics of its business and can affect the firm's performance. Organizational structure can vary among firms according to:

✦ Span of control

✦ Organizational height

✦ Use of line versus staff positions

**span of control**
the number of employees
managed by each manager

**Span of Control**   Top management determines the firm's **span of control**, or the number of employees managed by each manager. When an organizational structure is designed so that each manager supervises just a few employees, it has a narrow span of control. Conversely, when it is designed so that each manager supervises numerous employees, it has a wide span of control. When numerous employees perform similar tasks, a firm uses a wide span of control because these employees can be easily managed by one or a few managers. A firm with highly diverse tasks may need more managers with various skills to manage the different tasks, resulting in a narrow span of control.

Exhibit 8.1 illustrates how the span of control can vary among firms. The organizational structure at the top of the exhibit reflects a narrow span of control. Each employee oversees only one other employee. The nature of the business may require highly specialized skills in each position so that employees may focus on their own tasks and not have to monitor a large set of employees. The organizational structure at the bottom of the exhibit reflects a wide span of control. The president directly oversees all the other employees. Such a wide span of control is more typical of firms in which many employees have similar positions that can easily be monitored by a single person.

**Organizational Height**   The organizational structure can also be described by its height. A tall organizational structure implies that there are many layers from the bottom of the structure to the top. Conversely, a short (or flat) organizational structure implies that there is not much distance from the bottom of the structure to the top because there are not many layers of employees between the bottom and top. Many firms that are able to use a wide span of control tend to have a flat organizational structure because they do

**Exhibit 8.1**

Distinguishing Between a
Narrow and a Wide Span
of Control

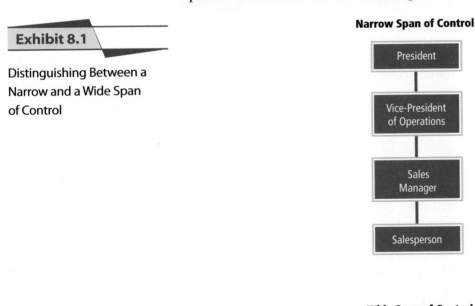

**Narrow Span of Control**

President

Vice-President
of Operations

Sales
Manager

Salesperson

*Suitable when the employees are performing similar jobs* →

**Wide Span of Control**

President

Sales-person 1 | Sales-person 2 | Sales-person 3 | Sales-person 4 | Sales-person 5 | Sales-person 6

not require many layers. Conversely, firms that need to use a narrow span of control tend to have a tall organizational structure with many layers. Notice that in Exhibit 8.1, the organizational structure with the narrow span of control is tall, while the organizational structure with the wide span of control is flat.

**line positions**

job positions established to make decisions that achieve specific business goals

**staff positions**

job positions established to support the efforts of line positions

**Line Versus Staff Positions**   The job positions in an organizational structure can be classified as line positions or staff positions. **Line positions** are established to make decisions that achieve specific business goals. **Staff positions** are established to support the efforts of line positions, rather than to achieve specific goals of the firm. For example, managers at Black & Decker who are involved in the production of power tools are in line positions. Employees in staff positions at Black & Decker offer support to the managers who are in line positions. Thus, the staff positions provide assistance to the line positions, and the authority to make decisions is assigned to the line positions.

**line organization**

an organizational structure that contains only line positions and no staff positions

**Line Organization**   An organizational structure that contains only line positions and no staff positions is referred to as a **line organization**. This type of organizational structure may be appropriate for a business that cannot afford to hire staff for support, such as a small manufacturing firm.

**line-and-staff organization**

an organizational structure that includes both line and staff positions and assigns authority from higher-level management to employees

**Line-and-Staff Organization**   Most firms need some staff positions to provide support to the line positions. An organizational structure that includes both line and staff positions and assigns authority from higher-level management to employees is referred to as a **line-and-staff organization**.

Exhibit 8.2 depicts a line organization and a line-and-staff organization. The line-and-staff organization in this exhibit includes a director of computer systems, who oversees the computer system, and a director of human resources, who is involved with hiring and training employees. These two positions are staff positions because they can assist the finance, marketing, and production departments but do not have the authority to make decisions that achieve specific business goals.

## 1.3  Impact of Information Technology on Organizational Structure

Whatever type of organizational structure a firm uses, technology facilitates communication among the job positions throughout the organizational structure. All parts of a firm use technology, and a wide variety of departments include technology experts among their employees. Information technology systems and technology professionals must support and connect every area of the organization. For example, videoconferencing and telecommuting allow members of project teams from different departments to work together regardless of their location or their department. Thus, technology enables departments within a firm to communicate more easily.

**Learning Objective 2**
Explain how accountability can be achieved in an organizational structure.

# 2. Accountability in an Organizational Structure

While the organizational structure indicates job descriptions and the responsibilities of employees and managers, the firm also needs to ensure that its employees and managers are accountable. One of the important

## Exhibit 8.2

Comparison of a Line
Organization with a
Line-and-Staff Organization

**Line Organization**

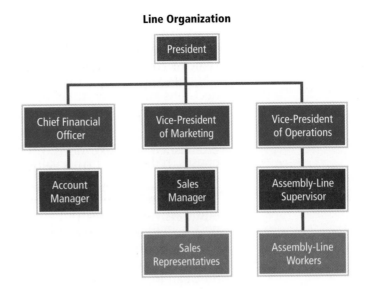

**Line-and-Staff Organization**

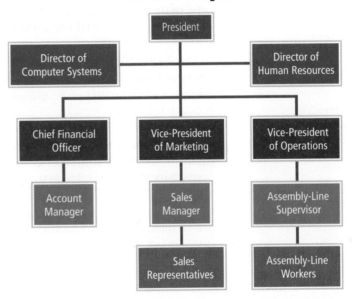

duties of the firm's managers is to evaluate the employees and make them accountable for fulfilling their responsibilities. The job descriptions provide direction for the job positions, but the managers above the positions must determine whether the employees performed according to their job descriptions.

The high-level managers of the firm, including the CEO and the vice-presidents, are accountable for the general performance of the firm. If they enforce a proper system of monitoring and accountability down through each layer of employees, they can ensure that the firm's employees are doing their jobs. These high-level managers also make many of the key decisions regarding the firm's product line, production process, compensation system, marketing, and financing. They tend to be well rewarded when the firm performs well, but they must also be held accountable if the firm has major problems. The board of directors, an internal auditor, and an internal control process can ensure that firms achieve accountability in the organizational structure.

## 2.1 Role of the Board of Directors

**board of directors**
a set of executives who are responsible for monitoring the activities of the firm's president and other high-level managers

Each firm has a **board of directors**, or a set of executives who are responsible for monitoring the activities of the firm's president and other high-level managers. Even the top managers of a firm may be tempted to make decisions that serve their own interests rather than those of the firm's owners. For example, the top managers may decide to use company funds to purchase private jets to use when they travel on business. This decision may be driven by their own self-interests. It may result in high expenses, reduce the firm's value, and therefore be detrimental to the firm's owners.

The board of directors is also responsible for supervising the business and affairs of the firm. In addition to attempting to ensure that the business is managed with the intent of serving its shareholders, the directors are also responsible for monitoring operations and ensuring that the firm complies with the law. They cannot oversee every workplace decision, but they can force the firm to have a process that guides some decisions about moral and ethical conduct. The directors can also ensure that the firm has a system for internal control and reporting. The directors are selected by the shareholders and serve as their representatives, as confirmed by a quotation from Sears' annual report:

*"The board of directors regularly reviews the corporation's structure to determine whether it supports optimal performance and thus serves the best interests of shareholders by delivering shareholder value."*

In general, the board focuses on major issues and normally is not involved in the day-to-day activities of the firm. Key business proposals, made by a firm's managers, such as acquisitions or layoffs, must be approved by the board. Directors may also initiate changes in a firm. For example, the board may decide that the firm's CEO needs to be replaced or that the firm's businesses should be restructured. Board meetings generally are scheduled every few months or are called when the directors' input is needed on an important issue. Board members of numerous firms have become more active in recent years.

The board of directors of a firm meets periodically to assess how the firm is performing and to offer guidance on key business issues, such as proposed changes in the strategic plan.

© SHUTTERSTOCK/YURI ARCURS

## SMALL BUSINESS SURVEY

### Who Are the Board Members of Small Firms?

A recent survey asked the CEOs of small firms (with less than $50 million in annual sales) about the background of their outside board members. The results of the survey follow.

| Background | Percentage of Firms Whose Board Members Have That Background |
|---|---|
| Executives of other firms | 69% |
| Major investors in the firm | 36% |
| Retired business executives | 30% |
| Attorneys | 29% |
| Accountants | 22% |
| Bankers | 18% |
| Business consultants | 13% |
| Customers | 2% |
| Others | 3% |

The results suggest that these firms rely heavily on executives and major investors to serve as their outside board members. The attorneys, accountants, and business consultants who are hired as outside board members typically also perform other duties (such as legal or banking duties) for the firm.

**inside board members**
board members who are also managers of the same firm

**outside board members**
board members who are not managers of the firm

**Inside Versus Outside Board Members**   The 1,000 largest U.S. firms have 12 directors on their boards on average. Board members who are also managers of the same firm (such as the CEO) are referred to as **inside board members**. Board members who are not managers of the firm are referred to as **outside board members**. Some firms, including General Electric and PepsiCo, provide directors with stock as partial compensation. This type of compensation may motivate the directors to serve the interests of the firm's shareholders because the board members will benefit if the firm's stock price rises.

**Conflicts of Interest Within the Board**   A board of directors is expected to ensure that top managers serve the interests of the firm rather than their own self-interests, but some directors also face conflicts of interest. As mentioned above, the board normally includes some insiders (employees) of the firm such as the CEO and some vice-presidents. These insiders will not be effective monitors of their own actions. For example, the insiders are not going to complain if the firm's managerial compensation is excessive, because they benefit directly as managers of the firm. In addition, some insider board members are not going to question the decisions of the CEO, because the CEO determines their compensation.

A board of directors may be more willing to take action if most of its members are outside directors (and therefore are not employees of the firm). The outside board members may suggest policies that will benefit shareholders, even if the policies are not supported by the firm's top managers. Therefore, shareholders tend to prefer that the board contain more outside directors.

Nevertheless, even outside directors may be subject to a conflict of interests that may inhibit their ability or willingness to make tough decisions for the firm. To illustrate these conflicts, consider the information about the board of directors of Gonzaga Company, shown in Exhibit 8.3. Notice from the exhibit that five of the eight board members are not employees of Gonzaga Company and therefore are outside directors. Yet, those five outside directors have conflicts of interest that may prevent them from making tough decisions about the top management. One of the outside directors is related to the CEO, while the other four outside directors receive money from Gonzaga Company in some form. Therefore, these outside directors will not be effective at representing the interests of Gonzaga's shareholders.

Recall the case of Enron, which distorted its financial statements to make its financial condition look better than it was. A committee from Enron's board was responsible for ensuring that the financial statements were properly checked. Of the six members on that committee, one received $72,000 per year from a consulting contract with Enron. Two other members were employed by universities that received large donations from

**Exhibit 8.3** Example of How Some Board Members Are Subject to a Conflict of Interest

| Name of Board Member | Job Position | Classified as Inside or Outside Director | Potential Conflict of Interest |
|---|---|---|---|
| Ed Martin | CEO of Gonzaga Co. | Inside | Since the CEO is a key decision maker of Gonzaga Co., he has a potential conflict of interest. A CEO is not an effective monitor of the decisions made by top management. |
| Lisa Kelly | Vice-President of Finance for Gonzaga Co. | Inside | Since the VP is a key decision maker of Gonzaga Co., she has a potential conflict of interest. A VP is not an effective monitor of the decisions made by top management. |
| Jerry Coldwell | Vice-President of Operations for Gonzaga Co. | Inside | Since the VP is a key decision maker of Gonzaga Co., he has a potential conflict of interest. A VP is not an effective monitor of the decisions made by top management. |
| Dave Jensen | Owner of a firm that is the key supplier of parts to Gonzaga Co. | Outside | Dave's company benefits directly from decisions of Gonzaga's top management to buy supplies from his firm. Thus, he is not likely to keep Gonzaga's top managers in line. |
| Sharon Martin (daughter-in-law of Ed Martin) | Vice-president of a real estate firm that does no business with Gonzaga Co. | Outside | Since Sharon is related to the CEO of Gonzaga, she is not likely to keep Gonzaga's top managers in line. |
| Karen Chandler | Independent consultant, who does a substantial amount of work for Gonzaga Co. | Outside | Karen relies on Gonzaga Co. for a large portion of her income, and therefore she is not likely to keep Gonzaga's top managers in line. |
| Terry Olden | Previous CEO of Gonzaga Co., now retired. | Outside | Terry no longer works at Gonzaga Co., but he is close to the top managers. Therefore, he is not likely to keep Gonzaga's top managers in line. |
| Mary Burke | CEO of a nonprofit health firm that receives large annual donations from Gonzaga Co. | Outside | Since Mary's firm receives donations from Gonzaga Co., she is not likely to keep Gonzaga's top managers in line. |

One or more outside board members of a publicly traded firm commonly meet with employees who are not on the board in order to listen to their broad views about the firm's operations and suggestions for improvement, as shown here. This allows the board members to develop more insight based on opinions of employees who are more closely tied to the firm's operations.

© SHUTTERSTOCK/MONKEY BUSINESS IMAGES

Enron. Thus, three of the committee members were subject to a conflict of interest and should not have been on this committee. Such conflicts of interest explain why many of the actions of Enron's top managers were not questioned.

**Resolving Conflicts of Interest**   The recent publicity about conflicts of interest within boards of directors has caused many firms to restructure their boards to ensure that the board is composed in a manner that effectively serves the shareholders. For example, eBay's corporate governance guidelines include the following:

> *"The Board should be composed of directors who are chosen based on integrity, judgment, and experience. The directors should have high-level managerial experience to deal with complex problems. They should represent the best interests of the stockholders."*

EBay usually attempts to have one or more former managers on its board. At the end of each board meeting, the outside board members have the option to meet separately without the inside directors. This gives the outside directors a chance to voice any concerns that the inside directors are making decisions to benefit themselves rather than the shareholders.

Similarly, Disney states in a recent annual report:

> *"We have established governance as a high priority at Disney for one simple reason—it's the right thing to do. By investing in Disney, shareholders are placing their trust in the board to help shape the overall course of the company's business and to hold management accountable for its performance."*

Intel Corporation has clearly defined the role of its board of directors:

*"The board is the company's governing body; responsible for hiring, oversee-ing and evaluating management, particularly the chief executive officer (CEO); and management runs the company's day-to-day operations. The end result is intended to be a well-run, efficient company that identifies and deals with its problems in a timely manner, creates value for its stockholders, and meets its legal and ethical responsibilities."*

*"We take our corporate governance seriously, expecting to achieve the same continuous improvement as in all of our business operations. Eight of our 11 directors are independent from the company except for their service to the board. They are not employees and do not have other business or consulting engagements with the company . . . . We expect that our directors will be en-gaged with us both inside and outside of board and committee meetings. Our directors meet with senior management on an individual basis, and attend and participate in employee forums. Unaccompanied by senior man-agement, individual directors visit Intel sites around the world—an excellent opportunity for them to assess local site issues directly. These activities help to keep the board better informed, and make the board's oversight and in-put more valuable . . . . Separating the roles of chairman (of the board) and CEO is an important step toward better corporate governance . . . . My job as chairman is to ensure it is organized to fulfill its responsibilities. I preside at the board meetings, make sure that the board receives the right informa-tion, set board meeting agendas, and ensure that the directors have suffi-cient time for discussion."*

— Intel Corporation

**Board Committees**   In recent years, committees made up of members of the board of directors have been given specific assignments to ensure proper oversight of the firm. Though every publicly traded firm has its own set of committees, the following committees are commonly formed:

+ **Compensation Committee**. Reviews existing salaries and com-pensation formulas for high-level managers, including the CEO.

+ **Nominating Committee**. Assesses whether the existing board members have the knowledge and skills necessary to be effective; makes recommendations to the board of directors about the size and composition of the board.

+ **Audit Committee**. Oversees the hiring and work of an external auditor that audits the firm's financial statements.

All three types of committees commonly consist of only independent board members to ensure that there will be no conflicts of interest. For example, J.C. Penney's policy is that its compensation committee will include only outside directors who are not employees or managers of the firm. Consequently, the committee can set the firm's compensation policy without being subjected to conflicts of interest.

## 2.2  Oversight of the Internal Auditor

**internal auditor**
responsible for ensuring that all departments follow the firm's guidelines and procedures

As another way to achieve accountability, many firms employ an **internal auditor**, who is responsible for ensuring that all departments follow the firm's guidelines and procedures. For example, an internal auditor may assess whether employees followed the firm's hiring procedures when filling job positions recently. The internal auditor is not attempting to interfere with managerial decisions, but is simply attempting to ensure that the procedures used to make those decisions are consistent with the firm's guidelines. Although the specific emphasis of an internal auditor varies among firms, some attention is commonly given to ensuring that employees' actions are consistent with the recommended procedures for hiring new employees, evaluating employees, maintaining safety, and responding to customer complaints.

## 2.3 Internal Control Process

As a result of the Sarbanes-Oxley Act, publicly traded firms were required to establish processes for internal control that enable them to more accurately monitor their financial performance over time. An internal control process complements the work of the internal and external auditors. It is a system that generates timely and accurate reporting of financial information and establishes controls over that information. Thus, it allows a firm's managers to more easily monitor the firm's financial condition. It also allows the firm to provide more accurate and timely disclosure of information to the public. Shareholders benefit from the firm's internal control process, because they want to be informed about the firm's recent performance and financial condition. The Sarbanes-Oxley Act caused firms to improve their internal control process by doing the following:

✦ Establishing a centralized database of information.

✦ Ensuring that all data reported by each division are reviewed for accuracy.

✦ Implementing a system that detects possible errors in the data.

✦ Acknowledging the risk associated with specific business operations.

✦ Ensuring that all departments are using consistent data.

✦ Speeding the process by which data are transferred among departments.

✦ Having their executives sign off (that is, take personal responsibility for) on specific financial statements to verify their accuracy.

The specific internal control process implemented varies among firms, but all of the systems use computer software that facilitates the reporting of financial information. All of them also require the work of employees to input data and evaluate the financial information.

One criticism of the Sarbanes-Oxley Act is that establishing an internal control process was a major expense for many firms. Some firms incurred a cost of $1 million or more to implement their system. Nevertheless, the internal control process may provide additional benefits because it not only allows for a better flow of information to the public, but also ensures that managers have up-to-date and reliable information when making decisions. Since many decisions are dependent on information, the improvement in the internal flow of information may allow managers to make better decisions.

# 3. Distributing Authority Among the Job Positions

A firm must determine how to distribute authority to make decisions among the job positions. Two firms may have the same organization chart, but the middle managers at one firm may be given much more authority than those at the other firm. The distribution of authority is often described by whether the firm is centralized or decentralized.

## 3.1  Centralization

**centralized**
most authority is held by the high-level managers

Some firms are **centralized**; that is, most authority is held by the high-level managers. In centralized firms, middle and supervisory managers are responsible for day-to-day tasks and for reporting to the top managers, but they are not allowed to make many decisions.

## 3.2  Decentralization

**decentralized**
authority is spread among several divisions or managers

**autonomy**
divisions can make their own decisions and act independently

In recent years, many firms have **decentralized**, meaning that authority is spread among several divisions or managers. An extreme form of decentralization is **autonomy**, in which divisions are permitted to make their own decisions and act independently. The trend toward decentralization is due to its potential advantages.

**Advantages**   A decentralized organizational structure can improve a firm's performance in several ways. First, decentralization reduces operating expenses because salaries of some employees who are no longer needed are eliminated.

Second, decentralization can shorten the decision-making process because lower-level employees are assigned more power. Decisions are made more quickly if the decision makers do not have to wait for approval from top managers. Many firms, including IBM, have decentralized to accelerate their decision making.

Third, delegation of authority can improve the morale of employees, who may be more enthusiastic about their work if they have more responsibilities. In addition, these managers become more experienced in decision making. Therefore, they will be better qualified for high-level management positions in the future. Decentralization has contributed to innovation at many technology firms, where many managers have become more creative. In addition, decentralization allows those employees who are closely involved in the production of a particular product to offer their input.

Johnson & Johnson is a prime example of a firm that has benefited from decentralization. It has numerous operating divisions scattered among more than 50 countries, and most of the decision making is done by the managers at those divisions. As a result, each unit can make quick decisions in response to local market conditions.

**Disadvantages**   A decentralized organizational structure can also have disadvantages. It could force some managers to make major decisions even though they lack the experience to make such decisions or prefer not to do so. Also, if middle and supervisory managers are assigned an excessive amount of responsibilities, they may be unable to complete all of their tasks.

**Proper Degree of Decentralization**    The proper degree of decentralization for any firm is dependent on the skills of the managers who could be assigned more responsibilities. Decentralization can be beneficial when the managers who are given more power are capable of handling their additional responsibilities. For example, assume that a firm's top managers have previously determined annual raises for all assembly-line workers but now decide to delegate this responsibility to the supervisors who monitor those workers. The supervisors are closer to the assembly line and are possibly in a better position to assess worker performance. Therefore, decentralization may be appropriate. The top managers may still have final approval of the raises that the supervisors propose for their workers.

As a second example, assume that top managers allow assembly-line supervisors to decide what price the firm will bid for a specific business that is for sale. Assembly-line supervisors normally are not trained for this type

# Self-Scoring Exercises

## How Decentralized Is Your Company?

Decentralization is one of the key design dimensions in an organization. It is closely related to several behavioral dimensions of an organization, such as leadership style, degree of participative decision making, teamwork, and the nature of power and politics within the organization.

The following questionnaire allows you to get an idea of how decentralized your organization is. (If you do not have a job, have a friend who works complete the questionnaire to see how decentralized his or her organization is.) Which level in your organization has the authority to make each of the following decisions? Answer the questionnaire by circling one of the following:

0 = The board of directors makes the decision.

1 = The CEO makes the decision.

2 = The division/functional manager makes the decision.

3 = A sub-department head makes the decision.

4 = The first-level supervisor makes the decision.

5 = Operators on the shop floor make the decision.

| Decision Concerning: | | Circle Appropriate Level | | | | | |
|---|---|---|---|---|---|---|---|
| a. | The number of workers required | 0 | 1 | 2 | 3 | 4 | 5 |
| b. | Whether to employ a worker | 0 | 1 | 2 | 3 | 4 | 5 |
| c. | Internal labor disputes | 0 | 1 | 2 | 3 | 4 | 5 |
| d. | Overtime worked at shop level | 0 | 1 | 2 | 3 | 4 | 5 |
| e. | Delivery dates and order priority | 0 | 1 | 2 | 3 | 4 | 5 |
| f. | Production planning | 0 | 1 | 2 | 3 | 4 | 5 |
| g. | Dismissal of a worker | 0 | 1 | 2 | 3 | 4 | 5 |
| h. | Methods of personnel selection | 0 | 1 | 2 | 3 | 4 | 5 |
| i. | Method of work to be used | 0 | 1 | 2 | 3 | 4 | 5 |
| j. | Machinery or equipment to be used | 0 | 1 | 2 | 3 | 4 | 5 |
| k. | Allocation of work among workers | 0 | 1 | 2 | 3 | 4 | 5 |

Add up all your circled numbers. Total = _____. The higher your number (for example, 45 or more), the more decentralized your organization. The lower your number (for example, 25 or less), the more centralized your organization.

# Global Business

## How Organizational Structure Affects the Control of Foreign Operations

A firm that has subsidiaries scattered around the world will find it more difficult to ensure that its managers serve the shareholders' interests rather than their own self-interests. In other words, the firm will experience more pronounced agency problems. It is difficult for the parent's top managers to monitor operations in foreign countries because of the distance from headquarters.

The magnitude of agency costs can vary with the management style of the multinational corporation. A centralized management style can reduce agency costs because it allows managers of the parent to control foreign subsidiaries and therefore reduces the power of subsidiary managers. However, the parent's managers may make poor decisions for the subsidiary because they are less familiar with its financial characteristics.

A decentralized management style is likely to result in higher agency costs because subsidiary managers may make decisions that do not focus on maximizing the value of the entire multinational corporation. Nevertheless, this style gives more control to the managers who are closer to the subsidiary's operations and environment.

Given the obvious tradeoff between centralized and decentralized management styles, some multinational corporations attempt to achieve the advantages of both styles. They allow subsidiary managers to make the key decisions about their respective operations, but the parent's management monitors the decisions to ensure that they are in the best interests of the entire firm.

The Internet makes it easier for the parent to monitor the actions and performance of foreign subsidiaries. Since the subsidiaries may be in different time zones, it is inconvenient and expensive to require frequent phone conversations. In addition, financial reports and designs of new products or plant sites cannot be easily communicated over the phone. The Internet allows the foreign subsidiaries to e-mail updated information in a standardized format to avoid language problems and to send images of financial reports and product designs. The parent can easily track inventory, sales, expenses, and earnings of each subsidiary on a weekly or monthly basis.

---

of task and should not be assigned to it. Determining the proper price to bid for a business requires a strong financial background and should not be delegated to managers without the proper skills.

As these examples demonstrate, high-level managers should retain authority for tasks that require their specialized skills but should delegate authority when the tasks can be handled by other managers. Routine decisions should be made by the employees who are closely involved with the tasks of concern. Decision making may improve because these employees are closer to the routine tasks and may have greater insight than top managers on these matters.

Some degree of centralization is necessary when determining how funds should be allocated to support various divisions of a firm. If managers of each division are given the authority to make this decision, they may request additional funds even though their division does not need to expand.

Centralized management of funds can prevent division managers from making decisions that conflict with the goal of maximizing the firm's value.

**Effect of Downsizing on Decentralization**    As firms expanded during the 1980s, additional management layers were created, resulting in taller organization charts. In the 1990s and 2000s, however, many firms have attempted to cut expenses by eliminating job positions. This so-called **downsizing** has resulted in flatter organization charts with fewer layers of managers. Continental Airlines, IBM, General Motors, Sears, and many other firms have downsized in recent years.

As some management positions are eliminated, many of those responsibilities are delegated to employees who previously reported to the managers whose positions have been eliminated. For example, consider a company that eliminates a middle layer of its organizational structure. When managers in the middle of the organization chart are removed, other employees must be assigned more power to make decisions. Thus, downsizing results in a greater degree of decentralization.

Downsizing has also affected each manager's span of control. When many middle managers are eliminated, the remaining managers have more diverse responsibilities. Consequently, the organizational structure of many firms now reflects a wider span of control, as illustrated in Exhibit 8.4.

In addition to removing some management layers and creating a wider span of control, downsizing has also led to the combination of various job responsibilities within the organizational structure. Whereas job assignments traditionally focused on production tasks, more attention is now given to customer satisfaction. Many firms recognize that they must rely on their current customers for additional business in the future and have revised their strategic plan to focus on achieving repeat business from their customers. In many cases, customers would prefer to deal with a single employee rather than several different employees. Consequently, employees are less specialized because they must have diverse skills to accommodate the customers.

**downsizing**
an attempt by a firm to cut expenses by eliminating job positions

**Exhibit 8.4**

Effect of Downsizing on Span of Control

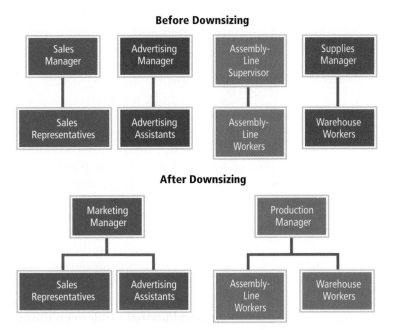

Out of Business

## 4. Structures That Allow More Employee Input

Firms commonly rely on the input of employees from various divisions for special situations. For this reason, they may need to temporarily adjust their formal organizational structure so that some extra responsibilities may be assigned. A firm may obtain employee input by using the following to complement its formal organizational structure:

✦ Matrix organization

✦ Intrapreneurship

✦ Informal organizational structure

Each of these methods is discussed in turn.

### 4.1 Matrix Organization

Firms are often confronted with special circumstances that require input from their employees. In a **matrix organization**, various parts of the firm interact to focus on specific projects. Because the projects may take up only a portion of the normal workweek, participants can continue to perform their normal tasks and are still accountable to the same boss for those tasks. For example, a firm that plans to install a new computer system may need input from each division on the specific functions that division will require from the system. This example is illustrated in Exhibit 8.5. As the exhibit shows, the finance, marketing, and production divisions each have one representative on the team; each representative can offer insight from the perspective of his or her respective division. The team of employees will periodically work on the assigned project until it is completed. Some employees may be assigned to two or more projects during the specific period. The lower horizontal line in Exhibit 8.5 shows the interaction among the representatives from different divisions. The manager of this project is a computer systems employee, who will report the recommendations of the matrix organization to the president or to some other top manager.

An advantage of the matrix approach is that it brings together employees who can offer insight from different perspectives. Each participant

As a business evolves, its organizational structure changes. Consequently, existing job assignments are commonly revised. In addition, new job positions are added, and the chain of command must be revised as well.

© SHUTTERSTOCK/HELDER ALMEIDA

who is assigned to a specific group (or team) has particular skills that can contribute to the project. By involving all participants in decision making, this teamwork may provide more employee satisfaction than typical day-to-day assignments. Firms such as Intel, IBM, and Boeing commonly use teams of employees to complete specific projects.

One possible disadvantage of a matrix organization is that no employee may feel responsible because responsibilities are assigned to teams of several employees. Therefore, a firm that uses teams to complete various tasks may designate one job position to have the responsibility of organizing the team and ensuring that the team's assignment is completed before the deadline. The person designated as project manager (or team leader) of a specific project does not necessarily have authority over the other participants for any other tasks.

Another disadvantage of the matrix organization is that any time used to participate in projects reduces the time allocated for normal tasks. In some cases, ultimate responsibility is not clear, causing confusion. Many firms eliminated their matrix structure for this reason.

**Exhibit 8.5**

A Matrix Organization for a Special Project to Design a New Computer System

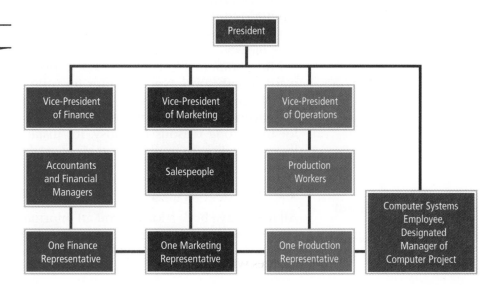

A matrix organization allows employees from various divisions of a business to offer input on a specific project, as shown here. Thus, the decisions about the project account for various perspectives.

© SHUTTERSTOCK/YURI ARCURS

*Apple and 3M encourage this.*

## 4.2 Intrapreneurship

Some firms not only seek input from employees on specific issues but also encourage employees to offer ideas for operational changes that will enhance the firm's value. These firms may even create a special subsidiary within their organizational structure in which particular employees are given the responsibility to innovate. In this way, the costs and benefits of innovation can be estimated separately from the rest of the business operations.

Particular employees of a firm can be assigned to generate ideas, as if they were entrepreneurs running their own firms. This process is referred to as **intrapreneurship**, as employees are encouraged to think like entrepreneurs within the firm. They differ from entrepreneurs, however, in that they are employees rather than owners of the firm. Some employees may even be assigned the responsibility of developing new products or ideas for improving existing products. A potential disadvantage of intrapreneurship is that it can pull employees away from normal, day-to-day production tasks. Nevertheless, it can also allow firms to be more innovative because employees are encouraged to search for new ideas. Many firms, including Apple and 3M Company, have used intrapreneurship to encourage new ideas.

Intrapreneurship is likely to be more successful if employees are rewarded with some type of bonus for innovations that are ultimately applied by the firm. The firm should also attempt to ensure that any ideas that employees develop are seriously considered. If managers shoot down ideas for the wrong reasons (jealousy, for instance), employees may consider leaving the firm to implement their ideas (by starting their own business).

**intrapreneurship**
the assignment of particular employees of a firm to generate ideas, as if they were entrepreneurs running their own firms

## 4.3 Informal Organizational Structure

All firms have both a formal and an informal organizational structure. The **informal organizational structure** is the informal communications network that exists among a firm's employees. This network (sometimes called the "grapevine") develops as a result of employee interaction over time. Some

**informal organizational structure**
an informal communications network among a firm's employees

A firm's informal organizational structure allows employees to exchange information about the firm on an informal basis.

*- often called the ~~Notice Unit~~ 'Grapevine'*

© SHUTTERSTOCK/YURI ARCURS

employees interact because they work on similar tasks. Employees at different levels may interact in a common lunch area or at social events.

**Communication** A firm may take steps to develop an informal organizational structure to encourage communication between managers and employees in a less formal environment. For example, the firm may organize social events within the firm. This does not affect the formal organizational structure, but it does create a complementary network to ensure more social interaction between employees at different levels. Consequently, the employees should have a better understanding of the managers who monitor them, and the managers should have a better understanding of their employees. In addition, the managers may receive informal feedback from their employees that they would not receive from the formal organizational structure. The feedback will be more informative than if a manager sends out a formal survey once a year asking employees for any concerns or suggestions that they may have. The employees may think that the manager was forced to send out the survey and is not really interested in their concerns. Assuming that it is just a formality and that their responses will be ignored, they will not make much of an effort to provide their opinions.

If a manager asks for feedback in an informal environment, however, the employees may be more willing to provide it because they realize that the manager is truly interested in their opinions. They may make suggestions about improving relations with employees, work conditions, salaries, or even product innovations. These types of suggestions could allow the firm to improve the level of employee job satisfaction, or improve the production process, and therefore could motivate employees to work more efficiently. Without an informal organizational structure, the firm might never receive these suggestions. Furthermore, with an informal structure information can travel quickly from the bottom to the top of the organization, so the higher-level managers will be tuned in to the morale of the employees.

Another advantage of an informal organizational structure is that employees who need help in performing a task may benefit from others. If employees had to seek help through the formal structure, they would have to go to the person to whom they report. If that particular person is not available, the production process could be slowed. An informal structure may also allow employees to substitute for one another, thereby ensuring that a task will be completed on time. In addition, an informal structure can reduce the amount of manager involvement.

An informal structure may also encourage friendships among employees, which may lead to employees being more satisfied with their jobs. On-the-job friendships could be the major factor that discourages them from looking for a new job. This is especially true of lower-level jobs that pay low wages. Because friendship can strongly influence employee satisfaction, firms commonly encourage social interaction by organizing social functions.

**Disadvantages**   Along with the advantages just described, an informal structure also has some disadvantages. Perhaps the main disadvantage is that employees may obtain incorrect or unfavorable information about the firm through the informal structure. Even if the information is untrue or is a gross exaggeration, it can have a major impact on employee morale. For example, when a boss meets with some employees on an informal basis, other employees who were left out of the meeting may become jealous or believe that they are not receiving as much attention. They may even start rumors about how the boss gives some employees more favorable treatment than others. Unfavorable information that has an adverse impact tends to travel faster and further throughout an informal structure than favorable information does.

<table>
<tr><td>

**Learning Objective** **5**

Identify methods that can be used to departmentalize tasks.

</td></tr>
</table>

**departmentalize**
assign tasks and responsibilities to different departments

# 5.  Methods of Departmentalizing Tasks

When developing or revising an organizational structure, high-level management must first identify all the different job assignments, tasks, and responsibilities. The next step is to **departmentalize** those tasks and responsibilities, which means to assign the tasks and responsibilities to different departments. The best way of departmentalizing depends on the characteristics of the business. By using an efficient method of departmentalizing tasks and responsibilities, a firm can minimize its expenses and maximize its value. The following are four of the more popular methods of departmentalizing:

✦ By function

✦ By product

✦ By location

✦ By customer

## 5.1  Departmentalize by Function

*functional structure*

When firms departmentalize by function, they allocate their tasks and responsibilities according to employee functions. The organization chart shown in Exhibit 8.6 is departmentalized by function. The finance, marketing and production divisions are separated. This system works well for firms that produce just one or a few products, especially if the managers communicate across the functions.

## 5.2  Departmentalize by Product

*Divisional structure*

In larger firms with many products, departmentalizing by product is common. Tasks and responsibilities are separated according to the type of

**Exhibit 8.6**

Departmentalizing
by Function

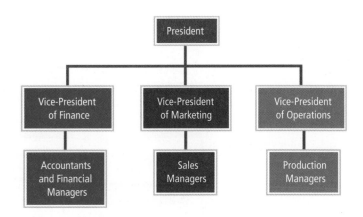

product produced. The organization chart shown in Exhibit 8.7 is departmentalized by product (soft drink, food, and restaurant). This type of organizational structure is used by General Motors, which has created divisions such as Buick, Cadillac, and Chevrolet.

Many large firms departmentalize by both product and function, as shown in Exhibit 8.8. The specific divisions are separated by product, and each product division is departmentalized by function. Thus, each product division may have its own marketing, finance, and production divisions. This system may appear to be inefficient because it requires several divisions. Yet, if the firm is large enough, a single division would need to hire as many employees as are needed for the several divisions. Separation by product allows employees to become familiar with a single product rather than having to keep track of several different products.

Departmentalizing by product enables a firm to more easily estimate the expenses involved in the production of each product. The firm can be viewed as a set of separate business divisions (separated by product), and each division's profits can be determined over time. This allows the firm to determine the contribution of each business division to its total profits, which is useful when the firm is deciding which divisions should be expanded.

For a small or medium-sized firm with just a few products, departmentalizing by product would lead to an inefficient use of employees, resulting in excessive expenses. A single financial manager should be capable of handling all financial responsibilities, and a single marketing manager should be capable of handling all marketing responsibilities. Thus, there is no reason to departmentalize by product.

**Exhibit 8.7**

Departmentalizing
by Product

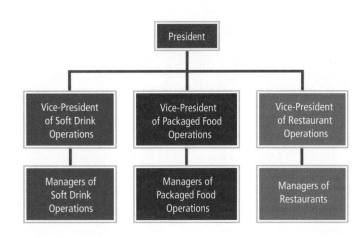

**Exhibit 8.8**

Departmentalizing
by Product and Function

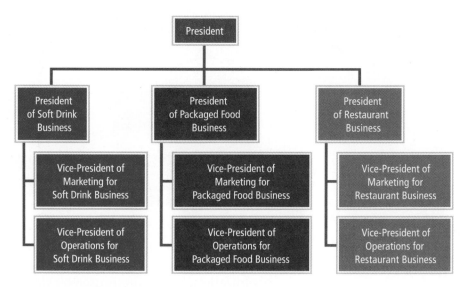

## 5.3 Departmentalize by Location

Tasks and responsibilities can also be departmentalized by location by establishing regional offices to cover specific geographic regions. This system may be appealing if corporate customers in particular locations frequently purchase a variety of the firm's products. Such customers would be able to contact the same regional office to place all of their orders. Large accounting firms departmentalize by location in order to be close to their customers.

When a firm is departmentalized by location, it can more easily estimate the expenses incurred at each location. The firm can be viewed as a

## Global Business

### Organizational Structure of a Multinational Corporation

The organizational structure of a multinational corporation is complex because responsibilities must be assigned not only to U.S. operations but also to all foreign operations. To illustrate, consider General Motors, which has facilities in Europe, Canada, Asia, Latin America, Africa, and the Middle East. It has departmentalized by location, so either a president or a vice-president is in charge of each foreign region.

Even when firms departmentalize their U.S. operations by product or by function, they commonly departmentalize their foreign operations by location. Normally, executives at the U.S. headquarters cannot easily monitor the foreign operations because they are not there on a daily or even a weekly basis. Consequently, it is more appropriate to assign an executive at the foreign facility the responsibility of overseeing a wide variety of products and functions at that facility.

In recent years, some multinational corporations have begun to select people who have international business experience for their boards of directors. Such directors are better able to monitor the firm's foreign operations. Furthermore, some multinational corporations have become more willing to promote managers within the firm who have substantial experience in international business. Sometimes a corporation will assign employees to its foreign facilities so that they can gain that experience.

# Responding to the Economy

## Revising Organizational Structure in Response to the Economy

An organizational structure is commonly revised over time in response to changing economic conditions. For example, if economic conditions weaken, a business may consider downsizing. It may allow for a greater degree of market coverage, whereby managers spend more time managing their existing operations, and less time planning for the future growth of the business. During a weak economy, managers may focus on retaining their existing business rather than increasing their business, as survival becomes a priority. When economic conditions improve, an organizational structure is commonly revised to include additional job responsibilities and a new chain of command.

A firm may also revise its departmentalization of tasks in response to changing economic conditions. For example, if transportation costs increase substantially due to high oil prices, a firm may attempt to departmentalize by location (with divisions scattered across locations) so that managers can travel less while managing their employees.

set of divisions separated by location, with each location generating its own profits. This allows the firm to identify the locations that have been performing well, which may help it determine which locations should attempt to expand their business.

## 5.4 Departmentalize by Customer

Some firms establish separate divisions based on the type of customer. For example, some airlines have a separate reservations division that focuses exclusively on group trips. Computer firms such as Dell have designated some salespeople to focus exclusively on selling computers to school systems. They also have some divisions that focus on online sales to individuals, while others focus on large corporate customers.

## COLLEGE HEALTH CLUB: DEPARTMENTALIZING TASKS AT CHC

Another decision that Sue Kramer needs to make as part of her business plan is how to departmentalize tasks at College Health Club (CHC). She first considers the main functions of CHC and who will perform these functions. She will decide on the marketing plan that will be implemented to attract new customers. The health club services will be provided by Sue and her part-time employees. Sue will make any future financing decisions for CHC. All services will be provided at one location. Sue needs to departmentalize tasks at CHC so that aerobics classes can be held in one part of the club while members can use exercise and weight machines in another area. She decides that she will establish a weekly aerobics schedule and assign a specific employee (or herself) to lead each class. When employees are not leading an aerobics class, they will be assigned to help members use the exercise and weight machines.

Although all health club services are currently provided at one location, Sue may open additional health clubs in the future. She then will departmentalize by location because any part-time employees will be assigned to only one of the health club locations.

# Cross-Functional Teamwork

## Interaction Among Departments

Although the organizational structure formally indicates to whom each employee reports, it still allows interaction among different departments. For example, a firm may departmentalize by function so that one executive is responsible for the management of operations, a second executive is responsible for the marketing function, and a third executive is responsible for the financing function.

Though each function appears independent of the others on the organization chart, executives in charge of their respective functions must interact with the other departments. The marketing department needs to be aware of any changes in the production of a product and the volume of the product that will be available before it finalizes its marketing strategies. The production department needs customer satisfaction information as it considers redesigning products. It also needs to receive forecasts of expected sales from the marketing department, which affect the decision of how much to produce. The marketing and production departments provide the finance department with their forecasts of funds needed to cover their expenses. The finance department uses this information along with other information to determine whether it needs to obtain additional financing for the firm.

# Summary of Learning Objectives

**1** The organizational structure of a firm identifies responsibilities for each job position within the firm and the relationships among those positions. The structure enables employees to recognize which job positions are responsible for the work performed by other positions.

The organizational structure can vary among firms according to the

✦ span of control, which determines the number of employees managed by each manager;

✦ organizational height, which determines the number of layers from the top to the bottom of the structure; and

✦ use of line positions (established to make decisions) versus staff positions (established to support the line positions).

**2** An organizational structure needs to ensure accountability at all levels including high-level managers. A firm's board of directors is responsible for overseeing the decisions made by the CEO and other high-level managers.

Firms also have internal control processes that ensure accountability by requiring frequent and accurate reporting of financial data; this information can be used to monitor the activities and performance of various divisions within the firm.

**3** Firms vary in the degree to which they distribute authority. Decentralized firms spread the authority among several divisions or managers. Decentralization is desirable because it can speed the

decision-making process and give employees more power and job satisfaction. However, firms must be careful to ensure that the managers who are given substantial authority are capable of handling the responsibilities that they are assigned.

**4** A firm can benefit from receiving frequent input from its employees regarding work conditions, salaries, or even product innovations. To obtain employee feedback, firms may implement the following to complement their organizational structure:

✦ matrix organization, which allows employees from different divisions of the firm to interact;

✦ intrapreneurship, which encourages employees to think like entrepreneurs by giving them some responsibility for offering suggestions about improving a specific product or part of the production process; and

✦ informal organizational structure, which encourages interaction between employees and managers at different levels so that employees have the opportunity to offer feedback to managers on an informal basis.

**5** The main methods of departmentalizing are by

✦ function, in which tasks are separated according to employee functions;

✦ product, in which tasks are separated according to the product produced;

✦ location, in which tasks are concentrated in a particular division to serve a specific area; and

✦ customer, in which tasks are separated according to the type of customer that purchases the firm's products.

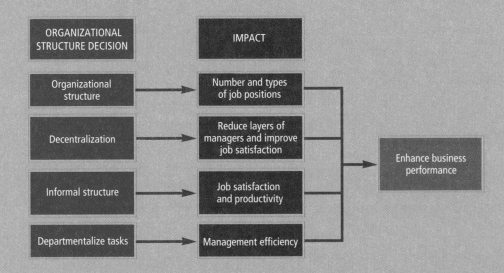

## Self-Test of Key Concepts

The following self-assessment allows you to test your understanding of the key concepts covered in this chapter. Answers are provided at the end of this exercise.

**True or False**

1. An organization chart shows the interaction among employee responsibilities.

2. An organizational structure identifies the responsibilities of each job position and the relationships among those positions.

3. A company's board of directors normally takes an active role in managing the firm's day-to-day activities.

4. Inside board members are more likely than outside members to support changes that will benefit the firm's stockholders, especially if the firm's top managers do not support the changes.

5. An organizational structure that is designed to have each manager supervise just a few employees has a narrow span of control.

6. In recent years, most firms have attempted to centralize authority in the hands of a few key executives.

7. Firms will have either a formal organizational structure or an informal organizational structure, but can never have both types of organizational structures at the same time.

8. An advantage of a firm's informal organizational structure is that it encourages the formation of friendships, which can improve morale and job satisfaction.

9. When a firm is departmentalized by location, its expenses involved in each location can be more easily estimated.

10. Most firms departmentalize their foreign operations by function.

**Multiple Choice**

11. The responsibilities of a firm's managers should be organized to achieve the:
    a) grapevine.
    b) formal contingency.
    c) strategic plan.
    d) chain of command.
    e) bureaucratic organization.

12. The president of a company:
    a) determines which members of the board of directors will be reappointed.
    b) coordinates the actions of all divisions and provides direction for the firm.
    c) directly supervises the actions of all other employees.
    d) seldom delegates managerial duties to other managers.
    e) operates independently of the board of directors.

13. The _____ for a firm identifies the job position to which each type of employee must report.
    a) chain of command
    b) job matrix
    c) staffing chart
    d) flow chart
    e) informal structure

14. The ultimate responsibility for the success of a firm lies with the:
    a) president.
    b) internal auditor.
    c) customer.
    d) competition.
    e) labor union.

15. The outside members of the board of directors of a company are those directors who:
    a) live outside the state in which the corporation received its charter.
    b) are not managers of the firm.
    c) are not stockholders in the firm.

d) serve on the board without direct compensation.
    e) were appointed by the president of the firm rather than selected by the firm's stockholders.

16. The board of directors has the responsibility of representing the interests of the firm's:
    a) top management.
    b) employees.
    c) customers.
    d) creditors.
    e) shareholders.

17. Members of a firm's board of directors are selected by the firm's:
    a) top management.
    b) management council.
    c) shareholders.
    d) creditors.
    e) employees.

18. The _____ refers to the number of employees managed by each manager.
    a) scope of authority
    b) management ratio
    c) employee limit
    d) span of control
    e) manager-employee multiplier

19. Span of control is determined by:
    a) consultants.
    b) staff.
    c) top management.
    d) employees.
    e) customers.

20. The _____ ensures that all departments follow the firm's guidelines and procedures.
    a) CEO
    b) internal auditor
    c) board of directors
    d) project manager
    e) inside director

21. A firm in which managers have narrow spans of control tends to have:
    a) a tall organizational structure.
    b) very decentralized decision making.
    c) a small number of employees.
    d) very few layers of management.
    e) a very large number of people serving on its board of directors.

22. The strategy of spreading authority among several divisions or managers is called:
    a) centralization.
    b) decentralization.
    c) decision rationing.
    d) abdication of authority.
    e) adjudication of authority.

23. An extreme form of decentralization in which divisions can make their own decisions and act independently is called:
    a) centralization.
    b) autonomy.
    c) span of control.
    d) span of management.
    e) departmentalization.

24. A possible disadvantage of decentralization is that it:
    a) may require inexperienced managers to make major decisions they are not qualified to make.
    b) usually increases the firm's operating expenses.
    c) slows down the decision-making process.
    d) harms employees' motivation by forcing them to take on more responsibilities.
    e) prevents employees from making creative decisions.

25. One outcome of the recent downsizing is:
    a) an increase in the layers of management.
    b) a narrower span of control for most managers.
    c) decentralization of authority.
    d) increased costs of production.
    e) a big reduction in the importance of the informal organizational structure.

26. Employees who serve in _____ positions provide assistance and support to employees who serve in line positions.
    a) secondary
    b) nominal
    c) reserve
    d) nonlinear
    e) staff

27. Jobs that are established to make decisions that achieve specific business goals are:
    a) staff positions.
    b) line positions.
    c) line-and-staff functions.
    d) temporary jobs.
    e) job placement.

28. Firms use a(n) _____ organization to allow the various parts of a firm to interact as they focus on a particular project.
    a) matrix
    b) quasi-linear
    c) tabular
    d) extracurricular
    e) cellular

29. One possible disadvantage of a matrix organization is that it:
    a) makes it difficult for different departments to communicate with each other.
    b) reduces employee satisfaction by requiring workers to perform monotonous tasks.
    c) reduces the time employees have to perform their normal duties.
    d) puts too much power in the hands of a small number of top managers.
    e) allows top management to make decisions without input from the board.

30. Firms are commonly departmentalized by all of the following except:
    a) function.
    b) product.
    c) customer.
    d) time period.
    e) location.

**True/False**

| 1. True | 7. False |
| 2. True | 8. True |
| 3. False | 9. True |
| 4. False | 10. False |
| 5. True | |
| 6. False | |

**Multiple Choice**

| 11. c | 18. d | 25. c |
| 12. b | 19. c | 26. e |
| 13. a | 20. b | 27. b |
| 14. a | 21. a | 28. a |
| 15. b | 22. b | 29. c |
| 16. e | 23. b | 30. d |
| 17. c | 24. a | |

# Self-Test of Key Terms

autonomy   260
board of directors   254
centralized   260
chain of command   250
decentralized   260
departmentalize   268
downsizing   263

informal organizational
    structure   266
inside board members   255
internal auditor   258
intrapreneurship   266
line organization   252
line positions   252

line-and-staff organization   252
matrix organization   264
organizational structure   250
outside board members   255
span of control   251
staff positions   252

Fill in each blank with the proper key term. To assess your understanding of the key terms, answers are provided at the end of this self-test.

1. A(n) _____ is an informal communications network that exists among a firm's employees.

2. The _____ is responsible for ensuring that employees follow the firm's guidelines and procedures.

3. The _____ identifies the job positions to which all types of employees must report.

4. The process of _____ assigns some employees to generate ideas as if they were running their own firms.

5. _____ are established to support the efforts of line positions.

6. Board members who are not managers of the company are referred to as _____.

7. In a(n) _____, various parts of the firm interact on specific projects.

8. A(n) _____ shows the interaction among employee responsibilities.

9. For firms that are _____, most authority is held by the high-level managers.

10. When firms are decentralized to an extreme level such that divisions are permitted to make their own decisions, this is referred to as _____.

11. _____ reflects efforts to cut expenses by eliminating job positions.

12. Board members who are managers of the company are referred to as _____.

13. _____ are established to make decisions that achieve specific business goals.

14. A(n) _____ identifies the responsibilities for each job position and the relationships among those positions.

15. The number of employees managed by each manager is described by the _____.

**Answers:**
1. informal organizational structure
2. internal auditor
3. chain of command
4. intrapreneurship
5. Staff positions
6. outside board members
7. matrix organization
8. organization chart
9. centralized
10. autonomy
11. Downsizing
12. inside board members
13. Line positions
14. organizational structure
15. span of control

# Concept Review Questions

1. **Organizational Structure.** How can a firm's organizational structure affect its value?

2. **Span of Control.** Explain how the span of control can vary among firms.

3. **Organizational Height.** Explain how the organizational height can vary among firms.

4. **Line Versus Staff.** Compare the role of line positions versus staff positions. Compare the structure of line organizations versus line-and-staff organizations.

5. **Board Composition.** Compare the role of inside board members with that of outside board members. Explain why conflicts can occur between them.

6. **Board Committees.** Describe the three main committees of the board of directors.

7. **Sarbanes-Oxley Act.** Explain how the Sarbanes-Oxley Act affected the internal control process of firms.

8. **Decentralization.** Compare centralization with decentralization. Explain the advantages and disadvantages of decentralization.

9. **Informal Structures.** Explain the various informal structures that allow more employee input.

10. **Departmentalizing.** Explain the methods of departmentalizing. What are the ways in which a firm can departmentalize?

# Class Communication Questions

1. **Span of Control Dilemma.** For a chain of clothing stores spread across the United States, do you think a narrow or wide span of control is optimal for each store manager?

2. **Outside Directors.** Do you think outside directors are more important for a small business in which most of the key managers are also the owners, or a large business that has thousands of shareholders?

3. **Sarbanes-Oxley Act.** The Sarbanes-Oxley Act requires that publicly traded firms establish more internal controls. Do you think that these controls are beneficial, or is this regulation causing businesses to waste money without any improvement?

# Small Business Case

## Organizational Structure Decisions

Mars Technology Company owns small production plants in four different cities that produce high-technology products such as digital cameras and miniature computers. The firm has four divisions, each of which includes a production plant served by its supervisors, who report to top-line managers. Every division has three vice-presidents—for finance, marketing, and production.

1. **Deciding a Span of Control.** At all levels above the supervisor, the organizational structure has a narrow span of control. What is a disadvantage of this structure?

2. **Impact on Efficiency.** How might the Mars Technology Company revise its organizational structure to increase its efficiency?

3. **Centralization Versus Decentralization.** Do you think factory workers at Mars Technology Company would be more satisfied if day-to-day production decisions were centralized or if they were made at each production plant? Why?

4. **Departmentalization Decision.** Mars Technology Company wants to departmentalize by product, but its divisions are in four different cities scattered across the United States. Why would it be costly for this firm to departmentalize by product?

# Web Insight

### Operational Structure at Schwinn

At the opening of the chapter, Schwinn was introduced. Go to the Schwinn website (www.schwinn.com) and review the products that Schwinn produces. Do you think that Schwinn should departmentalize tasks by product (have separate departments for bicycles, fitness equipment, and motor scooters)? Or should it departmentalize tasks by function (a marketing department would do the marketing for all products, a finance department would do the finance for all products, etc.)?

If Schwinn departmentalizes by product, it would need a separate marketing department for each product, a separate finance department for each product, etc. What type of organizational structure would be most appropriate for Schwinn? Explain your answer.

# Dell's Secret for Success

Go to Dell's website (www.dell.com) and click on the link "About Dell," near the bottom of the web page. You can also review a recent annual report to obtain more information.

1. **Functions of Executives.** Review Dell's organizational structure based on the position titles of its executives. What types of functions do these executives perform?

2. **Role of the Board.** What is the role of Dell's board of directors?

3. **Role of Executives.** What is the general role of Dell's top-level management?

# Video Exercise

### Lessons in Organizing an Effective Board of Directors

Many free business videos are available on websites such as YouTube (www.youtube.com), and more are added every day. Search for a recent video clip about an existing business that offers lessons on "board of directors" in YouTube or any other website that provides video clips.

1. **Main Lesson.** What is the name of the business in the video clip? Is the video clip focused on the creation of a board of directors, or an example of problems due to a particular board structure, or some other aspect of entrepreneurship? What is the main lesson of the video clip that you watched?

2. **Board Feedback.** Some videos stress that an entrepreneur who creates a board must ensure that the board is independent and willing to offer feedback. Why do you think some small businesses receive very little insight from the board?

3. **Entrepreneur-Board Conflict.** Why might some entrepreneurs prefer a board with members who do not offer much input?

# Projects

To encourage further comprehension of concepts covered in Chapter 8, the following five projects are available:

1. Analyzing Your Favorite Business

2. Building a Business Plan for Campus.com

3. Running Your Own Business

4. Planning Your Career

5. Stock Market Contest

All of these projects are provided in Appendix A at the end of the text. In addition, projects are available by part division at the end of each part.

A Word file for each project is also available at the textbook website (www.emcp.net/business5e) so that you may maintain one ongoing file for each project.

# Improving Productivity and Quality

© SHUTTERSTOCK/DRAGAN TRIFUNOV

## Chapter 9 Learning Objectives

**1** Identify the key resources used for production.

**2** Identify the factors that affect the plant site decision.

**3** Describe how various factors affect the design and layout decision.

**4** Describe the key tasks that are involved in production control.

**5** Describe the key factors that affect production efficiency.

# Chapter 9

## Productivity at MTV Network

Firms are created to produce products or services. Production management (also called operations management) is the management of the process in which resources are used to produce products or services. The specific process chosen by a firm to produce its products or services can affect its value. Consider the situation of the MTV network, which is owned by Viacom. MTV's production of television shows is intended to satisfy its viewers. Viewers' opinions of a show are highly influenced by how the show was produced. When MTV creates television shows, it must address the following questions:

◆ What are the key resources that the MTV network needs for production of its MTV television shows?

◆ How should the MTV network organize the layout when it produces MTV TV shows?

◆ How can the MTV network properly control its production to ensure that it produces quality programming?

◆ How can the MTV network produce its TV shows efficiently (at a relatively low cost)?

MTV incurs substantial expenses from its process of producing TV shows. However, it is rewarded when it produces shows that viewers like. If MTV attracts more viewers, it can generate more revenue from selling advertising time (commercials) and will earn higher profits.

All businesses must make the types of decisions described above. This chapter explains how the MTV network or any other firm can make production management decisions in a manner that maximizes the firm's value.

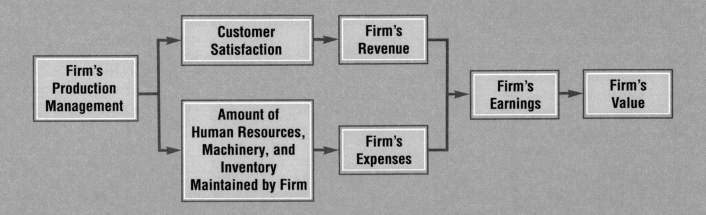

**production process (conversion process)**
a series of tasks in which resources are used to produce a product or service

**production management (operations management)**
the management of a process in which resources (such as employees and machinery) are used to produce products and services

# 1. Resources Used for the Production Process

Whether a firm produces products or services, it needs a **production process** (also called **conversion process**), or a series of tasks in which resources are used to produce a product or service. A process identifies the mixture of resources allocated for production, the assignment of tasks, and the sequence of tasks.

Many possible production processes can achieve the production of a specific product. Thus, effective **production management** (or **operations management**) attempts to develop an efficient (relatively low-cost) and high-quality production process for producing specific products and services. Specifically, production management can achieve efficiency by determining the proper amount of materials to use, the proper mix of resources to use, the proper assignments of the tasks, and the proper sequence of the tasks. Production management can contribute to the success of both manufacturing firms and service-oriented firms. For example, the success of Southwest Airlines, a service-oriented firm, is attributed to its low-cost production of air transportation for customers. Thus, the profits and value of each firm are influenced by its production management.

The main resources that firms use for the production process are human resources (employees), materials, and other resources (such as buildings, machinery, and equipment). Firms that produce products tend to use more materials and equipment in their production process. Firms that produce services (such as Internet firms) use more employees and information technology.

## 1.1 Human Resources

Firms must identify the type of employees needed for production. Skilled labor is necessary for some forms of production, but unskilled labor can be used for other forms. Some forms of production are labor-intensive in that they require more labor than materials. The operating expenses involved in hiring human resources are dependent both on the number of employees and on their skill levels. Because of the employee skill level required, an Internet firm incurs much larger salary expenses than a grocery store.

## 1.2 Materials

The materials used in the production process are normally transformed by the firm's human resources into a final product. Tire manufacturers rely on rubber, automobile manufacturers rely on steel, and book publishers rely on paper. Service firms such as travel agencies and investment advisers do not

Each employee (like the one shown here) involved in the production process has a major influence on the production output. An efficient production process requires that all employees do their assignments within the time allowed.

© SHUTTERSTOCK/PHOTOCREATE

Technology allows firms to produce products efficiently. The robotic hand (shown here) is commonly used for various types of production.

© SHUTTERSTOCK/BALONCICI

rely as much on materials because they do not engage in manufacturing.

## 1.3 Other Resources

A building is needed for most forms of production. Manufacturers use factories and offices. Service firms use offices. The site may be owned or rented by the firm. Since purchasing a building can be expensive, some firms simply rent the buildings they use. Renting also allows the firm to move at the end of the lease period without having to sell the building. Machinery and equipment are also needed by many manufacturing firms. Technology may also be a necessary resource for manufacturing and service firms.

## 1.4 Combining the Resources for Production

Managers attempt to utilize the resources just described in a manner that achieves production at a low cost. They combine the various resources with the use of work stations and assembly lines. A **work station** is an area in which one or more employees are assigned a specific task. A work station may require machinery and equipment as well as employees.

An **assembly line** consists of a sequence of work stations in which each work station is designed to cover specific phases of the production process. The production of a single product may require several work stations, with each station using employees, machinery, and materials. Since the cost of all these resources along with the building can be substantial, efficient management of the production process can reduce expenses, which can convert into higher profits.

An example of a typical production process is shown in Exhibit 9.1. Employees use buildings, machinery, and equipment to convert materials into a product or service. For example, employees of printing firms

**work station**
an area in which one or more employees are assigned a specific task

**assembly line**
a sequence of work stations in which each work station is designed to cover specific phases of the production process

**Exhibit 9.1**

Resources Used in Production

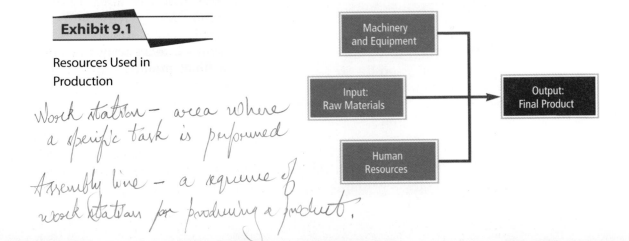

use machines for typesetting, printing, and binding to produce books. Employees of General Nutrition Centers (GNC) use its manufacturing plant (which is the size of four football fields) to produce more than 150,000 bottles of vitamins per day.

Most production processes are more efficient when different employees are assigned different tasks. In this way, employees can utilize their unique types of expertise to specialize in what they do best.

**Learning Objective**
Identify the factors that affect the plant site decision.

**2**

## 2. Selecting a Site

A critical decision in production management is the selection of a site (location) for the factory or office. Location can significantly affect the cost of production and therefore the firm's ability to compete against other firms. This is especially true for industrial firms such as U.S. Steel and Toyota, which require a large investment in plant and equipment.

### 2.1 Factors Affecting the Site Decision

Several factors must be considered when determining the optimal site. The most relevant factors are identified here.

**Cost of Workplace Space**  The cost of purchasing or renting workplace space (such as buildings or offices) can vary significantly among locations. Costs are likely to be high near the center of any business district where land costs are high. Costs also tend to be higher in certain regions. For example, office rental rates are generally higher in the northeastern states than in other areas. This is one major reason why companies located in northern cities have relocated to the South during the last 10 years.

**Cost of Labor**  The cost of hiring employees varies significantly among locations. Salaries within a city tend to be higher than salaries outside the city for a given occupation. Salaries are also generally higher in the North than the South for a given occupation. This is another reason why many companies have relocated to the South.

**Tax Incentives**  Some local governments may be willing to grant tax credits to attract companies to their area. The governments offer this incentive to increase the employment level and improve economic conditions in the area.

**Source of Demand**  If a firm plans to sell its product in a specific location, it may establish its plant there. The costs of transporting and servicing the product can be minimized by producing at a site near the source of demand.

**Access to Transportation**  When companies sell products across the nation, they may choose a site near their main source of transportation. They also need to be accessible so that materials can be delivered to them. Some factories and offices are established near interstate highways, rivers, or airports for this reason.

**Supply of Labor**  Firms that plan to hire specialized workers must be able to attract the labor needed. They may choose a location where a large supply of workers with that particular specialization exists. For instance, high-tech companies tend to locate near universities where there is an abundance of educated labor.

## 2.2 Evaluating Possible Sites

When a firm evaluates various sites, it must consider any factors that may affect the desirability of each site. The choice of the location within a city is also critical. A retail store may attract many customers simply because they are driving by and notice the store. Therefore, a retail store in an area without much traffic will need other ways (such as advertising) to attract customers. If the firm intends to rent space, it is important to meet with the landlord before deciding on a specific location. In some locations, leases are very restrictive and may require a large deposit that will be lost if the business decides to move.

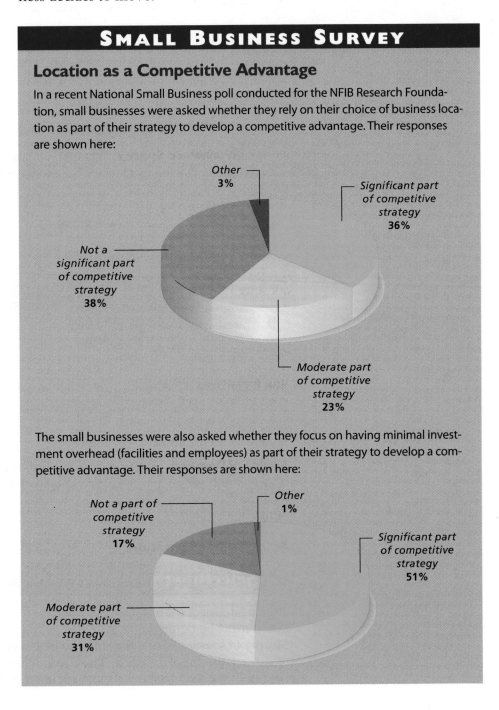

# SMALL BUSINESS SURVEY

## Location as a Competitive Advantage

In a recent National Small Business poll conducted for the NFIB Research Foundation, small businesses were asked whether they rely on their choice of business location as part of their strategy to develop a competitive advantage. Their responses are shown here:

Other
3%

Significant part
of competitive
strategy
36%

Not a
significant part
of competitive
strategy
38%

Moderate part
of competitive
strategy
23%

The small businesses were also asked whether they focus on having minimal investment overhead (facilities and employees) as part of their strategy to develop a competitive advantage. Their responses are shown here:

Not a part of
competitive
strategy
17%

Other
1%

Significant part
of competitive
strategy
51%

Moderate part
of competitive
strategy
31%

## Global Business

### Selecting a Foreign Production Site

The selection of a foreign production site by a U.S. firm is critical because location affects the firm's operating expenses and therefore its earnings. Consider the case of Pfizer, a U.S. firm that produces pharmaceutical and consumer products, including Listerine, Halls cough drops, Clorets mints, Certs mints, and Trident gum. Pfizer has operations in more than 100 countries. Its extensive development of foreign operations was motivated by global demand for its products. Pfizer attempts to offer "every product, everywhere." Consequently, it established production sites that were convenient to the foreign markets where it planned to sell products.

The selection of a production site by any multinational corporation is crucial because costs vary substantially among countries. Annual office rental rates per square foot are more than five times higher in Paris than in Mexico City and more than twice as high in Tokyo as in Paris. The cost of human resources is generally much lower in less-developed countries, but the supply of skilled labor in those countries may be inadequate. Furthermore, consumer demand for products in those countries may be low, so the products would have to be transported to other countries with much higher demand. Multinational corporations must assess the tradeoffs involved. If the products are light in weight (and therefore involve low transportation expenses), a multinational corporation might be willing to use facilities in less-developed countries and transport the products to areas where demand is higher.

When the firm has identified all of the factors that it should consider, it can create a site evaluation matrix, which accounts for the relative importance of each factor that could determine the optimal site. Specifically, it can assign a weight to each factor that reflects that factor's importance. Labor-intensive firms would likely place a high weight on the cost of human resources while other firms may be less concerned about this factor. Firms that sell products or services at the site will assign a high weight to the amount of traffic. Starbucks retail stores are commonly located in places where many people walk, such as downtown areas, suburban retail centers, office buildings, and university campuses. When Blockbuster opens new stores, it looks for areas with a high concentration of people but attempts to avoid areas already served by other Blockbuster stores so that it will not pull customers away from those stores.

Once the firm determines the weight assigned to each factor, it evaluates each possible site on all relevant factors to determine a weighted rating for each factor. Then, the ratings are combined to determine the overall rating for each possible site.

<table>
<tr><td>**Learning Objective**<br><br>Describe how various factors affect the design and layout decision.</td><td>**3**</td></tr>
</table>

## 3. Selecting the Design and Layout

Once a site for a manufacturing plant or office is chosen, the design and layout must be determined. The **design** indicates the size and structure of the plant or office. The **layout** is the arrangement of the machinery and equipment within the factory or office.

**design**
the size and structure of a plant
or office

**layout**
the arrangement of machinery
and equipment within a factory
or office

**product layout**
a layout in which tasks are positioned in the sequence that they
are assigned

**fixed-position layout**
a layout in which employees go to
the position of the product, rather
than waiting for the product to
come to them

**flexible manufacturing**
a production process that can be
easily adjusted to accommodate
future revisions

*Production process*

*1. Product layout*

*2. fixed position layout*

*3. flexible manufacturing*

Out of
Business
━━━━

## 3.1  Factors Affecting Design and Layout

Design and layout decisions are influenced by the following characteristics.

**Site Characteristics**  Design and layout decisions are dependent on some characteristics of the site selected. For example, if the site is in an area with high land costs, a high-rise building may be designed so that less land will be needed. The layout of the plant will then be affected by the design.

**Production Process**  Design and layout are also dependent on the production process to be used. If an assembly-line operation is to be used, all tasks included in this operation should be in the same general area. A **product layout** positions the tasks in the sequence that they are assigned. For example, one person may specialize in creating components, while the next person assembles the components, and the next person packages the product. A product layout is commonly used for assembly-line production.

Alternatively, some products (such as airplanes, ships, or homes) are completely produced in one fixed position, which requires a **fixed-position layout**. The employees go to the product, rather than having the product come to them.

Many firms now use **flexible manufacturing**, a production process that can be easily adjusted to accommodate future revisions. This enables the firm to restructure its layout as needed when it changes its products to accommodate customer demand. Many auto plants use flexible manufacturing so that they can produce whatever cars or trucks are in demand. A flexible layout normally requires that employees have flexible skills.

**Product Line**  Most firms produce more than one product or service at their site. Firms with a narrow product line focus on the production of one or a few products, which allows them to specialize. Firms with a broad product line offer a wide range of products.

As market preferences change, demand for products changes. The layout must be revised to accompany these changes. For example, the

popularity of hybrids has caused many automobile manufacturers to allocate more of their layout for the production of these vehicles. The allocation of more space for one product normally takes space away from others, unless the initial design and layout allowed extra space for expansion.

**Desired Production Capacity** When planning both design and layout, the firm's desired production capacity (maximum production level possible) must be considered. Most firms attempt to plan for growth by allowing flexibility to increase the production capacity over time. The design of the building may allow for additional levels to be added. The proper layout can open up more space to be used for increased production.

If firms do not plan for growth, they will be forced to search for a new site when demand for their product exceeds their production capacity. When a firm maintains its existing site and develops a second site to expand, it must duplicate the machinery and job positions assigned at the original site. Consequently, production efficiency tends to decrease. To avoid this problem, the firm may relocate to a site with a larger capacity.

Although having a layout that allows for growth is desirable, it is also expensive. A firm must invest additional funds to obtain additional land or floor space. This investment ties up funds that might be better used by the firm for other purposes. Furthermore, if growth does not occur, the layout will be inefficient because some of the space will continue to be unused.

A firm may achieve greater production capacity without changing its design and layout if employees can do some or all of their work at home. Given the improvements in telecommunications (computer networks, e-mail, and fax machines), employees of some businesses no longer need to be on site. When the employees who work at home need to come in to work, they use work spaces that are not permanently assigned to anyone. For example, a firm may keep an office available with a desk, a computer, and a telephone for any employee who normally works at home but needs to use temporary work space at the firm. This practice is referred to as **hotelling** (or **just-in-time office**). For example, hotelling may be appropriate for salespeople who travel frequently and generally work from a home office.

**hotelling (just-in-time office)**
providing an office with a desk, a computer, and a telephone for any employee who normally works at home but needs to use work space at the firm

---

**Learning Objective 4**
Describe the key tasks that are involved in production control.

**production control**
involves purchasing materials, inventory control, routing, scheduling, and quality control

# 4. Production Control

Once the plant and design have been selected, the firm can engage in **production control**, which involves the following:

✦ Purchasing materials

✦ Inventory control

✦ Routing

✦ Scheduling

✦ Quality control

## 4.1 Purchasing Materials

Managers perform the following tasks when purchasing supplies. First, they must select a supplier. Second, they attempt to obtain volume discounts. Third, they determine whether to delegate some production tasks to suppliers. These tasks are discussed next.

**Selecting a Supplier of Materials**   In selecting among various suppliers, firms consider characteristics such as price, speed, quality, servicing, and credit availability. A typical approach to evaluating suppliers is to first obtain prices from each supplier. Next, a sample is obtained from each supplier and inspected for quality. Then, these suppliers are asked to provide further information on their speed of delivery and their service warranties in case any delivery problems occur. The firm may then try out a single supplier and evaluate its reliability over time.

Alternatively, a firm may initially use a few suppliers and later select the supplier that has provided the best service. Some firms avoid depending on a single supplier so that if any problems occur with one supplier, they will not have a major impact on the firm.

Another consideration in selecting a supplier may be its ability to interact with an Internet-based order system. Many firms now rely on *e-procurement,* or the use of the Internet to purchase some of their materials. This reduces the time that employees must devote to orders and can reduce expenses. A basic system detects the existing level of supplies and automatically orders additional supplies once the quantity on hand falls to a specific level. Some systems are more sophisticated and can handle additional tasks.

**Obtaining Volume Discounts**   Firms that purchase a large volume of materials from suppliers may obtain a discounted price on supplies while maintaining quality. This practice has enabled firms such as AT&T and many automobile manufacturers to reduce their production expenses in recent years.

## SMALL BUSINESS SURVEY

### Why Do Firms Outsource Rather Than Produce Some Products Themselves?

A survey of the chief executive officers (CEOs) of 400 high-growth businesses asked what caused them to outsource rather than produce some products (including supplies) themselves. The results are summarized in the following chart:

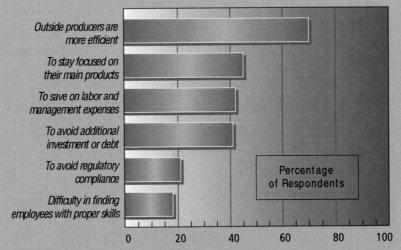

It appears from the survey that many firms recognize that they can benefit from specializing in what they do best and relying on other firms for supplies or parts needed for their production process.

**outsourcing**
purchasing parts from a supplier rather than producing the parts

**Delegating Production to Suppliers**   Manufacturers commonly use **outsourcing**; that is, they purchase parts from suppliers rather than producing the parts. Outsourcing can reduce a firm's expenses if suppliers can produce the parts at a lower cost than the firm itself. Some manufacturers have even begun delegating some parts of the production process to suppliers. Consider a manufacturing firm located in a city where wages are generally high. This firm has been ordering several components from a supplier and assembling them at its own plant. It may be better to have the supplier partially assemble the components before shipping them to the manufacturer. Some of the assembly task would thereby be shifted to the supplier. Partial assembly by the supplier may cost less than paying high-wage employees at the manufacturing plant.

Although outsourcing can be beneficial, it places much responsibility on other manufacturing companies. Thus, when a firm outsources, its ability to meet its production schedule depends on these other companies. For this reason, a firm that outsources must be very careful when selecting the suppliers on which it will rely.

**deintegration**
the strategy of delegating some production tasks to suppliers

The strategy of delegating some production tasks to suppliers is referred to as **deintegration** and is illustrated in Exhibit 9.2. The production process within the plant is no longer as integrated, because part of the production is completed by the supplier before the supplies or components are delivered to the manufacturing plant. Automobile manufacturers have deintegrated their production processes by delegating some production tasks to suppliers or other firms. For example, Ford Motor Company purchases fully assembled automobile seats from Lear Seating. By doing so, it saves hundreds of dollars per automobile because the supplier's cost of labor is lower than Ford's cost.

**Electronic Payments for Supplies**   Firms are increasingly paying for their supplies electronically instead of paying by check. This allows for a more efficient production system. To use electronic payments, a firm maintains a sufficient balance in its account. After receiving an order of supplies, it instructs its bank to transfer a payment from its account to the account of the supplier. Recent technology allows even small businesses to efficiently send payments in this manner rather than writing checks.

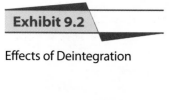

**Exhibit 9.2**

Effects of Deintegration

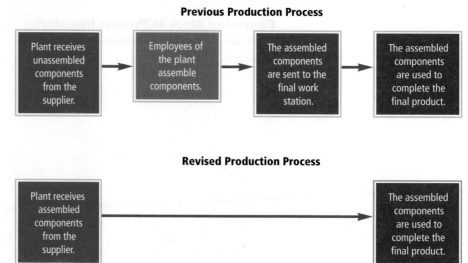

**Previous Production Process**

Plant receives unassembled components from the supplier. → Employees of the plant assemble components. → The assembled components are sent to the final work station. → The assembled components are used to complete the final product.

**Revised Production Process**

Plant receives assembled components from the supplier. → The assembled components are used to complete the final product.

## 4.2  Inventory Control

**inventory control**
the process of managing inventory at a level that minimizes costs

**Inventory control** is the process of managing inventory at a level that minimizes costs. It requires the management of materials inventories, work-in-process inventories, and finished goods inventories, as explained next.

**carrying costs**
costs of maintaining (carrying) inventories

**Control of Materials Inventories**   When firms carry excessive inventories of materials, they may need to borrow more funds to finance these inventories. This increases their **carrying costs**, or their costs of maintaining (carrying) inventories. Carrying costs include financing costs as well as costs associated with storing or insuring inventories. Although firms can attempt to reduce their carrying costs by frequently ordering small amounts of materials, this strategy increases the costs involved in placing orders (called **order costs**). Any adjustment in the materials purchasing strategy will normally reduce carrying costs at the expense of increasing order costs, or vice versa.

**order costs**
costs involved in placing orders for materials

**just-in-time (JIT)**
a system that attempts to reduce materials inventories to a bare minimum by frequently ordering small amounts of materials

A popular method for reducing carrying costs is the **just-in-time (JIT)** system originated by Japanese companies. This system attempts to reduce materials inventories to a bare minimum by frequently ordering small amounts of materials. It can reduce the costs of maintaining inventories. However, it also entails a cost of managerial time required for frequent ordering and a cost of frequent deliveries. In addition, the JIT system could result in a shortage if applied improperly. Nevertheless, U.S. firms such as Boeing Corporation, Oracle, and Black & Decker Corporation have improved their productivity by effectively using JIT inventory management.

**materials requirements planning (MRP)**
a process for ensuring that materials are available when needed

**Materials requirements planning (MRP)** is a process for ensuring that the materials are available when needed. Normally requiring the use of a computer, MRP helps managers determine the amount of specific materials that should be purchased at any given time. The first step in MRP is to work backward from the finished product toward the beginning and determine how long in advance materials are needed before products are completely produced. For example, if computers are to be assembled by a specific date, the computer components must arrive by a specific date before then, which means that they must be ordered even earlier. As the firm forecasts the demand for its product in the future, it can determine the time at which the materials need to arrive to achieve a production level that will accommodate the forecasted demand.

**work-in-process inventories**
inventories of partially completed products

**Control of Work-in-Process Inventories**   Firms must also manage their **work-in-process inventories**, which are inventories of partially completed products. Firms attempt to avoid shortages of all types of inventories. The direct consequence of a shortage in raw materials inventory or work-in-process inventory is an interruption in production. This can cause a shortage of the final product, and therefore results in forgone sales.

**Control of Finished Goods Inventories**   As demand for a firm's product changes over time, managers need to monitor the anticipated supply-demand differential. Consider the case of Amazon.com. It must maintain a sufficient stock of whatever books, DVDs, and other products may be ordered by customers. Maintaining an inventory of products uses up space, however. Therefore, Amazon.com attempts to accurately forecast the demand for its products so that its inventory is sufficient to accommodate demand without being excessive.

Blockbuster partially attributes its success to its efficient management of inventory. It effectively anticipates the demand for DVD rentals and therefore has a sufficient supply for customers. Autozone also attempts to manage its inventory of auto parts at all of its retail stores efficiently. Recently, it increased the size of its inventory to ensure that the stores will be able to accommodate the demand for any particular parts. This decision was based on the tradeoff of having to invest more funds to provide the inventory versus the lost sales that result when parts are not available.

Inventory decisions may adjust during the year due to seasonal demand. For example, stores that sell swimsuits experience their strongest demand during the summer. They need to maintain higher inventory levels in those months to ensure that they can accommodate demand.

If an excess supply of a product is anticipated, a firm can avoid excessive inventories by redirecting its resources toward the production of other products. For example, Ford Motor Company redirects resources away from the production of cars that are not selling as well as expected. Alternatively, a firm that experiences an excess supply of products can continue its normal production schedule and implement marketing strategies (such as advertising or reducing the price) that will increase demand.

If an increase in demand is anticipated, firms become concerned about possible shortages and must develop a strategy to boost production volume. They may schedule overtime for workers or hire new workers to achieve higher levels of production.

## 4.3 Routing

**routing**

the sequence (or route) of tasks necessary to complete the production of a product

**Routing** is the sequence (or route) of tasks necessary to complete the production of a product. Raw materials are commonly sent to various work stations so that they can be used as specified in the production process. A specific part of the production process is completed at each work station. For example, the production of a bicycle may require (1) using materials to produce a bike frame at one work station, (2) assembling wheels at a second work station, and (3) packaging the frames and wheels that have been assembled at a third work station.

The routing process is periodically evaluated to determine whether it can be improved to allow a faster or less expensive production process. General Motors and United Parcel Service have streamlined their routing process to improve production efficiency.

## 4.4 Scheduling

**scheduling**

the act of setting time periods for each task in the production process

**production schedule**

a plan for the timing and volume of production tasks

**Scheduling** is the act of setting time periods for each task in the production process. A **production schedule** is a plan for the timing and volume of production tasks. For example, the production schedule for a bicycle may set a time of two hours for each frame to be assembled and one hour for each wheel to be assembled. Scheduling is useful because it establishes the expected amount of production that should be achieved at each work station over a given day or week. Therefore, each employee understands what is expected. Furthermore, scheduling allows managers to forecast how much will be produced by the end of the day, week, or month. If a firm does not meet its production schedule, it will not be able to accommodate customer orders in a timely fashion and will lose some of its customers.

Firms use computer technology (like that shown here) to monitor the volume of various products that can be produced per hour or day. This information is useful for decisions regarding routing, scheduling, and determining the critical path.

© SHUTTERSTOCK/JEFFREY SCHMIEG

**Impact of Technology on Production Scheduling**   Many firms have used technology to improve their production scheduling. For example, a company that produces doors can allow customers to access its website where they can specify the features of the door they desire and receive instant pricing on a door with those features. Consequently, orders are now placed more quickly. In addition, there is less chance of error because the customers specify the desired features themselves rather than communicating the information to someone who would then have to communicate the information to the manufacturing department. Deliveries are now almost always on schedule.

Production scheduling is also being improved by the use of computer-based systems called *enterprise resource planning (ERP)* systems. These complex software packages can connect the computer systems from different departments. The goal is to automate accounting, production, order taking, and the other basic processes of the business. ERP achieves this by recording every transaction, from taking an order to delivering a finished product, and updating the entire system. The practical application allows the customer to place an order (either through traditional sales channels or electronically) that automatically schedules the items in the production line, adjusts raw materials inventories, and schedules the delivery. At the same time, the appropriate accounting entries are made and invoices sent. This high degree of integration allows every user at the firm to be better informed about its resources and commitments.

ERP systems can be expensive, however. The price depends on the complexity of the system and the number of users that will access it. Installation requires data to be reformatted and network systems to be overhauled.

**Scheduling for Special Projects**   Scheduling is especially important for special long-term projects that must be completed by a specific deadline. If

**Gantt chart**
a chart illustrating the expected timing for each task in the production process

many related tasks must be completed in a specific sequence, scheduling can indicate when each task should be completed.

One method of scheduling tasks for a special project is to use a **Gantt chart** (named after its creator, Henry Gantt), which illustrates the expected timing for each task within the production process. As an example of how a Gantt chart can be applied, assume that a chemical firm must produce 500 one-gallon containers of Chemical Z for a manufacturer. The production process involves creating large amounts of Chemicals X and Y, which are then mixed in a tank to produce Chemical Z. Next, Chemical Z must be poured into gallon containers and then packaged in cases to be delivered. Notice that while the first two tasks can be completed at the same time, each remaining task cannot begin until the previous task is completed.

The Gantt chart is shown in Exhibit 9.3. The bars can be marked when the respective tasks are completed to keep track of the production status.

Another method of scheduling tasks for a special project is the **program evaluation and review technique (PERT)**, which schedules tasks in a manner that will minimize delays in the production process. PERT involves the following steps:

**program evaluation and review technique (PERT)**
a method of scheduling tasks to minimize delays in the production process

1. The various tasks involved in the production process are identified.

2. The tasks are arranged in the order in which they must take place; this sequence may be represented on a chart with arrows illustrating the path or sequence of the production process.

3. The time needed for each activity is estimated.

An example of PERT as applied to the firm's production of Chemical Z is shown in Exhibit 9.4. The production of Chemical X (Task 1) and Chemical Y (Task 2) can be conducted simultaneously. The mixing of Chemicals X and Y (Task 3) cannot begin until Tasks 1 and 2 are completed.

Each sequence of tasks is referred to as a path. For example, the sequence of Tasks 1, 3, 4, and 5 represents one path. A second path is the sequence of Tasks 2, 3, 4, and 5. The accumulated time for this path is five weeks. The **critical path** is the path that takes the longest time to complete. In our example, the critical path is the sequence of Tasks 2, 3, 4, and 5; that path takes five weeks. It is important to determine the time necessary to complete the steps within the critical path, since the production process will take that long.

**critical path**
the path that takes the longest time to complete

**Exhibit 9.3**

Example of a Gantt Chart

| Production Tasks | Week 1 | Week 2 | Week 3 | Week 4 | Week 5 |
|---|---|---|---|---|---|
| 1. Produce Chemical X. | ▭ | | | | |
| 2. Produce Chemical Y. | ▭ | | | | |
| 3. Mix Chemicals X and Y in a tank to produce Chemical Z. | | | ▭ | | |
| 4. Pour Chemical Z into 500 one-gallon containers. | | | | ▭ | |
| 5. Package the one-gallon containers into cases. | | | | | ▭ |

## Responding to the Economy

### Revising Production Decisions in Response to the Economy

A firm may revise its production decisions in response to changing economic conditions. For example, an increase in the price of oil can increase some expenses of production when oil is used as a source of energy. The use of alternative sources of energy could affect the ideal layout for production. The decision regarding the production site might also be affected if oil prices increase, as firms may prefer to have a site near an energy source. Alternatively, they may prefer a site that is closer to their customers, depending on their specific business.

A weaker economy could affect production because the scheduled production may be reduced in anticipation of a reduction in future sales. Firms tend to reduce their inventory when economic conditions weaken so that do not have excessive inventory. Conversely, firms tend to anticipate higher sales during a stronger economy and may purposely allow for excess capacity so that they can increase production under such conditions.

Identifying the critical path and calculating the time it requires allows managers to estimate the slack time (extra time) on the other paths and reduce any inefficiencies that can be caused by that slack time. The five-week period has no slack time for the workers involved in the critical path. Since the other path in Exhibit 9.4 has a completion time of four weeks, it has slack time of one week over a five-week period. Therefore, some of the workers assigned to Task 1 may be assigned to help with the second task of the critical path sequence. This may reduce the time necessary to complete the critical path.

The tasks that are part of the critical path should be reviewed to avoid delays or increase production speed. Tasks estimated to take a long time are closely monitored because any delays in these tasks are more likely to cause a severe delay in the entire production process. Furthermore, firms attempt to determine whether these tasks can be performed more quickly so that the critical path is completed in less time.

**Exhibit 9.4**

Determining the Critical Path Based on a Sequence of Production Tasks

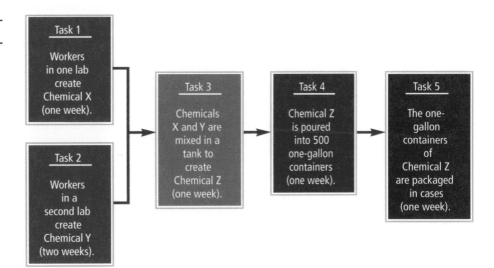

## 4.5 Quality Control

**quality**

the degree to which a product or service satisfies a customer's requirements or expectations

**Quality** can be defined as the degree to which a product or service satisfies a customer's requirements or expectations. Quality relates to customer satisfaction, which can have an effect on future sales and therefore on the future performance of the firm. Customers are more likely to purchase additional products from the same firm if they are satisfied with the quality. Firms now realize that it is easier to retain existing customers than it is to attract new customers who are unfamiliar with their products or services. Thus, firms are increasingly recognizing the impact that the quality of their products or services can have on their overall performance.

**quality control**

a process of determining whether the quality of a product meets the desired quality level

**Quality control** is a process of determining whether the quality of a product or a service meets the desired quality level and identifying improvements (if any) that need to be made in the production process. Quality can be measured by assessing the various characteristics (such as how long the product lasts) that enhance customer satisfaction. The quality of a computer may be defined by how well it works and how long it lasts. Quality may also be measured by how easy the computer is to use or by how quickly the manufacturer repairs a computer that experiences problems. All of these characteristics can affect customer satisfaction and therefore should be considered as indicators of quality.

The quality of services sold to customers must also be assessed. For example, Amazon.com produces a service of fulfilling orders of books, CDs, and other products ordered over the Internet by customers. Its customers assess the quality of the service in terms of the ease with which they can send an order over the Internet, whether they receive the proper order, and how quickly the products are delivered.

**total quality management (TQM)**

the act of monitoring and improving the quality of products and services provided

The act of monitoring and improving the quality of products and services produced is commonly referred to as **total quality management (TQM)**, which was developed by W. Edwards Deming. Among TQM's key guidelines for improving quality are the following: (1) provide managers and other employees with the education and training they need to excel in their jobs, (2) encourage employees to take responsibility and to provide leadership, and (3) encourage all employees to search for ways to improve the production process. Production quotas are discouraged so that employees can allocate more of their time to leadership and the improvement of the production process. Many firms use teams of employees to assess quality and offer suggestions for continuous improvement.

To ensure that quality is maintained, firms periodically evaluate the methods used to measure product or service quality. They rely on various techniques to assess quality, as described next.

**Control by Technology** Motorola and many other firms use computers to assess quality. The computers can determine whether each component of a product meets specific quality standards. Computer-controlled machinery has electronic sensors that can screen out defective parts.

Dell, Inc., uses custom configurations to ensure a high level of product quality and thereby fulfill its responsibility to its customers. It relies on its computer network to track its products from the point of initial sales contact to the time the product is sent to the customer, and beyond. Specifically, for a given order, Dell knows the date of the initial query by the customer, the date the order was placed, the date the order was delivered, the dates technical support was requested, and the types of support that were

# Cross-Functional Teamwork

## Interaction of Functions Involved in Total Quality Management

Total quality management requires an ongoing product assessment, beginning from the time product materials are ordered and continuing until the customer has purchased and used the product. Consequently, TQM requires an interaction of business functions. The key management functions involved in TQM are ordering the proper types and amounts of supplies, achieving efficient (low-cost) production of the product, and ensuring that the product satisfies the firm's production standards.

The key marketing functions involved in TQM are achieving efficient use of marketing strategies, ensuring customer satisfaction, and obtaining feedback from customers on how to improve the product. When marketing managers receive a similar criticism about a product from many customers, they should contact the production managers, who may redesign the product. This flow of information is shown in the diagram below.

The financing function is indirectly affected, as changes in expenses or revenue resulting from TQM may alter the amount of new financing that the firm needs.

Technological equipment (like that shown here) is commonly used by manufacturing firms to control the production process. It can be used to assess the specifications of partially finished or finished products to ensure that the products are produced properly.

© SHUTTERSTOCK/ILOSEVSKY PAVEL

provided. This tracking system offers several benefits. First, Dell can determine the speed at which it fills an order. Second, it has a history of its communications with the customer in case any dispute arises. Third, from the technical support communications, Dell can determine the type of support that was needed. When Dell redesigns its computers in the future, it can take these requests for support into consideration.

**Control by Employees**    Firms also use their employees to assess quality. Many firms such as IBM and Toyota use a **quality control circle**, which is a group of employees who assess the quality of a product and offer suggestions for improvement. Quality control circles usually allow for more interaction among workers and managers and provide workers with a sense of responsibility.

**Control by Sampling**    Firms also assess quality by **sampling**, or randomly selecting some of the products produced and testing them to determine whether they satisfy the quality standards. Firms may check one unit per 100 units produced and concentrate specifically on possible flaws that have been detected in previous checks.

**Control by Monitoring Complaints**    Quality should be assessed not only when the product is produced but also after it is sold. Some quality deficiencies may not become evident until after customers use the products. The quality of products that have been sold can be assessed by monitoring the proportion of products returned or by tracking customer complaints. Additional customer feedback can be obtained by conducting surveys. Firms can obtain customers' opinions on product quality by sending them a survey months after the sale.

**Correcting Deficiencies**    The purpose of the quality control process is not only to detect quality deficiencies but also to correct them. If quality is deficient, the problem was likely caused by one of the following factors: inadequate materials provided by suppliers, inadequate quality of work by employees, or malfunctioning machinery or equipment.

**quality control circle**
a group of employees who assess the quality of a product and offer suggestions for improvement

**sampling**
randomly selecting some of the products produced and testing them to determine whether they satisfy the quality standards

Customer service (shown here) can sometimes have a major influence on quality (and therefore on the satisfaction level of customers). In addition, it provides managers with a method of detecting deficiencies with existing products so that the problems can be corrected.

© SHUTTERSTOCK/KRISTIAN SEKULIC

## Global Business

### Global Quality Standards

Firms that conduct international business may attempt to satisfy a set of global quality standards. These standards have been established by the International Standardization Organization (ISO), which includes representatives from numerous countries. Firms are not required to meet these standards. By voluntarily meeting them, however, a firm can become certified, which may boost its credibility when selling products to foreign customers, who may be more comfortable if the firm has met the standards.

The certification process commonly costs at least $20,000 and takes at least one year. The standards focus on the design, manufacturing process, installation, and service of a product. Independent auditors review the firm's operations and decide whether to certify the firm.

Firms may also have to meet other standards to sell their products in specific foreign countries. For example, the Japanese government assesses any products that are sold in Japan to ensure that they are safe. Japan's safety standards have discouraged firms based in the United States and other countries from attempting to sell products in Japan. Thus, the standards may serve as a barrier that protects local firms in Japan from foreign competitors.

If inadequate materials caused the quality deficiency, the firm may require the existing supplier to improve the quality or may obtain materials from a different supplier in the future. If the cause is the work of employees, the firm may need to retrain or reprimand those employees. If the cause of quality deficiency is the machinery, the firm may need to to replace the machinery or make repairs.

While most production deficiencies cause a reduction in customer satisfaction, some deficiencies are worse than others. When a firm's product deficiency causes harm to a customer, the customer may bring a lawsuit against the firm claiming that it is liable for the harm caused by its product. The firm may incur major expenses if it must pay compensation to a customer as a result of a lawsuit. In addition, the firm may develop a bad reputation if there is publicity about its products causing harm to customers, and it may experience a loss in sales as a result. Quality control may ensure that products will not cause harm to customers.

**Winners of the Malcolm Baldrige National Quality Awards**    Firms that have recently won National Quality Awards used innovation to improve their quality. Cat Financial is a business that finances large orders of equipment from Caterpillar. Its services are available online, allowing customers to apply for financing and obtain information from the website without having to call a customer service representative. Stoner is the smallest business to ever win a Baldrige Quality Award. It has only 48 employees. Stoner created a software system to integrate its production, inventory, and distribution. Thus, its distribution decisions can be made with up-to-date information about production and inventory. Its decisions about future production can account for the latest inventory level. Though larger firms have used such technology, it is unusual for such a small company to have such an efficient system for integrating its production and distribution.

# SMALL BUSINESS SURVEY

## Exposure to Liability Lawsuits

In a recent National Small Business poll conducted for the NFIB Research Foundation, owners of small businesses were asked whether they believe liability laws favor those who file liability lawsuits or those who must defend against liability. Their responses are shown here:

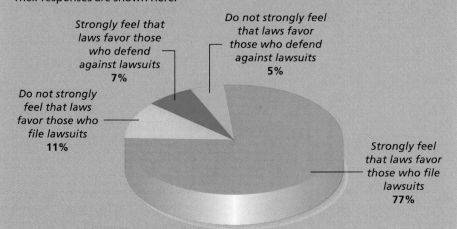

The small business owners were also asked if they were concerned about being subjected to a liability lawsuit. Their responses are shown here:

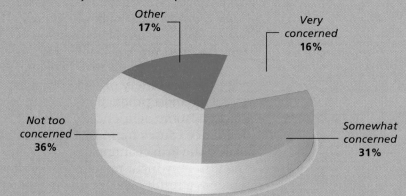

The owners of small businesses who participated in the survey and had been sued cited the following reason for the liability lawsuit:

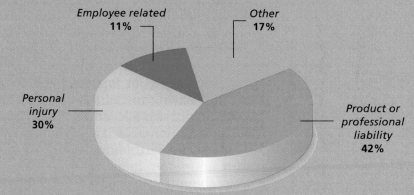

**production efficiency**
the ability to produce products at a low cost

**benchmarking**
a method of evaluating performance by comparison to some specified (benchmark) level, typically a level achieved by another company

**stretch targets**
production efficiency targets (or goals) that cannot be achieved under present conditions

**automated**
tasks are completed by machines without the use of employees

# 5.  Methods to Improve Production Efficiency

Firms strive to increase their **production efficiency**, which reflects a lower cost for a given amount of output and a given level of quality. Managers continually search for ways to manage human and other resources in a manner that improves production efficiency. Firms recognize the need to continually improve because other competitors may become more efficient and take their business away.

Production efficiency is important to service firms as well as manufacturing firms. For example, airlines need to be efficient in their service of flying passengers from one location to another so that they can achieve low expenses.

Many firms that set production efficiency goals use **benchmarking**, which is a method of evaluating performance by comparison to some specified (benchmark) level, such as a level achieved by another company. For example, a firm may set a goal of producing baseball caps at a cost of $6 per cap, which is the average cost incurred by the most successful producer of baseball caps.

The top managers of some firms set production efficiency targets (or goals) that cannot be achieved under present conditions. These targets are referred to as **stretch targets** because they are stretched beyond the ordinary. Stretch targets may be established in response to a decline in the firm's market share or performance. For example, 3M Company created a stretch target that 30 percent of its sales should be derived from sales of products created in the last four years. This target was intended to encourage more development of new products so that 3M did not rely on its innovations from several years ago.

Firms can improve production efficiency through the following methods:

✦ Technology

✦ Economies of scale

✦ Restructuring

Each of these methods is discussed in turn.

## 5.1  Technology

Firms may improve their production efficiency by adopting new technology. New machinery that incorporates improved technology can perform tasks more quickly.

Many production processes have become **automated**; that is, tasks are completed by machines without the use of employees. Since machinery can be less costly than human resources, automation may improve production efficiency. Guidelines for effective automation are summarized in Exhibit 9.5.

Many firms such as Albertson's (a grocery chain) and Home Depot have improved production efficiency with the use of computer technology. For example, computers can keep track of the daily or weekly volume of each type of product that is purchased at the cash register of a retail store. Therefore, the firm does not need an employee to monitor the inventory of these products. The computer may even be programmed to automatically reorder some products once the inventory is reduced to a specified level. Some hospitals use pharmacy robots that stock and

**Exhibit 9.5**

Guidelines for Effective Automation

To effectively capitalize on the potential benefits from automation, the following guidelines should be considered:

1. **Plan.** Automation normally does not simply speed up work; instead, it may require the elimination of some production steps. Planning is necessary to decide what type of automation will be most appropriate (computers versus other machinery).

2. **Use Automation Where the Benefits Are Greatest.** It may not be efficient to evenly allocate automation among all parts of the production process. Some workers will not be able to use a computer for their type of work.

3. **Train.** To make sure that the automation implemented is effectively utilized, any workers who use new computers or machinery should be trained.

4. **Evaluate Costs and Benefits over Time.** By assessing the costs and benefits of automation, a firm can decide whether to implement additional automation or revise its existing automation.

retrieve drugs. This technology increases production without additional labor expenses. Numerous manufacturing firms are using more powerful computers that have increased the speed at which various tasks can be completed.

**The Internet**  Much of the recent improvement in productivity is attributed to the Internet, in particular to its ability to improve the flow of information and communication between a firm's employees, and also between a firm and its customers and suppliers. A recent study by the University of California and the Brookings Institution found that almost half of the productivity improvements in U.S. firms are attributed to the use of Internet business solutions.

## 5.2 Economies of Scale

**economies of scale**
as the quantity produced increases, the cost per unit decreases

**fixed costs**
operating expenses that do not change in response to the number of products produced

**variable costs**
operating expenses that vary directly with the number of products produced

Firms may also be able to reduce costs by achieving **economies of scale**, which reflect a lower average cost incurred from producing a larger volume. To recognize how economies of scale can occur, consider that two types of costs are involved in the production of a product: fixed costs and variable costs. **Fixed costs** are operating expenses that do not change in response to the number of products produced. For example, the cost of renting a specific factory is not affected by the number of products produced there.

**Variable costs** are operating expenses that vary directly with the number of products produced. As output increases, the variable costs increase, but the fixed costs remain constant. The average cost per unit typically declines as output increases for firms that incur large fixed costs.

Automobile manufacturers incur a large fixed cost because they have to pay for their large facilities (including all the machinery) even if they do not produce many cars. Therefore, they need to produce a large number of cars to reduce the average cost per car produced.

Consider the production of a paperback book that requires some materials (ink and paper) and some manual labor. Assume that a printing company incurs a fixed cost (rent plus machinery) of $40,000 per month. These expenses exist regardless of the number of books printed. Assume that the variable cost of producing each book is $2 per book. The total cost of producing books each month is equal to the fixed cost plus the variable cost. The total cost is estimated for various production levels in Exhibit 9.6. The key measure of production efficiency is the average cost per unit, which is measured as the total cost divided by the number of units produced. Notice how the average cost declines when the production volume increases. This relationship exists because the fixed cost is not affected by the production volume. Therefore, the fixed costs can be spread over a larger production volume. No extra fixed cost is incurred when producing additional products.

Assume that each of the books produced can be sold for $10. Exhibit 9.7 shows the total revenue and total costs for various quantities of books produced. The total revenue is equal to the quantity produced times the price of $10 per book. The profits represent the difference between the total revenue and the total cost. Notice that the firm experiences losses at small

**Exhibit 9.6**

Relationship Between
Production Volume
and Costs

| Quantity of Books Produced | Fixed Cost | Variable Cost ($2 per Unit) | Total Cost | Average Cost per Unit |
|---|---|---|---|---|
| 1,000 | $40,000 | $2,000 | $42,000 | $42.00 |
| 3,000 | 40,000 | 6,000 | 46,000 | 15.33 |
| 5,000 | 40,000 | 10,000 | 50,000 | 10.00 |
| 10,000 | 40,000 | 20,000 | 60,000 | 6.00 |
| 15,000 | 40,000 | 30,000 | 70,000 | 4.67 |
| 20,000 | 40,000 | 40,000 | 80,000 | 4.00 |
| 25,000 | 40,000 | 50,000 | 90,000 | 3.60 |

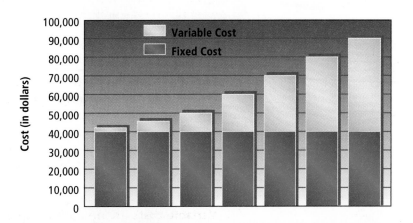

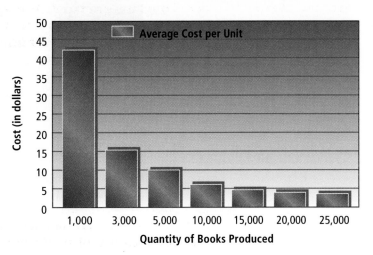

**break-even point**
the quantity of units sold at which total revenue equals total cost

quantities. This is because the fixed costs are incurred even though the production volume is low. At the quantity level of 5,000 books, the total revenue is equal to the total cost. The quantity of units sold at which total revenue equals total cost is referred to as the **break-even point**. At any quantity beyond 5,000 books, the firm earns profits. The profits are larger for larger quantities produced. This results from the lower average cost incurred from the production of more books.

Some firms strive to achieve a large market share so that they can achieve economies of scale. For example, Dell typically sets a goal to obtain a substantial market share for each of its products. This results in a large production volume so that Dell can achieve economies of scale. One of the largest expenses in the production of computers is the research and development to improve the computers. That expense is incurred whether Dell sells only 20 computers or 50,000 computers. Therefore, the average cost per unit is reduced when Dell produces a large amount of a specific computer.

## 5.3 Restructuring

**restructuring**
the revision of the production process in an attempt to improve efficiency

**Restructuring** involves the revision of the production process in an attempt to improve efficiency. When restructuring reduces the expense

**Exhibit 9.7**

Relationship Between Volume and Profitability

| Quantity of Books Produced | Total Revenue (= Quantity × Price) | Total Cost | Profits |
|---|---|---|---|
| 1,000 | $ 10,000 | $42,000 | $–32,000 |
| 3,000 | 30,000 | 46,000 | –16,000 |
| 5,000 | 50,000 | 50,000 | 0 |
| 10,000 | 100,000 | 60,000 | 40,000 |
| 15,000 | 150,000 | 70,000 | 80,000 |
| 20,000 | 200,000 | 80,000 | 120,000 |
| 25,000 | 250,000 | 90,000 | 160,000 |

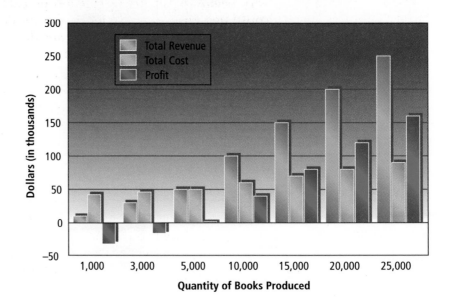

**reengineering**
the redesign of a firm's organizational structure and operations

of producing products or services, it can improve the firm's profits and therefore increase the firm's value. Many firms also engage in **reengineering**, which is the redesign of a firm's organizational structure and operations. The reengineering may result in some minor revisions, such as changes in the procedures used to take phone messages or to send packages. Alternatively, the revisions may be much larger, such as a new facility or a new assembly-line operation for production.

**downsizing**
an attempt by a firm to cut expenses by eliminating job positions

**Downsizing**    When firms restructure, they also typically engage in **downsizing**; that is, they reduce the number of employees. Firms identify various job positions that can be eliminated without affecting the volume or the quality of products produced. Some downsizing occurs as a result of technology because automated production processes replace human resources (as explained earlier). However, numerous firms downsize even when they have no plans to further automate their production process.

Although downsizing can help a firm achieve cost savings, downsizing also has its disadvantages. First, costs may be associated with the elimination of job positions, such as costs incurred to find other job positions within the firm or outside it for the employees whose jobs were cut. Second, costs may be associated with training some of the remaining employees whose responsibilities were expanded. Third, if the remaining employees believe their own positions may be cut, their morale may decline, reducing their performance. Fourth, downsizing may result in lower quality, as the remaining employees may be assigned more work and may not detect defects in the production process. Some firms become so obsessed with eliminating their inefficient components that they downsize too much. This is referred to as **corporate anorexia**.

**corporate anorexia**
the problem that occurs when firms become so obsessed with eliminating their inefficient components that they downsize too much

**supply chain**
the process from the beginning of the production process until the product reaches the customer

## 5.4  Integration of the Production Tasks

The production process described in this chapter consists of related tasks, such that each task can be accomplished only after other tasks have been completed. Thus, if any production task breaks down, the entire production schedule is affected. Furthermore, firms are unable to deliver their products to stores or to customers until all production tasks are completed. Therefore, firms monitor the so-called **supply chain**, or the process from the very beginning of the production process until the product reaches the consumer. Firms that produce products identify a site for production, hire employees, set up work stations, and determine the design and layout that will ensure efficient production. To recognize the integration required, consider the following example:

✦ After an automobile manufacturer identifies a site for production, it hires employees and assigns them to assembly lines.

✦ Machinery and tools (such as special wrenches) are placed along the assembly lines to help the employees assemble the automobiles.

✦ Materials (including steering wheels, seat cushions, engines, and tires) are delivered to different parts of the assembly line so that they can be installed during the production process. The design and layout are structured so that one task is completed before the automobile frame is moved to the next station on the assembly line, and so on. For example, the dashboard may be inserted at one station and the doors and windshield attached at the next station. The dashboard is installed first because inserting a dashboard is more difficult after the doors have been attached.

✦ A sufficient inventory of materials is ordered to accommodate the scheduled production.

✦ Tasks are scheduled so that each person who is assigned a task on the assembly line has enough time to complete it before the automobile frame is moved to the next station. Too much time should not be allocated for a specific task, however, because that would reduce the production volume.

✦ The quality control process takes place at different stations along the assembly line to ensure that each part of the production process is completed according to standards.

**How Breakdowns Disrupt the Production Process**   When production tasks are integrated, a breakdown in one part of the process may cause the entire production process to be slowed. Consider some examples. First, the machinery used by employees in the production process could break down, disrupting the entire process until the machinery is repaired or replaced. Second, materials needed at different stations along the assembly line may not arrive on time, halting production at those stations and at the stations that follow them on the assembly line. Third, some of the employees who were assigned tasks on the assembly line may become ill or quit, causing production to slow unless replacements are available. Fourth, the quality control process may require that a specific task be redone, disrupting the process because later tasks cannot be completed until the task in question is done properly.

The integration of tasks is not limited to assembly-line production. Firms such as Motorola, Johnson & Johnson, General Dynamics, and AT&T focus on coordinating all their production tasks in a manner that minimizes production cost while maintaining high quality. In fact, these firms frequently restructure their production process, continually searching for more efficient ways to produce their products.

**Integration of Tasks at Service Firms**   Even service firms use a production process that is integrated and therefore requires that the tasks described in this chapter are completed in a specific order. For example, Amazon.com hires employees to produce the service of fulfilling orders made by customers over a website. The production process for Amazon.com involves forecasting the future demand for books (or other items), ordering a sufficient number of each book to satisfy demand in a future period, storing books at warehouses, receiving orders, fulfilling orders, and ensuring that customers receive quality service (such as quick delivery). If Amazon.com does not order a sufficient amount of books relative to the amount customers order, it will not be able to accommodate all of the demand. Alternatively, if it has a sufficient inventory of the books but does not have enough employees and computer facilities to fulfill the orders, the production process will be disrupted.

## COLLEGE HEALTH CLUB: AVERAGE COST AT CHC

Sue Kramer wants to ensure that College Health Club is efficiently managed. Since CHC's expenses are mostly fixed, she recognizes the importance of generating economies of scale. She wants to determine the average cost per member served for various possible levels of membership. Since she expects CHC's total expenses over the first year to be $142,000, she estimates the cost per member served as follows:

**Impact of Membership Size on CHC's Average Cost per Member**

|  | If 280 Members Join in the First Year | If 300 Members Join in the First Year | If 320 Members Join in the First Year |
|---|---|---|---|
| (1) Total cost | $142,000 | $142,000 | $142,000 |
| (2) Number of members | 280 | 300 | 320 |
| (3) Cost per member = (1)/(2) | $507 | $473 | $444 |

If 280 members join, the average cost to CHC per member is $507, which exceeds the annual membership fee of $500. The higher the membership, the lower the average cost to CHC per member. This is why it is so important to attract a large membership at CHC.

# Summary of Learning Objectives

**1** The key resources used for production are human resources, materials, and other resources (such as the plant, machinery, and equipment).

**2** The plant site decision is influenced by

+ cost of workplace space,
+ cost of labor,
+ tax incentives,
+ source of demand for the product produced,
+ access to transportation, and
+ supply of labor.

A site evaluation matrix can be used to assign a rating to each relevant factor and derive a total rating for each possible site.

**3** The design and layout of a plant are influenced by the

+ site characteristics,
+ production process,
+ product line, and
+ desired production capacity.

**4** Production control involves

+ purchasing materials, which requires selecting a supplier, negotiating volume discounts, and possibly delegating production to suppliers;
+ inventory control, which involves managing various inventories at levels that minimize costs;
+ routing, which determines the sequence of tasks necessary to complete production;

+ scheduling, which sets time periods for the tasks required within the production process; and
+ quality control, which can be used to identify improvements (if any) that need to be made in the production process.

**5** The key methods used to improve production efficiency are

+ technology, which increases the speed of the production process;
+ economies of scale, which reduce the average cost per unit as a result of a higher production volume; and
+ restructuring, which is a revision of the production process to reduce production expenses.

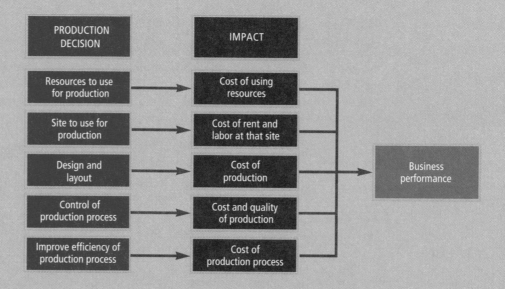

# Self-Test of Key Concepts

The following self-assessment allows you to test your understanding of the key concepts covered in this chapter. Answers are provided at the end of this exercise.

## True or False

1. A work station is an area in which one or more employees is assigned a specific task.

2. Design and layout decisions will have an impact on operating expenses.

3. A fixed-position layout is commonly used for assembly-line production.

4. Hotelling represents the sequence of tasks necessary to complete the production of a product.

5. A firm uses outsourcing so that it can hire additional employees at its main local facility.

6. The term "just-in-time" refers to a schedule that illustrates the expected timing for each task within a project.

7. Inventories of partially completed products are called work-in-process.

8. The critical path is the path that takes the shortest time to complete on a PERT diagram.

9. Quality control can be measured by assessing the various characteristics that enhance customer satisfaction.

10. Downsizing has enabled firms to reduce the amount of salary expense required.

## Multiple Choice

11. The goal of _____ is to develop an efficient, high-quality process for producing products or services.
    a) conversion management
    b) assembly-line control
    c) flexible manufacturing
    d) production management
    e) routing

12. A _____ represents a series of tasks in which resources are used to produce a product or service.
    a) layout chart
    b) Venn diagram
    c) organization chart
    d) production process
    e) chain of command

13. A sequence of work stations in which each work station is designed to cover specific phases of the production process is called a(n):
    a) assembly line.
    b) hotelling.
    c) deintegration.
    d) product location.
    e) Gantt chart.

14. The factors that affect a site decision include all of the following except:
    a) cost of workplace space.
    b) tax incentives.
    c) source of demand.
    d) access to transportation.
    e) quality assurance.

15. Once a site for the manufacturing plant is chosen, the next step to be determined is:
    a) design and layout.
    b) production control.
    c) hotelling.
    d) deintegration.
    e) inventory control.

16. Design and layout decisions are influenced by all of the following characteristics except the:
    a) production process.
    b) desired production capacity.
    c) product line.
    d) purchasing applications.
    e) site.

17. Which of the following production processes is most commonly used for assembly-line production?
    a) flexible manufacturing
    b) fixed-position layout
    c) product layout
    d) capacity layout
    e) cost-benefit layout

18. A production process where employees go to the position of the product, rather than waiting for the product to come to them, is a(n):
    a) assembly line.
    b) batch process.
    c) fixed-position layout.
    d) unit production process.
    e) mass production process.

19. Firms are forced to search for new sites once demand for their product exceeds their:
    a) quality control.
    b) production capacity.
    c) inspection requirements.
    d) routing schedules.
    e) purchase plans.

20. The development of temporary, shared office space for those employees who normally work at home is called:
    a) flexible manufacturing.
    b) deintegration.
    c) production control.
    d) hotelling.
    e) quality control.

21. All of the following are key tasks in production control except:
    a) layout and design.
    b) inventory control.
    c) routing.
    d) scheduling.
    e) quality control.

22. A system that attempts to reduce material inventories to a bare minimum by frequently ordering small amounts of materials from suppliers is called:
    a) routing.
    b) just-in-time.
    c) scheduling.
    d) quality control.
    e) deintegration.

23. The process of managing inventory at a level that minimizes costs is called:
    a) scheduling.
    b) routing.
    c) dispatching.
    d) production planning.
    e) inventory control.

24. Firms attempt to minimize the amount of inventory they have in order to reduce their:
    a) purchasing costs.
    b) production costs.
    c) carrying costs.
    d) quality control.
    e) human resources.

25. The sequence of tasks necessary to complete the production of a product is:
    a) dispatching.
    b) quality control.
    c) purchasing.
    d) routing.
    e) deintegration.

26. To minimize delays, the tasks that are part of the _____ are reviewed.
    a) purchasing applications
    b) Gantt chart
    c) critical path
    d) raw material inventory
    e) hotelling

27. Which of the following terms describes the process of monitoring the characteristics of a product to ensure that the firm's standards are met?
    a) expectation downsizing
    b) quality control
    c) critical path management
    d) program evaluation and review technique
    e) work-in-process control

28. A method of evaluating performance by comparison to some specified level, usually a level set by another company, is called:
    a) cost control.
    b) total quality management.
    c) targeting.
    d) benchmarking.
    e) goal setting.

29. The revision of the production process in an attempt to improve efficiency is called:
    a) restructuring.
    b) realignment.
    c) reintegration.
    d) downsizing.
    e) reengineering.

30. The supply chain is:
    a) the flow of inventory from raw materials to finished goods.
    b) the outsourcing process from supplier to firm.
    c) the marketing process from concept to consumption.
    d) the production process from beginning to consumer purchase.
    e) the conversion of resources to a product or service.

| True/False | | Multiple Choice | | |
|---|---|---|---|---|
| 1. True | 8. False | 11. d | 18. c | 25. d |
| 2. True | 9. True | 12. d | 19. b | 26. c |
| 3. False | 10. True | 13. a | 20. d | 27. b |
| 4. False | | 14. e | 21. a | 28. d |
| 5. False | | 15. a | 22. b | 29. a |
| 6. False | | 16. d | 23. e | 30. d |
| 7. True | | 17. c | 24. c | |

# Self-Test of Key Terms

assembly line   283
automated   301
benchmarking   301
break-even point   304
carrying costs   291
conversion process   282
corporate anorexia   305
critical path   294
deintegration   290
design   287
downsizing   305
economies of scale   302
fixed costs   302
fixed-position layout   287
flexible manufacturing   287
Gantt chart   294
hotelling   288

inventory control   291
just-in-time (JIT)   291
just-in-time office   288
layout   287
materials requirements
    planning (MRP)   291
operations management   282
order costs   291
outsourcing   290
product layout   287
production control   288
production efficiency   301
production management   282
production process   282
production schedule   292
program evaluation and review
    technique (PERT)   294

quality   296
quality control   296
quality control circle   298
reengineering   305
restructuring   304
routing   292
sampling   298
scheduling   292
stretch targets   301
supply chain   305
total quality management (TQM)
    296
variable costs   302
work-in-process inventories   291
work station   283

Fill in each blank with the proper key term. To assess your understanding of the key terms, answers are provided at the end of this self-test.

1. _____ is the sequence of tasks necessary to complete the production of a product.

2. _____ is the redesign of a firm's organizational structure and operations.

3. _____ involves randomly selecting some of the products produced and testing them.

4. The _____ indicates the size and structure of the plant or office.

5. The _____ is the process from the very beginning of the production process until the product reaches the consumer.

6. With _____, firms can adjust their production to accommodate future revisions.

7. _____ refers to the use of temporary office space by employees who normally work at home, but sometimes work at the firm's office.

8. _____ is the process in which a firm purchases parts from suppliers rather than producing its own parts.

9. The strategy of delegating some production tasks to suppliers is referred to as _____.

10. _____ represent the costs of maintaining inventories.

11. The _____ layout positions the tasks in the sequence that they are assigned.

12. _____ is a process for ensuring that the materials are available when needed.

13. A(n) _____ is an area in which one or more employees are assigned a specific task.

14. The _____ illustrates the expected timing for each task.

15. The _____ path is used to estimate slack time and identify inefficiencies in the production process.

16. In a(n) _____ layout, the employees go to the product to conduct their tasks.

17. _____ targets are production efficiency goals that cannot be achieved under present conditions.

18. Operating expenses that stay constant regardless of the number of products produced are called

_____.

19. A(n) _____ consists of a sequence of work stations in which each work station is designed to cover specific phases of the production process.

20. The _____ is the arrangement of machinery and equipment in the factory or office.

**Answers:**

1. Routing
2. Reengineering
3. Sampling
4. design
5. supply chain
6. flexible manufacturing
7. Hotelling
8. Outsourcing
9. deintegration
10. Carrying costs

11. product
12. Materials requirements planning
13. work station
14. Gantt chart
15. critical
16. fixed-position
17. Stretch
18. fixed costs
19. assembly line
20. layout

# Concept Review Questions

1. **Impact of Production Process on Value.** Explain why management of the production process can have a major impact on the valuation of a business.

2. **Resources.** Describe the resources used in the production process.

3. **Combining Resources.** Explain the use of work stations and assembly lines for combining resources.

4. **Site Location.** Explain the factors that should be considered in the site location decision.

5. **Production Layout.** Explain the common forms of layout in the production process.

6. **Delegating Production.** Explain how some firms may delegate a portion of the production process to suppliers.

7. **Materials Management.** Explain the tradeoff involved when managing the inventory of materials.

8. **PERT.** Explain the role of the program evaluation and review technique (PERT) in the production process.

9. **Quality Control.** Explain common methods used by managers to assess quality control.

10. **Production Efficiency.** Explain the common methods used to improve production efficiency.

# Class Communication Questions

1. **Managing Machinery versus People.** Do you think it is more difficult to manage an assembly line that relies heavily on machinery or on human resources?

2. **Tax Incentives for a Production Plant.** Would your city benefit from providing more tax incentives to attract new production plants? Or do you think these new tax incentives would be unfair to the existing businesses that are not able to benefit from the new incentives?

(Assume that your city cannot afford to offer tax incentives to all existing businesses.)

3. **Quality Control Issue.** Is quality control more important for a business that produces products or services?

# Small Business Case

## Production Decisions

Cell One Company must decide on the proper combination of resources to use for its production of its cell phones. When it developed its business, it initially used human resources for most of its production process. Now it relies more heavily on machinery for various phases of the production process in order to reduce its operating expenses. Advances in technology now allow some phases of the production process to be completed more efficiently by machines than by human resources. The human resources who were previously assigned to those production tasks have been reassigned to other jobs.

1. **Impact of Technology.** Some employees believe that Cell One Company should not use technology because then it could hire more employees to perform the tasks and this would improve employee morale and provide more jobs for unemployed people. Do you agree?

2. **Production Facility Decision.** Cell One Company has its production facility in Los Angeles, California. Explain why the cost of production is higher in Los Angeles than in smaller towns. What is an advantage of having a production facility in a big city such as Los Angeles?

3. **Decision to Allow Employees to Work at Home.** Cell One Company pays a very a high rent for its offices next to the production facility in Los Angeles. It wants to reduce office space and will let many of its office employees work at home. It will change the design of its offices so that any employees who need to be at the office can use whatever offices are available, and a specific office will not be designated to any employee. Is there a possible disadvantage of letting its employees work from home?

4. **Use of Quality Control.** Cell One Company pays close attention to quality control. It uses various machines to ensure that the cell phones it produces are made to fit the production specifications. Do you think this form of quality control will be ideal for detecting customer dissatisfaction?

# Web Insight

## Production at the MTV Network

At the opening of the chapter, the MTV network (owned by Viacom) was introduced. Go to the website (www.mtv.com) and review the types of television shows that MTV produces. What do you think are the key resources that are needed by the MTV network to create a TV show? How can the MTV network properly control its production to ensure that it produces quality programming?

# Dell's Secret for Success

Go to Dell's website (www.dell.com) and click on the link "About Dell" near the bottom of the web page. Review information about Dell's production quality. You can also review a recent annual report of Dell for more information.

1. **Quality Goals.** Describe Dell's goals regarding quality.

2. **Quality Monitoring.** How does Dell monitor quality?

3. **Quality Control.** How does customer satisfaction relate to Dell's quality control?

# Video Exercise

## Lessons in Production Quality

Many free business videos are available on websites such as YouTube (www.youtube.com), and more are added every day. Search for a recent video clip about an existing business that offers lessons on "production quality" in YouTube or any other website that provides video clips.

1. **Main Lesson.** What is the name of the business in the video clip?

Is the video clip focused on the use of technology for production, the quality control process, the customer satisfaction, or some other aspect of production quality? What is the main lesson of the video clip that you watched?

2. **Assessing Quality.** Some videos suggest that production quality begins with an understanding of customer preferences. Explain this point.

3. **Motives for Outsourcing.** Some related videos explain how outsourcing is necessary for the business to survive. Why do you think some businesses rely heavily on outsourcing?

# Projects

To encourage further comprehension of concepts covered in Chapter 9, the following five projects are available:

1. Analyzing Your Favorite Business
2. Building a Business Plan for Campus.com
3. Running Your Own Business
4. Planning Your Career
5. Stock Market Contest

All of these projects are provided in Appendix A at the end of the text. In addition, projects are available by part division at the end of each part.

A Word file for each project is also available at the textbook website (www.emcp.net/business5e) so that you may maintain one ongoing file for each project.

# Management

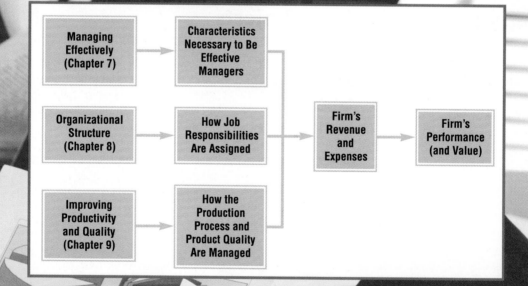

| Managing Effectively (Chapter 7) | → | Characteristics Necessary to Be Effective Managers |
| Organizational Structure (Chapter 8) | → | How Job Responsibilities Are Assigned | → | Firm's Revenue and Expenses | → | Firm's Performance (and Value) |
| Improving Productivity and Quality (Chapter 9) | → | How the Production Process and Product Quality Are Managed |

# Summary

Chapter 7 explains the key functions of management, while Chapter 8 applies management to the business organization and Chapter 9 applies management to the production process. In general, a business needs the management skills described in Chapter 8 to make the proper decisions, and an efficient organizational structure and production process to limit its expenses.

# Video on Managing a Business

## Managing for Success

The Small Business Administration plays a very important role in helping many small businesses. Its website, which offers a wide range of services and information for small businesses, has a section called Delivering Success (www.sba.gov/tools/audiovideo/deliveringsuccess/index.html) that provides video clips of small business success stories. Go to this website, and watch the video called "Top 10 Business Tips" (total time of clip is 4 minutes, 30 seconds).

Some of the tips discussed in this video clip are related to the key management concepts covered in this part of the text, as discussed below:

◆ Businesses need to hire good employees. If entrepreneurs have good employees, they can empower their employees with various responsibilities. This allows entrepreneurs more time to focus on the most important business decisions.

◆ Businesses need to keep their mission in mind when making their decisions; this will allow them to make decisions that are consistent with their ultimate goals.

◆ Businesses need to plan for the future. Business decisions today should be made with consideration to their impact in the future.

◆ Businesses should have goals, and these goals should be written down so that they can be documented. The goals can be separated into short-term goals and long-term goals.

Some of the desirable characteristics of managers (described in Chapter 7) are very similar to these characteristics of a successful business. The personality of the business reflects the personality of its managers.

1. **Impact of Management Skills on the Organization Chart.** Explain how effective planning, organizational, and leadership skills (Chapter 7) could affect the organization chart (Chapter 8) of a business.

2. **Impact of Planning Skills on Production Quality.** Explain how effective planning skills (Chapter 7) could affect the production quality (Chapter 9) of a business.

3. **Impact of Organizational Structure on Production Quality.** Explain how the organizational structure (Chapter 8) could affect the quality control process (Chapter 9).

# Self-Test for Part III

**Chapters 7–9.** Answers are provided at the end of the self-test.

1. The position of chief financial officer is considered to be a:
   a) supervisory position.
   b) top-management position.
   c) first-line management position.
   d) bottom-line position.
   e) middle-management position.

2. Middle- and high-level managers engage in short-term, small-scale plans that are consistent with the firm's strategic plan. These short-term, smaller-scale plans are known as:
   a) tactical plans.
   b) mission statements.
   c) leadership plans.
   d) bottom-up plans.
   e) contingency plans.

3. All of the following are typical goals that the management function can help to achieve except:
   a) high production efficiency.
   b) high production quality.
   c) limited competition.
   d) customer satisfaction.
   e) employee satisfaction.

4. Business firms develop and enforce _____ to prevent employees from conducting tasks in an inefficient, dangerous, or illegal manner.
   a) kickbacks
   b) reciprocity
   c) policies
   d) time management
   e) prioritizing tasks

5. The leading function of management should be conducted in a manner that is consistent with the firm's:
   a) competition.
   b) strategic plan.
   c) customers.
   d) industry demands.
   e) labor union.

6. The style of leadership that is the opposite extreme of the autocratic style is:
   a) free-rein.
   b) authoritative.
   c) manipulative.
   d) boss-centered.
   e) commanding.

7. The function of management that evaluates employee performance in comparison with established standards is:
   a) planning.
   b) controlling.
   c) organizing.
   d) leading.
   e) time management.

8. Using existing information, managers need _____ to determine how the firm's resources should be allocated.
   a) micro-skills
   b) interpersonal skills
   c) technical skills
   d) decision-making skills
   e) autocratic management skills

9. All of the following guidelines should be followed when using time management except:
   a) setting proper priorities.
   b) centralizing responsibility.
   c) scheduling long intervals of time for large tasks.
   d) minimizing interruptions.
   e) delegating some tasks to employees.

10. A manager faced with a large task that will take more than one day to complete should:
    a) demand help from other employees.
    b) take frequent breaks to refresh his/her concentration.
    c) retain sole responsibility for the project.
    d) set short-term goals.
    e) automatically assign the project top priority.

11. The responsibilities of a firm's managers should be organized to achieve the:
    a) grapevine.
    b) formal contingency.
    c) strategic plan.
    d) chain of command.
    e) bureaucratic organization.

12. The _____ for a firm identifies the job position to which each type of employee must report.
    a) chain of command
    b) job matrix
    c) staffing chart
    d) flow chart
    e) informal structure

13. The outside members of the board of directors of a company are those directors who:
    a) live outside the state in which the corporation received its charter.
    b) are not managers of the firm.
    c) are not stockholders in the firm.
    d) serve on the board without direct compensation.
    e) were appointed by the president of the firm rather than selected by the firm's stockholders.

14. The _____ refers to the number of employees managed by each manager.
    a) scope of authority
    b) management ratio
    c) employee limit
    d) span of control
    e) manager-employee multiplier

15. The _____ ensures that all departments follow the firm's guidelines and procedures.
    a) CEO
    b) internal auditor
    c) board of directors
    d) project manager
    e) inside director

16. The strategy of spreading authority among several divisions or managers is called:
    a) centralization.
    b) decentralization.
    c) decision rationing.
    d) abdication of authority.
    e) adjudication of authority.

17. A possible disadvantage of decentralization is that it:
    a) may require inexperienced managers to make major decisions they are not qualified to make.
    b) usually increases the firm's operating expenses.
    c) slows down the decision-making process.
    d) harms employees' motivation by forcing them to take on more responsibilities.
    e) prevents employees from making creative decisions.

18. Employees who serve in _____ positions provide assistance and support to employees who serve in line positions.
    a) secondary
    b) nominal
    c) reserve
    d) nonlinear
    e) staff

19. Firms use a(n) _____ organization to allow the various parts of a firm to interact as they focus on a particular project.
    a) matrix
    b) quasi-linear
    c) tabular
    d) extracurricular
    e) cellular

20. Firms are commonly departmentalized by all of the following except:
    a) function.
    b) product.
    c) customer.
    d) time period.
    e) location.

21. The goal of _____ is to develop an efficient, high-quality process for producing products or services.
    a) conversion management
    b) assembly-line control
    c) flexible manufacturing
    d) production management
    e) routing

22. A sequence of work stations in which each work station is designed to cover specific phases of the production process is called a(n):
    a) assembly line.
    b) hotelling.
    c) deintegration.
    d) product location.
    e) Gantt chart.

23. Once a site for the manufacturing plant is chosen, the next step to be determined is:
    a) design and layout.
    b) production control.
    c) hotelling.
    d) deintegration.
    e) inventory control.

24. Which of the following production processes is most commonly used for assembly-line production?
    a) flexible manufacturing
    b) fixed-position layout
    c) product layout
    d) capacity layout
    e) cost-benefit layout

25. Firms are forced to search for new sites once demand for their product exceeds their:
    a) quality control.
    b) production capacity.
    c) inspection requirements.
    d) routing schedules.
    e) purchase plans.

26. All of the following are key tasks in production control except:
    a) layout and design.
    b) inventory control.
    c) routing.
    d) scheduling.
    e) quality control.

27. The process of managing inventory at a level that minimizes costs is called:
    a) scheduling.
    b) routing.
    c) dispatching.
    d) production planning.
    e) inventory control.

28. The sequence of tasks necessary to complete the production of a product is:
    a) dispatching.
    b) quality control.
    c) purchasing.
    d) routing.
    e) deintegration.

29. Which of the following terms describes the process of monitoring the characteristics of a product to ensure that the firm's standards are met?
    a) expectation downsizing
    b) quality control
    c) critical path management
    d) program evaluation and review technique
    e) work-in-process control

30. The revision of the production process in an attempt to improve efficiency is called:
    a) restructuring.
    b) realignment.
    c) reintegration.
    d) downsizing.
    e) reengineering.

**Answers:**

| | | | | | |
|---|---|---|---|---|---|
| 1. b | 6. a | 11. c | 16. b | 21. d | 26. b |
| 2. a | 7. b | 12. a | 17. a | 22. a | 27. e |
| 3. c | 8. d | 13. b | 18. e | 23. a | 28. d |
| 4. c | 9. b | 14. d | 19. a | 24. c | 29. b |
| 5. b | 10. d | 15. b | 20. d | 25. b | 30. a |

# Projects

## PROJECT 1: ANALYZING YOUR FAVORITE BUSINESS

**Answering the Questions.** This entire project is provided in Appendix A. You can retrieve the Word file of this project from the textbook website (www.emcp.net/business5e), and insert your answer just below each question. The portion of the project that is related to the chapters in this part is provided here.

Using the annual report of the firm you selected, answer the following questions:

**Firm's Mission (related to Chapter 7).** What is the firm's mission?

**Firm's Strategic Plan (related to Chapter 7).** What is the firm's strategic plan?

**Firm's Organizational Structure (related to Chapter 8).** Briefly describe the firm's organizational structure. For example, does it appear to have many high-level managers?

**Firm's Production (related to Chapter 9).** Where are the firm's production facilities located? Have the operations been restructured to reduce expenses recently? What does the firm say about quality control in its annual report?

## PROJECT 2: BUILDING A BUSINESS PLAN FOR CAMPUS.COM

**Completing the Information.** You can complete the information on the Word file of this project from the textbook website (www.emcp.net/business5e). This allows you to insert all of your information on one file for this project by the end of the school term. The portion of the project that is related to the chapters in this part is provided here.

**Managing Effectively (related to Chapter 7).** The strategic plan for Campus.com is:

_____

_____

The tactical plans for Campus.com are:

_____

_____

_____

**Organizational Structure (related to Chapter 8).** Job positions required for Campus.com are:

_____

_____

_____

_____

_____

**Improving Productivity and Quality (related to Chapter 9).** The production process to produce Campus.com's service is:

_____

_____

_____

_____

The production process will be monitored (and possibly revised) over time, as explained here:

_____

_____

_____

_____

_____

**Quality Standards (related to Chapter 9).** Campus.com will maintain the quality of the service it provides by:

_____

_____

_____

_____

## PROJECT 3: RUNNING YOUR OWN BUSINESS

**Completing the Information.**
This entire project is provided in
Appendix A. You can retrieve the
Word file of this project from the
textbook website (www.emcp.net
/business5e), and insert your
answer just below each question.
The portion of the project that is
related to the chapters in this part is
provided here.

**Managing Effectively (related to
Chapter 7).** The strategic plan for
your business is:

_____

_____

The tactical plans for your business
are:

_____

_____

_____

**Organizational Structure
(related to Chapter 8).** Job positions required for your business are:

_____

_____

_____

_____

_____

_____

**Improving Productivity and
Quality (related to Chapter 9).**
The production process to produce
your products or services is:

_____

_____

_____

_____

_____

Your production process will be
monitored (and possibly revised)
over time, as explained here:

_____

_____

_____

_____

_____

**Quality Standards (related to
Chapter 9).** Your business will
maintain the quality of the service it
provides by:

_____

_____

_____

_____

_____

## PROJECT 4: PLANNING YOUR CAREER

This entire project is provided in Appendix A at the end of the text, and
you can access a Word file of this
project from the textbook website
(www.emcp.net/business5e), and
insert your answer just below each
question.

If you are very interested in the
topics covered in this section, you
may want to consider a major in
management. Some of the courses
commonly taken by management
majors are summarized here.

### Common Courses for Manage-
ment Majors

• **Organizational Behavior** Provides a broad overview of key managerial functions, such as organizing,
motivating employees, planning,
controlling, and teamwork.

• **Management Environment**
Focuses on the environment in
which managers work and the re-

sponsibilities of managers to society
and to regulators.

• **Human Resource Management** Focuses on the processes of
hiring, training, evaluating performance, and compensating
employees.

• **Labor Relations** Examines the
labor contract relationships among
managers, subordinates, and
unions; also covers the process of
negotiating.

• **Management Strategy** Focuses
on the competitive environment
faced by a firm and strategies used
by a firm's managers to increase its
growth or improve its performance.

• **Management Systems** Focuses
on the use of computer software and
systems to facilitate decision making.

• **Entrepreneurship** Deals with
the creation of business ideas,

methods of growing a small
business, and the challenges of
competing with larger firms.

• **Operations Management**
Examines the resources used in the
production process, the plant site
and layout decisions, alternative
production processes, and quality
control.

### Careers in Management

Information about job positions,
salaries, and careers for students
who major in management can be
found at the following websites:

• **Job position websites:**

**http://jobsearch.monster.com**
Administrative and Support Ser-
vices, Consulting Services, Human
Resources, Manufacturing, and
Production.

**http://careers.yahoo.com**
Management Consulting, Management Operations, Retail, Restaurant/ Food Service, Technology, and Transportation.

- **Salary website:**

**http://collegejournal.com /salarydata** Consulting, Hotel and Restaurant Management, Human

Resources, Logistics, Manufacturing, and Retailing.

## PROJECT 5: STOCK MARKET CONTEST

This entire project is provided in Appendix A at the end of the text, and you can access a Word file of the project from the textbook website (www.emcp.net/business5e). Your instructor may ask you to assess the performance of your investment up to this point, and whether the performance of your stock is attributed to any of the business concepts that were described in the chapters contained in this part.

# Part IV
# Managing Employees

Whereas Part III focused on organizational structure and production, Part IV focuses on human resources (employees), another critical component of management. Part IV contains two chapters that explain how managers can improve the performance of their employees. Chapter 10 describes the methods that can be used to motivate employees. Motivation may be necessary for many employees to perform well. To the extent that managers can effectively motivate employees, they can improve the performance of employees and therefore increase the performance of the firm.

Chapter 11 explains the proper methods for hiring, training, and evaluating the performance of employees. Proper hiring methods ensure that employees have the right background for the types of jobs they may be assigned. Proper training enables employees to apply their skills to perform specific tasks. Proper evaluation methods ensure that employees are rewarded when they perform well and that they are informed of any deficiencies so that they can correct them in the future. If managers can use these methods effectively, they should be able to improve the firm's performance.

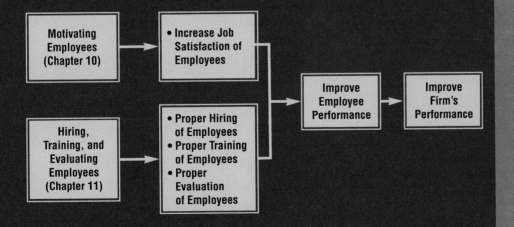

# Motivating Employees

## Chapter 10 Learning Objectives

**1** Explain how motivating employees can increase the value of a firm.

**2** Describe the theories on motivation.

**3** Discuss how a firm can motivate disgruntled employees.

**4** Explain how a firm can improve employee motivation.

## Motivating Employees at Google

A firm has a strategic plan that identifies opportunities and indicates the future direction of the firm's business. When the firm develops strategies to achieve the strategic plan, it relies on its employees to execute strategies that work. A pleasant work environment can motivate employees to work harder. Consider the situation of Google, which has experienced great success with its search engine service. To encourage employee interaction and creativity, Google's headquarters (called the Googleplex) in Menlo Park, California, has space where employees can work together. The Googleplex has a café for its employees, referred to as Charlie's café, which encourages social interaction among employees. It also has video games, a workout room, locker rooms, and showers on site. Massage and yoga services are provided at the Googleplex along with free snacks. Google's employees are more motivated to work because they enjoy their work environment.

Like any business that has employees, Google must address the following questions:

✦ How can it motivate employees to work hard?

✦ How can it motivate disgruntled employees?

✦ How can it improve employee motivation?

If Google can successfully motivate its employees, it benefits in two ways. First, employees who are motivated to work will be more productive. Second, Google will be able to retain employees for a longer period of time and will reduce the expenses associated with training new employees.

The types of decisions described above are necessary for all businesses. This chapter explains how a firm can motivate and satisfy employees in a manner that maximizes the firm's value.

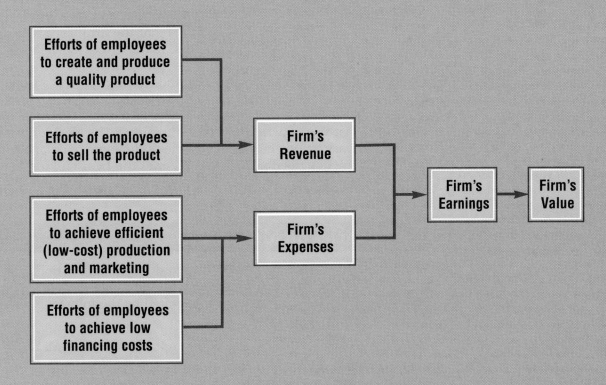

**Learning Objective**

**1**

Explain how motivating employees can increase the value of a firm.

# 1. The Value of Motivation

Many businesses are successful not just because of their business ideas, but also because of their employees. But employees need to be motivated as well as to have the proper skills to do their jobs. Employees at some firms have adequate skills for their jobs, but they lack the motivation to perform well. Consequently, these employees offer only limited help in the production process.

Some firms believe that if they can hire people who are naturally motivated, the employees will perform well in the workplace, but this will not always happen. Although some people naturally make more of an effort to perform well, they will still need a work environment that motivates them.

Consider Anna and Marie, who are equally intelligent and tend to exert the same amount of effort in the workplace. Anna and Marie are hired by two different firms in the same industry for the same type of job. They work the same number of hours and receive the same salary, but their workplaces differ as follows:

|  | **Firm A (which hires Anna)** | **Firm B (which hires Marie)** |
|---|---|---|
| Employee work interaction | Frequent | Seldom |
| Employee social interaction | Frequent | Seldom |
| Input provided by managers to employees | Frequent | Seldom |
| Input requested from employees by managers | Frequent | Seldom |

Given these conditions, Anna will be much more motivated to perform well than Marie. If Anna and Marie swap jobs, Marie will now be much more motivated than Anna. The point is that the firm has a major influence on the motivation of the employees. To the extent that a firm can motivate its employees, it can increase the productivity of each employee. Consequently, it can achieve a higher production level with a given number of employees, which results in higher profits.

How does a firm motivate its employees? There is no single motivational tool that works perfectly for all employees. The ideal form of motivation may vary among employees. Some of the more popular theories of motivation are described next. These theories can be useful for determining the advantages and limitations of various types of motivation.

**Learning Objective**

**2**

Describe the theories on motivation.

# 2. Theories on Motivation

The motivation of employees is influenced by **job satisfaction**, or the degree to which employees are satisfied with their jobs. Firms recognize the need to satisfy their employees, as illustrated by the following statements from recent annual reports:

*"You will see a greater focus on employee satisfaction . . . which will lead us to higher quality, better growth, and improved profitability."*

— Eastman Kodak

**job satisfaction**
the degree to which employees are satisfied with their jobs

*"To grow and be successful, Telecom must be able to attract, retain, and motivate capable employees."*

—Telecom Inc.

Since employees who are satisfied with their jobs are more motivated, managers can motivate employees by ensuring job satisfaction. Some of the more popular theories on motivation are summarized here, followed by some general guidelines that can be used to motivate workers.

## 2.1  Hawthorne Studies

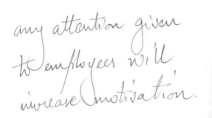

In the late 1920s, researchers studied workers in a Western Electric Plant near Chicago to identify how a variety of conditions affected their level of production. When the lighting was increased, the production level increased. Yet the production level also increased when the lighting was reduced. These workers were then subjected to various break periods; again, the production level increased for both shorter breaks and longer breaks. One interpretation of these results is that workers become more motivated when they feel that they are allowed to participate. Supervisors may be able to motivate workers by giving them more attention and by allowing them to participate. These Hawthorne studies, which ignited further research on motivation, are summarized in Exhibit 10.1 and suggest that human relations can affect a firm's performance.

**hierarchy of needs**
needs are ranked in five general categories. Once a given category of needs is achieved, people become motivated to reach the next category.

**physiological needs**
the basic requirements for survival

**safety needs**
job security and safe working conditions

**social needs**
the need to be part of a group

## 2.2  Maslow's Hierarchy of Needs

In 1943, Abraham Maslow, a psychologist, developed the **hierarchy of needs** theory. This theory suggests that people rank their needs into five general categories. Once they achieve a given category of needs, they become motivated to reach the next category. The categories are identified in Exhibit 10.2, with the most crucial needs on the bottom. **Physiological needs** are the basic requirements for survival, such as food and shelter. Most jobs can help achieve these needs.

Once these needs are fulfilled, **safety needs** (such as job security and safe working conditions) become the most immediate goal. Some jobs satisfy these needs. People also strive to achieve **social needs**, or the need to

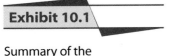

Exhibit 10.1

Summary of the Hawthorne Studies

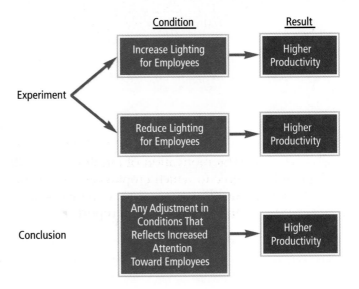

**Exhibit 10.2**

Maslow's Hierarchy of Needs

BSAES

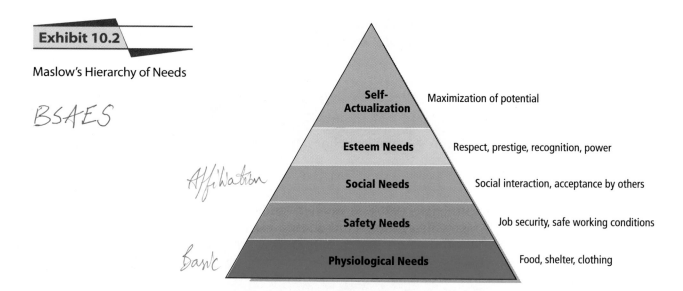

Affiliation

Basic

Self-Actualization — Maximization of potential

Esteem Needs — Respect, prestige, recognition, power

Social Needs — Social interaction, acceptance by others

Safety Needs — Job security, safe working conditions

Physiological Needs — Food, shelter, clothing

**esteem needs**
respect, prestige, and recognition

**self-actualization**
the need to fully reach one's potential

be part of a group. Some firms attempt to help employees achieve their social needs, either by grouping workers in teams or by organizing social events after work hours. People may also become motivated to achieve **esteem needs**, such as respect, prestige, and recognition. Some workers may achieve these needs by being promoted within their firms or by receiving special recognition for their work. The final category of needs is **self-actualization**, which represents the need to fully reach one's potential. For example, people may achieve self-actualization by starting and successfully running a specific business that fits their main interests.

The hierarchy of needs theory can be useful for motivating employees because it suggests that different employees may be at different places in the hierarchy. Therefore, their most immediate needs may differ. If managers can identify employees' needs, they will be better able to offer rewards that motivate employees.

## 2.3 Herzberg's Job Satisfaction Study

In the late 1950s, Frederick Herzberg surveyed 200 accountants and engineers about job satisfaction. Herzberg attempted to identify the factors that made them feel dissatisfied with their jobs at a given point in time. He also attempted to identify the factors that made them feel satisfied with their jobs. His study found the following:

**hygiene factors**
work-related factors that can fulfill basic needs and prevent job dissatisfaction

**motivational factors**
work-related factors that can lead to job satisfaction and motivate employees

| Common Factors Identified by Dissatisfied Workers | Common Factors Identified by Satisfied Workers |
|---|---|
| Working conditions | Achievement |
| Supervision | Responsibility |
| Salary | Recognition |
| Job security | Advancement |
| Status | Growth |

Employees become dissatisfied when they perceive work-related factors in the left column (called **hygiene factors**) as inadequate. Employees are commonly satisfied when the work-related factors in the right column (called **motivational factors**) are offered.

Managers commonly attempt various methods of motivating their employees, such as offering small rewards and recognition to employees who have achieved high performance (as shown here). Recognition can increase employee job satisfaction.

© SHUTTERSTOCK/YURI ARCURS

Herzberg's results suggest that factors such as working conditions and salary must be adequate to prevent workers from being dissatisfied. Yet better-than-adequate working conditions and salary will not necessarily lead to a high degree of satisfaction. Instead, a high degree of worker satisfaction is most easily achieved by offering additional benefits, such as responsibility. Thus, if managers assign workers more responsibility, they may increase worker satisfaction and motivate the workers to be more productive. Exhibit 10.3 summarizes Herzberg's job satisfaction study.

Notice how the results of Herzberg's study correspond with the results of Maslow's hierarchy. Herzberg's hygiene factors generally correspond with Maslow's basic needs (such as job security). This suggests that if hygiene factors are adequate, they fulfill some of workers' more basic needs. Fulfillment of these needs can prevent dissatisfaction as employees become

**Exhibit 10.3**

Summary of Herzberg's Job Satisfaction Study

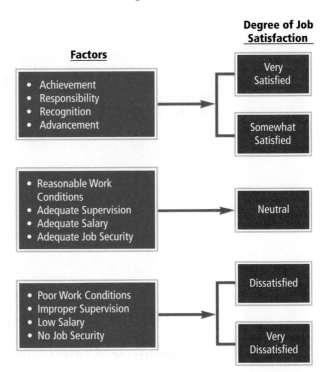

Although delegating responsibilities to employees can motivate them, delegating too much responsibility can increase their stress level (as shown here). Employees' productivity may be reduced if they know that they will not be able to complete all of their work on time regardless of how hard they try.

© SHUTTERSTOCK/VISI.STOCK

motivated to achieve a higher class of needs. Herzberg's motivational factors (such as recognition) generally correspond with Maslow's more ambitious hierarchy needs.

Several U.S. firms, including IBM, Wal-Mart, and Dell have implemented workshops to stress teamwork and company loyalty. These workshops build self-esteem by focusing on employees' worth to the company. In this way, the workshops may enable employees to achieve a higher class of needs, thereby increasing job satisfaction.

## 2.4 McGregor's Theory X and Theory Y

Another major contribution to motivation was provided by Douglas McGregor, who developed Theory X and Theory Y. Each of these theories represents supervisors' possible perception of workers. The views of Theories X and Y are summarized as follows:

| Theory X | Theory Y |
|---|---|
| Employees dislike work and job responsibilities and will avoid work if possible. | Employees are willing to work and prefer more responsibility. |

The way supervisors view employees can influence the way they treat the employees. Supervisors who believe in Theory X will likely use tight control over workers, with little or no delegation of authority. In addition, employees will be closely monitored to ensure that they perform their tasks. Conversely, supervisors who believe in Theory Y will delegate more authority because they perceive workers as responsible. These supervisors will also allow employees more opportunities to use their creativity. This management approach fulfills employees' needs to be responsible and to achieve respect and recognition. Consequently, these employees are likely to have a higher level of job satisfaction and therefore to be more motivated.

Exhibit 10.4 provides a summary of Theories X and Y. Most employees would prefer that their supervisors follow Theory Y rather than Theory X. Nevertheless, some supervisors may be unable to use Theory Y in specific situations, when they are forced to retain more authority over employees rather than delegate responsibility.

## 2.5 Theory Z

In the 1980s, a new theory on job satisfaction was developed. This theory, called Theory Z, was partially based on the Japanese style of allowing all employees to participate in decision making. Participation can increase job satisfaction because it gives employees responsibility. Job descriptions tend

**Exhibit 10.4**

Summary of McGregor's Theories X and Y

| | **Theory** | **Supervisors' View of Employees** | **Implications** |
|---|---|---|---|
| | Theory X | Employees dislike work and job responsibilities and will avoid work if possible. | Supervisors cannot delegate responsibilities. |
| | Theory Y | Employees are willing to work and prefer more responsibility. | Supervisors should delegate responsibilities, which will satisfy and motivate employees. |

to be less specialized, so employees develop varied skills and have a more flexible career path. To increase job satisfaction, many U.S. firms have begun to allow employees more responsibility.

## 2.6  Expectancy Theory

**expectancy theory**

holds that an employee's efforts are influenced by the expected outcome (reward) for those efforts

**Expectancy theory** suggests that an employee's efforts are influenced by the expected outcome (reward) for those efforts. Therefore, employees will be more motivated to achieve goals if they are achievable and offer some reward.

As an example, consider a firm that offers the salesperson who achieves the highest volume of annual sales a one-week vacation in Paris. This type of reward will motivate employees only if two requirements are fulfilled. First, the reward must be desirable to employees. Second, employees must believe they have a chance to earn the reward. If the firm employs 1,000 salespeople, and only one reward is offered, employees may not be motivated because they may perceive that they have little chance of being the top salesperson. Motivation may be absent even in smaller groups if all employees expect that a particular salesperson will generate the highest sales volume.

Motivational rewards are more difficult to offer for jobs where output cannot easily be measured. For example, employees who repair the firm's machinery or respond to customer complaints do not contribute to the firm in a manner that can be easily measured or compared with other employees. Nevertheless, their performance may still be measured by customer satisfaction surveys or by various other performance indicators.

## 2.7  Equity Theory

**equity theory**

suggests that compensation should be equitable, or in proportion to each employee's contribution

The **equity theory** of motivation suggests that compensation should be equitable, or in proportion to each employee's contribution. As an example, consider a firm with three employees: Employee 1 contributes 50 percent of the total output, Employee 2 contributes 30 percent, and Employee 3 contributes 20 percent. Assume that the firm plans to allocate $100,000 in bonuses based on the relative contributions of each employee. Using the equity theory, the $100,000 would be allocated as shown in Exhibit 10.5.

If employees believe that they are undercompensated, they may request greater compensation. If their compensation is not increased, employees may reduce their contribution. Equity theory emphasizes that employees can become dissatisfied with their jobs if they believe that they are not equitably compensated.

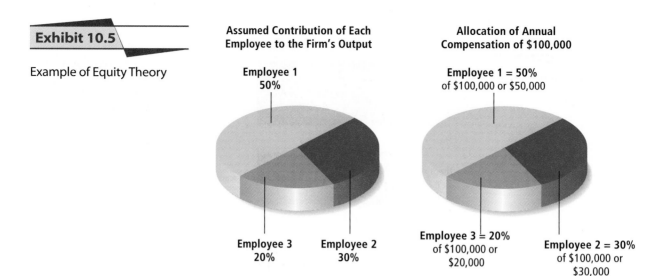

**Exhibit 10.5**

Example of Equity Theory

**Assumed Contribution of Each Employee to the Firm's Output**

Employee 1
50%

Employee 3
20%

Employee 2
30%

**Allocation of Annual Compensation of $100,000**

Employee 1 = 50%
of $100,000 or $50,000

Employee 3 = 20%
of $100,000 or
$20,000

Employee 2 = 30%
of $100,000 or
$30,000

Supervisors may prevent job dissatisfaction by attempting to provide equitable compensation. A problem, however, is that the supervisor's perception of an employee's contribution may differ from that of the employee. If a firm can define how employee contributions will be measured and compensate accordingly, its employees will be better satisfied and more motivated.

## 2.8 Reinforcement Theory

**reinforcement theory**
suggests that reinforcement can influence behavior

**positive reinforcement**
motivates employees by providing rewards for high performance

**negative reinforcement**
motivates employees by encouraging them to behave in a manner that avoids unfavorable consequences

**Reinforcement theory**, summarized in Exhibit 10.6, suggests that reinforcement can influence behavior. **Positive reinforcement** motivates employees by providing rewards for high performance. The rewards can range from an oral compliment to a promotion or large bonus. Employees may react differently to various forms of positive reinforcement. The more they appreciate the form of reinforcement, the more they will be motivated to continue high performance.

**Negative reinforcement** motivates employees by encouraging them to behave in a manner that avoids unfavorable consequences. For example, employees may be motivated to complete their assignments today to avoid having to admit the delay in a group meeting or to avoid negative evaluations by their supervisors.

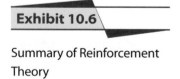

**Exhibit 10.6**

Summary of Reinforcement Theory

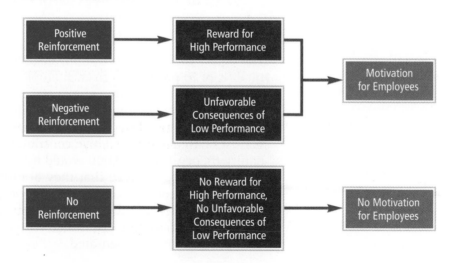

# Self-Scoring Exercises

## The Frazzle Factor

Read each of the following statements and rate yourself on a scale of 0 to 3, giving the answer that best describes how you generally feel (3 points for always, 2 points for often, 1 point for sometimes, and 0 points for never). Answer as honestly as you can, and do not spend too much time on any one statement.

### Am I Angry?

_____ 1. I feel that people around me make too many irritating mistakes.

_____ 2. I feel annoyed because I do good work or perform well in school, but no one appreciates it.

_____ 3. When people make me angry, I tell them off.

_____ 4. When I am angry, I say things I know will hurt people.

_____ 5. I lose my temper easily.

_____ 6. I feel like striking out at someone who angers me.

_____ 7. When a co-worker or fellow student makes a mistake, I tell him or her about it.

_____ 8. I cannot stand being criticized in public.

### Am I Overstressed?

_____ 1. I have to make important snap judgments and decisions.

_____ 2. I am not consulted about what happens on my job or in my classes.

_____ 3. I feel I am underpaid.

_____ 4. I feel that no matter how hard I work, the system will mess it up.

_____ 5. I do not get along with some of my co-workers or fellow students.

_____ 6. I do not trust my superiors at work or my professors at school.

_____ 7. The paperwork burden on my job or at school is getting to me.

_____ 8. I feel people outside the job or the university do not respect what I do.

To find your level of anger and potential for aggressive behavior, add your scores from both quiz parts.

40–48: The red flag is waving, and you had better pay attention. You are in the danger zone. You need guidance from a counselor or mental health professional, and you should be getting it now.

30–39: The yellow flag is up. Your stress and anger levels are too high, and you are feeling increasingly hostile. You are still in control, but it would not take much to trigger a violent flare of temper.

10–29: Relax, you are in the broad normal range. Like most people, you get angry occasionally, but usually with some justification. Sometimes you take overt action, but you are not likely to be unreasonably or excessively aggressive.

0–9: Congratulations! You are in great shape. Your stress and anger are well under control, giving you a laid-back personality not prone to violence.

Various forms of negative reinforcement can be used, ranging from a reprimand to job termination. Some supervisors may prefer to consistently offer positive reinforcement for high performance rather than penalize for poor performance. However, offering positive reinforcement for all tasks that are adequately completed may be difficult. Furthermore, if an employee who has performed poorly is not given negative reinforcement, others may think that employee was given preferential treatment, and their general performance may decline as a result.

## 2.9 Motivational Guidelines Offered by Theories

If supervisors can increase employees' job satisfaction, they may motivate employees to be more productive. All of the theories on motivation are briefly summarized in Exhibit 10.7. Based on these theories, some general conclusions can be offered on motivating employees and providing job satisfaction.

**Comparing Compensation to Contribution**   Employees commonly compare their compensation and perceived contribution with others. To prevent job dissatisfaction, supervisors should ensure that employees are compensated for their contributions.

**Other Needs**   Even if employees are offered high compensation, they will not necessarily be very satisfied. They have other needs as well, such as social needs, responsibility, and self-esteem. Jobs that can fulfill these needs may provide satisfaction and therefore provide motivation.

**Motivation Tied to Rewards**   Employees may be motivated if they believe that it is possible to achieve a performance level that will result in a desirable reward.

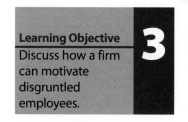

**Learning Objective**
Discuss how a firm can motivate disgruntled employees.

**3**

**Exhibit 10.7**

Comparison of Motivation Theories

# 3. Motivating Disgruntled Employees

A firm may not be able to motivate some employees, regardless of its efforts or the methods used to motivate them. If no form of motivation is effective, the threat of being fired may be used as a last resort to motivate

| Theory | Implications |
|---|---|
| Theory developed from Hawthorne studies | Workers can be motivated by attention. |
| Maslow's hierarchy of needs | Needs of workers vary, and managers can motivate workers to achieve these needs. |
| Herzberg's job satisfaction study | Compensation, reasonable working conditions, and other factors do not ensure job satisfaction but only prevent job dissatisfaction. Thus, other factors (such as responsibility) may be necessary to motivate workers. |
| McGregor's Theory X and Theory Y | Based on Theory X, workers will avoid work if possible and cannot accept responsibility. Based on Theory Y, workers are willing to work and prefer more responsibility. If Theory Y exists, managers can motivate workers by delegating responsibility. |
| Theory Z | Workers are motivated when they are allowed to participate in decision making. |
| Expectancy theory | Workers are motivated if potential rewards for high performance are desirable and achievable. |
| Equity theory | Workers are motivated if they are being compensated in accordance with their perceived contribution to the firm. |
| Reinforcement theory | Good behavior should be positively reinforced and poor behavior should be negatively reinforced to motivate workers in the future. |

these employees. If firms do not discipline disgruntled employees who are performing poorly, other employees will lose their enthusiasm, especially if they have to cover the work assignments that the disgruntled employees neglect.

If the disgruntled employees are not motivated, they may seek employment elsewhere, which would be beneficial to the firm. However, they may realize that they will be disgruntled wherever they work, and therefore decide not to quit, especially if they can avoid doing their work assignments. Firms should force disgruntled employees to do their jobs and should fire them if they are unwilling to perform, so their bad attitude will not have a negative effect on other employees.

## 4. How Firms Can Improve Employee Motivation

**Learning Objective**

**4**

Explain how a firm can improve employee motivation.

Many of the theories on motivation suggest that firms can motivate employees to perform well by ensuring job satisfaction. In general, the key characteristics that affect job satisfaction are money, security, work schedule, and involvement at work. To motivate employees, firms provide **job enrichment programs**, or programs designed to increase the job satisfaction of employees. The following are some of the more popular job enrichment programs:

**job enrichment programs**
programs designed to increase the job satisfaction of employees

✦ Adequate compensation program

✦ Job security

✦ Flexible work schedule

✦ Employee involvement programs

To the extent that firms can offer these job enrichment programs to employees, they may be able to motivate employees. Each program is discussed in turn.

### 4.1 Adequate Compensation Program

Firms can attempt to satisfy employees by offering adequate compensation for the work involved. However, adequate compensation will not necessarily motivate employees to make their best effort. Therefore, firms may attempt to ensure that those employees with the highest performance each year receive the highest percentage raises.

**merit system**
a compensation system that allocates raises according to performance (merit)

A **merit system** allocates raises according to performance (merit). For example, a firm may decide to give its employees an average raise of 5 percent, but poorly performing employees may receive 0 percent while the highest performing employees receive 10 percent. This system provides positive reinforcement for employees who have performed well and punishment for those who have performed poorly. A merit system is normally more effective than the alternative **across-the-board system**, in which all employees receive a similar raise. The across-the-board system provides no motivation because the raise is unrelated to employee performance.

**across-the-board system**
a compensation system that allocates similar raises to all employees

**incentive plans**
provide employees with various forms of compensation if they meet specific performance goals

Firms may attempt to reinforce excellent employee performance with other rewards as well as raises. **Incentive plans** provide employees with various forms of compensation if they meet specific performance goals. For example, a firm may offer a weekly or monthly bonus based on the number of components an employee produced or the dollar value of all products an employee sold to customers.

**Examples of Compensation Programs**   The compensation at some firms is composed of base pay and "reward" pay that is tied to specific performance goals. The base pay is set lower than the industry norm for a given job, but the additional reward pay (tied to specific goals) can allow the total compensation to exceed the norm. Employees are more motivated to perform well because they benefit directly from high performance.

Some employees of Enterprise Rent-A-Car Company are compensated according to the firm's profits. Steelworkers at Nucor can earn annual bonuses that exceed their annual base salary. Many salespeople earn bonuses based on their own sales volume.

Eastman Kodak uses an incentive plan that allows each executive to earn a bonus based on his or her performance. The performance targets are set by the outside board members who are not employees of Kodak. The bonuses are based on performance measures such as revenue and earnings. Procter & Gamble Company provides bonuses to executives based on some nonfinancial measures, such as integrity and leadership.

The bonuses of chief executive officers (CEOs) at General Electric, IBM, and many other firms are tied to the firm's performance. Performance measures may include revenue, earnings, production efficiency, and customer satisfaction. Firms recognize that tying compensation to performance may increase job satisfaction and motivate employees. The following descriptions of policies from recent annual reports confirm this:

*"A company lives or dies by results, and at Campbell, executive pay is linked directly to performance . . . and 100 percent of all incentive bonuses are tied to company performance."*

— Campbell's Soup Company

*"We are working hard to change the culture of the company by emphasizing and rewarding results, not activity."*

— IBM

In addition to linking compensation to performance, some firms also grant stock to their employees as partial compensation for their work. The value of this type of compensation depends on the firm's stock price. To the extent that employees can increase the firm's stock price with hard work, they can enhance their own compensation.

Initially, firms used stock as compensation only for CEOs. In recent years, however, other top managers of firms have been granted stock as well to keep them focused on enhancing the value of the stock. Some firms have extended this concept to all or most of their employees. For example, all employees of Avis receive some shares of Avis stock. This may motivate them to perform well because their performance may enhance the value of the stock they own. One limitation of this approach is that some employees who own only a small amount of stock may believe that their work habits will not have much influence on the firm's profits (and therefore on its stock price). Thus, they will not be motivated because they do not expect that their stock's price will increase as a result of their efforts. Stock options can also lead to conflicts of interest, as discussed in the next chapter.

As an illustration of how a firm's performance and value can improve when its employee compensation is linked to performance, consider the case of Paychex. In January 1998, Paychex announced its intent to tie

## Cross-Functional Teamwork

### Spreading Motivation Across Business Functions

When a firm uses compensation or other incentives to motivate employees, it must attempt to implement this program across all of its business functions. Since business functions interact, motivating employees who perform one type of function will have limited effects if employees performing other functions are not motivated.

For example, suppose that a firm's production employees are given new incentives to perform well, but marketing employees are not given any new incentives. The quality of the product achieved by the production department is somewhat dependent on the feedback it receives from marketing employees who conduct customer satisfaction surveys. Also, the production department's ability to produce an adequate supply of a product is dependent on the sales forecasts provided by the marketing department. If the sales forecast is too low, the production department may produce an insufficient volume, resulting in shortages.

Production tasks can also affect marketing tasks because effective marketing strategies will result in higher sales only if a sufficient volume of products is produced. Employees assigned to a specific function rely on employees assigned to other functions. Thus, employees who are assigned to a given function and are motivated can achieve high performance only if the other employees they rely on are motivated.

employee compensation to its performance. Over the next nine months, the firm's performance and its value (as measured by its stock price) increased substantially.

**Developing a Proper Compensation Plan**    Most compensation plans that tie pay to performance are intended to motivate employees to achieve high performance. The following guidelines can help in designing a compensation plan that motivates employees:

✦ **Align the Compensation Plan with Business Goals.** Compensation formulas for employees should be set only after the goals of the business are established. This ensures that employees are rewarded in line with their ability to satisfy the business's goals.

✦ **Align Compensation with Specific Employee Goals.** A compensation plan will motivate employees more successfully if it clearly specifies individual employee goals. Goals for an individual assembly-line employee should focus on specific job responsibilities that the employee can control. Conversely, individual goals that specify high performance for the entire production plant are not under the control of a single employee, and therefore the employee will not be as motivated to perform well.

Some firms compensate employees according to the performance of a group to which they belong within the firm. The groups are small enough that employees believe they have some control over the performance measurement.

✦ **Establish Achievable Goals for Employees.** The compensation plan will work better if the goals specified for each employee are achievable. By offering numerous achievable bonuses, managers can increase each employee's perception of the chance to earn a reward. Firms with limited budgets for bonuses can offer rewards that are less extravagant but still desirable.

Rewards that are desirable and achievable will motivate employees only if they are aware of the bonuses. Offering rewards at the end of the year is too late to motivate employees for that year. Levels of motivation will be higher if employees know about the potential for bonuses at the beginning of the year.

## 4.2 Job Security

Employees who have job security may be more motivated to perform well. They are less likely to be distracted at work because of concern about finding a more secure job.

Although firms recognize that job security can motivate their employees, they may not be able to guarantee job security. When a weakened U.S. economy lowers the demand for the goods and services provided by U.S. firms, these firms cannot afford to retain all of their employees. Even when the economy is strong, some firms are pressured to lay off employees to reduce expenses.

Firms can provide more job security by training employees to handle various tasks so that they can be assigned other duties if their usual assignments are no longer needed. Nevertheless, the firm may not have any job openings to which employees can be reassigned. Further, the job openings may be so different that reassignments are not possible. For example, workers on an assembly line normally would not be qualified to perform accounting or financial analysis jobs for an automobile manufacturer.

## 4.3 Flexible Work Schedule

**flextime programs**
programs that allow for a more flexible work schedule

**compressed workweek**
compresses the workload into fewer days per week

**job sharing**
two or more persons share a particular work schedule

Another method of increasing job satisfaction is to implement programs that allow for a more flexible work schedule (called **flextime programs**). Some firms have experimented with a **compressed workweek**, which compresses the workload into fewer days per week. Most commonly, a five-day, 8-hour-per-day workweek is compressed into four 10-hour days. The main purpose of this schedule is to allow employees to have three-day weekends. When employees are on a schedule that they prefer, they are more motivated to perform well.

Another form of a flexible work schedule is **job sharing**, where two or more persons share a particular work schedule. For example, a firm that needs a 40-hour workweek for deliveries may hire two people to share that position. This allows employees to work part-time and fulfill other obligations such as school or family.

Flexible work schedules are becoming increasingly popular, especially with employees who have specific time commitments involving their children such as attending school or social events. Technology allows many employees to attend these events and still complete their work without being at the workplace. For example, they can access updated data and information regarding their jobs through a special business website that is accessible only to employees. They can have their business e-mail forwarded to their home e-mail address or to some other address that they can access while they are away from the office. They may carry a cell phone for any necessary communication that cannot be handled by e-mail.

Technology can also give some employees more time with their families by allowing them to avoid a trip to the office on some days.

## 4.4 Employee Involvement Programs

As the theories summarized earlier indicate, employees are more motivated when they play a bigger role in the firm, either by being more involved in decisions or by being assigned more responsibility. Firms use various methods to allow more employee involvement and responsibility.

**job enlargement**
a program to expand (enlarge) the jobs assigned to employees

**Job Enlargement** One method of increasing employee responsibility is to use **job enlargement**, which is a program to expand (enlarge) the jobs assigned to employees. Job enlargement has been implemented at numerous firms such as Motorola and Xerox Corporation that have experienced downsizing. The program is aimed not only at motivating employees but also at reducing operating expenses.

**job rotation**
a program that allows a set of employees to periodically rotate their job assignments

**Job Rotation** **Job rotation** allows a set of employees to periodically rotate their job assignments. For example, an assembly-line operation may involve five different types of assignments. Each worker may focus on one assignment per week and switch assignments at the beginning of the next week. In this way, a worker performs five different assignments over each five-week period.

Job rotation not only may reduce boredom but also can prepare employees for other jobs if their primary job position is eliminated. In this way, employees can remain employed by the firm. For example, if the demand for a specific type of car declines, the manufacturer of that car may attempt to reassign the employees who worked on that car to work on other cars or trucks.

**empowerment**
allowing employees the power to make more decisions

**Empowerment and Participative Management** In recent years, supervisors at many firms have delegated more authority to their employees. This strategy is referred to as **empowerment**, as it allows employees the power to make more decisions. Empowerment is more specific than job enlargement because it focuses on increased authority, whereas job enlargement may not necessarily result in more authority. Empowerment may motivate those employees who are more satisfied when they have more authority. Also, they may be in a better position to make decisions on the tasks they perform than supervisors who are not directly involved in those tasks.

**participative management**
employees are allowed to participate in various decisions made by their supervisors or others

Empowerment is related to **participative management**, in which employees are allowed to participate in various decisions. For example, car manufacturers commonly have programs in which individual workers are asked for suggestions on cost cutting or improving quality. Managers review these suggestions and respond to the workers within a few days.

**management by objectives (MBO)**
allows employees to participate in setting their goals and determining the manner in which they complete their tasks

Empowerment assigns decision-making responsibilities to employees, whereas participative management simply allows for employee input in decisions. In reality, both terms are used to reflect programs that delegate more responsibilities to employees, whether they have complete or partial influence on decisions. The higher level of involvement by employees is supported by Theory Z, as discussed earlier.

A popular form of participative management is **management by objectives (MBO)**, in which employees work with their managers to set their goals and determine the manner in which they will complete their tasks.

Some managers use management by objectives (as shown here), in which they allow their employees to have input on the means by which they can achieve their objectives. Employees tend to be more motivated when they have influence on the process because they want to prove that their input was effective.

© SHUTTERSTOCK/YURI ARCURS

The employees' participation can be beneficial because they are closer to the production process. In addition, if their tasks can be completed in various ways, they may use their own creativity to accomplish the work.

MBO is commonly applied to salespeople by assigning a monthly sales quota (or goal) that is based on historical sales. The actual sales volume may be dependent on the state of the economy, however. Care must be taken to assign a goal that is achievable.

For production employees, a production volume goal is specified. Some employees may reduce the quality of their work to reach the goal, however, so the objective must specify adequate quality as well as quantity.

**teamwork**

a group of employees with varied job positions have the responsibility to achieve a specific goal

**Teamwork** Another form of employee involvement is **teamwork**, in which a group of employees with varied job positions have the responsibility to achieve a specific goal. Goodyear Tire and Rubber Company uses numerous project teams to achieve its goals. Car manufacturers encourage teamwork to generate new ideas. Employees at Yahoo! are encouraged to share their ideas with others to obtain feedback.

Car manufacturers commonly design cars with input from assembly-line workers. Executives establish general guidelines on a type of automobile that will satisfy consumers. The workers are then assembled in teams to work out the design details.

Out of Business

When employees work in teams (as shown here), they may enjoy their work to a greater degree. In addition, teams may lead to more social interaction, which can also increase job satisfaction.

© SHUTTERSTOCK/LISA F. YOUNG

When Jaguar (a subsidiary of Tata Motors, based in Mumbai, India) wanted to improve its customer service, its executives initially attempted to instruct employees on how to provide better service. However, motivating the employees was difficult because they were not satisfied with their jobs. The executives decided to create worker involvement teams to develop a plan for improved customer service. The employees were more willing to deal with the problem once they were allowed to search for the best solution.

A classic example of teamwork that all students can relate to is Belmont University's use of teamwork to resolve course registration hassles experienced by students. Students experienced difficulties when attempting to add a class, drop a class, submit a financial aid form, or any other task requiring service from the university. In addition, each task had to be completed at a different location on campus. Consequently, the university formed a team of administrators to find a solution that would make the process easier for students. The team proposed the creation of Belmont Central, a one-stop shop where students could accomplish all administrative tasks from registering for courses to applying for financial aid. For Belmont Central to work, its employees would have to be capable of handling all these tasks. Belmont University implemented the plan and trained the employees so that they were capable of handling a wide variety of tasks. As a result, a student now goes to one place and meets with one employee to perform all administrative tasks. The students are much more satisfied with the service than they were in the past, and the university has received an award from *USA Today* for its excellent use of teamwork to resolve its problems.

**open-book management**
a form of employee involvement that educates employees on their contribution to the firm and enables them to periodically assess their own performance levels

**Open-Book Management**   Another form of employee involvement is **open-book management**, which educates employees on their contribution to the firm and enables them to periodically assess their own performance levels. Open-book management educates employees on how they affect the key performance measures that are relevant for the firm's owners. In this way, it encourages employees to make decisions and conduct tasks as if they were the firm's owners.

Open-book management has three distinct characteristics:

✦ The firm educates all employees on the key performance measurements that affect the firm's profits and value and ensures that these performance measurements are widely available to employees over time (like an "open book" on the firm's performance). For example, various revenue, expense, and production figures may be displayed daily or weekly in the work area.

Managers of specific divisions of firms sometimes meet with their employees (as shown here) to summarize how the division has performed. They use techniques such as open-book management to indicate how the employees' performance influences the division's performance, and they may indicate performance-related goals of the division for the future.

© SHUTTERSTOCK/DOREEN SALCHER

✦ As employees are given the power to make decisions, they are trained to understand how the results of their decisions will affect the firm's overall performance. Thus, salespeople recognize how their efforts affect the firm's total revenue, while engineers recognize how their efforts reduce the cost of producing a product. Many job positions are not tied directly to revenue or total expenses. Therefore, it is helpful to break performance into segments that employees can relate to, such as number of customer complaints, proportion of

# SMALL BUSINESS SURVEY

## Do Employees Want More Influence in Business Decisions?

Employees may desire to be involved in business decision making because it increases their influence on the firm's performance. In recent years, the restructuring of firms has resulted in substantially more responsibilities for many employees. A survey of 4,500 workers of various firms was conducted to determine whether workers still wanted to have more influence in business decisions. The results are shown in the following chart:

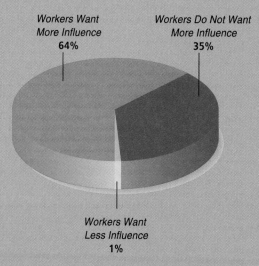

Workers Want
More Influence
64%

Workers Do Not Want
More Influence
35%

Workers Want
Less Influence
1%

The results suggest that even with the recent efforts of firms to give their employees more power and responsibility, employees would generally prefer more responsibility.

# Self-Scoring Exercises

## Are You an Empowered Employee?*

Read each of the following statements carefully. Then, indicate which answer best expresses your level of agreement (5 = strongly agree, 4 = agree, 3 = sometimes agree/sometimes disagree, 2 = disagree, 1 = strongly disagree, and 0 = undecided/do not know). Mark only one answer for each item, and be sure to respond to all items.

| | | |
|---|---|---|
| _____ | 1. I feel free to tell my manager what I think. | 5  4  3  2  1  0 |
| _____ | 2. My manager is willing to listen to my concerns. | 5  4  3  2  1  0 |
| _____ | 3. My manager asks for my ideas about things affecting our work. | 5  4  3  2  1  0 |
| _____ | 4. My manager treats me with respect and dignity. | 5  4  3  2  1  0 |
| _____ | 5. My manager keeps me informed about things I need to know. | 5  4  3  2  1  0 |
| _____ | 6. My manager lets me do my job without interfering. | 5  4  3  2  1  0 |
| _____ | 7. My manager's boss gives us the support we need. | 5  4  3  2  1  0 |
| _____ | 8. Upper management pays attention to ideas and suggestions from people at my level. | 5  4  3  2  1  0 |

To determine if you are an empowered employee, add your scores.

32–40: You are empowered! Managers listen when you speak, respect your ideas, and allow you to do your work.

24–31: You have some power! Your ideas are sometimes considered, and you have some freedom of action.

16–23: You must exercise caution. You cannot speak or act too boldly, and your managers appear to exercise close supervision.

8–15: Your wings are clipped! You work in a powerless, restrictive work environment.

*If you are not employed, discuss these questions with a friend who is employed. Is your friend an empowered employee?

product defects, or percentage of tasks completed on time. Each of these segments influences the total demand for the firm's product (and therefore the firm's revenue), as well as the expenses incurred.

✦ The compensation of employees is typically aligned with their contribution to the firm's overall performance. They may earn some stock so that they are shareholders as well as employees. This reinforces their focus on making decisions that will enhance the firm's value and therefore its stock price. In addition, the firm may provide annual pay raises only to employees who helped improve the firm's performance. Although educating employees on how their work affects the firm's value is useful, a firm may still need to compensate employees for their performance in order to motivate them. Firms may set specific annual performance targets for employees and then continually update the employees on their performance levels throughout the year.

## 4.5 Comparison of Methods Used to Enhance Job Satisfaction

The methods that can enhance job satisfaction and therefore motivate employees are compared in Exhibit 10.8. A combination of methods is especially useful for enhancing job satisfaction. When a firm succeeds in increasing employees' job satisfaction, it will be more effective in motivating the employees to achieve high performance. Therefore, putting emphasis on job satisfaction can improve a firm's profits and value.

## 4.6 Firms That Achieve the Highest Job Satisfaction Level

Many firms use a combination of methods to achieve high job satisfaction. Exhibit 10.9 lists some firms that have been frequently cited as the best firms to work for, along with the methods they use to achieve such high job satisfaction. Notice that each firm has its own way of satisfying employees.

**Exhibit 10.8**

Methods Used to Enhance Job Satisfaction

| Method | Description |
| --- | --- |
| 1. Adequate compensation program | ✦ Align raises with performance.<br>✦ Align bonuses with performance.<br>✦ Provide stock as partial compensation. |
| 2. Job security | ✦ Encourage employees to have a long-term commitment to the firm. |
| 3. Flexible work schedule | ✦ Allow employees flexibility on the timing of their work schedules. |
| 4. Employee involvement programs | ✦ Implement job enlargement.<br>✦ Implement job rotation.<br>✦ Implement empowerment and participative management.<br>✦ Implement teamwork.<br>✦ Implement open-book management. |

**Exhibit 10.9**

Firms That Were Recently Identified by Employees as Some of the Best Companies

| Firm | Method Used to Achieve High Job Satisfaction |
| --- | --- |
| Google | ✦ Free meals to employees.<br>✦ Free medical care at the workplace.<br>✦ Some employees are allowed to use 20 percent of their time to work on independent projects. |
| NepApp | ✦ Most employees are allowed flexible work schedules. |
| Starbucks | ✦ 85 percent of the employees are part-time, but they can qualify for full-time benefits. |
| Station Casinos | ✦ Employees receive discount on child care services. |

# Global Business

## Motivating Employees Across Countries

The techniques used to motivate employees in the United States may not necessarily be successful in motivating employees in other countries. For example, consider a U.S. firm that has just established a production plant in Eastern Europe. European employees' views on conditions necessary for job satisfaction may differ from those of U.S. production workers. In general, U.S. firms have successfully motivated production workers in the United States by giving them more responsibilities. Assigning additional responsibilities may not motivate production workers in Eastern Europe, however, especially if they have less experience and education.

In some situations, a U.S. firm may be more capable of motivating foreign workers than U.S. workers. For example, General Motors established a plant in what was then East Germany to produce automobiles. When it trained the workers at this plant, it explained the need for production efficiency to ensure the plant's survival. It asked the workers to provide suggestions on how the plant could increase its production efficiency. These workers offered 10 times as many suggestions as workers at other General Motors plants in Europe. The East German plant could assemble an entire automobile faster than any other General Motors plant. The efficiency of the workers at the East German plant may be attributed to their background. Although these workers did not have many years of experience on automobile assembly lines, they also had not learned any bad habits from working in less efficient assembly systems. Thus, these workers were more capable of learning an efficient production system.

Overall, a firm's ability to motivate workers in a specific country may depend on characteristics that are beyond the firm's control. Workers based in countries with fewer opportunities may be more motivated because they may appreciate their existing jobs more than workers in other countries. In general, a firm should attempt to determine what conditions will increase the job satisfaction of workers in a particular country and provide those conditions for workers who perform well.

## COLLEGE HEALTH CLUB: MOTIVATING EMPLOYEES AT CHC

One of the decisions that Sue Kramer needs to make as part of her business plan for College Health Club (CHC) is how to hire and motivate employees. Sue plans to hire capable employees who are currently exercise science majors at the college. She wants to ensure that the students are satisfied with their jobs and motivated to perform well. First, she plans to determine the typical compensation level for part-time jobs in the area and will offer wages slightly higher than the norm. Second, she plans to accommodate her employees by allowing them to work fewer hours in a week when they have a major exam or class project. Third, she will welcome employee involvement. As manager of CHC, she plans to interact with employees on a daily basis and ask them for suggestions on improving the club's performance. Fourth, if Sue opens an additional health club in the future, she plans to hire a manager to run that club. She will seriously consider hiring someone who has been an employee at CHC as the manager of the new health club after the person earns a college degree.

# Responding to the Economy

## Motivating Employees in Response to the Economy

Managers face the challenge of motivating employees under alternative economic conditions. When economic conditions are favorable, the job market is very competitive. Firms may struggle to retain good employees who may leave to take better job offers from other firms. Since some firms may not always be able to match higher salary offers by other firms, their managers must ensure that the employees are satisfied even when they could earn higher compensation at another firm. Consequently, the managers may rely on various methods of employee participation that may increase the job satisfaction level and discourage employees from seeking other jobs.

Another type of challenge for managers occurs when economic conditions are very weak. In this case, firms cannot afford to offer high compensation to their employees. In addition, the morale in the workplace could be low because of concerns about possible layoffs. Under these conditions, managers seek ways of motivating employees to perform well on the job. A popular strategy under these conditions is to allow employees more participation, so that they will enjoy their work even though the incentives such as pay raises and job promotions are limited.

# Summary of Learning Objectives

**1** If a firm can motivate its employees, it can increase the productivity of each employee. Consequently, it can achieve a higher production level with a given number of employees, which results in higher profits. The ideal form of motivation may vary among employees.

**2** The main theories on motivation are as follows:

✦ The Hawthorne studies suggest that employees are more motivated when they receive more attention.

✦ Maslow's hierarchy of needs theory suggests that employees are satisfied by different needs, depending on their position

within the hierarchy. Firms can motivate employees at the low end of the hierarchy by promising job security or safe working conditions. Firms can motivate employees whose basic needs are already fulfilled by allowing social interaction or more responsibilities.

✦ Herzberg's job satisfaction study suggests that the factors that prevent job dissatisfaction are different from those that enhance job satisfaction. Adequate salary and working conditions prevent job dissatisfaction, while responsibility and recognition enhance job satisfaction.

✦ McGregor's Theories X and Y suggest that when supervisors believe employees dislike work and responsibilities (Theory X),

they do not delegate responsibilities and employees are not motivated; when supervisors believe that employees prefer responsibilities (Theory Y), they delegate more responsibilities, which motivates employees.

✦ Theory Z suggests that employees are more satisfied when they are involved in decision making and therefore may be more motivated.

✦ Expectancy theory suggests that employees are more motivated if compensation is aligned with goals that are achievable and offer some reward.

✦ Equity theory suggests that employees are more motivated if their compensation is aligned with their relative contribution to the firm's total output.

◆ Reinforcement theory suggests that employees are more motivated to perform well if they are rewarded for high performance (positive reinforcement) and penalized for poor performance (negative reinforcement).

**3** A firm may not be able to motivate some employees, regardless of its efforts or the methods used to motivate them. If no form of motivation is effective, the threat of being fired may serve as a last resort to motivate these employees.

**4** Firms can enhance job satisfaction and therefore motivate employees by providing

◆ an adequate compensation program, which aligns compensation with performance;

◆ job security;

◆ a flexible work schedule; and

◆ employee involvement programs.

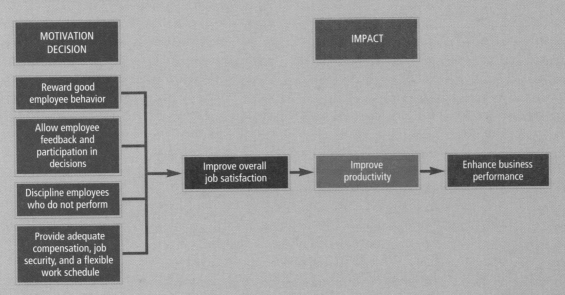

# Self-Test of Key Concepts

The following self-assessment allows you to test your understanding of the key concepts covered in this chapter. Answers are provided at the end of this exercise.

## True or False

1. Maslow's hierarchy of needs identifies superior compensation as the key to employee motivation.

2. According to Frederick Herzberg, hygiene factors are work-related factors that will motivate and please employees.

3. The management strategy of empowerment is favored by Theory X managers.

4. A supervisor who believes in McGregor's Theory Y will likely monitor employees closely to ensure that their work is completed.

5. Equity theory suggests that an employee's efforts are influenced by the expected outcome of those efforts.

6. Negative reinforcement motivates employees by encouraging them to behave in a manner that avoids unfavorable consequences.

7. Most compensation plans that tie pay to performance are intended to motivate employees to achieve high performance.

8. A merit system allocates raises for all employees according to sales of the firm.

9. Open-book management encourages employees to make decisions and conduct tasks as if they were the firm's owners.

10. The techniques of motivation can be similarly applied across countries.

**Multiple Choice**

11. One implication of the Hawthorne studies is that workers can be motivated by receiving:
    a) attention.
    b) money.
    c) stock.
    d) bonuses.
    e) profit sharing.

12. Maslow's hierarchy of needs theory can be useful for motivating employees because it suggests that:
    a) people are motivated to achieve their work-related hygiene factors.
    b) managers respond to the need for corporate profitability.
    c) employee needs are stable.
    d) employees are motivated by unsatisfied needs.
    e) money is the most important motivating factor.

13. Social interaction and acceptance by others are examples of:
    a) physiological needs.
    b) esteem needs.
    c) safety needs.
    d) social needs.
    e) self-actualization needs.

14. Needs that are satisfied with food, clothing, and shelter are called _____ needs.
    a) safety
    b) social
    c) affiliation
    d) self-esteem
    e) physiological

15. According to Herzberg, employees are commonly most satisfied when offered:
    a) adequate supervision.
    b) adequate salary.
    c) recognition.
    d) job security.
    e) safe working conditions.

16. All of the following are methods used to enhance job satisfaction except:
    a) employee involvement programs.
    b) Theory X management.
    c) job security.
    d) adequate compensation programs.
    e) flexible work schedules.

17. Which of the following theories of management suggests that workers will be motivated if they are compensated in accordance with their perceived contributions to the firm?
    a) expectancy theory
    b) equity theory
    c) need theory
    d) Theory Y
    e) reinforcement theory

18. The reinforcement theory that motivates employees by encouraging them to behave in a manner that avoids unfavorable consequences is _____ reinforcement.
    a) positive
    b) neutral
    c) equity
    d) negative
    e) expectancy

19. In an across-the-board system, all employees receive similar:
    a) raises.
    b) job assignments.
    c) offices.
    d) work schedules.
    e) performance appraisals.

20. Which of the following provides employees with various forms of compensation if specific performance goals are met?
    a) flextime programs
    b) job enlargement
    c) participative management
    d) job rotation
    e) incentive plans

21. Which of the following is not a guideline for designing a motivational compensation system?
    a) Align the system with business goals.
    b) Align the system with specific employee goals.
    c) Establish systems for rewarding employee seniority.
    d) Set achievable goals for employees.
    e) Allow employee input on the compensation system.

22. Two or more persons sharing a particular work schedule is called:
    a) job enlargement.
    b) job enrichment.
    c) job sharing.
    d) flextime.
    e) job rotation.

23. Even if the company cannot guarantee continuing employment, it can improve employees' sense of job security by:
    a) empowering employees.
    b) granting stock to employees.
    c) using open-book management.
    d) training employees in various tasks.
    e) instituting compressed workweeks.

24. A program to expand the jobs assigned to employees is called:
    a) hygiene theory.
    b) downsizing.
    c) positive reinforcement.
    d) equity theory of motivation.
    e) job enlargement.

25. An employee involvement program that periodically moves individuals from one job assignment to another is:
    a) job enlargement.
    b) job enrichment.
    c) job rotation.
    d) job sharing.
    e) flextime.

26. _____ can reduce boredom and prepare employees for other jobs if their primary job is eliminated.
    a) Job evaluation
    b) Job rotation
    c) Reengineering
    d) Performance appraisal
    e) Reinforcement

27. When firms delegate more authority to their employees, this strategy is referred to as:
    a) Theory X management.
    b) empowerment.
    c) the merit system.
    d) McGregor's hygiene theory.
    e) the equity system.

28. Which of the following allows employees to set their own goals and determine the manner in which they accomplish their tasks?
    a) equity theory of motivation
    b) expectancy theory of motivation
    c) management by objectives
    d) Theory X management
    e) Theory Y management

29. In open-book management, the compensation of employees is typically aligned with their contribution to the firm's:
    a) hierarchy of needs.
    b) industry demand.
    c) overall performance.
    d) reinforcement theory.
    e) hygiene theory.

30. In addition to linking compensation with performance, some firms grant employees _____ for good performance.
    a) internal satisfaction
    b) Theory X involvement
    c) Theory Y involvement
    d) corporate bonds
    e) common stock

**True/False**

| 1. False | 8. False |
| 2. False | 9. True |
| 3. False | 10. False |
| 4. False | |
| 5. False | |
| 6. True | |
| 7. True | |

**Multiple Choice**

| 11. a | 18. d | 25. c |
| 12. d | 19. a | 26. b |
| 13. d | 20. e | 27. b |
| 14. e | 21. c | 28. c |
| 15. c | 22. c | 29. c |
| 16. b | 23. d | 30. e |
| 17. b | 24. e | |

# Self-Test of Key Terms

across-the-board system   335
compressed workweek   338
empowerment   339
equity theory   331
esteem needs   328
expectancy theory   331
flextime programs   338
hierarchy of needs   327
hygiene factors   328
incentive plans   335

job enlargement   339
job enrichment programs   335
job rotation   339
job satisfaction   327
job sharing   338
management by objectives
  (MBO)   339
merit system   335
motivational factors   328
negative reinforcement   332

open-book management   341
participative management   339
physiological needs   327
positive reinforcement   332
reinforcement theory   332
safety needs   327
self-actualization   328
social needs   327
teamwork   340

Fill in each blank with the proper key term. To assess your understanding of the key terms, answers are provided at the end of this self-test.

1. _____ reinforcement motivates employees by providing rewards for high performance.

2. _____ provide employees with various forms of compensation if they meet specific performance goals.

3. According to Maslow's hierarchy of needs theory, _____ needs include respect, prestige, and recognition.

4. A form of employee involvement is _____, in which a group of employees with varied job positions have the responsibility to achieve a specific goal.

5. According to Herzberg's job satisfaction survey, _____ factors are work-related factors that fulfill basic needs and prevent job dissatisfaction.

6. _____ is a program designed to increase employee responsibilities.

7. According to _____ theory, an employee's efforts are influenced by the expected outcome or reward for efforts.

8. According to _____ theory, compensation should be in proportion to each employee's contribution.

9. According to Maslow's hierarchy of needs theory, _____ needs are satisfied first.

10. _____ reinforcement motivates employees by encouraging them to behave in a manner that avoids unfavorable consequences.

11. _____ programs are designed to increase job satisfaction.

12. The _____ of compensation allocates raises according to an employee's performance.

13. Programs that allow for a more flexible work schedule are referred to as _____.

14. _____ is an employee involvement program that educates employees on their contribution to the firm and enables them to periodically assess their own performance levels.

15. _____ allows a set of employees to periodically rotate their job assignments.

16. _____ is a form of participative management, in which employees to work with their managers to set their goals and determine the manner in which they will complete their tasks.

17. According to Maslow's hierarchy of needs theory, _____ represents the need to fully reach one's potential.

18. When two or more persons share a particular work schedule, it is referred to as _____.

**Answers:**

1. Positive
2. Incentive plans
3. esteem
4. teamwork
5. hygiene
6. Job enlargement
7. expectancy
8. equity
9. physiological

10. Negative
11. Job enrichment
12. merit system
13. flextime programs
14. Open-book management
15. Job rotation
16. Management by objectives
17. self-actualization
18. job sharing

# Concept Review Questions

1. **Impact of Motivation on Business Value.** Why would an increase in the motivation of employees increase the value of the business?

2. **Hawthorne Studies.** Explain the conclusion of the Hawthorne studies as it relates to the motivation of employees.

3. **Hierarchy of Needs.** Explain Maslow's hierarchy of needs theory as it relates to the motivation of employees.

4. **Herzberg's Job Satisfaction.** Briefly describe Herzberg's job satisfaction study on worker motivation.

5. **Theory X and Theory Y.** Compare McGregor's Theory X and Theory Y regarding supervisor perceptions of employees.

6. **Motivating Employees.** Based on the theories of motivation provided in this chapter, offer some general conclusions about how to motivate employees.

7. **Employee Compensation.** Explain how employee compensation can be aligned with changes in the value of a publicly traded firm. Also explain why this form of compensation is ineffective for some employees.

8. **Merit System.** Why does a merit system provide more motivation to employees than an across-the-board system?

9. **Employee Involvement Programs.** Describe some popular employee involvement programs and explain how they may motivate employees.

10. **Job Enlargement.** What is a possible disadvantage of job enlargement that could reduce the morale of employees?

# Class Communication Questions

1. **Motivation Theory in Reality.** Which theory of motivation reflects the employees where you currently work or most recently worked?

2. **Motivation Theory from a Manager's Perspective.** Which theory of motivation would you use in the environment where you currently work or most recently worked?

3. **Compensation Program in Reality.** Which compensation program is used where you currently work or most recently worked? If you were the owner of the business where you work, what compensation method would you use?

# Small Business Case

### How Not to Motivate Employees

Players Company produces and sells sporting goods. Last year it hired eight recent college graduates for various entry-level management positions. Each person was a business major with a high grade point average and very strong letters of recommendation. All of the new hires reported to Daniel Kemp. All of them quit their jobs within a year of being hired. Dawn St. Claire, the vice-president of human resources,

was shocked that all the new hires quit, so she contacted them to learn their reasons for quitting. They all suggested that their job positions lacked motivation. When Dawn told Daniel about the managers' comments, he replied "We paid them well. That should be enough motivation."

1. **Motivation Decision.** Daniel Kemp suggests that Players Company should hire a motivational speaker for a day after it hires its next batch of managers.

Do you think this will motivate the managers?

2. **Obtaining Employee Feedback.** Once new entry-level managers are hired, Dawn St. Claire plans to meet with Daniel Kemp frequently to determine how the new managers are performing. Will this strategy solve the lack of motivation of the new managers?

3. **Discipline as Motivation.** Dawn prefers not to discipline Daniel Kemp for his management style because she believes that Daniel would be upset if she told him that he needs to change. What is the problem with Dawn's reluctance to try to improve Daniel's poor management style?

4. **Empowerment as Motivation.** Dawn St. Claire has decided that the employees themselves should set workplace policies to ensure that they will be motivated. Are there any disadvantages to letting employees have this much power?

## Web Insight

### How Google Motivates Employees

At the opening of the chapter, Google was introduced. Go to the Google website (www.google.com) and go to the sections describing what it is like to work at Google. [You can also obtain this information by inserting the search term "Google Jobs" on a search engine.] Review the information about the work environment at Google. Identify the main features that in your opinion would make Google a great place to work.

## Dell's Secret for Success

Go to Dell's website (www.dell.com) and click on the link "About Dell," near the bottom of the web page. You can also review a recent annual report of Dell for more information.

1. **Motivation.** Explain how Dell's treatment of its employees motivates them to perform well.

2. **Employee Rewards.** Dell sometimes promotes some of its employees rather than hiring higher-level employees from other firms. Why is this beneficial?

## Video Exercise

### Lessons in Employee Motivation

Many free business videos are available on websites such as YouTube (www.youtube.com), and more are added every day. Search for a recent video clip about an existing business that offers lessons on "employee motivation" in YouTube or any other website that provides video clips.

1. **Main Lesson.** What is the name of the business in the video clip?

Is the video clip focused on motivating the executives, or motivating the other employees, or some other aspect of employee motivation? What is the main lesson of the video clip that you watched?

2. **Trusting Employees.** Some related videos suggest that an entrepreneur can improve the motivation of employees by trusting them. What does this mean?

3. **Motivation Methods.** What methods of motivation are suggested in the video clip that you watched? For example, does the business advocate high compensation, empowerment, job security, a flexible work schedule, or employee involvement programs?

# Projects

To encourage further comprehension of concepts covered in Chapter 10, the following five projects are available:

1. Analyzing Your Favorite Business
2. Building a Business Plan for Campus.com
3. Running Your Own Business
4. Planning Your Career
5. Stock Market Contest

All of these projects are provided in Appendix A at the end of the text. In addition, projects are available by part division at the end of each part.

A Word file for each project is also available at the textbook website (www.emcp.net/business5e) so that you may maintain one ongoing file for each project.

# Hiring, Training, and Evaluating Employees

## Chapter 11 Learning Objectives

**1** Explain human resource planning by firms.

**2** Explain how a firm can ensure equal opportunity and the benefits of doing so.

**3** Differentiate among the types of compensation that firms offer to employees.

**4** Describe the skills of employees that firms develop.

**5** Explain how the performance of employees can be evaluated.

## PepsiCo's Hiring, Training, and Evaluation of Employees

A firm's human resources (employees) are crucial to its performance. Therefore, a firm's performance is dependent on how its human resources are managed. The management of human resources involves recruiting employees, developing their skills, and evaluating their performance. The hiring, training, and evaluation of employees are a key to a firm's success. Consider the situation of PepsiCo, which has more than 185,000 employees. It is frequently hiring and training employees for a wide variety of positions and in many different countries. In regard to its employees, PepsiCo must address the following questions:

+ How should it recruit employees?

+ How can it ensure equal opportunity for its job positions?

+ What types of compensation should it provide to employees?

+ How can it ensure that its employees have the proper skills?

+ How should the employees that it hires be evaluated?

These types of questions must be addressed by all firms. This chapter explains how hiring, training, and evaluating can be conducted by PepsiCo or any other firm in a manner that maximizes its value.

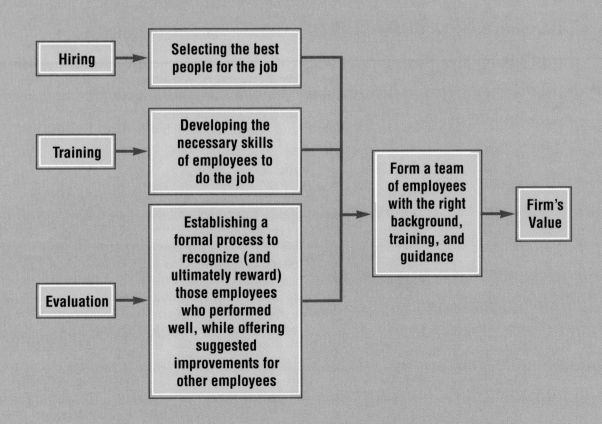

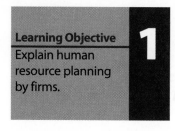

**Learning Objective**

Explain human resource planning by firms.

**1**

# 1. Human Resource Planning

**Human resource planning** involves planning to satisfy a firm's needs for employees. It consists of three tasks:

+ Forecasting staffing needs

+ Job analysis

+ Recruiting

**human resource planning**
planning to satisfy a firm's needs for employees

## 1.1 Forecasting Staffing Needs

If staffing needs can be anticipated in advance, the firm has more time to satisfy those needs. Some needs for human resources occur as workers retire or take jobs with other firms. Retirement can be forecasted with some degree of accuracy, but forecasting when an employee will take a job with another firm is difficult.

Additional needs for employees result from expansion. These needs may be determined by assessing the firm's growth trends. For example, if the firm is expected to increase production by 10 percent (in response to increased sales), it may prepare for the creation of new positions to achieve the projected production level. Positions that handle accounting and marketing-related tasks may not be affected by the increased production level.

If the firm foresees a temporary need for higher production, it may avoid hiring new workers, since it would soon have to lay them off. Layoffs not only affect the laid-off workers but also scare those workers who are still employed. In addition, firms that become notorious for layoffs will be less capable of recruiting people for new positions.

If firms avoid hiring during a temporary increase in production, they must achieve their objective in some other way. A common method is to offer overtime to existing workers. An alternative method is to hire temporary workers for part-time or seasonal work.

Once new positions are created, they must be filled. This normally involves job analysis and recruiting, which are discussed in turn.

## 1.2 Job Analysis

**job analysis**
the analysis used to determine the tasks and the necessary credentials for a particular position

**job specification**
states the credentials necessary to qualify for a job position

**job description**
states the tasks and responsibilities of a job position

Before a firm hires a new employee to fill an existing job position, it must decide what tasks and responsibilities will be performed by that position and what credentials (education, experience, and so on) are needed to qualify for that position. The analysis used to determine the tasks and the necessary credentials for a particular position is referred to as **job analysis**. This analysis should include input from the position's supervisor as well as from other employees whose tasks are related. The job analysis allows the supervisor of the job position to develop a job specification and job description. The **job specification** states the credentials necessary to qualify for the job position. The **job description** states the tasks and responsibilities of the job position. An example of a job description is provided in Exhibit 11.1. People who consider applying for the job position use the job specification to determine whether they could qualify for the position and use the job description to determine what the position involves.

**Exhibit 11.1**

Example of a Job Description

| | |
|---|---|
| Title: | Sales Representative |
| Department: | Sales |
| Location: | Southern Division, Atlanta, Georgia |

**Position Summary**

The sales representative meets with prospective customers to sell the firm's products and to ensure that existing customers are satisfied with the products they have purchased.

**Relationships**

◆ Reports to the regional sales manager for the Southern Division.

◆ Works with five other sales representatives, although each representative has responsibility for his or her own region within the Southern Division.

**Main Job Responsibilities**

1. Serve existing customers; call on main customers at least once a month to obtain feedback on the performance of products previously sold to them; take any new orders for products.

2. Visit other prospective customers and explain the advantages of each product.

3. Check on customers who are late in paying their bills; provide feedback to the billing department.

4. Meet with the production managers at least once a month to inform them about any product defects cited by customers.

5. Assess the needs of prospective customers; determine whether other related products could be produced to satisfy customers; provide feedback to production managers.

6. Will need to train new sales representatives in the future if growth continues.

7. Overnight travel is necessary for about eight days per month.

8. Sales reports must be completed once a month.

## 1.3  Recruiting

**human resource manager**
helps each specific department recruit candidates for its open positions

Firms use various forms of recruiting to ensure an adequate supply of qualified candidates. Some firms have a **human resource manager** (sometimes called the "personnel manager") who helps each specific department recruit candidates for its open positions. To identify potential candidates for the position, the human resource manager may check files of recent applicants who applied before the position was even open. These files are usually created as people submit their applications to the firm over time. In addition, the manager may place an ad in local newspapers. This increases the pool of applicants, as some people are unwilling to submit an application unless they know that a firm has an open position.

Increasingly, companies are also listing positions on their websites. Dell, Inc., uses the Internet extensively in its human resource planning. For example, the company allows potential employees to search for a specific job at its website. Dell also allows applicants to submit their résumés over the Internet. Furthermore, Dell uses its website to provide potential employees with information about benefits and about the areas where its plants and employment sites are located, such as cost-of-living estimates.

Most well-known companies receive a large number of qualified applications for each position. Many firms retain applications for only a few months so that the number of applications does not become excessive.

**internal recruiting**
an effort to fill open positions with persons already employed by the firm

**Internal Recruiting**   Recruiting can occur internally or externally. **Internal recruiting** seeks to fill open positions with persons already employed by the firm. Numerous firms post job openings so that existing employees can be informed. Some employees may consider the open positions more appealing than their current positions.

**promotion**
the assignment of an employee to a higher-level job with more responsibility and compensation

Internal recruiting can be beneficial because existing employees have already been proven. Their personalities are known, and their potential capabilities and limitations can be thoroughly assessed. Internal recruiting also allows existing workers to receive a **promotion** (an assignment of a higher-level job with more responsibility and compensation) or to switch to more desirable tasks. This potential for advancement can motivate employees to perform well. Such potential also reduces job turnover and therefore reduces the costs of hiring and training new employees. Many of the employees that Walt Disney hires for management positions are recruited internally. Wal-Mart has established a "first-in-line" program that it uses to promote its employees to managers, as explained in a recent annual report:

> *"The Customer-centered Wal-Mart culture must be embraced by thousands of new Associates if the Company is to keep growing. One way we'll retain that culture is by continuing to recruit nearly 70 percent of our management from the ranks of hourly workers. When room is available, college students who are working for Wal-Mart are the first considered for management jobs."*
>
> —Wal-Mart Corporation

Firms can do more internal recruiting if their employees are assigned responsibilities and tasks that train them for advanced positions. This strategy conflicts with job specialization because it exposes employees to more varied tasks. Nevertheless, it is necessary to prepare them for other jobs and to reduce the possibility of boredom. Even when a firm is able to fill a position internally, however, the previous position that the employee held becomes open, and the firm must recruit for that position.

**external recruiting**
an effort to fill positions with applicants from outside the firm

**External Recruiting**   **External recruiting** is an effort to fill positions with applicants from outside the firm. Some firms may recruit more qualified candidates when using external recruiting, especially for some specialized job positions. Although external recruiting allows the firm to evaluate applicants' potential capabilities and limitations, human resource managers do not have as much information as they do for internal applicants. The applicant's résumé lists previously performed functions and describes the responsibilities of those positions, but it does not indicate how the applicant responds to orders or interacts with other employees. This type of information is more critical for some jobs than others.

**Screening Applicants**   The recruiting process used to screen job applicants involves several steps.

✦ The first step is to assess each application to screen out unqualified applicants. Although the information provided on an application is limited, it is usually sufficient to determine whether the applicant has the minimum background, education, and experience necessary to qualify for the position.

Résumés that are not an appropriate match are discarded after a specified amount of time. Recruitment software has reduced costs by creating a more efficient system. Résumés are either received electronically or scanned into the computer and keywords are used to sort them. Human resource departments or the hiring manager can

Firms that conduct thorough interviews (as shown here) are more likely to hire employees who properly fit the job description.

use the software's searching capabilities to identify specific skill or experience requirements.

✦ The second step in screening applicants is the interview process. Some firms conduct initial interviews of college students at placement centers on college campuses. Other firms conduct initial interviews at their location. The human resource manager uses the personal interview to assess the personality of an applicant, as well as to obtain additional information that was not included on the application. Specifically, an interview can indicate an applicant's punctuality, communication skills, and attitude. Furthermore, an interview allows the firm to obtain more detailed information about the applicant's past experience.

A second interview may be necessary and may involve other employees of the firm who have some interaction with the position of concern. The input of these employees can often influence the hiring decision. A typical questionnaire for obtaining employee opinions about an applicant is shown in Exhibit 11.2.

✦ A third step in screening applicants is to contact the applicant's references. This screening method offers limited benefits, however, because applicants normally list only those references who are likely to provide strong recommendations. A survey by the Society for Human Resource Management found that more than 50 percent of the human resource managers surveyed sometimes receive inadequate information about a job applicant's personality traits. More than 40 percent of these managers said that they sometimes receive inadequate information about the applicant's skills and work habits.

**employment test**
a test of a job candidate's abilities

✦ Another possible step in the screening process is an **employment test**, which is a test of the candidate's abilities. Some tests are designed to assess intuition or willingness to work with others. Other tests are designed to assess specific skills, such as computer skills.

Until recently, some firms also requested a physical examination for candidates they planned to hire. Now, however, firms may request a

**Exhibit 11.2**

Example of a Questionnaire to Obtain Employee Opinions About a Job Applicant

Applicant's name _____

Position to be filled _____

| | Strongly Agree | Agree | Unsure | Disagree | Strongly Disagree |
|---|---|---|---|---|---|
| The applicant possesses the necessary skills to perform the tasks required. | | | | | |
| The applicant would work well with others. | | | | | |
| The applicant would be eager to learn new skills. | | | | | |
| The applicant has good communication skills. | | | | | |
| The applicant would accept responsibility. | | | | | |

Do you detect any deficiencies in the applicant? (If so, describe them.)

Do you recommend that we hire the applicant? Why, or why not?

Signature of employee who is assessing applicant: _____

physical examination only *after* a job offer has been made. This examination can determine whether the individual is physically able to perform the tasks that would be assigned. In addition, the examination can document any medical problems that existed before the individual was employed by the firm. This can protect the firm from being blamed for causing a person's medical problems through unsafe working conditions.

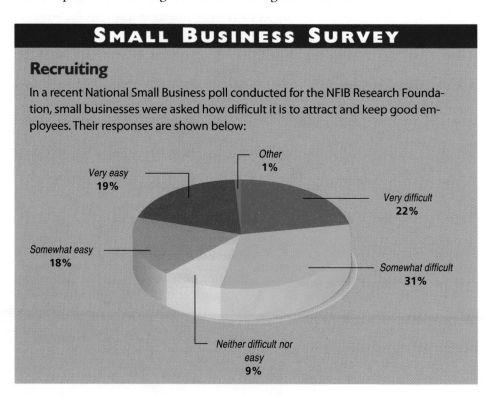

## SMALL BUSINESS SURVEY

**Recruiting**

In a recent National Small Business poll conducted for the NFIB Research Foundation, small businesses were asked how difficult it is to attract and keep good employees. Their responses are shown below:

Other 1%
Very easy 19%
Very difficult 22%
Somewhat easy 18%
Somewhat difficult 31%
Neither difficult nor easy 9%

Along with physical examinations, some firms ask new hires to take a drug test. Firms are adversely affected in two ways when their employees use illegal drugs. First, the firm may incur costs for health care and counseling for these employees. Second, the performance of these employees will likely be poor and may even have a negative effect on the performance of their co-workers.

**Make the Hiring Decision**   By the time the steps for screening applicants are completed, the application list should have been reduced to a small number of qualified candidates. Some firms take their hiring process very seriously because they recognize that their future performance is highly dependent on the employees that they select, as documented by the following statement:

> *"The past year's success is the product of a talented, smart, hard-working group, and I take great pride in being a part of this team. Setting the bar high [high standards] in our approach to hiring has been, and will continue to be, the single most important element of Amazon.com's success."*
>
> — Amazon.com

Careful screening enables firms to recruit people who turn out to be excellent employees. Consequently, careful recruiting can result in low turnover.

Once the screening is completed, the top candidate can be selected from this list and offered the job; the remaining qualified applicants can be considered if the top candidate does not accept the job offer. Exhibit 11.3 summarizes the steps used to screen job applicants. Notice that each step reduces the list of applicants who would possibly qualify for the position.

Once hired, the new employee is informed about the firm's health and benefits plans and additional details of the job. A summary of the various tasks necessary to fill a position is provided in Exhibit 11.4.

Before making the hiring decision, a manager may organize a meeting of existing employees to determine which job candidate the employees prefer. Employees like to have input on the hiring decision, especially when they will be working with the person to be hired for a new position.

© SHUTTERSTOCK/ANDRESR

**Exhibit 11.3**

Steps for Screening
Job Applicants

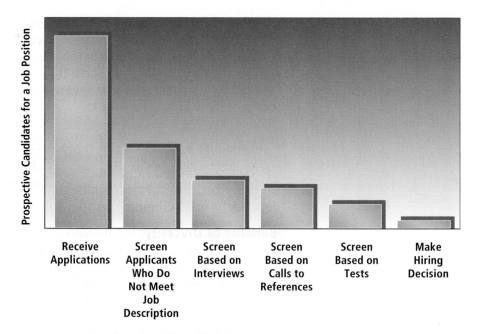

## 2. Providing Equal Opportunity

**Learning Objective**
Explain how a firm can ensure equal opportunity and the benefits of doing so.

**2**

When recruiting candidates for a job position, managers should base their assessment on the candidate's potential job performance. Basing hiring decisions on other factors may constitute discrimination. Not only is discrimination illegal, but it may reduce the efficiency of employees in the workplace.

### 2.1 Federal Laws Related to Discrimination

Federal laws prohibit discrimination in hiring. The following are some of the laws enacted to prevent discrimination or improper treatment:

+ The Equal Pay Act of 1963 mandates that men and women performing similar work must receive the same pay.

+ The Civil Rights Act of 1964 prohibits discrimination based on race, gender, religion, or national origin.

+ The Age Discrimination in Employment Act of 1967, amended in 1978, prohibits employers from discriminating against people who are 40 years old or older.

+ The Americans with Disabilities Act (ADA) of 1990 prohibits discrimination against people who are disabled.

+ The Civil Rights Act of 1991 enables women, minorities, and disabled people who believe that they have been subject to discrimination to sue firms. This act protects against discrimination in the hiring

**Exhibit 11.4**

Summary of Tasks Involved in
Human Resource Planning

process or the employee evaluation process. It also protects against sexual harassment in the workplace.

Overall, the federal laws have helped to encourage firms to make hiring decisions without discriminating.

## 2.2  Diversity Incentives

While the federal laws can penalize firms for discriminating, many firms now recognize the potential benefits of a more diverse workplace. These firms strive for diversity not just to abide by the laws, but because it can enhance their value.

**Benefits of Diversity**   Firms can benefit from diversity in three ways. First, studies have shown that employees who work in a diverse workplace tend to be more innovative. Second, employees in a diverse workplace are more likely to understand different points of view and be capable of interacting with a diverse set of customers. The proportion of a firm's customer base that consists of minorities will continue to increase. Third, a larger proportion of eligible employees will be from minority groups in the future.

Data from the U.S. Census Bureau illustrate how the number of minority customers and eligible minority employees has grown and will grow in the future. During the period 1990–2000, the white population in the United States increased by 3.4 percent; the African American population increased by 16 percent; the Native American population, by 15 percent; and the Hispanic population, by 50 percent. Thus, U.S. population growth is heavily dominated by minority groups. Together, these three minority groups represent 25 percent of the U.S. population now, and by the year 2050, they are expected to represent 38 percent.

By the year 2025, minority groups will in aggregate represent the majority of the population in some states. The total college-age population in the United States is expected to grow by 16 percent by the year 2015, and

The proportion of jobs held by women and minorities continues to increase. Moreover, women and minorities are increasingly serving in executive positions at corporations.

© SHUTTERSTOCK/ORANGE LINE MEDIA

minorities will account for 80 percent of this growth. Hispanics will account for half of the growth in the minority college-age population, while African Americans and Native Americans will make up the remainder. Thus, firms that create a diverse workplace will be able to match the more diverse customer base that will develop over time and will have better access to the pool of eligible employees.

**Firms Recognized for Achieving Diversity**  Exhibit 11.5 identifies some of the firms listed in *Fortune* magazine's best companies to work for based on the hiring of minorities. Some firms not only have recently hired minorities, but also have achieved diversity among their managers, and even among their board members. These firms demonstrate that diversity in the workplace can be accomplished and that firms with diverse sets of employees can be successful. Some of the largest firms in the United States, including American Express, Darden Restaurants, Aetna Inc., and Symantec, have minorities that are serving as chief executive officer (CEO).

Firms in the United States have also been making efforts to hire and promote more women. Women now occupy about 46 percent of all managerial and administrative positions in U.S. firms. In addition, they hold about 14 percent of all board member positions. These percentages are much higher than those in most other countries.

**Learning Objective**
Differentiate among the types of compensation that firms offer to employees.

**3**

# 3. Compensation Packages That Firms Offer

Firms attempt to reward their employees by providing adequate compensation. The level of compensation is usually established by determining what employees at other firms with similar job characteristics earn. Information on compensation levels can be obtained by conducting a salary survey or from various publications that report salary levels for different jobs. The wide differences in compensation among job positions are attributed to differences in the supply of people who have a particular skill and the demand for people with that skill. For example, demand for employees

**Exhibit 11.5**

Sampling of Firms That Are Known for Establishing a More Diverse Workplace

| Firm | Percentage of Employees Who Are Minorities | Percentage of Employees Who Are Women |
|---|---|---|
| Marriott International | 60% | 54% |
| Whole Foods Market | 45 | 44 |
| Yahoo! | 44 | 31 |
| Cisco Systems | 42 | 24 |
| Nordstrom | 41 | 73 |
| Publix Super Markets | 39 | 50 |
| Texas Instruments | 38 | 23 |
| Google | 36 | 31 |
| American Express | 34 | 67 |
| Timberland | 30 | 54 |
| Microsoft | 29 | 25 |
| Starbucks | 28 | 65 |

who have extensive experience in business financing decisions is high, but the supply of people with such experience is limited. Therefore, firms offer a high level of compensation to attract these people. Conversely, the supply of people who can qualify as a clerk is large, so firms can offer relatively low compensation to hire clerks.

**compensation package**
the total monetary compensation and benefits offered to employees

A **compensation package** consists of the total monetary compensation and benefits offered to employees. Some employees think of their compensation only in terms of their salary, but the benefits that some firms offer may be more valuable than the salary. The typical elements of a compensation package are salary, stock options, commissions, bonuses, profit sharing, benefits, and perquisites.

## 3.1  Salary

**salary (or wages)**
the dollars paid for a job over a specific period

**Salary (or wages)** is the dollars paid for a job over a specific period. The salary can be expressed per hour, per pay period, or per year and is fixed over a particular time period.

## 3.2  Stock Options

**stock options**
a form of compensation that allows employees to purchase shares of their employer's stock at a specific price

**Stock options** allow employees to purchase the firm's stock at a specific price. Consider employees who have been given stock options to buy 100 shares of stock at a price of $20 per share. This means that they can purchase the stock for this price, regardless of the stock's market price. Thus, even if the stock's market price rises to $30 per share, the employees can still buy the stock for $20 per share. They would need $2,000 (computed as 100 shares × $20 per share) to purchase 100 shares. If the firm performs well over time, the stock price will rise, and their 100 shares will be worth even more. Thus, these employees are motivated to perform well because they benefit directly when the firm performs well. As part-owners of the firm, they share in its profits.

Many firms provide stock options to their high-level managers, such as the CEO, vice-presidents, and other managers. Some firms, however, such as Starbucks and Microsoft, provide stock options to all of their employees. This can motivate all employees to perform well. Starbucks grants stock options to its employees in proportion to their salaries. An employee who received a salary of $20,000 in 1991 would have earned more than $50,000 by the year 2000 from owning the stock options.

Microsoft attributes much of its success to its use of stock options. Because of its strong performance (and therefore substantial increase in its stock price) since 1992, its managers who were hired in 1992 or before are now millionaires because their shares are worth more than $1 million.

A recent annual report of Wal-Mart summarized the potential benefits to a firm that uses stock options to compensate employees:

*"The ownership of Wal-Mart stock and options by directors and senior management is important because these individuals represent the Shareholders and should act in a manner consistent with the long-term interests of Shareholders. Making equity part of their compensation helps achieve this objective."*

In order to hire and retain talented employees, Amazon.com uses stock options as a major part of its compensation. By providing stock options, its employees have ownership in the firm, and their business decisions can affect the value of the shares they own. As the following comment indicates, Amazon believes that its success is highly influenced by its ability to motivate its employees:

*"We will continue to focus on hiring and retaining versatile and talented employees, and continue to weight their compensation to stock options rather than cash. We know our success will be largely affected by our ability to attract and retain a motivated employee base, each of whom must think like, and therefore must actually be, an owner."*

—Amazon.com

**How Options Can Cause a Conflict of Interests**    Stock options can also lead to problems for a firm's shareholders, however. When the top managers use their stock options to obtain the firm's stock, they want to sell that stock during a period when the stock's price is high. Although owning stock is supposed to encourage managers to improve the firm so that they benefit from a higher stock price, stock ownership may tempt them to manipulate the financial statements to boost the stock price. In some cases, a firm's managers have increased investor demand for the stock by using accounting methods that temporarily boosted the firm's earnings. The high demand caused the stock price to rise, allowing the managers to sell their holdings of stock at a high price. When investors learned that the firm's earnings were exaggerated, they sold their stock, causing the price to decline, but by that time the managers had already sold their shares. During the 2001–2002 period, managers of several firms, including Enron, Global Crossing, and WorldCom, were accused of using accounting to inflate their earnings and mislead investors in this way.

Some firms not only exaggerated their earnings, but failed to disclose financial problems. In several cases, managers knew of problems at a firm but withheld relevant information from the public until after they had sold their holdings of the firm's stock. The managers issued overly optimistic financial reports so that other shareholders would not sell the firm's stock and cause the price to decline until the managers had sold their shares. Thus, the managers were able to benefit at the expense of other investors who purchased the stock from them at a high price without realizing the firm's financial problems.

**Enron Example of Stock Option Compensation**    As an example, Enron manipulated its earnings so that they increased over 20 consecutive quarters leading up to 2001. Enron's stock price rose over time along with the earnings. When investors recognized that Enron was manipulating its earnings, however, they dumped the stock, and the stock price declined abruptly in 2001. In November 2001, Enron filed for bankruptcy. Yet, before Enron's price declined, 29 Enron executives or board members sold their holdings of Enron stock for more than $1 billion. In particular, Enron's CEO sold more than $100 million worth of Enron stock before the financial problems were disclosed. The CEO and other top managers were able to sell their shares at a high price because other shareholders did not know about Enron's problems. Thus, the managers benefited at the expense of the other shareholders. Similar abuses have occurred at other firms, although to a lesser extent.

## SMALL BUSINESS SURVEY

### What Benefits Are Offered by Small Businesses?

A survey was conducted by NFIB Research that investigated the bonuses and benefits offered by small businesses. The survey found that

- 52 percent pay employees periodic bonuses or profit sharing,
- 75 percent offer paid vacation to a majority of employees,
- 61 percent sponsor an employee health insurance plan,
- 59 percent provide paid sick leave,
- 30 percent provide a pension plan, and
- 29 percent provide life insurance.

The lesson of the Enron scandal is that managers who receive stock options as compensation may be tempted to manipulate the firm's stock price so that they can sell their shares at a high price. Although managers cannot control the stock's price directly, they can influence the price indirectly through the information that they release or withhold. Thus, they have an incentive to exaggerate the earnings, issue overly optimistic reports, or withhold bad news; by doing so, they can indirectly push the stock price higher and then sell their stock holdings at a high price.

A firm's board of directors should attempt to prevent such abuses. The board of directors can enact guidelines that allow the managers or board members to sell only a small amount of their stock holdings in any particular quarter or year. In this way, the managers will not have

## SMALL BUSINESS SURVEY

### Which Employee Benefits Are Most Important to Employees?

A recent survey by Transamerica asked employees of small businesses how important various employee benefits were to them. Their responses are shown here:

|  | Very Important | Somewhat Important | Not Very Important |
|---|---|---|---|
| Retirement contributions by employer | 44% | 40% | 16% |
| Retirement contributions by employee allowed | 58 | 33 | 8 |
| Health insurance coverage | 90 | 6 | 5 |
| Life insurance coverage | 48 | 32 | 20 |
| Disability insurance coverage | 59 | 32 | 9 |
| Stock options | 13 | 46 | 41 |

## Global Business

### Compensating Employees Across Countries

The manner in which firms compensate their employees may vary across countries. Salary may be perceived as less important in a country where personal income tax rates are high. If a large portion of the salary is taxed, employees may prefer other forms of compensation. The health benefits that a firm offers may be less important in countries that provide free medical services.

Some U.S. firms, such as PepsiCo, offer their employees opportunities to purchase their stock at below-market prices. Most employees in the United States perceive this form of employee compensation as desirable. Employees in other countries, however, perceive it as less desirable. The rules for individuals who purchase stock vary among countries. For example, individuals in Brazil, China, and India are restricted from purchasing or owning stock under some circumstances. The taxes imposed on the profits earned by individuals on their stocks also vary across countries, which makes stock ownership less desirable for employees based in certain countries. Furthermore, individuals in some countries are more comfortable investing in bank deposits rather than in stocks.

Since employees based in different countries may have varying views about compensation, a firm with employees in several countries should consider tailoring its compensation plans to fit the characteristics of each country. The firm may provide higher salaries in one country and more health benefits in another. Before establishing a compensation plan in a given country, the firm should assess the specific tax laws of that country and survey individuals to determine the types of compensation that are most desirable. When a firm designs a compensation plan to fit the country's characteristics, it can improve employee job satisfaction.

---

an incentive to create an artificially high stock price in any particular quarter or year because they will not be able to sell all of their stock at that time.

## 3.3 Commissions

**commissions**
compensation for meeting specific sales objectives

**Commissions** normally represent compensation for meeting specific sales objectives. For example, salespeople at many firms receive a base salary, plus a percentage of their total sales volume as monetary compensation. Commissions are not used for jobs where employee performance cannot be as easily measured.

## 3.4 Bonuses

**bonus**
an extra onetime payment at the end of a period in which performance was measured

A **bonus** is an extra onetime payment at the end of a period in which performance was measured. Bonuses are usually paid less frequently than commissions (such as once a year). A bonus may be paid for efforts to increase revenue, reduce expenses, or improve customer satisfaction. In most cases, the bonus is not set by a formula; thus, supervisors have some flexibility in determining the bonus for each employee. The total amount of bonus funds that are available for employees may be dependent on the firm's profits for the year of concern.

At Disney, 70 percent of the bonus compensation for executives is based on specific financial performance measures, such as earnings. The advantage of using these types of measures is that executives are encouraged to focus on specific financial goals that should also satisfy the company's shareholders.

## 3.5  Profit Sharing

**profit sharing**
a portion of the firm's profits is paid to employees

Some firms, such as Continental Airlines, Boeing, and J.P. Morgan Chase, offer employees **profit sharing**, in which a portion of the firm's profits is paid to employees. The goal of profit sharing is to provide an extra reward to the employees who are responsible for the firm's profits. This motivates employees to perform in a manner that improves profitability.

## 3.6  Employee Benefits

**employee benefits**
additional privileges beyond compensation payments, such as paid vacation time; health, life, or dental insurance; and pension programs

Employees may also receive **employee benefits**, which are additional privileges beyond compensation payments, such as paid vacation time; health, life, or dental insurance; and pension programs. Typically, these employee benefits are not taxed. Many firms provide substantial employee benefits to their employees. The cost of providing health insurance has soared in recent years. Many firms, such as Johnson & Johnson, have responded by offering preventive health-care programs. Some firms now give employees incentives to stay healthy by reducing the insurance premiums charged to employees who receive favorable scores on cholesterol levels, blood pressure, fitness, and body fat.

## 3.7  Perquisites

**perquisites**
additional privileges beyond compensation payments and employee benefits

Some firms offer **perquisites** (or "perks") to high-level employees; these are additional privileges beyond compensation payments and employee benefits. Common perquisites include free parking, a company car, club memberships, telephone credit cards, and an expense account.

## 3.8  Comparison across Jobs

The forms of compensation allocated to employees vary with their jobs, as shown in Exhibit 11.6. Employees who are directly involved in the production process (such as assembly-line workers) tend to receive most of their compensation in the form of salary. Low-level managers may also receive most of their compensation as salary but may receive a small bonus and profit sharing.

Many salespeople in the computer and technology sectors earn more compensation in the form of commissions than as salary. High-level managers, such as vice-presidents and CEOs, normally have a high salary and the potential for a large bonus. Their employee benefits are also relatively large, and they normally are awarded various perks as well.

**Learning Objective**

**4**

Describe the skills of employees that firms develop.

## 4.  Developing Skills of Employees

Firms that hire employees provide training to develop various employee skills. Motorola has established its own university where each employee receives at least one week of training per year. A study by the management

**Exhibit 11.6**

How Forms of
Communication
Can Vary Across Job
Descriptions

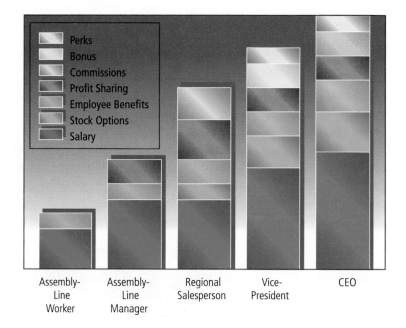

consulting firm Ernst & Young found that firms that invest in training programs are more profitable. To illustrate the attention that can be given to training, consider the case of The Home Depot Company. Its employees frequently interact with customers and need to have sufficient expertise to explain how various products can be used. The managers interact with the employees and with customers. The Home Depot Company has established an initiative focused on training, as explained in its recent annual report:

> *"We believe our greatest competitive advantage is our people. That's why we launched human resources initiatives designed to attract, motivate, and retain the best employees in the industry. Through learning programs for associates and leadership development of district and store managers, we will increasingly shift our store management focus from 'operating a box' to 'managing a business.'"*

Some of the more common types of training provided to employees are discussed next.

## 4.1 Technical Skills

Employees must be trained to perform the various tasks they engage in daily. Ace Hardware offers courses to train its employees in the use of the products that it sells. As factories owned by firms such as Toyota and Boeing incorporate more advanced technology, employees receive more training. These firms spend millions of dollars every year on training. With new development in computer technology, employees of travel agencies, mail-order clothing firms, retail stores, and large corporations must receive more training on using computers. In addition, employees who are assigned to new jobs will require extra training. Firms recognize that expenses may be incurred each year to continually develop each employee's skills.

Technical skills are needed by some employees (as shown here) to ensure that the firm's production process operates smoothly and to correct technical problems that occur.

© SHUTTERSTOCK/THOMAS SZTANEK

## 4.2 Decision-Making Skills

Firms can benefit from providing their employees with some guidelines to consider when making decisions and generating ideas. For example, Xerox trains all of its employees to follow a six-step process when generating ideas and making decisions. Eastman Kodak employees who recently created new products are asked to share their knowledge with other employees who are attempting to develop new products. Motorola trains its employees to apply new technology to develop new products. Ace Hardware offers courses on management skills for its managers.

# Responding to the Economy

## Hiring Employees in Response to the Economy

When firms are in the process of hiring employees, they face different challenges as economic conditions change. When economic conditions are favorable, firms are in a better financial position to pay higher compensation to their employees. However, other firms can also afford to pay higher compensation, and bidding wars for employees could occur. Firms may attempt to increase the quality of the work rather than offer higher compensation than all other firms. If employees are solely interested in achieving the maximum compensation without considering the quality of the job, they will probably leave the firm at some point anyway as soon as another firm makes a higher offer.

When economic conditions are weak, the pool of qualified job applicants for a given job position is much larger. This makes it easier for a firm to hire, but it creates a different type of challenge. Some job applicants will be overqualified for the job and will likely leave as soon as the economy improves and there are more jobs available for which they are qualified. Thus, managers involved in the screening process should consider whether applicants are overqualified. Managers might still consider hiring these applicants if they might be appropriate for other job positions that the firm will create once the economy improves.

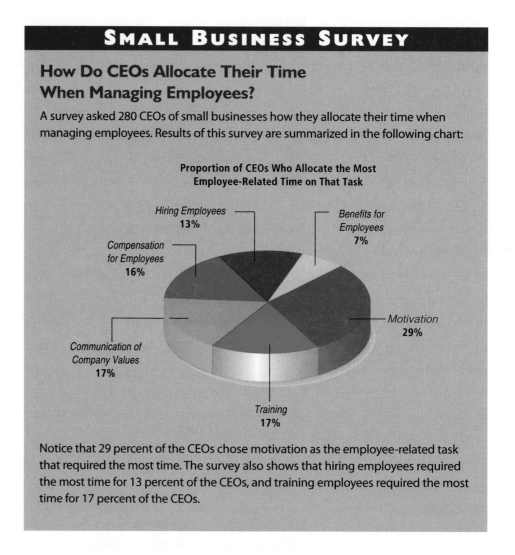

# SMALL BUSINESS SURVEY

## How Do CEOs Allocate Their Time When Managing Employees?

A survey asked 280 CEOs of small businesses how they allocate their time when managing employees. Results of this survey are summarized in the following chart:

**Proportion of CEOs Who Allocate the Most Employee-Related Time on That Task**

Hiring Employees 13%

Benefits for Employees 7%

Compensation for Employees 16%

Motivation 29%

Communication of Company Values 17%

Training 17%

Notice that 29 percent of the CEOs chose motivation as the employee-related task that required the most time. The survey also shows that hiring employees required the most time for 13 percent of the CEOs, and training employees required the most time for 17 percent of the CEOs.

## 4.3 Customer Service Skills

Employees who frequently deal with customers need to have customer service skills. Many employees in tourism industries such as airlines and hotels are trained to satisfy customers. The hotel chain Marriott International provides training on serving customers, with refresher sessions after the first and second months. The training is intended not only to ensure customer satisfaction but also to provide employees with an orientation that makes them more comfortable (and increases employee satisfaction). Ace Hardware offers courses for its managers to develop customer service skills. Walt Disney provides extensive training to its newly hired employees. Customer service skills are also necessary for employees hired by firms to sell products or deal with customer complaints.

## 4.4 Safety Skills

Firms also educate employees about safety within the work environment. This includes training employees on how to use machinery and equipment in factories owned by large manufacturing firms, such as Caterpillar and Goodyear Tire. United Parcel Service (UPS) implements training programs for its employees on handling hazardous materials.

Training programs not only reassure employees but also reduce health-care and legal expenses that could be incurred as a result of work-related injuries.

## 4.5  Human Relations Skills

Some training seminars may be necessary for supervisors who lack skills in managing other employees. In general, this type of training helps supervisors recognize that their employees not only deserve to be treated properly but also will perform better if they are treated well.

Firms commonly provide seminars on diversity to help employees of different races, genders, and religions become more sensitive to other views. Denny's offers employee training on diversity to prevent racial discrimination. Diversity training may enable a firm to create an environment in which people work together more effectively, thereby improving the firm's performance. It may also prevent friction between employees and thus can possibly prevent discrimination or harassment lawsuits against the firm.

Training seminars are also designed to improve relationships among employees across various divisions so that employees can work together in teams. For example, Motorola and Xerox provide seminars on teamwork for employees. Many small businesses organize regular meetings between employees and executives.

## 5.  Evaluation of Employee Performance

**Learning Objective 5**
Explain how the performance of employees can be evaluated.

Employees often perceive performance evaluation as only a method for allocating raises. Yet, if supervisors properly conduct the evaluation, it can also provide feedback and direction to employees. An evaluation should indicate an employee's strengths and weaknesses and may influence an employee's chances of being promoted within the firm in the future.

## 5.1 Segmenting the Evaluation

The overall performance of most employees is normally based on multiple criteria. Therefore, an evaluation can best be conducted by segmenting the evaluation into the criteria that are relevant for each particular job position. For example, consider employees who have excellent technical skills for their jobs, but are not dependable. Since they rate high on one criterion and low on another, their overall performance might be evaluated as about average. An average rating for overall performance, however, does not specifically pinpoint the employees' favorable or unfavorable work habits.

Segmenting performance evaluation into different criteria can help supervisors pinpoint specific strengths and weaknesses. Evaluating each criterion separately provides more specific information to employees about how they may improve. In our example, the employees who receive a low rating on dependability can focus on improving that behavior. Furthermore, these employees can see from their evaluation that their supervisor recognized their strong technical skills. Without a detailed evaluation, employees may not recognize what tasks they do well (in the opinion of supervisors) and what specific weaknesses need to be improved.

**Objective Versus Subjective Criteria**   Some performance criteria are objective, such as parts produced per week, number of days absent, percentage of deadlines missed, and proportion of defective parts caused by employee errors. Examples of direct measures of performance are provided for specific job positions in Exhibit 11.7 to illustrate how the measures vary by type of job. Other characteristics not shown in Exhibit 11.7 that are commonly assessed for some job positions include organization, communication, and decision-making skills.

Some criteria are less objective but still important. For example, sometimes the quality of work cannot be measured by part defects because many jobs do not focus on producing a single product. Therefore, quality of work may be subjectively assessed by a supervisor. Also, the willingness

**Exhibit 11.7**

Examples of Direct Measures of Performance

| Job Position | Direct Measures of Performance |
|---|---|
| Salesperson | Dollar volume of sales over a specific period |
| | Number of new customers |
| | Number of delinquent accounts collected |
| | Net sales per month in territory |
| Manager | Number of employee grievances |
| | Cost reductions |
| | Absenteeism |
| | Unit safety record |
| | Timeliness in completing appraisals |
| | Employee satisfaction with manager |
| | Division production |
| | Diversity of new hires |
| Administrative assistant | Number of letters prepared |
| | Word processing speed |
| | Number of errors in filing |
| | Number of tasks returned for reprocessing |
| | Number of calls screened |

## Cross-Functional Teamwork

### How Job Responsibilities Across Business Functions Can Complicate Performance Evaluations

Firms have increasingly encouraged employees to perform a variety of business functions to achieve higher levels of job satisfaction and efficiency. Although this form of job enlargement has been successful, it can complicate the evaluation of an employee's performance. Consider an employee of a sporting goods store whose only responsibility is stringing tennis rackets. The performance of this employee is judged by the number of tennis rackets strung and the quality of the stringing (as measured by customer feedback).

The employee's responsibilities are then enlarged to include visiting country clubs and selling tennis rackets to them. Whereas the employee's initial job focused on assembly of tennis rackets, new responsibilities involve marketing the tennis rackets. Furthermore, other employees are also involved in stringing rackets and making sales calls to country clubs. The performance evaluation of the employee has become more complicated for two reasons. First, more than one task now must be assessed. Second, other employees are also involved in completing these tasks, which makes it difficult to measure one employee's individual contribution. That is, a firm can easily assess the performance of a team of employees, but it cannot easily assess the performance of each employee within the team.

of an employee to help other employees is an important criterion that is subjective.

## 5.2  Using a Performance Evaluation Form

Supervisors are typically required to complete a performance evaluation form at the end of each year. An example of such a form is shown in Exhibit 11.8. When supervisors measure the performance of employees, they normally classify the employee in one of several categories such as the following: (1) outstanding, (2) above average, (3) average, (4) below average, and (5) poor. The set of criteria can be more specific for particular jobs within the firm. For example, assembly-line workers may be rated by the total components produced and production quality. A company salesperson may be evaluated by the number of computers sold and the quality of service provided to customers. It is important that supervisors inform employees of the criteria by which they will be rated. Otherwise, they may allocate too much time to tasks that supervisors view as less important.

## 5.3  Assigning Weights to the Criteria

An employee's ratings on all relevant criteria can be combined to determine the employee's overall performance level. Some firms use systems that weight and rate the criteria used to evaluate the employee. For example, bank tellers may be rated according to their speed in handling

**Exhibit 11.8** Example of Performance Appraisal Form

Employee Name _____ Date _____

Position _____

**Behavior Ratings: Check the one characteristic that best applies.**

**Quality of Work** (refers to accuracy and margin of error):

_____ 1. Makes errors frequently and repeatedly

_____ 2. Often makes errors

_____ 3. Is accurate; makes occasional errors

_____ 4. Is accurate; rarely makes errors

_____ 5. Is exacting and precise

**Quantity of Work** (refers to amount of production or results):

_____ 1. Usually does not complete workload as assigned

_____ 2. Often accomplishes part of a task

_____ 3. Handles workload as assigned

_____ 4. Turns out more work than requested

_____ 5. Handles an unusually large volume of work

**Timeliness** (refers to completion of task, within time allowed):

_____ 1. Does not complete duties on time

_____ 2. Is often late in completing tasks

_____ 3. Completes tasks on time

_____ 4. Usually completes tasks in advance of deadlines

_____ 5. Always completes all tasks in advance of deadlines

**Attendance and Punctuality** (refers to adhering to work schedule assigned):

_____ 1. Is usually tardy or absent

_____ 2. Is often tardy or absent

_____ 3. Normally is not tardy or absent

_____ 4. Makes a point of being on the job and on time

_____ 5. Is extremely conscientious about attendance

**Responsibility** (refers to completing assignments and projects):

_____ 1. Usually does not assume responsibility for completing assignments

_____ 2. Is at times reluctant to accept delegated responsibility

_____ 3. Accepts and discharges delegated duties willingly

_____ 4. Accepts additional responsibility

_____ 5. Is a self-starter who seeks out more effective ways to achieve results or seeks additional responsibilities

**Cooperation with Others** (refers to working and communicating with supervisors and co-workers):

_____ 1. Has difficulty working with others and often complains when given assignments

_____ 2. Sometimes has difficulty working with others and often complains when given assignments

_____ 3. Usually is agreeable and obliging; generally helps out when requested

_____ 4. Works well with others; welcomes assignments and is quick to offer assistance

_____ 5. Is an outstanding team worker; always assists others and continually encourages cooperation by setting an excellent example

**Performance Summary** (include strong areas and areas for future emphasis in improving performance or developing additional job skills):

**Employee Comments or Concerns:**

**Signatures:**

**Human Resource Manager** _____ Date _____

**Employee** _____ Date _____

**Supervisor** _____ Date _____

customer transactions, their quality (accuracy) in handling money transactions, and their ability to satisfy customers. The speed may be monitored by supervisors over time, while accuracy is measured by balancing the accounts at the end of each day, and customer satisfaction is measured from customer feedback over time.

The different criteria must also be weighted separately because some of the employee's assignments may be considered more important than others. Using our example, assume that the weights are determined as follows:

| | |
|---|---|
| Speed in handling customer transactions | 30% |
| Accuracy in handling customer transactions | 50% |
| Satisfying customers | 20% |
| | 100% |

The sum of the weights of all criteria should be 100 percent. The weighting system should be communicated to employees when they begin a job position so that they understand what characteristics are most important within the evaluation.

**Example**   To demonstrate how an overall performance measure is derived, assume that in our example the supervisor rated the bank teller as shown in Exhibit 11.9. The overall rating is the weighted average of 4.5; this rating is between "above average" and "outstanding." Other bank tellers could also be periodically rated in this manner. At the end of each year, the ratings may be used to determine the raise for each teller. The ratings may also be reviewed along with other characteristics (such as experience) when the employees are considered for a promotion.

**Limitations of Assigning Weights**   When employees have numerous job assignments, however, accounting for all types of assignments within the performance evaluation is more difficult. Nevertheless, some of the assignments may be combined into a single characteristic, such as "customer service" or "ability to complete tasks on time."

Some supervisors may believe that a weighted system is too structured and does not account for some relevant characteristics, such as ability to get along with other employees. Nevertheless, characteristics like these could be included within the weighting system.

## 5.4  Steps for Proper Performance Evaluation

Firms can follow specific steps for performance evaluation that demonstrate fairness and recognition of employees' rights and also satisfy legal guidelines.

**Exhibit 11.9**

Developing an Overall Rating

| Characteristic | Rating | Weight | Weighted Rating |
|---|---|---|---|
| Speed in handling customer transactions | 4 (above average) | 30% | 4 × 30% = 1.2 |
| Accuracy in handling customer transactions | 5 (outstanding) | 50% | 5 × 50% = 2.5 |
| Satisfying customers | 4 (above average) | 20% | 4 × 20% =  .8 |
| | | | Overall rating = 4.5 |

**Communication of Responsibilities**   Supervisors should communicate job responsibilities to employees when they are hired. Supervisors should also communicate any changes in employee job responsibilities over time. This communication can be done orally, but it should be backed up with a letter to the employee. The letters are not as personal as oral communication, but they provide documentation in case a disagreement arises in the future about assignments and responsibilities. The letters may not only provide support to defend against employee lawsuits, but they also force supervisors to pinpoint the specific tasks for employees in a particular job position.

**Communication of Deficiencies**   When supervisors notice that employees have deficiencies, they should inform the employees of those deficiencies. This communication may occur in the form of a standard periodic review. Supervisors may prefer to inform employees of deficiencies immediately, rather than wait for the review period. Employees should be given a chance to respond to the criticism. Supervisors may also allow a short period of time for employees to correct the deficiencies. Supervisors should also communicate with employees who were evaluated favorably so that those employees recognize that their efforts are appreciated.

**Communication of Evaluations**   Supervisors should be consistent when conducting performance evaluations. That is, two employees who have a similar deficiency should be treated equally in the evaluation process. Many supervisors find it easier to communicate deficiencies to employees who are more willing to accept criticism, but it is only fair to treat employees with the same deficiencies similarly.

## 5.5   Action Due to Performance Evaluations

Some performance evaluations require supervisors to take action. Employees who receive a very favorable evaluation may deserve some type of recognition or even a promotion. If supervisors do not acknowledge such outstanding performance, employees may either lose their enthusiasm and reduce their effort or search for a new job at a firm that will reward them for high performance. Supervisors should acknowledge high performance so that the employee will continue to perform well in the future.

Employees who receive unfavorable evaluations must also be given attention. Supervisors must determine the reasons for poor performance. Some reasons (such as a family illness) may have a temporary adverse impact on performance and can be corrected. Other reasons, such as a bad attitude, may not be temporary. When supervisors give employees an unfavorable evaluation, they must decide whether to take any additional actions. If the employees were unaware of their own deficiencies, the unfavorable evaluation can pinpoint the deficiencies that employees must correct. In this case, the supervisor may simply need to monitor the employees closely and ensure that the deficiencies are corrected.

If the employees were already aware of their deficiencies before the evaluation period, however, they may be unable or unwilling to correct them. This situation is more serious, and the supervisor may need to take action. The action should be consistent with the firm's guidelines and may include reassigning the employees to new jobs, suspending them temporarily, or firing them. A supervisor's action toward a poorly performing worker can affect the attitudes of other employees. If no penalty

Managers periodically meet with their employees on an individual basis (as shown here) in order to provide an evaluation of their progress and to pinpoint deficiencies (if any). The managers may provide a formal evaluation in writing, but it is also helpful to communicate the key points directly to employees and to allow them to respond to the evaluation.

© SHUTTERSTOCK/ANDREW TAYLOR

is imposed on an employee for poor performance, other employees may react by reducing their productivity as well.

Firms must follow certain procedures to fire an employee. These procedures are intended to prevent firms from firing employees without reason. Specifically, supervisors should identify deficiencies in employees' evaluations and give them a chance to respond.

## 5.6  Dealing with Lawsuits by Fired Employees

It is not uncommon for employees to sue the firm after being fired. Some lawsuits argue that the plaintiff—the fired employee—did not receive due process. Others argue that the firing occurred because of discrimination based on race, gender, age, religion, or national origin. Many firms with numerous employees have been sued for this reason, even when their supervisors have followed all proper procedures. Complaints of discrimination are first filed with the Equal Employment Opportunity Commission (EEOC), which is responsible for enforcing the discrimination laws. About 20 percent of the complaints filed with the EEOC are judged to state a reasonable cause for the fired employee to take action, while 80 percent of the complaints are considered to have no reasonable basis. Even when the EEOC believes the complaint is not valid, however, the fired employee can still sue the firm. Although the laws that prohibit discrimination have good intentions, the court system has not effectively separated the frivolous cases from the valid ones. Consequently, legal expenses for many firms have risen substantially.

A factor that contributes to firms' rising legal expenses is that plaintiffs have a right to a trial by jury. Juries are commonly perceived to be more sympathetic toward plaintiffs than judges are. Also, juries are perceived as more unpredictable, which can be a concern for firms that are sued by employees. In addition, since the enactment of the Civil Rights Act of 1991, plaintiffs can be awarded not only compensatory damages (such as back pay) but also punitive damages (to penalize the firm) and legal expenses. As a result, plaintiffs and their attorneys can be awarded substantial amounts of money.

Recognizing that employee lawsuits can be very costly, some firms have attempted to settle lawsuits before trial to reduce their legal expenses and avoid negative publicity. However, settling a lawsuit that has no merit may result in other frivolous lawsuits by employees.

Furthermore, a firm should not ignore an employee's deficiencies out of fear that the employee will sue. Doing so will reduce the motivation of other employees when they notice that one employee is receiving special treatment. Despite the increase in employee lawsuits, firms must still attempt to ensure that their employees are doing the jobs that they are paid to do. While firms cannot necessarily avoid employee lawsuits, they can attempt to establish training and performance evaluation guidelines that will reduce the chances of lawsuits or increase their chances of winning if a suit does occur. The court system has generally sided with firms in cases in which supervisors followed proper procedures in firing employees.

## 5.7 Employee Evaluation of Supervisors

**upward appraisals**
used to measure the managerial abilities of supervisors

Some firms allow employees to evaluate their supervisors. The evaluations can then be used to measure the managerial abilities of the supervisors. These so-called **upward appraisals** have been used by many firms, including AT&T and Dow Chemical. An upward evaluation is more effective if it is anonymous. Otherwise, workers may automatically submit a very favorable evaluation either in the hope that their supervisor will return the favor or to avoid retaliation. Evaluations of the supervisor may identify deficiencies, which can then be corrected so that the supervisor can more effectively manage employees in the future. The evaluation form should allow each criterion to be evaluated separately so that the supervisor can recognize which characteristics need to be improved.

## COLLEGE HEALTH CLUB: DEVELOPING EMPLOYEE SKILLS AND EVALUATING PERFORMANCE AT CHC

Sue Kramer realizes that if her employees are trained properly, they will serve the members better, and the members will be more satisfied with the health club.

Therefore, she plans to focus her employee training on three areas. First, when she hires her part-time employees, she will stress the need for safety. She wants to ensure that each employee understands the potential dangers in using the weight and exercise machines. Sue will provide all of her members with a booklet on safety, but she also wants her employees to understand the safety features so that they can help any members who are not using the machines properly. Second, Sue wants to make sure that her employees understand the importance of customer relations, especially in a service business like a health club. Third, she plans to emphasize human relations skills by explaining the need for the part-time employees to work together.

As Sue tries to decide on a method for evaluating the performance of her employees, she again recognizes that a key role of the employees is to satisfy CHC's members. Therefore, she will rate each employee's customer relations skills. To obtain feedback from members about CHC's services, Sue is asking them to complete survey forms. The survey forms will ask the members if they have any comments about the individual employees. In addition, Sue will rate employees according to how well they work with other employees. Now that she has identified the specific criteria to be used to evaluate the employees, she will communicate these criteria to the employees when she hires them so that they know how they will be evaluated. She will also remind them of these criteria during the training in customer relations and human relations skills.

# Summary of Learning Objectives

**1** The main functions involved in human resource planning are

✦ forecasting human resource needs;

✦ job analysis, which determines the tasks the job position involves and the credentials necessary to qualify for the position; and

✦ recruiting, which involves screening applicants and deciding who to hire.

**2** When recruiting, managers should ensure that they provide equal opportunity to all applicants. Some very well-known firms have made much progress in achieving diversity in recent years. Diversity can benefit firms because it may encourage innovation, it allows for different points of view, and a larger proportion of eligible employees will be from minority groups in the future.

**3** Compensation packages offered by firms can include salary, stock options, commissions, bonuses, profit sharing, employee benefits, and perquisites.

**4** After firms hire employees, they commonly provide training to enhance technical skills, decision-making skills, customer service skills, safety skills, and human relations skills.

**5** The performance of employees can be evaluated by segmenting the evaluation into different criteria, assigning an evaluation rating to each criterion, and weighting each criterion. The overall performance rating is the weighted average of all criteria that were assigned a rating.

Once supervisors evaluate employees, they should discuss the evaluations with the employees and identify any specific strengths, as well as any specific weaknesses that need to be improved.

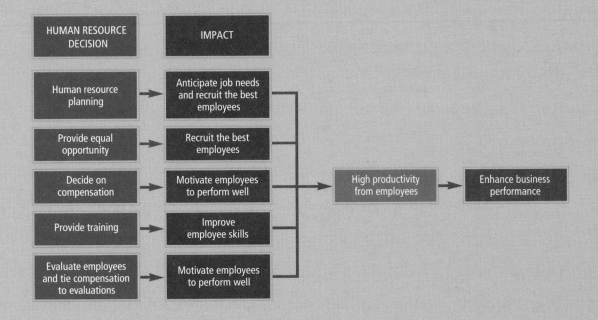

# Self-Test of Key Concepts

The following self-assessment allows you to test your understanding of the key concepts covered in this chapter. Answers are provided at the end of this exercise.

## True or False

1. Job analysis represents the forecasting of a firm's employee needs.

2. One task of human resource planning is recruiting.

3. Firms tend to avoid hiring new full-time workers to meet temporary needs for higher production levels.

4. A job specification states the credentials necessary to qualify for the position.

5. Federal laws make it illegal to discriminate on the basis of factors not related to potential job performance.

6. Employee benefits such as health insurance and dental insurance are taxed.

7. Firms should offer the same compensation package to their workers in foreign countries that they offer to employees in their home country.

8. The overall performance evaluation of most employees is based on multiple criteria.

9. Employees perceive performance evaluation as a method for allocating wage increases.

10. Each of the performance criteria must be weighted equally to avoid unbalancing the performance appraisal.

## Multiple Choice

11. The document that specifies the credentials necessary to qualify for a job position is a:
    a) job specification.
    b) job description.
    c) job analysis.
    d) job evaluation.
    e) performance evaluation.

12. A major responsibility of a human resource manager is to:
    a) help each specific department recruit candidates for its open positions.
    b) conduct the performance evaluations for all employees.
    c) establish the information system and local area network used by the firm's employees.
    d) help select the members of top management who will serve on the firm's board of directors.
    e) prevent the formation of labor unions.

13. The tasks and responsibilities of a job position are disclosed in a(n):
    a) job specification.
    b) indenture agreement.
    c) job description.
    d) organization chart.
    e) staffing report.

14. The process used to determine the tasks and the necessary credentials for a particular position is referred to as:
    a) job analysis.
    b) job screening.
    c) human resource planning.
    d) human resource forecasting.
    e) recruiting.

15. If firms wish to avoid hiring during a temporary increase in production, they can offer _____ to existing workers.
    a) overtime
    b) vacations
    c) training programs
    d) affirmative action
    e) orientation programs

16. When a firm attempts to fill job openings with persons it already employs, it is engaging in:
    a) intrapreneurship.
    b) internal recruiting.
    c) entrenchment.
    d) precruiting.
    e) focused recruiting.

17. A(n) _____ is an assignment to a higher-level job with more responsibility and greater pay.
    a) transfer
    b) lateral assignment
    c) perquisite
    d) upward appraisal
    e) promotion

18. A step in the recruiting process that involves screening applicants is the:
    a) training procedure.
    b) orientation procedure.
    c) upward appraisal.
    d) interview.
    e) probation period.

19. All of the following are advantages of diversity in the workplace except:
    a) increased innovation.
    b) less chance of discrimination lawsuits.
    c) enhanced ability to interact with customers.
    d) better access to the pool of eligible employees.
    e) a change in the production process.

20. A company gives employees the right to purchase its stock at a specified price when it provides them with:
    a) presumptive rights.
    b) an indenture agreement.
    c) stock options.
    d) a stock preference.
    e) a closed-end agreement.

21. The use of stock options as a means of compensation:
    a) legally can be provided only to top executives and members of the board of directors.
    b) is declining in popularity since options reduce the firm's profits.
    c) is opposed by labor unions, since options are available only to nonunion employees.
    d) may tempt managers to manipulate financial statements to boost stock prices.
    e) has allowed workers in many firms to control who serves on the board of directors of their firm.

22. An extra onetime payment at the end of a period in which performance was measured is a:
    a) salary.
    b) wage.
    c) stock option.
    d) piece rate.
    e) bonus.

23. _____ normally represent compensation for achieving specific sales objectives and often are part of the compensation received by people working in sales positions.
    a) Pensions
    b) Commissions
    c) Perquisites
    d) Stock options
    e) Dividends

24. Additional privileges given to high-level employees, such as a company car or membership in an exclusive club, are known as:
    a) professional privileges.
    b) commissions.
    c) executive options.
    d) perquisites.
    e) golden parachutes.

25. _____ are additional privileges, such as paid vacation time and health and dental insurance, given to most or all employees.
    a) Employee benefits
    b) Perquisites
    c) Commissions
    d) Implicit compensations
    e) Kickbacks

26. Employees who are directly involved in the production process (such as assembly-line workers) tend to receive most of their compensation in the form of a:
    a) bonus.
    b) commission.
    c) salary.
    d) stock option.
    e) perquisite.

27. A performance evaluation:
    a) should avoid subjective criteria because they are impossible to measure with any accuracy.
    b) is only useful as a means of determining whether employees qualify for pay raises.
    c) is typically based on multiple criteria, some of which are objective while others are subjective.
    d) is only necessary for workers who are likely candidates for higher-level positions.
    e) should be given only to workers who are experiencing job-related problems.

28. The following are objective criteria in performance evaluation except for:
    a) parts produced per week.
    b) number of days absent.
    c) percentage of deadlines missed.
    d) defective parts produced by employee errors.
    e) willingness of an employee to help other employees.

29. When firms allow employees to evaluate their supervisors, this process is known as a(n):
    a) management audit.
    b) upward appraisal.
    c) forward appraisal.
    d) peer review.
    e) executive evaluation.

30. When employees evaluate their supervisors, the results are likely to be more meaningful if the appraisal is done:
    a) verbally, with nothing put in writing.
    b) without the supervisor's knowledge.
    c) no more than once every two years.
    d) anonymously.
    e) only by employees who have known the supervisor for more than two years.

| True/False | | Multiple Choice | | |
|---|---|---|---|---|
| 1. False | 8. True | 11. a | 18. d | 25. a |
| 2. True | 9. True | 12. a | 19. e | 26. c |
| 3. True | 10. False | 13. c | 20. c | 27. c |
| 4. True | | 14. a | 21. d | 28. e |
| 5. True | | 15. a | 22. e | 29. b |
| 6. False | | 16. b | 23. b | 30. d |
| 7. False | | 17. e | 24. d | |

# Self-Test of Key Terms

bonus  368
commissions  368
compensation package  365
employee benefits  369
employment test  359
external recruiting  358

human resource manager  357
human resource planning  356
internal recruiting  357
job analysis  356
job description  356
job specification  356

perquisites  369
profit sharing  369
promotion  358
salary (or wages)  365
stock options  365
upward appraisals  380

Fill in each blank with the proper key term. To assess your understanding of the key terms, answers are provided at the end of this self-test.

1. _____ are completed by employees in order to assess their supervisors.
2. A(n) _____ consists of the total monetary compensation and benefits offered to employees.
3. The _____ provides the tasks and responsibilities involved in the position.
4. _____ represent compensation for meeting specific sales objectives.
5. A firm uses _____ when it attempts to fill positions with applicants from outside the firm.
6. A(n) _____ is a test of the job candidate's abilities.
7. The _____ lists the credentials that are necessary to qualify for a specific job position.

8. _____ granted to employees allow employees to purchase the firm's stock at a specific price.

9. The _____ involves determining the tasks and necessary credentials for a particular position.

10. A(n) _____ is an extra onetime payment at the end of a period in which performance was measured.

11. _____ occurs when employees are offered a portion of the firm's profits.

12. _____ represent additional privileges beyond compensation payments, such as paid vacation time and insurance.

13. The three major tasks of _____ are forecasting staffing needs, job analysis, and recruiting.

**Answers:**
1. Upward appraisals
2. compensation package
3. job description
4. Commissions
5. external recruiting
6. employment test
7. job specification
8. Stock options
9. job analysis
10. bonus
11. Profit sharing
12. Employee benefits
13. human resource planning

## Concept Review Questions

1. **Business Valuation.** Explain why the hiring, training, and evaluation of employees can affect the value of a business.

2. **Job Analysis.** Explain what is involved in a job analysis.

3. **Recruiting.** Describe the steps involved in the recruiting process.

4. **Internal Recruiting.** What is the benefit of internal recruiting? What is a potential disadvantage of internal recruiting?

5. **Diversity.** Describe the potential benefits to a firm that achieves diversity among its employees.

6. **Compensation Package.** Describe the key components of a compensation package.

7. **Stock Options.** Explain how stock options can align the goals of managers and shareholders. Explain why stock options are not always an effective method of compensation.

8. **Employee Skills.** Explain the key work skills that are needed by human resources.

9. **Employee Evaluations.** Explain the key steps of employee evaluations.

10. **Upward Appraisals.** What are upward appraisals? Why should firms encourage upward appraisals?

## Classroom Communication Questions

1. **Hiring Dilemma.** A small business has 40 employees and all six managers are males. The business wants to create more diversity by gender in its management. It currently has one managerial position open. Many of its existing employees quality for the position, and its top three internal applicants for this position are males. Should it hire a male applicant internally, hire a female applicant internally, or hire a female applicant who does not work for the business but whose qualifications are at least as high as those of any internal candidate?

2. **Commission Dilemma.** If you owned a small retail clothing store, would you pay your workers a commission based on how much clothing they sold? Is there a way that you could motivate them to sell, yet prevent them from giving bad advice to customers just to generate sales?

3. **Labor Union Issue.** Are labor unions (discussed in the appendix) beneficial to U.S. businesses?

# Small Business Case

## Hiring, Compensation, and Performance Evaluation Decisions

Web Czar Company develops websites for businesses. It recently received many orders from businesses that either want new websites or want to revise their existing websites. Brent Barber, the owner, forecasts that he needs to hire at least two more website designers on a full-time basis. He conducts a job analysis and develops the job specification stating the credentials that the designers need. The job openings are posted in the local newspaper. Brent engages in external recruiting by reviewing all the applications on file and new applications that arrive in response to the posted job openings.

1. **Interviewing Decision.** Brent would prefer to hire designers based on their credentials without conducting formal interviews. Why might this strategy backfire?

2. **Screening Applicants.** If many applicants have equally strong credentials, what characteristic could be used to select an applicant for a job?

3. **Hiring from Within the Business.** Some existing employees of Web Czar Company are upset with Brent because they want to be hired for the open job positions. They do not have the skills to be web designers, but they say that they have been loyal employees at the firm for more than five years and should be promoted to the position of web designer. Should Brent hire these employees for the web designer positions?

4. **Performance Evaluation.** The web designers of Web Czar Company are evaluated according to how well they satisfy the business's clients. The amount of time they spend on a web design project is not considered. Explain why the amount of time spent on a web design project deserves to be considered when assessing employee performance.

# Web Insight

## PepsiCo's Employee Diversity

At the opening of the chapter, PepsiCo was introduced. Go to the PepsiCo website (www.pepsico.com) and go to the section on Diversity. Summarize PepsiCo's comments about why it attempts to achieve diversity.

# Dell's Secret for Success

Go to Dell's website (www.dell.com) and click on the link "About Dell," near the bottom of the web page. You can also review a recent annual report of Dell for more information.

1. **Diversity.** Describe Dell's success in achieving a diverse workplace.

2. **Impact of Diversity.** How do you think diversity has resulted in higher performance at Dell?

3. **Stock Option Compensation.** Do you think Dell benefits from providing options to buy its stock at a low price as partial compensation to employees?

## Video Exercises

### Lessons in Hiring Employees

Many free business videos are available on websites such as YouTube (www.youtube.com), and more are added every day. Search for a recent video clip about an existing business that offers lessons on "hiring employees" in YouTube or any other website that provides video clips.

1. **Main Lesson.** What is the name of the business in the video clip? Is the video clip focused on the job description, the interviewing process, or some other aspect of the hiring process? What is the main lesson of the video clip that you watched?

2. **Attention to Hiring Process.** Many videos suggest that the success of a business is highly dependent on its employees. Most businesses attempt to hire good employees, but some businesses are much better at it than others.

Why do you think some businesses are better at hiring employees?

3. **Employee Attitude.** Some videos suggest that the most important characteristic of an applicant is attitude. What does this really mean? How can attitude make a difference?

## Projects

To encourage further comprehension of concepts covered in Chapter 11, the following five projects are available:

1. Analyzing Your Favorite Business

2. Building a Business Plan for Campus.com

3. Running Your Own Business

4. Planning Your Career

5. Stock Market Contest

All of these projects are provided in Appendix A at the end of the text. In addition, projects are available by part division at the end of each part.

A Word file for each project is also available at the textbook website (www.emcp.net/business5e) so that you may maintain one ongoing file for each project.

# Chapter 11 Appendix
# Labor Unions

**labor union**
an association established to represent the views, needs, and concerns of labor

A **labor union** is established to represent the views, needs, and concerns of labor. A union can attempt to determine the needs of its workers and then negotiate with the firm's management to satisfy those needs. The needs may include job security, safer working conditions, and higher salaries. The union may be able to negotiate for the workers better than they can themselves, because the workers do not have the time or the expertise for negotiating with management. Furthermore, management would not have the time to deal with each worker's needs separately. The union serves as the representative for all workers.

## A1. Background on Unions

**craft unions**
unions organized according to a specific craft (or trade), such as plumbing

**industrial unions**
unions organized for a specific industry

**local unions**
unions composed of members in a specified local area

**national unions**
unions composed of members throughout the country

**international unions**
unions that have members in several countries

Unions can be classified as either craft or industrial. **Craft unions** are organized according to a specific craft (or trade), such as plumbing. **Industrial unions** are organized for a specific industry. Unions can also be classified as either local or national. **Local unions** are composed of members in a specified local area. **National unions** are composed of members throughout the country. Some local unions are part of a national union. **International unions** have members in several countries.

## A1.1 History of Union Activities

The popularity of unions has been affected by various laws, summarized next.

**Norris-LaGuardia Act**
restricted the use of injunctions against unions and allowed unions to publicize a labor dispute

**The Norris-LaGuardia Act** Before 1932, the courts commonly accommodated employer requests to issue injunctions against unions. In 1932, Congress passed the **Norris-LaGuardia Act**, which restricted the use of injunctions against unions and allowed unions to publicize a labor dispute. It also prohibited employers from forcing workers to sign a **yellow-dog contract**, which was a contract requiring employees to refrain from joining a union as a condition of employment.

**yellow-dog contract**
a contract requiring employees to refrain from joining a union as a condition of employment

**Wagner Act**
prohibited firms from interfering with workers' efforts to organize or join unions

**The Wagner Act** Even with the Norris-LaGuardia Act, firms were able to discourage employees from joining or organizing unions. The **Wagner Act** (also referred to as the National Labor Relations Act) prohibited firms from interfering with workers' efforts to organize or join unions. Employers could not discriminate against employees who participated in union activities. In addition, the act required employers to negotiate with the union representing employees.

**Taft-Hartley Act**
an amendment to the Wagner Act that prohibited unions from pressuring employees to join

**right-to-work**
allows states to prohibit union shops

**Landrum-Griffin Act**
required labor unions to specify in their bylaws the membership eligibility requirements, dues, and collective bargaining procedures

**The Taft-Hartley Act**   Although the Wagner Act reduced employer discrimination against union participants, it was unable to reduce the number of strikes. The **Taft-Hartley Act**, an amendment to the Wagner Act, prohibited unions from pressuring employees to join. An exception is the union shop, where new employees are required to join the union. The **right-to-work** section of this act allows states to prohibit union shops (several states have used this power).

**The Landrum-Griffin Act**   In 1959, Congress passed the **Landrum-Griffin Act** (originally called the Labor-Management Reporting and Disclosure Act of 1959). This act required labor unions to specify in their bylaws the membership eligibility requirements, dues, and collective bargaining procedures.

## A1.2   Trends in Union Popularity

Union membership declined slightly in the early 1930s, as firms discouraged workers from participating in labor activities. After the Wagner Act was passed in 1935, union membership increased rapidly. By 1945, more than one-fourth of all workers were union members. During the 1980s and 1990s, however, union membership consistently declined. In 2008, only about 12 percent of all workers were union members. One of the reasons for the decline was the inability of some unionized firms to compete with nonunion firms whose expenses were lower.

## A2.   Negotiations Between Unions and Management

Contracts between unions and management commonly last for two to three years. An attempt is made to agree to a new contract before the existing contract expires. The union obtains feedback from its members on what working conditions need to be improved. The union also obtains data on existing wages and employee benefits provided for jobs similar to those of members. Management assesses existing conditions and determines the types of provisions it may be willing to make.

Before the actual negotiations begin, the union may offer a proposed revision of the existing contract. This proposal often includes very high demands, which management will surely refuse. Management may also offer a proposed revision of the existing contract that the union will surely refuse. Normally, the original gap between the two sides is very large. This establishes the foundation for negotiations.

When the union and management meet to negotiate a new contract, the more critical issues to be discussed include the following:

✦ Salaries

✦ Job security

✦ Management rights

✦ Grievance procedures

## A2.1   Salaries

A general concern of unions is to improve or at least maintain their members' standard of living. Unions are credited for negotiating high wages for their members. Unionized grocery store employees commonly receive at least double the salaries of nonunionized employees in the same job positions. Airline pilot captains of unionized airlines, such as American and Delta, earn more than $100,000 per year, while pilot captains of nonunionized airlines commonly earn less than $50,000 per year.

Unions attempt to negotiate for salary increases that will at least match expected increases in the cost of living. They also monitor salaries of workers at other firms to determine the salary increases that they will request. For example, the United Auto Workers (UAW) commonly uses the content of its contract with one car manufacturer to negotiate its new contract with another car manufacturer.

If the firm has experienced high profits in recent years, a union may use this as reason to negotiate for large wage increases. Conversely, firms that recently experienced losses will argue that they cannot afford to make pay increases. When pilots at Continental Airlines did not receive a salary increase over several years, poor relations developed between the pilots and management at Continental.

## A2.2  Job Security

Job security is a key issue from the perspective of workers. They want to be assured of a job until retirement. Management may not be willing to guarantee job security but may at least specify the conditions under which workers will be laid off. Workers with less seniority are more likely to be laid off.

Although unions are unable to force management to guarantee life-time jobs, they are somewhat successful at obtaining supplemental unemployment benefits for workers. Firms that offer these benefits contribute an amount for each hour worked into a fund. The fund is used to compensate workers who are laid off. This compensation is a supplement to the normal unemployment compensation workers receive.

Unions may also attempt to prevent management from replacing workers with machines. Management may agree to such demands if the unions reduce some of their other demands. Unions emphasize this issue in industries such as automobile manufacturing, where some tasks are highly repetitive and therefore workers are more likely to be replaced by machines.

For some workers, job security may be more important than higher wages. Therefore, firms that are willing to provide job security may not have to provide large increases in wages.

## A2.3  Management Rights

Management expects to have various rights as to how it manages its workers. For example, the union-management contract may state a specified number of work hours. Management may also retain the rights to make hiring, promotional, and transferring decisions without influence by unions.

## A2.4  Grievance Procedures

A grievance is a complaint made by an employee or the union. Contracts between a union and management specify procedures for resolving a grievance. The first step normally calls for a meeting between the employee, his or her supervisor, and a union representative. If this meeting does not resolve the grievance, the union normally meets with high-level managers.

## A3.  Conflicts Between Unions and Management

Unions use various methods to bargain for better working conditions or higher compensation. Employees may attempt to pressure management by **picketing**, or walking around near the employer's building with signs complaining of poor working conditions. Employees can also **boycott** the employer's products and services offered by refusing to purchase them.

### A3.1  Labor Strikes

A more dramatic method of bargaining is a **strike**, which is a discontinuation of employee services. Two recent well-publicized strikes were those by employees at UPS and at General Motors. The goal of the UPS strike was to achieve better wages. The objective of the General Motors strike was to ensure that some of GM's plants would not be closed.

The impact of a strike on a firm depends on the firm's ability to carry on operations during the strike. For example, if all machinists of a manufacturing firm strike, the firm's production will be severely reduced unless its other workers can substitute. Most firms carry an inventory of finished products that may be used to accommodate orders during the strike. However, even a large inventory will not be sufficient if the strike lasts long enough.

The publicity of a strike can reduce a firm's perceived credibility. Even though a strike is only temporary, it can create permanent damage. Some firms have long-term arrangements with other companies to provide a specified volume of supplies periodically. If these companies fear that their orders will not be satisfied because of a strike, they will search for a firm that is less likely to experience a strike.

To illustrate how the dissatisfaction of employees can affect a firm's value, consider the case of Caterpillar. About 14,000 of Caterpillar's workers went on strike on June 21, 1994. Exhibit 11A.1 shows the stock price

**picketing**

walking around near the employer's building with signs complaining of poor working conditions

**boycott**

refusing to purchase products and services

**strike**

a discontinuation of employee services

**Exhibit 11A.1**

Example of How a Strike Can Affect a Firm's Value

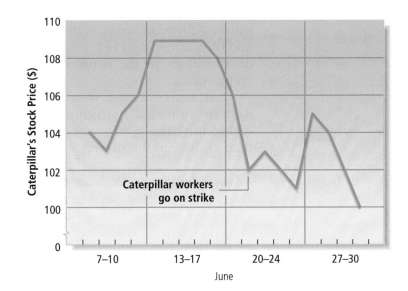

of Caterpillar around the time of the strike. Notice how the stock price declined by more than $4 per share in response to the strike. The strike lasted more than 17 months. Caterpillar replaced many of the strikers with temporary workers and experienced record earnings over the strike period. By the end of the strike, about one-third of the strikers returned to work without any compromise by Caterpillar.

## A3.2 Management's Response to Strikes

**injunction**
a court order to prevent a union from a particular activity such as picketing

**lockout**
prevents employees from working until an agreement between management and labor is reached

Management may respond to union pressure by obtaining an **injunction**, which is a court order to prevent the union from a particular activity such as picketing. Alternatively, it could use a **lockout**, which prevents employees from working until an agreement between management and labor is reached.

Another common response by management is to show how large benefits to workers will possibly result in the firm's failure, which would effectively terminate all jobs. The management of Northwest Airlines and US Air (now US Airways) used this approach in the mid-1990s to prevent excessive demands by the union. In 2005, Delta Airlines and Northwest Airlines used this strategy. Some airlines have recently offered their pilots partial ownership of the firm in place of salary increases.

The amount of bargaining power a union has is partially dependent on whether the firm can easily replace employees who go on strike. For example, an airline cannot easily replace pilots in a short period of time because of the extensive training needed. Other workers with specialized mechanical skills also have some bargaining power. When 33,000 machinists of Boeing (a producer of aircraft) went on strike in 1995, they forced Boeing to provide a larger salary increase as an incentive to end the strike. However, a strike by workers at Bridgestone/Firestone (a producer of tires) was not as successful, as the firm hired replacement workers.

## A3.3 Management's Criticism of Unions

Unions are criticized by management for several reasons, some of which are discussed here.

**Higher Prices or Lower Profits**  If unions achieve high wages for employees, firms may pass the increase on to consumers in the form of higher prices. If firms do not pass the increase on, their profits may be reduced, and the shareholders of the firm will be adversely affected. In essence, the disadvantages to the consumers or shareholders offset the benefits to employees.

A related criticism is that high wages resulting from the union can reduce the firm's ability to compete internationally. This was a major criticism during the 1980s, when many foreign competitors increased their market share in the United States.

**Adverse Impact on Economic Conditions**  A decision to strike by some unions can severely damage a given industry. Unions have the power to close large manufacturing plants, shut down an airline's operations, or even halt garbage collection. Some shutdowns can have a severe impact on the local area.

**Production Inefficiency**   Some unions have negotiated for a minimum number of workers to perform a specific task. In some cases, the number of workers has exceeded the number actually needed. A related criticism is that workers are sometimes perceived to be protected from being fired if they are in a union. A firm may be unwilling to fire an unproductive employee if it believes the union will file a grievance. If a firm retains unproductive workers, its efficiency is reduced, and its cost of production increases.

## A3.4  How Firms Reduce Employees' Desire for a Union

The management of some firms has consistently maintained good relations with labor. Consequently, labor has not attempted to organize a union. The following guidelines are some of the more common methods used to maintain good relations with employees:

1.  Management should promote employees from within so that employees are satisfied with their career paths.

2.  Management should attempt to avoid layoffs so that employees do not feel threatened whenever business slows down. This may be achieved by reassigning job positions to some employees who are no longer needed in their original positions.

3.  Management should allow employees responsibility and input into some decisions. Labor contracts between labor and management may require labor-management committees to be created at each plant to develop methods for improving efficiency. This is a classic example of considering input from employees.

4.  Management should maintain reasonable working conditions to demonstrate fairness to employees.

5.  Management should offer reasonable and competitive wages so that employees feel properly rewarded and are not continually quitting to take other jobs.

The points just listed represent the key provisions for which unions negotiate. If the firm adheres to these guidelines, workers may not need to organize a union. Reducing employees' desire to join a union may become increasingly important in the coming years if Congress passes legislation that was pending at the beginning of 2009. The proposed legislation would make it easier for employees to organize a union.

# Summary/Part IV

# Managing Employees

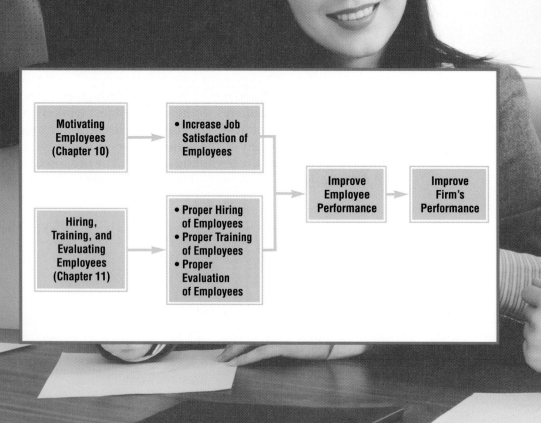

```
┌──────────────┐      ┌──────────────┐
│  Motivating  │      │• Increase Job│
│  Employees   │ ───▶ │  Satisfaction│
│ (Chapter 10) │      │  of          │
│              │      │  Employees   │
└──────────────┘      └──────────────┘ ──┐     ┌──────────────┐     ┌──────────────┐
                                          ├──▶  │   Improve    │ ──▶ │   Improve    │
┌──────────────┐      ┌──────────────┐   │     │   Employee   │     │    Firm's    │
│   Hiring,    │      │• Proper      │   │     │ Performance  │     │ Performance  │
│ Training, and│      │  Hiring      │   │     └──────────────┘     └──────────────┘
│  Evaluating  │ ───▶ │  of Employees│ ──┘
│  Employees   │      │• Proper      │
│ (Chapter 11) │      │  Training    │
│              │      │  of Employees│
└──────────────┘      │• Proper      │
                      │  Evaluation  │
                      │  of Employees│
                      └──────────────┘
```

# Summary

The chapters in Part IV focus on the management of employees. Chapter 10 explains various methods that can be used to motivate employees. Effective motivation can influence the effort of employees and therefore affects a firm's performance and value. Chapter 11 explains how to hire, train, and evaluate employees. Effective hiring methods may enable a firm to hire the best candidates for a job position. Effective training and evaluation methods may enable a firm to get the most out of its employees. Overall, motivation (Chapter 10) and training and evaluation (Chapter 11) can increase the job satisfaction level, which increases employee productivity and therefore enhances the performance of the firm.

# Video on Managing a Business

## Hiring the Best Employees

The Small Business Administration plays a very important role in helping many small businesses. Its website, which offers a wide range of services and information for small businesses, has a section called Delivering Success (www.sba.gov/tools/audiovideo/deliveringsuccess/index.html) that provides video clips of small business success stories. Go to this website, and watch the video called "Hiring and Developing Employees" (total time of clip is 9 minutes, 15 seconds).

This video contains advice from three entrepreneurs of very successful small businesses. All the entrepreneurs emphasize that the success of a small business is highly dependent on the employees that are hired. The insight provided by the entrepreneurs is summarized below:

✦ Entrepreneurs should give their employees more responsibilities. This not only allows entrepreneurs to focus on bigger decisions, but it also makes the job more enjoyable for employees.

✦ Businesses should take corrective action toward employees who are not performing well.

✦ Businesses should spend much time screening job applicants so that they are likely to hire the applicants who will be most effective.

✦ Businesses should devote considerable time to training their employees to make sure that the employees are well informed about the products that they are producing or selling.

✦ Some businesses can benefit from hiring prospective employees for a trial period so that the abilities and attitudes of the prospective employees can be fully assessed.

✦ Employees need to have goals that are aligned with those of the business.

1. **Interaction Between Motivation and Compensation.** Explain how employee motivation (Chapter 10) and compensation (Chapter 11) are indirectly related.

2. **Interaction Between Job Enrichment Programs and Compensation Package.** Explain how a firm's job enrichment program (Chapter 10) can affect the compensation package (Chapter 11) that it must offer in order to attract good employees.

3. **Interaction Between Motivation and Credentials.** Are businesses successful because they motivate employees (Chapter 10) or because they effectively screen their job applicants and hire the best employees?

# Self-Test for Part IV

**Chapters 10–11.** Answers are provided at the end of the self-test.

1. One implication of the Hawthorne studies is that workers can be motivated by receiving:
   a) attention.
   b) money.
   c) stock.
   d) bonuses.
   e) profit sharing.

2. Social interaction and acceptance by others are examples of:
   a) physiological needs.
   b) esteem needs.
   c) safety needs.
   d) social needs.
   e) self-actualization needs.

3. According to Herzberg, employees are commonly most satisfied when offered:
   a) adequate supervision.
   b) adequate salary.
   c) recognition.
   d) job security.
   e) safe working conditions.

4. Which of the following theories of management suggests that workers will be motivated if they are compensated in accordance with their perceived contributions to the firm?
   a) expectancy theory
   b) equity theory
   c) need theory
   d) Theory Y
   e) reinforcement theory

5. In an across-the-board system, all employees receive similar:
   a) raises.
   b) job assignments.
   c) offices.
   d) work schedules.
   e) performance appraisals.

6. Which of the following is not a guideline for designing a motivational compensation system?
   a) Align the system with business goals.
   b) Align the system with specific employee goals.
   c) Establish systems for rewarding employee seniority.
   d) Set achievable goals for employees.
   e) Allow employee input on the compensation system.

7. Even if the company cannot guarantee continuing employment, it can improve employees' sense of job security by:
   a) empowering employees.
   b) granting stock to employees.
   c) using open-book management.
   d) training employees in various tasks.
   e) instituting compressed workweeks.

8. An employee involvement program that periodically moves individuals from one job assignment to another is:
   a) job enlargement.
   b) job enrichment.
   c) job rotation.
   d) job sharing.
   e) flextime.

9. When firms delegate more authority to their employees, this strategy is referred to as:
   a) Theory X management.
   b) empowerment.
   c) the merit system.
   d) McGregor's hygiene theory.
   e) the equity system.

10. In open-book management, the compensation of employees is typically aligned with their contribution to the firm's:
    a) hierarchy of needs.
    b) industry demand.
    c) overall performance.
    d) reinforcement theory.
    e) hygiene theory.

11. A major responsibility of a human resource manager is to:
    a) help each specific department recruit candidates for its open positions.
    b) conduct the performance evaluations for all employees.
    c) establish the information system and local area network used by the firm's employees.
    d) help select the members of top management who will serve on the firm's board of directors.
    e) prevent the formation of labor unions.

12. The process used to determine the tasks and the necessary credentials for a particular position is referred to as:
    a) job analysis.
    b) job screening.
    c) human resource planning.
    d) human resource forecasting.
    e) recruiting.

13. When a firm attempts to fill job openings with persons it already employs, it is engaging in:
    a) intrapreneurship.
    b) internal recruiting.
    c) entrenchment.
    d) precruiting.
    e) focused recruiting.

14. A step in the recruiting process that involves screening applicants is the:
    a) training procedure.
    b) orientation procedure.
    c) upward appraisal.
    d) interview.
    e) probation period.

15. A company gives employees the right to purchase its stock at a specified price when it provides them with:
    a) presumptive rights.
    b) an indenture agreement.
    c) stock options.
    d) a stock preference.
    e) a closed-end agreement.

16. An extra onetime payment at the end of a period in which performance was measured is a:
    a) salary.
    b) wage.
    c) stock option.
    d) piece rate.
    e) bonus.

17. Additional privileges given to high-level employees, such as a company car or membership in an exclusive club, are known as:
    a) professional privileges.
    b) commissions.
    c) executive options.
    d) perquisites.
    e) golden parachutes.

18. Employees who are directly involved in the production process (such as assembly-line workers) tend to receive most of their compensation in the form of a:
    a) bonus.
    b) commission.
    c) salary.
    d) stock option.
    e) perquisite.

19. The following are objective criteria in performance evaluation except for:
    a) parts produced per week.
    b) number of days absent.
    c) percentage of deadlines missed.
    d) defective parts produced by employee errors.
    e) willingness of an employee to help other employees.

20. When employees evaluate their supervisors, the results are likely to be more meaningful if the appraisal is done:
    a) verbally, with nothing put in writing.
    b) without the supervisor's knowledge.
    c) no more than once every two years.
    d) anonymously.
    e) only by employees who have known the supervisor for more than two years.

**Answers:**

| | | | |
|---|---|---|---|
| 1. a | 6. c | 11. a | 16. e |
| 2. d | 7. d | 12. a | 17. d |
| 3. c | 8. c | 13. b | 18. c |
| 4. b | 9. b | 14. d | 19. e |
| 5. a | 10. c | 15. c | 20. d |

# Projects

## PROJECT 1:  ANALYZING YOUR FAVORITE BUSINESS

**Answering the Questions.** This entire project is provided in Appendix A. You can retrieve the Word file of this project from the textbook website (www.emcp.net /business5e), and insert your answer just below each question. The portion of the project that is related to the chapters in this part is provided here.

Using the annual report of the firm you selected, answer the following questions:

**Firm's Motivation of Employees (related to Chapters 10 and 11).** How does the firm motivate its employees? Does it offer special programs to enhance job satisfaction?

**Firm's Compensation for Employees (related to Chapters 10 and 11).** Does the firm offer bonuses or stock options to motivate its employees?

## PROJECT 2:  BUILDING A BUSINESS PLAN FOR CAMPUS.COM

**Completing the Information.** You can complete the information on the Word file of this project from the textbook website (www.emcp .net/business5e). This allows you to insert all of your information on one file for this project by the end of the school term. The portion of the project that is related to the chapters in this part is provided here.

**Motivating Employees (related to Chapter 10).** Working conditions for Campus.com employees will be:

_____

_____
_____
_____

Disadvantages of the working conditions that may limit employee effectiveness:

_____
_____
_____
_____

**Hiring, Training, and Evaluating Employees (related to Chapter 11).** Employees' performance will be assessed by:

_____
_____

The compensation plan for employees will be:

_____
_____
_____

## PROJECT 3:  RUNNING YOUR OWN BUSINESS

**Completing the Information.** This entire project is provided in Appendix A. You can retrieve the Word file of this project from the textbook website (www.emcp.net/ business5e), and insert your answer just below each question. The portion of the project that is related to the chapters in this part is provided here.

**Motivating Employees (related to Chapter 10).** You will motivate your employees by:

_____
_____
_____

**Hiring, Training, and Evaluating Employees (related to Chapter 11).** You will assess the performance of employees of your business by:

_____
_____

The compensation plan for your employees will be:

_____
_____

**Quality Standards (related to Chapter 9).** Your business will maintain the quality of the service it provides by:

_____
_____
_____
_____
_____
_____
_____
_____

## PROJECT 4:  PLANNING YOUR CAREER

This entire project is provided in Appendix A at the end of the text, and you can access a Word file of this project from the textbook website (www.emcp.net/business5e).

If you are very interested in the topics covered in this section, you may want to consider a major in human resources (sometimes referred to as "personnel management"). Some of the courses commonly taken by human resource majors are summarized here.

### Common Courses for Human Resource Majors

- **Organizational Behavior**  Provides a broad overview of key managerial functions, such as organizing, motivating employees, planning, controlling, and teamwork.

- **Management Environment**  Focuses on the environment in which managers work and the responsibilities of managers to society and to regulators.

- **Human Resource Management**  Focuses on the processes of hiring, training, evaluating performance, and compensating employees.

- **Labor Relations**  Examines the labor contract relationships among managers, subordinates, and unions; also covers the process of negotiating.

- **Management Strategy**  Focuses on the competitive environment faced by a firm and strategies used by a firm's managers to increase its growth or improve its performance.

- **Management Systems**  Explains the application of computer software and systems to facilitate decision making.

- **Psychology**  In particular, courses that attempt to explain human behavior and the human response to penalties, rewards, and incentives.

### Careers in Human Resources

Information about job positions, salaries, and careers for students who major in human resources can be found at the following websites:

- **Job position websites:**

**http://jobsearch.monster.com** Administrative and Support Services, Consulting Services, and Human Resources.

**http://careers.yahoo.com** Management Consulting.

- **Salary website:**

**http://collegejournal.com /salarydata** Consulting, Human Resources, and Logistics.

Some of the job positions described at these websites may require work experience or a graduate degree.

## PROJECT 5:  STOCK MARKET CONTEST

This entire project is provided in Appendix A at the end of the text, and you can access a Word file of the project from the textbook website (www.emcp.net/business5e). Your instructor may ask you to assess the performance of your investment up to this point, and whether the performance of your stock is attributed to any of the business concepts that were described in the chapters contained in this part.

# Part V
# Marketing

**12** Creating and Pricing Products

**13** Distributing Products

**14** Promoting Products

Marketing can be broadly defined as the actions of firms to plan and execute the design, pricing, distribution, and promotion of products. A firm's marketing mix is the combination of the product, pricing, distribution, and promotion strategies used to sell products.

In applying these strategies, a firm begins by using marketing research to define a consumer need. Once a product is developed to satisfy this need, a pricing decision is made. The pricing policy affects the demand for the product and therefore affects the firm's revenue. Then, a method of distributing the product to consumers must be selected. The use of intermediaries tends to make the product more accessible to customers but also results in higher prices. Finally, a promotion strategy must be designed to make consumers aware of the product or to convince them that this product is superior to others.

To recognize how all four strategies are used by a single firm, consider a computer firm that identifies a software package that consumers need. The firm develops the software (product strategy), sets a price for the software (pricing strategy), decides to sell the software through specific computer stores (distribution strategy), and decides to advertise the software in magazines (promotion strategy). These marketing strategies continue to be used as the product follows the typical life cycle. For example, the firm may conduct marketing research to determine whether the product should be revised or targeted toward a different market. The pricing policy could change if the target market is revised or if the production costs change. The decision regarding the channel of distribution will be reviewed periodically to determine whether some alternative channel is more feasible. The promotion strategy may be revised in response to changes in the target market, pricing, phase of the life cycle, or the channel of distribution. Chapter 12 focuses on the creation and pricing of products, Chapter 13 focuses on distributing products, and Chapter 14 focuses on promoting products.

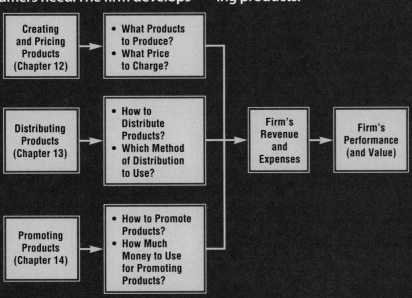

401

# Creating and Pricing Products

© SHUTTERSTOCK/STEPHEN COBURN

## Chapter 12 Learning Objectives

**1** Explain the product line, mix, and life cycle.

**2** Identify the main factors that affect a product's target market.

**3** Identify the steps involved in creating a new product.

**4** Explain the common methods used to differentiate a product.

**5** Identify the factors that influence the pricing decision.

**6** Discuss other pricing decisions that a firm may make.

# Chapter 12

## Product Strategies at Apple

Product strategies dictate the types of products that a firm creates to satisfy customers, whereas pricing strategies determine the prices to be charged for those products. Both strategies influence the demand for the products produced by the firm and therefore determine the amount of revenue that the firm will generate over a particular period. Consider Apple's creation of the iPod digital music player, which allows consumers to put their entire collection of music in their pocket. Apple's creation of this product was partially influenced by its assessment of what the market wanted and needed. Apple used its technology to create a new product that consumers wanted. When Apple creates products, it must make the following decisions:

✦ What types of products could it create that would fit within its existing line of products?

✦ How big will the target market be?

✦ What steps would be necessary to create a new product?

✦ How can it differentiate its product from those of competitors?

✦ What factors should it consider when deciding on the price of its products?

Apple incurs expenses when it develops ideas for new products, when it experiments with its ideas, and when it produces new products. However, it is rewarded when it successfully creates new products that satisfy consumers, because it generates more revenue from selling the new products. This chapter explains how the product and pricing decisions by Apple or any other firm can be conducted in a manner that maximizes the firm's value.

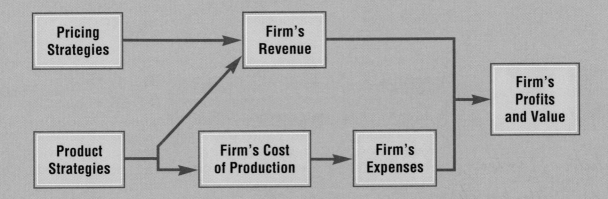

Pricing Strategies → Firm's Revenue → Firm's Profits and Value

Product Strategies → Firm's Cost of Production → Firm's Expenses

**Learning Objective**

Explain the product line, mix, and life cycle.

**1**

**product**
a physical good or service that can satisfy consumer needs

**convenience products**
products that are widely available to consumers, are purchased frequently, and are easily accessible

**shopping products**
products that are not purchased frequently

**specialty products**
products that specific consumers consider to be special and therefore make a special effort to purchase

**product line**
a set of related products or services offered by a single firm

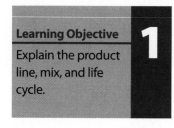

**product mix**
the assortment of products offered by a firm

# 1. Background on Products

The term **product** can be broadly defined to include both physical goods and services that can satisfy consumer needs. Firms must continually improve existing products and develop new products to satisfy customers over time. In this way, firms generate high sales growth, which normally increases their value.

Most products produced to serve consumers can be classified as convenience products, shopping products, or specialty products. **Convenience products** are widely available to consumers, are purchased frequently, and are easily accessible. Milk, newspapers, soda, and chewing gum are examples of convenience products.

**Shopping products** differ from convenience products in that they are not purchased frequently. Before purchasing shopping goods, consumers typically shop around and compare the quality and prices of competing products. Furniture and appliances are examples of shopping products.

**Specialty products** are products that specific consumers consider to be special and therefore make a special effort to purchase. A Rolex watch and a Jaguar automobile are examples of specialty products. When evaluating specialty products, consumers base their purchasing decision primarily on personal preference, not on comparative pricing.

## 1.1 Product Line

A **product line** is a set of related products or services offered by a single firm. For example, Coke, Diet Coke, Caffeine-Free Diet Coke, and Sprite are all part of a single product line at The Coca-Cola Company. Pepsi, Diet Pepsi, Mountain Dew, and Gatorade are all part of a single product line at PepsiCo.

A product line tends to expand over time as a firm identifies other consumer needs. The Coca-Cola Company recognizes that consumers differ with respect to their desire for a specific taste, caffeine versus no caffeine, and diet versus regular. It has expanded its product line of soft drinks to satisfy various needs. Procter & Gamble has added different versions of its Tide detergent such as Tide with Bleach to its product line over time, while Taco Bell has added various low-fat food items to its menus.

## 1.2 Product Mix

The assortment of products offered by a firm is referred to as the **product mix**. Most firms tend to expand their product mix over time as they identify other consumer needs or preferences. Before firms add more products to their product mix, they should determine whether a demand for new products exists and whether they are capable of efficiently providing those products. A firm may even decide to discontinue one of the products in its product mix.

**Examples of a Product Mix**   Quaker State originally focused on motor oil but added windshield washer fluid, brake fluid, and many other automobile products to its product mix. Amazon.com originally focused on selling books, but has added electronics, toys, music, kitchen products, drugs, and health and beauty products. The product mix of Liz Claiborne, Inc., includes clothing for women, jewelry, fashion accessories, and clothing for men.

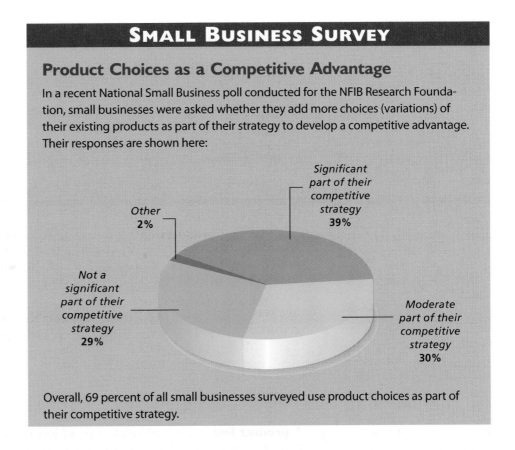

## SMALL BUSINESS SURVEY

### Product Choices as a Competitive Advantage

In a recent National Small Business poll conducted for the NFIB Research Foundation, small businesses were asked whether they add more choices (variations) of their existing products as part of their strategy to develop a competitive advantage. Their responses are shown here:

*Other*
**2%**

*Significant part of their competitive strategy*
**39%**

*Not a significant part of their competitive strategy*
**29%**

*Moderate part of their competitive strategy*
**30%**

Overall, 69 percent of all small businesses surveyed use product choices as part of their competitive strategy.

IBM's product mix includes software, hardware, and global services. The hardware segment generates more sales than either of the other segments, but its proportion of total sales is lower than in previous years. Meanwhile, the proportion of total sales generated by IBM's global services segment (which includes information technology) has increased substantially. This change in the relative proportions reflects IBM's shift away from its hardware product line and into other product lines related to information technology.

Service firms also have a product mix. For example, some commercial banks accept deposits, provide checking services, extend loans, and offer insurance products.

**Diversifying the Product Mix**   When their primary product is subject to wide swings in demand, firms tend to diversify their product mix so that they will not be completely dependent on one market. By diversifying, they are not as reliant on a single product whose performance is uncertain. Firms with flexible production facilities that allow for the production of additional goods are more capable of diversifying their product mix.

A common diversification strategy is for a firm to diversify products within its existing production capabilities. For example, hospital supply companies offer a wide variety of supplies that can be sold to each hospital. The Walt Disney Company, which had focused on producing films for children, now offers many gift products. Clothing manufacturers such as Donna Karan offer several types of clothes that can be sold to each retail outlet. A product mix that contains several related products can allow for more efficient use of salespeople.

To understand how firms can benefit from expanding their product mix, consider the case of Amazon.com, which initially focused on filling book orders requested over the Internet. First, it began to offer CDs as well, recognizing that if customers are willing to order books online, they may also order other products. Second, it had already proved that it could provide reliable service, so customers trusted that the additional services would be reliable as well. Third, it could use its existing technology to fill CD orders, which increased efficiency. Amazon.com also acquired a stake in Drugstore.com because it believed that it could fill drug orders requested over the Internet. The growth of Amazon.com demonstrates how a firm can expand by using the resources that initially made it successful to offer additional products.

Toyota Motor Corporation has diversified by producing a variety of trucks along with its cars. When demand for its cars is stagnant, it may still benefit from an increase in demand for trucks. Wells Fargo traditionally focused on commercial banking operations, but expanded its financial services over time to include mortgages, small business banking, brokerage services, and insurance. By diversifying its businesses, Wells Fargo has reduced its exposure to the traditional banking business. Exxon (now ExxonMobil) benefited from diversifying into the petrochemical businesses because the performance of its oil business was highly exposed to changes in the market price of crude oil. DuPont produces a wide variety of products, including nylon, coatings, pharmaceuticals, polyester, and specialty fibers. Dow Chemical Company has diversified across chemicals, plastics, and energy products. Wal-Mart diversified its retail business by also becoming a retailer of groceries.

The following comments from a recent annual report from Textron (a large diversified firm) confirm the potential benefits of diversification:

*"Textron's presence in diverse industries helps achieve balance and stability in a variety of economic environments by providing insulation from business and industry cycles. More specifically, we were able to maintain consistent growth . . . because the growth of our Aircraft, Automotive, Industrial and Finance businesses more than offset the downturns in the Systems and Components segment."*

After Starbucks became famous for its coffee, it diversified its product line to offer more flavors. Now it has added wireless Internet access in its stores for convenience purposes. In doing this, Starbucks established a new theme of providing a "third place" to customers beyond their home and their workplace. By offering Internet access, it not only diversified its sources of revenue, but its customers tend to stay longer, so it sells more coffee. Some of the stores were being transformed into Hear Music Coffeehouses, where customers could make custom CDs. Thus, Starbucks has expanded its services to the point that it may even be competing with Apple, Inc. Most importantly, it is providing other services so that if there is ever a sudden decline in the demand for coffee, it will still attract customers.

Dell historically focused on the production of personal computers (PCs), but recognizing that the growth in PC sales would be limited, it began to produce and sell printers and other related products in 2003. In its first year, it managed to capture 19 percent of the market for low-cost all-in-one inkjet printers. It even changed its name from Dell Computer to

Dell, Inc., to reflect its strategy of diversifying its products. Dell's sales of PCs still account for most of its revenue, but that may change over time as it continues to diversify its products.

Bookseller Barnes & Noble created superstores that offer DVDs as well as books. These stores also have an arrangement with Starbucks to serve coffee within the stores. By offering additional products, Barnes & Noble may attract more customers to its stores.

## 1.3  Product Life Cycle

**product life cycle**
the typical set of phases that a product experiences over its lifetime

Most products experience a **product life cycle**, or a typical set of phases over their lifetime. The marketing decisions made about a particular product may be influenced by the prevailing phase of the cycle. The typical product life cycle has four specific phases:

✦  Introduction

✦  Growth

✦  Maturity

✦  Decline

**introduction phase**
the initial period in which consumers are informed about a product

**Introduction**   The **introduction phase** is the initial period in which consumers are informed about a new product. The promotion of the product is intended to introduce the product and make consumers aware of it. In some cases, the product is first tested in particular areas to determine consumer reaction. For example, the concept of direct satellite television was tested in various locations. The initial cost of producing and advertising the product may exceed the revenue received during this phase. The price of the product may initially be set high if no other competing products are in the market yet. This strategy is referred to as **price skimming**.

**price skimming**
the strategy of initially setting a high price for a product if no other competing products are in the market yet

**growth phase**
the period in which sales of a product increase rapidly

**Growth**   The **growth phase** is the period in which sales of the product increase rapidly. The marketing of the product is typically intended to reinforce its features. Cellular telephones and direct satellite TVs are in the growth phase. Other firms that are aware of the product's success may attempt to create a similar or superior product. The price of the product may be lowered once competing products enter the market.

**maturity phase**
the period in which additional competing products have entered the market, and sales of a product level off because of competition

**Maturity**   The **maturity phase** is the period in which additional competing products have entered the market, and sales of the product level off because of the increased competition. At this point, most marketing strategies are used to ensure that customers are still aware that the product exists. Some marketing strategies may offer special discounts to maintain market share. The firm may also revise the design of the existing product (product differentiation) to maintain market share. Standard cable television service is an example of a product at the maturity phase.

**decline phase**
the period in which sales of a product decline, either because of reduced consumer demand for that type of product or because competitors are gaining market share

**Decline**   The **decline phase** is the period in which sales of the product decline, either because of reduced consumer demand for that type of product or because competitors are gaining market share. If firms do not prepare for a decline phase on some products, they may experience an abrupt decline in business. Some firms begin to prepare two or more years before the anticipated decline phase by planning revisions in their existing products or services.

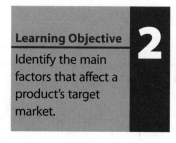

## Exhibit 12.1

Product Life Cycle Phases

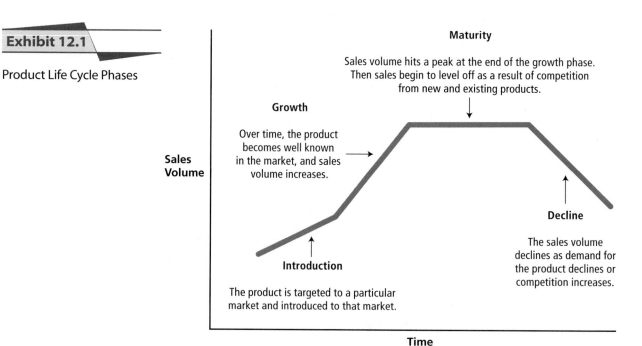

**Maturity**

Sales volume hits a peak at the end of the growth phase. Then sales begin to level off as a result of competition from new and existing products.

**Growth**

Over time, the product becomes well known in the market, and sales volume increases.

**Sales Volume**

**Decline**

The sales volume declines as demand for the product declines or competition increases.

**Introduction**

The product is targeted to a particular market and introduced to that market.

**Time**

The product life cycle is illustrated in Exhibit 12.1. The length of a cycle tends to vary among types of products. It also varies among the firms that sell a particular type of product because some firms lengthen the cycle by continually differentiating their product to maintain market share.

**Learning Objective 2**

Identify the main factors that affect a product's target market.

**target market**
a group of individuals or organizations with similar traits who may purchase a particular product

**consumer markets**
markets for various consumer products and services (such as cameras, clothes, and household items)

**industrial markets**
markets for industrial products that are purchased by firms (such as plastic and steel)

## 2. Identifying a Target Market

The consumers who purchase a particular product may have specific traits in common and thus also have similar needs. Firms attempt to identify these traits so that they can target their marketing toward people with those traits. Marketing efforts are usually targeted toward a particular **target market**, which is a group of individuals or organizations with similar traits who may purchase a particular product.

Target markets can be broadly classified as consumer markets or industrial markets. **Consumer markets** exist for various consumer products and services (such as cameras, clothes, and household items), while **industrial markets** exist for industrial products that are purchased by firms (such as plastic and steel). Some products (such as tires) can serve consumer markets or industrial markets (such as car manufacturers). Classifying markets as consumer or industrial provides only a broad description of the types of customers who purchase products, however. Consequently, firms attempt to describe their target markets more narrowly.

Common traits used to describe a target market include the consumer's gender, age, and income bracket. For example, the target market for dirt bikes may be males under 30 years of age, while the target market for three-month cruises may be wealthy males or females over 50 years of age. Eddie Bauer produces a line of casual clothes for a target market of customers between 30 and 50 years of age, while Carter's produces clothes for babies.

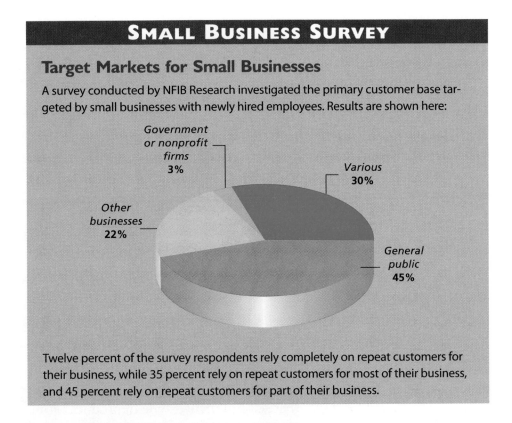

## SMALL BUSINESS SURVEY

### Target Markets for Small Businesses

A survey conducted by NFIB Research investigated the primary customer base targeted by small businesses with newly hired employees. Results are shown here:

Government or nonprofit firms
3%

Various
30%

Other businesses
22%

General public
45%

Twelve percent of the survey respondents rely completely on repeat customers for their business, while 35 percent rely on repeat customers for most of their business, and 45 percent rely on repeat customers for part of their business.

## 2.1  Factors That Affect the Size of a Target Market

As time passes, the demand for products changes. Firms attempt to be in a position to benefit from a possible increase in demand for particular products. For example, some hotels in Los Angeles and New York have anticipated an increase in Japanese guests and have offered new conveniences to capture that portion of the market. Common conveniences offered are Japanese translators, rooms with bamboo screens, and a Japanese language newspaper for these guests.

As consumer preferences change, the size of a particular target market can change. Firms monitor consumer preferences over time to anticipate how the size of their target market may be affected. The following are key factors that affect consumer preferences and therefore affect the size of the target market:

✦  Demographics

✦  Geography

✦  Economic factors

✦  Social values

**Demographics**   The total demand for particular products or services is dependent on the **demographics**, or characteristics of the human population or specific segments of the population. As demographic conditions change, so does the demand. For example, demographic statistics show an increase in the number of women who work outside the home. Firms have adjusted their product lines to capitalize on this change. Clothing stores have created more lines of business clothing for women. Food manufacturers have created easy-to-fix frozen foods to accommodate the busy schedules of wage-earning women. The tendency for people to

**demographics**
characteristics of the human population or specific segments of the population

If a business planned to set up a retail store where this photo was taken, it could determine if the demographics in this location match its customer profile. In particular, it would want to assess the typical age of people and the proportion of males versus females that walk in this location.

have less free time and more income has resulted in increased demand for more convenience services, such as quick oil changes and tire replacement services.

One of the most relevant demographic characteristics is age because target markets are sometimes defined by age levels. Demographic statistics show that the population is growing older. Consequently, the popularity of sports cars has declined as customers look for cars that are dependable and safe. Automobile manufacturers have adjusted to this demographic change by supplying fewer sports cars. Home Depot created an installation service business to capitalize on the growing number of mature customers who prefer not to do repair or installation work themselves.

Although the population has generally grown older, the number of children in the United States has recently increased. Many of these recently born children have two parents who work outside the home and spend large sums of money on their children. Firms such as OshKosh B' Gosh (a division of Carter's) and The Gap have capitalized on this trend by producing high-quality (and high-priced) children's clothing.

To illustrate how characteristics of the population can change over time, consider the changes over the 20-year period 1985–2005, shown in Exhibit 12.2. In general, the population has grown larger, while both the number of people age 65 or older and the number of households earning more than $60,000 annually have increased. Such information is relevant to firms because it suggests that the size of specific target markets may be changing over time.

**Geography**   The total demand for a product is also influenced by geography. Firms target snow tires to the northern states and surfboards to the east and west coasts of the United States. Tastes are also influenced by geography. The demand for spicy foods is higher in the southwestern states than in other states.

**Exhibit 12.2**

Changes in Consumer
Characteristics from
1985 to 2005

1. U.S. population has increased

2. Higher proportion of people age 65 or older

3. Higher proportion of households with income over $60,000

4. Higher proportion of minority households with income over $60,000

5. Higher proportion of high school students who enter college

6. Higher proportion of minority high school students who enter college

*Out of Business*

**Economic Factors**    As economic conditions change, so do consumer preferences. During a recessionary period, the demand for most types of goods declines. Specialty and shopping products are especially sensitive to these conditions. During a recession, firms may promote necessities rather than specialty products. In addition, their pricing may be more competitive. When the economy becomes stronger, firms have more flexibility to raise prices and may also promote specialty products more than necessities.

Interest rates can also have a major impact on consumer demand. When interest rates are low, consumers are more willing to purchase goods with borrowed money. The demand for products such as automobiles, boats, and homes is especially sensitive to interest rate movements because these products are often purchased with borrowed funds.

**Social Values**    As the social values of consumers change, so do their preferences. For example, the demand for cigarettes and whiskey has declined as consumers have become more aware of the dangers to health from using these products. If a firm producing either of these products anticipates a change in preferences, it can begin to shift its marketing mix. Alternatively, it could modify its product to capitalize on the trend. For example, it could reduce the alcohol content of its whiskey or the tar and nicotine content of its cigarettes. It may also revise its promotion strategy to inform the public of these changes.

# Global Business

## Targeting Foreign Countries

When firms sell their product mix in foreign countries, they must recognize that consumer characteristics vary across countries. They may use a global marketing strategy to penetrate any foreign markets where there is sufficient demand. They recognize that some products will be more successful than others in particular foreign markets. Thus, they consider the characteristics of the foreign country before deciding which products to market in that country.

Consider a U.S. producer of many types of food products. For each country, it reviews its list of products and attempts to sell the products that are popular there. It can determine the popularity of products in any country based on surveying consumers or reviewing the shelves of local grocery stores. For example, the company's mayonnaise may sell well in the Czech Republic and Slovakia but not in Latin American countries. Its cakes may sell in France, while its pudding may sell in the United Kingdom. Periodically, the company will reassess its offerings of products in each country, since consumer tastes can change over time. For example, ketchup has become more popular in some countries over time.

## 2.2 The Use of E-Marketing to Expand the Target Market

**e-marketing**
the electronic interaction with consumers in order to develop, improve, or promote products

The term **e-marketing** refers to the use of the Internet to execute the design, pricing, distribution, and promotion of products. E-marketing is part of *e-commerce,* which is the use of electronic technology to conduct business transactions, such as selling products and acquiring information about consumers, more efficiently. Amazon.com's use of e-marketing to differentiate itself from other book retailers demonstrates the importance of e-marketing. Amazon uses its website to accept orders and payment online from customers anywhere in the United States and delivers the products directly to the customers. By using the Internet, it offers customers convenience because they can purchase books without going to a store. Thus, Amazon has created a means by which it can reach a much broader target market than if it had simply opened bookstores in various locations, and it is able to offer lower prices by selling direct, without the need for retail outlets. Amazon has also personalized the website for each customer depending on what books the customer recently ordered. Thus, its "store" is structured to highlight the books that will fit the particular customer's interests.

Other retailers have noticed the popularity of ordering books online and have developed their own online systems to complement their "bricks and mortar" stores. In this way, they have also extended their target markets. Many firms that sell clothing, office supplies, travel services, electronic equipment, and many other products are using e-marketing to reach a larger target market.

The Internet also enables firms to target foreign markets. By establishing a foreign-language website that can accept orders and allow customers to pay by credit card, a firm can sell its products in foreign countries. It does not need to establish an office or hire employees in a foreign country to conduct this type of business. It can rely on its existing facilities to produce the products, use its website to market the product and accept payment, and deliver its product to the foreign customers via mail services.

In addition to allowing firms to receive orders at lower costs and to expand their target markets, e-marketing can enhance a firm's distribution (as described in Chapter 13) and its promotion of products (as described in Chapter 14).

# 3.  Creating New Products

In a given year, firms may offer more than 20,000 new products. The vast majority of these products will be discontinued within six months. These statistics suggest how difficult it is to create new products that are successful. Nevertheless, the profits from a single successful product may offset the losses resulting from several failed products.

A new product does not have to represent a famous invention. Most new products are simply improvements of existing products. Existing products become **obsolete**, or less useful than in the past, for two reasons. They may experience **fashion obsolescence** and no longer be in fashion. For example, the demand for some types of clothes declines over time because of fashion obsolescence.

Alternatively, products may experience **technological obsolescence** and be inferior to new products that are technologically more advanced. For example, when Hewlett-Packard creates faster printers, the old models are subject to technological obsolescence.

**obsolete**
less useful than in the past

**fashion obsolescence**
no longer being in fashion

**technological obsolescence**
being inferior to new products

Equipment such as copying machines (like that shown here) used by businesses and individuals is subject to technological obsolescence, as more advanced equipment is created over time.

© SHUTTERSTOCK/KONSTANTIN SHEVTSOV

Some products are created as an addition to the existing product line, rather than as a replacement for existing products. For example, Starbucks periodically adds new flavors to its existing coffee list, and Coca-Cola periodically adds new soft drinks to its existing product line.

Many additional products are created in response to customer feedback. For example, when customers frequently order a type of product that a firm does not sell, these requests prompt the firm to add that type of product to its product line. Clothing manufacturers rely heavily on customer requests to determine the types of new clothing that they produce. Many service firms expand their services in response to requests by customers.

## 3.1 Use of Marketing Research to Create Products

**marketing research**
the accumulation and analysis of data in order to make a particular marketing decision

When firms develop products, they assess the market to monitor the marketing strategies of their competitors. However, merely monitoring competitors may cause the firm to be a follower rather than a leader. Many firms prefer to make product decisions that are more innovative than those of their competitors. To obtain more insight on what consumers want, firms use **marketing research**, which is the accumulation and analysis of data in order to make a particular marketing decision.

Marketing research is useful for making product decisions. A marketing survey may find that many consumers desire a specific product that is not available. It may also identify deficiencies in the firm's existing products; this information can then be used to correct these deficiencies. The design and quality of a product may be revised to accommodate consumer preferences. For example, computer firms build computers and automobile manufacturers design their new cars to accommodate their perception of what consumers want. Firms' perceptions of consumer preferences are more accurate when backed by marketing research.

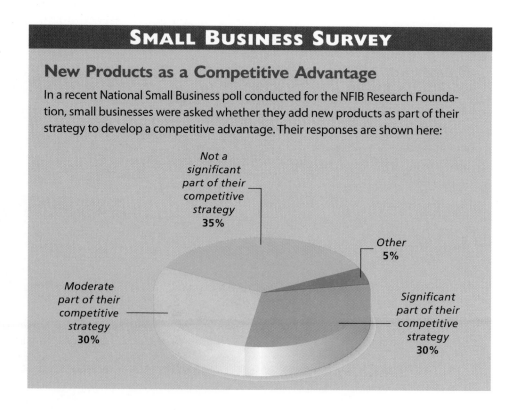

## SMALL BUSINESS SURVEY

### New Products as a Competitive Advantage

In a recent National Small Business poll conducted for the NFIB Research Foundation, small businesses were asked whether they add new products as part of their strategy to develop a competitive advantage. Their responses are shown here:

*Not a significant part of their competitive strategy*
**35%**

*Other*
**5%**

*Moderate part of their competitive strategy*
**30%**

*Significant part of their competitive strategy*
**30%**

To enable a firm to have confidence in the data obtained from marketing research, sample groups of consumers who represent the target market are studied. Many marketing research studies result in a marketing decision that will cost millions of dollars. If the marketing research leads to incorrect conclusions, the decision could result in a large loss for the firm.

One limitation of using marketing research to identify consumer preferences is that tastes change rapidly. Products, such as clothing, that were popular when the marketing research was conducted may be out of style by the time they are designed and distributed to the market.

**How E-Marketing Complements Marketing Research**   A key to developing or improving new products is to receive feedback on existing or experimental products. Many firms rely on e-marketing, which represents the electronic interaction with consumers in order to develop, improve, or promote products. The Internet is particularly useful for marketing research because it can quickly be revised and can generate quick feedback.

Firms can use the Internet for marketing research in several ways. First, by having a customer service e-mail system, a firm can obtain comments from customers about its existing products. Customers are more likely to provide feedback if they can simply send an e-mail than if they must send a letter. Second, because the firm has its customers' e-mail addresses, it can easily contact the customers to request feedback about a particular product or about their preferences. An online survey is a fast

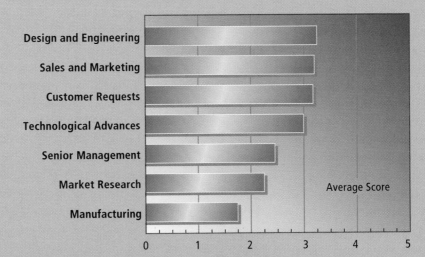

## SMALL BUSINESS SURVEY

### What Are the Keys to Creating Successful Products?

A survey asked 550 manufacturers of products to identify the sources of new product ideas. Each possible source listed in the following chart was rated 1 to 5, with 5 indicating that the source was frequently used by a firm for generating new product ideas. The chart shows the average score across the 550 manufacturers for each possible source of new product ideas.

The results indicate that new product ideas most frequently come from the engineering and marketing functions and are less frequently initiated by senior management or the manufacturing process.

way of gathering information. Third, a firm may even send out samples of an experimental product to customers who are willing to e-mail their assessment of the product to the firm. Samples have been so popular with many customers that some retailers have begun to offer online order services as well.

Procter & Gamble is well known for its extensive market research. In a recent year, about 50 percent of its huge market research budget was used for online market research. It can usually complete an online survey within 10 days, versus three or four weeks for a personal survey. In addition, an online survey costs substantially less than a personal survey. Another advantage is that some consumers are more open with their opinions online than when they are asked to respond to a survey conducted by a person.

## 3.2 Use of Research and Development to Create Products

Firms invest funds in research and development (R&D) to design new products or to improve the products they already produce. Manufacturing firms tend to invest more money in R&D than service firms because technology can improve manufactured products more easily than services.

Firms that spend money on R&D expect the benefits to exceed the expenses. Procter & Gamble's R&D resulted in its two-in-one shampoo and conditioner technology. It attributes the success of its Pantene Pro-V to its product technology. This product is now the leading shampoo in several countries. Procter & Gamble has improved the technology of Tide detergent more than 70 times. Technological development can also enable a firm to gain an advantage over its competitors. Many large firms typically spend more than $1 billion on R&D per year.

Because R&D can be so expensive, some firms have created alliances to conduct R&D. They share the costs and their technology in attempting to develop products. An alliance not only combines expertise from two or more firms, but it may also reduce the costs to each individual firm.

Many businesses such as pharmaceutical companies and technology firms rely heavily on research and development to create new product ideas.

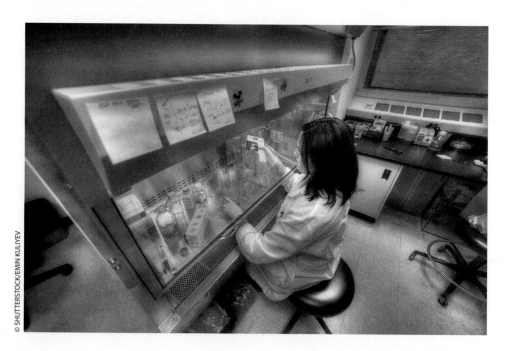

© SHUTTERSTOCK/EMIN KULIYEV

To expand their product line, many firms have recently increased their investment in R&D. For example, Abbott Laboratories has consistently increased its investment in R&D. Since Abbott Laboratories produces various medical drugs, its future performance is heavily dependent on its ability to create new drugs.

**Using Patents to Protect Research and Development**   One potential limitation of R&D is that a firm that creates a new product may not always be able to prevent its competitors from copying the idea. The potential to recover all the expenses incurred from R&D may depend on whether the ideas can be protected from competitors. To protect their ideas, firms apply for **patents**, which allow exclusive rights to the production and sale of a specific product. The U.S. Patent Office grants about 3,500 patents per week. Patents are pursued for a wide variety of products, ranging from medical drugs to special sunglasses and microwave popcorn.

Patents can enable firms that engage in extensive R&D, such as IBM and 3M, to benefit from their inventions because the patents prevent competitors from copying the ideas. The 3M Company, which created Post-it Notes, commonly obtains at least 400 patents per year. As an example of the importance of patents, consider the following comments from a recent annual report of Hewlett-Packard:

*"HP's R&D budgets and activity continue to ensure our leadership as one of the most productive product development and research institutes in the world. . . . HP was awarded nearly 1,000 patents in the United States and filed 5,000 patent applications worldwide. This essentially translates into protecting 20 new inventions every working day."*

Patents also have some disadvantages that should be recognized. Patent applications are quite tedious and may require a 20- to 40-page description of the product. Some technical patent applications are even more detailed and may contain more than 100 pages of description. Because of the large backlog of patent applications, the approval process can take several months. Many applications are not approved because the Patent Office decides that the ideas do not represent a new product. Even when a patent application is approved, it is difficult for the inventor to prevent other businesses from copying the idea in some form. Obtaining patents can also be expensive. To obtain a patent internationally, the cost is typically at least $100,000.

### 3.3  Steps Necessary to Create a New Product

The following steps are typically necessary to create a new product:

+ Develop a product idea.
+ Assess the feasibility of a product idea.
+ Design and test the product.
+ Distribute and promote the product.
+ Post-audit the product.

**Develop a Product Idea**   The first step in creating a new product is to develop an idea. When the focus is on improving an existing product, the idea already exists, and the firm simply attempts to make it better. When

**patents**
allow exclusive rights to the production and sale of a specific product

developing an entirely new product, a common method is to identify consumer needs or preferences that are not being satisfied by existing products. The ultimate goal is to develop a product that is superior to existing products in satisfying the consumer.

As firms attempt to improve existing products or create new products, they must determine what will satisfy customers. The commitment of some firms to customer satisfaction is confirmed by the following statements in recent annual reports:

*"Kodak's future is in total customer satisfaction."*

—Eastman Kodak

*"I [the CEO] want everyone in IBM to be obsessed with satisfying our customers."*

—IBM

*"We aim to redouble our efforts . . . toward one simple goal: meeting the needs of our customers."*

—Apple

Identifying consumer preferences so as to improve a product or create a new product may involve monitoring consumer behavior. For example, an airline may monitor flights to determine the most disturbing inconveniences, such as cramped seating. This leads to ideas for an improved product, such as wider seats. To satisfy consumer preferences, rental car companies at airports now allow their key customers to go straight from the airplane to their cars (rather than stand in line at the counter).

Technology can be used to monitor consumer behavior. When Amazon.com fills orders, it requests information about the customers. Thus, when Amazon considers expanding its product line, it knows the characteristics of the consumers who are buying its existing products. Based on this information about consumer preferences, it can attempt to identify other products that will sell over the Internet.

**Assess the Feasibility of a Product Idea**   Any idea for a new or improved product should be assessed by estimating the costs and benefits. The idea should be undertaken only if the benefits outweigh the costs. For example, American Airlines removed some seats to better satisfy customers by providing more leg room. The most obvious cost was the expense of removing the seats, but other costs were incurred as well. The strategy reduced the airline's seating capacity. The cost of this reduction was forgone revenue on those flights that were at full capacity. In addition, an airplane could not be used while the work was being performed. Any forgone revenue during that period also represented a cost of improving the product. Nevertheless, American hoped that the benefit of more leg room would lead to greater consumer satisfaction and thus to greater demand for its service, resulting in more revenue.

**Design and Test the Product**   If the firm believes the new (or revised) product is feasible, it must determine the design and other characteristics of the product. The new product may be tested before being fully implemented. For example, an airline such as American Airlines may first revise its seating structure in a few planes to determine consumer reaction. If the

# Cross-Functional Teamwork

## Interaction Among Product Decisions and Other Business Decisions

When marketing managers create a new product, they must design it in a manner that will attract customers. They must also decide the price at which the product will be sold. These marketing decisions require communication between the marketing managers and the managers who oversee production. Marketing managers explain to the production managers how they would like the product to be designed. The production managers may offer revisions that can improve the design. They also provide estimates on the costs of production. The cost per unit is typically dependent on the volume of products to be produced; therefore, the cost per unit can be estimated only after the marketing managers determine the volume that will need to be produced to satisfy the demand. Since the pricing decision is influenced by the cost of producing the product, the price cannot be determined by the marketing managers until they receive cost estimates from the production managers.

Once the marketing managers have received the necessary input from the production managers and have developed plans for the design and pricing of the product, a financial analysis by the financial managers is necessary to ensure that the proposal is feasible. The financial analysis involves estimating the revenue the firm will generate as a result of creating this product. It also involves estimating production expenses. Using these estimates, the financial managers can determine whether the new product will provide an adequate return to make the firm's investment in the development of this product worthwhile. The marketing managers should attempt to develop the product only if the financial analysis suggests that it will provide an adequate return to the firm. If the marketing managers decide to develop this product, they will inform the production managers, who may need to hire additional production employees. In addition, the financial managers must be informed because they may need to obtain funds to finance production.

Although the marketing managers may be responsible for the creation of new products, they rely on input from the production and financial managers when deciding whether each product is worthwhile and when determining the design and price of the new product.

actual costs exceed the benefits, the proposed changes will not be made on other airplanes. If the change has a favorable impact, however, it may be made throughout the entire fleet.

**Distribute and Promote the Product**   When firms introduce new products or improve existing products, they typically attempt to inform consumers. New or improved products are introduced to consumers through various marketing techniques. As an example, an airline that widens its seats may advertise this feature in the media. Additional expenses required to promote the revised design should be accounted for when determining whether it is worthwhile to create a new design.

**Post-Audit the Product**   After the new product has been introduced into the market, the actual costs and benefits should be measured and com-

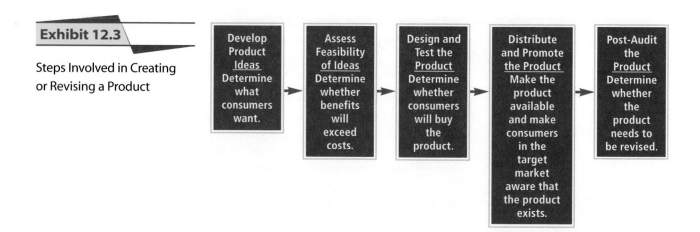

**Exhibit 12.3**

Steps Involved in Creating or Revising a Product

pared with the costs and benefits that were forecasted earlier. This comparison determines whether the cost-benefit analysis was reasonably accurate. If costs were severely underestimated or benefits were severely overestimated, the firm may need to adjust its method of analysis for evaluating other new products in the future. In addition, the post-audit of costs and benefits can be used for future development of the same product. For example, if the actual costs of improving the airplanes outweigh the benefits, the airline may revert to its original product design when new airplanes are needed.

**Summary of Steps Used to Create or Revise a Product**   A summary of the steps involved in creating or revising a product is shown in Exhibit 12.3. Notice that the whole process is initiated by attempting to satisfy consumer preferences.

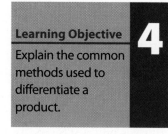

**Learning Objective 4**

Explain the common methods used to differentiate a product.

**product differentiation**
a firm's effort to distinguish its product from competitors' products in a manner that makes the product more desirable

# 4.  Product Differentiation

**Product differentiation** is the effort of a firm to distinguish its product from competitors' products in a manner that makes the product more desirable. Some products are differentiated from competing products by their quality. For example, Starbucks coffee has become popular around the country because of its quality, even though its price is high. KB Toys used a marketing strategy of specializing in a small selection of high-quality toys, rather than competing with Wal-Mart for the entire line of toys.

All firms look for some type of competitive advantage that will distinguish their product from the rest. The following are some of the more common methods used to differentiate the product:

✦  Unique product design

✦  Unique packaging

✦  Unique branding

## 4.1  Unique Product Design

Some products are differentiated by their design. Consider a homebuilder who builds homes and sells them once they are completed. The builder can attempt to build homes that will satisfy buyers by considering the following questions:

✦ Would consumers in this neighborhood prefer one- or two-story homes?

✦ Is a basement desirable?

✦ Is a fireplace desirable?

✦ What is a popular size for homes in this neighborhood?

✦ What type of architecture is popular in this neighborhood?

Once these and other issues are resolved, the builder can build homes with specifications that will attract buyers.

Various characteristics can make one product better than others, including safety, reliability, and ease of use. Firms such as AT&T, Eastman Kodak, and Audi have a reputation for reliability, which helps create a demand for their products. Producers attempt to improve reliability by using high-quality materials, providing service, and offering warranties. However, attempts to improve reliability usually result in higher costs.

**Differentiating the Design of a Service**   Just as firms that produce products attempt to create unique designs for their products, service firms attempt to develop unique services. For example, Southwest Airlines designed a differentiated service by focusing on many short routes that previously were not available to customers. Some grocery stores allow customers to purchase groceries online and provide a delivery service so that the customers do not have to shop at the store.

Most services can be differentiated by timing and efficiency. A firm that provides the service desired by customers on time and at a reasonable price has a good chance of being successful. Its method of differentiating itself from competitors is to prove that customers can trust it to provide what it promised and to do so on time. Firms that offer services commonly use a strategy of promising to provide service of a certain quality and then keeping their promises. A firm that delivers what it promised may not only receive additional business from those customers, but may also obtain other business from referrals.

Some products are primarily differentiated from others by their packaging, like the perfume in this photo. The packaging is intended to attract a particular target market.

## 4.2 Unique Packaging

A packaging strategy can determine the success or failure of a product, especially for products whose quality levels are quite similar. In an attempt to differentiate themselves from the competition, some firms have repackaged various grocery products in unbreakable or easily disposable containers.

Many packaging strategies focus on convenience. Motor oil is now packaged in containers with convenient twist-off caps, and many canned foods have pull-tabs. Tide detergent is packaged in both powder and liquid so that consumers can choose their preferred form.

Packaging can also provide advertising. For example, many food products such as microwave dinners are packaged with the preparation instructions on the outside. These instructions also demonstrate how simple the preparation is. Packaging also informs consumers about the nutrition of foods or the effectiveness of health-care products. The advertising on the package may be the key factor that encourages consumers to purchase one product instead of others.

## 4.3  Unique Branding

**branding**
a method of identifying products and differentiating them from competing products

**trademark**
a brand's form of identification that is legally protected from use by other firms

**Branding** is a method of identifying products and differentiating them from competing products. Brands are typically represented by a name and a symbol. A **trademark** is a brand's form of identification that is legally protected from use by other firms. Some trademarks have become so common that they represent the product itself. For example, "Coke" is often used to refer to any cola drink, and "Kleenex" is frequently used to refer to any facial tissue. Some symbols are more recognizable than the brand name. Levi's jeans, Nike, Pepsi, and Mercedes all have easily recognized symbols.

**family branding**
branding of all or most products produced by a company

**Family Versus Individual Branding**   Companies that produce goods assign either a family or an individual brand to their products. **Family branding** is the branding of all or most products produced by a company. The Coca-Cola Company sells Coca-Cola, Diet Coke, Cherry Coke, and other soft drinks. Ford, Disney, McDonald's, Microsoft, IBM, and Intel use family branding to distinguish their products from the competition.

**individual branding**
the assignment of a unique brand name to different products or groups of products

Companies that use **individual branding** assign a unique brand name to different products or groups of products. For example, Procter & Gamble produces Tide, Bold, and Era. General Mills produces numerous brands of cereal. Many clothing manufacturers use different brand names. One product line may be marketed to prestigious clothing shops. A second line may be marketed to retail stores. To preserve the prestige, the top quality brand may not be sold in retail stores.

**producer brands**
brands that reflect the manufacturer of the products

**store brands**
brands that reflect the retail store where the products are sold

**Producer Versus Store Brands**   Most products can be classified as either a producer brand, a store brand, or a generic brand. **Producer brands** reflect the manufacturer of the products. Examples of producer brands include Black & Decker, Frito-Lay, and Fisher Price. These brands are usually well known because they are sold to retail stores nationwide. **Store brands** reflect the retail store where the products are sold. For example, Sears and J. C. Penney offer some products with their own label. Even if store brands are produced by firms other than the retailer, the names of the producers are not identified. Store brand products do not have as much prestige as popular producer brands; however, they often have a lower price.

**generic brands**
products that are not branded by the producer or the store

Some products are not branded by either the producer or the store. These products have a so-called **generic brand**. The label on generic products simply describes the product. Generic brands have become increasingly popular over the last decade because their prices are relatively low. They are most popular for products that are likely to be similar among brands, such as napkins and paper plates. Customers are comfortable purchasing generic brands of these products because there is not much risk in buying a cheaper product.

**Benefits of Branding**    Branding continually exposes a company's name to the public. If the company is respected, its new products may be trusted because they carry the company brand name. If they carried a different name, new products introduced by the firm would likely not sell as well.

Many firms with a brand name use their name to enter new markets. The Coca-Cola Company uses its name to promote new soft drinks that it creates. Kraft Foods' Nabisco brand can more easily penetrate the market for various specialty foods because of its reputation for quality food products. These firms not only are able to offer new products but also may enter new geographic markets (such as foreign countries) because of their brand name.

A brand is especially useful for differentiating a product when there are only a few major competitors. For example, many consumers select among only two or three brands of some products, such as toothpaste or computers. The importance of branding is emphasized in a recent annual report of Procter & Gamble:

> *"Consumers have to trust that a brand will meet all their needs all the time. That requires superior product technology. And it also requires sufficient breadth of product choices. We should never give consumers a . . . reason to switch away from one of our brands."*

Having an established brand name is also often crucial to obtaining space in a store. For example, Coca-Cola and Pepsi often receive the majority of a store's soft drink shelf space. The same is true for some cereals, detergents, and even dog food. Retail stores normally allocate more space for products with popular brand names.

Branding also applies to services. When Southwest Airlines begins to serve a new route, it uses its brand (reliability, good service, low prices) to attract customers.

**co-branding**
firms agree to offer a combination of two noncompeting products at a discounted price

A recent trend in branding is **co-branding**, in which firms agree to offer a combination of two noncompeting products at a discounted price. For example, Blockbuster Entertainment Group has issued VISA cards. Blockbuster customers could get discounts on DVD rentals by using their VISA cards.

## 4.4  Summary of Methods Used to Differentiate Products

Exhibit 12.4 summarizes the methods used to achieve product differentiation. Firms sometimes combine several methods to differentiate their products. For example, if Kodak creates a product that is technologically superior to others, it may also differentiate the product by packaging it in a special manner and by using the Kodak family brand name.

To understand how some firms use all three methods to differentiate their products, consider the following comment from an annual report:

> *"Liz Claiborne, Inc., must work more diligently than ever to truly differentiate its brands, . . . applying product innovation [such as a unique design], canny brand marketing, . . . superb customer service and exceptional in-store presentation [unique packaging] to win over a consumer who has abundant choices."*

—Liz Claiborne, Inc.

**Exhibit 12.4**

Methods Used to
Differentiate Products

| Method | Achieve Superiority by: |
|---|---|
| Unique design | Higher level of product safety, reliability, or ease of use. |
| Unique packaging | Packaging to get consumers' attention or to improve convenience. |
| Unique branding | Using the firm's image to gain credibility, or using a unique brand name to imply prestige. |

**Learning Objective 5**

Identify the factors
that influence the
pricing decision.

# 5. Pricing Strategies

Whether a firm produces industrial steel, textbooks, or haircuts, it needs to determine a price for its product. Managers typically attempt to set a price that will maximize the firm's value. The price charged for a product affects the firm's revenue and therefore its earnings. Recall that the revenue from selling a product is equal to its price times the quantity sold. Although a lower price reduces the revenue received per unit, it typically results in a higher quantity of units sold. A higher price increases the revenue received per unit but results in a lower quantity of units sold. Thus, an obvious trade-off is involved when determining the price for a product.

Firms set the prices of their products by considering the following:

✦ Cost of production

✦ Supply of inventory

✦ Competitors' prices

## 5.1 Pricing According to the Cost of Production

**cost-based pricing**
estimating the per-unit cost of
producing a product and then
adding a markup

Some firms set a price for a product by estimating the per-unit cost of producing the product and then adding a markup. This method of pricing products is commonly referred to as **cost-based pricing**. If this method is used, the firm must also account for all production costs that are attributable to the production of that product. Pricing according to cost attempts to ensure that production costs are covered. Virtually all firms consider production costs when setting a price. The difference in price between a Cadillac and a Saturn is partially attributed to the difference in production costs. However, other factors may also influence the pricing decision.

**Economies of Scale** The per-unit cost of production may be dependent on production volume. For products subject to economies of scale, the average per-unit cost of production decreases as production volume increases. This is especially true for products or services that have high fixed costs (costs that remain unchanged regardless of the quantity produced), such as automobiles. A pricing strategy must account for economies of scale. If a high price is charged, not only does the sales volume decrease, but also the average cost of producing a small amount increases. For those products or services that are subject to economies of scale, the price should be sufficiently low to achieve a high sales volume (and therefore lower production costs).

## 5.2  Pricing According to the Supply of Inventory

Some pricing decisions are directly related to the supply of inventory. For example, computer firms such as Apple typically reduce prices on existing personal computers to make room for new models that will soon be marketed. Automobile dealerships frequently use this strategy as well. Most manufacturers and retailers tend to reduce prices if they need to reduce their inventory.

## 5.3  Pricing According to Competitors' Prices

Firms commonly consider the prices of competitors when determining the prices of their products. They can use various pricing strategies to compete against other products, as explained next.

**penetration pricing**
the strategy of setting a lower price than those of competing products to penetrate a market

**Penetration Pricing**   If a firm wants to be sure that it can sell its product, it may set a lower price than those of competing products to penetrate the market. This pricing strategy is called **penetration pricing** and has been used in various ways by numerous firms, including airlines, automobile manufacturers, and food companies.

The success of penetration pricing depends on the product's price elasticity, which reflects the responsiveness of consumers to a reduced price. When demand for a product is **price-elastic**, the demand is highly responsive to price changes. Some grocery products such as napkins and paper plates are price-elastic, as price may be the most important criterion that consumers use when deciding which brand to purchase. Many firms, such as TD Ameritrade, IBM, and Taco Bell have been able to increase their revenue by lowering prices.

**price-elastic**
the demand for a product is highly responsive to price changes

When Southwest Airlines entered the airline industry, its average fare was substantially lower than the average fare charged by other airlines for the same routes. Southwest not only pulled customers away from competitors but also created some new customer demand for airline services because of its low prices. Penetration pricing is not always successful, however. Allstate Insurance increased its market share by lowering its insurance prices (premiums), but its profits declined because it lowered its prices too much.

**price-inelastic**
the demand for a product is not very responsive to price changes

When demand for a product is **price-inelastic**, the demand is not very responsive to price changes. A firm should not use penetration pricing if its product is price-inelastic because most consumers would not switch to the product to take advantage of the lower price. For some products, such as deli products and high-quality automobiles, personalized service and perceived quality may be more important than price. The demand for many services is not responsive to price reductions because consumers may prefer one firm over others. For example, some consumers may be unwilling to switch dentists, hairstylists, or stockbrokers even if a competitor reduces its price.

**defensive pricing**
the strategy of reducing a product's price to defend (retain) market share

**Defensive Pricing**   Some pricing decisions are defensive rather than offensive. If a firm recognizes that the price of a competing product has been reduced, it may use **defensive pricing**, in which a product's price is reduced to defend (retain) market share. For example, airlines commonly reduce their airfares in response when a competitor lowers its airfares. This response tends to allow all airlines to retain their market share, but their revenue decreases (because of the lower price). Computer firms such as IBM

Boutique clothing shops, such as the one shown here, commonly charge relatively high prices to denote prestige and attract customers who want special designer clothing.

and Dell commonly reduce their prices in response to price reductions by their competitors.

Some firms lower their price to drive out new competitors that have entered the market. This strategy is called **predatory pricing**.

**Prestige Pricing** Firms may use a higher price if their product is intended to have a top-of-the-line image. This pricing strategy is called **prestige pricing**. For example, GapKids sells baby clothing at relatively high prices to create a high-quality image for customers who are not as concerned about price. Microbreweries use prestige pricing in an attempt to create a high-quality image for their beers.

Firms with a diversified product mix may use a penetration pricing strategy for some products and a prestige pricing strategy for others. For example, car manufacturers price some cars as low as possible to increase market share, but use prestige pricing on other models that have a top-of-the-line image.

**predatory pricing**
the strategy of lowering a product's price to drive out new competitors

**prestige pricing**
the strategy of using a higher price for a product that is intended to have a top-of-the-line image

## 5.4 Example of Setting a Product's Price

To show how a firm may set a product's price, assume that you move to New Orleans and start your own business as a hot dog vendor on the streets of the French Quarter (a tourist district). Assume that you plan to run this business for one year and that a hot dog cooker can be rented for $4,000 annually. This cost is referred to as a **fixed cost** because the cost of production remains unchanged regardless of how many units are produced. Also assume that your costs for hot dogs, buns, ketchup, and so on are about $.60 per hot dog. These costs are called **variable costs** because they vary with the quantity of hot dogs produced.

Other vendors in the area charge $2.00 per hot dog. After talking with several other vendors, you forecast that you can sell 20,000 hot dogs in one year as long as your price is competitive.

To determine an appropriate price, begin with the cost information and determine the total cost of production over the first year. The total cost is calculated as follows:

**fixed costs**
operating expenses that do not change in response to the number of products produced

**variable costs**
operating expenses that vary directly with the number of products produced

## SMALL BUSINESS SURVEY

### Pricing as a Competitive Advantage

In a recent National Small Business poll conducted for the NFIB Research Foundation, small businesses were asked whether they use pricing as part of their strategy to develop a competitive advantage. Their responses are shown here:

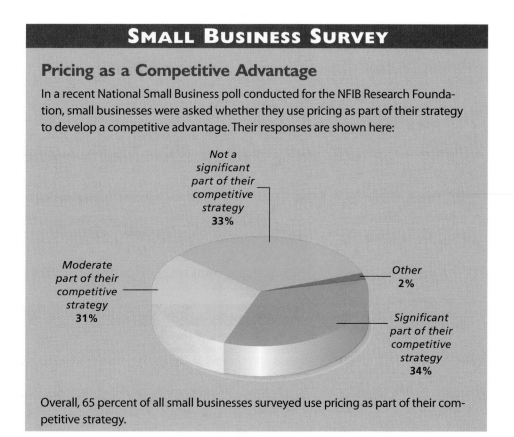

Not a significant part of their competitive strategy **33%**

Moderate part of their competitive strategy **31%**

Other **2%**

Significant part of their competitive strategy **34%**

Overall, 65 percent of all small businesses surveyed use pricing as part of their competitive strategy.

$$\text{Total Cost} = (\text{Fixed Cost}) + [(\text{Quantity}) \times (\text{Variable Cost per Unit})]$$
$$= \$4{,}000 + [(20{,}000) \times (\$.60)]$$
$$= \$4{,}000 + \$12{,}000$$
$$= \$16{,}000$$

Assume that you price the hot dogs at $1.80 so that your price is slightly lower than those of competitors. Since the total revenue is equal to price times the quantity sold, your total revenue is estimated to be:

$$\text{Total Revenue} = (\text{Quantity}) \times (\text{Price per Unit})$$
$$= (20{,}000) \times (\$1.80)$$
$$= \$36{,}000$$

Thus, your profits would be:

$$\text{Profits} = \text{Total Revenue} - \text{Total Cost}$$
$$= \$36{,}000 - \$16{,}000$$
$$= \$20{,}000$$

What if your forecast was too optimistic and you sell only 10,000 hot dogs? Then your total revenue and your profits would be:

$$\text{Total Revenue} = (\text{Quantity}) \times (\text{Price})$$
$$= (10{,}000) \times (\$1.80)$$
$$= \$18{,}000$$

$$\text{Profits} = \text{Total Revenue} - \text{Total Cost}$$
$$= \$18,000 - \$10,000$$
$$= \$8,000$$

The total cost and total revenue are depicted in Exhibit 12.5 for various quantities of hot dogs produced. Notice that the fixed cost remains unchanged for any quantity produced. The variable cost is equal to the quantity times $.60 per hot dog produced. The total cost is equal to the fixed cost plus the variable cost. The total revenue is equal to the price of $1.80 per hot dog times the quantity of hot dogs produced.

**break-even point**
the quantity of units at which total revenue equals total cost

**Break-Even Point.** The **break-even point** is the quantity of units at which total revenue equals total cost. At any quantity less than the break-even point, total costs exceed total revenue. For any quantity above the break-even point, total revenue exceeds total cost.

**Exhibit 12.5**

Estimation of Costs and Revenue at Various Quantities Produced

| Quantity (Q) | Fixed Cost | Variable Cost (Q × $.60) | Total Cost | Total Revenue (Q × $1.80) | Profits |
|---|---|---|---|---|---|
| 1,000 | $4,000 | $600 | $4,600 | $1,800 | −$2,800 |
| 3,000 | 4,000 | 1,800 | 5,800 | 5,400 | −400 |
| 4,000 | 4,000 | 2,400 | 6,400 | 7,200 | 800 |
| 7,000 | 4,000 | 4,200 | 8,200 | 12,600 | 4,400 |
| 10,000 | 4,000 | 6,000 | 10,000 | 18,000 | 8,000 |
| 15,000 | 4,000 | 9,000 | 13,000 | 27,000 | 14,000 |
| 20,000 | 4,000 | 12,000 | 16,000 | 36,000 | 20,000 |
| 25,000 | 4,000 | 15,000 | 19,000 | 45,000 | 26,000 |
| 30,000 | 4,000 | 18,000 | 22,000 | 54,000 | 32,000 |

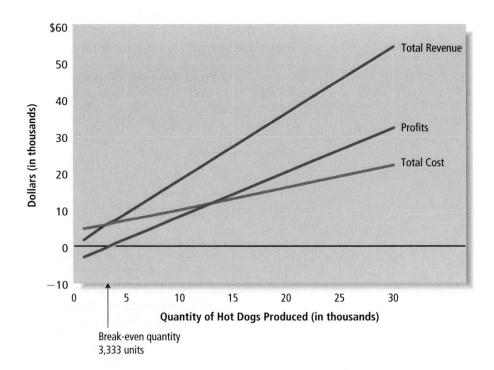

Break-even quantity
3,333 units

**contribution margin**

the difference between price and variable cost per unit

The break-even point can be determined by first estimating the **contribution margin**, which is the difference between price and variable cost per unit. In our example, the difference is as follows:

$$\text{Price} - \text{Variable Cost per Unit} = \$1.80 - \$.60 = \$1.20$$

For every unit sold, the price received exceeds the variable cost by $1.20. Given that each unit is priced above the variable cost, the break-even quantity of units that must be produced and sold to cover the fixed cost is as follows:

$$\text{Break-Even Quantity} = \frac{\text{Fixed Cost}}{\text{Price} - \text{Variable Cost per Unit}}$$

In our example, the break-even quantity is as follows:

$$\text{Break-Even Quantity} = \frac{\$4,000}{\$1.80 - \$.60}$$
$$= 3,333$$

If you charge a higher price for hot dogs, your contribution margin is higher, and you will break even at a lower quantity. However, a higher price may result in lower demand and therefore may be less profitable. This example is simplified in that only one product was produced. A hot dog vendor would likely offer other food or beverage products as well. Nevertheless, the example using a single product is sufficient to illustrate the factors that are considered when pricing a product.

## 5.5  Pricing Technology-Based Products

As information technology (IT) is increasingly incorporated into products, manufacturers are having to rethink their traditional pricing strategies. Traditionally, most product costs have come from labor and raw materials. This meant that the variable cost of each unit produced (the costs directly associated with a given unit) was a critical factor in the pricing decision. The IT components of products have a different cost structure, however. Although it may cost millions of dollars to design and test a single chip, once chips are in production, the variable cost of producing additional chips is very small (such as a few dollars or even pennies). The same is true for producing software. As a result, although incorporating IT into a product may dramatically improve product quality, it has little impact on the variable cost of that product. Therefore, variable cost is less useful in deciding on price. Firms with technology-based products need to spread the cost of the technology across their product and ensure that they properly price the product to cover the cost of the technology.

**Learning Objective** **6**

Discuss other pricing decisions that a firm may make.

## 6.  Additional Pricing Decisions

In addition to setting the price of a product, firms must decide whether to offer special discounts, periodic sales prices, and credit terms for specific customers. Each of these decisions is discussed separately.

## 6.1 Discounting

Since some consumers are willing to pay more for a product than others, a firm may attempt to charge different prices to different customers. For example, restaurants and hotels often offer discounts for senior citizens. Magazines offer student discounts on subscriptions. Airlines tend to charge business travelers at least twice the fares of customers who are paying for the flight themselves. Discounting can enable a firm to attract consumers who are more price conscious, while charging higher prices to other consumers who are less price conscious.

Some firms offer discounted prices to customers who submit orders via the Internet. In this way, the firms encourage more online orders, an advantage because a salesperson is not needed to take these orders. Some airlines and hotels offer special discounts when reservations are made through their websites.

## 6.2 Sales Prices

Many firms use sales prices as a means of discounting for those consumers who will make purchases only if the price is reduced. For example, retail stores tend to put some of their products on sale in any given week. This strategy not only attracts customers who may have been unwilling to purchase those products at the full price, but it also encourages them to buy other products while they are at the store.

Stores normally put high prices on many products, such as televisions and shoes, to allow for a major reduction in the prices when the products are on sale. Since most consumers recognize that these products may soon be priced at a 20 to 40 percent discount, they tend to purchase these products only when they are on sale.

## 6.3 Credit Terms

Regardless of the price charged for a product, firms must determine whether they will allow the product to be purchased on credit. Supplier firms commonly allow manufacturing firms to purchase supplies on credit. They would obviously prefer cash sales, since a cash payment avoids the possibility of bad debt and also provides an immediate source of funds. Nevertheless, they may still offer credit to attract some manufacturing firms that do not have cash available. Firms can encourage their customers to pay off their credit by offering a discount. For example, the terms "2/10 net 30" indicate that a 2 percent discount can be taken if the bill is paid within 10 days and that the bill must be paid in full within 30 days.

A change in credit terms can affect a firm's sales. Thus, firms may revise their credit terms as a marketing tool. If a firm desires to increase demand, it may offer an extended period to pay off the credit, such as 2/10 net 60. A disadvantage of this strategy is that many credit balances will be paid off at a slower rate. In addition, the level of bad debt tends to be higher for firms that offer such loose credit terms.

Many retail stores offer credit to customers through MasterCard and VISA credit cards. Retailers pay a percentage of their credit sales (usually around 4 percent) to the sponsor of the card. The advantage of these cards is that the credit balance is paid by a bank, which in turn is responsible for collecting on customer credit.

# Responding to the Economy

## Revising Product Plans in Response to the Economy

A firm may need to revise its decisions regarding its products in response to changes in economic conditions. During a weak economy, the consumer demand for shopping products may decrease as consumers focus more on basic needs. A weaker economy might also make a firm reconsider whether to implement new product ideas. The decision to produce and sell a new product may be feasible when economic conditions are strong, but not when the economy is weak. Thus, the firm has to carefully assess potential economic conditions before it devotes resources to the production of a new product. Once the resources are committed and a production process is established, it is difficult to reverse this decision even if economic conditions deteriorate.

When economic conditions are strong, firms are more willing to increase the offerings of new products. However, they will face more intense competition as other firms enter the market to capitalize on favorable conditions. Thus, while firms may attempt to expand their product line under these conditions, they still need to defend the market share of their existing products.

A firm's pricing decision is also dependent on the economic conditions. It may need to set a lower price if economic conditions are weak, because consumers are more price conscious under these conditions. Conversely, a firm may be able to charge higher prices when the economy is stronger, although its prices must still be in line with those set by its competitors.

Many companies, such as Sears, issue their own credit cards to consumers. These companies frequently use the Internet to make customers aware of the benefits associated with owning a credit card issued by the company. Advertising the card on the company's website allows customers to assess the potential benefits of owning the credit card.

## COLLEGE HEALTH CLUB:  CHC'S PRODUCT DIFFERENTIATION, DISCOUNTING, AND CREDIT DECISIONS

Services such as aerobics classes, weight machines, and exercise machines are somewhat similar among health clubs. Nevertheless, Sue Kramer, the president of College Health Club (CHC), thinks that she can differentiate CHC from other health clubs. For college students, CHC offers several advantages. Perhaps the most important advantage is its location. It is located across from the college campus, so students can walk to the club. Since many students do not have cars, this location is a major advantage over other health clubs for the students who live on campus. In addition, CHC's membership fee is lower than that of other health clubs in the area, which is important to college students.

Sue also considers various types of discounting strategies to increase membership at CHC. First, she considered offering a 10 percent discount to any students who signed up in the first week of the fall semester. She decided against that strategy, however, because she was afraid that existing members might become upset that they were not offered the discount.

She also considered increasing the annual membership fee to $525 and offering a student discount so that students could still become members for $500. Nonstudents could more easily afford to pay a slightly higher membership fee. She decided against this policy, however, because she wants to attract more nonstudent members.

Sue also considered offering credit terms to members as a way of increasing memberships. For example, she could allow them to sign up for a membership and then pay three or six months later. She decided against this strategy because some members who receive credit might not ever pay their bill.

# Summary of Learning Objectives

**1** A product line is a set a related products or services offered by a single firm. The assortment of products offered by a firm is its product mix. The phases of the product life cycle are
+ introduction phase, in which consumers are informed about the product;
+ growth phase, in which the product becomes more popular and increases its share of the market;
+ maturity phase, in which the sales volume levels off as a result of competition; and
+ decline phase, in which the sales volume is reduced as a result of competition or reduced consumer demand.

**2** The main factors affecting the size of a product's target market are
+ demographic trends, such as age and income levels;
+ geography;
+ economic factors, such as economic growth; and
+ changes in social values, such as a decline in demand for products perceived to be unhealthy.

**3** The main steps involved in creating a new product are
+ develop a product idea, which may be in response to changes in consumer needs or preferences;
+ assess the feasibility of the product idea, which entails comparing the expected benefits with the costs of the product;
+ design the product and test it with some consumers in the target market;
+ distribute the product so that it is accessible to the target market, and promote the product to ensure that consumers are aware of it; and
+ post-audit the product to determine whether the product needs to be revised in any way.

**4** Some common methods used to differentiate a product are
+ unique design, in which the product produced is safer, more reliable, easier to use, or has some other advantages;
+ unique packaging, which can enhance convenience or contain advertising; and
+ unique branding, which may enhance consumers' perception of the product's quality.

**5** The key factors that influence the pricing decision are
+ cost of production, so the price charged can recover costs incurred;
+ inventory supply, so the price can be lowered to remove excess inventory; and
+ prices of competitors, so the price may be set below those of competitors to gain an advantage (penetration pricing) or above those of competitors to create an image of high quality (prestige pricing).

**6** In addition to setting a price for each product, firms need to make these other pricing decisions:
+ discounting, which involves deciding whether to give discounts to specific customers;
+ sales prices, which entails deciding whether to put some products on sale for all customers periodically, and what the sales price should be; and
+ credit terms, which involves deciding whether to provide credit to large customers that buy the product in bulk, and what the credit terms should be.

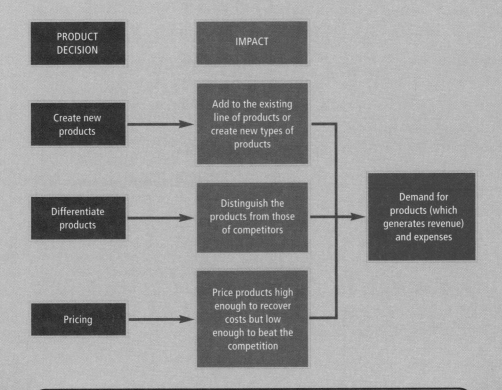

## Self-Test of Key Concepts

The following self-assessment allows you to test your understanding of the key concepts covered in this chapter. Answers are provided at the end of this exercise.

### True or False

1. Consumers purchasing convenience goods will shop around and compare quality and price of similar products.

2. As new consumer needs are identified, firms tend to expand both their product lines and their product mix.

3. Demographics can be used to identify a target market.

4. During a recession, the demand for specialty goods tends to increase.

5. Price skimming is a strategy commonly used in highly competitive markets.

6. A change in interest rates can have a major impact on consumer demand.

7. E-marketing is highly successful in domestic (U.S.) markets, but the high cost of shipping has prevented U.S. companies from using it successfully in foreign markets.

8. A change in credit terms can affect a firm's sales.

9. Warranties can be used to achieve product differentiation.

10. Firms should use penetration pricing if their products are price-inelastic.

### Multiple Choice

11. A Rolex watch and a Jaguar automobile are considered:
    a) convenience products.
    b) shopping goods.
    c) industrial products.
    d) specialty products.
    e) priority products.

12. When a hospital supply company offers a wide variety of products to its customers, the firm is:
    a) offering quantity price discounts in order to attract price-conscious customers.
    b) encouraging customers to pay their outstanding debts in order to take advantage of discounts.
    c) practicing product differentiation.
    d) diversifying its product mix.
    e) responding to the needs of a diverse labor force.

13. All of the following are key factors that influence consumer preferences and the size of a target market except:
    a) social values.
    b) anthropology.
    c) economic factors.
    d) geography.
    e) demographics.

14. Cameras, clothes, and household items are examples of products that exist in:
    a) industrial markets.
    b) business markets.
    c) consumer markets.
    d) government markets.
    e) foreign industrial markets.

15. The size of a particular target market is most likely to change in response to a change in:
    a) inflation.
    b) consumer preferences.
    c) interest rates.
    d) the number of competitors.
    e) the size of the largest competitor.

16. E-marketing supports marketing research in all the following ways except:
    a) low cost of personal surveys.
    b) speed of receiving marketing information.
    c) customer openness with opinions.
    d) access to customers of varied income levels.
    e) face-to-face interviews.

17. Which of the following can be used by a firm to protect its investments in research and product development?
    a) marketing research
    b) patents
    c) demographics
    d) target market selection
    e) product mix

18. The first step in creating a new product is to:
    a) assess the feasibility of the product.
    b) develop a product idea.
    c) design the product.
    d) test the product.
    e) distribute and promote the product.

19. New and revised products may be tested through:
    a) commercialization.
    b) geographic sales.
    c) product life cycle.
    d) family brands.
    e) marketing research.

20. All of the following are methods commonly used to differentiate products from those of competitors except:
    a) quality.
    b) design.
    c) tax policies.
    d) packaging.
    e) branding.

21. The Coca-Cola Company sells Coca-Cola, Diet Coke, Cherry Coke, and other soft drinks, which is an example of a(n):
    a) family brand.
    b) individual brand.
    c) corporate brand.
    d) trademark.
    e) copyright.

22. Products that are not branded by the producer or retail store are called:
    a) manufacturer brands.
    b) national brands.
    c) store brands.
    d) obsolete brands.
    e) generic brands.

23. The process of combining two noncompeting products at a discounted price is called:
    a) complementary advertising.
    b) multiple discounts.
    c) co-branding.
    d) sales promotion double.
    e) quantity pricing.

24. Sales of the product increase rapidly during the _____ phase of the product life cycle.
    a) maturity
    b) introduction
    c) saturation
    d) growth
    e) declining

25. Which of the following pricing strategies would likely be used in a market where no other competitive products are available?
    a) cost-based pricing
    b) penetration pricing
    c) predatory pricing
    d) price skimming
    e) defensive pricing

26. Managers typically attempt to set a price that will maximize a firm's:
    a) value.
    b) cost.
    c) production.
    d) advertising.
    e) promotion.

27. When a firm lowers its price and total revenue increases, it tells us that:
    a) the demand for the product is price-inelastic.
    b) a penetration pricing strategy is being followed.
    c) consumers are not very responsive to price changes.
    d) the demand for the product is price-elastic.
    e) the firm is using a price-skimming strategy.

28. Which of the following pricing strategies adds a profit markup to the per-unit cost of production?
    a) prestige pricing
    b) cost-based pricing
    c) defensive pricing
    d) profit pricing
    e) penetration pricing

29. When a cost of production remains unchanged regardless of how many units are produced, it is referred to as:
    a) variable.
    b) semifinished.
    c) fixed.
    d) in process.
    e) terminal.

30. (Fixed Cost) + (Quantity × Variable Cost per Unit) describes:
    a) Total Cost.
    b) Total Revenue.
    c) Break-Even Point.
    d) Profits.
    e) Average Cost per Unit.

| True/False | | Multiple Choice | | |
| --- | --- | --- | --- | --- |
| 1. False | 9. True | 11. d | 19. e | 27. d |
| 2. True | 10. False | 12. d | 20. c | 28. b |
| 3. True | | 13. b | 21. a | 29. c |
| 4. False | | 14. c | 22. e | 30. a |
| 5. False | | 15. b | 23. c | |
| 6. True | | 16. e | 24. d | |
| 7. False | | 17. b | 25. d | |
| 8. True | | 18. b | 26. a | |

## Self-Test of Key Terms

branding   422
break-even point   428
co-branding   423
consumer markets   408
contribution margin   429
convenience products   404
cost-based pricing   424
decline phase   407
defensive pricing   425
demographics   409
e-marketing   412
family branding   422
fashion obsolescence   413
fixed costs   426

generic brands   422
growth phase   407
individual branding   422
industrial markets   408
introduction phase   407
marketing research   414
maturity phase   407
obsolete   413
patents   417
penetration pricing   425
predatory pricing   426
prestige pricing   426
price skimming   407
price-elastic   425

price-inelastic   425
producer brands   422
product   404
product differentiation   420
product life cycle   407
product line   404
product mix   404
shopping products   404
specialty products   404
store brands   422
target market   408
technological obsolescence   413
trademark   422
variable costs   426

Fill in each blank with the proper key term. To assess your understanding of the key terms, answers are provided at the end of this self-test.

1. _____ is the accumulation and analysis of marketing data in order to make a decision.

2. _____ brands reflect the manufacturer of the merchandise.

3. With _____, two firms agree to sell two noncompeting products together at a discounted price.

4. _____ products are considered to be unique, and consumers make an extra effort to purchase them.

5. _____ brands reflect the retail store where the product is sold.

6. The _____ is a set of phases that a product typically experiences over its life.

7. A firm can use _____ by setting the price high it wants to achieve a top-of-the-line image.

8. During the _____ phase of the product life cycle, sales of a product level off.

9. _____ is the common branding of all or most products produced by a single company.

10. The _____ is the difference between price and variable cost per unit.

11. When demand for a product is _____, the demand is highly responsive to price changes.

12. The term _____ refers to the electronic interaction with consumers in order to develop, improve, or promote products.

13. When products experience _____, they are no longer in style.

14. A firm uses _____ pricing to sell its product at a lower price than those of competing products for the purpose of entering the market.

15. _____ products are widely available to consumers and are purchased frequently.

16. _____ is the effort of a firm to distinguish its product from competitors' products.

17. A(n) _____ market is a group of individuals or organizations with similar traits who may purchase a particular product.

18. _____ products are not purchased frequently, and consumers compare prices before purchasing them.

19. A(n) _____ is the assortment of products offered by a firm.

20. A(n) _____ is a set of related products or services offered by a single firm.

**Answers:**

1. Marketing research
2. Producer
3. co-branding
4. Specialty
5. Store
6. product life cycle
7. prestige pricing
8. maturity
9. Family branding
10. contribution margin

11. price-elastic
12. e-marketing
13. fashion obsolescence
14. penetration
15. Convenience
16. Product differentiation
17. target
18. Shopping
19. product mix
20. product line

# Concept Review Questions

1. **Business Valuation.** Explain how the decisions regarding the creation and pricing of products can affect the value of a business.

2. **Product Line Versus Mix.** Explain the difference between a product line and a product mix.

3. **Product Life Cycle.** Describe the phases of the product life cycle.

4. **Target Market.** Explain the factors that affect the size of the target market.

5. **e-Marketing.** Explain how e-marketing can be used by a firm to expand its target market.

6. **New Product.** Describe the steps necessary to create a new product.

7. **Product Differentiation.** Explain how a firm can differentiate its product.

8. **Cost-Based Pricing.** Compare cost-based pricing with setting the price of products in response to changes in inventories.

9. **Pricing Response to Competitors.** Explain how a firm may price a product in response to prices of competitors' products.

10. **Other Pricing Decisions.** Explain the decisions to use discounting, sales prices, or credit terms for products.

# Class Communication Questions

1. **Target Market Dilemma.** If you open a clothing store at the local mall, do you think your target market should be children, teenagers, consumers older than age 20, or all age groups?

2. **Product Versus Pricing.** Assume that you work in a cloth-ing store and that your task is to increase the sales to students at your college. Do you think the product (type of clothing, brand name) or the price would be the key factor that influences the demand for the clothing?

3. **Pricing Dilemma.** A famous pro basketball player is about to launch new basketball shoes. The price must be at least $50 to cover the expenses of producing the shoes. Do you think the revenue from selling the shoes will be highest if the shoes are sold at your local mall for $50, $70, or $90?

# Small Business Case

## Product Decisions

NightLife Film Company is a movie production firm that wants to expand its product offerings. It currently has a good reputation for producing science fiction films. It could expand its product line by offering new types of science fiction films that might appeal to different age groups. Another possibility is to produce comedies or other types of films. It must also decide how to expand its product mix. It currently produces films for theaters and sells DVDs of the films several months after they have been in theaters.

1. **Product Line Decision.** What would be an advantage to NightLife Film Company if it keeps its product line focused on science fiction films?

2. **Product Line Tradeoff.** What would be a disadvantage to NightLife Film Company if it keeps its product line focused on science fiction films?

3. **Target Market Decision.** NightLife Film Company re-cently produced a new movie. It needs to advertise this movie to consumers. Why must it decide on its target market for this movie before it advertises the movie?

4. **Impact of Customer Feed-back.** NightLife Film Company commonly allows consumers to complete an online survey about any of its movies. Why may this feedback be useful, even though the movies have already been produced and cannot be changed?

# Web Insight

## Product Differentiation at Apple

At the opening of the chapter, Apple was introduced. Go to Apple's web-site (www.apple.com) and go to a section where you can view the products. Select any product and re-view its description. Summarize Apple's comments about that product and how that product is differ-entiated from those produced by competitors.

# Dell's Secrets for Success

Go to Dell's website (www.dell.com) and click on the link "About Dell," near the bottom of the web page. You can also review a recent annual report of Dell to obtain more information.

1. **Target Market.** Describe Dell's target markets.

2. **Product Line.** How has Dell expanded its products?

3. **Product Line Expansion.** Why do you think Dell benefited from expanding its products to include printers?

# Video Exercise

## Lessons in Creating New Products

Many free business videos are available on websites such as YouTube (www.youtube.com), and more are added every day. Search for a recent video clip about an existing business that offers lessons on "creating new products" in YouTube or any other website that provides video clips.

1. **Main Lesson.** What is the name of the business in the video clip? Is the video clip focused on the skills needed to create a new product, or the technical applications of creating a new product, or the typical profile of entrepreneurs who create new products? What is the main lesson of the video clip that you watched?

2. **Constructive Criticism.** Some related videos suggest that the first step in creating a new product is to determine what you do not like about an existing product. What does this mean?

3. **Impact of Pricing.** Some related videos suggest that a business should determine the price range of a new product before the product is fully developed, even though the total cost of production is not yet clear. Why?

# Projects

To encourage further comprehension, of concepts covered in Chapter 12, the following five projects are available:

1. Analyzing Your Favorite Business

2. Building a Business Plan for Campus.com

3. Running Your Own Business

4. Planning Your Career

5. Stock Market Contest

All of these projects are provided in Appendix A at the end of the text. In addition, projects are available by part division at the end of each part. A Word file for each project is also available at the textbook website (www.emcp.net/business5e) so that you may maintain one ongoing file for each project.

# Distributing Products

© SHUTTERSTOCK/PRISM_68

## Chapter 13 Learning Objectives

**1** Explain the advantages and disadvantages of a direct channel of distribution, and identify factors that could determine the optimal channel of distribution.

**2** Differentiate between types of market coverage.

**3** Describe the various forms of transportation used to distribute products.

**4** Explain how the distribution process can be accelerated.

**5** Describe the characteristics of retailers.

**6** Explain how wholesalers can serve manufacturers and retailers.

**7** Explain the strategy and potential benefits of vertical channel integration.

## Distribution by Urban Outfitters

A distribution channel represents the path of a product from the producer to the consumer. The channel often includes marketing intermediaries, or firms that participate in moving the product toward the customer. Consider the case of Urban Outfitters, which illustrates how retail stores and wholesalers may be created to distribute products. Urban Outfitters has established many retail stores throughout the United States. It has also established a wholesale business called Urban Wholesale that designs and produces clothes that can be distributed to the retail stores and to other unrelated stores. The retail stores obtain some of their clothes from other manufacturers. Thus, the wholesale business and the retail stores are run independently, but benefit each other. In addition, Urban Outfitters created a website where customers can buy clothing online. Urban Outfitters must address these questions about distributing products to consumers:

✦ What should be its role in the distribution of products from the producer to the consumer?

✦ What forms of transportation should it use when transporting products from the wholesaler to the retail stores?

✦ How can it accelerate its process of distributing products from the wholesaler to the retail stores?

✦ How can its wholesaler and retail stores help each other?

These types of decisions are necessary for all businesses. This chapter explains how various distribution decisions can be made by Urban Outfitters or any other firm in a manner that maximizes its value.

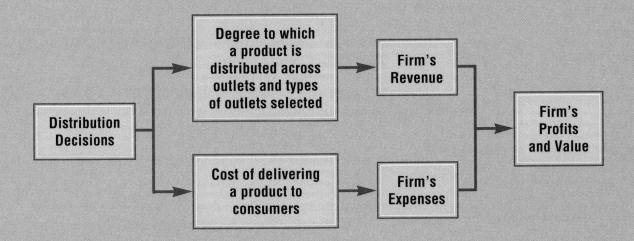

# 1. Channels of Distribution

**Learning Objective** **1**

Explain the advantages and disadvantages of a direct channel of distribution, and identify factors that could determine the optimal channel of distribution.

A firm's distribution decision determines the manner by which its products are made accessible to its customers. Firms must develop a strategy to ensure that products are distributed to customers at a place convenient to them. Firms consider using **marketing intermediaries**, which are firms that help move the product from the producer to consumer. Black & Decker distributes its power tools at various retail stores where customers shop for power tools. Liz Claiborne distributes its clothing at upscale clothing stores where customers shop for quality clothing. Ralston Purina distributes its dog food to grocery stores where customers shop for dog food.

**marketing intermediaries**
firms that participate in moving the product from the producer toward the customer

**direct channel**
the situation when a producer of a product deals directly with customers

## 1.1 Direct Channel

When a producer of a product sells the product directly to customers, it is using a **direct channel**. An example of a direct channel is a firm such as Land's End that produces clothing and sells some clothing directly to customers. Land's End distributes catalogs in the mail to customers, who can call in their orders. It also has a website where consumers can place orders online.

**Advantages of a Direct Channel**  The advantage of a direct channel is that the full difference between the manufacturer's cost and the price paid by the consumer goes to the producer. When manufacturers sell directly to customers, they have full control over the price to be charged to the consumer. Conversely, when they sell their products to marketing intermediaries, they do not control the prices charged to consumers. Manufacturers also prefer to avoid intermediaries because the prices of their products are increased at each level of the distribution channel, and the manufacturers do not receive any of the markup.

Another advantage of a direct channel is that the producer can easily obtain firsthand feedback on the product. This allows the producer to respond quickly to any customer complaints. Customer feedback also informs the producer about potential problems in the product design and therefore allows for improvement.

Use of a direct channel of distribution is becoming more popular as a result of the Internet. Many manufacturers advertise their products online, take orders on their website, and deliver the products directly to the customers. Dell, Inc., is a good example of a firm that uses the Internet in this way. Although Dell now sells its products through retailers such as Wal-Mart and Best Buy, it still relies heavily on direct sales to consumers online.

Dell justifies its use of a direct channel of distribution in a recent annual report:

*"The direct model eliminates the need to support an extensive network of wholesale and retail dealers, thereby avoiding dealer markups; avoids the higher inventory costs associated with the wholesale/retail channel and the competition for retail shelf space. . . . In addition, the direct model allows the Company to maintain, monitor, and update a customer database that can be used to shape the future product offerings. . . . This*

Retail stores such as this one serve as marketing intermediaries, as they distribute products from the manufacturer to the consumer.

© SHUTTERSTOCK/IOFOTO

*direct approach allows the Company to rapidly and efficiently deliver relevant technology to its customers."*

When Dell sells its computers online, there is no additional markup by intermediaries, so customers get what they want at a lower price, and Dell can still be very profitable. Dell relies heavily on the Internet to facilitate its direct channel of distribution and to receive customer questions. About half of the technical support communication between customers and Dell occurs online.

Dell continues the direct relationship with its customers after they purchase their computers. If the customers have complaints, they contact Dell directly. Consequently, Dell can identify any deficiencies and correct them when it designs the next generation of computers. For example, assume that Dell sells a computer model that is popular but would be even more desirable with a redesigned keyboard. When Dell deals directly with customers online, it will receive frequent feedback from the customers about the keyboard. When Dell sells computers to marketing intermediaries, it does not have such direct access to customer opinions because the intermediaries are dealing with the customers.

**Disadvantages of a Direct Channel**   A direct channel also has some disadvantages. First, manufacturers that use a direct channel need more employees. If a company that produces lumber wants to avoid intermediaries, it has to hire sales and delivery people to sell the lumber directly to consumers. By using intermediaries, the company can specialize in the production of lumber rather than be concerned with selling the lumber directly to consumers. In addition, producers that use a direct channel may have to incur more expenses to promote the product. Intermediaries can promote products through advertisements or even by placing the product in a place where consumers will see it.

Another disadvantage of a direct channel is that the manufacturer may have to sell its products on credit when selling to customers directly. By selling to intermediaries, it may not have to provide credit.

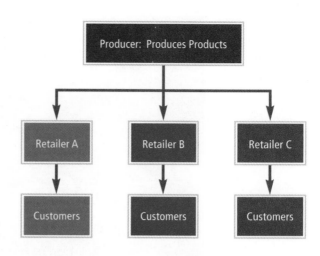

Example of a One-Level Channel of Distribution

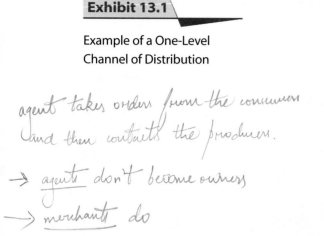

*agent takes orders from the consumer and then contacts the producer.*

*→ agents don't become owners*

*→ merchants do*

## 1.2 One-Level Channel

**one-level channel**
one marketing intermediary is between the producer and the customer

**merchants**
marketing intermediaries that become owners of products and then resell them

**agents**
marketing intermediaries that match buyers and sellers of products without becoming owners

In a **one-level channel**, one marketing intermediary is between the producer and the customer, as illustrated in Exhibit 13.1. Some marketing intermediaries (called **merchants**) become owners of the products and then resell them. For example, wholesalers act as merchants by purchasing products in bulk and reselling them to other firms. In addition, retail stores (or "retailers") such as Wal-Mart and Sears act as merchants by purchasing products in bulk and selling them to consumers. GNC (General Nutrition Centers) uses its chain of more than 4,200 retail stores to distribute its vitamins and related products. Foot Locker has more than 2,700 retail outlets that sell athletic shoes produced by Nike, Reebok, and other shoe producers. Other marketing intermediaries, called **agents**, match buyers and sellers of products without becoming owners.

Time Warner commonly uses a one-level channel of distribution for its films and CDs. Its film company distributes films to movie theaters (the retailer), while its record companies distribute CDs to retail music shops.

## 1.3 Two-Level Channel

**two-level channel**
two marketing intermediaries are between the producer and the customer

Some products go through a **two-level channel** of distribution, in which two marketing intermediaries are between the producer and the customer. This type of distribution channel is illustrated in Exhibit 13.2. As an example, consider a company that produces lumber and sells it to a wholesaler, who in turn sells the lumber to various retailers. Each piece of lumber goes through two merchants before it reaches the customer.

As an alternative, an agent could take orders for lumber from retail stores; then, the agent would contact the lumber company and arrange to have the lumber delivered to the retailers. In this case, the merchant wholesaler is replaced with an agent, but there are still two intermediaries.

Anheuser-Busch typically uses a two-level channel to distribute Budweiser and its other brands of beer. It relies on 900 beer wholesalers to distribute its beer to retail outlets such as grocery and convenience stores.

**Benefits for Small Producers** Small businesses that produce one or a few products commonly use a two-level channel of distribution. Because these businesses are not well known, they may not receive orders from retail outlets. Therefore, they rely on agents to sell the

*agent takes orders from the retailer and contacts the producer and gets it delivered to the retailer.*

*Producer*
*↓*
*Agent*
*↓*
*Retailer*
*↓*
*Consumer*

**Exhibit 13.2**

Example of a Two-Level
Channel of Distribution

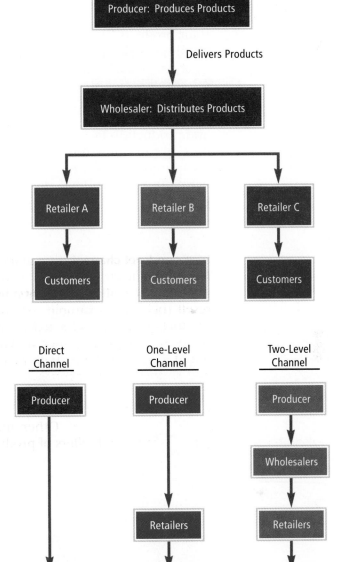

**Exhibit 13.3**

Comparison of Common
Distribution Systems

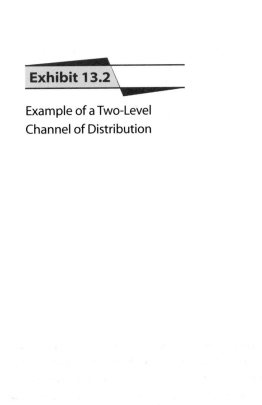

products to retailers. Consider all the products that a retailer like Home Depot sells. If an entrepreneur creates a new paint product or other home improvement product, it may use an agent to meet with a representative (called a buyer) of Home Depot who will decide whether Home Depot should carry this product in its stores. A small business that creates only a few products may have a much better chance of succeeding if it can convince a large retailer to carry its products. Thus, an agent can be critical to the success of such a firm.

## 1.4  Comparison of Distribution Systems

The most common distribution systems are compared in Exhibit 13.3. Firms can use more than one distribution system. For example, Gillette's shaving products are produced at 32 facilities in 14 countries.

They are distributed through wholesalers and retailers through different distribution systems that cover more than 200 countries. Many firms sell products directly to customers through their websites but also sell their products through intermediaries. When firms can avoid a marketing intermediary, they may be able to earn a higher profit per unit on their products, but they will likely sell a smaller quantity unless they use other marketing strategies.

A firm may change its distribution system as circumstances change. For example, in 2006 Dell, Inc., opened an integrated customer center and production facility in Xiamen, China. The facility gave Dell a major presence in the world's most populous country, where it had marketed computers through distributors for several years. Thus, Dell has converted from a two-level distribution channel in China to a direct distribution channel, which is perfect for a product that may be damaged during transport and is not standardized.

## 1.5 Factors That Determine the Optimal Channel of Distribution

The optimal channel of distribution depends on the product's characteristics, such as its ease of transporting and degree of standardization. The firm's ability to fulfill Internet orders is also a factor. The effects of these characteristics are described next.

**Ease of Transporting** If a product can be easily transported, the distribution channel is more likely to involve intermediaries. If the product cannot be transported, the producer may attempt to sell directly to consumers. For example, a manufacturer of built-in swimming pools must deal directly with the consumer, since the product cannot be channeled to the consumer. Conversely, aboveground pools are transportable and are more likely to involve intermediaries.

**Degree of Standardization** Products that are standardized are more likely to involve intermediaries. When specifications are unique for each consumer, the producer must deal directly with consumers. For example, specialized office furniture for firms may vary with each firm's preferences. Specialized products cannot be standardized and offered at retail shops.

**Internet Orders** Firms that fill orders over the Internet tend to use a direct channel because their website serves as a substitute for a retail store. For example, Amazon.com provides a menu of books and other products that it can deliver to customers so that customers do not need to go to a retail store to purchase these products. Amazon fills orders by having products delivered directly from its warehouses to customers. In fact, Amazon recently built new warehouses in additional locations so that it can ensure quick delivery to customers throughout the United States and in many foreign countries.

The Gap uses the Internet to sell clothes directly to customers, but it still maintains its retail stores for customers who wish to shop at the mall rather than online.

**Learning Objective**

**2**

Differentiate between types of market coverage.

**market coverage**
the degree of product distribution among outlets

**intensive distribution**
the distribution of a product across most or all possible outlets

**selective distribution**
the distribution of a product through selected outlets

# 2. Selecting the Degree of Market Coverage

Any firm that uses a marketing intermediary must determine a plan for **market coverage**, or the degree of product distribution among outlets. Firms attempt to select the degree of market coverage that can provide consumers with easy access to their products, but they may also need to ensure that the outlets are capable of selling their products. Market coverage can be classified as intensive distribution, selective distribution, or exclusive distribution.

## 2.1 Intensive Distribution

To achieve a high degree of market coverage for all types of consumers, **intensive distribution** is used to distribute a product across most or all possible outlets. Firms that use intensive distribution ensure that consumers will have easy access to the product. Intensive distribution is used for products such as chewing gum and cigarettes that do not take up much space in outlets and do not require any expertise for employees of outlets to sell.

For example, PepsiCo uses intensive distribution to distribute its soft drinks and snacks. PepsiCo's products are sold through retail outlets that focus on food and drinks. The company distributes its soft drinks and snack foods to virtually every supermarket, convenience store, and warehouse club in the United States and in some foreign countries.

## 2.2 Selective Distribution

**Selective distribution** is used to distribute a product through selected outlets. Some outlets are intentionally avoided. For example, some specialized computer equipment is sold only at outlets that emphasize computer sales because some expertise may be necessary. Some college textbooks are sold only at college bookstores and not at retail bookstores. Liz Claiborne distributes its clothing only to upscale clothing stores.

Some retail stores (such as this one) are very selective about the brands that they will sell. Consequently, only clothes that have a selective distribution and a prestigious image would be considered by this store. By following this selective distribution strategy, the store tends to attract higher-income consumers who are more willing to pay higher prices.

© SHUTTERSTOCK/ZASTOL'SKIY VICTOR LEONIDOVICH

## 2.3  Exclusive Distribution

**exclusive distribution**
the distribution of a product through only one or a few outlets

With **exclusive distribution**, only one or a few outlets are used. This is an extreme form of selective distribution. For example, some luxury items are distributed exclusively to a few outlets that cater to very wealthy consumers. By limiting the distribution, the firm can create or maintain the prestige of the product. Some Nike brands are sold exclusively to Foot Locker's retail stores.

Some products that have exclusive distribution require specialized service. A firm producing high-quality jewelry may prefer to distribute exclusively to one particular jewelry store in an area where the employees receive extensive training.

## 2.4  Selecting the Optimal Type of Market Coverage

Exhibit 13.4 compares the degrees of market coverage achieved by different distribution systems. The optimal degree of coverage depends on the characteristics of the product.

**How Marketing Research Can Influence the Market Coverage Decision**
Marketing research can help a firm determine the optimal type of coverage by identifying where consumers desire to purchase products or services. A firm may attempt to get customer feedback before it determines its market coverage. For example, a producer of DVDs could conduct a marketing survey to determine whether consumers would purchase its DVDs at grocery stores and retail stores as well as through video stores. If the survey leads to a decision to distribute through grocery stores, the firm can then use additional marketing research to compare the level of sales at its various outlets. This research will help determine whether the firm should continue distributing DVDs through grocery stores. Nike has used marketing research to determine the types of outlets where it may be able to sell its shoes. When research showed that Foot Locker attracts teenagers who are often willing to spend at least $80 on shoes, Nike decided that Foot Locker was a feasible retail outlet for its shoes.

**Exhibit 13.4**

Alternative Degrees of Market Coverage

|  | Advantage | Disadvantage |
|---|---|---|
| Intensive distribution | Gives consumers easy access. | Many outlets will not accept some products if consumers are unlikely to purchase those products there. |
| Selective distribution | The distribution is focused on outlets where there will be demand for the products and/or where employees have expertise to sell the products. | Since the distribution is selective, the products are not as accessible as they would be if intensive distribution were used. |
| Exclusive distribution | Since the distribution is focused on a few outlets, the products are perceived as prestigious. Also the producer can ensure that the outlets where the products are distributed are able to service the product properly. | The product's access to customers is limited. |

© SHUTTERSTOCK/ROBERT ASENTO

**Learning Objective**

Describe the various forms of transportation used to distribute products.

# 3. Selecting the Transportation Used to Distribute Products

Any distribution of products from producers to wholesalers or from wholesalers to retailers requires transportation. The cost of transporting some products can exceed the cost of producing them. An inefficient form of transportation can result in higher costs and lower profits for the firm. For each form of transportation, firms should estimate timing, cost, and availability. This assessment allows the firm to choose an optimal method of transportation. The most common forms of transportation used to distribute products are described next.

## 3.1 Truck

Trucks are commonly used for transport because they can reach any destination on land. They can usually transport products quickly and can make several stops. For example, The Coca-Cola Company uses trucks to distribute its soft drinks to retailers in a city.

## 3.2 Rail

Railroads are useful for heavy products, especially when the producer and the marketing intermediary are located close to railroad stations. For example, railroads are commonly used to transport coal to electricity-generating plants. If a firm is not adjacent to a station, however, it must reload the product onto a truck. Because the road system allows much more accessibility than railroad tracks, railroads are not useful for short distances. For long distances, however, rail can be a cheaper form of transportation than trucks.

## 3.3 Air

Transportation by air can be quick and relatively inexpensive for light items such as computer chips and jewelry. For a large amount of heavy

Trains commonly facilitate the distribution process by transporting products within containers as shown here.

products such as steel or wood, truck or rail is a better alternative. Even when air is used, trucks are still needed for door-to-door service (to and from the airport).

### 3.4 Water

For some coastal or port locations, transportation by water deserves to be considered. Shipping is necessary for the international trade of some goods such as automobiles. Water transportation is often used for transporting bulk products.

### 3.5 Pipeline

For products such as oil and gas, pipelines can be an effective method of transportation. However, the use of pipelines is limited to only a few types of products.

### 3.6 Additional Transportation Decisions

The selection of the proper form of transportation (such as truck, rail, and so on) is only the first step in developing a proper system for transporting products. Consider the transportation decisions faced by Toyota, which sends cars from its factory in Kentucky to various dealerships around the country. It used to let its finished cars sit until it had a large batch to send by rail to a specific city. Now it immediately sends its finished vehicles by rail to a sorting dock, where they are sorted and then delivered to various cities nearby. Consequently, the cars no longer sit at the factory. This process has reduced the distribution time by two days.

Also, consider the distribution decisions faced by PepsiCo, which may receive orders for its snack foods and soft drinks from 100 stores in a single city every week. It must determine an efficient way to load the products and then create a route to distribute those products among stores. It must decide the best route and the number of trucks needed to cover the 100 stores. It must also decide whether to distribute snack foods and soft drinks simultaneously or have some trucks distribute snack foods and others distribute soft drinks.

In reality, no formulas are available to determine the ideal distribution system. Most firms attempt to estimate all the expenses associated with each possible way of delivering products that are ordered. Firms compare the total estimated expenses of each method and select the one that is most efficient.

**Learning Objective 4**

Explain how the distribution process can be accelerated.

## 4. How to Accelerate the Distribution Process

The structure of a firm's distribution system affects its performance. A lengthy distribution process has an adverse effect. First, products will take longer to reach customers, which may allow competitors to supply products to the market sooner. As a result, retail stores or customers may order their products from other firms.

A slow distribution process will also result in a lengthy period from the time the firm invests funds to produce the product until it receives revenue from the sale of the product. In most cases, firms will not receive payment until after customers receive the products. Consequently, firms are forced to invest their funds in the production process for a longer period of time.

To illustrate the importance of speed in the distribution process, consider that the actual time required to distribute a typical cereal box from the producer to the retailer (the grocery store) is about 100 days. Now consider a cereal firm that receives $100 million per year in revenue from the sale of cereal and finds a way to reduce its distribution time from 100 days to 60 days on average. In a typical year, this firm will receive its $100 million of revenue 40 days earlier than before, meaning that it will have 40 extra days to reinvest those funds in other projects. Thus, a reduction in distribution time can enhance a firm's value.

## 4.1  Streamline the Channel of Distribution

Many firms are attempting to streamline the channel of distribution so that the final product reaches customers more quickly. For example, by eliminating some of its six regional warehouses, National Semiconductor reduced its typical delivery time by 47 percent and its cost of distribution by 2.5 percent. It now sends its microchips directly to customers around the world from its distribution center. This restructuring has removed one level of the distribution process, as shown in Exhibit 13.5.

Restructuring a distribution process commonly results in the elimination of warehouses. When products are light (such as microchips) and can be easily delivered by mail to customers, warehouses may not be needed. Heavy products (such as beverages), however, cannot be easily delivered by mail, so warehouses are necessary.

## 4.2  Use of the Internet for Distribution

Electronic business has streamlined the distribution by providing information on websites so that customers can compare prices and quality of products. For example, Autobytel.com provides information about new car purchases, offers suggestions about leasing, gives access to dealer invoices, and enables the consumer to find a low-cost car dealer in the area. Paperexchange.com acts as a broker for paper products and equipment. The way consumers make their purchases is gradually changing. The result is more competition among firms and less brand loyalty.

**Exhibit 13.5**

Example of a Restructured Distribution Process

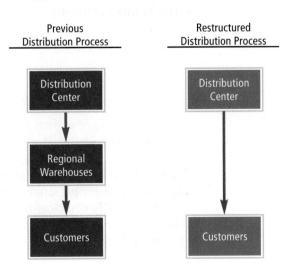

**Exhibit 13.6**

Relationship Between
Production and Distribution

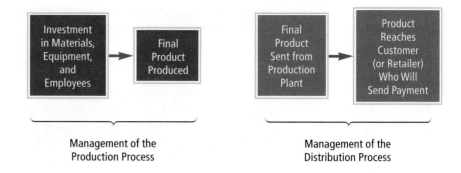

As the Internet eliminates the distance between producers and consumers, it also eliminates the need for wholesalers, distributors, and retailers. Amazon.com is a classic example of a company that has prospered without traditional retail outlets.

When firms sell their products directly to customers without using retail stores, they can improve their efficiency. They may be able to sell their product at a lower price as a result. Another significant change occurs in firms' relationships with suppliers and freight haulers.

## 4.3 Integrate the Production and Distribution Processes

The distribution process can also be accelerated by improving its interaction with the production process. Notice in Exhibit 13.6 how the production process interacts with the distribution process. As an example, if a firm produces automobiles but does not distribute them quickly, it may have to halt the production process until it has room to store the newly produced automobiles. Alternatively, if an insufficient quantity of automobiles is produced, the manufacturer will not be able to distribute as many automobiles as dealers desire, no matter how efficient its distribution process is.

Saturn ensures that its production and distribution processes interact. Its factories must always have the supplies and parts needed to produce a large volume of automobiles. Then, the automobiles are distributed to

Out of
Business

Many clothing stores like this one now offer their products online as well. In this way, they serve the market of consumers who prefer to order products online, while their store still serves consumers who enjoy shopping in stores.

© SHUTTERSTOCK/ANDRE BLAIS

numerous dealerships around the country. Local or economic conditions can cause the amount of new automobiles that dealerships periodically need to change abruptly. Thus, Saturn's production and distribution processes must be able to respond quickly to abrupt changes in the demand by dealerships. Since Saturn allows interaction between its production process and its distribution process, it can adjust to satisfy demand.

Compaq Computer (a division of Hewlett-Packard) also used interaction between production and distribution to accelerate its process of distributing computers to more than 30,000 wholesalers and retail stores. It significantly reduced the time from when a final product was produced until it left the production plant. Computer technology was used to indicate which products should be loaded onto specific trucks for delivery purposes.

Exhibit 13.7 provides another perspective on the tasks involved from the time supplies and materials used to produce a product are ordered until the product is delivered to retailers. This exhibit shows how the distribution of products relies on production. If any step in the production process breaks down and lengthens the production period, products will not be distributed on a timely basis.

Assuming that the production process is properly conducted, the firm still needs an efficient distribution system to ensure that products are consistently available for customers. One of the keys to an efficient distribution system is to ensure that any intermediaries used to transfer products from producers to consumers maintain an adequate inventory. The producer must maintain sufficient inventory in anticipation of orders from wholesalers, retailers, or customers. If it does not, it will experience shortages. This task is especially challenging when the firm produces a wide variety of products and sells them to several different intermediaries or customers.

**Role of E-Marketing**   E-marketing can facilitate the integration between a firm's production and distribution processes. The firm's volume of orders should be updated online and be accessible to both the intermediaries and the production facilities. Consider a manufacturer of video games that has a sales force assigned to sell its games to retail stores. Each salesperson can use the same online ordering service to transmit new orders. The online service continuously updates the total orders received by the entire sales force. The firm fills these orders from its existing inventory. Thus, by checking the orders, the firm can determine where future

**Exhibit 13.7**

Steps Involved in the
Production and Distribution
of Products

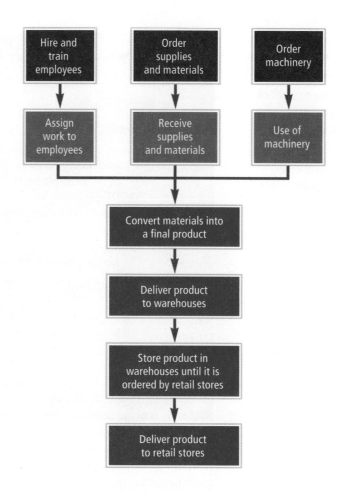

inventory shortages may occur and can increase its production of whatever video games have a low inventory.

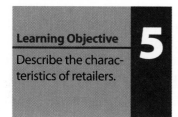

**Learning Objective 5**

Describe the charac-
teristics of retailers.

# 5. Characteristics of Retailers

Retailers serve as valuable intermediaries by distributing products directly to customers. One of the most successful retailers in the world is
Wal-Mart. It explains that its distribution network is a key to its success
in a recent annual report:

*"Wal-Mart is in the business of serving customers. In the United States,
our operations are centered on operating retail stores and membership
warehouse clubs. . . . We have built our business by offering our customers quality merchandise at low prices. We are able to lower the cost of
merchandise through our negotiations with suppliers (wholesalers) and
by efficiently managing our distribution network."*

— Wal-Mart Corporation

Most retailers can be described by the following characteristics:

✦ Number of outlets
✦ Quality of service

## Cross-Functional Teamwork

### Interaction Between Distribution Decisions and Other Business Decisions

When marketing managers decide how to distribute a product, they must consider the existing production facilities. Firms that have production facilities scattered around the United States can more easily distribute their products directly from those facilities to the retailer or to the customer. Conversely, firms that use a single manufacturing plant may rely on intermediaries to distribute the product. When a large production facility is needed to achieve production efficiency (as in automobile manufacturing), intermediaries are used to distribute the product.

When a firm creates a new product that will be demanded by customers throughout the United States, it must decide where to produce and how to distribute the product. The two decisions are related. Financial managers of the firm use input provided by production managers on estimated production costs and from marketing managers on estimated distribution costs. If the product is to be produced at a single manufacturing plant, the production cost can be minimized, but the distribution costs are higher. Conversely, if the product is produced at several small manufacturing plants, the production costs are higher, but the distribution costs are relatively low. The financial analysis conducted by financial managers can determine the combination of production and distribution that is most efficient.

Many firms use a single manufacturing plant in the United States and distribute their products throughout the country. If they experience some demand from foreign customers, they may initially attempt to export the products. The cost of distributing products to foreign countries can be very high, however, so U.S. firms often establish a foreign production facility to accommodate the foreign demand.

+ Variety of products offered
+ Store versus nonstore

### 5.1  Number of Outlets

**independent retail store**
a retailer that has only one outlet

**chain**
a retailer that has more than one outlet

An **independent retail store** has only one outlet, whereas a **chain** has more than one outlet. Although there are more independent stores than chain stores, the chain stores are larger on average. Chain stores such as Home Depot, Ace Hardware, and Wal-Mart can usually obtain products at a lower cost because they can buy in bulk from the producer (or its intermediaries). Wal-Mart typically deals with the manufacturer so that it can avoid any markup by marketing intermediaries. Chain stores often have a nationwide reputation, which usually provides credibility. This is a major advantage over independent stores.

### 5.2  Quality of Service

**full-service retail store**
a retailer that generally offers much sales assistance to customers and provides servicing if needed

A **full-service retail store** generally offers much sales assistance to customers and provides servicing if needed. Some products are more appropriate for full service than others. For example, a men's formal wear store offers advice on style and alters the fit for consumers. An elec-

**self-service retail store**

a retailer that does not provide sales assistance or service and sells products that do not require much expertise

tronics store such as Radio Shack provides advice on the use of its products. A **self-service retail store** does not provide sales assistance or service and sells products that do not require much expertise. Examples of self-service stores are Publix Supermarkets and 7-Eleven.

Some retail stores are adapting to the varied preferences of their customers. For example, stores such as Sears and Best Buy offer personalized sales service for customers who need that service. At the same time, they also allow other customers who do not want personalized service to place orders online and pick up the merchandise from the stores. By placing their orders online, the customers avoid time in the store; by picking up the merchandise, they avoid a delivery fee. In addition, they receive the products quicker by picking them up than if they waited for delivery.

## 5.3 Variety of Products Offered

**specialty retail store**

a retailer that specializes in a particular type of product

**variety retail store**

a retailer that offers numerous types of goods

A **specialty retail store** specializes in a particular type of product, such as sporting goods, furniture, or automobile parts. Kinney's Shoes, which specializes in shoes, is an example of a specialty store. These stores tend to focus on only one or a few types of products but have a wide selection of brands available. A **variety retail store** offers numerous types of goods. For example, KMart, J. C. Penney, and Sears are classified as variety stores because they offer a wide variety of products, including clothes, household appliances, and even furniture.

The advantage of a specialty store is that it may carry a certain degree of prestige. If an upscale clothing store begins to offer other types of products, it may lose its prestige. The disadvantage of a specialty store is that it is not as convenient for consumers who need to purchase a variety of goods. Some consumers may prefer to shop at a store that sells everything they need.

Specialty shops in a shopping mall can retain their specialization and prestige while offering consumers more convenience. Because the mall contains various specialty shops, consumers may perceive it as one large outlet with a variety of products.

Several of these characteristics can be used to describe a single retailer. For example, consider Blockbuster. It is a chain, a self-service

Specialty stores specialize in a particular type of product. The store shown here specializes in sales of DVDs. It has a wide selection of DVDs, and serves customers who are primarily shopping for DVDs.

store, and a specialty store. The Athlete's Foot is a chain, a full-service store, and a specialty store.

## 5.4  Nonstore Retailers

**nonstore retailer**

retailer that does not use a store to offer its products or services

A **nonstore retailer** is a retailer that does not use a store to offer its products or services. The three most common types of nonstore retailers are mail-order retailers, websites, and vending machines.

**Mail-Order Retailers**    A mail-order retailer receives orders through the mail or over the phone. It then sends the products through the mail. Mail-order retailers have become very popular in recent years because many consumers have less leisure time than before and desire shopping convenience. In particular, mail-order clothing retailers have been extremely successful, as consumers find it more convenient to order by phone than to shop in stores. Mail order is more likely to work for products that are light, are somewhat standardized, and do not need to be serviced.

Home shopping networks are a form of mail-order retailing. They have become very popular for specialized items such as jewelry.

**Websites**    Many firms have established websites where their products can be ordered. One of the main advantages of this method over mail order is that the firm does not have to send out catalogs. In addition, changes can be made easily and frequently.

Most mail-order firms have transformed their business to allow online orders as well. Lands' End is a typical example. Since Lands' End was acquired by Sears, its clothing is available in a large number of Sears stores, and it has a small number of retail stores of its own. Nonetheless, Lands' End continues to do substantial business as a catalog retailer, accepting phone orders for clothing and fulfilling the orders by mail. When the Internet emerged, Lands' End decided to set up a website and accept online orders. The website can reach customers who do not have a catalog available, and Lands' End can easily change the website at any time, whereas any changes to its catalog will require another distribution to customers by mail. Lands' End's online orders account for a substantial amount of its total sales.

**Vending Machines**    Vending machines have also become popular as a result of consumer preferences for convenience. They are often accessible at all hours. Although they were initially used mainly for cigarettes, candy, and soft drinks, some machines are now being used for products such as over-the-counter medications, razors, and travel insurance.

**Learning Objective**

**6**

Explain how wholesalers can serve manufacturers and retailers.

## 6.  Services Offered by Wholesalers

Wholesalers are intermediaries that purchase products from manufacturers and sell them to retailers. They are useful to both manufacturers and retailers, as explained next.

## 6.1  How Wholesalers Serve Manufacturers

Wholesalers offer five key services to manufacturers:

✦  Warehousing

✦  Sales expertise

+ Delivery to retailers
+ Assumption of credit risk
+ Information

**Warehousing** Wholesalers purchase products from the manufacturer in bulk and maintain these products at their own warehouses. Thus, manufacturers do not need to use their own space to store the products. In addition, manufacturers can maintain a smaller inventory and therefore do not have to invest as much funds in inventory.

To illustrate how manufacturers can benefit from this warehousing, consider Jandy Industries, which produces equipment for swimming pools. Jandy sells its products in bulk to wholesalers that are willing to maintain an inventory of parts. Jandy focuses on maintaining its own inventory of uncommon parts that are not carried by wholesalers.

**Sales Expertise** Wholesalers use their sales expertise when selling products to retailers. The retailer's decision to purchase particular products may be primarily due to the wholesaler's persuasion. Once a wholesaler persuades retailers to purchase a product, it will periodically contact the retailers to determine whether they need to purchase more of that product.

**Delivery to Retailers** Wholesalers are responsible for delivering products to various retailers. Therefore, manufacturers do not need to be concerned with numerous deliveries. Instead, they can deliver in bulk to wholesalers.

**Assumption of Credit Risk** When the wholesaler purchases the products from the manufacturer and sells them to retailers on credit, it normally assumes the credit risk (risk that the bill will not be paid). In this case, the manufacturer does not need to worry about the credit risk of the retailers.

For a manufacturer, one benefit of using a wholesaler is that the wholesaler may be willing to store large inventories in its warehouse. Consequently, the manufacturer does not have to worry about storage.

**Information**   Wholesalers often receive feedback from retailers and can provide valuable information to manufacturers. For example, they can explain to the manufacturer why sales of the product are lower than expected and can inform the manufacturer about new competing products that are being sold in retail stores.

## 6.2  How Wholesalers Serve Retailers

Wholesalers offer five key services to retailers:

✦ Warehousing

✦ Promotion

✦ Displays

✦ Credit

✦ Information

**Warehousing**   Wholesalers may maintain sufficient inventory so that retailers can order small amounts frequently. Thus, the retailers do not have to maintain a large inventory because the wholesalers have enough inventory to accommodate orders quickly.

**Promotion**   Wholesalers sometimes promote their products, and these efforts may increase the sales of those products by retail stores. The promotional help comes in various forms, including posters or brochures to be displayed in retail stores.

**Displays**   Some wholesalers set up a display of the products for the retailers. The displays are often designed to attract customers' attention but take up little space. This is important to retailers because they have a limited amount of space.

# Responding to the Economy

### Revising Distribution Decisions in Response to the Economy

A firm's distribution decisions change in response to changing economic conditions. For example, high gasoline prices increase transportation costs and increase the cost of distribution. Under these conditions, some producers may be more willing to sell products through wholesalers so that they will not have to incur the cost of delivering products directly to retailers or directly to the consumers.

High gas prices may also encourage some consumers to purchase more products online in order to reduce the amount they drive. Consequently, firms may attempt to attract these consumers by selling their products though a website; then the products that are ordered online can be delivered directly to consumers. When firms recognize that consumers want to shop more online, they dedicate more resources to the development of websites that effectively display their products and accept and fulfill orders.

**Credit** Wholesalers sometimes offer products to retailers on credit. This provides a form of financing for retailers, who may have to borrow funds if they are required to make payment when receiving the products.

**Information** Wholesalers can inform retailers about policies implemented by other retailers regarding the pricing of products, special sales, or changes in the hours their stores are open. A retailer can use this type of information when it establishes its own related policies.

**Learning Objective**

**7**

Explain the strategy and potential benefits of vertical channel integration.

**vertical channel integration**
two or more levels of distribution are managed by a single firm

# 7. Vertical Channel Integration

Some firms use **vertical channel integration**, in which two or more levels of distribution are managed by a single firm. This strategy can be used by manufacturers or retailers, as explained next.

## 7.1 Vertical Channel Integration by Manufacturers

Manufacturers may decide to vertically integrate their operations by establishing retail stores. Consider a producer of clothing that has historically sold its clothes to various retailers. It notices that the retailers' prices are typically about 90 percent above what they paid for the clothes. Consequently, the clothing manufacturer may consider opening its own retail shops if it can achieve higher sales by selling its clothes through these shops.

L. L. Bean has established its own outlet stores that sell the clothing it produces. In this way, the firm serves as the producer and as an intermediary. The intermediaries (outlets) allow the product to be widely distributed. Meanwhile, all earnings generated by the producer or the outlets are beneficial to the owners of L. L. Bean.

When a producer or wholesaler considers expanding into retailing operations, it must address the following questions:

✦ Can it absorb the cost of leasing store space and employing workers? These costs can be substantial.

✦ Can the firm offer enough product lines to make full use of a store? If the firm specializes in producing pullover shirts, it will not have a sufficient variety to attract consumers.

✦ Will the additional revenue to be earned cover all additional costs incurred?

✦ Will the firm lose the business that it had developed with other retail firms once it begins to compete with those firms on a retail level?

The idea of expansion may become less appealing when the wholesaler addresses these questions.

## 7.2 Vertical Channel Integration by Retailers

Just as a producer may consider establishing retail outlets, a retailer may consider producing its own products. Consider a clothing retailer that has historically purchased its clothes from several different producers. It believes that the producer's cost is about 50 percent less than the price charged to retailers. Consequently, it begins to consider producing the

## Global Business

### Global Distribution

In the United States, the distribution network is well organized. Manufacturers of most products are able to find distributors that have the knowledge and relationships with retailers to distribute the products. In many foreign countries, however, distribution networks are not well organized. Many products have simply not been marketed in some less-developed countries, so a distribution network has never been established for these products. Now that U.S. firms have begun to market numerous products to these countries, they recognize that they cannot necessarily rely on intermediaries to distribute the products. U.S. firms have responded to this dilemma by selling their product directly to retail stores rather than rely on a wholesaler. However, they may have to rent a warehouse so that they can store the products. In addition, they must deliver the products to the retailers if they cannot rely on a wholesaler. Overall, their role as producer expands because they must also perform some duties that are performed by wholesalers in the United States. One benefit of avoiding the wholesaler in foreign countries is that the U.S. firms can provide the product to retailers at a lower price because the wholesaler would have added a markup. The firms may charge a higher price to the retailers to reflect the markup that the wholesaler would have included. In this way, they can cover their costs of warehousing and delivering products to the retailers.

clothes itself. This is the reverse of the previous example. Yet it also involves a firm that is considering vertical integration.

When a retailer considers expanding into production of products, it must address the following questions:

✦ Can it absorb the expenses resulting from production, including the cost of a production plant and new employees?

✦ Does it have the expertise to adjust the production process as consumer tastes change over time? If a clothing manufacturer cannot adjust, it may be stuck with a large inventory of out-of-date clothing.

In general, the firm must decide whether the benefits from producing the clothes itself are greater than the additional costs.

### COLLEGE HEALTH CLUB: CHC's DISTRIBUTION

As Sue Kramer develops her business plan for College Health Club (CHC), she must determine her method of distribution. Her business will provide health club services. Like most services, health club services will be distributed directly to the customer.

Sue also plans to use CHC as a retailer for vitamin supplements. CHC will purchase jars of supplements from a vitamin wholesaler and then sell them to its members. In addition, she considers serving as a retailer of exercise clothing for CHC's members. She met with a wholesaler of exercise clothing to learn what types of clothing she could purchase and at what prices. The retail price charged at CHC would be higher than the wholesale price, resulting in a profit for CHC.

# Summary of Learning Objectives

**1** A direct channel of distribution allows the producers to easily obtain feedback on the product and the opportunity to correct any deficiencies. The disadvantages of a direct channel of distribution, however, are

- the producer must employ more salespeople;

- the producer must provide all product promotions (some intermediaries might be willing to promote the products for producers); and

- the producer may have to provide credit to customers and incur the risk of bad debt (some intermediaries might be willing to incur this risk).

The optimal channel of distribution is dependent on the product's ease of transportation: the greater the ease, the more likely that intermediaries could be used. It is also dependent on the product's degree of standardization: the more standardized the product, the more likely that intermediaries could be used.

**2** The three types of market coverage are

- intensive distribution, which is used to distribute the product across most or all outlets;

- selective distribution, which is used to intentionally avoid some outlets; and

- exclusive distribution, which uses only one or a few outlets.

**3** The most common forms of transportation are truck, rail, air, water, and pipeline. Trucks can reach any destination on land with the ability to make multiple stops. Railroads are useful for heavy products being transported over long distances. Air transportation can be quick and relatively inexpensive for light items.

**4** Firms may accelerate their distribution process by reducing the channels of distribution. Alternatively, they may improve the integration between the distribution and production processes. The distribution process relies on the production process to have products ready when needed.

**5** Retailers serve as intermediaries for manufacturers by distributing products directly to customers. Each retailer is distinguished by its characteristics, such as number of outlets (independent versus chain), quality of service (self-service versus full-service), variety of products offered (specialty versus variety), and whether it is a store or a nonstore retailer.

**6** Wholesalers serve manufacturers by

- maintaining the products purchased at their own warehouse,

which allows manufacturers to maintain smaller inventories;

- using their sales expertise to sell products to retailers; and

- delivering the products to retailers;

Wholesalers serve retailers by

- maintaining sufficient inventory so that retailers can order small amounts frequently;

- sometimes promoting the products they sell to the retailers;

- setting up product displays for retailers;

- offering products on credit to retailers; and

- informing retailers about policies implemented by other retailers regarding the pricing of products, allocation of space, and so on.

**7** Vertical channel integration is the managing of more than one level of the distribution system by a single firm. A manufacturer of a product may create an intermediary such as a retail store to distribute the product. Alternatively, an intermediary may decide to produce the product instead of ordering it from manufacturers.

| DISTRIBUTION DECISION | IMPACT |
|---|---|

**Channels of distribution** → The more levels used, the lower the price that should be charged so that the intermediaries can add markups.

**Type of market coverage** → When pursuing broad market coverage, the product should be priced low.

**Type of transportation** → When using retailers (or other intermediaries) that are spread out, transportation costs are higher.

**Accelerating the distribution** → May result in additional sales, but may also result in higher expenses.

**Choice of retailers** → Use of more intermediaries allows greater potential sales, but the price must be set low so that the intermediaries can add a markup.

→ **Business performance**

# Self-Test of Key Concepts

The following self-assessment allows you to test your understanding of the key concepts covered in this chapter. Answers are provided at the end of this exercise.

**True or False**

1. Retailers sell primarily to wholesalers.

2. Manufacturers that use a direct distribution channel need fewer employees than they would need if they used a one-level or two-level channel.

3. Small business firms that produce only a few products typically use a two-level channel of distribution.

4. Products that are standardized are more likely to involve intermediaries.

5. One reason firms may choose an exclusive distribution strategy is to create or maintain prestige for their product.

6. Distribution decisions do not affect the cost of delivering a product.

7. A zero channel of distribution is always the ideal distribution system.

8. A lengthy distribution process adversely affects a firm's performance.

9. Wholesalers commonly offer manufacturers sales expertise.

10. Manufacturers can vertically integrate their operations by establishing retail stores.

## Multiple Choice

11. The manner by which a firm's products are made accessible to its customers is determined by its:
    a) advertising strategies.
    b) product decisions.
    c) pricing strategies.
    d) distribution decisions.
    e) package designs.

12. A distribution channel represents the path of a product from producer to:
    a) retailer.
    b) wholesaler.
    c) consumer.
    d) manufacturer.
    e) industrial distributor.

13. With a direct channel of distribution, the full difference between the manufacturer's cost and the price paid by the consumer goes to the:
    a) manufacturer.
    b) wholesaler.
    c) retailer.
    d) intermediary.
    e) merchant.

14. Wholesalers are marketing intermediaries who purchase products from manufacturers and sell them to:
    a) final users.
    b) retailers.
    c) other manufacturers.
    d) primary customers.
    e) secondary customers.

15. Marketing intermediaries that match buyers and sellers of products without becoming the owners of the products themselves are known as:
    a) single-service marketers.
    b) agents.
    c) commission-based wholesalers.
    d) stockers.
    e) mediators.

16. Products that are standardized and easily transported are likely to:
    a) be sold at a high markup.
    b) have limited market areas.
    c) use intermediaries in their distribution channels.
    d) be sold at steep discounts.
    e) use a direct channel of distribution.

17. _____ refers to the degree of product distribution among outlets.
    a) The marketing mix
    b) Demographic distribution
    c) Market coverage
    d) Channelization
    e) The retail ratio

18. Firms that fill orders over the Internet tend to use a(n) _____ channel of distribution.
    a) one-level
    b) unidirectional
    c) multimodal
    d) direct
    e) intrinsic

19. _____ distribution is used when a producer distributes its products through certain chosen outlets while intentionally avoiding other possible outlets.
    a) Restrictive
    b) Exclusive
    c) Intensive
    d) Narrow
    e) Selective

20. An advantage of exclusive distribution is that it:
    a) makes the product widely available to consumers at a variety of outlets.
    b) eliminates all market intermediaries.
    c) allows the firm to avoid charging a sales tax on the goods.
    d) may allow the firm to create and maintain an image of prestige.
    e) provides the goods to consumers at the lowest possible cost.

21. Newspaper publishers have their papers available in grocery stores, convenience stores, and vending machines and at many other locations throughout a city. This is an example of a(n) _____ distribution of a product.
    a) nonspecific
    b) specialized
    c) geographically dispersed
    d) intensive
    e) decentralized

22. Exclusive distribution can be viewed as an extreme form of:
    a) intensive distribution.
    b) the one-channel approach.
    c) selective distribution.
    d) price discrimination.
    e) mass merchandising.

23. A(n) _____ is a retailer with only one outlet.
    a) exclusive retailer
    b) independent retail store
    c) wholesaler
    d) franchise retailer
    e) sole proprietorship

24. _____ are usually the best way to ship goods when the goods must be delivered quickly to several different locations in a local area.
    a) Trucks
    b) Barges
    c) The railroads
    d) Pipelines
    e) Containerized modules

25. One way to accelerate the distribution process is to make sure that it is integrated with the _____ process.
    a) marketing
    b) financing
    c) credit approval
    d) advertising
    e) production

26. A camera shop that has knowledgeable salespeople who can provide advice to purchasers and also offers to service and repair the cameras it sells is an example of a(n):
    a) mass merchandiser.
    b) agent-seller.
    c) one-stop shopping outlet.
    d) distribution chain.
    e) full-service retailer.

27. When the wholesaler purchases the products from the manufacturer and sells them to retailers on credit, it normally assumes the:
    a) package design.
    b) credit risk.
    c) promotional expenses of the manufacturer.
    d) manufacturer's guarantee.
    e) producer's risk.

28. A wholesaler provides all of the following services to manufacturers except:
    a) production.
    b) warehousing.
    c) delivery to retailers.
    d) sales expertise.
    e) feedback from retailers.

29. A situation in which two or more levels of distribution are managed by a single firm is called:
    a) vertical channel integration.
    b) horizontal channel integration.
    c) multilevel marketing.
    d) wheel of retailing.
    e) conglomeration.

30. When a _____ considers vertical integration, it must be concerned about whether it will lose its established business with retail firms.
    a) retailer
    b) producer
    c) service provider
    d) retailer
    e) chain store

| True/False | | Multiple Choice | | |
|---|---|---|---|---|
| 1. False | 7. False | 11. d | 18. d | 25. e |
| 2. False | 8. True | 12. c | 19. e | 26. e |
| 3. True | 9. True | 13. a | 20. d | 27. b |
| 4. True | 10. True | 14. b | 21. d | 28. a |
| 5. True | | 15. b | 22. c | 29. a |
| 6. False | | 16. c | 23. b | 30. b |
| | | 17. c | 24. a | |

# Self-Test of Key Terms

agents  444
chain  455
direct channel  442
exclusive distribution  448
full-service retail store  455
independent retail store  455

intensive distribution  447
market coverage  447
marketing intermediaries  442
merchants  444
nonstore retailer  457
one-level channel  444

selective distribution  447
self-service retail store  456
specialty retail store  456
two-level channel  444
variety retail store  456
vertical channel integration  460

Fill in each blank with the proper key term. To assess your understanding of the key terms, answers are provided at the end of this self-test.

1. A(n) _____ retail store offers a single or specific type of product, such as sporting goods.

2. With _____, two or more levels in the channel of distribution for a product are managed by a single firm.

3. With _____, only one or a few outlets are used.

4. In a _____ channel of distribution, one marketing intermediary is between the producer and customers.

5. _____ retail stores offer a wide assortment of products, including clothes, household appliances, and furniture.

6. _____ represents the degree of product distribution among outlets.

7. To achieve a high degree of market coverage for all types of consumers, _____ is used to distribute a product across most or all possible outlets.

8. When a firm sells its product to individuals through its website rather than through a retail store, it may be referred to as a(n) _____.

9. _____ are marketing intermediaries that match buyers and sellers of products without becoming the owner.

10. A(n) _____ retail store has only one outlet.

11. A(n) _____ retail store does not provide sales assistance and generally offers products that do not require much expertise to use.

12. When a producer of a product sells the product directly to its customers, it is using a(n) _____ channel of distribution.

13. In a(n) _____ channel of distribution, two marketing intermediaries are between the producer and customers.

14. _____ is used to distribute a product through selected outlets.

15. _____ are marketing intermediaries that become owners of the products and then resell them.

**Answers:**

1. specialty
2. vertical channel integration
3. exclusive distribution
4. one-level
5. Variety
6. Market coverage
7. intensive distribution
8. nonstore

9. Agents
10. independent
11. self-service
12. direct
13. two-level
14. Selected distribution
15. Merchants

# Concept Review Questions

1. **Impact of Distribution on Business Valuation.** Explain how distribution decisions of a firm can enhance its performance and value.

2. **Direct Channel.** Explain the advantages and disadvantages of direct channel distribution.

3. **Merchants Versus Agents.** Compare the role of merchants

versus agents in the distribution process.

4. **Channels of Distribution.** Explain the difference between a one-level channel and a two-level channel of distribution.

5. **Optimal Channel.** Describe the factors that determine the optimal channel of distribution for distributing a product.

6. **Market Coverage.** Describe the different types of market coverage that can be used by firms that produce products.

7. **Methods of Transportation.** List the common methods of transporting products.

8. **Accelerating Distribution.** Explain how to accelerate the distribution process.

9. **Retailer Characteristics.** Identify the various characteris-

tics that can be used to describe retailers.

10. **Vertical Integration.** If a manufacturer of a product considers vertical integration, what questions must the firm address to determine whether it is worthwhile?

# Class Communication Questions

1. **Intensive Versus Selective Distribution.** If you owned a business that produced electronic games, would you use intensive or selective distribution?

2. **Intermediary Dilemma.** When intermediaries of sporting goods are involved in the

distribution process, the price of the product is higher to compensate for their services. Are the intermediaries necessary, or should they be circumvented by the manufacturers?

3. **Retail Store Dilemma.** A publisher of books that ap-

pealed only to scientists is attempting to determine its distribution strategy. Should it attempt to sell its books through retail book stores? What alternative method of distribution may be more appropriate?

# Small Business Case

## Distribution Decisions by Lada, Inc.

Lada, Inc. produces office supplies and used to sell them to wholesalers. The wholesalers would then sell the supplies to retailers at a price of about 40 percent more than what they paid Lada for the supplies. This year, Lada created a website so that it could receive orders directly from the retail stores that sell office supplies. It now ships the office supplies

directly to the retail stores. It is able to offer the stores a lower price for its supplies than what these stores were paying when a wholesaler was involved. Consequently, the demand for its supplies has increased substantially. By eliminating the intermediary, Lada has been able to generate more sales and improve its performance.

1. **Disadvantage of Eliminating Wholesalers.** What is the

disadvantage to Lada, Inc. of dealing directly with retailers?

2. **Advantage of Eliminating Wholesalers.** What is the advantage to Lada of dealing directly with retailers?

3. **Market Coverage.** Why might Lada be able to reach more retail stores across the United States with its new distribution system?

# Web Insight

## Urban Outfitters' Reliance on Producers

At the opening of the chapter, Urban Outfitters was introduced. Go to

(www.urbanoutfitters.com) and review the types of clothes that are available. Summarize what you learn from a quick review of clothes

that you might consider purchasing. Specifically, does the store rely on one producer of clothing or many producers?

## Dell's Secrets for Success

Go to Dell's website (www.dell.com) and click on the link "About Dell," near the bottom of the web page. You can also review a recent annual report for more information.

1. **Distribution System.** Review Dell's comments about its distribution. How does it distribute its products to its customers?

2. **Direct Channel.** Describe the advantages of Dell's direct channel of distribution. What is a possible disadvantage of Dell's distribution system?

3. **Website Sales.** Dell has had success with its website sales. Why is Dell's website so important for its particular type of business?

## Video Exercise

### Lessons in Distributing Products

Many free business videos are available on websites such as YouTube (www.youtube.com), and more are added every day. Search for a recent video clip about an existing business that offers lessons on "distributing products" in YouTube or any other website that provides video clips.

1. **Main Lesson.** What is the name of the business in the video clip? Is the video clip focused on the type of market coverage, the type of transportation used to distribute the products, accelerating the distribution process, or some other aspect of entrepreneurship? What is the main lesson of the video clip that you watched?

2. **Reliance of Wholesalers.** Some videos explain the benefits of wholesaling. Based on the pros and cons of using a wholesaler, do you think the business in the video you watched relies on wholesalers?

3. **Reliance on Retailers.** Some videos explain the benefits of retailing. Based on the pros and cons of using a retailer, do you think the business in the video you watched relies on retailers?

## Projects

To encourage further comprehension of concepts covered in Chapter 13, the following five projects are available:

1. Analyzing Your Favorite Business

2. Building a Business Plan for Campus.com

3. Running Your Own Business

4. Planning Your Career

5. Stock Market Contest

All of these projects are provided in Appendix A at the end of the text. In addition, projects are available by part division at the end of each part. A Word file for each project is also available at the textbook website (www.emcp.net/business5e) so that you may maintain one ongoing file for each project.

# Promoting Products

© SHUTTERSTOCK/EMIN KULIYEV

## Chapter 14 Learning Objectives

**1** Explain the benefits of promotion.

**2** Describe how advertising is used.

**3** Describe the steps involved in personal selling.

**4** Describe the sales promotion methods that are used.

**5** Describe how firms can use public relations to promote products.

**6** Explain how firms select the optimal mix of promotions to use.

## The Coca Cola Company's Promotional Strategy

Firms regularly engage in promotion, which is the act of informing or reminding consumers about a specific product or brand. They can use promotion to increase the demand for the product and thereby increase the value of the firm. Consider the situation of The Coca-Cola Company, producer of Minute Maid, Powerade, and many other drink products. Its success is partially attributed to its effective promotions.

Although The Coca-Cola Company incurs expenses from its promotion efforts, it is rewarded for using effective promotions that increase the demand for its products and therefore increase its revenue.

To achieve this revenue increase, The Coca Cola Company must determine how to allocate its funds to various promotional strategies in a manner that reaches the target market and attracts customers.

When The Coca-Cola Company considers promotions for its existing drink products or new drink products, it must address the following questions:

✦ What type of advertising should it use?

✦ What other promotion methods should it use?

✦ How it can use public relations to promote its business?

✦ What is the optimal mix of promotions to use?

The types of decisions described above are necessary for all businesses. This chapter explains how promotion decisions by The Coca Cola Company or any other firm can be made in a manner that maximizes its value.

While The Coca-Cola Company incurs expenses from its promotion efforts, it is rewarded for using effective promotions that increase the demand for its products and therefore increase its revenue.

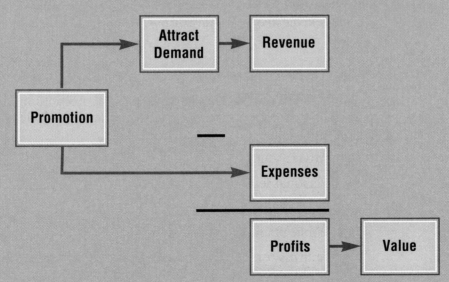

471

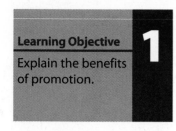

**promotion**

the act of informing or reminding consumers about a specific product or brand

# 1. Benefits of Promotion

Even if a firm's product is properly produced, priced, and distributed, it still needs to be promoted. **Promotion** represents the act of informing or reminding consumers about a specific product or brand. Firms commonly use promotion to supplement the other marketing strategies (product, pricing, and distribution strategies) described in the previous two chapters. For example, an automaker supplements its strategy of improving product quality with promotions that inform consumers about the strategy. An airline typically supplements its strategy to lower prices with promotions that inform consumers about the pricing strategy. A quality product that is reasonably priced may not sell unless it is promoted to make customers aware of it.

To make consumers aware of a new product, promotion can be used when the product is introduced. Promotion can also remind consumers that the product exists. Furthermore, promotion reminds consumers about the product's qualities and the advantages it offers over competing products. Promotion may also include special incentives to induce consumers to purchase a specific product. Promotion may also be used on a long-term basis to protect a product's image and retain its market share.

Effective promotion should increase demand for the product and generate a higher level of sales. To recognize how promotions can enhance product sales, consider the following statement in a recent annual report by Procter & Gamble:

> *"Our leading brands begin with world-class product technology, but it's advertising that gets consumers' attention and persuades them to use our products again and again. 'Advertising is the lifeblood of our brands.' . . . [A]dvertising is the key driver in all our businesses, but it's especially important for health care products—because consumers want a brand they know and trust. Advertising helps establish the trust."*

## 1.1 Promotion Mix

**promotion mix**

the combination of promotion methods that a firm uses to increase acceptance of its products

The **promotion mix** is the combination of promotion methods that a firm uses to increase acceptance of its products. The four methods of promotion are:

✦ Advertising

✦ Personal selling

✦ Sales promotion

✦ Public relations

Some firms use one of these promotion methods to promote their products, while other firms use two or more. The optimal promotion mix for promoting the product depends on the characteristics of the target market. Each of the four promotion methods is discussed in detail next.

# 2. Advertising

**Advertising** is a nonpersonal sales presentation communicated through media or nonmedia forms to influence a large number of consumers. It is a common method for promoting products and services. Although advertising is generally more expensive than other methods, it can reach many consumers. Large firms commonly use advertising agencies to develop their promotion strategies for them. Many firms such as Anheuser-Busch, General Motors, and ExxonMobil spend more than $100 million per year on advertising. Procter & Gamble spends more than $3 billion a year on advertising.

Although advertising can be expensive, it can increase a product's market share. One reason for Frito-Lay's increase in market share over time is its heavy use of advertising. Frito-Lay typically spends more than $50 million a year on advertising.

## 2.1 Reasons for Advertising

Advertising is normally intended to enhance the image of a specific brand, institution, or industry. The most common reason is to enhance the image of a specific brand. Common reasons for advertising are described below.

**Brand Advertising**   **Brand advertising** is a nonpersonal sales presentation about a specific brand. Some brands are advertised to inform consumers about changes in the product. GNC (General Nutrition Centers) spends more than $80 million per year on brand advertising. The Gap and The Coca-Cola Company also spend heavily on brand advertising. Amazon.com uses extensive brand advertising on its own website.

**Comparative Advertising**   **Comparative advertising** is intended to persuade customers to purchase a specific product by demonstrating a brand's superiority by comparison with other competing brands. Some soft drink makers use taste tests to demonstrate the superiority of their respective soft drinks. Volvo advertises its superior safety features, while Saturn advertises that its price is lower than that of its competitors and that its quality is superior.

**Reminder Advertising**   **Reminder advertising** is intended to remind consumers of a product's existence. It is commonly used for products that are already successful and are at the maturity stage of their life cycle. This type of advertising is frequently used for grocery products such as cereal, peanut butter, and dog food.

**Institutional Advertising**   **Institutional advertising** is a nonpersonal sales presentation about a specific institution. For example, firms such as IBM and ExxonMobil sometimes advertise to enhance their overall image, without focusing on a particular product they produce. Utility companies also advertise to enhance their image.

**Industry Advertising**   **Industry advertising** is a nonpersonal sales presentation about a specific industry. Industry associations advertise their respective prod-ucts (such as orange juice, milk, or beef) to increase demand for these products.

---

**advertising**
a nonpersonal sales presentation communicated through media or nonmedia forms to influence a large number of consumers

**brand advertising**
a nonpersonal sales presentation about a specific brand

**comparative advertising**
intended to persuade customers to purchase a specific product by demonstrating a brand's superiority by comparison with other competing brands

**reminder advertising**
intended to remind consumers of a product's existence

**institutional advertising**
a nonpersonal sales presentation about a specific institution's product

**industry advertising**
a nonpersonal sales presentation about a specific industry's product

## 2.2  Forms of Advertising

Firms can advertise their products through various means. The most effective advertising varies with the product and target market of concern. Most types of advertising can be classified as follows:

- ✦ Newspapers
- ✦ Magazines
- ✦ Radio
- ✦ Television
- ✦ Internet
- ✦ E-mail
- ✦ Direct mail
- ✦ Telemarketing
- ✦ Outdoor ads
- ✦ Transportation ads
- ✦ Specialty ads

**Newspapers**   Many small and large businesses use newspaper advertising. It is a convenient way to reach a particular geographic market. Because many stores generate most of their sales from consumers within a 10-mile radius, they use a local newspaper for most of their ads. Newspaper ads can be inserted quickly, allowing firms to advertise only a few days after the idea was created. Best Buy, Publix, and other stores frequently use newspapers as a means of advertising.

**Magazines**   Because most magazines are distributed nationwide, magazine advertising is generally used for products that are distributed nationwide. Some magazines such as *BusinessWeek* have the flexibility to include regional ads that are inserted only in magazines distributed to a certain area.

**Radio**   An advantage of radio advertising is that, unlike magazines and newspapers, it talks to the audience. However, it lacks any visual effect. Because most radio stations serve a local audience, radio ads tend to focus on a particular local area. Furthermore, the particular type of music or other content on each radio station attracts consumers with similar characteristics. Therefore, each station may be perceived to reach a particular target market.

**Television**   Television ads combine the advantages of print media (such as newspapers and magazines) and radio. They can talk to the audience and provide a visual effect. Ads can be televised locally or nationwide. McDonald's, Sears, Duracell, and AT&T commonly run a commercial more than 20 times in a given week. Although television ads are expensive, they reach a large audience and can be highly effective. Some large firms, such as McDonald's and AT&T, run more than 1,000 television ads per year.

Firms attempt to use television advertising during shows that attract their target market. For example, lipstick and fashion firms may focus on the annual Academy Awards because more than 40 million women are watching. Beer and snack food producers focus on football games, which attract mostly men. A thirty-second ad during the 2009 Super

Bowl cost $3 million. The rates are much cheaper for ads that are only televised locally or are run on less-popular shows.

In recent years, many firms (including Procter & Gamble) have created **infomercials**, or commercials that are televised separately rather than within a show. Infomercials typically run for 30 minutes or longer and provide detailed information about a specific product promoted by the firm.

Together, television, radio, magazines, and newspapers account for more than 50 percent of total advertising expenditures. The allocation is shown in Exhibit 14.1.

**Internet**   The Internet has become a popular way for firms to advertise their products and services. It is a form of nonpersonal communication that can create awareness and persuade the customer.

Initially, firms questioned whether people surfing the Internet would pay attention to ads. There is now much evidence that the Internet can be an effective way to advertise. Consider the case of Bristol-Myers Squibb Company, which experimented with an ad on some financial websites offering a free sample of Excedrin (one of its products) to all viewers who typed in their name and address next to the ad on the website. Bristol-Myers Squibb expected that it would receive 10,000 responses at the very most over a one-month period. Yet, in one month, 30,000 people responded. Thus, the Internet ad experiment was a success. Furthermore, the Internet ads cost less than traditional methods of advertising. Other firms have experienced similar results with ads on the Internet.

Today, Internet advertising can potentially reach a large audience. Yahoo!, AOL, and MSN are viewed by more than 50 million people a day. In 2007, firms spent about $21 billion for paid advertising on the Internet. Firms such as Microsoft and IBM spend more than $10 million per year on technology-based Internet ads.

Some firms use their own websites to advertise all of their products. When a firm advertises its products on its own website, it attempts to ensure that the website is easily accessible to potential customers, both in the United States and in foreign countries. Some websites are very visible because they are given high priority by search engines, but the number of competing websites is making it difficult for some firms to reach potential customers. For example, more than a million websites are listed in response to a Web search for "clothing," so a firm that wants to sell clothing on the Internet may not receive much attention.

**infomercials**
commercials that are televised separately rather than within a show

## Exhibit 14.1

Allocation of Advertising Expenditures

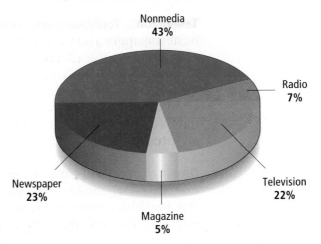

Nonmedia
**43%**

Radio
**7%**

Television
**22%**

Magazine
**5%**

Newspaper
**23%**

A firm can use various strategies to ensure that its website is noticed. First, a website that sells unusual items may be more visible because it may fit specific searches. For example, a website that is focused on ski clothing would have a better chance of being noticed by customers who do a search for "ski clothing" than a general clothing store, because the website fits that specific search. Second, some firms pay the search engines to receive a higher priority in response to a search term. These sponsored sites appear at the top of the list of all websites that fit a particular search term. The firm may pay the search engine a monthly fee for this priority or pay per click (each time the search engine has led someone to click on the website to visit it). Third, a firm may hire a Web marketing firm to help it receive higher priority from the search engines. The search engines determine the order of the websites provided in response to a search term by using various criteria such as the number of times that the search terms are used on the website's pages. By ensuring that its website meets the criteria, a firm can improve the position of its website on the list. Fourth, a firm can arrange link exchanges from its website to other websites that serve similar types of customers. For example, a website focused on selling skis may be willing to insert a link on its site that will direct viewers to a website focused on selling ski clothing. In return, the website focused on selling ski clothing will insert a link on its site that will direct viewers to the website focused on selling skis.

Firms may also promote their products on other websites that are commonly viewed by people who may purchase their products. One of the most popular types of Internet ads is a "banner ad," which is usually rectangular and placed at the top of a Web page. Toyota, which frequently uses banner ads, found that more than 150,000 Internet users typed in their name and address next to the ad to get more information in a 12-month period. More than 5 percent of those users purchased a Toyota. An alternative type of Internet ad is the "button ad," which takes the viewer to the website of the firm advertised there if the viewer clicks on the ad. When a firm advertises on a website other than its own, it may pay a set fee to the firm that owns the website. Alternatively, the fee may be based on the number of clicks (by viewers) on the ad itself (to learn more about the advertised product) or on the number of orders of the product by viewers (if the ad results in viewers ordering the product).

Some film producers spend millions of dollars on websites dedicated to promote films that they produce. They attract potential customers who visit the websites, and attempt to create interest among people who frequently use the Internet.

**E-Mail**   Many firms send e-mail messages to their customers to promote products. Some e-mail promotions are general and apply to all customers on the e-mail list. Other e-mail promotions are personalized to fit the customer's interests. For example, Amazon.com sends promotions about specific books to customers who have previously expressed an interest on that topic. Marriott International sends promotions about hotels in specific locations to customers who have previously expressed an interest in those locations.

**Direct Mail**   Direct-mail advertising is frequently used by local service firms, such as realtors, home repair firms, and lawn service firms. It is also used by cosmetic firms (including Avon Products), as well as numerous clothing firms that send catalogs directly to homes.

If a firm plans to advertise through the mail, it should first obtain a mailing list that fits its target market. For example, Ford Motor Company sends ads to previous Ford customers. Talbots (a clothing firm) sends ads to a mailing list of its previous customers. Another common approach is for a firm to purchase the subscriber list of a magazine that is read by its targeted consumers. Many mailing lists can be separated by state or even zip code. As the price of paper and postage has increased, advertising by direct mail has become more expensive.

**telemarketing**
the use of the telephone for promoting and selling products

**Telemarketing**    **Telemarketing** uses the telephone for promoting and selling products. Many local newspaper firms use telemarketing to attract new subscribers. Phone companies and cable companies also use telemarketing to sell their services.

**Outdoor Ads**    Outdoor ads are shown on billboards and signs. Such ads are normally quite large because consumers are not likely to stop and look at them closely. Vacation-related products and services use outdoor advertising. For example, Disney World ads and Holiday Inn Hotel ads appear on billboards along many highways.

**Transportation Ads**    Advertisements are often displayed on forms of transportation, such as buses and the roofs of taxi cabs. These ads differ from the outdoor ads just described because they are moving rather than stationary. The ads generally attempt to provide a strong visual effect that can be recognized by consumers while the vehicle is moving.

**Specialty Ads**    Other forms of nonmedia advertising are also possible, such as T-shirts, hats, and bumper stickers. T-shirts advertise a wide variety of products, from shoes such as Adidas and Nike to soft drinks such as Coca-Cola and Pepsi.

## 2.3  Summary of Forms of Advertising

Exhibit 14.2 summarizes the forms of advertising. It also indicates whether each form targets the national market (nationwide advertising) or a local market.

**Exhibit 14.2**

Forms of Advertising

| Forms of Advertising | Typical Area Targeted |
|---|---|
| Newspaper | Local |
| Magazine | National |
| Radio | Local |
| Television | National or local |
| Internet | National |
| E-mail | National |
| Direct mail | National or local |
| Telemarketing | Local |
| Outdoor | Local |
| Transportation | Local |
| Specialty | National or local |

**Learning Objective 3**

Describe the steps involved in personal selling.

**personal selling**
a personal sales presentation used to influence one or more consumers

# 3. Personal Selling

**Personal selling** is a personal sales presentation used to influence one or more consumers. It requires a personal effort to influence a consumer's demand for a product. Salespeople conduct personal selling on a retail basis, on an industrial basis, and on an individual basis. The sales effort on a retail basis is usually less challenging because it is addressed mostly to consumers who have already entered the store with plans to purchase. Many salespeople in retail stores do not earn a commission and thus may be less motivated to make a sale than other salespeople.

Selling on an industrial basis involves selling supplies or products to companies. Salespeople in this capacity are normally paid a salary plus commission. The volume of industrial sales achieved by a salesperson is highly influenced by that person's promotional efforts.

Selling on an individual basis involves selling directly to individual consumers. Some insurance salespeople and financial planners fit this description. Their task is especially challenging if they do not represent a well-known firm, because they must prove their credibility.

Salespeople who sell on an industrial or individual basis generally perform the following steps:

✦ Identify the target market.

✦ Contact potential customers.

✦ Make the sales presentation.

✦ Answer questions.

✦ Close the sale.

✦ Follow up.

## 3.1 Identify the Target Market

An efficient salesperson first determines the type of consumers interested in the product. In this way, less time is wasted on consumers who

A key to personal selling is a presentation that focuses on the potential customer's needs and how the product will satisfy them better than competing products will.

© SHUTTERSTOCK/ANDREW TAYLOR

will not purchase the product, regardless of the sales effort. If previous sales have been made, the previous customers may be an obvious starting point.

Industrial salespeople can identify their target market by using library references and the Yellow Pages of a phone book. If they sell safety equipment, they will call almost any manufacturer in their area. If they sell printing presses, their market will be much more limited.

Individual salespeople have more difficulty identifying their market because they are unable to obtain information on each household. Thus, they may send a brochure to the "resident" at each address, asking the recipient to call if interested. The target market initially includes all households but is then reduced to those consumers who call back. Specific subdivisions of households that fit the income profile of typical consumers may be targeted.

### 3.2  Contact Potential Customers

Once potential customers are identified, they should be contacted by phone, e-mail, direct mail, or in person and provided with a brief summary of what the firm can offer them. Interested customers will make an appointment to meet with salespeople. Ideally, the salespeople should schedule appointments so that their time is used efficiently. For example, an industrial salesperson working the state of Florida should not make appointments in Jacksonville (northeast Florida), Miami (southeast), and Pensacola (northwest) within the same week. Half the week would be devoted to travel alone. The most logical approach is to fill the appointment schedule within a specific area. Individual salespeople should also attempt to schedule several appointments in the same area on a specific day.

### 3.3  Make the Sales Presentation

A sales presentation can range from demonstrating how a printing press is used to explaining the benefits of an insurance policy. Industrial salespeople usually bring equipment with them. They also provide free samples of some products to companies. The sales presentation generally describes the use of each product, the price, and the advantages

## SMALL BUSINESS SURVEY

### What Skills Are Needed to Be Successful in Sales?

A survey asked 1,500 sales managers and sales representatives to rank 14 different skills in order of importance for their success. The following table shows the percentage of respondents who ranked each skill as being one of the top four skills in importance:

| Skill | Percentage of Respondents |
|---|---|
| Planning before the sales call | 54 |
| Sales approach | 48 |
| Assessing the potential customer's needs | 47 |
| Managing time | 45 |
| Overcoming concerns about the product | 42 |
| Closing the sale | 36 |
| Initiating sales calls (cold calling) | 30 |
| Making presentations | 26 |
| Handling problems with the product | 20 |
| Negotiating | 19 |
| Following up after sales calls | 16 |
| Using the telephone to make sales calls | 15 |
| Managing paperwork | 7 |
| Demonstrating the product | 4 |

Notice that the four activities that were perceived to be most important are conducted before the sales call. This confirms the need for salespeople to plan and organize if they are to be successful.

over competing products. The presentation should focus on how a particular product satisfies customer needs.

### 3.4 Answer Questions

Potential customers normally raise questions during the course of the sales presentation. Salespeople should anticipate common questions and prepare responses to them.

### 3.5 Close the Sale

Most salespeople prefer to make (or "close") a sale right after the sales presentation, while the product's advantages are still in the minds of potential customers. For this reason, they may offer some incentive to purchase immediately, such as a discounted price.

## 3.6  Follow Up

A key to long-term selling success is the attention given to purchasers after the sale is made. This effort increases the credibility of salespeople and encourages existing customers to call again when they need additional products. Salespeople should also follow up on potential customers who did not purchase the product after a sales presentation. These potential customers may experience budget changes and become more interested in purchasing the product over time. E-mail facilitates the follow-up communication between the purchasers and the salespeople. Exhibit 14.3 summarizes the steps in personal selling.

## 3.7  Managing Salespeople

**sales manager**
an individual who manages a group of sales representatives

A common goal of many sales representatives is to become a **sales manager** and manage a group of sales representatives. For example, a company with 40 sales representatives around the country may split the geographic markets into four regions. Each region would have 10 sales representatives who are monitored by a sales manager.

Sales managers require some of the same skills as sales representatives. They need to have knowledge of the product and the competition. In addition, they must be able to motivate their representatives to sell. They must also be able to resolve customer complaints on the service provided by representatives and reprimand representatives when necessary. Some people are better suited to selling than managing salespeople. There is a distinct difference between motivating consumers to purchase a product and motivating employees to sell a product.

Since sales managers do not perform the daily tasks of selling the product, they can concentrate on special projects, such as servicing a major customer's massive order of products. They should evaluate the long-term prospects of the product and consider possible plans for expanding the geographic market. Information from their sales representatives may help their assessments.

---

**Exhibit 14.3**

Summary of Tasks Involved in Personal Selling

| Task | Description |
|---|---|
| Identify target market | Focus on types of customers most likely to purchase the product; contact these potential customers by phone or mail. |
| Contact potential customers | Schedule appointments with potential customers who are located in the same area on the same days. |
| Make sales presentation | Demonstrate the use and benefits of the product. |
| Answer questions | Prepare for typical questions and allow potential customers to ask questions. |
| Close the sale | Close the sale after the presentation, perhaps by offering a discount if a purchase is made immediately. |
| Follow up | Call customers who recently purchased the product to ensure their satisfaction. Call other potential customers who decided not to purchase the product to determine whether they would like to reconsider. |

**sales promotion**
the set of activities that is intended to influence consumers

# 4. Sales Promotion

**Sales promotion** is the set of activities that is intended to influence consumers. It can be an effective means of encouraging consumers to purchase a specific product. The following are the most common sales promotion strategies:

✦   Rebates

✦   Coupons

✦   Sampling

✦   Displays

✦   Premiums

## 4.1 Rebates

**rebate**
a potential refund by the manufacturer to the consumer

A **rebate** is a potential refund by the manufacturer to the consumer. When manufacturers desire to increase product demand, they may offer rebates rather than lowering the price charged to the retail store. Lowering the price to the retail store does not guarantee that the store will pass on the discount. Thus, this strategy could result in lower profit per unit without increasing demand. A rebate ensures that consumers receive the manufacturer's discount. Automobile manufacturers frequently offer rebates of $500 or more.

## 4.2 Coupons

**coupons**
a promotional device used in newspapers, magazines, and ads to encourage the purchase of a product

**Coupons** are used in newspapers, magazines, and ads to encourage the purchase of a product. They are also commonly packaged with a product so that consumers can use the coupon only if they purchase this same product again. Coupons used in this way can encourage consumers to repeatedly purchase the same brand. Consequently, consumers may become loyal to that brand.

Coupons allow consumers to purchase products at a reduced price and therefore may attract more consumers. They are frequently offered by manufacturers of household products.

© SHUTTERSTOCK/CARSTEN REISINGER

Some coupons are not available until consumers make repeated purchases. For example, airlines offer free flights to frequent fliers, and some hotels offer a free night's stay to frequent customers.

Promoting with coupons may be inefficient for some firms. General Mills had historically used coupons to promote its cereals. However, after learning from marketing research that 98 percent of all cereal coupons are not used, it decided to cut back on this promotion strategy. It reduced annual spending on some promotions by $175 million and focused on improving its product.

## 4.3  Sampling

**sampling**
offering free samples to encourage consumers to try a new brand or product

**Sampling** involves offering free samples to encourage consumers to try a new brand or product. The intent is to lure customers away from competing products. For example, Clinique samples are available in cosmetics departments of retail stores. Food samples are offered in grocery stores. Manufacturing firms also provide samples so that consumers can try out equipment. Samples are even sent through direct mail.

Samples are most commonly used to introduce new products. Firms recognize that once customers become accustomed to a particular brand, they tend to stick with that brand. Thus, the free sample is intended to achieve **brand loyalty**, or the loyalty of consumers to a specific brand over time.

**brand loyalty**
the loyalty of consumers to a specific brand over time

**Sampling of Services**    Sampling is used for services as well as products. For example, in 1999 America Online (AOL) provided a limited amount of free online time to potential customers. This strategy allowed customers to experience the service that AOL provides and resulted in a large number of subscriptions to AOL's online service. Subsequently, AOL merged with media giant Time Warner.

## 4.4  Displays

Many stores create special displays to promote particular products. The displays are used to attract consumers who are in the store for other

Displays like this can feature specific products that a firm wants to promote. Display products tend to sell more readily than other products because they are more likely to be noticed by consumers.

© SHUTTERSTOCK/DUNDANIM

Out of Business

reasons. Products are more likely to get attention if they are located at a point of purchase, such as by the cash registers where consumers are waiting in line. Because there is limited room for displays, companies that want retail stores to display their products are typically willing to set up the display themselves. They may even offer a reduced price to retail stores that allow a display.

## 4.5 Premiums

**premium**
a gift or prize provided free to consumers who purchase a specific product

A **premium** is a gift or prize provided free to consumers who purchase a specific product. For example, *Sports Illustrated* magazine may offer a free sports DVD to new subscribers. A boat manufacturer may offer a free fishing rod to anyone who purchases its boats. Premiums offer an extra incentive to purchase products.

## 4.6 Summary of Sales Promotion Strategies

Exhibit 14.4 provides a summary of sales promotion methods. The ideal strategy is dependent on the features of the product. Sampling and displays are intended to make the consumer aware of the product's qualities, while other sales promotion strategies are intended to make the price of the product appear more reasonable.

**Exhibit 14.4**

Comparison of Sales Promotion Strategies

| Strategy | Description |
|---|---|
| Rebates | Firm sends refund directly to consumers after product is purchased. |
| Coupons | Product is sold at a discounted price to consumers with coupons. |
| Sampling | Free samples of products are distributed to consumers. |
| Displays | Products are placed in a prominent area in stores. |
| Premiums | Gifts or prizes are provided free to consumers who purchase a specific product. |

# 5. Public Relations

**Learning Objective** **5**

Describe how firms can use public relations to promote products.

The term **public relations** refers to actions taken with the goal of creating or maintaining a favorable public image. Firms attempt to develop good public relations by communicating to the general public, including prospective customers. Public relations can be used to enhance the image of a product or of the firm itself. It may also be used to clarify information in response to adverse publicity. Many firms have a public relations department that provides information about the firm and its products to the public. Public relations departments typically use the media to relay their information to the public.

**public relations**
actions taken with the goal of creating or maintaining a favorable public image

Firms commonly attempt to be very accessible to the media because they may receive media coverage at no charge. When employees of a firm are quoted by the media, the firm's name is mentioned across a large audience. Some banks assign employees to provide economic forecasts because the media will mention the bank's name when reporting the forecast. Some public relations are not planned but result from a response to circumstances. For example, during the tragedy of September 11, Home Depot offered its support and was recognized by the media for its efforts.

The following are the most common types of public relations strategies:

+ Special events
+ News releases
+ Press conferences

## 5.1  Special Events

Some firms sponsor a special event such as a race. Anheuser-Busch (producer of Budweiser) supports many marathons and festivals where it promotes its name. 7UP promotes local marathons and has even printed the marathon logo and running figures on 7UP cans, which may attract consumers who run or exercise.

## 5.2  News Releases

**news release**
a brief written announcement about a firm provided by that firm to the media

A **news release** is a brief written announcement about a firm provided by that firm to the media. It enables the firm to update the public about its products or operations. It may also be used to clarify information in response to false rumors that could adversely affect the firm's reputation. The news release may include the name and phone number of an employee who can provide more details if desired by the media. There is no charge for providing a news release, but the firm incurs an indirect cost for hiring employees to promote news releases. Also, there is no guarantee that a news release will be publicized by the media.

## 5.3  Press Conferences

**press conference**
an oral announcement about a firm provided by that firm to the media

A **press conference** is an oral announcement about a firm provided by that firm to the media. Like a news release, a press conference may be intended to enhance the firm's image or to eliminate any adverse effects caused by false rumors. A press conference is more personal than a news release because an employee of the firm makes the announcement

Firms commonly call a press conference when they have important news to disclose to the public. For example, a firm may use a press conference to announce the hiring of a new CEO or the introduction of a new product that it is going to sell.

© SHUTTERSTOCK/STEVE YAGER

directly to the media and may even be willing to answer questions from the media. There is no charge for organizing a press conference, but there is an indirect cost of hiring employees to perform the necessary tasks.

# Global Business

## Promoting Products Across Countries

When firms promote products, they tend to emphasize the features that give those products an advantage over others. Yet consumers in different countries may base their purchase decisions on different features. A product may be popular in the United States because it is durable, but it may be popular in another country because of its low price. Therefore, a firm may need to revise its promotional strategy according to the country. In addition, the manner in which a feature is promoted may vary with the country. Television commercials may not reach a large audience in some less-developed countries, where they may be seen by only the relatively wealthy consumers. Some television commercials may still be effective in these countries if the ads are seen by the type of people who would likely purchase the product. U.S. firms must recognize that the typical profile of the people in foreign countries who watch television or read specific newspapers may vary from the profile in the United States.

Furthermore, a commercial that is acceptable in one country may be restricted in another country. The United Kingdom prohibits commercials from directly comparing one product with a competing product. Therefore, commercials that compared Pepsi with Coca-Cola had to be revised to compare Pepsi against Brand X.

Given the different perceptions of products by consumers across countries and different government regulations, a firm may have to create a different promotion for a particular product in each country where the product is sold. Just as firms create products that are tailored to the unique characteristics of consumers in a specific country, they should also promote products in a manner that appeals to specific consumers.

# 6. Determining the Optimal Promotion Mix

Exhibit 14.5 provides a brief summary of the various promotion methods. Each method has its own advantages and disadvantages, so no single method is ideal for all products. Firms must decide whether to use advertising, personal selling, sales promotion, publicity, or some mix of these promotion methods to promote their products. Firms must consider the characteristics of their target market and their promotion budget when determining the optimal promotion mix, as explained next.

## 6.1 Target Market

If a firm's target market is made up of a wide variety of customers throughout a specific region, it may use advertising to promote its product. If a firm produces a surgical device for a target market of hospital surgeons, it may consider using some advertising to make surgeons aware of the device, along with personal selling to explain how the device is used. If the target market is made up of consumers on tight budgets (such as retired people), the firm may use sales promotion methods such as coupons or rebates.

Any of these promotion methods may be complemented with public relations such as sponsoring a special event for consumers who are in the target market for the product. For example, to promote its women's athletic shoes, Reebok sponsored a Sports Training Challenge for female high school athletes.

Firms typically attempt to direct their promotion to the target market. Miller Brewing, Anheuser-Busch, and other beer producers run commercials during sports events and direct the ads at a target market of men. Women's clothing ads are placed in fashion magazines and directed at a target market of women. Procter & Gamble promotes its household products on television shows watched by women because women generally make most of the household purchases.

**Pull Strategy**   When firms direct their promotion directly at the target market, they provide information to the consumers who would most likely purchase the products. Consumers become aware of the product without hearing about it from a retailer. They may then request the product from retailers, who in turn request it from wholesalers or

**Exhibit 14.5**

Summary of Methods That Make Up the Promotion Mix

| Promotion Method | Advantages | Disadvantages |
|---|---|---|
| Advertising | Reaches a large number of customers. | Can be expensive; is not personalized. |
| Personal selling | Provides personalized attention. | Difficult to reach a large number of customers. |
| Sales promotion | Offers various incentives for consumers to purchase products. | May not reach as many consumers as advertising. |
| Public relations | Inexpensive method of enhancing the image of the firm or its products. | Provides only a limited amount of promotion because news releases and press conferences may not always be covered by the media. |

Clothing manufacturers commonly use a pull strategy when targeting young women. They advertise their clothing to young women, who shop at clothing stores in search of clothing that was advertised. Clothing stores order the type of clothing from manufacturers that young women prefer.

© SHUTTERSTOCK/KONSTANTIN TAVROV

**pull strategy**
firms direct their promotion directly at the target market, and consumers in turn request the product from wholesalers or producers

**push strategy**
producers direct their promotion of a product at wholesalers or retailers, who in turn promote it to consumers

producers. This strategy is called a **pull strategy**, because the product is pulled through the distribution channel as a result of consumer demand. For example, suppose that a firm develops a new type of DVD player and advertises it to consumers. As consumers become aware of the product, their demand at retail outlets pulls the product through the distribution channel.

**Push Strategy** Some producers direct their promotion at wholesalers or retailers instead of their target market. When producers promote their products to wholesalers or retailers, their promotion effort is called a **push strategy**. Wholesalers promote the product to retailers, who in turn promote it to consumers. Thus, the product is pushed through the distribution channel. For example, assume that a manufacturer of a new DVD player has representatives demonstrate its advantages to all wholesalers. The wholesalers then promote the DVD player to retailers so that they can inform consumers. The difference between a push strategy and a pull strategy is illustrated in Exhibit 14.6. Personal selling is commonly used to apply a push strategy.

**Exhibit 14.6**

Comparison of Pull and Push Strategies

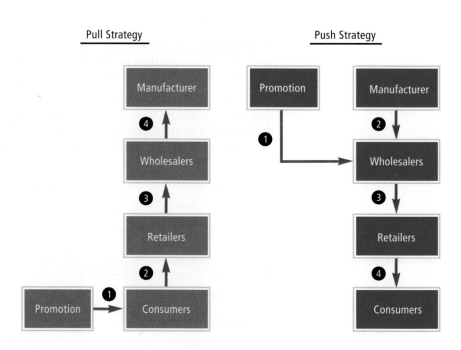

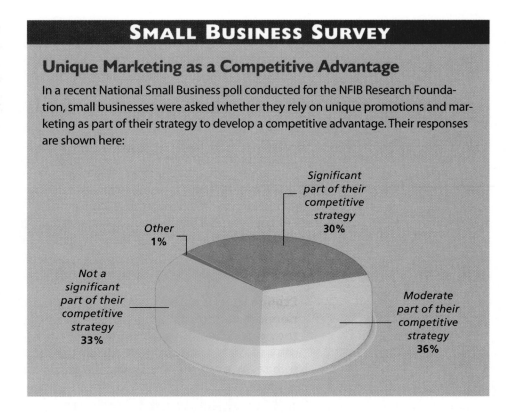

## SMALL BUSINESS SURVEY

### Unique Marketing as a Competitive Advantage

In a recent National Small Business poll conducted for the NFIB Research Foundation, small businesses were asked whether they rely on unique promotions and marketing as part of their strategy to develop a competitive advantage. Their responses are shown here:

Significant part of their competitive strategy **30%**

Other **1%**

Not a significant part of their competitive strategy **33%**

Moderate part of their competitive strategy **36%**

**Surveying the Target Market**  Marketing research can enhance a firm's promotion decisions by determining the types of promotions that are favorably received by the target market of concern. For example, a firm that sells clothing to teenagers may survey a sample of teenagers for feedback on various promotions that it may offer. The firm will implement the promotion strategy that is likely to result in the highest level of sales (assuming each promotion strategy has the same cost), based on the feedback from the teenagers surveyed.

## 6.2  Promotion Budget

**promotion budget**
the amount of funds that have been set aside to pay for all promotion methods over a specified period

A **promotion budget** is the amount of funds that have been set aside to pay for all promotion methods over a specified period. Firms may establish a promotion budget for each product that they produce. The budget may be large if the firm believes that promotion will have a major effect on sales or is necessary to prevent a substantial decline in sales. If the promotion budget for a specific product is small, advertising on television or in widely distributed magazines may not be possible. The firm may have to rely on inexpensive advertising (such as local newspapers) and inexpensive sales promotion methods (such as displays). Perhaps no single type of promotion will be as effective by itself.

The promotion budget varies substantially across firms and may even vary for each firm's product line over time. The promotion budget for a specific product is influenced by the following characteristics:

✦  Phase of the product life cycle

✦  Competition

✦  Economic conditions

**Phase of the Product Life Cycle**   Products that are just being introduced to the market will require more promotions to inform customers about the products. Products that are in the growth phase are promoted to inform and remind customers. Products in the maturity or decline phases of the life cycle may not require as much promotion. Nevertheless, they may still need some promotion to remind customers and retain their market share. The amount of promotion typically used for different phases of the life cycle is shown in Exhibit 14.7. Firms that revise their products in an effort to extend the life cycle may use a large amount of promotion even in the maturity phase.

**Competition**   A firm whose competitors frequently advertise may feel compelled to match their advertising with its own promotional campaign. This is a defensive strategy. As this illustrates, firms use advertising not only as an aggressive strategy to increase market share but also as a defensive strategy to retain existing market share.

**Economic Conditions**   Firms respond in different ways to favorable economic conditions. Some firms may increase their promotion because they can better afford it. Others will cut back, expecting the strong economy to carry their products. In a stagnant economy, firms may attempt to heavily promote their products in an attempt to maintain demand.

## 6.3  Evaluating and Revising a Firm's Promotions

Firms recognize that marketing can have a major impact on sales, but they also want to make sure that their promotion efforts are worth the cost. They view marketing as an investment, not just an expense, and they want to see the results of that investment. Thus, an important part of promotions involves determining whether the promotion strategy was successful. Many companies, including Home Depot, Procter & Gamble, and Kraft Foods, are working to make their marketing strategies more accountable. They are attempting to determine the precise impact of their promotions so that they can decide whether to use similar promotions in the future. For example, Chrysler has shifted some of its promotions to special events so that it can monitor the responses of

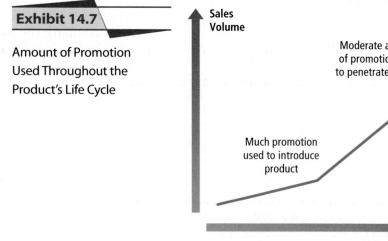

**Exhibit 14.7**

Amount of Promotion Used Throughout the Product's Life Cycle

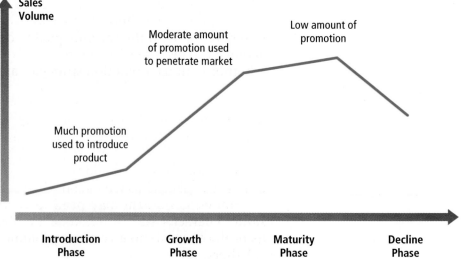

Sales Volume

Much promotion used to introduce product

Moderate amount of promotion used to penetrate market

Low amount of promotion

Introduction Phase

Growth Phase

Maturity Phase

Decline Phase

# Cross-Functional Teamwork

## Interaction Between Promotion Decisions and Other Business Decisions

When marketing managers make promotion decisions, they must interact with other managers of the firm. The amount of promotion that is used for a particular product will influence demand for that product. If marketing managers anticipate a larger demand for the product in response to new promotion strategies, they must inform the production department. The production managers must be aware of the anticipated demand so that they can produce a sufficient volume of products. Promotions that increase demand will increase sales only if the firm produces a larger volume in anticipation of the larger demand. Otherwise, the firm will experience shortages, and customers who are unable to purchase the product may purchase it from a competitor. In some cases, production may already be at full capacity, which means that the promotion may not be worthwhile until the manufacturing process can be revised to increase capacity.

Marketing managers also interact with financial managers about promotion decisions for the following reasons. First, when marketing managers estimate the costs of a specific promotion and the extra revenue that will be generated over time as a result of that promotion, they may rely on financial managers to assess whether the promotion will provide an adequate return to make it worthwhile to the firm. Second, when marketing managers decide to implement large promotions, they may need a substantial amount of funds; they can inform the financial managers, who may determine the best method to obtain those funds. Thus, marketing managers rely on input from both the production managers and the financial managers when making their promotion decisions.

the potential customers who were targeted during the events. Some websites that allow Internet advertising are capable of determining how many times customers clicked on an ad for more details or ordered products online (when available) in response to an ad.

If a firm establishes measurable objectives at the time of the promotion, it can assess whether the objectives were achieved. For example, consider a strategy that is intended to increase revenue by 10 percent over the next year. Once the year is over, the firm can compare the actual revenue with the revenue goal to determine whether the goal was achieved. This type of comparison can be useful for determining whether various promotion strategies are successful over time.

If the objectives of the promotion strategy are not accomplished, the firm may revise its strategy. Sometimes a marketing plan fails because the objectives were overly optimistic. In this situation, the firm may need to revise its objectives rather than its strategies. Firms must also recognize that changes in other conditions may affect revenue. For example, poor economic conditions may cause a firm's revenue to be less than the goal established even if the promotion strategy was effective.

Sometimes a firm may need to change its promotion mix. If consumer characteristics or market conditions change, the firm may revise its promotion mix to give more prominence to some strategies and less to others.

# Responding to the Economy

## Revising Promotion Decisions in Response to the Economy

Weak economic conditions could encourage some firms to cut back on their marketing budgets. But it could also cause other firms to spend more on marketing, because they need to retain their market share. Promotion strategies will focus more on products that sell better during a weak economy. In addition, the message within the promotion strategies may focus on the price of the product because consumers are more price conscious during a weak economy.

When gas prices are high and are a major concern to consumers, some firms attempt promotion strategies that offer free delivery or some other method of lowering the cost of driving. In general, the promotion strategy aims to address consumers' concerns and how the product or service will satisfy them. As economic conditions change, consumers' needs change, and promotions are adapted to focus on consumers' most important concerns. If a firm recognizes what is most important to consumers, it not only provides the product to fit those needs, but also communicates with its promotions how the product will satisfy them.

## COLLEGE HEALTH CLUB: PROMOTION AT CHC

As Sue Kramer develops her business plan for College Health Club (CHC), she must decide on the mix of different strategies that she will use to promote CHC. She decides to use a promotion mix consisting of (1) advertising through the Texas College newspaper, (2) coupons for vitamin supplements and a free day pass inserted in the Texas College newspaper, and (3) personal selling through monthly presentations about exercise and health to students on campus. All three parts of her promotion mix are focused on the students at the college, who are CHC's target market.

Sue has decided to advertise in the Texas College newspaper because she needs to reach a large number of potential members without spending too much money. Sue ruled out magazines, local television, radio, and the Internet because they are too expensive. She did not think that telemarketing, outdoor ads, transportation ads, or specialty ads would attract many members. Sue has decided that advertising in the college's newspaper is the easiest way to reach her target market. This weekly newspaper is free to students, and most students read it or at least skim it. Sue has decided on an ad that takes up one-quarter of a page and plans to run it for the next 10 weeks. Then she will determine the impact the ad has had on memberships and decide whether to continue running it.

To determine whether her promotion mix is effective, Sue also plans to monitor how the number of memberships changes after implementing her promotion mix. She realizes, however, that memberships may increase for reasons other than the promotion strategies. Therefore, she has included a question on the membership application asking what caused the applicant to purchase a membership. The choices are (1) referral from a friend, (2) advertising in the student newspaper, (3) coupons in the student newspaper, (4) the exercise and health presentations on campus, or (5) other. She can determine from the membership applications which promotion strategies are attracting the most members. This information can help her decide how to use her promotion budget in the future.

# Summary of Learning Objectives

**1** Promotional efforts can increase sales or at least prevent a decrease in sales because the brand name stays in the consumer's mind, consumers are informed about the product's advantages, and the product's perceived credibility may be enhanced.

**2** The key forms of advertising are newspapers, magazines, radio, television, the Internet, e-mail, direct mail, telemarketing, outdoor ads, transportation ads, and specialty ads.

**3** The main steps involved in personal selling are to

+ identify the target market,
+ contact potential customers,
+ make the sales presentation,
+ answer questions,
+ close the sale, and
+ follow up.

**4** The most common sales promotion methods include

+ rebates, in which firms give refunds directly to consumers after the product is purchased;
+ coupons, which allow products to be sold to specific consumers at discounted prices;
+ sampling, in which consumers receive free samples of products;
+ displays, in which products are placed in prominent areas of stores; and
+ premiums, in which gifts or prizes are provided free to consumers who purchase a specific product.

**5** Firms can use public relations to enhance a product's or a firm's image. The most common types of public relations strategies are

+ special events, which can be sponsored by a firm to promote a specific product;

+ news releases, which are brief written announcements about a firm provided by the firm to the media; and
+ press conferences, which are oral announcements about a firm provided by that firm to the media.

**6** When a firm selects the optimal promotion mix to use for promoting a product, it considers the

+ target market, so that it can use a promotion method that properly reaches that target market; and
+ promotion budget, since only those promotion methods that are affordable can be considered.

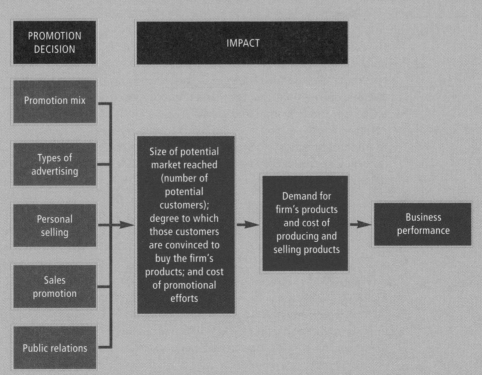

# Self-Test of Key Concepts

The following self-assessment allows you to test your understanding of the key concepts covered in this chapter. Answers are provided at the end of this exercise.

**True or False**

1. Comparative advertising is intended to enhance the image of a firm without focusing on a particular product.

2. The promotion mix is the combination of promotion methods that a firm uses to increase the acceptance of its products.

3. The Internet, magazines, direct mail, and television are all forms of advertising.

4. A key to successful selling is the follow-up service to customers provided by salespeople.

5. Television advertising is the most widely used form of personal selling for medium and large businesses.

6. Rebates are used to offer a price discount from retailers to their customers.

7. A firm using a push strategy will aim its promotional message directly at the target market customers.

8. Public relations is one of the most expensive forms of sales promotion.

9. One factor that will influence the size of the promotion budget for a product is the phase of the product in the product life cycle.

10. Sales managers perform the daily tasks of selling the product.

**Multiple Choice**

11. Even if a firm's product is properly produced, priced, and distributed, it still needs to be:
    a) manufactured.
    b) inspected.
    c) graded.
    d) promoted.
    e) market tested.

12. All of the following are methods of promotion except:
    a) target marketing.
    b) personal selling.
    c) advertising.
    d) sales promotion.
    e) public relations.

13. The act of informing or reminding consumers about a specific product or brand is referred to as:
    a) personal selling.
    b) production.
    c) finance.
    d) promotion.
    e) research and development.

14. Which of the following promotion strategies is a nonpersonal sales promotion aimed at a large number of consumers?
    a) advertising
    b) public relations
    c) telemarketing
    d) retail selling
    e) mega-marketing

15. A nonpersonal sales presentation about a specific brand is:
    a) institutional advertising.
    b) personal selling.
    c) brand advertising.
    d) comparative advertising.
    e) reminder advertising.

16. Ads that show consumers choosing between Pepsi and Coca-Cola are examples of _____ advertising.
    a) comparative
    b) institutional
    c) industry
    d) reminder
    e) generic

17. All of the following are forms of advertising except:
    a) direct mail.
    b) outdoor ads.
    c) personal selling.
    d) online banner ads.
    e) transportation ads.

18. Ads that are televised separately rather than within a show are called:
    a) commercials.
    b) specialty ads.
    c) infomercials.
    d) institutional ads.
    e) direct-mail ads.

19. The use of the telephone for promoting and selling products is known as:
    a) telepromotion.
    b) telemarketing.
    c) online sales promotion.
    d) telecommunication mix.
    e) annoying phone calls.

20. Salespeople generally perform all of the following steps except:
    a) identify the target market.
    b) follow up.
    c) contact potential customers.
    d) make the sales presentation.
    e) advertising.

21. A visual method that retail stores use in promoting particular products is a:
    a) display.
    b) rebate.
    c) coupon.
    d) premium.
    e) market.

22. The promotion strategy of sampling is most often used to:
    a) provide customers with a premium as an incentive to purchase more of the product.
    b) introduce new products.
    c) give customers a discount if a larger quantity is purchased.
    d) serve as a reminder for former customers to buy the product again.
    e) unload surplus inventory.

23. The main, immediate goal of public relations is to:
    a) remind customers of the firm's existence.
    b) compare the firm's brand to a competitor's brand.
    c) identify the firm's target market.
    d) enhance the image of the firm.
    e) increase sales.

24. Which of the following sales promotion strategies provides a gift or prize to consumers who purchase a specific product?
    a) pull
    b) push
    c) sampling
    d) rebates
    e) premiums

25. When firms promote products, they highlight the advantages over all other products. They emphasize the product's:
    a) publicity.
    b) features.
    c) sales promotion.
    d) labeling.
    e) life cycle.

26. Which of the following is a public relations strategy in which an organization provides the media with a written announcement?
    a) special events
    b) press conference
    c) concert sponsorship
    d) direct mail
    e) news release

27. If a firm's target market is made up of a wide variety of customers throughout a specific region, it would likely use _____ to promote its product.
    a) personal selling
    b) advertising
    c) door-to-door sales
    d) one-on-one communication
    e) target marketing

28. When producers promote their products to wholesalers or retailers, their promotion effort is called a:
    a) push strategy.
    b) premium price strategy.
    c) sales promotion.
    d) market segmentation.
    e) pull strategy.

29. Which of the following is a strategy where firms focus their promotional messages on the target market customers, who in turn request the product from wholesalers or producers?
    a) push
    b) co-branding
    c) product life cycle
    d) sponsorship
    e) pull

30. The promotion budget varies substantially across firms and may even vary for each firm's product line over time. Its characteristics are influenced by all of the following except:
    a) size of human resource department.
    b) competition.
    c) phase of the product life cycle.
    d) economic conditions.

**True/False**

| | |
|---|---|
| 1. False | 8. False |
| 2. True | 9. True |
| 3. True | 10. False |
| 4. True | |
| 5. False | |
| 6. False | |
| 7. False | |

**Multiple Choice**

| | | |
|---|---|---|
| 11. d | 18. c | 25. b |
| 12. a | 19. b | 26. e |
| 13. d | 20. e | 27. b |
| 14. a | 21. a | 28. a |
| 15. c | 22. b | 29. e |
| 16. a | 23. d | 30. a |
| 17. c | 24. e | |

# Self-Test of Key Terms

advertising  473
brand advertising  473
brand loyalty  483
comparative advertising  473
coupons  482
industry advertising  473
infomercials  475
institutional advertising  473
news release  485

personal selling  478
premium  484
press conference  485
promotion  472
promotion budget  489
promotion mix  472
public relations  485
pull strategy  488
push strategy  488

rebate  482
reminder advertising  473
sales manager  481
sales promotion  482
sampling  483
telemarketing  477

Fill in each blank with the proper key term. To assess your understanding of the key terms, answers are provided at the end of this self-test.

1. A(n) _____ strategy directs the promotion of a product at consumers, who in turn request the product from retailers.

2. _____ uses the telephone for promoting and selling products.

3. _____ a nonpersonal sales presentation communicated through the media or nonmedia forms to influence a large number of consumers.

4. A(n) _____ is a gift or prize provided to consumers who purchase a specific product.

5. _____ is intended to demonstrate a brand's superiority over other products.

6. A(n) _____ is an oral announcement about a firm provided by that firm to the media.

7. _____ commercials that are televised separately rather than within a show and promote a specific product for a firm.

8. The _____ is the combination of methods that a firm uses to increase acceptance of its products.

9. _____ is a personal presentation used to influence one or more consumers.

10. _____ refers to actions taken with the goal of creating or maintaining a favorable public image.

11. A(n) _____ is a potential refund by the manufacturer to the consumer.

12. _____ are used in newspapers, magazines, and ads to encouage the purchase of a product.

13. _____ is intended to remind consumers of the product's existence.

14. A(n) _____ is a brief written announcement about a firm provided by that firm to the media.

15. Firms use a(n) _____ strategy by directing their promotion of a product at wholesalers or retailers, who in turn promote it to consumers.

16. A(n) _____ is the amount of funds that have been set aside to pay for all promotion methods over a specified period.

17. _____ a nonpersonal sales presentation about a specific brand.

**Answers:**

1. pull
2. telemarketing
3. Advertising
4. premium
5. Comparative advertising
6. press conference
7. Infomercials
8. promotion mix
9. Personal selling
10. Public relations
11. rebate
12. Coupons
13. Reminder advertising
14. news release
15. push
16. promotion budget
17. Brand advertising

# Concept Review Questions

1. **Impact of Promotion on Business Valuation.** Explain how promotion strategies can enhance the performance and valuation of a business.

2. **Promotion Mix.** Identify the key components of a firm's promotion mix.

3. **Reasons for Advertising.** What are the common reasons for advertising?

4. **Forms of Advertising.** What are the common forms of advertising?

5. **E-Mail Advertisements.** Why do you think e-mail advertisements have limited effectiveness?

6. **Sales Promotion Strategies.** Identify commonly used sales promotion strategies.

7. **Optimal Promotion Mix.** Explain why the target market affects the optimal promotion mix. Explain why the promotion budget affects the optimal promotion mix.

8. **Pull Versus Push Strategies.** Explain the difference between a pull strategy and a push strategy.

9. **Promotion Budget.** Why is the promotion budget influenced by the product's present phase in the product life cycle?

10. **Evaluating Promotion Strategies.** How can firms evaluate the performance of a particular promotion strategy that they apply in a particular period?

# Class Communication Questions

1. **Target for Advertisements.** If your business produces toys that are sold to children between the ages of five and ten years of age, would you advertise the product to the children or to their parents?

2. **Promotion Dilemma.** If you owned a retail store that sells electronic games, what would be an affordable and effective method of advertising that you could use to increase your sales?

3. **Internet Advertising Dilemma.** Do you think that a retail store in the local mall would benefit from advertising on the main web page of Google or Yahoo?

# Small Business Case

## Promotion Decisions

Karma Coffee Company was recently opened in downtown Boston. The owner, Stephanie Logan, wants to attract many of the people who work in major office complexes nearby. Stephanie is hoping that they will stop in Karma for coffee before they start work, after they leave work in the evening, or during breaks for informal meetings with business associates or friends. She decides that the local business people represent her target market.

1. **Spending Money for Promotion.** Explain why Stephanie may benefit from spending money to promote her business.

2. **Advertising Decision.** Television advertising reaches a very large audience, but it is very expensive. Would this form of advertising be worthwhile for Karma Coffee?

3. **Sales Presentation Advantage.** Stephanie contacted the special events director of each firm in the vicinity of Karma Coffee, and made a sales presentation about how her coffee house may be the ideal place for their events. What is an advantage of personal selling over advertising?

4. **Sales Promotion Advantage.** Stephanie decides to provide all business employees in the area with brochures about her coffee house. Each brochure contains a coupon for a free coffee. What benefit does this sales promotion provide that Karma Coffee would not obtain from advertising?

# Web Insight

## Coca Cola's Web Promotions

At the opening of the chapter, The Coca Cola Company was introduced. Go to the website (www.cocacola.com) and review a section that has promotions (such as the section called "Rewards.") Summarize the type of promotions that The Coca Cola Company uses on its website.

# Dell's Secrets for Success

Go to Dell's website (www.dell.com) and click on the link "About Dell," near the bottom of the web page. You can also review a recent annual report for more information.

1. **Degree of Advertising.** Dell does not use excessive advertising. It tends to use more of its funds to focus on high-quality production and customer satisfaction. Does this strategy make sense?

2. **Product Life Cycle.** Dell is beyond the introduction phase of the product life cycle. Why might Dell have to change its promotion strategy when it enters the decline phase of the product life cycle?

# Video Exercise

**Lessons in Promotion**

Many free business videos are available on websites such as YouTube (www.youtube.com), and more are added every day. Search for a recent video clip about an existing business that offers lessons on "promotion" in YouTube or any other website that provides video clips.

1. **Main Lesson.** What is the name of the business in the video clip? Is the video clip focused on the firm's use of advertising, its personal selling, sales promotion methods, public relations, or some other aspect of promotion? What is the main lesson of the video clip that you watched?

2. **Benefits of Public Relations.** Some entrepreneurs say that they attempt to interact with customers every chance they get, regardless of the event. Why?

3. **Ideal Method of Advertising.** Some businesses mention in videos that direct mail is their ideal method of advertising. Yet, other businesses say that radio or television is their ideal method of advertising. Who is right?

# Projects

To encourage further comprehension of concepts covered in Chapter 14, the following five projects are available:

1. Analyzing Your Favorite Business

2. Building a Business Plan for Campus.com

3. Running Your Own Business

4. Planning Your Career

5. Stock Market Contest

All of these projects are provided in Appendix A at the end of the text. In addition, projects are available by part division at the end of each part.

A Word file for each project is also available at the textbook website (www.emcp.net/business5e) so that you may maintain one ongoing file for each project.

# Summary/Part V

# Marketing

# Summary

The chapters in Part V explain the key marketing decisions made by a business. Chapter 12 focuses on identifying products (or services) that can be provided, making those products unique from those offered by competitors, identifying a target market, and pricing the products. These functions essentially determine the firm's product line. Chap-ter 13 describes alternative methods of distributing products. No distribu-tion method is ideal for all firms. The most effective method is depen-dent on the characteristics of the business. A business that selects the most effective distribution method for its particular product line can re-duce expenses and may even en-hance revenue. Chapter 14 explains alternative methods of promoting products. As with distribution, the most effective promotion method is dependent on the characteristics of the business. If applied properly, promotion can substantially en-hance the revenue generated by a business.

# Video on Managing a Business

## Marketing for Success

The Small Business Administration plays a very important role in help-ing many small businesses. Its web-site, which offers a wide range of services and information for small businesses, has a section called Delivering Success (www.sba.gov/tools/audiovideo/deliveringsuccess/index.html) that provides video clips of small business success sto-ries. Go to this website, and watch the video called "Planning and Re-search" (total time of clip is 6 min-utes, 40 seconds).

In this video clip, two entrepre-neurs with successful businesses summarize their marketing re-search experience. Many small businesses are not necessarily known by consumers.

Therefore, marketing may be crucial for them. When determining the ideal marketing strategy to use, businesses should attempt to put themselves in the position of a con-sumer and assess how they would respond to the various advertising methods that could be applied. A business may initially experiment with various advertising methods, and monitor the results to deter-mine which method led the cus-tomers to the business. The marketing strategy of a small busi-ness can affect the key components of a business plan. The revenue of a business may be influenced by the marketing strategy, and the amount of financing that a business can ob-tain can be influenced by the esti-mated revenue.

1. **Interaction Between Target Market and Advertising Strategy.** Explain how the marketing strategy (Chapter 14) of a small business is related to the target market identified by the business (Chapter 12).

2. **Interaction Between Distri-bution and Advertising Methods.** Explain how the dis-tribution strategy (Chapter 13) and the marketing strategy (Chapter 14) of a small business are related.

3. **Interaction Between Pricing and Promotion.** Explain how the pricing of a product (Chap-ter 12) is related to promotion (Chapter 14).

# Self-Test for Part V

**Chapters 12-14.** Answers are provided at the end of the self-test.

1. A Rolex watch and a Jaguar automobile are considered:
   a) convenience products.
   b) shopping goods.
   c) industrial products.
   d) specialty products.
   e) priority products.

2. When a hospital supply company offers a wide variety of products to its customers, the firm is:
   a) offering quantity price discounts in order to attract price-conscious customers.
   b) encouraging customers to pay their outstanding debts in order to take advantage of discounts.
   c) practicing product differentiation.
   d) diversifying its product mix.
   e) responding to the needs of a diverse labor force.

3. The size of a particular target market is most likely to change in response to a change in:
   a) inflation.
   b) consumer preferences.
   c) interest rates.
   d) the number of competitors.
   e) the size of the largest competitor.

4. Which of the following can be used by a firm to protect its investments in research and product development?
   a) marketing research
   b) patents
   c) demographics
   d) target market selection
   e) product mix

5. All of the following are methods commonly used to differentiate products from those of competitors except:
   a) quality.
   b) design.
   c) tax policies.
   d) packaging.
   e) branding.

6. The process of combining two noncompeting products at a discounted price is called:
   a) complementary advertising.
   b) multiple discounts.
   c) co-branding.
   d) sales promotion double.
   e) quantity pricing.

7. Which of the following pricing strategies would likely be used in a market where no other competitive products are available?
   a) cost-based pricing
   b) penetration pricing
   c) predatory pricing
   d) price skimming
   e) defensive pricing

8. When a firm lowers its price and total revenue increases, it tells us that:
   a) the demand for the product is price-inelastic.
   b) a penetration pricing strategy is being followed.
   c) consumers are not very responsive to price changes.
   d) the demand for the product is price-elastic.
   e) the firm is using a price-skimming strategy.

9. Which of the following pricing strategies adds a profit markup to the per-unit cost of production?
   a) prestige pricing
   b) cost-based pricing
   c) defensive pricing
   d) profit pricing
   e) penetration pricing

10. (Fixed Cost) + [(Quantity × Variable Cost per Unit)] describes:
    a) Total Cost.
    b) Total Revenue.
    c) Break-Even Point.
    d) Profits.
    e) Average Cost per Unit.

11. The manner by which a firm's products are made accessible to its customers is determined by its:
    a) advertising strategies.
    b) product decisions.
    c) pricing strategies.
    d) distribution decisions.
    e) package designs.

12. With a direct channel of distribution, the full difference between the manufacturer's cost and the price paid by the consumer goes to the:
    a) manufacturer.
    b) wholesaler.
    c) retailer.
    d) intermediary.
    e) merchant.

13. Marketing intermediaries that match buyers and sellers of products without becoming the owners of the products themselves are known as:
    a) single-service marketers.
    b) agents.
    c) commission-based wholesalers.
    d) stockers.
    e) mediators.

14. _____ refers to the degree of product distribution among outlets.
    a) The marketing mix
    b) Demographic distribution
    c) Market coverage
    d) Channelization
    e) The retail ratio

15. _____ distribution is used when a producer distributes its products through certain chosen outlets while intentionally avoiding other possible outlets.
    a) Restrictive
    b) Exclusive
    c) Intensive
    d) Narrow
    e) Selective

16. Newspaper publishers have their papers available in grocery stores, convenience stores, and vending machines and at many other locations throughout a city. This is an example of a(n) _____ distribution of a product.
    a) nonspecific
    b) specialized
    c) geographically dispersed
    d) intensive
    e) decentralized

17. A(n) _____ is a retailer with only one outlet.
    a) exclusive retailer
    b) independent retail store
    c) wholesaler
    d) franchise retailer
    e) sole proprietorship

18. One way to accelerate the distribution process is to make sure that it is integrated with the _____ process.
    a) marketing
    b) financing
    c) credit approval
    d) advertising
    e) production

19. When the wholesaler purchases the products from the manufacturer and sells them to retailers on credit, it normally assumes the:
    a) package design.
    b) credit risk.
    c) promotional expenses of the manufacturer.
    d) manufacturer's guarantee.
    e) producer's risk.

20. A situation in which two or more levels of distribution are managed by a single firm is called:
    a) vertical channel integration.
    b) horizontal channel integration.
    c) multilevel marketing.
    d) wheel of retailing.
    e) conglomeration.

21. All of the following are methods of promotion except:
    a) target marketing.
    b) personal selling.
    c) advertising.
    d) sales promotion.
    e) public relations.

22. Which of the following promotion strategies is a nonpersonal sales promotion aimed at a large number of consumers?
    a) advertising
    b) public relations
    c) telemarketing
    d) retail selling
    e) mega-marketing

23. Ads that show consumers choosing between Pepsi and Coca-Cola are examples of _____ advertising.
    a) comparative
    b) institutional
    c) industry
    d) reminder
    e) generic

24. Ads that are televised separately rather than within a show are called:
    a) commercials.
    b) specialty ads.
    c) infomercials.
    d) institutional ads.
    e) direct-mail ads.

25. Salespeople generally perform all of the following steps except:
    a) identify the target market.
    b) follow up.
    c) contact potential customers.
    d) make the sales presentation.
    e) advertising.

26. The promotion strategy of sampling is most often used to:
    a) provide customers with a premium as an incentive to purchase more of the product.
    b) introduce new products.
    c) give customers a discount if a larger quantity is purchased.
    d) serve as a reminder for former customers to buy the product again.
    e) unload surplus inventory.

27. Which of the following sales promotion strategies provides a gift or prize to consumers who purchase a specific product?
    a) pull
    b) push
    c) sampling
    d) rebates
    e) premiums

28. Which of the following is a public relations strategy in which an organization provides the media with a written announcement?
    a) special events
    b) press conference
    c) concert sponsorship
    d) direct mail
    e) news release

29. When producers promote their products to wholesalers or retailers, their promotion effort is called a:
    a) push strategy.
    b) premium price strategy.
    c) sales promotion.
    d) market segmentation.
    e) pull strategy.

30. Which of the following is a strategy where firms focus their promotional messages on the target market customers, who in turn request the product from wholesalers or producers?
    a) push
    b) co-branding
    c) product life cycle
    d) sponsorship
    e) pull

**Answers:**

| | | | |
|---|---|---|---|
| 1. d | 9. b | 17. b | 25. e |
| 2. d | 10. a | 18. e | 26. b |
| 3. b | 11. d | 19. b | 27. e |
| 4. b | 12. a | 20. a | 28. e |
| 5. c | 13. b | 21. a | 29. a |
| 6. c | 14. c | 22. a | 30. e |
| 7. d | 15. e | 23. a | |
| 8. d | 16. d | 24. c | |

# Projects

## PROJECT 1: ANALYZING YOUR FAVORITE BUSINESS

**Answering the Questions.** This entire project is provided in Appendix A. You can retrieve the Word file of this project from the textbook website at (www.emcp.net/business5e), and insert your answer just below each question. The portion of the project that is related to the chapters in this part is provided here.

Using the annual report of the firm you selected, answer the following questions:

**Firm's Product Line and Mix (related to Chapter 12).** Describe the firm's product line and product mix.

**Firm's Target Market (related to Chapter 12).** Describe the firm's target market.

**Distribution (related to Chapter 13).** How does the firm distribute its products?

**Promotion (related to Chapter 14).** How does the firm promote its products?

## PROJECT 2: BUILDING A BUSINESS PLAN FOR CAMPUS.COM

**Completing the Information.** You can complete the information on the Word file of this project from the textbook website at (www.emcp.net/business5e). This allows you to insert all of your information on one file for this project by the end of the school term. The portion of the project that is related to the chapters in this part is provided here.

**Creating and Pricing Products (related to Chapter 12).**
Campus.com can expand its product line by:

_____

_____

_____

_____

_____

Campus.com can expand its target market by:

_____

_____

_____

_____

**Pricing (related to Chapter 12).** Campus.com's pricing plan is:

_____

_____

_____

_____

Campus.com will offer these types of discounts:

_____

_____

_____

**Distributing Products (related to Chapter 13).** Campus.com's distribution plan is:

_____

_____

_____

_____

**Promoting Products (related to Chapter 14).** Campus.com's advertising plan is (include explanation of the target market and the types of media used):

_____

_____

_____

_____

_____

## PROJECT 3: RUNNING YOUR OWN BUSINESS

**Completing the Information.** This entire project is provided in Appendix A. You can retrieve the Word file of this project from the textbook website (www.emcp.net/business5e), and insert your answer just below each question. The por-

tion of the project that is related to the chapters in this part is provided here.

**Creating and Pricing Products (related to Chapter 12).** Your business can expand its product line by:

_____

_____

_____

_____

_____

Your business can expand its target market by:

_____
_____
_____
_____

**Pricing (related to Chapter 12).** Your business will price its products based on (cost? competitor prices?):

_____
_____
_____
_____

Your business will offer these types of discounts:

_____
_____
_____
_____

**Distributing Products (related to Chapter 13).** The distribution plan of your business is:

_____
_____
_____
_____

Explain whether the cost of distributing your product will be affected substantially if there is a large increase in the price of gasoline or in postal rates.

_____
_____
_____

**Promoting Products (related to Chapter 14).** The advertising plan of your business is (include explanation of the target market and the types of media used):

_____
_____
_____
_____

## PROJECT 4: PLANNING YOUR CAREER

This entire project is provided in Appendix A at the end of the text, and you can access a Word file of this project from the textbook website (www.emcp.net/business5e), and insert your answer just below each question.

If you are very interested in the topics covered in this section, you may want to consider a major in marketing. Some of the more common courses taken by marketing majors are summarized here.

### Common courses for marketing majors

• **Advertising** Focuses on methods of promoting products, alternative types of advertising, the use of the media for advertising, and the role of advertising agencies.

• **Marketing Environment** Discusses the impact of social, technological, and other environmental conditions on marketing decisions and looks at how marketing decisions have changed in response to changes in the marketing environment.

• **Distribution Systems** Examines the role of inventory maintenance for distribution, channels of distribution, and transportation methods used for distribution.

• **Promotional Management** Examines how consumers make purchasing decisions, what factors drive their decisions, and how firms can capitalize on this information.

• **Marketing Research** Focuses on methods of assessing consumer purchases and the effects of marketing

strategies; discusses gathering data, analysis, and deriving implications from the analysis.

• **Marketing Strategy** Explains how marketing concepts can be applied to solve marketing problems and make marketing decisions.

• **Services Marketing** Describes the application of marketing strategy to services.

• **Marketing Planning** Focuses on the process of developing a marketing plan, including the creation of a product, the identification of a target market, and the creation of a structure for distribution and promotion.

• **Psychology Courses** Especially those courses that explain human behavior as related to consumption, preferences, and needs.

## PROJECT 5: STOCK MARKET CONTEST

This entire project is provided in Appendix A at the end of the text, and you can access a Word file of the project from the textbook website (www.emcp.net/business5e). Your instructor may ask you to assess the performance of your investment up to this point, and whether the performance of your stock is attributed to any of the business concepts that were described in the chapters contained in this part.

# Part VI
# Financial Management

Financial management involves the analysis of financial data, as well as the determination of how to obtain and use funds. Chapter 15 explains how a financial analysis of a firm can be conducted to determine how it is performing, and why. This type of analysis is used to detect a firm's deficiencies so that they can be corrected.

Finance is the means by which firms obtain funds (financing) and invest funds in business projects. Firms may obtain funds to build a new factory, purchase new machinery, purchase more supplies, or even purchase an existing business owned by another company. Chap-ter 16 describes the common financing methods that firms use and also identifies the types of financial institutions that provide financing. It also explains the factors that influence the ideal type of financing. Chapter 17 describes the tasks that are necessary when a firm determines whether to invest in a particular business project. In addition, it explains why firms sometimes use their funds to acquire other firms. The chapters on financing and business investment are closely related because financing supports the firm's investment in new business projects.

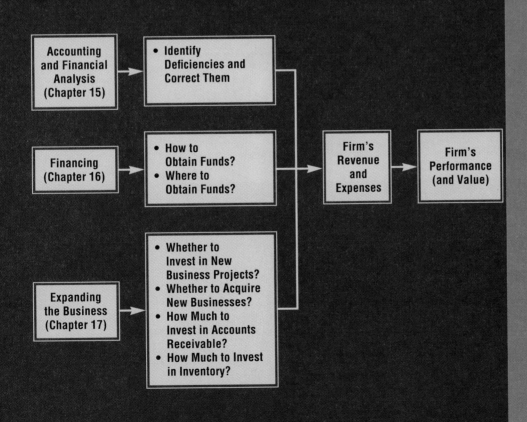

# Accounting and Financial Analysis

## Chapter 15 Learning Objectives

**1** Explain how firms use accounting.

**2** Discuss how firms can ensure proper financial reporting.

**3** Explain how to interpret financial statements.

**4** Explain how to evaluate a firm's financial condition.

### Financial Analysis at Cheesecake Factory

Accounting is the summary and analysis of a firm's financial condition. The accounting process generates financial statements, which provide detailed information about a firm's recent performance and its financial condition. Managers of all types of firms use financial statements to assess their performance and to make business decisions. Consider the situation of The Cheesecake Factory, which has established many restaurants in the U.S. It can use financial analysis to compare its financial performance among its restaurants. This would allow it to determine which of its

restaurants are the most popular, which is useful information when planning to build more restaurants in the future. The financial analysis would also allow The Cheesecake Factory to detect any unusually high expenses at a particular restaurant that need to be reduced. In addition, The Cheesecake Factory may also want to assess the financial performance following a particular promotion (or other strategy) so that it can determine whether the promotion was successful. This analysis indicates whether to use such a promotion at its other restaurants.

When The Cheesecake Factory engages in accounting and finan-

cial analysis, it must address the following questions:

✦ How can it measure its recent performance?

✦ How can it ensure that its financial statements are accurate?

✦ How can it assess its present financial condition?

These questions must be addressed by all businesses. This chapter explains how the accounting and financial analysis functions described here can be used by The Cheesecake Factory or by any other firm in a manner that maximizes its value.

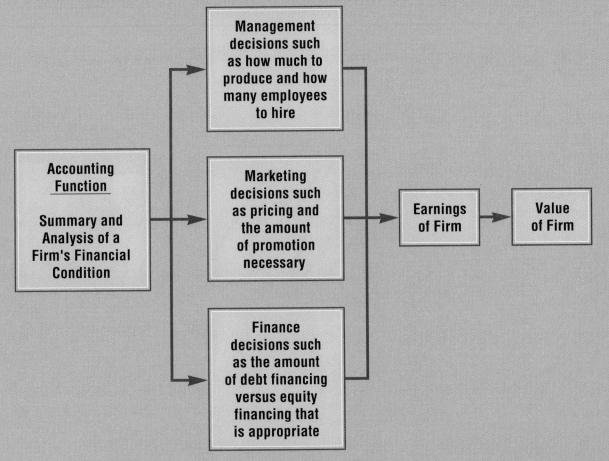

**accounting**
summary and analysis of a firm's financial condition

**public accountants**
accountants who provide accounting services for a variety of firms for a fee

**certified public accountants (CPAs)**
accountants who meet specific educational requirements and pass a national examination

**bookkeeping**
the recording of a firm's financial transactions

**financial accounting**
accounting performed for reporting purposes

# 1. How Firms Use Accounting

Firms use **accounting** to report their financial condition, support decisions, and control business operations, as explained in this order next. The accounting process itself is performed by accountants who may be private or public accountants. Private accountants provide accounting services for the firms where they are employed. Although they usually have an accounting degree, they do not have to be certified.

**Public accountants** provide accounting services for a variety of firms for a fee. A license is required to practice public accounting. Accountants who meet specific educational requirements and pass a national examination are referred to as **certified public accountants (CPAs)**.

## 1.1 Reporting

One accounting task is to report accurate financial data. **Bookkeeping** is the recording of a firm's financial transactions. For example, the recording of daily or weekly revenue and expenses is part of the book-keeping process.

Firms are required to periodically report their revenue, expenses, and earnings to the Internal Revenue Service (IRS) so that their taxes can be determined. The type of accounting performed for reporting purposes is called **financial accounting**.

Financial accounting must be conducted in accordance with generally accepted accounting principles (GAAP) that explain how financial information should be reported. The Financial Accounting Standards Board (FASB), Securities and Exchange Commission (SEC), and IRS establish the accounting guidelines. The use of a common set of guidelines allows for more consistency in reporting practices among firms. Consequently, a comparison of financial statements between two or more different firms may be more meaningful.

Financial reporting commonly involves a graphic comparison of a firm's revenue during the last year and its expenses. This allows stockholders to determine how the earnings have changed over the last year.

## SMALL BUSINESS SURVEY

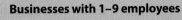

### Responsibility for Financial Reporting

In a recent National Small Business poll conducted for the NFIB Research Foundation, small business owners were asked who is responsible for their financial reporting. Their responses are shown below:

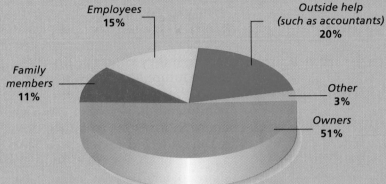

**Businesses with 1–9 employees**

Employees 15%

Outside help (such as accountants) 20%

Family members 11%

Other 3%

Owners 51%

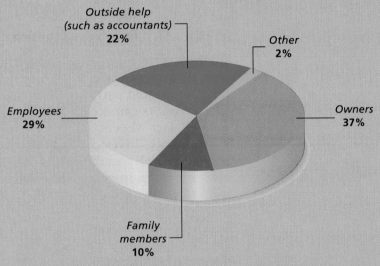

**Businesses with 10–19 employees**

Outside help (such as accountants) 22%

Other 2%

Employees 29%

Owners 37%

Family members 10%

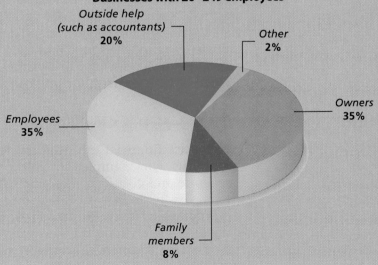

**Businesses with 20–249 employees**

Outside help (such as accountants) 20%

Other 2%

Employees 35%

Owners 35%

Family members 8%

**Reporting to Investors**   Publicly owned firms are required to periodically report their financial condition for investors who either already own the firm's stock or may purchase it in the future. Most shareholders of a publicly owned firm are not employees of the firm, but simply invest in its stock in an effort to earn a high return on their investment. The market price of the firm's stock tends to move in line with the firm's performance. The price rises when the firm performs well, but declines when the firm performs poorly. Thus, the return on an investment in the firm's stock in a future period is dependent on the firm's performance over that period. Investors assess the firm's recent earnings and other financial information to predict how the firm will perform in the future. If they conclude that the price of the stock will rise substantially in the future, they may buy the stock.

If the financial statements indicate that the firm has performed poorly and do not offer any clear evidence that the performance will improve, investors will not buy the firm's stock, and existing shareholders may decide to sell their stock. Alternatively, if they own a large amount of shares, they may attempt to join with other disgruntled shareholders in demanding that some high-level managers or board members be fired as a result of the firm's poor performance. This activist role is intended to result in more effective management of the firm in the future, which would lead to a higher stock price and a decent return on their investment.

**Online Reporting**   Many firms use the Internet to make their financial information available. For example, Dell, Inc., provides its investors and other interested parties with detailed financial information via its website. Investors can access Dell's most recent annual report, quarterly "financial fact sheets," and earnings estimates for the coming year. Furthermore, investors can request specific financial information using the website. By making this information available over the Internet, Dell provides investors and other parties with current, up-to-the-minute feedback on its financial performance.

**Reporting to Creditors**   Firms also report their financial condition to existing and prospective creditors. The creditors assess firms' financial statements to determine the probability that the firms will default on loans. Creditors that consider providing short-term loans assess financial statements to determine the firm's liquidity (ability to sell existing assets). Creditors that consider providing long-term loans may assess the financial statements to determine whether the firm is capable of generating sufficient income in future years to make interest and principal payments on the loan far into the future.

## 1.2  Decision Support

Firms use financial information developed by accountants to support decisions. For example, a firm's financial managers may use historical revenue and cost information for budgeting decisions. The marketing managers use sales information to evaluate the impact of a particular promotion strategy. The production managers use seasonal sales information to determine the necessary production level in the future. The type of accounting performed to provide information to help managers make decisions is referred to as **managerial accounting**. Financial

**managerial accounting**
accounting performed to provide information to help managers of the firm make decisions

accounting also reports information, but to shareholders and the IRS (outside the firm). To provide a complete set of information, the information generated by managerial accounting can be combined with other information (such as industry characteristics). For example, Blockbuster maintains information on revenue, current and historical sales and rental activity, demographics of store customers, and rental patterns. It can use this information to predict the types of DVDs that may be popular in the future.

## 1.3  Control

In addition to providing information to support decisions, managerial accounting helps managers maintain control. By reviewing financial information, managers monitor the performance of individuals, divisions, and products. Accounting information on sales is used to monitor the performance of various products and the salespeople who sell them. Information on operating expenses is used to monitor production efficiency.

**auditing**
an assessment of the records that were used to prepare a firm's financial statements

**internal auditors**
specialize in evaluating various divisions of a business to ensure that they are operating efficiently

Managers evaluate their firm's financial statements to monitor operations and to identify the firm's strengths and weaknesses. Financial statements can be generated and analyzed as frequently as necessary to identify problems and resolve them quickly before they become serious.

Another accounting task used for control is **auditing**, which is an assessment of the records that were used to prepare the firm's financial statements. **Internal auditors** specialize in evaluating various divisions within a firm to ensure that they are operating efficiently.

**Learning Objective**

**2**

Discuss how firms can ensure proper financial reporting.

# 2.  Responsible Financial Reporting

Firms have some flexibility when accounting for their financial condition. Some firms tend to use whatever method of accounting will inflate their earnings because they know that their stockholders will be better satisfied if earnings are high. Moreover, some of a firm's top managers who own the firm's stock may want a favorable financial report to ensure that the stock value stays high until they sell their stock holdings. Enron, Inc., used accounting gimmicks to inflate its revenue and its earnings until 2001 when investors finally realized that the financial statements were distorted. Enron filed for bankruptcy in November 2001. WorldCom used accounting gimmicks to reduce its expenses. In June 2002, it admitted that its expenses over the previous five quarters were underestimated by $3.9 billion. In July 2002, it went bankrupt.

A firm should use whatever method of accounting provides the most accurate indication of its financial condition. By doing so, the firm may benefit in two ways. First, it may gain some credibility with existing and prospective stockholders by providing clear and consistent reports that are easily understood. Second, using an understandable and logical accounting method makes it easier for the firm's managers to detect and correct deficiencies.

## 2.1  The Role of Auditors in Ensuring Proper Reporting

Publicly traded firms are required to have their annual financial reports audited by an independent accounting firm of public accountants,

Out of Business

I AM PLEASED TO SAY THAT I HAVE TOLD OUR ACCOUNTANTS WHAT EARNINGS TO REPORT FOR THE NEXT SIX YEARS AND WE ARE ALL GOING TO RECEIVE VERY GOOD BONUSES BASED ON THESE FUTURE EARNINGS REPORTS.

BOARD MEMBERS

known as an independent auditor. The auditor's role is to certify that the financial statements are accurate and within the generally accepted reporting guidelines. An auditor's stamp of approval does not imply anything about a firm's performance; the auditor is certifying only that the information contained within the financial statements is accurate. Nevertheless, some auditors have certified financial reports that were misleading. Perhaps the best-known example was the audit of Enron by the accounting firm Arthur Andersen in the year 2000. Andersen certified some of Enron's financial reports that were very questionable. Auditors are sometimes tempted to certify financial reports because they want to be hired by the firm again in the future. In 2000, Arthur Andersen earned more than $50 million in fees for its auditing and other work provided to Enron. The auditors knew that if they did not certify the financial reports, Enron would hire another accounting firm instead. This ethical dilemma does not absolve Arthur Andersen from blame, but it does explain why auditors sometimes certify financial reports that should not be certified. Arthur Andersen was also the auditor of WorldCom during the period when WorldCom's expenses were underestimated.

Given the conflict of interest that may arise, auditors cannot always be trusted to ensure that a firm properly reports financial information to its stockholders. The publicity surrounding the demise of Enron and WorldCom has caused investors to be more cautious when interpreting financial statements. Some firms have responded by disclosing more details about their financial condition to demonstrate that they have nothing to hide.

## 2.2 The Role of Directors in Ensuring Proper Reporting

Since a firm's board of directors represents the shareholders, it can try to prevent the firm from providing misleading financial reports. However, some boards do not effectively represent the stockholders. For example, a problem may arise when board members are compensated with the firm's stock. Like the firm's top managers who own its stock, the board members might benefit from misleading financial reporting that artificially inflates the stock's price because they too could sell their shares while the stock is priced artificially high. The board members may be more willing to enforce proper disclosure if they cannot sell any of their stock holdings while serving on the board. If forced to hold on to their shares for a long-term period, directors may be more likely to make decisions that benefit the long-term performance of the firm.

## 2.3  The Role of the Sarbanes-Oxley Act

In response to the accounting fraud at Enron and other firms, regulators are attempting to ensure more accurate financial disclosure by firms. Stock exchanges have instituted new regulations for the firms that list on the exchange. The Securities and Exchange Commission has been granted more resources and power to monitor financial reporting.

Perhaps the most important regulatory changes to ensure accurate financial disclosure are the result of the Sarbanes-Oxley Act of 2002. Some of the act's more important provisions are summarized here.

+ An auditing firm is allowed to provide nonaudit services when auditing a client only if the client's audit committee preapproves these services before the audit begins. This provision is intended to prevent a firm from requesting extra nonaudit work in an attempt to entice the auditor to approve its financial statements.

+ Auditing firms may not audit companies whose chief executive officer (CEO), chief financial officer (CFO), or other managers in similar roles were employed by the auditing firm in the one-year period prior to the audit. This provision prevents an audit by auditors who may still have close ties to the firm.

+ Those board members of the firm who are assigned to oversee the audit to ensure that it is done properly should not receive consulting or advising fees or other compensation from the auditing firm. This provision prevents audit committee members from being paid off to ignore their oversight duties.

+ The CFO and other managers of the firm must file an internal control report along with each annual report. The internal control report must explain the controls that the firm has established to ensure that its financial reporting is accurate.

+ The CEO and CFO must certify that the audited statements fairly represent the operations and financial condition of the firm. This prevents them from later saying that they were unaware of accounting gimmicks that were used to inflate earnings.

+ Major fines or prison terms are imposed on employees who mislead investors or hide evidence. This provision attempts to ensure that a firm's employees will be penalized for their role in distorting the accounting statements.

The act should result in more accurate accounting. However, it requires publicly traded firms to complete substantial paperwork and increases their reporting costs. For some firms, the cost to ensure that they are following the guidelines of the Sarbanes-Oxley Act exceeds $1 million per year. Consequently, some small publicly traded firms have decided to revert back to privately held ownership to avoid the substantial costs of reporting. In addition, some firms will likely continue to use creative accounting methods (within the guidelines) that mislead investors. Therefore, investors will still have to be cautious when making investment decisions based on the financial information provided by firms.

## 3. Interpreting Financial Statements

**income statement**
indicates the revenue, costs, and earnings of a firm over a period of time

**balance sheet**
reports the book value of all assets, liabilities, and owner's equity of a firm at a given point in time

**net sales**
total sales adjusted for any discounts

**cost of goods sold**
the cost of materials used to produce the goods that were sold

The most important financial statements are the income statement and the balance sheet. The **income statement** indicates the firm's revenue, costs, and earnings over a period of time (such as a quarter or year), and the **balance sheet** reports the book value of all the firm's assets, liabilities, and owner's equity at a given point in time.

It is possible for a firm to show high earnings on its income statement while being financially weak according to its balance sheet. It is also possible for a firm to show low earnings or even losses on its income statement while being financially strong according to its balance sheet. Because the two statements reveal different financial characteristics, both financial statements must be analyzed along with other information to perform a complete evaluation.

Understanding the information reported on income statements and balance sheets is a necessary part of financial analysis. These financial statements are explained briefly next.

### 3.1 Income Statement

The annual income statement for Taylor, Inc., a manufacturing firm, is presented in Exhibit 15.1. The income statement items shown in Exhibit 15.1 are disclosed in the income statements of most manufacturing firms.

**Revenue and Expenses**   **Net sales** reflect the total sales adjusted for any discounts. The net sales number is commonly referred to as revenue. **Cost of goods sold** is the cost of the materials used to produce the goods that were sold. For example, the cost of steel used to produce automo-

**Exhibit 15.1**

Example of Income Statement: Taylor, Inc.

| | | |
|---|---|---|
| Net Sales | | $20,000,000 |
| Cost of Goods Sold | | 16,000,000 |
| Gross Profit | | $4,000,000 |
| Selling Expense | $1,500,000 | |
| General & Administrative Expenses | 1,000,000 | |
| Total Operating Expenses | | 2,500,000 |
| Earnings Before Interest and Taxes (EBIT) | | $1,500,000 |
| Interest Expense | | 500,000 |
| Earnings Before Taxes | | $1,000,000 |
| Income Taxes (at 30%) | | 300,000 |
| Net Income | | $700,000 |

Firms obtain materials (shown here) that are used to produce products. The cost of these materials is listed on the income statement as "cost of goods sold."

© SHUTTERSTOCK/NATULRICH

**gross profit**
net sales minus the cost of goods sold

**operating expenses**
composed of selling expenses and general and administrative expenses

**earnings before interest and taxes (EBIT)**
gross profit minus operating expenses

**earnings before taxes**
earnings before interest and taxes minus interest expenses

**net income (earnings after taxes)**
earnings before taxes minus taxes

biles is part of the cost of goods sold for an automobile manufacturer. **Gross profit** is equal to net sales minus the cost of goods sold. Thus, gross profit measures the degree to which the revenue from selling products exceeded the cost of the materials used to produce them.

**Operating expenses** are composed of selling expenses and general and administrative expenses. For example, the cost of labor and utilities and advertising expenses of manufacturers are part of operating expenses.

**Measures of Earnings** Gross profit minus a firm's operating expenses equals **earnings before interest and taxes (EBIT)**. Earnings before interest and taxes minus interest expenses equals **earnings before taxes**. Finally, earnings before taxes minus taxes equals **net income** (sometimes referred to as **earnings after taxes**).

**Percentage of Sales Measurement** Firms commonly measure each income statement item as a percentage of total sales, as illustrated in Exhibit 15.2 for Taylor, Inc. The exhibit shows how each dollar of sales is used to cover various expenses that were incurred to generate the sales. Notice that 80 cents of every dollar of sales is used to cover the cost of the goods sold, while 12.5 cents of every dollar of sales is needed to cover operating expenses; 2.5 cents of every dollar of sales is needed to cover interest expense, and 1.5 cents of every dollar of sales is needed to pay taxes. That

**Exhibit 15.2**

Income Statement Items as a Percentage of Net Sales for Taylor, Inc.

| | | |
|---|---|---|
| Net Sales | | 100.0% |
| Cost of Goods Sold | | 80.0% |
| Gross Profit | | 20.0% |
| Selling Expense | 7.5% | |
| General & Administrative Expenses | 5.0% | |
| Total Operating Expenses | | 12.5% |
| Earnings Before Interest and Taxes (EBIT) | | 7.5% |
| Interest Expense | | 2.5% |
| Earnings Before Taxes | | 5.0% |
| Income Taxes (at 30%) | | 1.5% |
| Net Income | | 3.5% |

Fixed assets on the firm's balance sheet include machinery as shown here. To account for deterioration in the machinery over time, the balance sheet includes an entry for "depreciation" of the fixed assets, which reduces their book value.

© SHUTTERSTOCK/PHOTOCREATE

leaves 3.5 cents of every dollar of sales as net income. This breakdown for a firm can be compared with other firms in the industry. Based on this information, the firm may notice that it is using too much of its revenue to cover the cost of goods sold (relative to other firms in the industry). Therefore, it may search for ways to reduce the cost of producing its goods.

## 3.2  Balance Sheet

**asset**
anything owned by a firm

**liability**
anything owed by a firm

**basic accounting equation**
Assets = Liabilities + Owner's Equity

Anything owned by a firm is an **asset**. Anything owed by a firm is a **liability**. Firms normally support a portion of their assets with funds of the owners, called "owner's equity" (also called "stockholder's equity"). The remaining portion is supported with borrowed funds, which creates a liability. This relationship is described by the following **basic accounting equation**:

$$\text{Assets} = \text{Liabilities} + \text{Owner's Equity}$$

For example, consider a person who purchases a car repair shop for $200,000. Assume that the person uses $40,000 of savings for the purchase and borrows the remaining $160,000 from a local bank. The accounting statement for this business will show assets of $200,000, liabilities of $160,000, and owner's equity of $40,000. As the business acquires equipment and machinery, its total asset value will increase. The funds used to purchase more assets will be obtained through either additional borrowing or additional support from the owner. Any increase in assets will therefore be matched by an equal increase in liabilities and owner's equity.

The balance sheet for Taylor, Inc., as of the end of the year, is shown in Exhibit 15.3. The assets listed on a balance sheet are separated into current assets and fixed assets.

**current assets**
assets that will be converted into cash within one year

**Current Assets**   **Current assets** are assets that will be converted into cash within one year. They include cash, marketable securities, accounts receivable, and inventories. Cash typically represents checking account balances. Marketable securities are short-term securities that can easily

**Exhibit 15.3**

Example of Balance Sheet for Taylor, Inc.

**Taylor, Inc.**

### Assets

| | |
|---|---|
| **Current Assets:** | |
| Cash | $200,000 |
| Marketable Securities | 300,000 |
| Accounts Receivable | 500,000 |
| Inventory | 1,000,000 |
| Total Current Assets | $2,000,000 |
| **Fixed Assets:** | |
| Plant and Equipment | $10,000,000 |
| Less: Accumulated Depreciation | 2,000,000 |
| Net Fixed Assets | $8,000,000 |
| Total Assets | $10,000,000 |

### Liabilities & Owner's Equity

| | |
|---|---|
| **Current Liabilities:** | |
| Accounts Payable | $600,000 |
| Notes Payable | 400,000 |
| Total Current Liabilities | $1,000,000 |
| Long-Term Debt | $5,000,000 |
| **Owner's Equity:** | |
| Common Stock ($5 par value, 200,000 shares) | $1,000,000 |
| Additional Paid-In Capital | 2,000,000 |
| Retained Earnings | 1,000,000 |
| Total Owner's Equity | $4,000,000 |
| Total Liabilities and Owner's Equity | $10,000,000 |

be sold and quickly converted to cash if additional funds are needed. Marketable securities earn interest for the firm until they are sold or redeemed at maturity. Accounts receivable reflect sales that have been made but for which payment has not yet been received. Inventories are composed of raw materials, partially completed products, and finished products that have not yet been sold.

**fixed assets**
assets that will be used by a firm for more than one year

**depreciation**
a reduction in the value of fixed assets to reflect deterioration in the assets over time

**accounts payable**
money owed by a firm for the purchase of materials

**notes payable**
short-term loans to a firm made by creditors such as banks

**Fixed Assets**   **Fixed assets** are assets that the firm will use for more than one year. They include the firm's plant and equipment. In Exhibit 15.3, depreciation is subtracted from plant and equipment to arrive at net fixed assets. **Depreciation** represents a reduction in the value of fixed assets to reflect deterioration in the assets over time. Specific accounting rules are used to measure the depreciation of fixed assets.

**Liabilities and Owner's Equity**   Liabilities and owner's equity are also shown in Exhibit 15.3. Current (short-term) liabilities include accounts payable and notes payable. **Accounts payable** represent money owed by the firm for the purchase of materials. **Notes payable** represent short-term loans to the firm made by creditors such as banks. Long-term

**Exhibit 15.4**

Breakdown of Balance Sheet for Taylor, Inc.

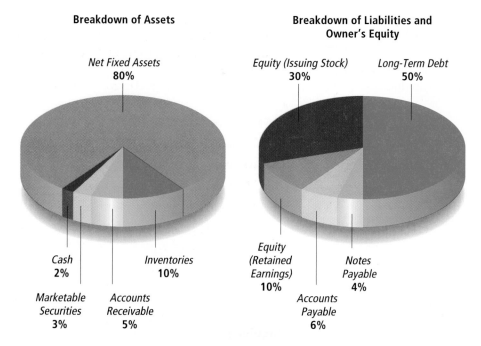

**Breakdown of Assets**

Net Fixed Assets
80%

Cash
2%

Marketable
Securities
3%

Accounts
Receivable
5%

Inventories
10%

**Breakdown of Liabilities and Owner's Equity**

Equity (Issuing Stock)
30%

Long-Term Debt
50%

Equity
(Retained
Earnings)
10%

Accounts
Payable
6%

Notes
Payable
4%

liabilities (debt) are liabilities that will not be repaid within one year. These liabilities commonly include long-term loans provided by banks and the issuance of bonds.

**owner's equity**
includes the par (or stated) value of all common stock issued, additional paid-in capital, and retained earnings

**Owner's equity** includes the par (or stated) value of all common stock issued, additional paid-in capital, and retained earnings. Additional paid-in capital represents the dollar amount received from issuing common stock that exceeds par value. Retained earnings represent the accumulation of the firm's earnings that are reinvested in the firm's assets rather than distributed as dividends to shareholders.

**Percentage of Total Assets Measurement** A firm can use its balance sheet to determine the percentage of its investment in each type of asset. An example is provided in Exhibit 15.4. Notice that 80 percent of the firm's assets are allocated to net fixed assets. Most manufacturing firms allocate a large portion of their funds to net fixed assets because these are the assets used in the production process.

The liabilities and owner's equity can also be broken down to determine where the firm is obtaining most of its financial support. Notice that the firm obtained 50 percent of its funds by issuing long-term debt and another 30 percent from issuing stock. Retained earnings made up 10 percent of the firm's funds.

**Learning Objective** **4**

Explain how to evaluate a firm's financial condition.

**ratio analysis**
an evaluation of the relationships between financial statement variables

## 4. Ratio Analysis

A firm's financial managers can use the financial statements to assess the financial condition of the firm. An important part of this assessment is **ratio analysis**, an evaluation of the relationships between financial statement variables. Firms can assess their financial characteristics by comparing their financial ratios with those of other firms in the same industry. In this way, they can determine how their financial condition differs from that of other firms that conduct the same type of business.

Firms can also assess the ratios over time to determine whether financial characteristics are improving or deteriorating. The industry average serves as a benchmark for what would be considered normal for the firm. Differences from the norm can be favorable or unfavorable, depending upon the size and direction of the difference.

Financial ratios are commonly classified according to the characteristics they measure. These include the following:

+ Measures of liquidity
+ Measures of efficiency
+ Measures of financial leverage
+ Measures of profitability

The ratios that are used to assess each of these characteristics are defined and discussed next. Each ratio is computed for Taylor, Inc., based on its financial statements in Exhibits 15.1 and 15.3.

## 4.1  Measures of Liquidity

**liquidity**

a firm's ability to meet short-term obligations

**Liquidity** refers to a firm's ability to meet short-term obligations. Since short-term assets are commonly used to pay short-term obligations (which are current liabilities), most liquidity measures compare current assets with current liabilities. The greater the level of current assets available relative to current liabilities, the greater the firm's liquidity.

A high degree of liquidity can enhance the firm's safety, but an excessive degree of liquidity can reduce the firm's return. For example, holding an excessive amount of cash is a waste and can reduce a firm's returns. Firms that have excessive cash, marketable securities, accounts receivable, and inventories could have invested more funds in assets such as machinery or buildings (fixed assets) that are used for production. Firms attempt to maintain sufficient liquidity to be safe, but not excessive liquidity. Two common liquidity measures are identified next.

**Current Ratio**   The current ratio compares current assets with current liabilities in ratio form. It is defined as:

$$\text{Current Ratio} = \frac{\text{Current Assets}}{\text{Current Liabilities}}$$

For Taylor:

$$\text{Current Ratio} = \frac{\$2,000,000}{\$1,000,000}$$

$$= 2.00$$

For most manufacturing firms, the current ratio is between 1.0 and 2.0. For Taylor, current assets are twice the amount of its current liabilities. A more detailed comparison of Taylor's liquidity and other financial ratios to the industry norms is conducted later in this chapter after all financial ratios have been discussed.

**Quick Ratio**   The quick ratio requires a slight adjustment in the current ratio. Inventory may not be easily converted into cash and therefore may be excluded when assessing liquidity. To get a more conservative

Until the clothes shown here are sold, they represent inventory for the clothing store and therefore currently are an asset to the store. Firms have an investment in their inventory of products, which means that they used funds to finance the production (or purchase) of products that have not yet been sold. They earn a return on their investment in inventory only after the products have been sold.

indication of a firm's liquidity, the quick ratio does not include inventory in the numerator:

$$\text{Quick Ratio} = \frac{\text{Cash} + \text{Marketable Securities} + \text{Accounts Receivable}}{\text{Current Liabilities}}$$

For Taylor:

$$\text{Quick Ratio} = \frac{\$1,000,000}{\$1,000,000}$$
$$= 1.00$$

Since the quick ratio does not include inventory in the numerator, it is smaller than the current ratio for any firm that has some inventory. The larger the firm's quick ratio, the greater its liquidity.

## 4.2 Measures of Efficiency

Efficiency ratios measure how efficiently a firm manages its assets. Two of the more popular efficiency ratios are described next.

**Inventory Turnover** Firms prefer to generate a high level of sales with a low investment in inventory because fewer funds are tied up. However, very low levels of inventory can also be unfavorable because they can result in shortages, which can reduce sales. To assess the relationship between a firm's inventory level and sales, the inventory turnover ratio can be used:

$$\text{Inventory Turnover} = \frac{\text{Cost of Goods Sold}}{\text{Inventory}}$$

For Taylor:

$$\text{Inventory Turnover} = \frac{\$16,000,000}{\$1,000,000}$$
$$= 16.00$$

Firms assess their asset turnover ratio to determine whether they are using their assets (such as the newspaper printing machinery shown here) efficiently. Firms strive to have a high asset turnover ratio (relative to their corresponding industry average) because that suggests that they are using their assets efficiently.

© SHUTTERSTOCK/ANDREW PARK

This ratio suggests that Taylor turns its inventory over 16 times during the year. The cost of goods sold is used instead of sales in the numerator to exclude the markup that is reflected in sales.

The average inventory over the period of concern should be used in the denominator when it is available, since inventory can change substantially during that period. When the average inventory is not available, the year-end inventory is used.

**Asset Turnover**    Firms prefer to support a high level of sales with a relatively small amount of assets so that they efficiently utilize the assets they invest in. Firms that maintain excess assets are not investing their funds wisely. To measure the efficiency with which firms use their assets, the asset turnover ratio can be calculated. It is defined and computed for Taylor as follows:

$$\text{Asset Turnover} = \frac{\text{Net Sales}}{\text{Total Assets}}$$

$$= \frac{\$20,000,000}{\$10,000,000}$$

$$= 2.00$$

Taylor's sales during the year were two times the level of its total assets. Like all other financial ratios, the asset turnover should be evaluated over time and in comparison with the industry norm.

## 4.3  Measures of Financial Leverage

Financial leverage represents the degree to which a firm uses borrowed funds to finance its assets. Firms that borrow a large proportion of their funds have a high degree of financial leverage. This can favorably affect the firm's owners when the firm performs well, because the earnings generated by the firm can be spread among a relatively small group of owners. When the firm experiences poor performance, however, a high degree of financial leverage is dangerous. Firms with a high degree of financial leverage incur higher fixed financial costs (interest expenses) that must be paid regardless of their levels of sales. These firms are more likely to experience debt repayment problems and therefore are perceived as having more risk. Conversely, firms that obtain a larger proportion of funds from equity financing incur smaller debt payments and therefore have less risk.

Although a high proportion of equity financing reduces risk, it may also force earnings to be widely distributed among many shareholders. Firms that rely heavily on equity typically have a large number of shareholders who share the firm's earnings. This may dilute the earnings that are distributed to each shareholder as dividends.

**debt-to-equity ratio**
a measure of the amount of long-term financing provided by debt relative to equity

**Debt-to-Equity Ratio**  A measure of the amount of long-term financing provided by debt relative to equity is called the **debt-to-equity ratio**. This ratio is defined and computed for Taylor as follows:

$$\text{Debt-to-Equity Ratio} = \frac{\text{Long-Term Debt}}{\text{Owner's Equity}}$$

$$= \frac{\$5,000,000}{\$4,000,000}$$

$$= 1.25$$

For Taylor, long-term debt is 1.25 times the amount of owner's equity.

**times interest earned ratio**
measures the ability of a firm to cover its interest payments

**Times Interest Earned**  The **times interest earned ratio** measures a firm's ability to cover its interest payments. If a firm has a low level of earnings before interest and taxes (EBIT) relative to the size of its interest expense, a small decrease in EBIT in the future could force the firm to default on the loan. Conversely, a high level of EBIT relative to the annual interest expense suggests that even if next year's EBIT declines substantially, the firm will still be able to cover the interest expense. The times interest earned ratio is defined and computed for Taylor as follows:

$$\text{Times Interest Earned} = \frac{\text{Earnings Before Interest and Taxes (EBIT)}}{\text{Annual Interest Expense}}$$

$$= \frac{\$1,500,000}{\$500,000}$$

$$= 3.0$$

A times interest earned ratio of 3.0 indicates that Taylor's earnings before interest and taxes were three times its interest expense.

## 4.4 Measures of Profitability

Profitability measures indicate the performance of a firm's operations during a given period. The dollar amount of profit generated by the firm can be measured relative to the firm's level of sales, assets, or equity. The ratios that measure these relationships are discussed next.

**net profit margin**

a measure of net income as a percentage of sales

**Net Profit Margin**   The **net profit margin** is a measure of net income as a percentage of sales. This ratio measures the proportion of every dollar of sales that ultimately becomes net income. The net profit margin is computed for Taylor as follows:

$$\text{Net Profit Margin} = \frac{\text{Net Income}}{\text{Net Sales}}$$

$$= \frac{\$700,000}{\$20,000,000}$$

$$= 3.50\%$$

Even with a low profit margin, firms with a high volume of sales can generate a reasonable return for their shareholders. However, firms with a low volume of sales may need a higher profit margin to generate a reasonable return for their shareholders.

**return on assets (ROA)**

measures a firm's net income as a percentage of the total amount of assets utilized by the firm

**Return on Assets**   A firm's **return on assets (ROA)** measures the return (net income) of the firm as a percentage of the total amount of assets utilized by the firm. It is defined and computed for Taylor as follows:

$$\text{Return on Assets} = \frac{\text{Net Income}}{\text{Total Assets}}$$

$$= \frac{\$700,000}{\$10,000,000}$$

$$= 7.00\%$$

The ROA provides a broad measure of a firm's performance. The higher the ROA, the more efficiently the firm utilized its assets to generate net income.

**return on equity (ROE)**

measures the return to the common stockholders (net income) as a percentage of their investment in the firm; earnings as a proportion of the firm's equity

**Return on Equity**   The **return on equity (ROE)** measures the return to the common stockholders as a percentage of their investment in the firm. Existing and potential investors monitor this ratio closely because it indicates the recent return on the investment of the existing shareholders. The ROE measures the firm's performance from using the equity provided. The return on equity is defined and computed for Taylor as follows:

$$\text{Return on Equity} = \frac{\text{Net Income}}{\text{Owner's Equity}}$$

$$= \frac{\$700,000}{\$4,000,000}$$

$$= 17.50\%$$

Stockholders prefer ROE to be very high because a high ROE indicates a high return relative to the size of their investment. Using high levels of financial leverage can increase ROE (because less equity is used), so the net income is distributed among fewer shareholders, but high levels of financial leverage increase the firm's exposure to risk.

## 4.5 Comparison of Ratios with Those of Other Firms

Exhibit 15.5 provides the common interpretations for ratios that deviate substantially from what is normal in the industry. Note, however, that there may be a perfectly acceptable reason why a ratio deviates from the norm. For example, consider a firm that has an abnormally large amount of cash according to a comparison with the industry average. Common stockholders may interpret this as evidence of inefficient use of assets. However, further investigation may reveal that the firm has built up its cash because it plans to purchase machinery in the near future. Financial analysis based on an assessment of financial ratios does not necessarily lead to immediate conclusions, but it does lead to questions about a firm that deserve further investigation.

Exhibit 15.6 provides a general summary of the financial ratios commonly used for ratio analysis. Comparing a firm's ratios with an industry average can help identify the firm's strengths and weaknesses. Columns 1 and 2 of Exhibit 15.6 identify and define the financial ratios presented in this chapter. Column 3 lists Taylor's ratios, and the industry averages are provided in column 4. Column 5 uses the information in columns 3 and 4 to provide an evaluation of Taylor's ratios relative to those of the industry average.

| **Exhibit 15.5** | Interpretation of Financial Ratios That Differ from the Industry Norm | |
|---|---|---|
| **Ratios** | **Common Interpretation if Ratio Is Significantly Lower than Normal** | **Common Interpretation if Ratio Is Significantly Higher than Normal** |
| **Liquidity Ratios** | | |
| Current ratio | Insufficient liquidity | Excessive liquidity |
| Quick ratio | Insufficient liquidity | Excessive liquidity |
| **Efficiency Ratios** | | |
| Inventory turnover | Excessive inventory | Insufficient inventory |
| Asset turnover | Excessive level of assets relative to sales | Insufficient assets based on existing sales |
| **Leverage Ratios** | | |
| Debt-to-equity ratio | Low level of long-term debt | Excessive long-term debt |
| Times interest earned | Potential cash flow problems because required interest payments are high relative to the earnings available to pay interest | The firm can easily make its debt payments. |
| **Profitability Ratios** | | |
| Net profit margin | Expenses are high relative to sales. | Expenses are low relative to sales. |
| Return on assets | Net income is low relative to the amount of assets maintained by the firm. | Net income is high relative to the amount of assets maintained by the firm. |
| Return on equity | Net income is low relative to the amount of equity invested in the firm. | Net income is high relative to the amount of equity invested in the firm. |

A firm's financial managers not only create financial statements for reporting purposes, but they apply ratio analyses and monitor trends in order to predict the future financial condition of the firm.

© SHUTTERSTOCK/FERNANDO BLANCO CALZADA

**Exhibit 15.6**

Evaluation of Taylor, Inc., Based on Ratio Analysis

| Ratio | Calculation | Ratio for Taylor | Average for Industry | Evaluation of Taylor Based on the Ratio |
|---|---|---|---|---|
| **Liquidity** | | | | |
| Current | Current Assets / Current Liabilities | 2.00 | 1.60 | Too high |
| Quick | Cash + Marketable Securities + Accts. Receivable / Current Liabilities | 1.00 | 0.90 | Too high |
| **Efficiency** | | | | |
| Inventory Turnover | Cost of Goods Sold / Inventory | 16.00 | 16.22 | OK, unless shortages are occurring |
| Asset Turnover | Net Sales / Total Assets | 2.00 | 4.11 | Too low |
| **Financial Leverage** | | | | |
| Debt-to-Equity Ratio | Long-Term Debt / Owner's Equity | 1.25 | 0.60 | Too high |
| Times Interest Earned | Earnings Before Interest and Taxes / Annual Interest Expense | 3.0 | 7.4 | Too low |
| **Profitability** | | | | |
| Net Profit Margin | Net Income / Net Sales | 3.5% | 4.00% | Too low |
| Return on Assets | Net Income / Total Assets | 7.00% | 16.44% | Too low |
| Return on Equity | Net Income / Owner's Equity | 17.50% | 26.30% | Too low |

**Liquidity**  In terms of liquidity, Taylor's current and quick ratios are above the industry average. This suggests that although Taylor probably has sufficient liquidity, it may have an excessive amount of current assets.

## Global Business

### Effect of Exchange Rate Movements on Earnings

A U.S. firm that has subsidiaries (including offices and factories) in foreign countries typically generates earnings in the local currencies of the countries where those subsidiaries are located. Any firm with foreign subsidiaries must consolidate the financial data from all subsidiaries when preparing its financial statements. Because of the consolidation process, changes in exchange rates can have an impact on the firm's reported earnings, as illustrated next.

Consider a U.S. firm that has a subsidiary in the United Kingdom that generated £10 million in earnings last year. Also assume that the firm's U.S. operations generated $12 million in earnings. The firm must consolidate the £10 million with the $12 million when preparing its income statement. The £10 million cannot simply be added to the $12 million because the British and U.S. currencies have different values. Therefore, the British earnings must be "translated" by determining the dollar amount of those earnings. The average exchange rate of the currency of concern over the period in which income was generated is used to translate the foreign earnings.

If the foreign currency has a high value over the period of concern, the foreign earnings will be translated into a higher amount of dollar earnings reported on the income statement. Many U.S. firms with foreign subsidiaries may report unusually high earnings when the values of foreign currencies are high in that period (when the dollar is weak). Under these conditions, the foreign earnings are translated into a large amount of dollar earnings on the income statement. If the values of foreign currencies decline over a particular year (when the dollar strengthens), the foreign earnings will translate into a smaller amount of dollar earnings, which will reduce the level of consolidated earnings reported on the firm's income statement.

**Efficiency**  Taylor's inventory turnover ratio is similar to the industry average. This suggests that Taylor maintains the normal amount of inventory.

Taylor's asset turnover ratio is below the industry average. This suggests that Taylor is not using all of its assets efficiently. That is, it has an excessive investment in assets, given the level of sales. Taylor might consider either taking steps to increase sales (which would force more production from its assets) or selling some of its assets.

**Financial Leverage**  With regard to financial leverage, the debt-to-equity ratio is higher than the industry average. This suggests that Taylor has a relatively high proportion of long-term financing provided by debt relative to equity. The times interest earned ratio for Taylor is lower than the industry norm. Other firms of the same size and in the same industry have lower interest expenses (because they use a lower proportion of debt financing). Since Taylor already has a relatively high proportion of debt, it may be less able to borrow additional funds.

**Profitability**  Regarding profitability, Taylor's net profit margin is lower than the industry norm, which suggests that Taylor is not generating adequate net income based on its level of sales. Also, its return on assets is too low, which is partially attributed to its inefficient use of assets.

| Exhibit 15.7 |
| --- |

Example of How
Management, Marketing, and
Finance Deficiencies
Can Be Detected with
Ratio Analysis

**Management Decisions**

One of a firm's relevant management decisions is the production process used to produce products. An efficient production process can result in a relatively higher amount of production and sales with a given level of assets. The asset turnover ratio is an indicator of the efficiency of production because it measures the level of sales generated with a given level of assets. Taylor has a low asset turnover ratio, implying an inefficient use of assets.

**Marketing Decisions**

Since Taylor's asset turnover ratio is low, it should either eliminate those assets that are not efficiently utilized or maintain its assets but produce and sell a higher volume of products. If it decides to maintain its assets and increase production, it will need effective marketing strategies to sell the extra amount of products produced. Thus, proper marketing strategies may help Taylor to improve its asset turnover ratio.

**Finance Decisions**

Taylor's debt-to-equity ratio is higher than the norm, which reflects its high degree of financial leverage. Its high proportion of debt financing may make it difficult for Taylor to cover its interest payments. Taylor may use more equity financing in the future, but this will reduce its return on equity. Given its poor utilization of assets, Taylor might consider selling some of its assets and using the proceeds to reduce its debt level. This would allow for a more acceptable degree of financial leverage.

Since Taylor is not using its assets efficiently to generate sufficient sales, it cannot generate a sufficient amount of net income.

Taylor's ROE is too low, which means that it is not generating an adequate net income, given the size of the equity investment in the firm. If Taylor could more efficiently utilize its assets, it could increase its net income and therefore increase its ROE.

**Conclusion**   Exhibit 15.7 illustrates how the financial analysis identifies different business functions that may need improvement. Taylor's management, marketing, and finance functions may need to be reassessed to improve its performance. In general, management strategies may be revised to improve production efficiency, marketing strategies may be revised to increase sales, and financing strategies may be revised to establish a more appropriate degree of financial leverage.

## 4.6   Limitations of Ratio Analysis

Ratio analysis is useful for detecting a firm's strengths and weaknesses. Nevertheless, it has some limitations, which can result in misleading conclusions. The major limitations of ratio analysis are discussed next.

**Firms Operate in Multiple Industries**   Comparing some firms with an industry average can be difficult because the firms operate in more than one industry. Consider a firm that produces gas grills, machinery, and aluminum panels. The firm's ratios may deviate from a specific industry norm as a result of the characteristics of the other industries in which the firm operates. Also, the industry used as a benchmark for comparison may include firms that are involved in a variety of other businesses. This distorts the average ratios for the industry.

**Firms Use Different Accounting Practices**   Accounting practices vary among firms. A firm's financial ratios can deviate from the norm because of differences in accounting methods rather than differences in operations. For example, one firm may have used an accounting method that inflates its revenue or defers the reporting of some expenses until the following quarter. Consequently, this quarter's earnings will be inflated, and ratios such as ROA or ROE will be inflated. The firm's performance is essentially exaggerated in the quarter because of the accounting method used. Investors may overvalue a firm when its reported earnings are inflated.

**Seasonal Variation** Firms with seasonal swings in sales may show large deviations from the norm at certain times but not at others. Normally, however, the seasonal swings should not distort annual financial statements.

## 4.7 Sources of Information for Ratio Analysis

To help perform ratio analysis, industry data can be obtained from a variety of sources. The following are two of the more common sources.

**Robert Morris Associates** The booklet *Annual Statement Studies,* published by Robert Morris Associates, provides financial ratios for many different industries. Ratios for firms of various sizes are included so that a firm's ratios can be compared with those of similar-sized firms in the same industry.

**Dun and Bradstreet** Dun and Bradstreet provides financial ratios for industries and for groups of firms within industries classified by size.

# Responding to the Economy

## Financial Analysis in Response to the Economy

Firms engage in financial analysis so that they can detect deficiencies and implement corrections in business operations in response. When firms detect a decline in their revenue, it could be due to poor management or a weak economy. A firm may experience a decline in revenue due to a decline in market share. A firm will attempt to revise its business operations when its market share declines, because this means that other competitors are taking part of its business. Conversely, a firm may experience a decline in revenue simply because of a weak economy. In this case, the decline is due to a drop-off in consumer demand, so the firm still retains its market share even though its revenue is lower. However, even in this case, the firm may attempt to improve its revenue by implementing new strategies, such as lowering its prices or increasing its promotions.

Financial analysis is also useful for detecting changes in expenses over time. Higher expenses are assessed to determine if they are caused by managerial inefficiencies or by factors outside the firm's control. For example, if the higher expenses occur because the firm is using too many employees for a given level of production, it may need to reorganize its production process and job assignments. Conversely, if the increased expenses are primarily caused by high transportation costs (due to higher gas prices), this is not management's fault. Nevertheless, the firm may still look for ways to reduce its transportation costs, such as transporting products to a wholesaler every two weeks instead of every week.

## COLLEGE HEALTH CLUB: FINANCIAL CONDITION OF CHC

Sue Kramer is conducting a financial analysis of College Health Club (CHC). Her analysis raises two concerns. First, her expenses may exceed her income for several months, which will result in a loss (negative profits) over that period. Sue realizes, however, that as CHC's memberships increase, its revenue will increase. In addition, many of CHC's expenses are fixed and should not change significantly. Thus, CHC's revenue should exceed its expenses once the memberships increase.

Sue is also concerned that CHC's financial leverage (based on the debt-to-equity ratio) is high. Since Sue is investing $20,000 of her own money (equity) and is borrowing an additional $40,000 (debt), CHC's initial debt-to-equity ratio is 2.0, indicating that its debt is twice its equity. Since Sue plans to reinvest any profits back into the business, CHC's equity will increase over time as profits accumulate. By increasing the equity over time without borrowing additional funds, she will be able to reduce CHC's degree of financial leverage.

Overall, Sue's financial analysis helps her realize that her concerns about CHC's profitability and its financial leverage should be alleviated over time. If CHC's memberships increase as expected, its profitability and financial leverage ratios will improve.

## Summary of Learning Objectives

**1** A firm's financial condition is important to financial managers, to the firm's creditors, and to investors. Financial managers evaluate the firm to detect weaknesses that can be corrected and strengths that can be exploited. Creditors evaluate the firm with a view toward determining its creditworthiness, and investors evaluate the firm's performance to determine whether they should buy or sell the firm's stock.

**2** Firms are responsible for reporting accurate financial information to their existing shareholders, prospective investors, and creditors. Under the Sarbanes-Oxley Act (SOX), any managers or auditors who were responsible for a firm's misleading financial statements are subject to more severe penalties. The act was intended to protect the interests of investors who may make investment decisions based on information disclosed in financial statements.

**3** The key financial statements necessary to perform a thorough evaluation are the income statement and balance sheet. The income statement reports costs, revenue, and earnings over a specified period. The balance sheet reports the book value of assets, liabilities, and owner's equity at a given point in time.

**4** Most financial ratios help evaluate one of four characteristics: liquidity, efficiency, financial leverage, and profitability. The liquidity ratios measure a firm's ability to meet its short-term obligations. Efficiency ratios measure how efficiently a firm utilizes its assets. Financial leverage ratios measure the firm's relative use of debt financing versus equity financing and indicate the firm's ability to repay its debt. Profitability ratios measure the firm's net income relative to various size levels. In evaluating a firm's financial ratios, it is useful to compare them with an industry norm. This approach can help detect any deficiencies that exist so that corrective action can be taken. Furthermore, it provides useful input for implementing new policies.

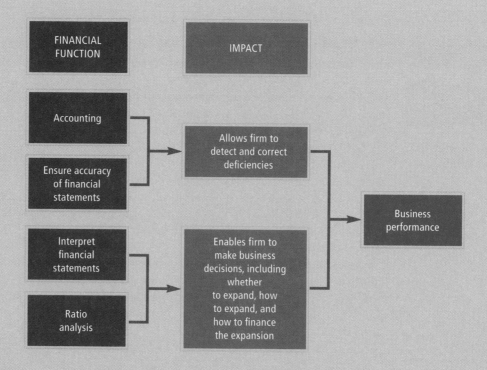

# Self-Test of Key Concepts

The following self-assessment allows you to test your understanding of the key concepts covered in this chapter. Answers are provided at the end of this exercise.

**True or False**

1. Accounting is the summary and analysis of a firm's financial condition.

2. Financial accounting is primarily used to help managers make decisions.

3. Bookkeeping is the recording of a firm's financial transactions.

4. An accountant working for Microsoft, a publicly owned corporation, is an example of a public accountant.

5. The two primary financial statements for a firm are the balance sheet and the bookkeeping statement.

6. Inventory and accounts receivables are shown as fixed assets on a firm's financial statements.

7. A balance sheet reports the book value of a firm's assets, liabilities, and owner's equity.

8. Firms are encouraged to design their financial accounting reports to best satisfy their managers' need for information.

9. The debt-to-equity ratio measures the liquidity of a firm.

10. Financial leverage represents the degree to which a firm uses borrowed funds to finance its assets.

**Multiple Choice**

11. Publicly owned firms are required to periodically report their financial condition for existing or potential:
    a) suppliers.
    b) customers.
    c) employees.
    d) shareholders.
    e) unions.

12. The type of accounting performed for reporting purposes is referred to as:
    a) ratio analysis.
    b) financial accounting.
    c) managerial accounting.
    d) cost accounting.
    e) payroll accounting.

13. Which of the following groups are primarily concerned with the risk of default on a loan?
    a) owners
    b) certified public accountants
    c) creditors
    d) auditors
    e) stockholders

14. Individuals who provide accounting services to a variety of firms for a fee are:
    a) master accountants.
    b) managerial accountants.
    c) internal auditors.
    d) corporate controllers.
    e) public accountants.

15. The type of accounting performed to provide information to help managers of the firm make decisions is referred to as:
    a) certified public accounting.
    b) external auditing.
    c) public accounting.
    d) government accounting.
    e) managerial accounting.

16. Which of the following financial statements summarizes a firm's revenues, costs, and earnings for a specific period of time?
    a) balance sheet.
    b) income statement.
    c) cash budget.
    d) retained earnings statement.
    e) sources and uses of funds statement.

17. The statement that reports the book value of all assets, liabilities, and owner's equity of a firm at a given point in time is the:
    a) income statement.
    b) cash budget.
    c) profit and loss statement.
    d) revenue statement.
    e) balance sheet.

18. A firm's operating expenses are subtracted from gross profit to determine its:
    a) net sales.
    b) cost of goods sold.
    c) profit or loss.
    d) balance sheet.
    e) earnings before interest and taxes (EBIT).

19. The value of materials used in the production of goods that are then sold is called:
    a) net sales.
    b) cost of goods sold.
    c) sales return and allowances.
    d) gross profit.
    e) net income.

20. Which of the following represents funds provided by the owners of a business?
    a) revenue.
    b) cost of goods sold.
    c) gross profit.
    d) net income.
    e) owner's equity.

21. The firm's assets are financed with its:
    a) cost of goods sold.
    b) earnings before interest and taxes.
    c) liabilities and owner's equity.
    d) plant and equipment.
    e) net sales.

22. If a firm has $1,000 in assets and $300 in liabilities, the owner's equity must be:
    a) $700.
    b) $333.
    c) $1,300.
    d) $3,000.
    e) $0.30.

23. Assets that will be converted into cash within one year are:
    a) fixed assets.
    b) current assets.
    c) plant and equipment.
    d) owner's equity.
    e) liabilities.

24. A reduction in the value of fixed assets to reflect deterioration in the assets over time is:
    a) cost of goods sold.
    b) gross profit.
    c) sales revenue.
    d) depreciation.
    e) owner's equity.

25. In order to encourage board members to enforce proper financial disclosures:
    a) all board members should be certified public accountants or financial analysts.
    b) all board members should be inside members.
    c) board members should not be allowed to own the firm's stock.
    d) all board members should be officers of the corporation.
    e) board members should not be able to sell the firm's stock while serving on the board.

26. All of the following are characteristics commonly used to classify financial ratios except for:
    a) revenue.
    b) liquidity.
    c) efficiency.
    d) leverage.
    e) profitability.

27. Which of the following categories of financial ratios measures how well management uses its assets to generate sales?
    a) liquidity.
    b) profitability.
    c) efficiency.
    d) financial leverage.
    e) sales leverage.

28. Long-term borrowing undertaken by a firm can be assessed through:
    a) liquidity ratios.
    b) profitability ratios.
    c) current ratios.
    d) efficiency ratios.
    e) leverage ratios.

29. A ratio that measures net income as a percentage of sales is the:
    a) net profit margin.
    b) leverage ratio.
    c) liquidity ratio.
    d) activity ratio.
    e) asset turnover.

30. Any firm with foreign subsidiaries must consolidate the financial data from all subsidiaries when preparing its:
    a) mission statement.
    b) foreign exchange.
    c) balance of payment.
    d) financial statements.
    e) domestic policy.

| True/False | | Multiple Choice | | |
|---|---|---|---|---|
| 1. True | 7. True | 11. d | 18. e | 25. e |
| 2. False | 8. False | 12. b | 19. b | 26. a |
| 3. True | 9. False | 13. c | 20. e | 27. c |
| 4. False | 10. True | 14. e | 21. c | 28. e |
| 5. False | | 15. e | 22. a | 29. a |
| 6. False | | 16. b | 23. b | 30. d |
| | | 17. e | 24. b | |

# Self-Test of Key Terms

accounting 512
accounts payable 521
asset 520
auditing 515
balance sheet 518
basic accounting equation 520
bookkeeping 512
certified public accountants (CPAs) 512
cost of goods sold 518
current assets 520
debt-to-equity ratio 526

depreciation 521
earnings before interest and taxes (EBIT) 519
earnings before taxes 519
financial accounting 512
fixed assets 521
gross profit 519
income statement 518
internal auditors 515
liability 520
liquidity 523
managerial accounting 514

net income (earnings after taxes) 519
net profit margin 527
net sales 518
notes payable 521
operating expenses 519
owner's equity 522
public accountants 512
ratio analysis 522
return on assets (ROA) 527
return on equity (ROE) 527
times interest earned ratio 526

Fill in each blank with the proper key term. To assess your understanding of the key terms, answers are provided at the end of this self-test.

1. _____ represent money owed by a firm for the purchase of materials.

2. The _____ measures the return to common stockholders as a percentage of their investment.

3. The type of accounting performed to provide information to managers is _____.

4. _____ are assets that the firm will use for more than one year.

5. _____ represents a reduction in the value of fixed assets to reflect deterioration in assets over time.

6. A firm's _____ measures the net income to the firm as a percentage of the total amount of assets utilized by the firm.

7. The _____ reports the book value of all assets, liabilities, and owner's equity of a firm at a given point in time.

8. _____ represent short-term loans to the firm made by creditors.

9. _____ are composed of selling expenses and general and administrative expenses.

10. The _____ is the cost of the materials used to produce the products that were sold.

11. The _____ is equal to net sales minus the cost of goods sold.

12. Anything owed by a firm is a(n) _____.

13. _____ includes the par value of all common stock issued, additional paid-in capital, and retained earnings.

14. _____ are assets that will be converted into cash within one year.

15. A firm's _____ indicates the firm's revenue, costs, and earnings over a period of time.

16. _____ is an assessment of a firm's records that were used to prepare its financial statements.

17. Firms use _____ to report their financial condition, support decisions, and control operations.

18. _____ is the recording of a firm's financial transactions.

19. The _____ is measured as net income as a percentage of sales.

20 _____ reflect the total sales adjusted for any discounts.

**Answers:**

| | |
|---|---|
| 1. Accounts payable | 11. gross profit |
| 2. return on equity | 12. liability |
| 3. managerial accounting | 13. Owner's equity |
| 4. Fixed assets | 14. Current assets |
| 5. Depreciation | 15. income statement |
| 6. return on assets | 16. Auditing |
| 7. balance sheet | 17. accounting |
| 8. Notes payable | 18. Bookkeeping |
| 9. Operating expenses | 19. net profit margin |
| 10. cost of goods sold | 20. Net sales |

# Concept Review Questions

1. **Business Valuation.** What is accounting? Explain how managerial accounting can enhance the value of a firm.

2. **Auditing.** Explain the role of auditing and why it is necessary.

3. **Sarbanes-Oxley Act.** Describe the key provisions of the Sarbanes-Oxley Act that attempt to ensure the accuracy of financial statements created by publicly traded firms.

4. **Financial Statements.** What is the difference between a balance sheet and an income statement?

5. **Income Statement.** Show how an income statement can be broken down to determine a firm's gross profit. Once a firm has determined its gross profit, how would it compute its earnings before interest and taxes?

6. **Motive for Assessing the Income Statement.** What is the benefit of assessing an income statement?

7. **Financial Leverage.** What do measures of financial leverage indicate? Why are they useful?

8. **Profitability.** How can a firm's profitability be measured?

9. **Efficiency.** Explain how a firm can use its reported sales and its assets to measure its efficiency.

10. **Ratio Analysis.** What are the limitations of ratio analysis?

# Class Communication Questions

1. **Sarbanes-Oxley Act.** Some firms suggest that there is too much government regulation. The Sarbanes-Oxley Act has many rules that have increased the cost of reporting by more than $1 million per publicly traded firm on average. Do you think that these provisions are necessary?

2. **Board Member Monitoring.** The board members of a firm are sometimes given shares of the firm's stock as compensation. Board members are supposed to monitor the firm to ensure that managers serve the interests of shareholders. Do you think that board members can be trusted to monitor the firm's reporting process to ensure proper financial reporting?

3. **Balance Sheet Information.** Why do you think creditors rely so heavily on a firm's balance sheet information when determining whether to provide the firm with a loan? Shouldn't the income statement be sufficient, since it indicates the firm's profitability?

# Small Business Case

### Use of Financial Reporting for Business Decisions

Eight years ago Sue and Jim Williams established the Surf Clothing Company, which produces clothing and then sells the clothing through their retail stores. Sue and Jim use an accounting system to keep track of revenue and expenses. First, the revenue and expenses are summed across all stores to provide an overall report. Second, revenue and expenses are reported per retail store so that an individual store's performance can be monitored. Third, revenue and expenses are reported per category of clothing (categorized by age group and gender)

so that the performance of each clothing category can be monitored. This helps Sue and Jim to identify the underlying reasons for the overall performance of the business.

1. **Use of Accounting to Assess Consumer Demand.** How can the accounting system be used to compare consumer demand across the stores?

2. **How Financial Reporting Can Help Assess Managers.** How can the accounting system be used to determine which stores deserve extra funding to support expansion?

3. **How Financial Reporting Can Help Plan for Expan-**

sion. Sue and Jim Williams are planning to establish new clothing stores. First, they want to assess the performance of two stores that they opened earlier this year to detect any deficiencies in those stores that could be avoided in the new stores. How can accounting information be used to detect such deficiencies?

4. **How Ratio Analysis Can Guide Production Decisions.** Explain how ratio analysis may affect the decision regarding the amount of clothing to order for the stores each month.

# Web Insight

### Financial Analysis at The Cheesecake Factory

At the opening of the chapter, The Cheesecake Factory was introduced. Use a search engine with the search terms "Cheesecake Factory" and "Investor Relations." This search will

take you to the website where annual reports and other financial information are disclosed about The Cheesecake Factory. Summarize the type of financial information that is provided. Do you think most of this information reflects financial ac-

counting (for the purpose of reporting to existing or prospective investors) or managerial accounting (for the purpose of helping the firm's managers make decisions)?

## Dell's Secrets for Success

Go to Dell's website (www.dell.com) and review the financial statements.

1. **Income Statement.** What items on the income statement would Dell closely monitor to ensure that it was achieving its goals?

2. **Balance Sheet.** What balance sheet items would be very important to Dell?

3. **Financial Reporting.** Review Dell's comments about its financial reporting. Why is it important for Dell to inform investors about its efforts to monitor and control its financial reporting?

## Video Exercise

### Lessons in Financial Analysis

Many free business videos are available on websites such as YouTube (www.youtube.com), and more are added every day. Search for a recent video clip about an existing business that offers lessons on "company financial analysis" or "company financial accounting" in YouTube or any other website that provides video clips.

1. **Main Lesson.** What is the name of the business in the video clip? Is the video clip focused on why the firm conducts a financial analysis of its business, or how it conducts an analysis, or some other aspect of financial analysis? What is the main lesson of the video clip that you watched?

2. **Recording Financial Information.** Some small companies maintain only enough financial information to determine what taxes they owe on their income. Explain how financial information could be used by even small (private) businesses to improve their performance.

3. **Use of Financial Information for Planning.** How can a firm use financial information to assess the accuracy of its business plan?

## Projects

To encourage further comprehension of concepts covered in Chapter 15, the following five projects are available:

1. Analyzing Your Favorite Business

2. Building a Business Plan for Campus.com

3. Running Your Own Business

4. Planning Your Career

5. Stock Market Contest

All of these projects are provided in Appendix A at the end of the text. In addition, projects are available by part division at the end of each part. A Word file for each project is also available at the textbook website (www.emcp.net/business5e) so that you may maintain one ongoing file for each project.

# Financing

© SHUTTERSTOCK/SAIM NADIR

## Chapter 16 Learning Objectives

**1** Identify the common methods of debt financing for firms.

**2** Identify the common methods of equity financing for firms.

**3** Explain how firms issue securities to obtain funds.

**4** Explain how firms may obtain financing through suppliers or leasing.

**5** Describe how firms determine the composition of their financing.

**6** Describe the remedies for firms that are unable to repay their debts.

# Chapter 16

## Financing Decisions by eBay

Firms obtain capital (long-term funds) in the form of debt or equity. With debt financing, the firm borrows funds. With equity financing, the firm receives investment from owners (by issuing stock or retaining earnings). The manner in which a firm decides to finance its business can affect its financing costs and thus can affect its value.

Consider the case of eBay, the auction website created in 1995. In September 1998, eBay raised $63 million from its initial public offering of stock, which allowed it to expand its business and improve its website. In 1999, it issued additional stock and raised more than $1 billion, so that it had funding to acquire other companies and improve its own business. In 2006, eBay created additional financing flexibility by negotiating a credit arrangement so that it could borrow up to $1 billion from various commercial banks. Whenever eBay wants to obtain more funds to finance its expansion, it addresses the following questions:

✦ What methods of debt financing could it use to finance its expansion?

✦ What methods of equity financing could it use to finance its expansion?

✦ How could it issue securities to obtain funds?

✦ What is the optimal composition of the financing for its expansion?

The types of decisions described here are necessary for all businesses. This chapter explains how eBay or any other firm can make financing decisions in a manner that maximizes its value.

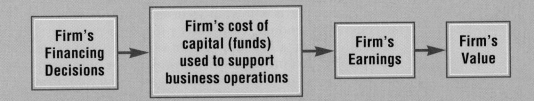

**Learning Objective** 1

Identify the common methods of debt financing for firms.

**debt financing**
the act of borrowing funds

**capital**
long-term funds

# 1. Methods of Debt Financing

Businesses commonly rely on **debt financing** as a means of funding business operations. Most businesses rely on debt financing to some degree at most stages of their life. The disadvantage of debt financing, however, is that interest must be paid on the loan. An interest payment on a loan is like any other expense. The higher the interest paid in a given month, the higher are the firm's expenses, and the lower are its profits. Thus, it is important for a firm to rely on debt financing only to the degree that it is necessary. In addition, the firm should understand the various sources of debt financing so that it can obtain funding at the lowest possible interest rate.

When a business is first established, its owners may rely on their savings to finance the operations. They may borrow from family members or friends or from a credit card. Or they may allow family members or friends to become part-owners by investing in the firm as a form of equity. At some point, though, the business will likely need more funding than can be provided by family members or friends. It may need funds to invest in assets.

Firms borrow funds to invest in assets such as buildings, machinery, and equipment. Those firms that invest in more assets typically need to borrow more funds. Service firms spend more money on employees and less on machinery and factories. Thus, they may not need to borrow as much because they do not have to purchase machinery for production purposes. In contrast, industrial firms tend to have large investments in assets such as buildings and machinery and therefore need to obtain more long-term funds (referred to as **capital**). The common methods of debt financing are described next.

## 1.1 Borrowing from Financial Institutions

Firms commonly attempt to obtain financing from financial institutions such as commercial banks, savings institutions, and finance companies (the different financial institutions will be discussed in more detail later in the chapter). Commercial banks are the biggest lenders to businesses. They are known for their low loan rates and their useful advice to businesses that borrow from them. Before a commercial bank will provide a loan, however, it will want to be certain that the business is capable of generating enough cash each month to cover its loan payments. Therefore, when a firm applies for a loan, it must present a detailed financial plan that includes specific projections of future revenue and expenses. The plan should demonstrate how the firm will generate sufficient revenue over time to repay the loan. Newly established businesses may not be able to obtain a commercial loan because they do not have a business history to demonstrate that they will have sufficient cash to make monthly loan payments.

**Creditworthiness** Because many loans are for three years or longer, lenders assess the creditworthiness of a firm according to several factors. These include (1) the firm's planned use of the borrowed funds, (2) the financial condition of the firm's business, (3) the outlook for the industry or environment surrounding the firm's business, and (4) available collateral of the business that can be used to back the loan. To perform

When a business has a new building built (like the one shown here), much of the funding for that building is commonly borrowed from a commercial bank. The building serves as a form of collateral for the bank in the event that the business does not repay the loan. The collateral reduces the risk to the bank and therefore enables the bank to charge a lower rate on the loan.

© SHUTTERSTOCK/MARK WINFREY

**collateral**

assets of the borrower that are transferred to the lender if the borrower defaults on the loan

this assessment and determine whether the firm will be able to repay its loan on schedule, the lender will want to examine the firm's financial statements. In addition, the lender will want to assess the firm's business plan so that it can determine whether the firm has a reasonable strategy for expanding its market share in the future or at least for preventing competitors from taking its market share.

If the lender determines that the firm is creditworthy, it will attempt to establish terms of the loan that are acceptable to the firm. The terms of the loan specify the amount to be borrowed, the maturity, the collateral, and the rate of interest on the loan. Several different types of loans are generally available.

**Pledging Collateral**  Firms that need to borrow may be asked to pledge a portion of their assets as **collateral** to back the loan. Lenders are more comfortable providing loans when the loans are backed by collateral. A common form of collateral is the asset for which the borrowed funds will be used. For example, a firm that is borrowing funds to purchase a machine may offer that machine as collateral. If the lender expects that it could sell the machine for 70 percent of its existing value, the lender may finance 70 percent of the purchase and require the machine to be used as collateral. If the firm defaults on the loan, the lender can sell the machine for an amount that covers the loan.

A firm may also pledge its accounts receivable (payments owed to the firm for previous sales of products) as collateral. If the firm defaults on the loan, the lender takes control of the accounts receivable. To ensure that the accounts receivable collateral sufficiently covers the loan balance, the lender will provide a loan amount that is just a fraction (say, 65 percent) of the required collateral. Thus, even if some customers never pay off their accounts receivable, the collateral may still cover the full amount of the loan.

**Loan Rate**  When setting the loan rate, banks determine the average rate of interest that they pay on their deposits (which represents their cost of funds) and add on a premium. Since deposit rates change over time in response to general interest rate movements, loan rates change as well.

The premium is dependent on the credit risk of the loan or the probability of default. If the firm appears to be in good financial condition and the collateral covers the loan amount, the premium may be about 4 percentage points. For example, if the lender's cost of funds is 6 percent, the loan rate may be 10 percent. If the borrowing firm is perceived to have more credit risk, however, the premium may be more than 4 percentage points. The rate of interest typically charged on loans to the most creditworthy firms that borrow is called the **prime rate**.

**prime rate**
the rate of interest typically charged on loans to the most creditworthy firms that borrow

**Fixed-Rate Versus Floating-Rate Loans**   When firms need funds, they must choose between a fixed-rate loan and a floating-rate loan. Most commercial loans charge floating interest rates that move in tandem with market interest rates. Consider a firm that can obtain a five-year floating-rate loan with an interest rate that is adjusted by the bank once a year according to changes in the prime rate. Assume that the initial loan rate of interest is 8 percent (based on the prevailing prime rate) and will be adjusted once a year. Alternatively, the firm can obtain a fixed-rate loan of 10 percent. Which loan is preferable? The answer depends on future interest rate movements, which are uncertain. Firms that expect interest rates to rise consistently over the five-year period will prefer a fixed-rate loan so that they can avoid the upward adjustments on a floating-rate loan. Firms that expect interest rates to decline or remain stable over the five-year period will prefer a floating-rate loan.

Exhibit 16.1 shows the interest rates that would be charged under three different scenarios. If the firm has a fixed-rate loan, the interest rate charged on its loan is $I_1$, regardless of how market interest rates move over time. If the firm has a floating-rate loan, the interest rate charged on its loan will be $I_2$ if market interest rates increase over time, or $I_3$ if market interest rates decrease over time. Rising interest rates adversely affect firms that obtain floating-rate loans because the interest rate on their loans will increase.

The interest rate charged on a new loan is based on the general level of interest rates at that time. The top part of Exhibit 16.2 shows how the prime rate has changed over time. The lower part of the exhibit shows the interest expense that a firm would have incurred if it was charged the prime rate on a $1 million loan at that time.

**Types of Business Loans**   Several different types of business loans are generally available. The specific type of loan that a firm obtains may depend on its reasons for needing funding or the length of time the funds are required. A common type of business loan is intended to support ongoing business operations. There is a lag between the time when a firm incurs costs for producing and marketing a product and the time when the firm receives revenue from selling the product. The loan can provide necessary funding to cover expenses until the product is sold and cash is received.

Another type of business loan is a term loan, which is used to finance the purchase of fixed assets such as machinery. The maturity on a term loan is typically between 3 and 10 years.

A more flexible lending arrangement is a line of credit, which allows the firm to borrow up to a specified amount of money within a specified

**Exhibit 16.1**

Interest Rate Charged on Loans Under Three Different Scenarios

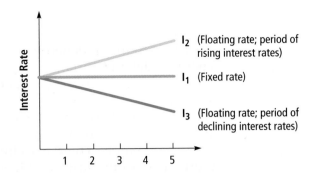

**Exhibit 16.2**

Effect of Interest Rates on Interest Expenses Incurred by Firms

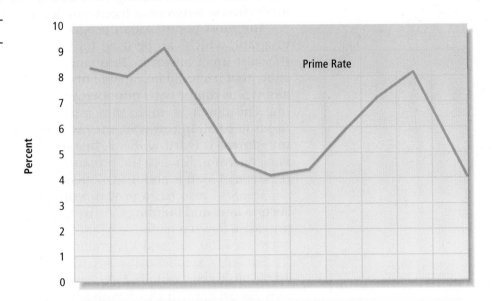

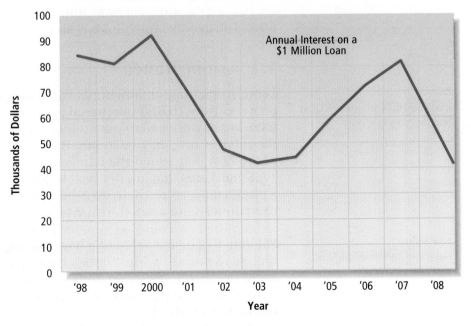

period of time. For example, a line of credit may allow a firm to borrow up to $100,000, but it would have to pay off the credit within one year. A line of credit is especially useful when a firm expects that it will need funding in the future, but does not know exactly when it will need funds or how much it will need.

**Loans Backed by the U.S. Government**   The Small Business Administration (SBA) backs loans provided by lenders to small businesses under various programs. When a loan is backed by the SBA, a financial institution is more willing to lend because it is less exposed to the risk that the business will be unable to repay the loan. The SBA guarantees that a large portion (such as 75 percent) of the loan will be repaid, so the lender has less to lose if the business is unable to repay the loan.

The most popular loan program sponsored by the SBA is the 7(a) program, which can be used for a wide variety of purposes, including the start-up of business. To qualify for this program, the business must show that it should be capable of repaying the loan and must also make a down payment with nonborrowed funds to partially cover the funding. This down payment may amount to about 25 percent of the total funds needed. In this way, the owners demonstrate their belief that the investment is worthwhile. A financial institution such as a commercial bank agrees to finance the remainder of the project. The average size of this type of loan is about $167,000.

The SBA also has a program to finance the purchase of fixed assets such as land and buildings. As with the 7(a) program, the business must provide a down payment toward the purchase. The size of these loans is between $200,000 and $10 million.

For very small businesses, the SBA offers a microloan program. These businesses usually have fewer than five employees, and the business owner qualifies as low income, minority, or disabled. These loans are made by nonprofit community groups that are granted funds by the SBA. The average microloan is about $14,000.

## 1.2 Issuing Bonds

**bonds**
long-term debt securities (IOUs) purchased by investors

Large firms may obtain funds by issuing **bonds**, which are long-term debt securities (IOUs) purchased by investors. Some large firms prefer to issue bonds rather than obtain loans from financial institutions because the interest rate may be lower. Bondholders are creditors, not owners, of the firm that issued the bonds.

Small firms that are not well known are unable to issue bonds. Even if they could issue their own bonds, a bond issuance typically raises more funds than a small firm would need.

**par value**
the amount that bondholders receive at maturity

**Par Value**   The **par value** of a bond is the amount that the bondholders receive at maturity. Most bonds have a maturity of between 10 and 30 years.

**Coupon Payments**   The coupon (interest) payments paid per year are determined by applying the so-called coupon rate to the par value. If the coupon rate is 10 percent, the coupon payments paid per year will be $100 for every $1,000 of par value. The coupon payments are normally paid semiannually and are fixed over the life of the bond. The coupon rate of bonds is influenced by the general level of interest rates at the time

Exhibit 16.3

**Summary of Risk Ratings Assigned by Bond Rating Agencies**

| | Rating Assigned by: | |
|---|---|---|
| | **Moody's** | **Standard & Poor's** |
| Highest quality | Aaa | AAA |
| High quality | Aa | AA |
| High-medium quality | A | A |
| Medium quality | Baa | BBB |
| Medium-low quality | Ba | BB |
| Low quality (speculative) | B | B |
| Poor quality | Caa | CCC |
| Very poor quality | Ca | CC |
| Lowest quality (in default) | C | DDD, D |

the bonds are issued. Firms typically prefer to issue bonds at a time when interest rates are relatively low. By doing so, they can lock in a relatively low coupon rate over the life of the bond. Forecasting interest rates is difficult, however, so firms cannot easily time a bond issue to take place when interest rates have hit their bottom. Also, firms that need funds immediately cannot wait until interest rates are at a more desirable level.

**Indenture**   When a firm plans to issue bonds, it creates an **indenture**, which is a legal document that explains its obligations to bondholders. For example, the indenture will state what collateral (if any) is backing the bonds. **Secured bonds** are backed by collateral, whereas **unsecured bonds** are not backed by collateral. The indenture also states whether the bonds have a **call feature**, which provides the issuing firm with the right to repurchase the bonds before maturity. To recognize the benefits of a call feature, consider a firm that issued bonds when interest rates were very high. If interest rates decline a few years later, the firm could issue new bonds at the lower interest rate and use the proceeds to repay the old bonds. Thus, the call feature gives the firm the flexibility to replace old bonds with new bonds that have a lower interest rate. Bonds that have a call feature typically need to pay a higher rate of interest.

**Default Risk of Bonds**   The interest rate paid on bonds is influenced not only by prevailing interest rates but also by the issuing firm's risk level. Firms that have more risk of default must provide higher interest to bondholders to compensate for the risk involved. Rating agencies such as Moody's Investor Service and Standard & Poor's Corporation rate the bonds according to their quality (safety). The rating agencies assign ratings after evaluating the financial condition of each firm. They closely assess the amount of debt that a firm has and the firm's ability to cover interest payments on its existing debt. Firms are periodically reevaluated since their ability to repay debt can change in response to economic or industry conditions, or even conditions unique to the firm.

Exhibit 16.3 provides a summary of the different ratings that can be assigned. Although each rating agency uses its own criteria for rating bonds, most bonds are rated within a similar risk level by the agencies. Investors may prefer to rely on the rating agencies rather than develop their own evaluations of the firms that issue bonds. At a given point in time, bonds with higher ratings offer lower interest rates.

**indenture**
a legal document that explains the firm's obligations to bondholders

**secured bonds**
bonds backed by collateral

**unsecured bonds**
bonds that are not backed by collateral

**call feature**
provides the issuing firm with the right to repurchase its bonds before maturity

The larger the amount of resources a business requires for production, the more funding the business needs. If its resources are not sufficient to achieve the production level needed to satisfy consumer demand, the business may obtain additional debt financing so that it can acquire more resources.

© SHUTTERSTOCK/MIKHAIL MALYSHEV

If a firm's financial condition weakens, the rating agencies may lower their ratings on the bonds it has issued. As a firm's bond ratings decline, it is less able to issue new bonds because investors will be concerned about the lower rating (higher risk).

Bondholders may attempt to limit the risk of default by enforcing **protective covenants**, which are restrictions imposed on specific financial policies of the firm. The purpose of these covenants is to ensure that managers do not make decisions that could increase the firm's risk and therefore increase the probability of default. For example, some protective covenants may restrict the firm from borrowing beyond some specified debt limit until the existing bonds are paid off.

**protective covenants**
restrictions imposed on specific financial policies of a firm that has issued bonds

### 1.3 Issuing Commercial Paper

**commercial paper**
a short-term debt security normally issued by firms in good financial condition

Many firms also issue **commercial paper**, which is a short-term debt security normally issued by firms in good financial condition. Its normal maturity is between three and six months. Thus, the issuance of commercial paper is an alternative to obtaining loans directly from financial institutions. The minimum denomination of commercial paper is usually $100,000. Typically, denominations are in multiples of $1 million. Various financial institutions commonly purchase commercial paper. The interest rate on commercial paper is influenced by the general market interest rates at the time of issuance.

### 1.4 Impact of the Debt Financing Level on Interest Expenses

To illustrate how the level of debt financing (whether by borrowing from financial institutions or by issuing IOUs) affects interest expenses, consider a firm that borrows $1 million for a five-year period at an interest rate of 9 percent. This firm will pay $90,000 in interest in each of the next five years (computed as $1,000,000 × 9%). Thus, the firm will need sufficient revenue to cover not only its operating expenses (such as salaries) but also its interest expenses. If the firm had borrowed

$2 million, it would have to pay $180,000 in annual interest (computed as $2,000,000 × 9%). When firms borrow money excessively, they have large annual interest payms that are difficult to cover. For this reason, the firms have a higher probability of defaulting on the loans than they would if they had borrowed less funds.

## 1.5 Common Creditors That Provide Debt Financing

Various types of creditors can provide debt financing to firms.

**Commercial Banks**   **Commercial banks** obtain deposits from individuals and use the funds primarily to provide business loans.

**Savings Institutions**   **Savings institutions** (also called "thrift institutions") also obtain deposits from individuals and use some of the deposited funds to provide business loans. Although savings institutions lend most of their funds to individuals who need mortgage loans, they have increased their amount of business loans in recent years.

**Finance Companies**   **Finance companies** typically obtain funds by issuing debt securities (IOUs) and lend most of their funds to firms. In general, finance companies tend to focus on loans to less established firms that have a higher risk of loan default. The finance companies charge a higher rate of interest on these loans to compensate for the higher degree of risk.

**Pension Funds**   **Pension funds** receive employee and firm contributions toward pensions and invest the proceeds for the employees until the funds are needed. They commonly invest part of their funds in bonds issued by firms.

**Insurance Companies**   **Insurance companies** receive insurance premiums from selling insurance to customers and invest the proceeds until the funds are needed to pay insurance claims. They also commonly invest part of their funds in bonds issued by firms.

**Mutual Funds**   **Mutual funds** are investment companies that receive funds from individual investors; the mutual funds pool the amounts and invest them in securities. Mutual funds can be classified by the type of investments that they make. Some mutual funds (called **bond mutual funds**) invest the funds received from investors in bonds that are issued by firms.

**commercial banks**
financial institutions that obtain deposits from individuals and use the funds primarily to provide business loans

**savings institutions**
financial institutions that obtain deposits from individuals and use the deposited funds primarily to provide mortgage loans

**finance companies**
financial institutions that typically obtain funds by issuing debt securities (IOUs) and lend most of their funds to firms

**pension funds**
receive employee and firm contributions toward pensions and invest the proceeds for the employees until the funds are needed

**insurance companies**
receive insurance premiums from selling insurance to customers and invest the proceeds until the funds are needed to pay insurance claims

**mutual funds**
investment companies that receive funds from individual investors and then pool and invest those funds in securities

**bond mutual funds**
investment companies that invest the funds received from investors in bonds

**Learning Objective 2**
Identify the common methods of equity financing for firms.

**equity financing**
the act of receiving investment from owners (by issuing stock or retaining earnings)

## 2. Methods of Equity Financing

The common methods of **equity financing** are retaining earnings and issuing stock, as explained next.

## 2.1 Retaining Earnings

A firm can obtain equity financing by retaining earnings rather than by distributing the earnings to its owners. The board of directors of each firm decides how much of the firm's quarterly earnings should be retained (reinvested in the firm) versus distributed as dividends to owners.

**dividend policy**
the decision regarding how much of the firm's quarterly earnings should be retained (reinvested in the firm) versus distributed as dividends to owners

This decision, referred to as the firm's **dividend policy**, is important because it influences the amount of additional financing the firm must obtain. For example, consider a firm that earned $30 million after taxes. Assume that it will need $40 million for various expenses in the near future. If it retains all of the earnings, it will need an additional $10 million. At the other extreme, if it pays out the entire $30 million as dividends, it will need to obtain an additional $40 million.

Managers may want to retain earnings to provide financial support for the firm's expansion. For example, if a firm needs $10 million for expansion and has just earned $6 million after taxes, it may retain the $6 million as equity financing and borrow the remaining $4 million. Many small firms retain most of their earnings to support expansion. Larger corporations tend to pay out a portion of their earnings as dividends and retain only part of what they earned. Large firms can more easily obtain debt financing, so they can afford to pay out a portion of their earnings as dividends.

**Factors That Affect a Firm's Dividend Policy**   There is no optimal dividend policy to be used by all firms. Some firms establish their dividend payment as a percentage of future earnings. For example, General Mills sets a dividend target of 50 percent of earnings, and Philip Morris International set an initial dividend payout ratio of 65 percent when it was spun off from Altria in 2008. Each firm's unique characteristics may influence its dividend policy.

A firm's shareholders may expect to receive dividends if they have historically been receiving them. If the firm discontinues or reduces the dividend payment, shareholders could become dissatisfied. Thus, many firms such as ConAgra and Campbell's Soup make an effort to either maintain or increase dividends from year to year.

A firm that has no need for additional funds may distribute most of its earnings as dividends. However, it may be concerned that if it pays high dividends, shareholders will come to expect them. Thus, instead of trying to maintain its high dividend payment, the firm may decide to use a portion of the earnings for another purpose. For example, it may consider replacing old assets or expanding part of its business.

## 2.2  Issuing Stock

**common stock**
a security that represents partial ownership of a particular firm

A firm can also obtain equity financing by issuing stock. **Common stock** is a security that represents partial ownership of a particular firm. Only the owners of common stock are permitted to vote on certain key matters concerning the firm, such as the election of the board of directors, whether to issue new shares of common stock, and whether to accept a merger proposal. Firms can issue common stock to obtain funds. When new shares of stock are issued, the number of shareholders who own the firm increases.

**preferred stock**
a security that represents partial ownership of a particular firm and offers specific priorities over common stock

**Preferred stock** is a security that represents partial ownership of a particular firm and offers specific priorities over common stock. If a firm does not pay dividends over a period, it must pay preferred stockholders all dividends that were omitted before paying any dividends to common stockholders. Also, if the firm goes bankrupt, the preferred stockholders have priority claim to the firm's assets over common stockholders. If a firm goes bankrupt, however, there may not be any assets left for preferred stockholders, because creditors (such as lenders

When a business needs some equity funding, but not enough to engage in a public stock offering, its owners may meet with representatives from venture capital firms. The owners will present their plan for how they would use the funds provided. The venture capital firms may extend funding if they think that they would receive a good return on their investment in the business.

© SHUTTERSTOCK/ARNE TRAUTMANN

or bondholders) have first claim. Preferred stockholders normally do not have voting rights. Firms issue common stock more frequently than preferred stock.

**Issuing Stock to Venture Capital Firms**   Firms can issue stock privately to a **venture capital firm**, which is a firm composed of individuals who invest in small businesses. These individuals act as investors in firms rather than as creditors. They expect a share of the businesses in which they invest. Their investments typically support projects that have potential for high returns but also have high risk.

Entrepreneurs who need equity financing can attend venture capital forums, where they are allowed a short time (15 minutes or so) to convince the venture capital firms to provide them with equity financing. If an entrepreneur's presentation is impressive, venture capital firms may arrange for a longer meeting with the entrepreneur to learn more about the business that needs financing.

Providers of venture capital recognize that some of the businesses they invest in may generate little or no return. They hope that the successful businesses will more than make up for any unsuccessful ones. Venture capital firms commonly assess businesses that require an equity investment of between $200,000 and $2 million. Small projects are not popular because their potential return is not worth the time required to assess their feasibility.

**Going Public**   If a small privately held business desires to obtain additional funds, it may consider an **initial public offering (IPO)** of stock (also called "going public"), which is the first issue of stock to the public. Firms such as Google, Yahoo!, and Amazon.com went public so that they would have sufficient funds to support their expansion.

Insurance companies and pension funds commonly purchase large amounts of stocks issued by firms. In addition, **stock mutual funds** (investment companies that invest pooled funds received from individual investors in stocks) purchase large amounts of stocks issued by firms. An IPO allows a firm to obtain additional funds without boosting its existing debt level and without relying on retained earnings. Firms can obtain a

**venture capital firm**
a firm composed of individuals who invest in small businesses

**initial public offering (IPO)**
the first issue of stock to the public

**stock mutual funds**
investment companies that invest funds received from individual investors in stocks

Out of Business

WE HAVE A UNIQUE FINANCIAL STRATEGY... BORROW UNTIL ALL THE BANKS CUT US OFF THEN LOOK FOR NAÏVE INVESTORS WHO ARE WILLING TO INVEST EQUITY

FINANCIAL MEETING IN PROGRESS

large amount of funds by going public without increasing future interest payments to creditors.

Along with the advantages, IPOs have some disadvantages. First, firms that go public are responsible for informing shareholders of their financial condition. All firms that issue stock to the public must file periodic financial reports with the Securities and Exchange Commission, and preparing these reports can be expensive. Furthermore, the financial information then is accessible to investors. Some firms may prefer not to disclose information that would reveal the success (and perhaps the wealth) of the owners.

A second disadvantage is that when a small business attempts to obtain funding from the public, it may have difficulty convincing investors that its business plans are feasible. This limits the amount of funding that can be obtained from an IPO. It also forces the firm to sell part of the ownership at a relatively low cost. If a firm goes public and cannot obtain funding at a reasonable price, its original owners may feel that they gave away part of the firm for nothing.

A third disadvantage of an IPO is that the firm's ownership structure is diluted. Once shares are sold to the public, the proportion of the firm owned by the original owners is reduced. Thus, the original owners have less control of the firm, and other investors have more influence on the firm's board of directors and therefore on major decisions. Also, the profits earned by the firm that are distributed among owners as dividends must be allocated among more owners.

A fourth disadvantage of an IPO is that investment banks charge high fees for advising and placing the stock with investors. The firm also incurs legal fees, accounting fees, and printing fees. The fees may be about 10 percent of the total amount of funds received from the IPO. Thus, an IPO of $20 million may result in fees of $2 million.

IPOs are generally more popular when most stock prices are high, as firms may receive a higher price for their newly issued stock under these conditions. For example, stock prices were very high in the late 1990s, and there were numerous IPOs in that period.

**Listing the Stock**   Once a firm has issued stock to the public, it lists its stock on a stock exchange. This allows the investors to sell the stock

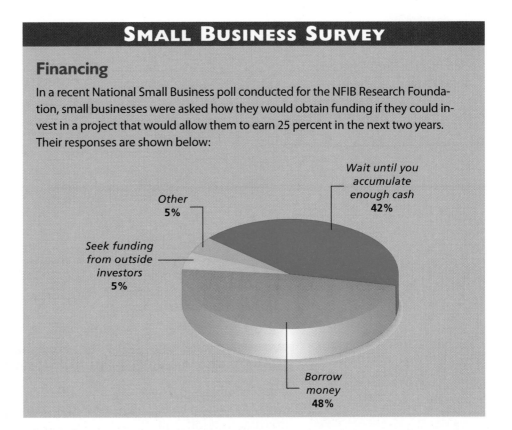

**Financing**

In a recent National Small Business poll conducted for the NFIB Research Foundation, small businesses were asked how they would obtain funding if they could invest in a project that would allow them to earn 25 percent in the next two years. Their responses are shown below:

*Wait until you accumulate enough cash* **42%**

*Other* **5%**

*Seek funding from outside investors* **5%**

*Borrow money* **48%**

---

**secondary market**
a market where existing securities can be traded among investors

they purchased from the firm to other investors over time. The stock exchange serves as a **secondary market**, or a market where existing securities can be traded among investors. Thus, investors have the flexibility to sell stocks that they no longer wish to hold.

The most popular stock exchanges in the United States are the New York Stock Exchange (NYSE), the American Stock Exchange (AMEX), and the over-the-counter (OTC) market. Stocks in the OTC market trade via an electronic network known as the National Association of Securities Dealers Automated Quotations (Nasdaq). Each exchange has a set of listing requirements that firms must satisfy to have their stocks listed on that exchange.

## 2.3  Comparison of Equity Financing with Debt Financing

Equity financing and debt financing are compared in Exhibit 16.4. Notice from the exhibit that the forms of debt financing (loans and bonds) require the firm to make interest and principal payments. Conversely, the forms of equity financing (retained earnings and stock) do not require any payments. Financing with stock may result in dividend payments, but only if the firm can afford them. Also, there are no principal payments to the stockholders, as the stock has no maturity.

Firms typically use a variety of financing methods to obtain funds. 3M Company, ChevronTexaco Corporation, Motorola, and many other firms frequently obtain funds by borrowing from banks, issuing bonds, and issuing new stock.

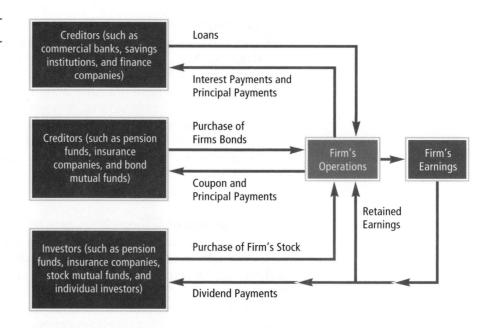

**Exhibit 16.4**

Summary of Firm's Debt and
Equity Financing Methods

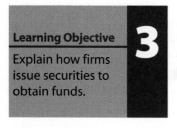

**Learning Objective**

**3**

Explain how firms
issue securities to
obtain funds.

**public offering**
the selling of securities
to the public

**underwritten**
the investment bank guarantees
a price to the issuing firm, no
matter what price the securities
are sold for

**best-efforts basis**
the investment bank does not
guarantee a price to the firm
issuing securities

**underwriting syndicate**
a group of investment banks that
share the obligations of underwriting securities

**prospectus**
a document that discloses relevant financial information about
securities and about the firm
issuing them

# 3. How Firms Issue Securities

A **public offering** of securities (such as bonds or stocks) represents the
selling of securities to the public. Public offerings include both IPOs and
offerings of additional securities by firms that went public earlier. A firm
that plans a public offering of securities can receive help from investment banks, which originate, underwrite, and distribute the securities.
Today, most investment banks operate as divisions within bank holding
companies that also have commercial banking operations.

## 3.1 Origination

Investment banks advise firms on the amount of stocks or bonds they
can issue. The issuance of an excessive amount of securities can cause a
decline in the market price because the supply of securities issued may
exceed the demand. Also, the issuance of bonds requires the determination of a maturity date, a coupon rate, and collateral.

## 3.2 Underwriting

When securities offerings are **underwritten**, the investment bank guarantees a price to the issuing firm, no matter what price the securities are
sold for. In this way, the investment bank bears the risk that the securities may be sold only at low prices. Alternatively, the investment bank
may attempt to sell the securities on a **best-efforts basis**; in this case, it
does not guarantee a price to the issuing firm.

For large issues of securities, the investment bank may create an
**underwriting syndicate**, which is a group of investment banks that share
the obligations of underwriting the securities. Each investment bank in
the syndicate is allocated a portion of the securities and is responsible
for selling that portion.

## 3.3 Distribution

The issuing firm must register the issue with the Securities and Exchange
Commission (SEC). It provides the SEC with a **prospectus**, which is a

document that discloses relevant financial information about the securities (such as the amount) and about the firm.

Once the SEC approves the registration, the prospectus is distributed to investors who may purchase the securities. Some of the more likely investors are pension funds and insurance companies that have large amounts of funds to invest. Some issues are completely sold within hours. When an issue does not sell well, the investment bank may lower the price of the securities to increase demand.

Firms that issue securities incur **flotation costs**, which include fees paid to investment banks for advice and for selling the securities, printing expenses, and registration fees.

**flotation costs**
costs of issuing securities; include fees paid to investment banks for their advice and efforts to sell the securities, printing expenses, and registration fees

**private placement**
the selling of securities to one or a few investors

**Private Placement**   Some firms may prefer to use a **private placement**, in which the securities are sold to one or a few investors. An investment bank may still be used for advisory purposes and for help in identifying a financial institution (such as an insurance company) that may purchase the entire issue. The selling costs are lower with a private placement because only one or a few investors are involved. A disadvantage, however, is that many investors cannot afford to purchase an entire issue. Consequently, privately placing the securities may be difficult.

**Learning Objective**
Explain how firms may obtain financing through suppliers or leasing.

**4**

## 4.  Other Methods of Obtaining Funds

In addition to debt financing and equity financing, firms may obtain funds in other ways, as discussed next.

### 4.1  Financing from Suppliers

When a firm obtains supplies, it may be given a specific period to pay its bill. The supplier is essentially financing the firm's investment over that period. If the firm is able to generate adequate revenue over that time to pay the bill, it will not need any more financing. Even if it needs

Some suppliers will deliver supplies to a manufacturer but not require payment until a few months later. This provides a form of temporary financing to the manufacturer.

© SHUTTERSTOCK/KENNETH V. PILON

How Firms Can Benefit from
Supplier Financing

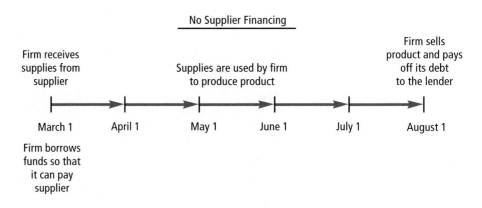

more financing, the supplier's willingness to wait for payment saves the firm some financing costs.

Exhibit 16.5 shows the benefits of supplier financing. In the top diagram, the firm receives supplies on March 1, but does not have to pay its bill until August 1. By August 1, the firm will have sold the product that required the use of the supplies. Thus, it can use a portion of the revenue received from selling the product to pay the supplier.

The lower diagram shows that with no supplier financing, the firm must obtain funds from another source. For example, it may borrow funds from a commercial bank on March 1 to pay the supplier at that time. When the firm receives its payment for the product on August 1, it can use a portion of the revenue received to pay off the debt. In this case, the firm had to borrow funds for five months and incurred interest expenses over that period. The difference between these two scenarios is that the firm incurs only the expense of the supplies when it obtains supplier financing, but it incurs the expense of supplies plus interest expenses if supplier financing is not available.

## 4.2 Leasing

**leasing**

renting assets for a specified period of time

Some firms prefer to finance the use of assets by **leasing**, or renting the assets for a specified period of time. These firms rent the assets and have full control over them over a particular period. They return the assets at the time specified in the lease contract. Many firms that lease assets cannot afford to purchase them. By leasing, they must make periodic lease payments but do not need to make a large initial outlay.

Some firms prefer to lease rather than purchase when they may need the assets for only a short period of time. For example, consider a new firm that does not know how much factory space it will need until it can assess the demand for its product. This firm may initially lease factory space so that it can switch factories without having to sell its existing factory if it needs more space.

When a business opens a store in a mall, it typically leases the space. Leasing space is beneficial for many businesses that could not afford to purchase land or a building for a store.

© SHUTTERSTOCK/IGOR STEPOVIK

## SMALL BUSINESS SURVEY

### Leasing

In a recent National Small Business poll conducted for the NFIB Research Foundation, small businesses were asked to identify the most important advantage of leasing assets rather than purchasing them. Their responses are provided here:

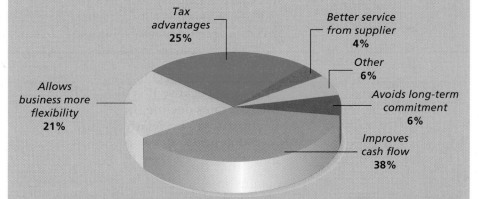

Tax advantages 25%
Better service from supplier 4%
Other 6%
Avoids long-term commitment 6%
Improves cash flow 38%
Allows business more flexibility 21%

They were also asked to identify the most important advantage of purchasing assets instead of leasing them. Their responses are shown below:

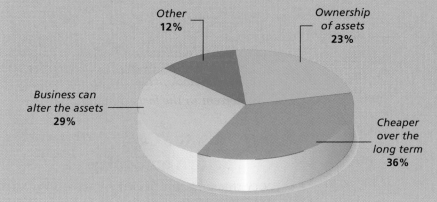

Other 12%
Ownership of assets 23%
Business can alter the assets 29%
Cheaper over the long term 36%

**Learning Objective**

Describe how firms
determine the
composition of their
financing.

**5**

**capital structure**
the amount of debt versus
equity financing

# 5. Deciding the Capital Structure

All firms must decide on a **capital structure**, or the amount of debt versus equity financing. No particular capital structure is perfect for all firms. However, some characteristics should be considered when determining the appropriate capital structure. The use of debt (such as bank loans or bonds) as a source of funds is desirable because the interest payments made by the firm on its debt are tax-deductible. Firms can claim their interest payments during the year as an expense, thereby reducing their reported earnings and their taxes. When firms use equity as a source of funds, they do not benefit in this way.

Although debt offers the advantage of tax deductibility, too much debt can increase the firm's risk of default on its debt. A higher level of debt results in a higher level of interest payments each year, which can make it difficult for a firm to cover all its debt payments. When creditors are concerned about the firm's ability to make future interest payments, they are less willing to provide additional credit. A firm's ability to increase its debt level is also constrained by the amount of collateral available.

Firms tend to retain some earnings as an easy and continual form of equity financing. When they need additional funds to support their operations, they typically use debt financing if they have the flexibility to do so. When they approach their debt capacity, however, they may have to retain more earnings or issue stock to obtain additional capital.

## 5.1 Revising the Capital Structure

Many firms revise their capital structure in response to changes in economic conditions, such as economic growth and interest rates. If economic growth declines and their earnings decline, they may reduce their debt because it is more difficult to cover interest payments. When interest rates decline, firms may increase their debt because the interest payments will be relatively low.

Sometimes firms revise their capital structure by changing the amount of stock they have outstanding. As described earlier, a firm can obtain equity financing by issuing additional shares of stock. Firms may also decrease the amount of stock outstanding by repurchasing shares issued previously. This strategy may have a favorable impact on the firm's stock price. To illustrate how the repurchasing of stock can improve a firm's value (and therefore its stock price), consider the following statements from a recent annual report of Wal-Mart:

*"In a move to improve shareholder value, the Board of Directors authorized a $2 billion share repurchase program. . . . We started buying (when the stock price was) in the low 20s, and the stock ended up rising 73 percent in the last calendar year."*

## 5.2 How the Capital Structure Affects the Return on Equity

A firm's earnings performance (as measured by its return on equity) can be significantly influenced by the capital structure decision. Consider a

**Exhibit 16.6**

How a Firm's Return on
Equity Is Dependent
on Financial Leverage
*Note:* Assume that the
firm had a net income of
$1 million last year and has
$10 million in assets.

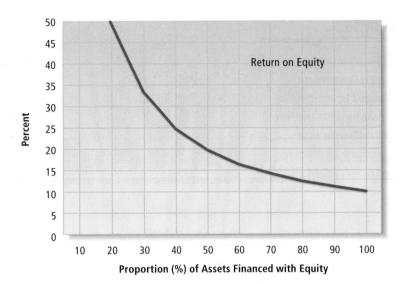

firm that had earnings of $1 million last year and has $10 million in assets. The firm's return on equity (measured as earnings divided by owner's equity) depends on the amount of the firm's assets that was financed with equity versus debt. Exhibit 16.6 shows how the firm's return on equity is dependent on its financial leverage. If the firm used all equity to finance its $10 million in assets, its return on equity (ROE) would be:

$$\text{ROE} = \frac{\$1,000,000}{\$10,000,000}$$

$$= 10\%$$

At the other extreme, if the firm used only 20 percent equity ($2 million) to finance its assets, its ROE would be:

$$\text{ROE} = \frac{\$1,000,000}{\$2,000,000}$$

$$= 50\%$$

Although using little equity (mostly debt) can achieve a higher return on equity, it exposes a firm to the risk of being unable to cover its interest payments. To illustrate the risk, Exhibit 16.7 shows how the annual interest expense incurred by a firm (with $10 million in assets) is dependent on the firm's degree of financial leverage. This exhibit assumes a 10 percent interest rate. For example, if the firm uses all equity, it does not incur any interest expenses. At the other extreme, if it uses only 20 percent ($2 million) of equity financing and relies on 80 percent ($8 million) of debt financing, it will incur an interest expense of $800,000 per year.

The relationship shown in Exhibit 16.7 is intended simply to illustrate how a high degree of financial leverage can result in high interest expenses. In reality, the impact of high financial leverage may be even more pronounced than in Exhibit 16.7, because lenders may charge a higher interest rate to firms that wish to borrow an excessive amount.

**Exhibit 16.7**

How a Firm's Interest Expense Is Dependent on Financial Leverage
*Note:* Assume that the firm has $10 million in assets; also assume a 10 percent interest rate on debt.

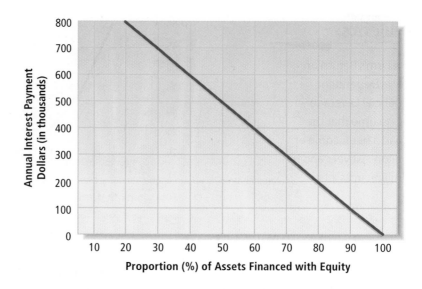

## SMALL BUSINESS SURVEY

### Financing Choices of Small Firms

A recent survey asked small firms how they are financing their businesses, with the results as shown:

| | Proportion of Firms That Recently Used This Type of Financing |
|---|---|
| Commercial bank loans | 36% |
| Credit cards | 27 |
| Retained earnings | 24 |
| Private loans | 18 |
| Personal bank loans | 17 |
| Supplier credit | 14 |
| Leasing | 10 |
| Other | 13 |

The results of this survey show that small firms use a wide variety of methods to obtain funds. The commercial bank loans, credit cards, and private loans reflect debt financing, while the use of retained earnings reflects equity financing.

The extra premium on the interest rate compensates the lenders for the risk that the firm may be unable to repay its debt.

Firms weigh the potential higher return on equity that results from using mostly debt financing against the risk resulting from high interest payments. Many firms compromise by balancing their amounts of equity and debt financing. For example, a firm might finance its $10 million in assets by using $5 million of equity and the remaining $5 million of debt. Assuming an interest rate of 10 percent on debt, the interest expense would be $500,000 (computed as 10% × $5,000,000), as shown in Exhibit 16.7.

## Global Business

### Global Financing

When a U.S. firm establishes businesses in foreign countries (called "foreign subsidiaries"), it must obtain sufficient funds to support them. The firm must decide not only whether the foreign subsidiaries should use debt or equity but also what currency they should use. A common strategy is to have a subsidiary borrow funds locally so that the subsidiary's interest expense will be in the same currency as its revenue. Consequently, the subsidiary will not need to exchange its local currency into another currency to pay off the debt.

## Cross-Functional Teamwork

### Interaction Between Financing Decisions and Other Business Decisions

When financial managers make financing decisions, they rely on input from other managers. The amount of financing is dependent on the difference between the amount of cash outflows resulting from the payment of expenses and the cash inflows resulting from sales. The larger the difference, the more financing will be needed. Financial managers can ask production managers to estimate the salaries and other production expenses that will be incurred by the firm in the future. They can ask marketing managers to estimate the marketing expenses to be incurred by the firm. They can also ask marketing managers to estimate the future demand for each of the firm's products; this information can be used to estimate the firm's future revenue.

When financial managers decide whether to finance with debt or equity, they rely on input from marketing managers. If the future revenue to be received by the firm is somewhat stable over time, the firm may be willing to finance with debt because cash inflows each month will be sufficient to cover its interest payments on debt. If the monthly revenue is expected to be erratic, however, cash inflows each month may not be sufficient to make interest payments. In this case, the firm may use equity financing instead of debt financing. The marketing managers can offer useful input on this topic because they should know whether the demand for the product will be somewhat stable over time.

# Responding to the Economy

## Financing Decisions in Response to the Economy

When economic conditions are weak, a firm faces the risk that its revenue may decline and that it may not be able to cover its debt repayment obligations. Creditors can force a firm into bankruptcy if they do not receive their payments in a timely manner. Therefore, some firms are more willing to use equity funding during weak economic conditions, perhaps by inviting additional owners to invest in the firm. A portion of the additional equity can be used to pay off some debt, so that the firm can still make its debt payments even if its revenue declines.

During strong economic conditions, firms are less concerned about a decline in their revenue. However, they face a different type of challenge. Interest rates typically rise during periods of strong economic growth (as explained in the appendix to this chapter). Since many business loans have interest rates that adjust over time to the prevailing market rate, an increase in interest rates can result in higher interest expenses. Firms that rely heavily on debt will be more vulnerable to an increase in interest expenses due to higher interest rates. Consequently, firms attempt to forecast economic conditions, as their capital structure decision is dependent on their expectations of economic growth and interest rates.

---

**Learning Objective 6**

Describe the remedies for firms that are unable to repay their debts.

# 6. Remedies for Debt Problems

The ultimate danger to taking on too much debt is that the firm may be unable to make its payments to its creditors. The extreme consequence of this situation is business failure, in which the firm's assets are sold to pay creditors part of what they are owed. In this case, a formal bankruptcy process is necessary. First, however, the firm should consider alternative informal remedies, which could avoid some legal expenses. Common remedies include the following:

✦ Extension

✦ Composition

✦ Private liquidation

✦ Formal remedies

## 6.1 Extension

**extension**

provides additional time for a firm to generate the necessary cash to cover its payments to its creditors

If a firm is having difficulty covering the payments it owes, its creditors may allow an **extension**, which provides additional time for the firm to obtain the necessary cash to cover its payments. An extension is feasible only if the creditors believe that the firm's financial problems are temporary. If formal bankruptcy is inevitable, an extension may only delay the liquidation process and possibly reduce the liquidation value of the firm's assets.

If creditors allow an extension, they may require that the firm abide by various provisions. For example, they may prohibit the firm from making dividend payments until the firm retains enough funds to repay its loans. The firm will likely agree to any reasonable provisions because the extension gives the firm a chance to survive.

A creditor cannot be forced to go along with an extension. Creditors who prefer some alternative action must be paid off in full if an extension is to be allowed. If too many creditors disapprove, an extension will not be feasible, as the firm would first have to pay all disapproving creditors what they are owed.

## 6.2  Composition

**composition**
specifies that a firm will provide its creditors with a portion of what they are owed

If the failing firm and its creditors do not agree on an extension, they may attempt to negotiate a **composition** agreement, which specifies that the firm will provide its creditors with a portion of what they are owed. For example, the agreement may call for creditors to receive 40 cents on every dollar owed to them. This partial repayment may be as much as or more than the creditors would receive from formal bankruptcy proceedings. In addition, the firm may be able to survive, since its future interest payments will be eliminated after paying off the creditors. As with an extension, creditors cannot be forced to go along with a composition agreement. Any dissenting creditors must be paid in full.

## 6.3  Private Liquidation

**private liquidation**
creditors may informally request that a failing firm liquidate (sell) its assets and distribute the funds received from liquidation to them

If an extension or composition is not possible, the creditors may informally request that the failing firm liquidate (sell) its assets and distribute the funds received from liquidation to them. Although this can be achieved through formal bankruptcy proceedings, it can also be accomplished informally outside the court system. An informal agreement will typically be accomplished more quickly than formal bankruptcy proceedings and is less expensive as it avoids many legal fees. All creditors must agree to this so-called **private liquidation**, or an alternative remedy will be necessary.

To carry out a private liquidation, a law firm with expertise in liquidation will normally be hired to liquidate the debtor firm's assets. Once the assets are liquidated, the remaining funds are distributed to the creditors on a pro rata basis.

## 6.4  Formal Remedies

If creditors cannot agree to any of the informal remedies, the solution to the firm's financial problems will be worked out formally in the court system. The formal remedies are either reorganization or liquidation under bankruptcy. Whether a firm should reorganize or liquidate depends on its estimated value under each alternative.

**liquidation value**
the amount of funds that would be received as a result of the liquidation of a firm.

**Reorganization**   Reorganization of a firm can include the termination of some of its businesses, an increased focus on its other businesses, revisions of the organizational structure, and downsizing. Consider a firm whose value as a "going concern" (a continuing business) would be $20 million after it reorganizes. Now consider the **liquidation value** of that firm, which is the amount of funds that would be received from liquidating all of the firm's assets. If the firm's liquidation value exceeds $20 million, it should be liquidated. The creditors would receive more funds from liquidation than they would expect to receive if the firm were reorganized. Conversely, if its liquidation value is less than $20 million, the firm should be reorganized.

In the case of reorganization, the firm or the creditors must file a petition. The bankruptcy court then appoints a committee of creditors to work with the firm in restructuring its operations. The firm is protected against any legal action that would interrupt its operations. The firm may revise its capital structure by using less debt so that it can reduce its periodic interest payments owed to creditors. Once the restructuring plan is completed, it is submitted to the court and must be approved by the creditors.

**Liquidation Under Bankruptcy**  If the firm and its creditors cannot agree on some informal agreement, and if reorganization is not feasible, the firm will file for bankruptcy. A petition for bankruptcy may be filed by either the failing firm or the creditors.

The failing firm is obligated to file a list of creditors along with up-to-date financial statements. A law firm is appointed to sell off the existing assets and allocate the funds received to the creditors. Secured creditors are paid with the proceeds from selling off any assets serving as their collateral.

## COLLEGE HEALTH CLUB: FINANCING AT CHC

One of the decisions that Sue Kramer needs to make as part of her business plan for College Health Club (CHC) is how to finance the business. Sue has obtained a loan for $40,000 to finance CHC. One advantage of using debt rather than obtaining additional equity is that the interest payments are tax-deductible. A second advantage is that since Sue has not accepted an equity investment from another person, she has full control over the business. The disadvantage of using debt rather than equity financing is that CHC will incur an interest expense each month as long as the loan exists. Sue expects that the annual interest expense will be $4,000, which means that CHC's earnings before taxes will be $4,000 less than if it had no debt. Sue decided to use debt financing rather than additional equity financing because she prefers to be the sole owner and feels confident that CHC can afford the $4,000 interest payment.

Sue also has to decide whether to purchase the land and facilities for the health club or lease the space. The advantage of owning assets such as the weight and exercise machines and the facilities is that they would be hers to keep, unless she sold them. In addition, she would not have to make lease payments. The disadvantage, however, is the expense associated with purchasing the equipment and facilities. To purchase them, she would need a very large loan. Creditors might not be willing to extend such a large amount. Even if they did, her interest payments would be much higher because of the large loan. Also, leasing gives her flexibility. If Sue decides to discontinue the business, for example, she will not need to find a buyer for the equipment or facilities. Given the advantages of leasing, Sue has decided to lease the equipment and the facilities. If she accumulates substantial funds in the future, she will reconsider whether to purchase these assets.

# Summary of Learning Objectives

**1** The common sources of debt financing are obtaining bank loans, issuing bonds, or issuing commercial paper.

The financial institutions that provide loans to firms are commercial banks, savings institutions, and finance companies. The financial institutions that commonly purchase the corporate bonds issued by firms are insurance companies, pension funds, and bond mutual funds.

**2** The common sources of equity financing are retaining earnings and issuing stock. The financial institutions that purchase stocks issued by firms are insurance companies, pension funds, and stock mutual funds.

**3** When firms issue debt securities or stocks, they normally hire an investment bank. The invest-

ment bank may provide advice on the amount of securities the firm should issue (origination), underwrite the securities, and find buyers of the securities that the firm issues (distribution).

**4** Firms may also obtain financing from suppliers. If the firm is not required to pay for the supplies immediately, it is essentially receiving funding from the supplier. However, such an arrangement with a supplier does not provide long-term financing.

Firms may also be able to finance investments in their business by leasing. By leasing assets rather than buying them, a firm does not need to obtain funding. It only needs to make the monthly lease payment for the use of those assets.

**5** Firms may prefer to use debt financing over equity financing because the interest payments are

tax-deductible. However, a high level of debt financing results in a high level of interest payments, which could make it difficult for the firm to make those payments. With equity financing, the firm does not have to make periodic payments.

**6** When a firm performs poorly, it may not have sufficient funds to repay its debt. It may need to consider selling all of its assets and use the proceeds to pay off part of the debt. Alternatively, it could attempt to obtain an extension from its creditors so that it has additional time to cover its debt payments. Another possibility is that it may negotiate a composition agreement, in which the creditors accept a portion of what they are owed, and the firm may be able to stay in business.

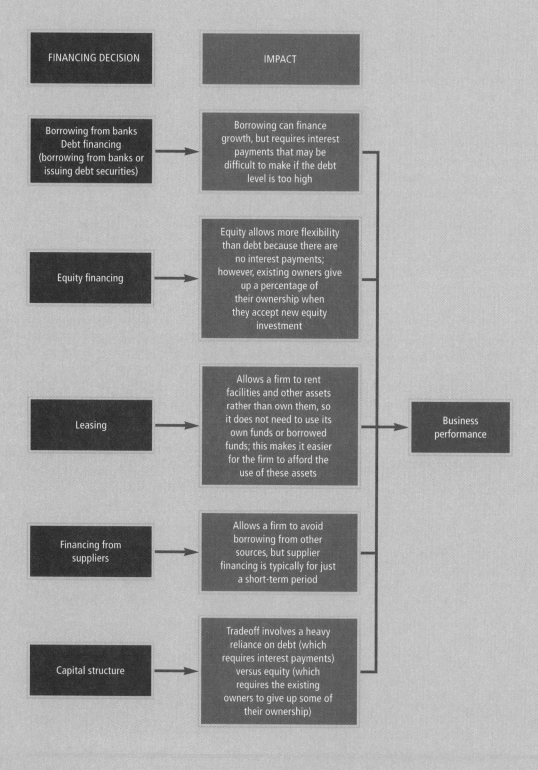

FINANCING DECISION

IMPACT

Borrowing from banks
Debt financing
(borrowing from banks or
issuing debt securities)

Borrowing can finance
growth, but requires interest
payments that may be
difficult to make if the debt
level is too high

Equity financing

Equity allows more flexibility
than debt because there are
no interest payments;
however, existing owners give
up a percentage of
their ownership when
they accept new equity
investment

Leasing

Allows a firm to rent
facilities and other assets
rather than own them, so
it does not need to use its
own funds or borrowed
funds; this makes it easier
for the firm to afford the
use of these assets

Business
performance

Financing from
suppliers

Allows a firm to avoid
borrowing from other
sources, but supplier
financing is typically for just
a short-term period

Capital structure

Tradeoff involves a heavy
reliance on debt (which
requires interest payments)
versus equity (which
requires the existing
owners to give up some of
their ownership)

# Self-Test of Key Concepts

The following self-assessment allows you to test your understanding of the key concepts covered in this chapter. Answers are provided at the end of this exercise.

## True or False

1. Debt financing is the act of issuing stock or retaining earnings.

2. A common form of collateral is the asset purchased with the borrowed funds.

3. Both bonds and commercial paper represent debt financing sources for a firm.

4. The higher a firm's probability of default, the lower the interest rate charged for a loan.

5. A call feature on a bond allows the issuing firm to repurchase the bond before maturity.

6. Par value represents the rate of interest charged on loans to the most creditworthy firms.

7. Preferred stock is a security that represents partial ownership of a particular firm and offers specific priorities over common stock.

8. When firms obtain all new financing by going public, they do not increase future interest payments to creditors.

9. The issuance of an excessive amount of securities by a firm can cause a decline in the market price of the securities because the supply issued may exceed the demand.

10. A firm can increase its financial leverage by increasing the proportion of equity financing in its capital structure.

## Multiple Choice

11. Firms obtain capital (funds) in the form of:
    a) inventory and accounts receivable.
    b) revenues and expenses.
    c) equity and assets.
    d) working capital and cost of goods sold.
    e) debt and equity.

12. Compared to service businesses, manufacturing firms:
    a) borrow more funds.
    b) have fewer dollars invested in assets.
    c) pay larger dividends.
    d) use less financial leverage.
    e) accumulate less retained earnings.

13. When assessing the creditworthiness of a business, a lender will consider all of the following factors except:
    a) planned use of the borrowed funds.
    b) financial condition of the firm.
    c) industry outlook.
    d) voting rights of preferred stockholders.
    e) availability of collateral.

14. When a firm applies for a loan, it must organize and project its future revenue and expenses in a detailed:
    a) marketing mix.
    b) production plan.
    c) accounting plan.
    d) financial plan.
    e) production schedule.

15. Long-term debt securities purchased by investors are called:
    a) corporate bonds.
    b) common stock.
    c) preferred stock.
    d) accounts payable.
    e) notes payable.

16. Firms that need funds and expect interest rates to fall will likely:
    a) pay dividends to their stockholders.
    b) borrow funds at double the prime rate.
    c) borrow funds with a fixed-rate loan.
    d) borrow funds with a floating-rate loan.
    e) default on their existing bonds.

17. When a firm plans to issue bonds, it explains its obligations to bondholders in a legal document known as a(n):
    a) equity ownership.
    b) asset acquisition.
    c) sales revenue.
    d) indenture.
    e) note payable.

18. The interest rate paid on bonds issued by firms is influenced not only by prevailing interest rates but also by the firm's:
    a) retained earnings.
    b) risk level.
    c) dividend policy.
    d) earnings per share.
    e) return on equity.

19. Moody's and Standard & Poor's:
    a) rate the firm's ability to cover interest payments on its existing debt.
    b) organize investor syndicates.
    c) issue initial public offerings.
    d) evaluate the credibility of the firm's financial statements.
    e) predict the amount of dividends the firm will pay in the future.

20. Creditors that can provide debt financing to firms include all of the following except:
    a) commercial banks.
    b) insurance companies.
    c) management consultants.
    d) pension funds.
    e) mutual funds.

21. Investment companies that invest pooled funds from individual investors are:
    a) mutual funds.
    b) bond indentures.
    c) new primary issues.
    d) retained earnings.
    e) cash dividends.

22. _____ represent(s) earnings of the firm that are reinvested into the business.
    a) Dividends
    b) Collateral
    c) Retained earnings
    d) Working capital
    e) Capital structure

23. If a privately held firm desires to obtain additional funds and "go public," it will:
    a) borrow funds from a commercial bank.
    b) sell bonds in the primary market.
    c) merge with a multinational corporation.
    d) engage in a public commercial paper offering.
    e) engage in an initial public offering.

24. A group of investment banks that share the obligations of underwriting the securities is a(n):
    a) bond indenture.
    b) corporate charter.
    c) savings and loan institution.
    d) mutual savings bank.
    e) underwriting syndicate.

25. Fees charged by investment banks for their efforts in selling a firm's securities are called:
    a) coupon payments.
    b) best-effort fees.
    c) cost of capital.
    d) interest fees.
    e) flotation costs.

26. Corporate stock and bond issues must be registered with the:
    a) Federal Trade Commission.
    b) Securities and Exchange Commission.
    c) Internal Revenue Service.
    d) Department of Commerce.
    e) Bureau of Labor.

27. Some firms prefer to finance the use of assets by renting the assets for a specified period of time. This is referred to as:
    a) capital structure.
    b) leasing.
    c) retained earnings.
    d) sales revenue.
    e) notes payable.

28. The composition of debt versus equity financing is known as:
    a) retained earnings.
    b) revenue.
    c) asset composition.
    d) working capital.
    e) capital structure.

29. A firm with mostly debt in its capital structure will likely have:
    a) low inventory turnover.
    b) high accounts receivable.
    c) high retained earnings.
    d) a large amount of preferred stock.
    e) high interest payments.

30. Shareholder expectations and the firm's financing needs are two characteristics that can influence the firm's:
    a) exchange rates.
    b) governmental relationships.
    c) dividend policy.
    d) foreign exchange.
    e) counter trade.

**True/False**

| | |
|---|---|
| 1. False | 6. False |
| 2. True | 7. True |
| 3. True | 8. True |
| 4. False | 9. True |
| 5. True | 10. False |

**Multiple Choice**

| | | |
|---|---|---|
| 11. e | 18. b | 25. e |
| 12. a | 19. a | 26. b |
| 13. d | 20. c | 27. b |
| 14. d | 21. a | 28. e |
| 15. a | 22. c | 29. e |
| 16. d | 23. e | 30. c |
| 17. d | 24. e | |

## Self-Test of Key Terms

best-efforts basis   554
bond mutual funds   549
bonds   546
call feature   547
capital   542
capital structure   558
collateral   543
commercial banks   549
commercial paper   548
common stock   550
composition   563
debt financing   542
dividend policy   550
equity financing   549

extension   562
finance companies   549
flotation costs   555
indenture   547
initial public offering (IPO)   551
insurance companies   549
leasing   556
liquidation value   563
mutual funds   549
par value   546
pension funds   549
preferred stock   550
prime rate   544
private liquidation   563

private placement   555
prospectus   554
protective covenants   548
public offering   554
savings institutions   549
secondary market   553
secured bonds   547
stock mutual funds   551
underwriting syndicate   554
underwritten   554
unsecured bonds   547
venture capital firm   551

Fill in each blank with the proper key term. To assess your understanding of the key terms, answers are provided at the end of this self-test.

1. Some firms prefer to finance the use of assets by _____, or renting the assets for a specified period of time.

2. The rate of interest typically charged on loans to the most creditworthy firms is called the _____.

3. Creditors may allow firms a(n) _____, which provides additional time for the firm to generate the necessary cash to cover its payments.

4. A(n) _____ of stock is the selling of stock to the public.

5. _____ bonds are backed by collateral.

6. A firm's _____ is the amount of its debt versus equity financing.

7. A(n) _____ provides the issuing firm with the right to repurchase bonds before maturity.

8. A firm's decision regarding how much of its earnings should be retained versus distributed to shareholders is referred to as the firm's _____.

9. _____ are fees paid to investment banks for selling securities issued by the firm.

10. _____ is a security that represents partial ownership of a particular firm.

11. A(n) _____ of stock represents the first issue of stock to the public by a firm.

12. In a(n) _____ agreement, a failing firm will provide its creditors with a portion of what they are owed.

13. A(n) _____ is a legal document that explains the firm's obligations to its bondholders.

14. A(n) _____ is the selling of securities to one or a few investors.

15. Firms that need to borrow money may be asked to pledge their assets as _____ to back the loan.

16. _____ is a short-term debt security normally issued by firms in good financial condition.

17. The _____ of a bond is the amount of money that bondholders receive when the bond matures.

18. _____ are restrictions imposed by creditors on specific financial policies of the firm.

**Answers:**

1. leasing
2. prime rate
3. extension
4. public offering
5. Secured
6. capital structure
7. call feature
8. dividend policy
9. Flotation costs
10. Common stock
11. initial public offering
12. composition
13. indenture
14. private placement
15. collateral
16. Commercial paper
17. par value
18. Protective covenants

# Concept Review Questions

1. **Collateral.** Explain the role of collateral and how it can make it easier for a business to obtain a loan.

2. **Prime Rate.** What is the prime rate, and how is it used to set rates on loans to businesses?

3. **Floating-Rate Loan.** Explain how a firm's interest expenses would change during a four-year period of rising interest rates if it obtains a floating-rate loan at the beginning of the period.

4. **Bonds.** Explain why firms issue bonds. What is par value? hat are protective covenants?

5. **Secured Versus Unsecured Bonds.** Explain the difference between secured and unsecured bonds.

6. **Indenture.** When a firm plans to issue bonds, what is the role of an indenture?

7. **Financial Institutions.** Identify the common types of financial institutions that serve as creditors for firms.

8. **Equity Financing.** What are the two common methods that firms use to obtain equity financing?

9. **Initial Public Offering.** What is an initial public offering (IPO)? What are some disadvantages of engaging in an IPO?

10. **Debt Financing.** Why might owners of a firm prefer to use debt financing rather than equity financing?

# Class Communication Questions

1. **Going Public.** You are one of 10 owners of a business that has expanded substantially and has performed very well. You and the other owners have complete control of the business and are very focused on making the business efficient. Some of the owners want to go public so that they can sell their ownership shares to other investors. There are many small investors who do not know the business very well, but who nonetheless would in-

vest in shares in the hope of earning a high return on their investment. Do you think going public will improve the performance of the business?

2. **Dividends.** You are a financial manager of a publicly traded firm. You expect that the firm will expand its business substantially in the future, but it already has a lot of debt. Do you think the firm should dis-tribute most of its future earnings as dividends? Explain.

3. **Funding Dilemma.** Your friend wants to expand his small business. There is considerable risk that his business could fail if economic conditions weaken. Your friend has very little of his own money invested in the business. A financial institution is willing to provide him with a loan, but at a very high interest rate. Your friend thinks that he should accept the loan. He says that if the business fails, the lender will be the loser because he does not have much money invested in the business. Will you advise your friend to accept the loan?

# Small Business Case

## Financing Decisions

Rock-On Company produces musical instruments, including guitars and drum sets, and sells them to retail stores in North Carolina. It currently has 30 owners who have already invested a total of $4 million in the firm. It used the equity to invest in its operations. Now Rock-On wants to purchase an additional manufacturing plant that will cost about $4 million. It has about $1 million in cash retained from recent earnings, so it will need to borrow the remaining $3 million to purchase this plant. If Rock-On obtains a loan, it will have to make loan payments of about $300,000 a year.

1. **Use of a Business Plan to Obtain a Loan.** If Rock-On Company pursues a loan, why would a lender require it to provide a financial plan showing how the funds would be used?

2. **Impact of Firm's Condition on Its Loan Rate.** Why would the interest rate charged on a loan to Rock-On Company be dependent on its financial condition?

3. **Equity Financing Tradeoff.** Instead of borrowing to obtain the funds to purchase an additional manufacturing plant, Rock-On Company is considering using equity funding to finance this investment. It could obtain additional equity from a venture capital firm. What is the potential advantage of obtaining equity rather than borrowing funds? What is the disadvantage of using equity financing?

4. **Leasing Decision.** If Rock-On Company wants the flexibility to expand a specific production facility it is using, would it prefer to purchase (own) or lease the facility?

# Web Insight

## eBay's IPO

At the opening of the chapter, eBay was introduced. Recall that eBay engaged in an initial public offering (IPO) in September 1998. Investors who were able to purchase eBay's stock at the time of the IPO earned a very high return on their investment in eBay in a single day. Conduct an online search using the search terms "eBay" and "IPO" and review information about eBay's IPO. By how much did eBay's price rise on the day of the IPO?

# Dell's Secrets for Success

Go to Dell's website (www.dell.com) and click on the link "About Dell," near the bottom of the web page. You can also review an annual report to obtain more information.

1. **Capital Structure.** Some firms rely more on debt than on eq-uity as a source of funds. Dell tends to use a relatively small amount of debt compared to its equity. Describe the advantage of this strategy.

2. **Initial Public Offering.** Dell's website describes its initial pub-lic offering in 1988, just four years after its business was cre-ated. It raised $30 million from its offering. Why do you think Dell needed to issue stock?

# Video Exercise

## Lessons in Business Financing

Many free business videos are avail-able on websites such as YouTube (www.youtube.com), and more are added every day. Search for a recent video clip about an existing business that offers lessons on "business fi-nancing" in YouTube or any other website that provides video clips.

1. **Main Lesson.** What is the name of the business in the video clip? Is the video clip fo-cused on why financing is criti-cal to the business, or how much financing it needs, or how it determines the compo-sition of its financing, or some other aspect of business financ-ing? What is the main lesson of the video clip that you watched?

2. **Debt Financing.** Some related videos illustrate how a business can experience problems if it obtains only debt financing and no equity financing. Explain why a business could experi-ence financial problems when most of its financing is with debt.

3. **Excessive Financing.** Some re-lated videos explain how firms that recently experienced strong growth engage in stock offerings to support future growth. Is it possible for a busi-ness to obtain more funds than it needs? If so, how could this adversely affect the business?

# Projects

To encourage further compre-hension of concepts covered in Chapter 16, the following five projects are available:

1. Analyzing Your Favorite Business

2. Building a Business Plan for Campus.com

3. Running Your Own Business

4. Planning Your Career

5. Stock Market Contest

All of these projects are provided in Appendix A at the end of the text. In addition, projects are available by part division at the end of each part. A Word file for each project is also available at the textbook website (www.emcp.net/business5e) so that you may maintain one ongoing file for each project.

# Chapter 16 Appendix
# How Interest Rates Are Determined

Firms closely monitor interest rates because they affect the cost of borrowing money. The interest rate is the price charged for borrowing money. Managers of firms should understand how interest rates change and should recognize the factors that can cause interest rates to change, as explained by this appendix.

## A1. How Interest Rates Change

The interest rate on funds to be borrowed is influenced by the supply of loanable funds (provided by depositors) and the demand for those loanable funds by borrowers. The interaction between demand and supply causes interest rates to change, as explained next.

### A1.1 Demand for Loanable Funds

To illustrate the effects of demand on interest rates, assume that the United States has only one commercial bank. The bank receives all deposits from depositors and uses all the funds to make loans to borrowers. Demand for loans by borrowers will vary with the interest rate the bank charges on loans. The higher the interest rate it charges, the lower the amount of loanable funds demanded (requested for loans). This is because some firms (and other borrowers) are unwilling to pay a high interest rate. If the interest rate is too high, firms may simply not borrow the funds they were hoping to use for expansion. Consider the demand schedule for loanable funds shown in the second column of Exhibit 16A.1. The demand schedule for loanable funds is also shown on the graph in Exhibit 16A.1 and is labeled $D_1$. This schedule shows the inverse relationship between the interest rate and the quantity of loanable funds demanded.

### A1.2 Supply of Loanable Funds

The quantity of funds supplied (by depositors) to the bank is also related to possible interest rate levels, but in a different manner. The higher the interest rate offered on deposits, the higher the quantity of loanable funds (in the form of deposits) that will be supplied by depositors to banks. The supply schedule for loanable funds to be supplied by depositors is shown in the third column of Exhibit 16A.1. It is also shown on

**Exhibit 16A.1**

How the Demand for and Supply of Loanable Funds Affect Interest Rates

| At an Interest Rate of: | The Quantity of Loanable Funds Demanded by Borrowers Would Be: | The Quantity of Loanable Funds Supplied by Savers Would Be: |
|---|---|---|
| 12% | $300 billion | $500 billion |
| 10% | 350 billion | 450 billion |
| 8% | 400 billion | 400 billion |
| 6% | 450 billion | 350 billion |

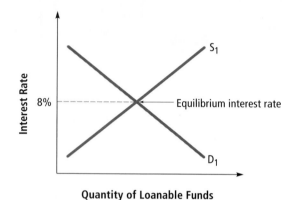

the accompanying graph and is labeled $S_1$. This schedule shows the positive relationship between the interest rate and the quantity of funds supplied.

## A1.3 Combining Demand and Supply

Interest rates are determined by the interaction of the demand and supply schedules for loanable funds. Notice in Exhibit 16A.1 that at relatively high interest rates (such as 12 percent), the quantity of loanable funds supplied exceeds the quantity of loanable funds demanded, resulting in a surplus of loanable funds. When the interest rate is relatively low (such as 6 percent), the quantity of loanable funds supplied is less than the quantity of loanable funds demanded, resulting in a shortage of funds.

Notice from Exhibit 16A.1 that at the interest rate of 8 percent, the quantity of loanable funds supplied by depositors is $400 billion, which is equal to the quantity of loanable funds demanded by borrowers. At this interest rate, there is no surplus or shortage of loanable funds. The interest rate at which the quantity of loanable funds supplied is equal to the quantity of loanable funds demanded is called the **equilibrium interest rate.**

**equilibrium interest rate** the interest rate at which the quantity of loanable funds supplied is equal to the quantity of loanable funds demanded

## A1.4 Effect of a Change in the Demand Schedule

As time passes, conditions may change, causing the demand schedule of loanable funds to change. Consequently, a change will occur in the equilibrium interest rate. Reconsider the previous example and assume that most firms suddenly decide to expand their business operations. This decision may result from optimistic news about the economy. Those firms that decide to expand will need to borrow additional funds

| | | |
|---|---|---|
| | | **But the Quantity of Loanable Funds Demanded Would Now Be:** |
| **At an Interest Rate of:** | **The Quantity of Loanable Funds Demanded Was:** | |
| 12% | $300 billion | $400 billion |
| 10% | 350 billion | 450 billion |
| 8% | 400 billion | 500 billion |
| 6% | 450 billion | 550 billion |

**Exhibit 16A.2**

Effect of a Change in the Demand for Loanable Funds on Interest Rates

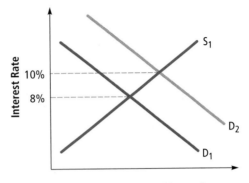

from the bank. Assume that the demand schedule for loanable funds changes, as shown in Exhibit 16A.2. The graph in the exhibit shows that the demand curve shifts outward from $D_1$ to $D_2$.

Now consider the effect of this change in the demand for loanable funds on the equilibrium interest rate, as shown in Exhibit 16A.2. Assuming that the supply schedule of loanable funds remains unchanged, there is now a shortage of loanable funds at the equilibrium interest rate. However, at an interest rate of 10 percent, the quantity of loanable funds supplied by savers will once again equal the quantity of loanable funds demanded by borrowers. Therefore, the new equilibrium interest rate is 10 percent. The graph in Exhibit 16A.2 confirms that the new equilibrium interest rate is 10 percent.

## A1.5   Effect of a Change in the Supply Schedule

Just as the demand schedule for loanable funds may change, so may the supply schedule. To illustrate how a change in the supply schedule can affect the interest rate, reconsider the original example in which the equilibrium interest was 8 percent. Now assume that savers decide to save more funds than they did before, which results in a new supply schedule of loanable funds, as shown in Exhibit 16A.3. At any given interest rate, the quantity of loanable funds supplied is now higher than it was before. The graph in Exhibit 16A.3 shows how the supply curve shifts out from $S_1$ to $S_2$.

Now consider the effect of the shift in the supply schedule on the equilibrium interest rate. Assuming that the demand schedule remains unchanged, the supply of loanable funds will exceed the demand for loanable funds at the previous equilibrium interest rate of 8 percent. However, at an equilibrium interest rate of 6 percent, the quantity of loanable funds supplied by savers will equal the quantity of loanable

Effect of a Change in the Supply of Loanable Funds on Interest Rates

| At an Interest Rate of: | The Quantity of Loanable Funds Supplied by Savers Was: | But the Quantity of Loanable Funds Supplied by Savers Would Now Be: |
|---|---|---|
| 12% | $500 billion | $600 billion |
| 10% | 450 billion | 550 billion |
| 8% | 400 billion | 500 billion |
| 6% | 350 billion | 450 billion |

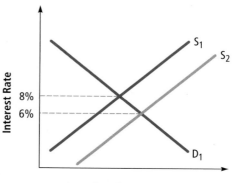

**Quantity of Loanable Funds**

funds demanded by borrowers. The graph in Exhibit 16A.3 confirms that the shift in the supply schedule from $S_1$ to $S_2$ causes a new equilibrium interest rate of 6 percent.

This discussion of interest rates has assumed just one single commercial bank that receives all deposits from savers and provides those funds as loans to borrowers. In reality, many commercial banks and other financial institutions provide this service. Nevertheless, this does not affect the general discussion of interest rates. The equilibrium interest rate in the United States is determined by the interaction of the total demand for loanable funds by all U.S. borrowers and the total supply of loanable funds provided by all U.S. savers.

## A2. Factors That Can Affect Interest Rates

Several factors can cause shifts in the demand schedule or supply schedule of loanable funds and therefore can cause shifts in equilibrium interest rates. Firms monitor these factors so that they can anticipate how interest rates may change in the future. In this way, firms can anticipate how their interest owed on borrowed funds may change.

### A2.1 Monetary Policy

Recall that the Federal Reserve System can affect interest rates by implementing monetary policy. As the money supply is adjusted, so is the supply of funds that can be lent out by financial institutions. When the Fed increases the supply of funds, interest rates decrease (assuming no change in demand for funds). Conversely, when the Fed reduces the supply of funds, interest rates increase.

## A2.2    Economic Growth

When economic conditions become more favorable, firms tend to make more plans for expansion. They borrow more money, which reflects an increase in their demand for loanable funds. Assuming that the supply of loanable funds remains unchanged, the increased demand for loanable funds will result in a higher equilibrium interest rate.

The *Wall Street Journal, BusinessWeek,* and other business publications frequently monitor the indicators of economic growth and suggest how interest rates may be affected. A typical headline might be something like this: "Economic Growth Increases; Higher Interest Rates Expected." When firms read this headline, they may interpret it as both good news and bad. The good news is higher economic growth, which may increase the demand for the firm's products, thereby increasing the firm's revenue. The bad news is that if the higher economic growth leads to higher interest rates, it may also increase the annual interest expenses owed by the firm on its borrowed funds.

Conversely, a decline in economic growth can cause firms to reduce their plans for expansion. If firms expect poor economic conditions, they may decide not to expand because they anticipate that the demand for their products may decline. If firms demand (borrow) less loanable funds, and the supply of loanable funds remains unchanged, the equilibrium interest rate will decline.

As an example of the relationship just described, consider the effects of the weak economy during 2008 and 2009. In that period, firms lowered their demand for loans because of pessimism about the future, and interest rates decreased substantially.

## A2.3    Expected Inflation

When consumers and firms expect a high rate of inflation, they tend to borrow more money. To understand why, assume you plan to purchase a Ford Mustang in two years, once you have saved enough money to pay for it with cash. However, if you believe that the price of the Mustang you wish to purchase will rise substantially by then, you may decide to use borrowed funds to buy it now before the price rises. So, when the rate of inflation in the United States is high (or is expected to be high in the near future), many consumers attempt to purchase automobiles, homes, or other products before the prices rise. Firms may also purchase machinery or buildings before the prices rise. These conditions cause an increase in the demand for loanable funds by consumers and firms, which results in higher interest rates. This explains why U.S. interest rates tend to be high when U.S. inflation is high.

Expectations of lower inflation can have the opposite effect. Consumers and firms may be more willing to defer making some purchases if they cannot afford them. They may wait until they are in a better financial situation. When planned purchases are put off until the future, consumers and firms do not need to borrow as much money. Given a lower demand for loanable funds, the interest rate should decline.

Changes in expected inflation could also affect the supply of loanable funds. However, the demand for loanable funds tends to be much more sensitive than the supply of loanable funds to changes in expected inflation.

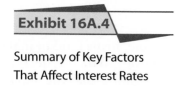

**Exhibit 16A.4**

Summary of Key Factors
That Affect Interest Rates

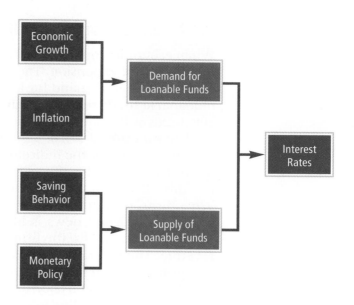

## A2.4 Saving Behavior

As the saving behavior of people changes, so does the supply schedule of loanable funds, and so does the interest rate. For example, if people become more willing to save money, this increases the amount of money that will be deposited in banks at any possible interest rate. Since the amount of funds that can be loaned out by banks to borrowers has increased, a surplus of funds is available at the previous equilibrium interest rate. Therefore, the new equilibrium interest rate will decline to the level at which the quantity of funds supplied equals the quantity of funds demanded.

## A2.5 Summary of Factors That Affect Interest Rates

Four factors that influence interest rates have been identified and are illustrated in Exhibit 16A.4. The main effects of economic growth and inflation on interest rates occur as a result of influencing the demand for loanable funds. The main effects of saving behavior and monetary policy on interest rates occur as a result of influencing the supply of loanable funds.

The factors that affect interest rates can all change at the same time. One factor may be pushing interest rates up while the others are pushing interest rates down. The final effect on interest rates may depend on which factor has the biggest impact.

# Expanding the Business

© SHUTTERSTOCK/NACI YAVUZ

## Chapter 17 Learning Objectives

**1** Explain capital budgeting and identify the types of investment decisions that a firm may make.

**2** Describe the capital budgeting tasks that are necessary to make business investment decisions.

**3** Describe the motive for investing in other firms (acquisitions), explain the merger process, and identify other types of restructuring that firms may use.

**4** Explain how firms make decisions for investing in short-term assets.

# Chapter 17

## Expansion Decisions by Netflix

Whereas the previous chapter focused on how firms obtain funds (financing), this chapter focuses on how firms utilize funds (business investment). A firm makes short-term investment decisions when it considers investing in accounts receivable and inventory. It makes long-term investment decisions when it considers investing in long-term assets. Consider the situation of Netflix, which has quickly become the world's largest online entertainment subscription service. It offers DVD rentals by delivery or online. The business was created in 1999, and just three years later, Netflix raised $82.5 million from its initial public offering of stock. It used the funds to support its growth. Netflix now generates revenue of more than $1 billion per year. As Netflix expands its business, it must address the following questions:

✦ What types of investments should it consider?

✦ What tasks are necessary to make business investment decisions?

✦ How can it conduct an analysis of proposed investments to decide whether they are feasible?

✦ How should it make decisions to invest in short-term assets?

If Netflix can make investment decisions properly, it will use its funds in a manner that benefits its owners. In other words, the benefits from expansion will exceed the costs. Netflix's decisions on investing in short-term assets are also intended to enhance its business performance by using funds in an efficient manner.

The types of decisions described here are necessary for all businesses. This chapter explains how Netflix or any other firm can make investment decisions in a manner that maximizes the firm's value.

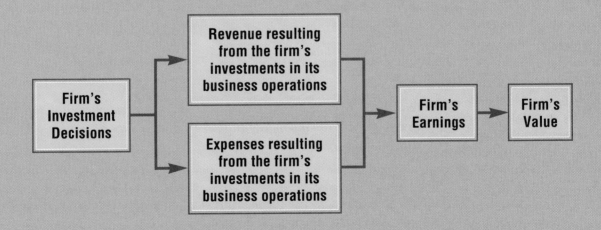

**Learning Objective**

**1**

Explain capital budgeting and identify the types of investment decisions that a firm may make.

**capital budgeting**
a comparison of the costs and benefits of a proposed project to determine whether it is feasible

# 1. Investment Decisions

Firms continually evaluate potential projects in which they may invest, such as the construction of a new building or the purchase of a machine. Many firms plan for growth every year. DuPont, IBM, and 3M Company expand by continually creating new products. Retailers such as The Gap and Abercrombie & Fitch expand by establishing new stores. To decide whether proposed projects should be implemented, firms such as The Gap conduct **capital budgeting**, which is a comparison of the costs and benefits of a proposed project to determine whether it is feasible. The costs of a project include the initial outlay (payment) for the project, along with the periodic costs of maintaining the project. The benefits of a project are the revenue it generates.

For example, when McDonald's establishes a new restaurant, the initial outlay includes the construction of the building, the furniture needed, utensils, and cooking facilities. It also includes costs of food as well as labor. The benefits of this project are the revenue that the restaurant will generate over time. In most cases, the precise amounts of a project's costs and benefits are not known in advance and can only be estimated.

Many decisions that result from capital budgeting are irreversible. That is, if the project does not generate the benefits expected, it is too late to reverse the decision. For example, if a restaurant is unsuccessful, its selling price will likely be much lower than the cost of establishing it.

To illustrate how an inaccurate budgeting analysis can affect the firm, consider the case of Converse, which invested in a company called Apex One. Unfortunately, Converse underestimated the expenses involved in this project and overestimated the revenue. Consequently, just three months after the initial outlay, Converse terminated the project and incurred a $41.6 million loss. As an illustration of how firms focus on each project's return versus its cost, consider the following statements from recent financial reports:

*"The company's strategic plan continues to focus on capital efficiency and return on investment."*

—Wal-Mart

*"With a return on capital roughly three times our cost of capital, this strategy [of borrowing more funds to expand] makes even more sense now than before."*

—The Coca-Cola Company

*"All of our divisions use the measurement of return on invested capital relative to the cost of capital as their standard."*

—Textron

## 1.1 How Interest Rates Affect Investment Decisions

Interest rates determine the cost of borrowed funds. A change in interest rates can affect the cost of borrowing as well as the project's feasibility. Firms require a return on projects that exceeds their cost of funds. If

Businesses need financing in order to invest in new office buildings (like the one shown here), new machinery, or new equipment. A firm's investments are constrained by its capital budget, which is typically influenced by how much funding it can obtain. Some firms lease their workplace space so that they do not need to make such a large investment.

**capital budget**
a targeted amount of funds to be used for purchasing assets such as buildings, machinery, and equipment that are needed for long-term projects

© SHUTTERSTOCK/UKRPHOTO

they use borrowed funds to finance a project and pay 15 percent on those funds, they would require a return of at least 15 percent on that project. If interest rates decrease, the cost of financing decreases, and the firm's required rate of return decreases. Thus, a project once perceived by the firm as unfeasible may be feasible once the firm's required rate of return is lowered.

## 1.2  Capital Budget

Firms plan a **capital budget**, or a targeted amount of funds to be used for purchasing assets such as buildings, machinery, and equipment that are needed for long-term projects. The annual capital budget for firms such as PepsiCo, The Coca-Cola Company, IBM, and ExxonMobil commonly exceeds $1 billion. The size of a firm's capital budget is influenced by the amount and size of feasible business projects.

A firm's capital budget can be allocated across its various businesses. PepsiCo distributes its capital budget across snack foods and beverages.

A capital budget can also be segmented by geographic markets. PepsiCo allocates its capital budget for projects in the United States and for projects in foreign countries.

## 1.3  Classification of Capital Expenditures

The types of potential capital expenditures considered by a firm can be broadly classified into the following three categories.

**Expansion of Current Business**    If the demand for a firm's products increases, a firm invests in additional assets (such as machinery or equipment) to produce a large enough volume of products to accommodate the increased demand. For example, many health-care firms have increased their capital budgets as they anticipate an increase in demand for their products.

**Development of New Business**    When firms expand the line of products that they produce and sell, they need new facilities for production. They may also need to hire employees to produce and sell the new products. Car manufacturers may invest millions of dollars per year to add new products such as hybrid cars and to improve their exporting capabilities.

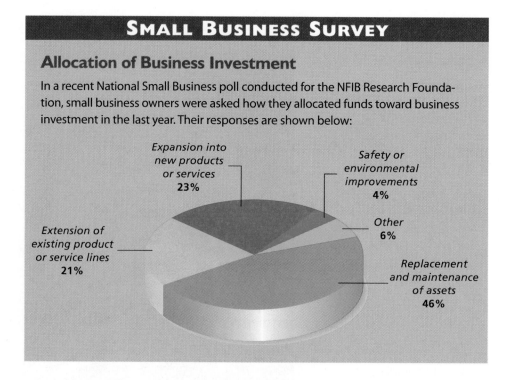

## SMALL BUSINESS SURVEY

### Allocation of Business Investment

In a recent National Small Business poll conducted for the NFIB Research Foundation, small business owners were asked how they allocated funds toward business investment in the last year. Their responses are shown below:

- Expansion into new products or services **23%**
- Safety or environmental improvements **4%**
- Other **6%**
- Extension of existing product or service lines **21%**
- Replacement and maintenance of assets **46%**

**Investment in Assets That Will Reduce Expenses**  Machines and equipment wear out or become technologically obsolete over time. Firms replace old machines and equipment to capitalize on new technology, which may allow for lower expenses over time. For example, a new computer may be able to generate a firm's financial reports more economically than an older computer. The benefits of lower expenses may outweigh the initial outlay needed to purchase the new computer.

Firms also purchase machines that can perform the work of employees. For example, machines rather than employees could be used on an assembly line to package a product. The benefits of these machines are the cost savings that result from employing fewer workers. To

Businesses commonly invest funds in technologically advanced machinery so that they can reduce expenses. They will purchase new machinery if they believe that the cost is less than the amount of money saved by using this machinery to produce products.

determine whether the machines are feasible for this purpose, the cost savings must be compared with the price of the machines.

**2** 

# 2.   Capital Budgeting Tasks

The process of capital budgeting involves five tasks:

✦  Proposing new projects

✦  Estimating cash flows of projects

✦  Determining whether projects are feasible

✦  Implementing feasible projects

✦  Monitoring projects that were implemented

## 2.1   Proposing New Projects

New projects are continually proposed within the firm as various departments or divisions offer input on new projects to consider.

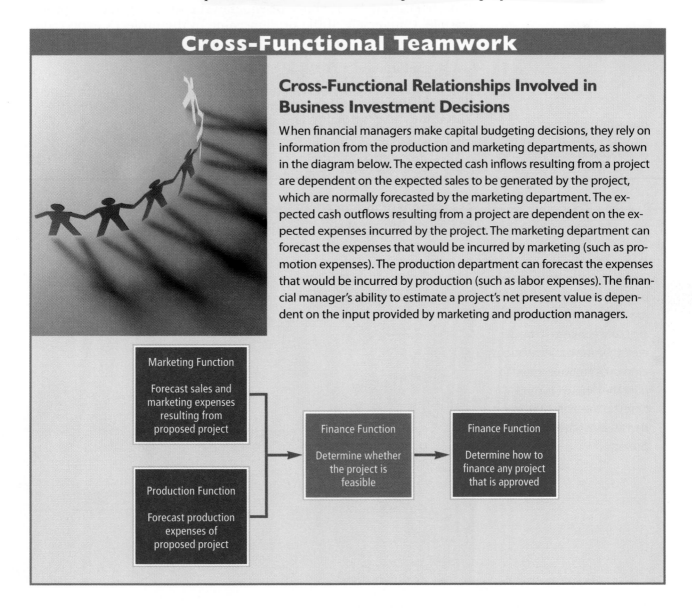

# Cross-Functional Teamwork

### Cross-Functional Relationships Involved in Business Investment Decisions

When financial managers make capital budgeting decisions, they rely on information from the production and marketing departments, as shown in the diagram below. The expected cash inflows resulting from a project are dependent on the expected sales to be generated by the project, which are normally forecasted by the marketing department. The expected cash outflows resulting from a project are dependent on the expected expenses incurred by the project. The marketing department can forecast the expenses that would be incurred by marketing (such as promotion expenses). The production department can forecast the expenses that would be incurred by production (such as labor expenses). The financial manager's ability to estimate a project's net present value is dependent on the input provided by marketing and production managers.

**Marketing Function**

Forecast sales and marketing expenses resulting from proposed project

**Production Function**

Forecast production expenses of proposed project

**Finance Function**

Determine whether the project is feasible

**Finance Function**

Determine how to finance any project that is approved

## 2.2 Estimating Cash Flows of Projects

Each potential project affects the cash flows of the firm. Estimating the cash flows that will result from the project is a critical part of the capital budgeting process. Revenue received from the project represents cash inflows, while payments to cover the project's expenses represent cash outflows. The decision whether to make a capital expenditure is based on the size of the periodic cash flows (defined as cash inflows minus cash outflows per period) that are expected to occur as a result of the project.

## 2.3 Determining Whether Projects Are Feasible

Once potential projects are proposed and their cash flows estimated, the projects must be evaluated to determine whether they are feasible. Specific techniques are available to assess the feasibility of projects. One popular method is the net present value technique, which compares the expected periodic cash flows resulting from the project with the initial outlay needed to finance the project. If the present value of the project's expected cash flows is above or equal to the initial outlay, the project is feasible. Conversely, if the present value of the project's expected cash flows is below the initial outlay, the project is not feasible.

**mutually exclusive**
the situation in which only one of two projects designed for the same purpose can be accepted

**Assessment of Mutually Exclusive Projects**   In some cases, the evaluation involves deciding between two projects designed for the same purpose. When only one of the projects can be accepted, such projects are referred to as **mutually exclusive**. For example, a firm may be considering two machines that perform the same task. The two alternative machines are mutually exclusive because the purchase of one machine precludes the purchase of the other.

**Assessment of Independent Projects**   When the decision of whether to adopt one project has no bearing on the adoption of other projects, the

The proposal and assessment of a project typically involve projections of the revenue, cost, and earnings to be generated by the project. Various employees may be asked to offer their input (as shown here) on the estimated expenses associated with the project.

© SHUTTERSTOCK/ZSOLT NYULASZI

**independent project**
a project whose feasibility can be assessed without consideration of any others

project is said to be **independent**. For example, the purchase of a truck to enhance delivery capabilities and the purchase of a large computer system to handle payroll processing are independent projects. That is, the acceptance (or rejection) of one project does not influence the acceptance (or rejection) of the other project.

## 2.4  Implementing Feasible Projects

Once the firm has determined which projects are feasible, it must focus on implementing those projects. All feasible projects should be given a priority status so that those projects that fulfill immediate needs can be implemented first. As part of the implementation process, the firm must obtain the necessary funds to finance the projects.

## 2.5  Monitoring Projects That Were Implemented

After a project has been implemented, it should be monitored over time. The project's actual costs and benefits should be compared with the estimates made before the project was implemented. The monitoring process may detect errors in the previous estimation of the project's cash flows. If any errors are detected, the employees who were responsible for project evaluation should be informed of the problem so that future projects can be evaluated more accurately.

A second purpose of monitoring is to detect and correct inefficiencies in the current operation of the project. Furthermore, monitoring can help determine if and when a project should be abandoned (liquidated) by the firm.

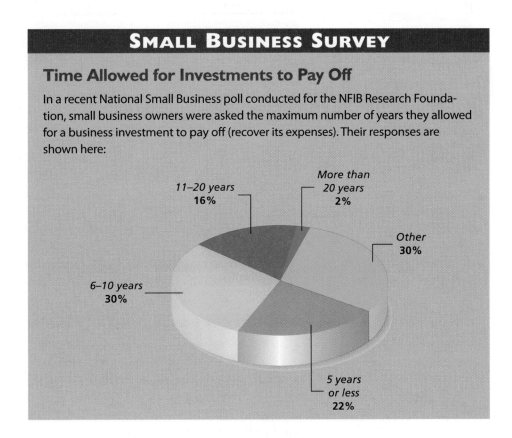

## SMALL BUSINESS SURVEY

### Time Allowed for Investments to Pay Off

In a recent National Small Business poll conducted for the NFIB Research Foundation, small business owners were asked the maximum number of years they allowed for a business investment to pay off (recover its expenses). Their responses are shown here:

11–20 years
**16%**

More than 20 years
**2%**

Other
**30%**

6–10 years
**30%**

5 years or less
**22%**

# Global Business

## Global Investing

U.S. firms frequently consider investing funds in foreign projects. The Coca-Cola Company commonly invests more than $1 billion per year to expand its worldwide business. It typically invests the bulk of its capital budget overseas, because international markets offer more opportunities for the company.

When U.S. firms such as Coca-Cola consider the purchase of a foreign company, they conduct a capital budgeting analysis to determine whether the project is feasible. The capital budgeting analysis required to assess a foreign project is more complex than the analysis for a domestic project because of the need to assess specific characteristics of the foreign country. For example, the initial outlay required to purchase the foreign firm will depend on the exchange rate between the dollar and the currency of the foreign country at that time. The lower the value of the foreign currency, the lower the initial outlay required to invest in that country. Firms prefer to invest in foreign companies (or any other foreign projects) when the dollar is strong and the foreign currency is weak.

Another consideration is political risk. Foreign projects in developing countries are especially risky because they could be terminated by the governments of those countries. This point is especially important in light of the recent trend U.S. firms investing in large projects based in developing countries. For example, in 2008 PepsiCo announced that it plans to invest $500 million in India over the next three years and $1 billion in China over the next four years. The large amount that PepsiCo plans to invest in these countries suggests that it expects the projects to generate very high returns, making them worthwhile even though they are riskier than projects in the United States.

---

**Exhibit 17.1**

Summary of Capital Budgeting Tasks

| Task | Description |
|------|-------------|
| Propose new projects. | Propose new projects that require expenditures necessary to support expansion of existing businesses, development of new businesses, or replacement of old assets. |
| Estimate cash flows of projects. | Cash flows in each period can be estimated as the cash inflows (such as revenue) resulting from the project minus cash outflows (expenses) resulting from the project. |
| Determine whether projects are feasible. | A project is feasible if the present value of its future cash flows exceeds the initial outlay needed to purchase the project. |
| Implement feasible projects. | Feasible projects should be implemented, with priority given to those projects that fulfill immediate needs. |
| Monitor projects that were implemented. | Projects that have been implemented need to be monitored to determine whether their cash flows were estimated properly. Monitoring may also detect inefficiencies in the project and can help determine when a project should be abandoned. |

## 2.6  Summary of Capital Budgeting Tasks

The five tasks necessary to conduct capital budgeting are summarized in Exhibit 17.1. The most challenging task is the estimation of cash flows, because it is difficult to accurately measure the revenue and expenses that will result from a particular project.

**Learning Objective** **3**

Describe the motives for investing in other firms (acquisitions), explain the merger process, and identify other types of restructuring that firms may use.

**merger**
two firms are merged (or combined) to become a single firm owned by the same owners (shareholders)

**horizontal merger**
the combination of firms that engage in the same types of business

**vertical merger**
the combination of a firm with a potential supplier or customer

**conglomerate merger**
the combination of two firms in unrelated businesses

# 3. Mergers

Among the most expensive projects that a firm may consider are investments in other firms through acquistions. The different types of mergers that firms may engage in are described here, followed by an examination of the motives for mergers and the merger process. Firms may also engage in other forms of restructuring including leveraged buyouts and divestitures, and those are described as well.

## 3.1  Types of Mergers

A firm may invest in another company by purchasing all the stock of that company. This results in a **merger**, in which two firms are merged (or combined) to become a single firm owned by the same owners (shareholders). A merger may be feasible if it can increase a firm's value either by increasing the return to the firm's owners or by reducing the firm's risk without a reduction in return. Mergers can be classified as one of three types, as explained below.

**Horizontal Mergers**   A **horizontal merger** is the combination of firms that engage in the same types of business. For example, the merger between Wells Fargo & Company and Wachovia Corporation was a horizontal merger, as it combined two large commercial banks.

**Vertical Mergers**   A **vertical merger** is the combination of a firm with a potential supplier or customer, such as General Motors' acquisition of a battery manufacturer that could produce the batteries for many of its automobiles.

**Conglomerate Mergers**   A **conglomerate merger** is the combination of two firms in unrelated businesses. For example, a merger between a book publisher and a steel manufacturer would be a conglomerate merger. The term *conglomerate* is sometimes used to describe a firm that is engaged in a variety of unrelated businesses.

## 3.2  Corporate Motives for Mergers

Mergers are normally initiated as a result of one or more of the following motives.

**Immediate Growth**   A firm that plans for growth may prefer to achieve its objective immediately through a merger. Consider a firm whose production capacity cannot fully satisfy demand for its product. The firm would need two years to build additional production facilities. To achieve an immediate increase in production, the firm may search for a company that owns the appropriate facilities. By acquiring either part or all of such a company, the firm can achieve immediate growth in its production capacity, thereby allowing for growth in its sales. When Walt Disney Company purchased Capital Cities/ABC, it created more growth potential than if it had simply attempted to expand its existing businesses.

**Economies of Scale**   Growth may also be desirable to reduce the production cost per unit. Products that exhibit economies of scale can be

**Exhibit 17.2**

Illustration of How an Acquisition Can Generate Economies of Scale

| Firm | Total Output Produced | Variable Cost per Unit | Variable Cost | Fixed Cost (Rent) | Total Cost | Average Cost per Unit |
|---|---|---|---|---|---|---|
| A | 500 units | $10 | $5,000 | $6,000 | $11,000 | ($11,000/500) = $22.00 |
| B | 400 units | $10 | $4,000 | $6,000 | $10,000 | ($10,000/400) = $25.00 |
| A & B Combined | 900 units | $10 | $9,000 | $6,000 | $15,000 | ($15,000/900) = $16.67 |

produced at a much lower cost per unit if a large amount is produced. A merger may allow a firm to combine two production facilities and thereby achieve a lower production cost per unit.

For example, assume that Firm A and Firm B produce a similar product. Also assume that each firm uses an assembly-line operation for about eight hours per day and sells its product to its own set of customers. Firm A sells 500 units per month, while Firm B sells 400 units per month. The variable cost per unit is $10 for each firm. Each firm pays $6,000 per month to rent its own factory. This rent is a fixed cost because it is not affected by the amount of the product produced. If Firm A acquires Firm B, it will be able to serve both sets of customers, which will result in a higher production level. The factory can be used for 16 hours a day by running a second shift for the assembly line.

Based on the initial assumptions, the average cost per unit for each firm is shown in Exhibit 17.2. Notice that when Firm A acquires Firm B, the average cost per unit is lower than it was for either individual firm. This occurs because only one factory is needed when the firms are merged. Thus, the average cost per unit declines when Firm A makes more efficient use of the factory.

There may be additional ways for the combination of firms to reduce costs, beyond the savings resulting from renting only one factory. For example, assume each firm has its own accountant. Each firm pays a salary for this position, which reflects a fixed cost. However, Firm A's accountant may be able to cover all the accounting duties for the combined firm, which means that it need not incur the cost of Firm B's accountant. Therefore, it can further reduce costs by removing any job positions in Firm B that can be handled by Firm A's existing employees.

Horizontal mergers are more likely to achieve economies of scale than vertical or conglomerate mergers because they involve firms that produce similar products. Firms with similar operations can eliminate similar positions once the firms are combined.

**Managerial Expertise** The performance of a firm is highly dependent on the managers who make the decisions for the firm. Since the firm's value is influenced by its performance, its value is influenced by its managers. To illustrate this point, consider a firm called "Weakfirm" that has had weak performance recently because of its managers. This firm's value should be low if its performance has been weak and is not expected to improve.

Also assume, however, that another firm in the same industry, called "Strongfirm," has more competent managers. If the managers of Strongfirm had been managing the operations of Weakfirm, the performance of Weakfirm might have been much higher. Given this information, Strongfirm may consider purchasing Weakfirm. The price for

Weakfirm should be relatively low because of its recent performance. Yet, once Strongfirm purchases Weakfirm, it can improve Weakfirm's performance. The owners (shareholders) of Strongfirm will benefit because their firm is able to acquire another firm at a relatively low price and turn it into something more valuable. In other words, the additional earnings generated by Strongfirm following the acquisition may exceed the cost of the acquisition.

The example just described occurs frequently. Some firms that have had relatively weak performance (compared with other firms in the industry) become targets. Consequently, weak firms are always in danger of being acquired.

Some mergers can be beneficial when each firm relies on the other firm for specific managerial expertise. For example, consider Disney's acquisition of the ABC television network. Disney produced movies that were sold to television networks. When television networks began to produce their own movies, Disney could have had difficulty selling its movies to various networks. By acquiring the ABC network, Disney could rely on the network to show some of its movies, while the ABC network was assured that it would be supplied with various popular Disney movies. Disney had expertise as the producer of the product (movies), and ABC had expertise as the distributor of that product. Both firms benefited as a result of the acquisition.

**Tax Benefits**    Firms that incur negative earnings (losses) are sometimes attractive candidates for mergers because of potential tax advantages. The previous losses incurred by the company prior to the merger can be carried forward to offset positive earnings of the acquiring firm. Although the losses of the acquired firm have occurred prior to the acquisition, they reduce the taxable earnings of the newly merged corporation. To illustrate the potential tax benefits, consider an acquisition in which the acquiring firm applies a $1 million loss of the acquired firm to partially offset its earnings. If the acquiring firm is subject to a 30 percent tax rate, it can reduce its taxes by $300,000 (computed as 30 percent times the $1 million in earnings that is no longer subject to tax because of applying the $1 million loss).

### 3.3  Merger Analysis

When a firm plans to engage in a merger or acquisition, it must conduct the following tasks:

+ Identify potential merger prospects.

+ Evaluate potential merger prospects.

+ Make the merger decision.

**Identify Potential Merger Prospects**    Firms attempt to identify potential merger prospects that may help them achieve their strategic plan. If the firm plans for growth in its current line of products, it will consider purchasing (or "acquiring") companies in the same business. If it needs to restructure its production process, it may attempt to acquire a supplier. If it desires a more diversified product line, it may attempt to acquire companies in unrelated businesses. The firm's long-run objectives influence the selection of merger prospects that are worthy of evaluation.

The size of the firm is also a relevant criterion, as some firms may be too small to achieve the desired objectives while others may be too large to acquire. The location is another possible criterion because a firm's product demand and production costs are dependent on its location.

**Evaluate Potential Merger Prospects** Once merger prospects have been identified, they must be analyzed thoroughly, using publicly available financial statements. The financial analysis may detect problems that will eliminate some prospects from further consideration. Prospects with deficiencies that can be corrected should still be considered, however. Along with the firm's financial condition, additional characteristics of each prospect must be assessed, including its reputation and labor-management relations. From this assessment, potential problems that may not be disclosed on financial statements can be detected.

The firm planning the acquisition needs to evaluate the prospect's specific characteristics, such as its facilities, its dependence on suppliers, and pending lawsuits. Unfortunately, a full evaluation of such specific characteristics may not be possible unless the prospect provides the information. The firm planning the acquisition may contact the prospect to request more detailed information. The prospect may comply if it is willing to consider the possibility of a merger.

**Make the Merger Decision** Once the firm has identified a specific prospect it wishes to acquire, it can assess the feasibility of acquiring that prospect by using capital budgeting analysis. Thus, the acquisition prospect can be evaluated just like any other project. The cost of this project is the outlay necessary to purchase the firm. The benefits are the extra cash flows that will be generated over time as a result of the acquisition. If the present value of the future cash flows to be received by the acquiring firm exceeds the initial outlay, the acquisition is feasible.

Mergers commonly require negotiations by representatives of the two companies.

© SHUTTERSTOCK/MARCIN BALCERZAK

## 3.4 Merger Procedures

If an attempt is made to acquire a prospect, that prospect becomes the "target." It is set apart from all the other prospects that were considered. To carry out the acquisition, firms will normally hire an investment bank for guidance. Investment banking functions are conducted by the investment banking divisions of bank holding companies such as Goldman Sachs and Bank of America, which acquired Merrill Lynch. Some firms that continuously acquire or sell businesses may employ their own investment banking department to handle many of the necessary tasks. The main tasks of a merger are:

✦ Financing the merger

✦ Bidding process

✦ Integrating the businesses

✦ Postmerger evaluation

**Financing the Merger**    A merger normally requires a substantial amount of long-term funds, as one firm may purchase the existing stock of another firm. In a common method of financing a merger, a firm issues more of its own stock to the public. As new stock is sold to the public, the proceeds are used to purchase the target's stock. Alternatively, the acquiring firm may trade its new stock to the shareholders of the target firm in exchange for their stock. Instead of issuing new stock, the acquiring firm may also borrow the necessary funds to purchase the target's stock from its shareholders. Some mergers, called **leverage buyouts**, are financed completely with debt (financial leverage) of the bidding firm.

**leveraged buyout (LBO)**
the purchase of a company by a firm or group of investors with borrowed funds

**Bidding Process**    The bidding firm first contacts the management of the target firm to negotiate a merger. The bidding firm normally pays a premium on the target firm's stock to make the deal worthwhile to the target firm's stockholders.

When two firms cannot come to terms, the bidding firm may attempt a **tender offer**. This is a direct bid by the bidding firm for the shares of the target firm. It does not require prior approval of the target firm's management. Thus, a tender offer could accomplish a merger even if the management of the target firm disapproves.

**tender offer**
a direct bid by an acquiring firm for the shares of a target firm

The bidding firm must decide the price at which it is willing to purchase the target firm's shares and then officially extend this tender offer to the shareholders. The tender offer normally represents a premium of 20 percent or more above the prevailing market price, which may be necessary to encourage the shareholders of the target firm to sell their shares. The bidding firm can achieve control of the target firm only if enough of the target firm's shareholders are willing to sell.

**Integrating the Businesses**    If a merger is achieved, various departments within the two companies may need to be restructured. The key to successfully integrating the management of two companies is to clearly communicate the strategic plan of the firm. In addition, the organizational structure should be communicated to clarify the roles of each department and position. This includes identifying to whom each position will report and who is accountable for various tasks. If the roles are not clearly defined up front, the newly integrated management will not function properly. Tensions are especially high in the beginning stages of a merger, as the employees of the acquired firm are not fully aware of the acquiring firm's plans. Once the merger has occurred, the personnel involved in the initial evaluation of the target firm should guide the integration of the two firms. For example, if the primary reason for a horizontal merger was to reduce the duplication of some managerial functions (to increase production efficiency), management of the newly formed firm should make sure that these reasons for initiating the merger are realized.

A newly formed merger typically requires a period in which the production, financing, inventory management, capital structure, and dividend policies are reevaluated. Policies are commonly revised to conform to the newly formed firm's characteristics. For example, to deal with the larger volume of sales, inventory of the combined firm may need to be larger than for either original business (although perhaps not as large as the sum of both businesses).

Although identifying ways in which a merger could be beneficial is often easy, it may not be as easy to achieve those benefits without creating any new problems. As a final point, the process of creating the merger can also be much more expensive than originally anticipated and can often impose a financial strain on the acquiring company (especially when the target fights the takeover effort). Therefore, firms that are considering acquisitions should attempt to anticipate all types of expenses that may be incurred as a result of the acquisitions.

**Postmerger Evaluation**   After the merger, the firm should periodically assess the merger's costs and benefits. Were the benefits as high as expected? Did the merger involve unanticipated costs? Was the analysis of the target firm too optimistic? Once the merger takes place, it cannot easily be reversed. Thus, any errors detected from the analysis that led to the merger cannot be washed away. Nevertheless, the firm can learn lessons from any errors so that it will be able to evaluate future merger prospects more accurately.

**divestiture**
the sale of an existing business by a firm

When a firm conducts a postmerger evaluation, it may determine that some segments of the target that was purchased are not performing well or do not really fit in with the rest of the business. Under these conditions, the firm may consider engaging in a **divestiture**, which is the sale of an existing business by a firm. A firm may divest (sell) businesses that are not part of its core operations so that it can focus on what it does best. For example, Eastman Kodak, Ford Motor Company, and many other firms have sold various businesses that were not closely related to their core businesses. Divestitures generate funds for the firm because it is selling one of its businesses in exchange for cash. A firm may even sell a business that is performing well as long as the price is more than what it believes the business is worth.

## 3.5  Target's Defense Against Takeover Attempts

In some cases, managers of a target firm may not approve of the takeover attempt by the acquiring firm. They may believe that the price offered for their firm is less than it is worth or that their firm has higher potential if it is not acquired. They may view the potential acquiring firm as a shark approaching for the kill (takeover). Under such conditions, management of the target firm can choose from a variety of "shark repellents" to defend it against the hostile takeover attempt.

**Convince Shareholders to Retain Shares**   A common defensive tactic against a takeover attempt is to try to convince shareholders to retain their shares. If shareholders retain (do not sell) their shares, the bidding firm cannot obtain control of the target.

**Private Placement of New Shares**   Another tactic to avoid a merger is a private placement of stock. By selling shares directly (privately) to specific institutions, the target firm can reduce the acquiring firm's chances of obtaining enough shares to gain a controlling interest. The more shares outstanding, the larger the amount of shares that must be purchased by the acquiring firm to gain a controlling interest.

**Find a White Knight**   A third defensive tactic is for the target firm to find a more suitable company (called a **white knight**) that is willing to acquire the firm and rescue it from the hostile takeover efforts of some other firm. The white knight rescues the target firm by acquiring the target firm itself. Although the target firm no longer retains its independence, it may prefer being acquired by the white knight firm.

**white knight**

a more suitable company that is willing to acquire a firm and rescue it from the hostile takeover efforts of some other firm

---

**Learning Objective 4**

Explain how firms make decisions for investing in short-term assets.

## 4. Short-Term Investment Decisions

**Working capital management** involves the management of a firm's short-term assets and liabilities. A firm's short-term assets include cash, short-term securities, accounts receivable, and inventory. Its short-term liabilities include accounts payable and short-term loans. Working capital management is typically focused on the proper amount of investment in a firm's cash, short-term securities, accounts receivable, and inventory. All of these strategies can be classified as a firm's investment strategies. Working capital management can be segmented into liquidity management, accounts receivable management, and inventory management.

**working capital management**

the management of a firm's short-term assets and liabilities

### 4.1  Liquidity Management

Firms that are **liquid** have adequate access to funds to pay bills when they come due. **Liquidity management** involves the management of short-term assets and liabilities to ensure adequate liquidity. To remain liquid, firms may maintain cash and short-term securities. For example, they may invest in **Treasury bills**, which are short-term debt securities issued by the U.S. Treasury. Treasury bills have maturities of 13 weeks, 26 weeks, and one year. Treasury bills offer a relatively low return. They provide a firm with easy access to funds because they can easily be sold to other investors. When firms need funds to cover expenses, they sell the Treasury bills and use the proceeds to pay expenses. Firms such as DuPont and The Coca-Cola Company hold hundreds of millions of dollars worth of short-term securities to maintain liquidity.

Firms normally attempt to limit their holdings of cash and short-term securities so that they can use their funds for other purposes that generate higher returns. They can be liquid without holding cash and short-term securities if they have easy access to borrowed funds. Most firms have a **line of credit** with one or more banks, which is an agreement that allows access to borrowed funds upon demand over some specified period (usually one year). If a firm experiences a temporary shortage of funds, it

**liquid**

having access to funds to pay bills when they come due

**liquidity management**

the management of short-term assets and liabilities to ensure adequate liquidity

**Treasury bills**

short-term debt securities issued by the U.S. Treasury

**line of credit**

an agreement with a bank that allows a firm access to borrowed funds upon demand over some specified period

## Out of Business

BUSINESS INVESTMENT MEETING IN PROGRESS

WHAT IS GOING ON HERE?

YOU TOLD US THAT WE SHOULD INCREASE OUR LEVEL OF LIQUID ASSETS

WE ARE NOW HEAVILY INVESTED IN LIQUID ASSETS

can use its line of credit to obtain a short-term loan immediately. The interest charged by the banks on the loan is normally tied to some specified market-determined interest rate. Thus, the interest rate will be consistent with existing market rates at the time of the loan. Firms with a line of credit do not need to go through the loan application process. They can normally reapply for a new line of credit each year.

Because of its line of credit, its cash, and its short-term securities, The Coca-Cola Company always has access to a sufficient amount of funds to pay its bills.

When firms build up an excessive amount of cash, they search for ways to use the excess. For example, they commonly use excess cash to repurchase some of their existing stock. Alternatively, they may use excess cash to pay off some of their existing debt.

Retailers commonly allow consumers to use credit cards to purchase products. Manufacturers of products benefit when retailers accept credit cards because customers purchase more when they are allowed to use credit.

### 4.2 Accounts Receivable Management

Firms have accounts receivable when they grant credit to customers. By granting credit, firms may generate more sales than if they required an immediate cash payment. Allowing credit has two potential disadvantages,

## SMALL BUSINESS SURVEY

### Investment Decisions by Small Businesses

About 300 Entrepreneur of the Year award winners were surveyed by the accounting firm Ernst & Young to determine how they would invest funds if they received the ideal level of financing. The respondents were allowed to select more than one type of investment. Their responses are shown in the following chart:

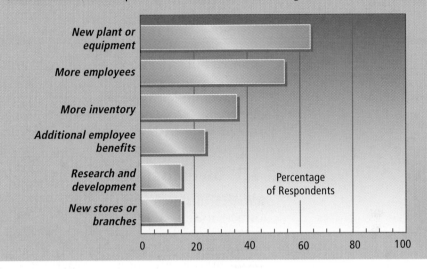

## SMALL BUSINESS SURVEY

### Extending Credit

In a recent National Small Business poll conducted for the NFIB Research Foundation, small businesses were asked if they extend credit to business customers, to individual customers, or to both types of customers. Their responses are shown here:

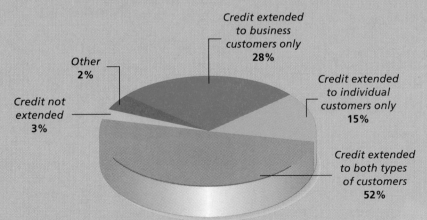

Clearly, businesses recognize that they need to provide credit in order to attract customers.

however. The first is that the customers may not pay the credit balance for a long time. Thus, the firm does not have use of the cash until several months after the sale was made. Consequently, the firm may have to borrow funds until the cash is received and will have to pay interest on those funds.

The second potential disadvantage of extending credit to customers is that the customers may default on the credit provided. In this case, the firm never receives payment for the products it sold to customers.

**Accounts receivable management** sets the limits on credit available to customers and the length of the period in which payment is due. The goal is to be flexible enough so that sales increase as a result of credit granted but strict enough to avoid customers who would pay their bills late (beyond the period specified) or not at all.

Given the possibilities of late payments or no payments (default) on the credit, firms need to closely assess the creditworthiness of any customers who wish to pay their bills with credit.

## 4.3 Inventory Management

When firms maintain large amounts of inventory, they can avoid stockouts (shortages). By holding so much inventory, however, they invest a large amount of funds that they could have used for other purposes. Consider the case of Wal-Mart, which continuously attempts to order enough of each product to satisfy customers. Yet, it does not want to order an excessive amount of any product, which would be an inefficient use of its funds.

**Inventory management** determines the amount of inventory that is held. Managers attempt to hold just enough inventory to avoid stockouts, without tying up funds in excess inventories. This task is complicated because it requires forecasts of future sales levels, which can be erratic. If sales are more than expected, stockouts may occur unless the firm has excess inventory.

**accounts receivable management**
sets the limits on credit available to customers and the length of the period in which payment is due

**inventory management**
determines the amount of inventory that is held

Businesses maintain an inventory of products so that they can accommodate demand. They maintain an inventory level that exceeds the expected sales so that they can avoid stockouts.

© SHUTTERSTOCK/TONIS VALING

# Responding to the Economy

## Business Investment Decisions in Response to the Economy

When assessing the feasibility of proposed projects, firms need to revise the projects' estimated revenue or expenses in response to changing economic conditions. Expectations of a weaker economy may lead to a downward revision in revenue to be received from a project. Expectations of higher inflation may lead to an upward revision in the expenses incurred by a project. Thus, a new product that is feasible to implement when economic conditions are expected to be favorable may not be feasible under more adverse economic conditions.

The decision to invest in a project should be reassessed for existing projects as well as for new projects. Thus, a firm should periodically reassess its existing business projects to determine whether it should continue each project. For example, a firm may decide to stop producing some products if it expects that these products will generate less revenue than in the past or incur higher costs than in the past due to changing economic conditions.

Firms cannot predict the future economic conditions with complete accuracy. However, they can identify various possible economic scenarios that may occur; then they can estimate the revenue and expenses of a project based on each scenario. This analysis allows a firm to determine how sensitive a project's performance may be in response to various possible economic conditions. In this way, the firm can at least prepare for a variety of possible outcomes.

A firm can also benefit from correctly anticipating an increase in economic growth because it may want to expand its product line when consumers are likely to be spending more money. In addition, the firm may wish to increase its inventory of existing products during a strong economy so that it will have an adequate supply of products to accommodate orders by customers.

## COLLEGE HEALTH CLUB: ACCOUNTS RECEIVABLE MANAGEMENT AT CHC

One of the decisions that Sue Kramer needs to make as part of her business plan for College Health Club (CHC) is whether to implement a credit policy for her members. Recall that she expects that CHC will attract 300 members in its first year. Sue knows that some students who may want to become members cannot afford CHC's annual membership fee. She thinks that by implementing a credit policy that would allow members to pay later in the year, she could increase the membership to 330 members in the first year. However, Sue also thinks that 40 of those members would never pay their membership fee if they were not required to pay when they first joined the club. Her analysis of the impact of a credit policy on CHC's first-year performance is shown in the following table:

| | CHC's Performance If . . . | |
| --- | :---: | :---: |
| | **Credit Is Not Offered** | **Credit Is Offered** |
| (1) Price per membership | $500 | $500 |
| (2) Number of members in first year | 300 | 330 |
| (3) Number of members who pay their fees | 300 | 290 |
| (4) Revenue = (1) × (3) | $150,000 | $145,000 |
| (5) Total operating expenses | $138,000 | $138,000 |
| (6) Interest expenses | $4,000 | $4,000 |
| (7) Earnings before Taxes = (4) − (5) − (6) | $8,000 | $3,000 |

Although the number of members would be higher if Sue allows credit, fewer members would pay their fees. Based on this analysis, Sue decides not to allow credit. However, she will consider an alternative plan that would allow a student to purchase a three-month membership for $150. This price is slightly higher (on a monthly basis) than the annual membership fee. This plan would attract students who could not afford the annual membership. In addition, it does not involve an extension of credit, as these students will not be allowed to continue receiving health club services unless they renew their membership.

The entire business plan developed throughout this text by Sue Kramer is shown in the appendix of this chapter. Among other things, the plans for the business determine how funds are to be invested, which influences the amount of financing that is needed.

# Summary of Learning Objectives

**1** Capital budgeting involves a comparison of the costs and benefits of a proposed project to determine whether it is feasible. A capital budget is a targeted amount of funds to be used for purchasing assets that are needed for long-term projects. Firms consider three types of potential capital expenditures: expansion of a current business, development of a new business, and investment in assets that will reduce expenses.

**2** The process of capital budgeting involves five tasks:

✦ Proposing new projects that deserve to be assessed.

✦ Estimating cash flows of projects, which represent the cash inflows (derived from revenue) minus cash outflows (derived from expenses) per period.

✦ Determining which projects are

✦ Implementing feasible projects based on a priority status.

✦ Monitoring projects that were implemented.

**3** Firms consider investing funds to acquire other companies based on one or more of the following motives:

✦ A firm can achieve immediate growth by acquiring another firm.

✦ Mergers can create a higher volume of sales for a firm, which allows it to achieve economies of scale.

✦ Mergers can allow firms to combine resources and contribute those resources in which they have the most managerial expertise.

✦ Mergers can allow the acquiring firm to reduce its taxable earnings when it acquires a company that recently incurred a loss.

**4** Firms invest in short-term assets such as cash, short-term securities, accounts receivable, and inventory. They invest in a sufficient amount of cash and short-term securities to maintain adequate liquidity. However, excessive investment in cash and short-term securities represents an inefficient use of funds.

Firms desire to invest in sufficient accounts receivable so that they can increase revenue over time. They must impose adequate credit standards, however, so that they can avoid excessive defaults on credit they have provided.

Firms desire to invest in a sufficient amount of inventory so that they can avoid stockouts. However, excessive investment in inventory represents an inefficient use of funds.

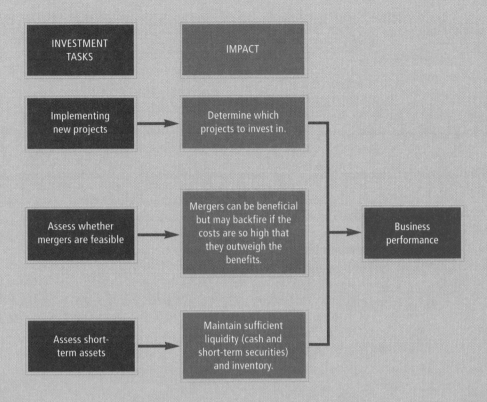

# Self-Test of Key Concepts

The following self-assessment allows you to test your understanding of the key concepts covered in this chapter. Answers are provided at the end of this exercise.

**True or False**

1. Capital budgeting involves the comparison of assets and revenue.

2. Many decisions that result from capital budgeting decisions are irreversible.

3. One of the most popular methods available to assess the feasibility of projects is the net present value (NPV) technique.

4. Projects are mutually exclusive if the acceptance of one results in the acceptance of another.

5. Projects are referred to as independent when they have no impact on the firm's performance or value.

6. A tender offer is a method used by a firm to issue new stock.

7. The amount of money that a firm can receive from selling a project is referred to as the net present value.

8. Capital budgeting analysis for investment projects in foreign countries tends to be more complex than analysis for domestic projects.

9. Firms can merge only if they are producing similar products.

10. Firms can be liquid even if they are not holding large amounts of cash and short-term securities.

**Multiple Choice**

11. A firm's _____ is a targeted amount of funds to be used for purchasing assets such as buildings, machinery, and equipment that are needed for long-term projects.
    a) master budget
    b) capital budget
    c) working capital projection
    d) escrow account
    e) sinking fund

12. All of the following are motives for capital budgeting expenditures except:
    a) expansion of current business.
    b) development of new business.

c) acquisition of assets that will reduce expenses.

d) acquisition of liabilities.

13. If the adoption of investment A has no bearing on whether other investments should be adopted, investment A is said to be:

a) redundant.

b) irrelevant.

c) independent.

d) expedient.

e) unrestricted.

14. All of the following are tasks involved in capital budgeting except:

a) estimating cash flows from the investment.

b) determining which projects are feasible.

c) monitoring projects that are implemented.

d) determining the appropriate size of the line of credit.

e) implementing feasible projects.

15. A merger between a tire manufacturer and a firm that produces clocks and watches is:

a) illegal.

b) a horizontal merger.

c) a diagonal merger.

d) a vertical merger.

e) a conglomerate merger.

16. The three general types of mergers are horizontal, conglomerate, and:

a) cooperative.

b) vertical.

c) divestiture.

d) bureaucratic.

e) parallel.

17. The result of a firm investing in another company by purchasing all the stock of that company is a(n):

a) divestiture.

b) net present value.

c) economies of scale.

d) line of credit.

e) merger.

18. Which of the following is the best example of a vertical merger?

a) A chain of fast-food restaurants merges with a firm that produces electronic components for computers.

b) A small book publisher that specializes in travel and history books merges with a larger book publisher that specializes in biographies and popular fiction.

c) A golf club manufacturer merges with a firm that helps people prepare their income taxes.

d) A firm that publishes a newspaper in the St. Louis area merges with a firm that publishes a newspaper in the Chicago area.

e) A firm that sells flour, sugar, and spices merges with a firm that bakes pies and cakes.

19. If the per unit cost of producing a good decreases as a greater quantity is produced, the production process exhibits:

a) economies of scale.

b) diminishing returns.

c) higher fixed costs than variable costs.

d) an exception to the law of supply.

e) a very high break-even point.

20. Economies of scale are more likely to be achieved by:

a) vertical mergers.

b) horizontal mergers.

c) conglomerate mergers.

d) divestitures.

e) accounts receivable management.

21. Firms that incur negative earnings are sometimes attractive candidates for mergers because of potential:

a) tax advantages.

b) cash advantages.

c) profit exploitation.

d) retained earnings.

e) divestitures.

22. A purchase of a company by a firm or group of investors with borrowed funds is a(n):

a) common stock purchase.

b) purchase from retained earnings.

c) equity purchase.

d) preferred stock purchase.

e) leveraged buyout.

23. When a firm sells off one of its existing businesses, the process is known as a:
    a) reverse merger.
    b) leveraged buyout.
    c) corporate downsizing.
    d) conglomeration strategy.
    e) divestiture.

24. A firm's short-term assets include all of the following except:
    a) cash.
    b) accounts receivable.
    c) machinery.
    d) inventory.
    e) short-term securities.

25. Firms are said to be _____ if they have adequate access to funds so that they can pay their bills as they come due.
    a) leveraged
    b) fully endowed
    c) vested
    d) bonded
    e) liquid

26. _____ are short-term debt securities offered by the U.S. Treasury that provide firms with easy access to funds since they can be sold to other investors.
    a) Federal warrants
    b) Treasury trust certificates
    c) Treasury stock
    d) Treasury bills
    e) Federal Reserve notes

27. The management of a firm's short-term assets and liabilities is:
    a) accounts receivable management.
    b) working capital management.
    c) sales management.
    d) plant and equipment management.
    e) fixed asset management.

28. An agreement that allows a firm access to borrowed funds upon demand over some specified period of time is a:
    a) bond indenture.
    b) stock flotation.
    c) note receivable.
    d) line of credit.
    e) note payable.

29. The goal of _____ management is to be flexible enough to increase sales to credit customers while being strict enough to limit losses due to customers who pay their bills late or not at all.
    a) leverage
    b) accounts receivable
    c) trade credit
    d) accounts payable
    e) invoice

30. Firms try to maintain a large enough inventory to avoid:
    a) stockouts.
    b) the need for trade credit.
    c) leveraged financing.
    d) default on bonds.
    e) undiversified portfolios.

| True/False | | Multiple Choice | | |
|---|---|---|---|---|
| 1. False | 8. True | 11. b | 18. e | 25. e |
| 2. True | 9. False | 12. d | 19. a | 26. d |
| 3. True | 10. True | 13. c | 20. b | 27. b |
| 4. False | | 14. d | 21. a | 28. d |
| 5. False | | 15. e | 22. e | 29. b |
| 6. False | | 16. b | 23. e | 30. a |
| 7. False | | 17. e | 24. c | |

## Self-Test of Key Terms

accounts receivable management  598
capital budget  583
capital budgeting  582
conglomerate merger  589
divestiture  594
horizontal merger  589

independent project  587
inventory management  598
leveraged buyout (LBO)  593
line of credit  595
liquid  595
liquidity management  595
merger  589

mutually exclusive  586
tender offer  593
Treasury bills  595
vertical merger  589
white knight  595
working capital management  595

Fill in each blank with the proper key term. To assess your understanding of the key terms, answers are provided at the end of this self-test.

1. _____ are short-term securities issued by the U.S. Treasury.

2. If a firm is _____, it has adequate access to funds so that it can pay bills when they come due.

3. When the capital budgeting decision is to choose between two proposed projects, the projects are _____.

4. In a(n) _____, a group of investors borrow funds in order to purchase a company.

5. A(n) _____ involves the combination of two firms into one.

6. A(n) _____ merger involves the combination of a firm with a potential supplier or customer.

7. A(n) _____ is an agreement that allows a firm access to borrowed funds within a specified period of time.

8. _____ management involves the management of short-term assets and liabilities to ensure adequate liquidity.

9. A(n) _____ is a direct bid by the acquiring firm for the shares of the target firm.

10. When the decision to adopt or reject one project has no bearing on the adoption of another project, the projects are _____.

11. A target firm may attempt to prevent a hostile takeover by finding a more suitable firm called a(n) _____ that would be willing to acquire it.

12. A(n) _____ is the sale of an existing business by a firm.

13. _____ is the management of a firm's short-term assets and liabilities.

14. A(n) _____ is a targeted amount of funds to be used for purchasing assets such as buildings.

15. A(n) _____ merger is the combination of unrelated businesses.

16. _____ sets the limits on credit available to customers and the length of the period in which payment is due.

17. _____ is used to compare of the costs and benefits of a proposed project.

18. A(n) _____ merger represents the combination of two firms in the same business.

**Answers:**

1. Treasury bills
2. liquid
3. mutually exclusive
4. leveraged buyout
5. merger
6. vertical
7. line of credit
8. Liquidity management
9. tender offer
10. independent
11. white knight
12. divestiture
13. Working capital management
14. capital budget
15. conglomerate
16. Accounts receivable management
17. Capital budgeting
18. horizontal

# Concept Review Questions

1. **Feasibility of a Project.** Explain how a capital budgeting decision determines whether a proposed business project is feasible. Why might the prevailing interest rate influence a firm's decision to invest in a project?

2. **Capital Expenditures.** Describe the common types of capital expenditures by a business.

3. **Capital Budgeting Tasks.** Describe the tasks involved in capital budgeting.

4. **Mutually Exclusive Projects.** Explain the difference between mutually exclusive projects and independent projects that are considered by businesses.

5. **Types of Mergers.** Describe the common types of mergers.

6. **Motives for Mergers.** What are common motives for corporate mergers?

7. **Methods to Finance a Merger.** Explain common methods used to finance a merger.

8. **Divestiture Motives.** Why might a firm divest some of its assets?

9. **Liquidity Management.** Describe a firm's liquidity management.

10. **Credit Policy.** Describe a firm's accounts receivable management and explain the tradeoff involved when a firm allows no credit versus when it uses a liberal credit policy.

## Class Communication Questions

1. **Merger Strategy.** A firm notices that one of its competitors has performed well. To improve its own performance, it decides to acquire this other firm. Why might this effort backfire?

2. **Credit Policy.** In an effort to increase sales, a firm decides to extend credit to all customers and not to require payment until one year after the products are purchased. Does this liberal credit policy makes sense? Justify your opinion.

3. **Inventory Policy.** A retail firm wants to ensure that it will not run out of inventory of televisions. It usually sells about 100 televisions per week. The firm decides to build a huge warehouse that can store 3,000 televisions so that it will not experience stockouts. Does this inventory policy make sense? Justify your opinion.

## Small Business Case

### Deciding Whether to Acquire a Business

Benson, Inc., is a publisher that sells books to retail bookstores in the United States. Judith Benson, the owner, is concerned because her suppliers continue to increase the price of paper and other materials that her company purchases from them weekly. One supplier to Benson, Inc., is Hill Company, which provides high-quality supplies but has experienced financial problems recently because of inefficient management.

Judith believes that Benson, Inc., could benefit from merging with Hill Company. She believes that she could acquire (purchase) Hill Company at a low price because it has performed poorly in the past. She also believes that she could improve Hill Company's performance by reorganizing its business. In addition, the merger with Hill Company would give Benson, Inc., more control over the cost of its supplies. It could obtain supplies from Hill Company, which would now be part of Benson, Inc. Therefore, it would not be subject to increased prices by other suppliers. Meanwhile, Hill Company would not only produce supplies for Benson, Inc., but would also sell them to other customers, as it did in the past.

1. **Type of Merger.** What type of merger is Judith considering?

2. **Pricing the Target.** Explain the key factors that Judith should consider when deciding on the price to offer for the target (Hill Company).

3. **Risk of a Merger.** How could the purchase of Hill Company backfire?

## Web Insight

### Business Expansion at Netflix

At the opening of the chapter, Netflix was introduced. Go to the website (http://ir.netflix.com/annuals.cfm) to retrieve a recent annual report [or you can find the information by using the search terms "Netflix" and "annual report" on a search engine]. Review Netflix's most recent letter to shareholders, which is at the beginning of its annual report. Summarize the comments made by Netflix about its recent growth and plans for future expansion.

## Dell's Secrets for Success

Go to Dell's website (www.dell.com) and click on the link "About Dell," near the bottom of the web page. You can also review a recent annual report to obtain more information.

1. **Type of Expansion.** Dell has expanded its operations in re-cent years. Review how the size of Dell's assets has in-creased over time.

2. **Reasons for Growth.** Why do you think Dell has been able to grow at a much faster rate than other firms in its industry?

3. **Dell's Potential Growth.** Do you think Dell is reaching its peak level, or does it have more potential for growth?

## Video Exercise

### Lessons in Business Acquisitions

Many free business videos are avail-able on websites such as YouTube (www.youtube.com), and more are added every day. Search for a recent video clip about an existing business that offers lessons on "company's acquisition" in YouTube or any other website that provides video clips.

1. **Main Lesson.** What is the name of the business in the video clip? Is the video clip fo-cused on the potential benefits of merging with another busi-ness, or the process the firm used to engage in an acquisi-tion, or some other aspect of business acquisitions? What is the main lesson of the video clip that you watched?

2. **Why Acquisitions Can Back-fire.** Some acquisitions have backfired, as the performance of the acquiring firm deterio-rated after it acquired the tar-get. Why do you think some acquisitions backfire?

3. **Benefits of Communication.** Some businesses that have merged emphasize the impor-tance of communicating to all employees the plans following the acquisition. Why is com-munication so important?

## Projects

To encourage further compre-hension of concepts covered in Chapter 17, the following five projects are available:

1. Analyzing Your Favorite Business

2. Building a Business Plan for Campus.com

3. Running Your Own Business

4. Planning Your Career

5. Stock Market Contest

All of these projects are provided in Appendix A at the end of the text. In addition, projects are available by part division at the end of each part. A Word file for each project is also available at the textbook website (www.emcp.net/business5e) so that you may maintain one ongoing file for each project.

# Chapter 17 Appendix
# Consolidating All
# Major Strategies in
# the Business Plan

Each chapter of the text has explained specific strategies, each of which represents a portion of the business plan. A complete business plan consolidates all of the firm's major strategies. Exhibit 17A.1 shows the complete business plan for College Health Club (CHC), which consolidates the various business plan segments that were discussed in each chapter. Notice that every major business function is covered, in the order that it was discussed in the text. As time passes, Sue Kramer may change various strategies in CHC's business plan, and each change could affect other parts of the business plan. If Sue decides on an investment plan of expanding the club, she will have to revise the financial plan to finance the additional investment. If CHC needs additional financing, Sue will have a better chance of obtaining funds from a creditor if she can present a revised business plan showing how CHC will efficiently use those funds.

**Exhibit 17A.1**

Example of a Business Plan

### Business Plan for College Health Club (CHC)

**Part I. Business Environment**

**1. Business Idea**

The business is a health club called College Health Club (CHC) that will be located in a shopping mall just across from the Texas College campus. The health club should appeal to the students because it is convenient and will be affordable to them.

**2. Business Responsibilities**

CHC has a responsibility to its customers, its employees, its owners, its creditors, and the environment. It intends to offer its customers excellent service at reasonable prices. It will encourage feedback from customers and attempt to continually improve its services to satisfy customers. It intends to offer its employees a safe working environment and equal opportunities without bias. The firm will be managed in a manner that will maximize the value of the business for any owners who are invited to invest in the firm over time. CHC recognizes its responsibility to make timely payments on debt owed to creditors. It also pledges to conduct its business in a manner that will not harm the environment. By satisfying customers, employees, and creditors, CHC should establish a good reputation and attract more customers in the future.

**3. Exposure to Economic Conditions**

CHC's membership is exposed to local economic conditions. If a weaker economy causes some students to lose their part-time jobs in the local area, the number of memberships will likely decline. Consequently, CHC's revenue and its earnings will also decline. A stronger economy will allow for more part-time jobs and will result in more memberships at CHC. Consequently, CHC's revenue and earnings will increase.

#### 4. *Exposure to Global Conditions*

CHC serves the local community and is not directly affected by global conditions. It will sell vitamin supplements (which are imported from Mexico), and the cost of the supplements will rise when the dollar weakens against the Mexican peso. Since vitamins are not expected to be a primary source of revenue, CHC's exposure to global conditions is negligible.

### Part II. Business Ownership and Plan

#### 5. *Business Ownership*

CHC is structured as a proprietorship, with Sue Kramer as the sole proprietor. She will invest $20,000 in the business. An additional $40,000 is needed and will be obtained in the form of a loan.

CHC's earnings are expected to be a low level in the first year, but its earnings should increase over the years as the number of memberships increases. The main source of risk of the firm is uncertainty regarding the number of future memberships, which is the key to the success of the business. However, given the strong interest by the local students in joining a health club, the membership level is expected to increase rapidly over time.

#### 6. *Exposure to Competition*

Currently, no other health clubs are convenient to the Texas College campus. New health clubs may be established over time and could pull some of CHC's customers away. Nevertheless, because most of CHC's business is expected to come from students at the college, CHC should not be significantly affected by other health clubs that focus on customers who have full-time jobs and are not currently enrolled at the college. CHC needs to develop a strategy for retaining its members over time. The overall demand for health club services is expected to remain strong because of the desire by people to stay in shape.

### Part III. Management

#### 7. *Strategic Plan*

CHC must attract a large number of members to fully utilize the health club space and achieve high performance. As memberships increase, CHC's earnings will increase.

A longer-term objective is to expand over time by capitalizing on the same business concept by establishing other health clubs near college campuses. CHC will assess other college campuses to determine whether there is sufficient demand for health club services. If students appear to want these services and no health club is located nearby, CHC will conduct a more thorough analysis of the expenses and potential revenue associated with establishing a new health club near that campus. CHC will open additional health clubs near other college campuses only if and when it is feasible to do so.

#### 8. *Organizational Structure*

CHC uses a wide span of control, as all employees report directly to Sue Kramer. Tasks at CHC are departmentalized: some employees conduct aerobics classes in one part of the club while others assist members with the exercise and weight machines. Sue Kramer sets up a weekly aerobics schedule and assigns a specific employee (or herself) to lead each class. When employees are not leading an aerobics class, they are assigned to help members use the exercise and weight machines.

If CHC expands by opening new health clubs over the long term, it will departmentalize by location. A manager will be hired for each new health club and will be responsible for managing all of its operations. The manager of each new health club will be trained by Sue Kramer, so that she can ensure that the manager is trained in the procedures that have made CHC successful.

#### 9. *Production*

Resources Used at CHC
CHC's resources are combined to produce health club services. First, human resources are used to lead aerobics classes and interact with customers. Second, equipment such as exercise and weight machines is provided for customers' use. A health club facility is available to the customers. The main expenses of providing these resources are salaries to the human resources and the rental cost of equipment and the facilities.

Site
CHC is located in a shopping mall across the street from the Texas College campus. Since the goal of the business is to target students at this college who want to join a health club, the site selection serves those students. The rent at this facility is reasonable. The health club has easy access to labor because it hires exercise science majors on internships to work part-time.

### Design and Layout
The production of health club services is organized by type of service. Aerobics classes are offered in one part of the health club, and exercise and weight machines are available in another part. While Sue Kramer leads aerobics classes, another employee is responsible for overseeing the machines in case the members need any assistance. The facilities are large enough to allow for some expansion. The layout of the facilities allows flexibility so that the exercise and weight machines can be rearranged.

### Production Control
CHC engages in production control to ensure that its services are provided in a timely manner and achieve the desired level of quality. CHC purchases vitamin supplements from its supplier every month and attempts to have a sufficient number of jars of each type of supplement available for its customers. Since the jars are inexpensive and do not take up much space, CHC maintains a large inventory of all of its supplements.

Routing for CHC involves the sequence of tasks necessary to complete the production of health club services. Sue Kramer has a daily schedule of aerobics classes that she teaches. She also posts a weekly schedule of aerobics classes so that members know when they are offered. The main preparation is to ensure that equipment (e.g., a step for step aerobics) and towels are available for the participants. The exercise and weight machines are always available to members.

### Production Quality and Efficiency
Total quality management is needed to ensure customer satisfaction. Survey cards will be periodically distributed to members to obtain their feedback about the services. In particular, members will be asked to rate the aerobics classes they take at CHC and the quality of the exercise and weight machines. They will also be asked for suggestions on any other services that they would like CHC to provide.

Production efficiency is needed for CHC to achieve a high level of earnings. Many of its expenses are fixed. Therefore, CHC needs a large number of members to achieve production efficiency. To the extent that CHC offers a membership at an attractive price and provides the types of health club services that students desire, it should attract a large number of members. With a large number of members, CHC's revenue will be high, and since many of its expenses are fixed, they will not be affected by the high membership level.

## Part IV. Managing Employees

### 10. *Motivating Employees*

Part time employees tend to like working in a health club. CHC can easily find qualified part-time employees by recruiting students who are majoring in exercise science at Texas College. CHC offers compensation that is slightly higher than other local employers of part-time college students. It allows flexible work schedules so that students can work fewer hours in a particular week if they have a major exam or class project. CHC welcomes employee involvement.

### 11. *Human Resource Planning*

CHC's part-time staffing needs are filled by hiring students who are currently majoring in exercise science at the Texas College. Ads are posted in that department to recruit new applicants. The typical tasks of part-time employees include leading aerobics classes, helping members use the weight and exercise machines, washing towels, and responding to phone inquiries. Students submit applications online.

### Developing Employees Skills
When part-time employees are hired at CHC, they are told that the focus is on safety in using the weight and exercise machines. Although all members are given a booklet on safety, employees should understand the safety features in case they see a member who is not using the machines properly. Second, employees are trained on the importance of customer relations. Third, employees are trained to work together.

### Employee Evaluation
Part-time employees are evaluated according to their customer relations and their employee relations. The survey forms that request feedback from members ask if they have any comments about the individual part-time employees.

## Part V. Marketing

### 12. *Product and Pricing*

### Product Mix
CHC's product mix includes the provision of aerobics classes, weight machines, and exercise machines. All of these services are provided at no charge to customers who pay

an annual membership fee. In addition, CHC sells vitamin supplements to members. It may expand its product mix over time by selling workout clothing.

Target Market
The target market is the set of students enrolled at Texas College who want to join a health club. CHC also wants to retain the students as members after they graduate if they continue to live in the local area. Since the health club is not on the campus but in a shopping mall across the street from the campus, CHC should also be able to attract local people who are not affiliated with the college.

Product Differentiation
The main appeal of CHC to the students at Texas College is its location. It is located across from the college campus, so students can walk to the club. Since many of them do not have a car, this location is ideal and separates CHC from all other health clubs.

Pricing Policy
The membership fee is influenced by the cost of production and by competitors' prices. CHC's annual expenses are expected to be about $142,000. Assuming that CHC can attract 300 members, an annual membership fee of $500 will be sufficient to cover the cost of production and will also be competitive. The number of members is expected to grow over time.

### 13. Distribution

Since CHC provides its services directly to members, channels of distribution are not needed. However, CHC does serve as a retailer for vitamin supplements and may serve as a retailer for a limited amount of exercise clothing CHC purchases its vitamin supplements from a vitamin wholesaler and may purchase exercise clothing from a clothing wholesaler.

### 14. Promotion

Advertising
CHC reaches its target market by advertising in the college's school newspaper. This weekly newspaper is free to students, and most students read it or at least skim it.

Personal Selling
CHC offers presentations about exercise and health to students at the auditorium on one Friday afternoon each month. The presentations do not directly advertise CHC's services, but they provide some name recognition for CHC.

Sales Promotion Strategy
CHC distributes coupons for the vitamin supplements in the Texas College newspaper. The intent is to attract nonmember students who will come to CHC to buy the vitamin supplements at a discounted price (with the coupon) and will look at the health club facilities while they are there. CHC also distributes coupons in the student newspaper that allow a free pass for a day to try out an aerobics class or the weight machines. These coupons may entice some students who will try out the facilities and later become members. A display of the vitamin supplements is set up near the door of CHC so that they are visible to anyone who walks into the health club.

Promotion Mix
CHC uses a promotion mix consisting of (1) advertising in the Texas College newspaper, (2) a sales promotion of coupons for vitamin supplements and a free day pass in the Texas College newspaper, and (3) personal selling through monthly presentations about exercise and health to students on campus. All three parts of the promotion mix are focused on the students.

Evaluating the Effects of Promotion
The membership application requests information about what caused the person to purchase a membership. The choices are (1) referral from a friend, (2) advertising in the student newspaper, (3) coupons in the student newspaper, (4) the exercise and health presentations on campus, or (5) other. A review of the information provided by applicants indicates what promotion strategy was effective. This information will be considered when deciding what sales promotion strategies should be used in the future.

**Part VI. Financial Plan**

### 15. Financial Plan at CHC

Revenue from annual memberships, sales of vitamin supplements, and sales of exercise clothing is expected to be about $150,000 at the end of the first year. CHC's expenses in the first year are expected to be $142,000, as shown below. Its main expenses are the rent for the facilities ($60,000 per year), salaries ($48,000), rental expenses for the weight and exercise machines ($7,200), and marketing expenses ($3,600). Other expenses are expected to be $23,200 over the first year.

| Operating Expenses | Monthly Expenses | Total Expenses in First Year |
|---|---|---|
| Rent of facilities | $5,000 | $60,000 |
| Salaries | 4,000 | 48,000 |
| Utilities | 700 | 8,400 |
| Rent of exercise and weight machines | 600 | 7,200 |
| Marketing expenses | 300 | 3,600 |
| Liability insurance | 800 | 9,600 |
| Miscellaneous | 100 | 1,200 |
| Total operating expenses | | $138,000 |
| Interest expenses | | 4,000 |
| Total expenses | | $142,000 |

Given the estimated revenue of $150,000 and total expenses of $142,000, CHC's estimated earning before taxes are $8,000 in the first year. In the following years, the expenses are expected to be about the same, but memberships are expected to increase, so revenue should be higher. In addition, sales of vitamin supplements and exercise clothing are expected to increase.

### 16. *Financing*

**Equity Financing**
Sue Kramer, president of CHC, invests $20,000 of her own money as an equity investment in CHC. She will reinvest any earnings in the business over time. Sue has no plans to rely on additional equity funding from venture capital firms.

**Debt Financing**
CHC needs a loan for $40,000 to finance this business. The prevailing interest rate for small business loans is about 10 percent. The desired loan maturity is seven years. At the end of seven years. CHC will repay the loan. Given a 10 percent interest rate on the loan amount of $40,000, CHC's annual interest expense is $4,000.

**Leasing**
The exercise and weight machines will be leased. The facilities for the health club will also be leased. Thus, in the event that the business is discontinued, there will be no need to find a buyer for the machines or the facilities. This flexibility makes CHC a more favorable opportunity for lenders because they are less exposed to the possibility of failure by the business. If CHC has substantial funds in the future, it will reconsider whether to purchase these assets.

**Dividend Policy**
Once CHC begins to generate positive earnings, it will retain the earnings and reinvest them rather than pay dividends. This will allow for more expansion.

### 17. *Business Investment and Expansion*

**Investment of Funds**
CHC will lease its equipment and facilities rather than purchase them, so it does not need funds to make such purchase. However, CHC needs to have sufficient funds on hand to cover the monthly lease payments. It will initially use its funds to cover operating expenses such as salaries, utility expenses, insurance, and marketing expenses. As time passes. CHC should generate sufficient revenue to cover these operating expenses.

If CHC accumulates substantial funds over time, it may purchase the exercise and weight machines that it leases. Second, it may purchase the facilities that it currently leases. Third, it may acquire an existing health club as a means of expanding its business. It would likely need some additional financing if it purchases its present facilities or acquires another health club.

**Credit Policy**
CHC will not extend credit to its members. To make its membership more affordable to students who want credit, it will offer shorter-term memberships, such as a three-month membership for $150.

# Summary/Part VI

## Financial Management

| | | | |
|---|---|---|---|
| **Accounting and Financial Analysis (Chapter 15)** → | • Identify Deficiencies and Correct Them | | |
| **Financing (Chapter 16)** → | • How to Obtain Funds? <br> • Where to Obtain Funds? | **Firm's Revenue and Expenses** → | **Firm's Performance (and Value)** |
| **Expanding the Business (Chapter 17)** → | • Whether to Invest in New Business Projects? <br> • Whether to Acquire New Businesses? <br> • How Much to Invest in Accounts Receivable? <br> • How Much to Invest in Inventory? | | |

# Summary

The chapters in Part VI focus on financial reporting, financing, and business investment. Chapter 15 explains how financial reporting can be used internally to make better decisions, and therefore to enhance business performance. It is also used for financial disclosure to shareholders or creditors. Chapter 16 explains the alternative methods by which firms can obtain financing for their business. The proper method of financing is dependent on the characteristics of the business. Firms that make proper financing decisions can reduce their costs of financing and therefore enhance business performance. Chapter 17 explains how firms assess proposed business projects. Proper decisions on how to expand can substantially increase the performance and value of a business.

# Video on Managing a Business

### Financing for Success

The Small Business Administration (SBA) plays a very important role in helping many small businesses. Its website, which offers a wide range of services and information for small businesses, has a section called Delivering Success (www.sba.gov/tools/audiovideo/deliveringsuccess/index.html) that provides video clips of small business success stories. Go to this website, and watch the video called "Entrepreneurial Spirit" (total time of clip is 5 minutes, 49 seconds).

In this video clip, an entrepreneur of a successful business summarizes his experience and offers advice about financing a small business. A small business needs to develop a well-organized plan to obtain a loan from a bank. The future revenue and some expenses of a business cannot be forecasted with perfect accuracy, so the small business owner must consider how the business's performance might change under alternative conditions (such as an increase in competition, a weakening of the economy, etc.). The entrepreneur obtained financing for his small business with the help of an SBA guarantee backing his business. That is, if his business defaulted on the loan, the SBA would pay off the loan. Thus, the commercial bank was more willing to offer financing for the small business.

1. **Interaction Between Accounting and Financing.** Explain the relationship between the accounting function (Chapter 15) of a business and the financing function (Chapter 16). Why is the accounting function necessary for a business to obtain financing?

2. **How Short-term Investment Decisions Are Influenced by Access to Financing.** Explain how the firm's short-term investment decisions (Chapter 17) are related to its access to financing (Chapter 17).

3. **How Acquisition and Financing Decisions Are Related.** Explain how acquisitions (Chapter 17) are dependent on financing (Chapter 16).

# Self-Test for Part VI

**Chapters 15-17.** Answers are provided at the end of the self-test.

1. Publicly owned firms are required to periodically report their financial condition for existing or potential:
   a) suppliers.
   b) customers.
   c) employees.
   d) shareholders.
   e) unions.

2. The type of accounting performed for reporting purposes is referred to as:
   a) ratio analysis.
   b) financial accounting.
   c) managerial accounting.
   d) cost accounting.
   e) payroll accounting.

3. Individuals who provide accounting services to a variety of firms for a fee are:
   a) master accountants.
   b) managerial accountants.
   c) internal auditors.
   d) corporate controllers.
   e) public accountants.

4. Which of the following financial statements summarizes a firm's revenues, costs, and earnings for a specific period of time?
   a) balance sheet
   b) income statement
   c) cash budget
   d) retained earnings statement
   e) sources and uses of funds statement

5. A firm's operating expenses are subtracted from gross profit to determine its:
   a) net sales.
   b) cost of goods sold.
   c) profit or loss.
   d) balance sheet.
   e) earnings before interest and taxes (EBIT).

6. Which of the following represents funds provided by the owners of a business?
   a) revenue
   b) cost of goods sold
   c) gross profit
   d) net income
   e) owner's equity

7. If a firm has $1,000 in assets and $300 in liabilities, the owner's equity must be:
   a) $700.
   b) $333.
   c) $1,300.
   d) $3,000.
   e) $0.30.

8. A reduction in the value of fixed assets to reflect deterioration in the assets over time is:
   a) cost of goods sold.
   b) gross profit.
   c) sales revenue.
   d) depreciation.
   e) owner's equity.

9. All of the following are characteristics commonly used to classify financial ratios except for:
   a) revenue.
   b) liquidity.
   c) efficiency.
   d) leverage.
   e) profitability.

10. Any firm with foreign subsidiaries must consolidate the financial data from all subsidiaries when preparing its:
    a) mission statement.
    b) foreign exchange.
    c) balance of payment.
    d) financial statements.
    e) domestic policy.

11. Firms obtain capital (funds) in the form of:
    a) inventory and accounts receivable.
    b) revenues and expenses.
    c) equity and assets.
    d) working capital and cost of goods sold.
    e) debt and equity.

12. When assessing the creditworthiness of a business, a lender will consider all of the following factors except:
    a) planned use of the borrowed funds.
    b) financial condition of the firm.
    c) industry outlook.
    d) voting rights of preferred stockholders.
    e) availability of collateral.

13. Long-term debt securities purchased by investors are called:
    a) corporate bonds.
    b) common stock.
    c) preferred stock.
    d) accounts payable.
    e) notes payable.

14. When a firm plans to issue bonds, it explains its obligations to bondholders in a legal document known as a(n):
    a) equity ownership.
    b) asset acquisition.
    c) sales revenue.
    d) indenture.
    e) note payable.

15. Moody's and Standard & Poor's:
    a) rate the firm's ability to cover interest payments on its existing debt.
    b) organize investor syndicates.
    c) issue initial public offerings.
    d) evaluate the credibility of the firm's financial statements.
    e) predict the amount of dividends the firm will pay in the future.

16. Investment companies that invest pooled funds from individual investors are:
    a) mutual funds.
    b) bond indentures.
    c) new primary issues.
    d) retained earnings.
    e) cash dividends.

17. If a privately held firm desires to obtain additional funds and "go public," it will:
    a) borrow funds from a commercial bank.
    b) sell bonds in the primary market.
    c) merge with a multinational corporation.
    d) engage in a public commercial paper offering.
    e) engage in an initial public offering.

18. Fees charged by investment banks for their efforts in selling a firm's securities are called:
    a) coupon payments.
    b) best-effort fees.
    c) cost of capital.
    d) interest fees.
    e) flotation costs.

19. Some firms prefer to finance the use of assets by renting the assets for a specified period of time. This is referred to as:
    a) capital structure.
    b) leasing.
    c) retained earnings.
    d) sales revenue.
    e) notes payable.

20. A firm with mostly debt in its capital structure will likely have:
    a) low inventory turnover.
    b) high accounts receivable.
    c) high retained earnings.
    d) a large amount of preferred stock.
    e) high interest payments.

21. A firm's _____ is a targeted amount of funds to be used for purchasing assets such as buildings, machinery, and equipment that are needed for long-term projects.
    a) master budget
    b) capital budget
    c) working capital projection
    d) escrow account
    e) sinking fund

22. If the adoption of investment A has no bearing on whether other investments should be adopted, investment A is said to be:
    a) redundant.
    b) irrelevant.
    c) independent.
    d) expedient.
    e) unrestricted.

23. A merger between a tire manufacturer and a firm that produces clocks and watches is:
    a) illegal.
    b) a horizontal merger.
    c) a diagonal merger.
    d) a vertical merger.
    e) a conglomerate merger.

24. Which of the following is the best example of a vertical merger?
    a) A chain of fast-food restaurants merges with a firm that produces electronic components for computers.
    b) A small book publisher that specializes in travel and history books merges with a larger book publisher that specializes in biographies and popular fiction.
    c) A golf club manufacturer merges with a firm that helps people prepare their income taxes.
    d) A firm that publishes a newspaper in the St. Louis area merges with a firm that publishes a newspaper in the Chicago area.
    e) A firm that sells flour, sugar, and spices merges with a firm that bakes pies and cakes.

25. If the per unit cost of producing a good decreases as a greater quantity is produced, the production process exhibits:
    a) economies of scale.
    b) diminishing returns.
    c) higher fixed costs than variable costs.
    d) an exception to the law of supply.
    e) a very high break-even point.

26. Firms that incur negative earnings are sometimes attractive candidates for mergers because of potential:
    a) tax advantages.
    b) cash advantages.
    c) profit exploitation.
    d) retained earnings.
    e) divestitures.

27. When a firm sells off one of its existing businesses, the process is known as a:
    a) reverse merger.
    b) leveraged buyout.
    c) corporate downsizing.
    d) conglomeration strategy.
    e) divestiture.

28. Firms are said to be _____ if they have adequate access to funds so that they can pay their bills as they come due.
    a) leveraged
    b) fully endowed
    c) vested
    d) bonded
    e) liquid

29. The management of a firm's short-term assets and liabilities is:
    a) accounts receivable management.
    b) working capital management.
    c) sales management.
    d) plant and equipment management.
    e) fixed asset management.

30. The goal of _____ management is to be flexible enough to increase sales to credit customers while being strict enough to limit losses due to customers who pay their bills late or not at all.
    a) leverage
    b) accounts receivable
    c) trade credit
    d) accounts payable
    e) invoice

**Answers:**

| | | | |
|---|---|---|---|
| 1. d | 9. a | 17. e | 25. a |
| 2. b | 10. d | 18. e | 26. a |
| 3. e | 11. e | 19. b | 27. e |
| 4. b | 12. d | 20. e | 28. e |
| 5. e | 13. a | 21. b | 29. b |
| 6. e | 14. d | 22. c | 30. a |
| 7. a | 15. a | 23. e | |
| 8. d | 16. a | 24. e | |

# Projects

## PROJECT 1: ANALYZING YOUR FAVORITE BUSINESS

**Answering the Questions.** This entire project is provided in Appendix A. You can retrieve the Word file of this project from the textbook website (www.emcp.net/business5e), and insert your answer just below each question. The portion of the project that is related to the chapters in this part is provided here.

Using the annual report of the firm you selected, answer the following questions:

**Firm's Financial Performance (related to Chapter 15).** Review the financial summary. Did the firm achieve strong performance last year based on its financial statements?

**Firm's Financing (related to Chapter 16).** When the firm finances its business, how does it typically obtain funds? By borrowing or by issuing stock?

**Firm's Expansion (related to Chapter 17).** Does the firm plan to expand in the future? If so, how?

**Stock Price Performance During the Semester (related to Chapter 17).** Go to the financial website of Google (http://finance.google.com). Insert the name of your company in the box that says "Search Finance." How has the firm's stock price changed during your school term? You can assess the stock price by going to Yahoo's financial website and inserting the ticker symbol of the firm's stock. Why do you think this firm's performance was strong or weak during this semester? Is its performance attributed to its recent management strategies? Or its marketing strategies? Or to something else? Explain.

## PROJECT 2: BUILDING A BUSINESS PLAN FOR CAMPUS.COM

**Completing the Information.** You can complete the information on the Word file of this project from the textbook website (www.emcp.net/business5e). This allows you to insert all of your information on one file for this project by the end of the school term. The portion of the project that is related to the chapters in this part is provided here.

**Accounting and Financial Analysis (related to Chapter 15)** Campus.com's performance over time will be monitored by assessing the following financial ratios:

**Financing (related to Chapter 16)** Alternative choices to obtain funds to support expansion are:

The best alternative is:

_____

_____

_____

The disadvantages of this alternative are:

_____

_____

_____

**Expanding the Business (related to Chapter 17)** Campus.com will determine whether future expansion is feasible by:

_____

_____

_____

_____

_____

_____

_____

## PROJECT 3: RUNNING YOUR OWN BUSINESS

**Completing the Information.** This entire project is provided in Appendix A. You can retrieve the Word file of this project from the textbook website (www.emcp.net/business5e), and insert your answer just below each question. The portion of the project that is related to the chapters in this part is provided here.

**Accounting and Financial Analysis (related to Chapter 15)** The performance of your business over time will be monitored by assessing the following financial ratios:

_____

_____

_____

_____

**Financing (related to Chapter 16)** Alternative choices to obtain funds to support expansion of your business are:

_____

_____

_____

_____

The best alternative is:

_____

_____

_____

_____

_____

The disadvantages of this alternative are:

_____

_____

_____

_____

_____

**Expanding the Business (related to Chapter 17)** Your business will determine whether future expansion is feasible by:

_____

_____

_____

_____

## PROJECT 4: PLANNING YOUR CAREER

This entire project is provided in Appendix A at the end of the text, and you can access a Word file of this project from the textbook website (www.emcp.net/business5e), and insert your answer just below each question.

If you are very interested in the topics covered in this section, you may want to consider a major in accounting or finance. Some of the more common courses taken by accounting and finance majors are summarized here.

### Common Courses for Accounting Majors

• **Principles of Accounting** Focuses on the creation and interpretation of the income statement and the balance sheet.

• **Intermediate Accounting** Deals with the accounting for inventory, fixed assets, and operating expenses.

• **Cost Accounting** Focuses on internal accounting related to management decisions.

• **Accounting Information Systems** Deals with the design and application of information systems used to facilitate accounting.

• **Auditing** Provides an overview of the concepts and methods used to ensure the accuracy of accounting reports and financial statements.

• **Internal Auditing** Focuses on the evaluation of internal tasks, procedures, and guidelines.

### Common Courses for Finance Majors

• **Financial Management** Emphasizes managerial decisions about financing and investing.

• **Personal Finance** Focuses on individuals' financial decisions about budgeting, the use of credit, insurance, investments, and retirement planning.

• **Financial Institutions** Examines the sources and uses of funds of financial institutions; also covers the management, performance, and regulation of financial institutions.

• **Financial Management of Institutions** Discusses decision making by financial institutions, exposure of institutions to risk, and how the risk can be managed.

• **Financial Markets** Provides an overview of securities that are traded in financial markets, with emphasis on how financial markets facilitate security transactions.

• **Advanced Financial Management** Provides an in-depth analysis of decisions by financial managers, including dividend policy, capital structure, and capital budgeting.

• **Investment Analysis** Focuses on valuation of securities, investment

strategies, and managing the risk of investment portfolios.

• **International Financial Management** Discusses financial management from the perspective of a firm in an international environment, with emphasis on how financial decisions account for exchange rate movements.

• **Real Estate** Provides a survey of real estate investments, the valuation of real estate, and the risk of real estate investments.

### Careers in Accounting and Finance

The following websites provide information about job positions, salaries, and careers for students who major in accounting or finance:

• **Job position websites:**

**http://jobsearch.monster.com** Accounting/Auditing, Banking, Finance, Insurance, and Real Estate

**http://careers.yahoo.com** Accounting/Finance, Banking/ Mortgage, Insurance, and Real Estate

• **Salary website:**

**http://collegejournal.com/ salarydata** Accounting, Banking, Consulting, Insurance, and Real Estate

## PROJECT 5: STOCK MARKET CONTEST

This entire project is provided in Appendix A at the end of the text, and you can access a Word file of the project from the textbook website (www.emcp.net/business5e). Your instructor may ask you to assess the performance of your investment up to this point, and whether the performance of your stock is attributed to any of the business concepts that were described in the chapters contained in this part.

# Appendix A

# Projects

## Project 1: Analyzing Your Favorite Business

## Part I

The following exercise allows you to apply the key concepts covered in each chapter to your favorite business. Select a publicly traded business in which you have a strong interest, perhaps a business in which you would like to work someday. By the end of the school term, you will have a complete report about this firm. This project will not only help you learn more about your favorite business, but it will reinforce the key concepts covered in this text.

**Obtain the Annual Report.** You will need access to the firm's annual report, which can often be found on the firm's website. You can do an Internet search to access the most recent annual report (use the name of the firm as your search term along with "annual report"). Or you may

be able to access the annual report from Yahoo's financial website.

**Answering the Questions.** You can retrieve the Word file of this project from the textbook website (www.emcp.net /business5e), and insert your answer just below each question. The portion of the project that is related to the chapters in this part is provided here.

Using the annual report of the firm you selected, answer the following questions:

**Business Description (related to Chapter 1).** Describe the business of the firm that you selected. What products does it produce?

**Ethics Policy (related to Chapter 2).** Many firms disclose their policies on ethics and social responsibilities

within their annual reports. Briefly summarize the firm's policy.

**Exposure to Economic Conditions (related to Chapter 3).** Firms commonly summarize how their recent performance was affected by economic conditions. How was the firm affected by economic conditions last year?

**Firm's International Business (related to Chapter 4).** Does the firm export products? Does it import products? Does it have any subsidiaries in foreign countries?

**Firm's Exposure to International Conditions (related to Chapter 4).** Was the firm affected by international economic conditions last year? If so, how?

## Part II

**Answering the Questions.** You can retrieve the Word file of this project from the textbook website (www.emcp.net /business5e), and insert your answer just below each question. The portion of the project that is related to the chapters in this part is provided here.

Using the annual report of the firm you selected, answer the following questions:

**Firm's Competition (related to Chapter 6).** Briefly summarize any industry conditions (such as competition) that affected the firm's performance last year.

**Competitive Advantage (related to Chapter 6).** Does the firm have a competitive advantage?

# Part III

**Answering the Questions.** You can retrieve the Word file of this project from the textbook website (www.emcp.net /business5e), and insert your answer just below each question. The portion of the project that is related to the chapters in this part is provided here.

Using the annual report of the firm you selected, answer the following questions:

**Firm's Mission (related to Chapter 7).** What is the firm's mission?

**Firm's Strategic Plan (related to Chapter 7).** What is the firm's strategic plan?

**Firm's Organizational Structure (related to Chapter 8).** Briefly describe the firm's organizational structure. For example, does it appear to have many high-level managers?

**Firm's Production (related to Chapter 9).** Where are the firm's production facilities located? Have the operations been restructured to reduce expenses recently? What does the firm say about quality control in its annual report?

# Part IV

**Answering the Questions.** You can retrieve the Word file of this project from the textbook website (www.emcp.net /business5e), and insert your answer just below each question. The portion of the project that is related to the chapters in this part is provided here.

Using the annual report of the firm you selected, answer the following questions:

**Firm's Motivation of Employees (related to Chapters 10 and 11).** How does the firm motivate its employees? Does it offer special programs to enhance job satisfaction?

**Firm's Compensation for Employees (related to Chapters 10 and 11).** Does the firm offer bonuses or stock options to motivate its employees?

# Part V

**Answering the Questions.** You can retrieve the Word file of this project from the textbook website (www.emcp.net/business5e), and insert your answer just below each question. The portion of the project that is related to the chapters in this part is provided here.

Using the annual report of the firm you selected, answer the following questions:

**Firm's Product Line and Mix (related to Chapter 12).** Describe the firm's product line and product mix.

**Firm's Target Market (related to Chapter 12).** Describe the firm's target market.

**Distribution (related to Chapter 13).** How does the firm distribute its products?

**Promotion (related to Chapter 14).** How does the firm promote its products?

# Part VI

**Answering the Questions.** You can retrieve the Word file of this project from the textbook website (wwwemcp.net /business5e), and insert your answer just below each question. The portion of the project that is related to the chapters in this part is provided here.

Using the annual report of the firm you selected, answer the following questions:

**Firm's Financial Performance (related to Chapter 15).** Review the financial summary. Did the firm achieve strong performance last year based on its financial statements?

**Firm's Financing (related to Chapter 16).** When the firm finances its business, how does it typically obtain funds? By borrowing or by issuing stock?

**Firm's Expansion (related to Chapter 17).** Does the firm plan to expand in the future? If so, how?

**Stock Price Performance During the Semester (related to Chapter 17).** Go to the financial website of Google (http://finance.google.com). Insert the name of your company in the box that says "Search Finance." How has the firm's stock price changed during your school term? You can assess the stock price by going to Yahoo's financial website and inserting the ticker symbol of the firm's stock. Why do you think this firm's performance was strong or weak during this semester? Is its performance attributed to its recent management strategies? Or its marketing strategies? Or to something else? Explain.

# Project 2:  Building a Business Plan for Campus.com

## Part I

### Instructions

Create a business plan for Campus .com by filling in the blank sections below. Your instructor will provide you with additional guidelines, such as whether you work on this individually or in teams, and the deadline for completing your business plan.

**Complete the Information.** You can complete the information on the Word file of this project from the textbook website (www.emcp.net /business5e). This allows you to insert all of your information on one file for this project by the end of the school term. The portion of the project that is related to the chapters in this part is provided here.

### Business Idea

Campus.com will provide an information service for high school students who are assessing different colleges to which they may apply. It will provide information on the lifestyles of any college that they select. High school students might find this service useful for several reasons. First, many books compare academic requirements at colleges, but provide very limited information on student lifestyles. Second, some high school students do not rely on the lifestyle information in these books because they question whether the authors really understand students. Third, students do not necessarily want to purchase an entire volume on all colleges across the country just to obtain information on the few colleges to which they may apply. Fourth, students recognize that the material in these books can become outdated.

Campus.com will show a directory of all colleges. Customers (high school students) will then click on those colleges for which they want information. They must submit a credit card number and will be charged $1 for each college that they select. They will receive immediate information on their computer about the campus lifestyles of each college selected.

The main expenses for Campus .com are (a) the creation of the website and (b) gathering information about every college campus from reliable sources. Initially, this information will be gathered by ordering back issues of campus newspapers for the last year and then summarizing the campus activities for each college. In addition, the plan is to send a brief survey to about thirty students at each school (offering $20 to each respondent who fills out the survey), asking them to answer general questions about their opinions of the activities and to rate the campus in terms of its sports activities, entertainment on campus, and nightlife. You hope to receive responses from at least twenty students before you summarize the information for each college. The information will be updated every three months by paying some of the same students who filled out the first survey to fill out an updated survey. Thus, the information that you provide to customers is frequently updated, which is an advantage over any books they could buy in stores.

### Business Environment

**Main Sources of Revenue and Expenses (related to Chapter 1).** The main source of Campus.com's revenue will be:

_____

_____

_____

_____

_____

The main source of Campus.com's expenses will be:

_____

_____

_____

_____

How the earnings of the firm will be used (to pay owners? to be reinvested?):

_____

_____

_____

_____

**Ethics and Social Responsibilities (related to Chapter 2).** What is the mission of Campus.com? Include statements on how the business will fulfill its responsibilities to its customers, its employees, and· its owners:

_____

_____

_____

_____

**Economic Conditions (related to Chapter 3).** Campus.com's performance will be affected in the following ways if economic conditions change:

_____

_____

_____

**Global Conditions (related to Chapter 4).** Campus.com may expand outside the United States by:

_____

_____

_____

A logical choice of a foreign country to target would be:

_____

_____

_____

# Part II

**Completing the Information.** You can complete the information on the Word file of this project from the textbook website (www.emcp .net/business5e). This allows you to insert all of your information on one file for this project by the end of the school term. The portion of the project that is related to the chapters in this part is provided here.

**Form of Business Ownership (related to Chapter 5).** The optimal form of ownership for Campus.com is:

_____

_____

_____

Reasons for choosing that type of ownership:

_____

_____

_____

_____

_____

_____

_____

_____

_____

_____

**Entrepreneurship (related to Chapter 6).** Campus.com's existing competition is:

_____

_____

_____

_____

_____

_____

_____

_____

_____

_____

# Part III

**Completing the Information.** You can complete the information on the Word file of this project from the textbook website (www.emcp. net/business5e). This allows you to insert all of your information on one file for this project by the end of the school term. The portion of the project that is related to the chapters in this part is provided here.

**Managing Effectively (related to Chapter 7).** The strategic plan for Campus.com is:

_____

_____

_____

_____

The tactical plans for Campus.com are:

_____

_____

_____

_____

**Organizational Structure (related to Chapter 8).** Job positions required for Campus.com are:

_____

_____

_____

_____

**Improving Productivity and Quality (related to Chapter 9).** The production process to produce Campus.com's service is:

_____

_____

_____

_____

The production process will be monitored (and possibly revised) over time, as explained here:

_____

_____

_____

_____

**Quality Standards (related to Chapter 9).** Campus.com will maintain the quality of the service it provides by:

_____

_____

_____

_____

_____

_____

_____

_____

_____

# Part IV

### Completing the Information.
You can complete the information on the Word file of this project from the textbook website (www.emcp.net/business5e). This allows you to insert all of your information on one file for this project by the end of the school term. The portion of the project that is related to the chapters in this part is provided here.

### Motivating Employees (related to Chapter 10). Working conditions for Campus.com employees will be:

_____

_____

_____

_____

_____

Disadvantages of the working conditions that may limit employee effectiveness:

_____

_____

_____

_____

### Hiring, Training, and Evaluating Employees (related to Chapter 11). Employees' performance will be assessed by:

_____

_____

_____

_____

The compensation plan for employees will be:

_____

_____

_____

_____

_____

_____

_____

_____

_____

# Part V

### Completing the Information.
You can complete the information on the Word file of this project from the textbook website (www.emcp.net/business5e). This allows you to insert all of your information on one file for this project by the end of the school term. The portion of the project that is related to the chapters in this part is provided here.

### Creating and Pricing Products (related to Chapter 12). Campus.com can expand its product line by:

_____

_____

_____

Campus.com can expand its target market by:

_____

_____

_____

**Pricing (related to Chapter 12).** Campus.com's pricing plan is:

_____

_____

_____

_____

_____

_____

Campus.com will offer these types of discounts:

_____

_____

_____

_____

_____

_____

_____

**Distributing Products (related to Chapter 13).** Campus.com's distribution plan is:

_____

_____

_____

_____

**Promoting Products (related to Chapter 14).** Campus.com's advertising plan is (include explanation of

the target market and the types of media used):

_____

_____

_____

_____

_____

_____

_____

## Part VI

**Completing the Information.** You can complete the information on the Word file of this project from the textbook website (www.emcp .net/business5e). This allows you to insert all of your information on one file for this project by the end of the school term. The portion of the project that is related to the chapters in this part is provided here.

**Accounting and Financial Analysis (related to Chapter 15).** Campus.com's performance over time will be monitored by assessing the following financial ratios:

_____

_____

_____

**Financing (related to Chapter 16).** Alternative choices to obtain funds to support expansion are:

_____

_____

_____

_____

_____

The best alternative is:

_____

_____

_____

_____

The disadvantages of this alternative are:

_____

_____

_____

**Expanding the Business (related to Chapter 17).** Campus.com will determine whether future expansion is feasible by:

_____

_____

_____

_____

# Project 3: Running Your Own Business

## Part I

### Instructions

Create a business plan for your own business by filling in the blank sections below. You may want to fill in each section after completing each chapter or part of the text, while the information is fresh on your mind. Your instructor will provide you

with additional guidelines, such as whether you work on this individually or in teams, and the deadline for completing your business plan.

**Completing the Information.** You can complete the information on the Word file of this project from the textbook website (www.emcp

.net/business5e). This allows you to insert all of your information on one file for this project by the end of the school term. The portion of the project that is related to the chapters in this part is provided here.

## Your Business Environment

**Business Idea (related to Chapter 1).** The main idea of your business is:

_____

_____

_____

**Main Sources of Revenue and Expenses (related to Chapter 1).** Your main source of revenue will be:

_____

_____

_____

Your main sources of expenses resulting from your business will be:

_____

_____

_____

_____

How will the earnings of the business be used?  (to pay yourself? to be reinvested?)

_____

_____

_____

_____

_____

**Establishing Ethics and Social Responsibilities (related to Chapter 2).** How will your business fulfill responsibilities to your customers, your employees, and other owners (if any)?

_____

_____

_____

_____

_____

_____

**Assessing Economic Conditions (related to Chapter 3).** How will the performance of your business be affected if economic conditions change?

_____

_____

_____

_____

_____

_____

**Assessing Global Conditions (related to Chapter 4).** Will your business expand outside the United States? If so, what foreign country will you target?

_____

_____

_____

_____

_____

# Part II

**Completing the Information.** You can retrieve the Word file of this project from the textbook website (www.emcp.net /business5e), and insert your answer just below each question. The portion of the project that is related to the chapters in this part is provided here.

**Selecting a Form of Business Ownership (related to Chapter 5).** The optimal form of ownership for your business is:

_____

_____

_____

_____

Reasons for choosing that type of ownership:

_____

_____

_____

_____

**Entrepreneurship (related to Chapter 6).** Your business will target these industry segments:

_____

_____

_____

_____

Describe the existing competition that your business must face:

_____

_____

_____

_____

_____

_____

_____

_____

_____

_____

# Part III

**Completing the Information.**
You can retrieve the Word file of
this project from the textbook
website (www.emcp.net /busi-
ness5e), and insert your answer just
below each question. The portion of
the project that is related to the
chapters in this part is provided
here.

**Managing Effectively (related to
Chapter 7).** The strategic plan for
your business is:

_____

_____

_____

The tactical plans for your business
are:

_____

_____

_____

_____

**Organizational Structure (re-
lated to Chapter 8).** Job positions
required for your business are:

_____

_____

_____

_____

_____

**Improving Productivity and
Quality (related to Chapter 9).**
The production process to produce
your products or services is:

_____

_____

_____

_____

_____

Your production process will be
monitored (and possibly revised)
over time, as explained here:

_____

_____

_____

_____

_____

**Quality Standards (related to
Chapter 9).** Your business will
maintain the quality of the service it
provides by:

_____

_____

_____

_____

_____

_____

_____

_____

_____

_____

# Part IV

**Completing the Information.**
You can retrieve the Word file of
this project from the textbook
website (www.emcp.net /busi-
ness5e), and insert your answer just
below each question. The portion of
the project that is related to the
chapters in this part is provided
here.

**Motivating Employees (related
to Chapter 10).** You will motivate
your employees by:

_____

_____

_____

_____

_____

**Hiring, Training, and Evaluating
Employees (related to Chapter
11).** You will assess the performance
of employees of your business by:

_____

_____

_____

The compensation plan for your employees will be:

_____

_____

_____

_____

_____

**Quality Standards (related to
Chapter 9).** Your business will
maintain the quality of the service it
provides by:

_____

_____

_____

_____

_____

_____

_____

# Part V

**Completing the Information.**
You can retrieve the Word file of this project from the textbook website (www.emcp.net /business5e), and insert your answer just below each question. The portion of the project that is related to the chapters in this part is provided here.

**Creating and Pricing Products (related to Chapter 12).** Your business can expand its product line by:

———————————————

———————————————

———————————————

———————————————

Your business can expand its target market by:

———————————————

———————————————

———————————————

———————————————

**Pricing (related to Chapter 12).** Your business will price its products based on (cost? competitor prices?):

———————————————

———————————————

———————————————

———————————————

Your business will offer these types of discounts:

———————————————

———————————————

———————————————

———————————————

**Distributing Products (related to Chapter 13).** The distribution plan of your business is:

———————————————

———————————————

———————————————

———————————————

Explain whether the cost of distributing your product will be affected substantially if there is a large increase in the price of gasoline or in postal rates.

———————————————

———————————————

———————————————

———————————————

**Promoting Products (related to Chapter 14).** The advertising plan of your business is (include explanation of the target market and the types of media used):

———————————————

———————————————

———————————————

———————————————

# Part VI

**Completing the Information.**
You can retrieve the Word file of this project from the textbook website (www.emcp.net /business5e), and insert your answer just below each question. The portion of the project that is related to the chapters in this part is provided here.

**Accounting and Financial Analysis (related to Chapter 15).** The performance of your business over time will be monitored by assessing the following financial ratios:

———————————————

———————————————

———————————————

———————————————

**Financing (related to Chapter 16).** Alternative choices to obtain funds to support expansion of your business are:

———————————————

———————————————

———————————————

———————————————

The best alternative is:

———————————————

———————————————

———————————————

The disadvantages of this alternative are:

———————————————

———————————————

———————————————

———————————————

**Expanding the Business (related to Chapter 17).** Your business will determine whether future expansion is feasible by:

———————————————

———————————————

———————————————

———————————————

# Project 4: Planning Your Career

## Goal of Project

The goal of this project is to help you learn about specific career opportunities that fit your specific interests, and to help you recognize what you need to accomplish over time in order to qualify for the career that you desire. Your instructor may provide you with some guidance on how long your project should be.

## Sources of Information

Many websites are available to guide you toward careers that may fit your interests or skills, including:

- www.khake.com
- http://online.onetcenter.org/skills
- www.jobprofiles.org
- www.careerexplorer.net /descriptions.asp
- www.bls.gov/oco
- www.careerplanner.com

You may also retrieve more specific information if you do an Internet search based on the industry in which you are interested. For example, if you are interested in computer technology, or health care, or pharmaceuticals, you can do a search of "Career plan" and that industry and you will find web sites that provide specific information about job positions in that industry.

## Answering the Questions

You can answer the questions related to this project on the Word file from the textbook website (www .emcp.net/business5e). This allows you to insert all of your information on one file for this project by the end of the school term.

## Questions

**1. Career Goal.** What type of business career do you plan to pursue after you complete your education? Mention the industry and the job position (for example, manager of an automobile assembly line, sales manager of a publishing company, technology specialist for a cell phone company, or analyst for a health care firm).

**2. Job Title.** Identify the specific job title that you would like to achieve right after you graduate. If your primary goal is to achieve a position one level above what you can achieve immediately after graduating, you may identify that position as well. Do not specify an executive position such as president unless you plan to own your own business or would likely have a chance to achieve that position. Select a career that you seriously consider pursuing. For example, do not select heart surgeon just because the salary is high if you have no plans to invest the time and effort in medical school.

**3. Job Description.** What is the job description of the job title that you wish to pursue? That is, what are the key tasks for people in the business career that you wish to pursue?

**4. Skills Required.** What types of skills are critical to excel in the business career that you wish to pursue? Possible answers include communication skills, working with other people, managing people, selling, writing skills, and reading skills. Some skills are more critical than others, depending on the business career that you selected.

**5. Reasons for Your Career Goal.** Why do you think the career that you identified would be ideal for you? Your answer should focus on why you would enjoy the work that is involved in this particular career and why you would perform well within that career. You can consider the potential benefits of a specific career (high salary, flexible working hours, expense account) but focus more on why the work (rather than the benefits) would be pleasing to you.

**6. Concerns About Your Career Goal.** Are there any parts of this job that you may not like (such as long work hours, having to deal with angry customers, low salary)? Explain. Even jobs that are very desirable may have some characteristics that you might not like. You should be aware of these characteristics before you pursue your career.

**7. Educational Background Required.** What is the typical required educational background for people who have the career you wish to pursue? What is the typical work experience required for people who have the career that you wish to pursue?

**8. What You Need to Achieve Your Goal.** Given your existing situation, what would it take for you to have the typical background to qualify for the career that you wish to pursue? For example, do you need to complete more courses or degrees? Do you need to major in a specific field? Do you need more years of work experience in that field? Specify how much more education and work experience you need to achieve your goal.

# Project 5:  Stock Market Contest

## Goal of Project

This project allows you to simulate investing $10,000 in a selected stock, monitoring its value, and documenting how good business decisions can enhance the value of a business. You select a publicly-traded company, monitor its value (stock price), and monitor how specific publicized business decisions by the company affect the company's stock price. You learn from this project how stock prices move as a result of this project. More importantly for this course, you will realize how the value of a company can be enhanced by good business decisions, and how it can be adversely affected by bad business decisions.

## Obtaining Stock Price and Dividend Information

Go to the financial website of Google (http://finance.google.com). Insert the name of the stock that you selected in the box that says "Search Finance." Just after the menu of the firm, the stock exchange is identified followed by the ticker symbol of the stock. Many investors refer to a stock by its ticker symbol. Notice that the dividend is listed within the financial information that is given. If the dividend says N/A, this means that the firm does not pay its shareholders a dividend (it reinvests all of its earnings). The dividend quoted on the Google finance website reflects the dividend provided per quarter.

## Completing the Information

You can answer the questions related to this project on the Word file from the textbook website (www.emcp.net/business5e). This allows you to insert all of your information on one file for this project by the end of the school term.

## Enter the Stock Market Contest

1. Identify a stock in which you wish to invest:

_____

2. Ticker symbol of stock:

_____

3. Price per share of your stock at this time:

$_____ per share

4. Number of shares that you purchased with $10,000:

_____ shares

5. Dividend per share paid per quarter:

$_____ per share

Your professor may want you to submit this information at the beginning of the school term when you enter the stock market contest, and will also explain how many points you may earn on this project and how many bonus points you would receive (if any) if you win the contest.

## Determine Your Gain over the School Term

Near the end of the semester, you can determine your gain (or loss) from your investment in a stock. The end date for the project should be specified by your professor. Your professor may ask you to compare your results with other students in the class.

6.  Price per share of your stock on the end date:

$_____ per share

7.  Total dollar value of your shares on the end date (number of shares multiplied by price per share):

$_____

8.  Total dollar amount of dividends received (dividend per share multiplied by number of shares):

$_____

9.  Total dollar amount that you have on the end date:

$_____

10. Return on your investment (total amount above minus $10,000 divided by $10,000):

_____%

## Explaining Your Gain

Near the end of the semester, you may go to http://finance.google.com and insert the name of your selected stock in the search box. The website will then provide a chart that shows the stock price movement of this stock. Click on "3m" above the chart in order to review the stock price movements over the last three months. Notice that major news announcements about the stock are provided during this period. Focus on any announcements that occurred shortly before large stock price movements. Summarize the news announcements that had a large impact on your stock and explain how these announcements relate to the material in the text. That is, do the announcements reflect management, marketing, finance, or the economic environment?

## Comparing Your Stock to the General Market

A common benchmark used to measure general stock market conditions is the S&P 500 index. After you click on "3m" in the stock price chart to review a three-month period, check the small S&P 500 box just above the chart. The website will provide a trend of the S&P 500 index on the same chart as your stock. This allows you to compare the performance of your stock to the stock market in general. Did your stock move in the same direction as the market for most of the school term? Did your stock perform better or worse than the market in general?

## Team Project

If students were divided into teams of equal size, each team can determine its total gain and compare it against other teams. The total gain is the total dollars that all students on the team have from their investment at the end of the school term.

# How to Invest in Stocks

As a firm's business performance changes, so does its stock price. Since performance levels vary among firms, so do stock price movements. Investors who select high-performing firms will typically earn higher returns on their investments. Some stocks have increased by as much as 1,500 percent in one year. Thus, an investor who invested $10,000 in the stock at the beginning of this period and sold the stock one year later would have received $150,000. Meanwhile, the stock prices of some other firms may have declined by 100 percent over that same period. Thus, investors who invested $10,000 in these stocks at the beginning of the period would have lost their entire investment. Investors who understand how stock prices are affected by various factors may be better able to select stocks that will generate high returns.

## 1. How a Firm's Stock Price and Value Are Related

A stock's price should represent the value of the firm on a per-share basis. For example, if a firm is valued at $600 million and has 20 million shares, its stock price is:

$$\text{Stock Price} = \frac{\text{Value of Firm}}{\text{Number of Shares}}$$

$$= \frac{\$600,000,000}{20,000,000 \text{ Shares}}$$

$$= \$30 \text{ per Share}$$

As the performance of the firm improves, investors' demand for the stock will increase. Consequently, the stock price will rise.

A stock price by itself does not clearly indicate the firm's value. Consider Firms A and B, each with stock priced at $40 per share. Assume, however, that Firm A has 10 million shares outstanding and Firm B has 20 million shares. Thus, the value of Firm A is $400 million, while the value of Firm B is $800 million.

## 2. Understanding Stock Quotations

Financial newspapers such as *The Wall Street Journal*, *Barron's*, and *Investors' Business Daily* publish stock quotations, as do *USA Today* and local newspapers. Although the format of stock quotations varies among newspapers,

Example of a Stock Quotation for IBM

| 52-Week | | | | | | | | | | | |
| Hi | Lo | Stock | Symbol | DIV | YLD | PE | Vol. in 100s | Hi | Lo | Close | Change |
| --- | --- | --- | --- | --- | --- | --- | --- | --- | --- | --- | --- |
| 134 | 110 | IBM | IBM | $2.00 | 1.67% | 15 | 76,520 | 121 | 118 | 120 | +.40 |

most quotations provide similar information. Stock prices are always quoted on a per-share basis. Some of the more relevant characteristics that are quoted are summarized next. Use the stock quotations for IBM shown in Exhibit B.1 to supplement the following discussion.

## 2.1  52-Week Price Range

The stock's highest price and lowest price over the last 52 weeks are commonly quoted just to the left of the stock's name. The high and low prices indicate the range for the stock's price over the last year. Some investors use this range as an indicator of how much the stock fluctuates. Other investors compare this range with the prevailing stock price, as they purchase a stock only when its prevailing price is not at its 52-week high.

Notice that IBM's 52-week high price was $134 and its low price was $110 per share. The low price is about 18 percent below the high price. At the time IBM's stock price hit its 52-week low price, IBM's market value was about 18 percent less than its market value at the time its stock price reached its 52-week high.

## 2.2  Symbol

Each stock has a specific symbol that is used to identify the firm. This symbol may be used to communicate trade orders to brokers. Ticker tapes displayed in brokerage firms or on financial news television shows use the symbol to identify each firm. The symbol is normally placed just to the right of the firm's name if it is shown in the stock quotations. The symbol is usually composed of two to four letters for each firm. For example, IBM's symbol is IBM, Home Depot's is HD, Motorola's is MOT, and Yahoo!'s is YHOO.

## 2.3  Dividend

The annual dividend (DIV) is commonly listed just to the right of the firm's name and symbol. It indicates the dividends distributed to stockholders over the last year on a per-share basis. For example, a dividend quotation of $2 for IBM indicates that annual dividends of $2 per share were distributed, or an average of $0.50 per share for each quarter. The annual dollar amount of dividends paid can be determined by multiplying the dividends per share times the number of shares outstanding. If a firm that paid dividends of $4 per share had 100 million shares of stock outstanding during the last year, it paid out annual dividends of $400 million.

Some stock quotation tables also show a dividend yield (YLD) next to the annual dividend, which represents the annual dividend per share as a percentage of the stock's prevailing price. For example, if IBM's annual dividend is $2 per share and the stock's prevailing price is $120 per share, the stock's dividend yield is:

$$\text{Dividend Yield} = \frac{\text{Dividends Paid per Share}}{\text{Prevailing Stock Price}}$$

$$= \frac{2}{120}$$

$$= 1.67\%$$

Some firms (such as General Electric) attempt to provide a somewhat stable dividend yield over time, while other firms do not. For other firms (such as Nike), the dividend yield varies substantially over time. Some other firms (such as Yahoo!) reinvest all of their earnings rather than pay dividends.

## 2.4  Price-Earnings Ratio

Most stock quotations include the stock's price-earnings (PE) ratio, which represents the firm's prevailing stock price per share divided by the firm's earnings per share (earnings divided by number of existing shares of stock) generated over the last year. For example, if IBM's stock is currently priced at $120 per share, and its earnings over the last year were $8 per share, the stock's price-earnings ratio is:

$$\text{Price-Earnings Ratio} = \frac{\text{Stock Price per Share}}{\text{Earnings per Share}}$$

$$= \frac{\$120}{\$8}$$

$$= 15$$

The price-earnings ratio is closely monitored by some investors who believe that a low PE ratio (relative to other firms in the same industry) signals that the prevailing price is too low based on the firm's earnings. That is, they perceive the stock as undervalued.

## 2.5  Volume

The volume (referred to as "Vol" or "Sales") of shares traded on the previous day is commonly included in stock quotations. The volume is normally quoted in hundreds of shares. It is not unusual for 1 million shares of a large firm's stock to be traded on a single day. Some newspapers also show the percentage change in the volume of trading from the day before.

## 2.6  Previous Day's Price Quotations

The high price (Hi) and low price (Lo) for the previous trading day are normally included in stock quotations, along with the closing price (Close) at the end of the day. In addition, the change in the price is also typically provided and indicates the increase or decrease in the stock price from the closing price on the previous trading day.

## 2.7  Stock Index Quotations

Most financial news reports on the general performance of the stock market over a given day mention how particular stock indexes changed. Each stock index represents a particular set of stocks. For example, the following indexes are commonly quoted:

| Index | Description |
|---|---|
| Standard & Poor's (S&P) 500 Index | 500 large firms |
| Dow Jones Industrial Average (DJIA) | 30 large industrial firms |
| Standard & Poor's (S&P) 600 Small Cap | 600 small publicly traded firms |
| Nasdaq 100 | 100 firms traded on the Nasdaq |

The two most commonly cited indexes are the S&P 500 Index and the Dow Jones Industrial Average, which are monitored to assess general market performance for the previous day or a previous period. The S&P 500 and Dow Jones Industrial Average indexes are not proper indicators for specific industries or for smaller stocks, however.

## 3. Measuring the Return on Stocks

Stockholders can earn a return from a particular stock through a dividend or an increase in the stock's price. Over a given period, the return to stockholders who invest in the stock can be measured as:

$$\text{Return} = \frac{(\text{Selling Price} - \text{Purchase Price}) + \text{Dividend}}{\text{Purchase Price}}$$

Notice that the numerator reflects a dollar amount composed of the difference between the sales price and purchase price, plus the dividend. This dollar amount is divided by the purchase price to measure the return.

For example, consider a stock that was purchased for $40 per share at the beginning of the year. Assume that a dividend of $2 per share was paid to the investor and that the stock was sold for $44 at the end of the year. The return on this stock over the year is:

$$\text{Return} = \frac{(\text{Selling Price} - \text{Purchase Price}) + \text{Dividend}}{\text{Purchase Price}}$$
$$= \frac{(\$44 - \$40) + \$2}{\$40}$$
$$= .15, \text{ or } 15\%$$

Since the return on the stock is made up of dividends plus the increase in the stock's price, investors cannot assess a stock's performance just by its dividends. Some firms that tend to pay out a higher proportion of their earnings as dividends have less ability to grow in the future, which may limit the potential increase in the stock price. Conversely, firms that retain (reinvest) most of their earnings pay low or no dividends but are more capable of growing. Therefore, investors who are willing to invest in growth firms that do not pay dividends may benefit from larger increases in the stock price.

## 3.1 Return-Risk Tradeoff for Small Stocks

Some investors prefer to invest in stocks of small firms that have potential for a large increase in the stock price. They may attempt to invest before the firms have had much success, because they can purchase the stock at a relatively low price. If these firms become successful, the share price should increase substantially. Many investors realize that if they had purchased shares of successful growing firms such as Microsoft and Dell when those firms went public, they would be millionaires now. For every huge success story, however, there are many other firms that failed. Investors who invested in these other unsuccessful firms may have lost 100 percent of their investment. Stocks of small firms tend to have potential for high returns but also tend to have high risk. In addition, many stocks of small firms are not traded frequently, which means that investors who wish to sell their shares may have difficulty finding a buyer. This can force the investors to sell the stock at a lower price.

## 4. Factors That Influence Stock Price Movements

The perceived value of a firm (and therefore the stock's price) can change in response to several factors as explained next.

### 4.1  Economic Effects

Any factor that enhances the expected performance of the firm can increase its value. For example, when economic conditions are expected to improve, the firm's performance may be expected to increase, and so should the firm's value. Some firms are more sensitive to economic conditions, as a change in economic conditions affects the demand for some products more than others. A retail store such as Wal-Mart is more sensitive to economic conditions than a utility company. Therefore, the stock price of Wal-Mart should be more sensitive to economic conditions than the stock price of a utility company.

### 4.2  Market Effects

**bullish**
periods in which there is considerable demand for stocks because investors have favorable expectations about the performance of firms

**bearish**
periods in which investors are selling their stocks because of unfavorable expectations about the performance of firms

A stock's price may ride along with the general trend of the stock market. During some so-called **bullish** periods, there is considerable demand for stocks because investors have favorable expectations about the performance of firms. During other so-called **bearish** periods, investors are selling their stocks because of unfavorable expectations about the performance of firms. As an extreme example, the prices of many stocks declined by more than 40 percent from September 2008 to November 2008 when the credit crisis intensified. Most stocks declined by at least 20 percent over that period. The major decline was at least partially attributed to a more pessimistic outlook about economic conditions.

### 4.3  Industry Effects

Stock prices are also driven by industry factors. For example, expectations of future performance in the computer industry may be very favorable in a specific period, while expectations may be less favorable for the steel industry. Stock prices in the oil industry are driven by the market price for oil.

### 4.4  Characteristics of the Firm

In addition to market and industry effects, stock prices can also be affected by characteristics of the firm. For example, one firm may have better management than others in the same industry, which could result in higher earnings and higher stock returns. Alternatively, a firm could experience a labor strike, which could cause its earnings and stock return to be lower than those of other firms in the industry. Stock price movements of firms in the same industry vary over time, even though these firms are affected by the same industry conditions.

A given firm may use many strategies that could cause its stock price return to be different from those of other firms in the industry. In general, any strategy that is likely to improve earnings will result in a higher stock price. The stock price of IBM rose after IBM restructured its operations and eliminated thousands of jobs. Investors may have expected that operating expenses would be reduced as a result of the restructuring.

## 4.5 How Stock Prices Respond to New Information

The price of a stock adjusts in response to changes in the demand for the stock or in the supply of the stock for sale by investors. The price may change throughout the day. For example, a stock's price tends to increase substantially if investors are confident that the company is about to be acquired by another firm, because firms commonly bid up the share price of a target by 30 to 50 percent in order to acquire all of its shares. Alternatively, a stock's price might decline substantially if there is news that the company's medical patents were rejected or that its main product has a defect.

## 5. Identifying Undervalued Firms

Investors recognize that any new information about a firm's performance (especially its earnings) will affect its stock price. Consequently, they would like to anticipate the information before other investors so that they can take their investment position before others become aware of the information. For example, investors may attempt to forecast whether firms are implementing any major policies, such as acquisitions or layoffs. They use such forecasts to estimate future earnings. If their estimate of the firm's earnings is higher than that of most other investors, they may believe the firm is undervalued.

As explained earlier, some investors closely monitor PE ratios to determine whether a firm's stock is undervalued. Consider Firm Z with a stock price of $20 per share and recent annual earnings of $4 per share. This firm's PE ratio is 20/4, or 5. Assume that most firms in Firm Z's industry have a PE ratio of 9, which means that their stock prices are nine times their recent annual earnings, on average. Since Firm Z's stock price is only five times its recent earnings, some investors may believe that Firm Z's stock is undervalued. They may argue that its price should be nine times its annual earnings, or about $36.

## 5.1 Stock Market Efficiency

**stock market efficiency**
a term used to suggest that stock prices reflect all publicly available information

The term **stock market efficiency** is used to suggest that stock prices reflect all publicly available information. That is, the prevailing prices have not ignored any publicly available information that could affect the firms' values. Consequently, stocks should not be overvalued or undervalued. The

# Self-Scoring Exercises

## How Much Risk Can You Take?

Investing in the stock market isn't for those with queasy stomachs or short time horizons. The money you've earmarked for emergencies should be in liquid investments with relatively steady returns, such as money market funds. But stocks are the backbone of a long-term portfolio for retirement or other goals that are at least 10 to 15 years away.

This simple, self-scoring risk-tolerance test is designed to help you decide what percentage of your long-term money should go into stocks. As you (and your stomach) become more accustomed to the market's ups and downs, you might want to retake the test. Questions come from VALIC (The Variable Annuity Life Insurance Company) and other sources.

_____ 1. Which of the following would worry you the most?
   a) My portfolio may lose value in one of every three years.
   b) My investments won't stay even with inflation.
   c) I won't earn a premium over inflation on my long-term investments.

_____ 2. How would you react if your stock portfolio fell 30 percent in one year?
   a) I would sell some or all of it.
   b) I would stop investing money until the market came back.
   c) I would stick with my investment plan and consider adding more to stocks.

_____ 3. You've just heard that the stock market fell by 10 percent today. Your reaction is to:
   a) consider selling some stocks.
   b) be concerned, but figure the market is likely to go up again eventually.
   c) consider buying more stocks because they are cheaper now.

_____ 4. You read numerous newspaper articles over several months quoting experts who predict stocks will lose money in the coming decade. Many argue that real estate is a better investment. You would:
   a) consider reducing your stock investments and increasing your investment in real estate.
   b) be concerned, but stick to your long-term investments in stocks.
   c) consider the articles as evidence of unwarranted pessimism over the outlook for stocks.

_____ 5. Which of the following best describes your attitude about investing in bonds as compared with stocks?
   a) The high volatility of the stock market concerns me, so I prefer to invest in bonds.
   b) Bonds have less risk but they provide lower returns, so I have a hard time choosing between the two.
   c) The lower return potential of bonds leads me to prefer stocks.

_____ 6. Which of the following best describes how you evaluate the performance of your investments?
   a) My greatest concern is the previous year's performance.
   b) The previous two years are the most important to me.
   c) Performance over five or more years is most significant to me.

*(continued)*

# Self-Scoring Exercises

_____ 7. Which of the following scenarios would make you feel best about your investments?
   a) Being in a money market fund saves you from losing half your money in a market downturn.
   b) You double your money in a stock fund in one year.
   c) Over the long term, your overall mix of investments protects you from loss and outpaces the rate of inflation.

_____ 8. Which of the following statements best describes you?
   a) I often change my mind and have trouble sticking to a plan.
   b) I can stay with a strategy only as long as it seems to be going well.
   c) Once I make up my mind to do something, I tend to carry through with it, regardless of the obstacles.

_____ 9. If you won $20,000 in the lottery, you would:
   a) spend it on a new car.
   b) invest it in a safe municipal bond fund.
   c) invest it in the stock market.

_____10. How much experience do you have investing in stocks or stock funds?
   a) None.
   b) A little.
   c) A comfortable amount.

**SCORING:** For each a, give yourself 4 points; for each b, 6 points; and for each c, 10 points. Your total score tells you the percentage you should invest in stocks. Put the rest in bonds or other fixed-income investments.

rationale for stock market efficiency is that there are numerous stock analysts who closely monitor stocks. If any stock was undervalued based on existing information, investors would purchase those stocks. The stock's price would be pushed higher in response to the strong demand by all the investors who recognized that the stock was undervalued. Conversely, investors holding overvalued stock would sell that stock once they recognized that it was overvalued. This action would place downward pressure on the stock's price, causing it to move toward its proper level.

Even if the stock market is efficient, investors differ on how to interpret publicly available information. For example, investors may react differently to information that IBM's earnings increased by 20 percent over the last year. Some investors may view that information as old news, while others may believe it is a signal for continued strong performance in the future. Such differences in interpretation are why some investors purchase a stock and others sell that same stock, based on the same information.

## 6. Problems in Valuing Stocks

As just explained, investors buy a stock when they believe it is undervalued and sell a stock when they believe it is overvalued. To decide whether a stock is over- or undervalued, they commonly rely on financial statements provided by firms. In particular, they derive the value of a stock from the firm's reported earnings because earnings serve as an estimate of cash flows. When a firm's revenue is in cash, and its expenses are paid in cash, the earnings are a good measure of cash flow.

Although earnings can be a very useful indicator of a firm's performance, investors must recognize that the reported earnings are subject to manipulation. A firm has some flexibility in the rules it uses when estimating its revenue and its expenses. Thus, it can inflate its reported earnings by using accounting methods that inflate its reported revenue or reduce its reported expenses.

Various accounting methods are used to inflate revenue. For example, if a firm has a multi-year contract with a client, it may record all the revenue in the first year of the contract, even though it receives payment only for the first year. Some firms report all of their sales as revenue even though the cash has not yet been received. If some of the sales are credit sales, the firm may never receive cash from those sales.

Firms also have some flexibility when accounting for expenses, which means that some firms underestimate their expenses. One of the most common ways to underestimate expenses is to separately report some types of expenses that will not occur again (such as expenses that result from closing a manufacturing plant). The firm can exclude these from its normal operating expenses. Thus, when it subtracts its normal operating expenses from revenue to estimate earnings, the earnings level will appear to be relatively high.

## 6.1  Investor Reliance on Analyst Ratings

Many investors make decisions about buying or selling stocks based on ratings by stock analysts, who are supposed to be experts at analyzing stocks. Although some analysts may offer valuable advice, many analysts offer poor advice. Most of the analysts provide very optimistic ratings on most stocks. That is, the analysts are unwilling to discriminate between good and bad stocks. If investors took the analysts' advice literally, they would buy most stocks.

Many analysts are employed by investment firms that hope to be hired to perform other services for the firms that are being rated. Thus, there is an obvious conflict of interests. Analysts may be implicitly pressured to rate most firms highly.

## 7.  Stock Transactions

**stockbroker**
a person who facilitates desired stock transactions

**floor traders**
people on the trading floor of a stock exchange who execute transactions

Investors who wish to purchase stocks use a **stockbroker** who facilitates the stock transactions desired. Brokers receive requests for trades from investors and then communicate these requests to people on the trading floor of a stock exchange (called **floor traders**) who execute the transactions.

A typical stock transaction order specifies the name of the stock, whether the stock is to be bought or sold, the amount of shares to be traded, and the investor's desired price. For example, one investor may call a broker and request: "Purchase 100 shares of IBM; pay no more than $110 per share." A second investor who is holding IBM stock may call a different broker and request: "Sell 100 shares of IBM at the highest price possible." Both brokers will send this information to the stock exchange. One floor trader will accommodate the buyer, while another floor trader will accommodate the seller. The two traders can agree on a transaction in which 100 shares of IBM are sold for $110 per share.

## 7.1  Market Orders Versus Limit Orders

**market order**
an investor's order requesting a transaction at the best possible price

**limit order**
an investor's order that places a limit on the price at which the investor is willing to purchase or sell a stock

Investors can place a **market order**, which means they request a transaction at the best possible price. They can also place a **limit order**, which puts a limit on the price at which they are willing to purchase or sell a stock. Examples of a market order are (1) "Purchase 200 shares of Microsoft stock at the best [lowest] price available" and (2) "Sell 300 shares of Cisco stock at the best [highest] price available." Examples of a limit order are (1) "Purchase 300 shares of Disney; pay no more than $30 per share" and (2) "Sell 100 shares of PepsiCo; sell for no less than $70 per share."

## 7.2  Purchasing Stocks on Margin

**on margin**
purchasing a stock by providing cash for only a portion of the funds needed and borrowing the remainder from the brokerage firm

Investors can purchase stocks **on margin**, which means that they provide cash for only a portion of the funds needed to purchase stock. Many brokerage firms extend loans to investors who wish to buy on margin. For example, an investor may place an order to purchase 100 shares of Wells Fargo stock at $34 per share. The transaction is priced at $3,400. An investor who has only $3,000 available may borrow the remaining $400 from the brokerage firm. There are limits on the amount that investors can borrow, however. Normally, the amount borrowed cannot exceed 50 percent of the amount of the investment.

## 7.3  Types of Brokers

**discount brokers**
brokers who ensure that a transaction desired by an investor is executed but do not offer advice

**full-service brokers**
brokers who provide advice to investors on stocks to purchase or sell and also ensure that transactions desired by investors are executed

Different types of brokers provide services that investors need. **Discount brokers** ensure that a transaction desired by an investor is executed but do not offer advice. Popular discount brokers include E*Trade and TD Ameritrade. **Full-service brokers** provide advice to investors on stocks to purchase or sell and also ensure that transactions desired by investors are executed. Popular full-service brokers include Merrill Lynch (part of Bank of America) and Morgan Stanley.

## 7.4  Commissions on Stock Transactions

**commission**
sales fee

Brokers charge a **commission**, or sales fee, to execute a stock transaction. The commissions charged by full-service brokers are typically higher than those charged by discount brokers. Commissions are sometimes set according to the number of shares traded. Other discount and full-service brokers set their commissions according to the dollar value of the transaction.

Many stock transactions are now executed online through online brokerage websites (see Exhibit B.2). The commissions for these trades are very low, such as $10 per trade.

**round lots**
multiples of 100 shares

**odd lots**
less than 100 shares

Investors typically purchase stocks in **round lots**, or multiples of 100 shares. They may also purchase stocks in **odd lots**, or less than 100 shares, but the transaction cost may be higher.

| **Exhibit B.2** | Websites with Online Trading Information |
| --- | --- |
| NYSE Euronext | www.amex.com |
| Fidelity Investors | https://www.fidelity.com |
| E*Trade | www.etrade.com |
| Charles Schwab | www.schwab.com |
| Merrill Lynch | http://ml.com |
| TD Ameritrade | www.ameritrade.com |

## 8.  Stock Exchanges

The main stock exchange in the United States is the New York Stock Exchange (NYSE). The NYSE has a trading floor where traders exchange stocks. Many traders represent brokerage firms and execute the transactions that their customers desire. Other traders execute transactions for their own accounts. The trading resembles an auction, as traders selling a stock attempt to receive the highest possible price. Each trader may serve as a buyer for some transactions and a seller for others.

Many of the largest firms in the United States (such as Procter & Gamble and IBM) have their stocks listed on the NYSE. Firms that list their stocks on this exchange must satisfy various requirements on their earnings, size, the number of shareholders who own their stock, and the number of their shares outstanding. They also must pay fees to list on the exchange. More than 1 billion shares are traded per day on the NYSE.

Some firms list on other exchanges in the United States, such as the the Midwest Stock Exchange and the Pacific Stock Exchange. Each of these exchanges also has a trading floor. The listing requirements to list a stock on these exchanges are not as restrictive as the NYSE's requirements. Consequently, many smaller firms that might not meet the NYSE's requirements can list their stocks on these stock exchanges.

### 8.1  Over-the-Counter Market

**National Association of Security Dealers Automated Quotation (Nasdaq)**
a computerized network within the OTC market for firms that meet specific size and capital requirements

In addition to the exchanges just described, there is also an over-the-counter (OTC) market. The OTC market is most commonly used by smaller firms, some of which do not meet the size requirements to trade on the NYSE. Stock transactions on the OTC market are executed by traders through a telecommunications network rather than on a trading floor. Stocks of firms that meet specific size and capital requirements are traded through a computerized network within the OTC market, called the **National Association of Security Dealers Automated Quotation (Nasdaq)**. This system provides immediate stock price quotations. The network allows transactions to be executed without the need for a trading floor. Stocks of about 5,000 firms are traded on the Nasdaq. More than 1 billion shares are traded daily in the Nasdaq market. Nevertheless, the market value of these trades is less than that of the NYSE, because the transactions on the NYSE are larger. Although most firms listed in the Nasdaq market are smaller than those listed on the NYSE, some (such as Microsoft and Intel) are very large. Many technology firms are listed in the Nasdaq market.

## 8.2  Regulation of Stock Exchanges

The Securities and Exchange Commission (SEC) was created in 1934 to regulate security markets such as the stock exchanges. It enforces specific trading guidelines to prevent unethical trading activities. For example, it attempts to prevent **insider trading**, or transactions initiated by people (such as employees) who have information about a firm that has not been disclosed to the public (called **insider information**). Consider an executive of an engineering firm that has just completed a contract to do work for the government that will generate a large amount of revenue for the firm. If the executive calls a broker to buy shares of the firm, this executive has an unfair advantage over other investors because of the inside information that has not yet been disclosed to the public.

## 9.  Investing in Foreign Stocks

U.S. investors can also purchase foreign stocks. When foreign stocks are not listed on a U.S. exchange, the U.S. broker may need to call a broker at a foreign subsidiary, who communicates the desired transaction to the foreign stock exchange where the stock is traded. The commissions paid by U.S. investors for such transactions are higher than those paid for transactions on U.S. exchanges. Many of the larger foreign stocks are listed on U.S. stock exchanges as **American depository receipts (ADRs)**. An ADR is a certificate representing ownership of a stock issued by a non-U.S. firm. The more popular ADRs include British Airways and Sony.

## 10.  Investing in Mutual Funds

Mutual funds sell shares to individual investors and use the proceeds to invest in various securities. They are attractive to investors because they employ portfolio managers with expertise in making investment decisions. Thus, individual investors can leave the responsibility for investment decisions with these portfolio managers. Second, individual investors with a small amount of money (such as $500 or $1,000) can invest in mutual funds. In this way, they can be part owners of a widely diversified portfolio with a small amount of money.

The **net asset value (NAV)** of a mutual fund is the market value of the fund's securities after subtracting any expenses incurred (such as portfolio manager salaries) by the fund, on a per-share basis. As the values of the securities contained in a mutual fund rise, so does the mutual fund's NAV.

### 10.1  Types of Mutual Funds

**Open-end mutual funds** stand ready to repurchase their shares at the prevailing NAV if investors decide to sell the shares. Conversely, shares of **closed-end funds** are funds that are sold on stock exchanges.

**growth funds**
mutual funds that invest in stocks of firms with high potential for growth

**income funds**
mutual funds that invest in stocks that pay large dividends or in bonds that provide coupon payments

**international stock funds**
mutual funds that invest in stocks of foreign firms

**load mutual funds**
open-end mutual funds that can be purchased only by calling a broker

**no-load funds**
open-end mutual funds that can be purchased without the services of a broker

**expense ratio**
for a mutual fund, expenses divided by assets

Most mutual funds tend to focus on particular types of securities so that they can attract investors who wish to invest in those securities. For example, **growth funds** invest in stocks of firms with high potential for growth. **Income funds** invest in stocks that pay large dividends or in bonds that provide coupon payments. **International stock funds** invest in stocks of foreign firms. Each mutual fund has a prospectus that describes its investment objectives, its recent performance, the types of securities it purchases, and other relevant financial information.

## 10.2  Load Versus No-Load Mutual Funds

Open-end mutual funds that can be purchased only by calling a broker are referred to as **load mutual funds**. The term load refers to the transaction fees (commissions) charged for the transaction. Other open-end mutual funds that can be purchased without the services of a broker are referred to as **no-load funds**. These mutual funds are purchased by requesting a brief application from the funds and sending it in with the investment.

All mutual funds incur expenses from hiring portfolio managers to select stocks and from serving clients (mailing fees and so on). A mutual fund's **expense ratio** (defined as expenses divided by assets) can be assessed to determine the expenses incurred by the fund per year. Some mutual funds have an expense ratio of less than .5 percent, while others have an expense ratio above 2 percent. The mutual fund's prospectus will include its expense ratio. Since high expenses can cause lower returns, investors closely monitor the expense ratio.

## Key Terms

American depository receipts (ADRs)  644
bearish  636
bullish  637
closed-end mutual funds  644
commission  642
discount brokers  642
expense ratio  645
floor traders  641
full-service brokers  642
growth funds  645

income funds  645
insider information  644
insider trading  644
international stock funds  645
limit order  642
load mutual funds  645
market order  642
National Association of Security Dealers Automated Quotation (Nasdaq)  643

net asset value (NAV)  644
no-load funds  645
odd lots  642
on margin  642
open-end mutual funds  644
round lots  642
stockbroker  641
stock market efficiency  638

# College and Career Guide

This guide is designed to help you maximize your success in college and in your career. Accordingly, it is divided into three parts:

✦ How to make the most of this course

✦ How to apply this course to your career

✦ How to maximize your chances of success in your career

Topics discussed include time management for college students, choosing a particular business major, the kinds of jobs that are available for various business majors, selecting a career, and pursuing a job after graduation.

## 1. How to Make the Most of This Course

You may wonder how you can use this course to prepare for your future. Even if you do not get a job in the business world, you can apply the concepts in this book to many different areas of your life. You can use human resource management techniques to improve your relationships with your coworkers and friends. You can use marketing concepts to promote yourself in your workplace. You can use finance concepts to maximize your retirement funds. You can use accounting techniques to budget your personal finances. Thus, you can apply the knowledge you acquire in this class to improve your life in many ways. Even if you are returning to school after working in the business world, there is still more to learn about the diverse business disciplines.

How can you optimize your chances for success in this course? Several concepts in this course can be applied to enhance your college career. They include time management, organization and professional behavior.

### 1.1 Manage Your Time

Do you often turn in course assignments late, or cram for exams at the last minute? If so, your time management skills may not be as strong as they should be to be successful in college. In the business world, you will be expected to organize your time efficiently and to finish projects before the deadline. College differs from high school in that it is necessary to budget your time more carefully. You can use many techniques to manage your time effectively.

If you have a weakness in time management, you can begin to correct the deficiency by appraising what you do on a day-to-day basis. Often, people do not realize how much time they waste. To reduce the amount of time that you spend on activities, do a self-assessment of a typical day in your life. What time do you typically wake up in the morning? How much time do you spend on the Internet? Do you spend a great deal of time watching television? If you are honest with yourself, you will most likely identify many ways that you can spend your time more efficiently so that you are able to complete assignments on time, study for exams in an effective manner, and still participate in other activities.

Regardless of your major, your decisions about how you use your time will largely determine how successful you will be. If you accept a job in the business world, you will be expected to follow behavioral norms that will affect your chances for success and promotion. Therefore, you should use your college experience to develop the skills you will need on the job after your graduate.

**Create and Stick to a Schedule**   Many students do not schedule their time effectively. They procrastinate and end up cramming when exam time arrives. They could avoid this last-minute panic by simply establishing a study schedule and sticking to it. Ideally, you should avoid deadline-based scheduling, where you do work only when it is required in the near future. Scheduling is very relevant to the business world, where you will have to collect, interpret, and organize information in advance of deadlines in order to make professional presentations. You should work on maintaining a schedule now so that you will be accustomed to doing so when you get a job.

**Be on Time**   Many college students view time casually and walk into the classroom after the class has started. This reflects poorly on the student and often results in poor performance due to the material missed. In the business world, you will have to be at meetings and conferences on time or risk losing your job. Most managers consider being late to work unprofessional and undesirable. While you are in college, establish a routine of arriving at class on time so that you will not have to adjust to being on time at work. You also will get more out of your classes if you get there on time.

## 1.2   Organize Your Materials

Businesspeople and students run into problems simply because of disorganization. It is important that you establish a method of organizing notes and handouts now so that you will be prepared to do so in the future. You can easily set up a system for storing information by using binders for all your course notes and handouts and a filing cabinet to store information regarding potential job leads and materials from past courses. This way, when you need to access information from current and past classes, the material will be available at your fingertips.

## 1.3   Get the Most out of Your Classes

College students often do not learn as much as they could from their classes because they skip class, fail to pay attention to details presented in class, and fail to develop good study habits. These suggestions can help you get the most out of your classes.

**Go to Class**   Most students take several classes each semester, so they may be tempted to "blow off class" with the excuse that work in other classes is piling up. By missing class, you will miss important information, and you will also get further behind in the class. If you know that you will miss class in advance, make sure to get the e-mail address and phone number of a classmate so that you can make up the material that you missed.

**Take the Course Content Seriously**    It is easy to take a course and study for exams without really absorbing the material. In a class such as this, however, it is important to understand what you are reading and to think about how you can apply the knowledge that you acquire to your own life. You will know more about business and have an advantage over other students and competitors in the job market if you take the class seriously, work through the end-of-chapter questions even if they are not assigned, and take good notes based on class lectures.

**Take Good Notes**    Do you often daydream in class and fail to pay attention? Do you stay up late at night and then nearly fall asleep in your morning classes? If so, you will not be able to take good notes, which is essential for maximizing your performance in class. You should make sure to get a good night's sleep before class and be prepared to take notes, either on a laptop computer or by hand. You may also want to borrow a classmate's notes and compare them to yours to make sure that you did not miss anything.

**Use the Self-Assessment Section**    Even if you take good notes and organize your materials, you may still need practice in mastering the concepts presented in class. For this reason, after you finish a chapter in the text, you should turn to the self-assesssment section and make sure that you can answer all of the questions. This allows you to detect any concepts that deserve additional review.

## 1.4  Maintain a Professional Appearance

In the business world, you typically will be expected to follow a dress code. For many firms, the dress code is "business casual": generally, this means khakis and a dress shirt for men and dress pants or a skirt for women. Jeans and T-shirts are not permitted in most workplaces. Generally, when you attend a job interview, you are expected to dress formally. Consider investing in a suit that you can wear to job interviews and to your workplace.

**Behave Professionally with E-mail**    In college and in the workplace, e-mail is an important means of communication. When writing messages to your professors or to other staff in a college environment, write in a professional manner. Avoid slang and use complete sentences. This format is good practice for using e-mail in the business world.

## 2.  How to Apply This Course to Your Career

You may be wondering if a career in business might be right for you or what is involved with working in a business discipline. This textbook highlights the basics of business management, from understanding the economic environment to marketing strategies that businesses use. In other words, by utilizing your professors and this book, you should be able to begin the process of discovering what your interests are as they relate to business.

Your first steps toward gaining the education you need to get the career you want are to select a college and a major. If you choose a business major, many different types of careers may be available to you.

## 2.1  Choosing a College

People who decide to pursue a college degree must also select the proper college or university. If you will be working while pursuing your degree, the choice of a college may be dictated by the location of your job. If you have the flexibility to relocate, several criteria are worth considering. The first step is to identify the colleges that offer a degree in your main field of interest. Review college catalogs (available at many libraries) to compare the courses offered. Then, you can more closely assess each college that offers a degree in your desired field to determine the course requirements, possible elective courses, and minor fields available. Other factors such as tuition and locations should also be considered. Several colleges offer a degree in any given field.

Some colleges are more prestigious than others, which can be important in attaining a good job. Colleges' reputations tend to vary, however. One college may have a strong program in one field but a weak program in others.

If you plan to find a job in the local area, the college does not need to have a national reputation. Specialized jobs are scarce in many college towns, however. Therefore, even if the college is not nationally recognized, it should be reputable from the perspective of potential employers who may hire its graduates.

When considering colleges, obtain information about the admission criteria, cost, reputation, types of majors offered, job placement data, and financial aid. Guidance on selecting a college is available at various websites, including the following:

| Website | Offers |
| --- | --- |
| **www.careersandcolleges.com** | Advice on applying, student life, comparison of private versus public schools. |
| **www.finaid.org** | Advice on applying for loans and scholarships |
| **www.college.org** | Information about types of colleges, financial aid, and types of degrees offered. |

## 2.2  Selecting a Major

You are probably at the beginning of your college career and may be uncertain about what kind of career you want. At your college or university, there are so many options to choose from for your major and minor. How can you make the decision about whether to be a business major? Your decision should be made based on your particular skill set—your strengths and your personality.

## 2.3  Careers for Business Majors

After taking this class, you will have a better understanding of each area of business. If you pursue a career in business, your salary and level of job satisfaction will depend on the type of job you select. The job satisfaction level for any given career varies among people. Thus, you may not know whether you like a particular type of job until you have worked at it. This is a major dilemma because it is difficult to properly assess job satisfaction without on-the-job experience, which normally occurs after graduation. To measure your present level of job satisfaction, go to (http://hotjobs.yahoo.com).

Every field offers different career paths that can be chosen, and each field has different educational requirements. Some of the jobs that are available for graduates of business programs are described next.

**Accounting Majors**   Accounting is mainly concerned with the collection and analysis of information about a company. For example, an accountant will create balance sheets and income statements for a firm that comply with generally accepted accounting principles (GAAP) and report this information to the executives and shareholders of the firm. Accounting is very important for companies because accountants collect and interpret information about revenue, expenses, and profits in particular periods. Accountants also analyze financial information provided by the company and certify that the information is correct. Publicly traded companies must disclose this information to the government to be in compliance with Securities and Exchange Commission regulations. Chapter 15 in the text provides more information about the concepts that accounting majors study.

Accounting majors may get several types of jobs after graduation. Often, companies hire them to provide information regarding the profitability of the firm as well as auditing, budgeting, and cash flow analysis. Most accounting jobs, however, require an advanced degree such as a master's degree and certification as a certified public accountant (CPA). So, if you decide to become an accountant, you should anticipate that you will have to continue your education.

**Economics Majors**   Economics majors study supply and demand conditions in the economy, as well as microeconomics and labor economics. Many economics courses, such as macroeconomics, international economics, monetary theory, and public policy, use a country perspective. Jobs for economics majors include economic forecasting of exchange rates, interest rates, and commodity prices, as well as finance-related jobs in banking and stock analysis. Chapters 3 and 4 in the text provide more information regarding the subject matter that an economics major would study.

**Finance Majors**   Finance is the study of how firms raise funds and how they make investments. Finance courses, such as investments, financial institutions, corporate finance, and international finance, focus on the decisions that managers and investors make. Chapters 16 and 17 provide an overview of the topics that a finance major would study.

A person with a degree in finance may decide to work for a company, doing cash flow analysis, or for a bank or financial institution, analyzing potential investments. One specific type of finance major is financial planning, which involves helping clients make the most of their personal finances, including retirement and wealth management planning. Often, new finance graduates take these jobs and receive commissions when they attract new customers for their employers.

**Insurance Majors**   Insurance majors specialize in risk management. They may be hired by corporations to forecast changes in economic conditions and determine the best ways to avoid risk. For personal finance jobs, they advise clients on the kinds of life insurance that would be most favorable for them and sell other types of insurance products, such as car insurance and property insurance.

**Management Majors**   Management includes several areas of specialization, which are covered in Chapters 7 to 11. One area is organizational behavior, which describes how managers work with other employees to ensure that the firm performs well. This area is described in Chapters 7 and 8. A second important area of management is production management, which is focused on managing the manufacturing process. This topic is discussed in Chapter 9. A third important area of management is human resource management, which involves handling relationships between the firm and its employees. It also addresses the optimal compensation structure of employees, ways of motivating employees, and discipline of employees. Human resource majors may find jobs as hiring managers at large companies. They may also be in charge of designing compensation packages for a company's employees. Chapters 10 and 11 in the text provide more information on human resource management.

**Marketing Majors**   Marketing is the study of consumer demand. Marketing majors take courses such as consumer behavior, advertising, and placement of goods in the markets in which they are sold. Marketing majors typically find jobs in companies, identifying and implementing strategies related to product, price, promotion, and distribution. They may also be hired as purchasing managers for retail stores. Chapters 12, 13, and 14 in the text provide more information regarding the subjects that marketing majors consider.

**International Business Majors**   International business majors learn about business practices in foreign countries, as well as about how to manage cultural differences in various settings. Their courses include international culture, international relations, global marketing, and international finance. In terms of careers, international business majors typically work for large companies with many operations overseas or for the government in establishing trade relationships. Chapter 4 discusses topics that international business majors study.

**Information Technology Majors**   Information technology is the study of how to access and manage information in a firm. Information technology majors take courses in programming. As a career, information technology majors may find work setting up networks, coordinating information across divisions of a firm, or implementing new designs of human interface with technology. Appendix B at the end of the text provides more information regarding information technology.

# 3. How to Maximize Your Chances of Success in Your Career

When you are close to graduation, you will need to conduct a job search. You may have several interviews for jobs that do not appeal to you because of the salary or working conditions. Some recommendations for maximizing your likelihood of getting a job that you would like are presented here. Though this information is specific to jobs in the business world, it can be applied to a job search in any field.

## 3.1  Make Decisions About Your Career

If you are taking this course, you most likely have thought about the kind of career you want and are working toward achieving the goal of a new career or a better job than you currently have. Your costs of college represent an investment in the future.

What is the difference between a job and a career? A *job* is short-term employment until something fulfilling comes along, whereas a *career* implies a lifelong, satisfying work experience. We all want to have careers that meet our personal goals and objectives over the course of our lives. You most likely are taking this course because you want some insights into what a career in business entails.

Before embarking on a career, consider the growth of the industry in which you are considering work. In many industries, the opportunities for career advancement are limited, which means that it will be difficult to remain in that profession for a long period of time. If unemployment is high in a given profession, then you should seek one where unemployment is relatively low. Another factor that should play a role in your decision making is your ability to adapt to other jobs if the industry you are in begins to lay off workers. While no one can predict the future, you should do research on forecasts of job availability over time. You should also consider if you will need any further education once you have completed your associates or undergraduate degree program.

## 3.2  Get Your Résumé in Order

When you go on the job market, you will need to create a résumé, which is a document that highlights your skills and accomplishments. It is critically important that your résumé tells potential employers that you are qualified to take a job with their company. Your résumé needs to stand out from all of the other résumés that the hiring manager sees. What can you do to make your résumé attractive to potential employers?

1. Begin with a job objective. To alert the hiring manager regarding the specific position you are seeking, it is important to start off your résumé with a job objective.

2. List all of your previous jobs. This lets the hiring manager or business owner know what kind of experience you have had. It also informs the potential employer that you have been responsible enough to hold a job in the past, thereby increasing the employer's comfort level with you as a potential employee. Even minimum-wage jobs you held as a student or unpaid internships you have completed should be featured on your résumé because they signify responsibility.

3. List your educational accomplishments. You spent a great deal of time and money to get your degree, and you will want potential employers to be impressed with the education you have received. You can highlight some of the courses that you have taken that relate to the job want and "customize" your résumé to indicate that you are qualified. You may also want to include your grade point average in college, if you feel that it is high enough to impress an employer.

4. Provide contact information clearly. You should put your contact information, such as your address, phone number, and e-mail address, at the top of your résumé, so that companies can contact you to set up an interview.

5. Highlight skill sets. Are you well trained in spreadsheet use, or have you taken a programming class? Are you bilingual? If so, you should include this information on your résumé so that employers know that you are uniquely qualified for a position in their company.

6. Include extracurricular activities. Perhaps you participated in student government or a sport. Putting this on your résumé lets hiring managers know that you have leadership experience and also tells employers that you can handle the responsibilities of working with others as a "team player."

7. Ask your professors if they will provide recommendations for you. It is standard practice to include "references provided upon request," in a résumé and allow the potential employer to ask for the contact information of a reference. You should plan for references before going on the job market and alert the people you have chosen, so that they will not be surprised by a phone call from a potential employer.

8. Check spelling and grammar. A well-organized and accurate résumé signals that you pay close attention to details. Make sure to use whatever spelling and grammar check software you have available to ensure that there are no errors in your résumé.

9. If necessary, have a professional write your résumé for you. Professional résumé-writing services will create a résumé based on your job experience and education. Such services have a great deal of experience in creating professional-looking documents, and by using one, you will minimize the likelihood that there will be errors in your résumé.

A sample résumé is shown in Exhibit C.1. Notice the contact information, job objective, educational accomplishments, and list of previous jobs. When you are putting together your résumé, you can refer to the exhibit and also to the questionnaire in the Self-Scoring Exercise to make sure your résumé looks professional and contains all the necessary information.

**Post Your Résumé Online**   Once you have completed your résumé, you can maximize your visibility so that potential employers can find you and contact you by posting your résumé online at a site like www.monster .com. In this way, your résumé is available to many hiring managers who can identify your skill set easily and quickly.

## 3.3  Create a Cover Letter

When you apply for a job and submit a résumé, you will need to write a "cover letter" that accompanies your résumé. The purpose of the cover

Exhibit C.1

Example of a Résumé

**Résumé**
Robert Smith
1022 N. Main Street
Tallahassee, FL 32306
Phone: 999-555-1234

**Job Objective:**  Entry-level accountant

**Education:**  Florida State University, Sept. 2005–May 2009. B.S. in Accounting received May 2009; grade point average 3.1 on a 4-point scale.

**Work Experience:**  Intern at Mega Accountants, Inc., April 2008 to April 2009.

❑ Assisted tax accountants in compiling information submitted by clients to be used to file their tax returns.

❑ Researched previous Tax Court cases to provide information needed to answer clients' specific tax questions.

❑ Met with prospective clients to explain the tax services offered by the firm.

Lantern Clothing Store, March 2006 to March 2008.

❑ Responsible for ordering clothing, monitoring deliveries of clothing, and selling clothing.

**Professional:**  Treasurer of the Accounting Association at Florida State University,

**Organizations:**  Member of Business Club.

**Extracurricular Activities:**  Volunteer for Salvation Army, Intramural Sports (Baseball and Basketball).

**References:**  Provided upon request.

# Self-Scoring Exercises

## Evaluating Your Résumé

|  | Evaluation | Suggestions |
|---|---|---|
| Clearly communicates your experience? |  |  |
| Clearly communicates your skills? |  |  |
| Clearly communicates your potential? |  |  |
| Clearly communicates your comparative advantages over new applicants? |  |  |
| Length of résumé |  |  |
| Clearly communicates how you could benefit the firm? |  |  |
| Focus of résumé |  |  |
| Grammar in résumé |  |  |

letter is to market yourself to the potential employer and to demonstrate your interest in the position. In the cover letter, you should introduce yourself, indicate the position you are interested in, and explain why you are qualified for the job. Your cover letter should also tell potential employers why you are interested in their firm. Be sure to use spelling and grammar checks to make sure that your letter does not have any errors because you want to make a good first impression. A sample cover letter is shown in Exhibit C.2.

## 3.4 Identify Job Positions Available

When you have completed your résumé, you are ready to apply for jobs. How can you find information about positions that are available to you? At any given time, there are likely to be several jobs in the geographic area you prefer, but it is not always easy to find out about jobs that are available.

**Exhibit C.2**

Example of a Cover Letter

1022 N. Main Street
Tallahassee, FL 32306

June 9, 2009

Mr. Raymond Jones
President
Jones Manufacturing Co.
550 East 1st Street
Orlando, FL 32816

Dear Mr. Jones:

**[State the specific job you are pursuing.]**
I noticed that you have a job opening for a tax accountant. I just recently earned my accounting degree from Florida State University. I worked as an intern at Mega Accountants, Inc., in its tax department. Much of the intern work focused on tax accounting for manufacturing firms. I believe that my educational and intern experience has prepared me for your tax accountant position. I have enclosed my résumé, which provides more details about my education and intern background.

**[Describe when you are available for work and how you can be reached.]**
I am available for work immediately. Please call me at 999-555-1234 if you would like to interview me. I can be reached at that number during the morning on any day of the week. I look forward to hearing from you.

Sincerely,

***Robert Smith***

Robert Smith

Many firms advertise positions in newspapers, on their company websites, or on job listing websites such as the following:

| Website | Offers |
| --- | --- |
| **http://hotjobs.yahoo.com/jobs** | Job listings by category; features companies |
| **www.careermag.com** | Job listings by profession |
| **www.techjobs.com** | Job listings for high-tech firms; career advice |
| **www.monster.com** | Job listings in the field you specify |
| **www.career.com** | Career advice |

Some websites, including the following, also provide information about the salaries that are paid by various types of jobs:

| Website | Offers |
| --- | --- |
| **http://hotjobs.yahoo.com/jobs** | Salaries for various job positions |
| **www.careermag.com** | Salaries for various job positions |
| **www.monster.com** | Salaries for various job positions |

Often, though, firms do not advertise positions and prefer to rely on their applicant files to fill openings. Therefore, it may be worthwhile to send your résumé to many companies, even if they are not currently advertising a position.

Other resources for learning about available jobs are discussed next.

**Campus Placement**    Many colleges allow employers to interview students on campus. Therefore, it is very important that you familiarize yourself with the campus placement department at your school. The placement center will typically have potential employers on file, as well as information on any upcoming career fairs. Career fairs are forums where many potential employers gather on campus to provide information about jobs at their companies. The fairs allow students to find out about the business environment at different companies. Students often fill out applications at the career fair and schedule interviews based on personal interactions at the fair.

**Headhunters**    Headhunters are people who bring together employers looking to hire for a job position and potential employees. A headhunter can line up interviews at companies. Typically, the headhunters are paid by the company who is seeking employees rather than by the person who is seeking a job. Headhunters may be very useful because they act as an intermediary between the companies and job seekers and bring particular job seekers to the attention of hiring managers.

**Temp Agencies**    Many people do not realize that they may be able to get their foot in the door at a company by using a temp agency. Temp agencies, such as Workforce One, find people to meet the temporary employment needs of businesses. Job assignments typically last for a couple of months. During that time, both you and your employer can see if you are suited to each other in terms of a permanent job. Some temp agencies specialize in "temp to hire" jobs, where good performance during the temp job means that the temp worker will be considered for a permanent position. You can find out more information about temp agencies at www.net-temps.com.

**Open Houses**  Sometimes, companies advertise "open houses" for their companies, where representatives of the company hold informal meetings for the purpose of identifying potential employees. The open house will typically be held at a hotel. If you decide to attend an open house, make sure to dress professionally so that you create a good impression with the company's representatives.

**Internships**  Another way to get your foot in the door is through an internship. You can pursue internships while you are still in college. Some internships are paid, and others are unpaid. If you do not have financial constraints, you may consider an unpaid internship to see if you would be happy working in the particular job where you intern.

Some firms offer internships that enable students to gain on-the-job experience while pursuing a degree. Information about internships may often be found on a firm's website. In addition, many colleges have internship programs designed for various majors. For example, a specified number of business majors may work at local firms each semester under a college's internship program.

Internships provide many benefits to students. First, students may receive college credit for internships at some colleges. Second, internships may enhance students' understanding of coursework by allowing them to see how the theory in the classroom is applied in the real world. Third, internships enable students to learn more about a particular career. Thus, they either reinforce the students' desire to pursue a particular major or career or make the students realize that they need to rethink their major or career plans.

Fourth, some students receive letters of recommendation from the firm where they worked. When they complete their degree, they have experience along with an endorsement from the firm where they interned. This type of letter of recommendation is very valuable because it describes performance in the workplace and thus can complement other letters of recommendation that focus on performance in the classroom.

Finally, internships allow employers to assess interns for future job openings. The information firms obtain from observing an intern's work habits is often more useful than information obtained from a job interview. Some interns ultimately are offered jobs at the firms where they interned. Numerous firms, including AT&T, Apple Computer, and Boeing, frequently hire interns.

These obvious benefits have made internships very desirable. Consequently, many more students apply for internships than the number of internships available. For more information about internships, go to http://collegejournal.com.

**Previous Employers**  If you have work experience, or if you had an internship at a company that you like, you may want to apply for any job openings at your previous workplace. Most likely, you know the kinds of jobs that are available and may have the "inside track" for getting a job because the managers at the company know you and are familiar with your skill set. Even if you are not interested in a job at a previous employer, you should still contact previous coworkers in order to network and to see if they have any leads on available jobs elsewhere.

**Networking**  Networking is often very important in terms of meeting potential employers. Often, people get jobs because they know someone who works for a potential employer and can recommend you for a job, or at least inform you about opportunities that may be available. You can network while you are still in college by joining an honor society or student organization related to the kind of career you want. In this way, you can expand your circle of connections before going on the job market.

## 3.5  Practice Your Interviewing Skills

A potential employer has called you and wants to interview you next week. What can you do to be ready for the interview? First, to make a good impression on the hiring manager, you should find out as much as you can about the company. You should also do some research on the job position for which you are interviewing. By doing this, you will be prepared for the interview and will be able to answer any questions that arise about your qualifications for the specific position. You also show your enthusiasm for the position, which will please the hiring manager. Often you can find information about a company on the Internet. Next, you should practice going through an interview with a friend. Have your friend ask you the kinds of questions that you might be asked in the interview, such as what your long-term goals are, why you are qualified for the job, and what you can bring to the job in terms of experience and knowledge.

In preparing for the interview, keep in mind that firms conduct interviews to evaluate applicants more thoroughly. Various characteristics, such as the applicant's personality, cannot be evaluated from résumés alone. Personal interviews allow firms to assess these characteristics. Many firms screen applications and résumés to identify a pool of qualified applicants. Then the qualified applicants are interviewed to determine the optimal applicant for the position. Although strong qualifications on a résumé enable an applicant to be interviewed, they do not guarantee a job. A person who interviews well may be preferable to one with a stronger résumé who interviews poorly.

Firms design most interviews to provide the applicant with additional information about the position and to determine the following:

1. Is the applicant neat and presentable?

2. Would the applicant get along with customers?

3. Does the applicant have good communication skills?

4. Does the applicant have a genuine interest in the position?

5. Would the applicant work well with others?

You cannot prepare for all possible questions that may be asked during an interview, but you should at least prepare for some of the more obvious types of questions that may be asked:

1. Why do you want to work for our company?

2. What do you know about our company?

3. Why do you plan to leave your present employer?

4. Why should our company hire you?

5. What are your strengths?

6. What are your weaknesses?

7. What are your salary requirements?

8. When would you be ready to begin this job?

Although you cannot guarantee the outcome of the interview, a few simple but critical rules should be followed:

1. Dress properly.

2. Be on time.

3. Send a follow-up thank-you letter to the persons who interview you.

**What to Ask in an Interview**   A person who is being interviewed is normally allowed time to ask questions about the firm that is conducting the interview. These questions may be just as important as your answers in determining whether the job is offered. The questions show your interest in the firm and intelligence about the job. Some possible questions are:

1. How much interaction is there between this position and related divisions?

2. How much responsibility is delegated by the supervisor of this position?

3. What is the typical educational background for this position?

4. Who is involved in the performance evaluation for this position?

5. To what extent does the position involve public relations or contact with customers?

A second set of questions would ask for more details about the position, which could show your competence in the area. These questions would vary with the type of position, but a few examples can be provided:

1. What type of computer is used in the department?

2. Which companies are your key suppliers or customers?

3. What are the projected sales for the division over the next year?

Although asking questions can be valuable, you must recognize the amount of time allocated for the interview and make sure that the interviewer has sufficient time to ask questions. For more information on how to interview, go to http://hotjobs.yahoo.com.

## 3.6  Comparing Job Offers

After your interviews, you may be offered more than one job and will have to decide which one to accept. In making your decision, you should consider the total package offered by the firms.

**Salary**   The salary is important, especially when you are supporting yourself. However, many other factors should influence your decision about where you go to work.

**Benefits**   Many employers provide noncash benefits for their employees. These benefits should be weighed carefully when making a decision about where to work, For example, some companies offer on-site day care and exercise facilities. Given the cost of child care, this noncash benefit may be very valuable. Other possible benefits include health care coverage, contributions to retirement funds, paid vacation time, stock option plans, compensation for further education, and flexible working hours. A salary calculator that you can use to take into account the value of various benefits can be found at www.salary.com.

**Location**   Many people face limitations in their job search because they have a specific geographic area where they want to live. Perhaps you have family obligations in the city in which you live. You would then restrict your job search to firms in the same city or start your own business locally. Although this would limit your job opportunities, you may not have any alternative.

If you have no geographic limitations, you may consider other factors. For example, you may be attracted to a particular geographic location due to quality-of-life factors, such as cultural aspects, access to a major airport, the size of the city, the quality of the school system, and opportunities for your spouse to find a job if you are married.

**Cost of Living**   You should also consider the cost of living when making career decisions. The cost of living differs dramatically across cities, and it is important to consider your salary in light of the cost of renting or owning your own home. To compare the cost of living, you can use a calculator that tells you how much a given salary in one city differs from that in another city. There are several online calculators for determining the cost of living:

www.datamasters.com

www.cityrating.com/costofliving.asp

http://cgi.money.cnn.com/tools/costofliving/costofliving.html

## 3.7  Planning a Career Path

Even after a job is offered and accepted, you will have to make career decisions. On-the-job experience may affect your desired career job. Aspiring to a position above the present position is natural. The planned career path to that position may involve either a series of promotions within the firm or switching to a different firm. Although planning a career path is a useful motivator, your plans should be achievable. If everyone planned to be president of a company, most plans would not be achieved. This can lead to frustration. A preferable career path would include short-term goals, since some ultimate goals may take 20 years or longer. Setting short-term goals can also reinforce your confidence as you achieve the goals.

## 3.8  Career Versus Further Education

Students who receive their associate's degree are faced with a decision of whether to pursue a bachelor's degree or a full-time career. Students who receive their bachelor's degree must then decide whether to pursue a master's degree or a full-time career. Both decisions involve weighing an additional degree versus a career. The following discussion suggests some factors to consider when making these decisions.

Although the appropriate decision varies among students, some general guidelines deserve consideration. You should conduct a cost-benefit analysis of the decision to pursue an additional degree. Some of the more obvious costs are tuition, the forgone income that could have been earned by working instead of going to school, and the forgone on-the-job experience that could have been earned by working instead of going to school. Some possible benefits of pursing an additional degree are more marketability in the job market, a higher starting salary, and greater potential for promotion.

The costs and benefits of attaining an additional degree can vary significantly among majors. In addition to the costs and benefits just identified, other factors also deserve to be considered. For example, some people may need a break from school and prefer to begin their career right away. Others may perform best in school by continuing their education while the previous coursework is still fresh in their minds.

It is often suggested that people get more out of an additional degree if they work full-time for a few years and then return to school. The on-the-job experience may allow for a greater understanding and appreciation of coursework. Such a strategy can have a high cost, however. It is difficult to feel motivated on a job when you know you will quit in a few years to pursue an additional degree. If you are thinking about graduate school, you can obtain information about finding a graduate school and practice tests for graduate admission tests at http://www.collegejournal.com.

**Pursuing a Career and Degree**   A popular compromise for those facing the career-versus-degree dilemma is to begin a career and pursue the degree part-time. Many firms will even pay an employee's tuition if the coursework could enhance the employee's performance on the job. This strategy allows people to obtain a degree without giving up the income and on-the-job experience they would forgo if they pursued a degree full-time. The disadvantage is that it may take five or more years to achieve the degree part-time. In addition, taking coursework at night after a long day on the job can lead to fatigue and stress.

Furthermore, an extra degree does not automatically guarantee immediate success. The number of people receiving bachelor's and master's degrees has increased dramatically in recent years. Therefore, competition for existing jobs can be fierce even with additional education. An additional degree can be especially marketable when it complements existing skills. For example, many engineers have pursued master's degrees in business administration so that they can pursue management-level positions at engineering firms.

**Starting Your Own Business**   You may have thought about what it would be like to be an entrepreneur and work for yourself. During the course of a career, many people wonder whether they should continue working for a firm or start their own business. Some people recognize the potential benefits of owning their own firm, such as being their own boss or the potential to earn a high level of income. However, the decision to start a business requires an idea for a product or service that will generate sufficient sales. A successful business also requires proper planning, production, marketing, and financing decisions, as will be explained throughout the text. Some general guidelines for developing a successful business, which apply to most firms, are listed here:

1.  *Create a product (or service) that the market wants.*  A new business is typically created when the owner recognizes a product or service desired by customers that is not being offered by a sufficient number of (or by any) existing firms.

2. *Prepare for adverse conditions.* An owner of a business should have enough financial backing to prepare for adverse conditions, such as a decline in economic growth or more intense competition. Even if the business is based on a good product (or service) idea, it may experience weak performance in some periods because of factors beyond your control.

3. *Capitalize on new opportunities.* A business should use a flexible strategic plan that adjusts in response to new business opportunities. Businesses that remain flexible are more likely to capitalize on new opportunities.

4. *Ensure customer satisfaction.* The long-run success of many businesses is based on the quality of a product, which leads to customer satisfaction.

5. *Ensure employee satisfaction.* When owners of businesses create conditions that satisfy employees, they motivate employees to perform well and also avoid a high level of employee turnover.

6. *Promote the product.* A good product will not sell unless the market is aware of it. Promotion may be necessary to ensure that the market is informed about the product.

# Lessons in Business as a Result of the Credit Crisis

A review of the credit crisis identifies how some businesses made bad decisions, because they did not follow some of the most important principles in business. This appendix provides a summary of the credit crisis with a focus on the lessons in business that can be learned from this crisis.

A mortgage company plays an important role in the housing market. It receives applications from prospective homeowners who wish to purchase a home. The mortgage company assesses the financial condition of the prospective homeowners, based on their income and how much cash they can use to make a down payment on the home. The mortgage amount is the difference between the price to be paid for the home and the down payment. The mortgage company determines the amount of the monthly payment that the prospective homeowners would pay on their mortgage and attempts to assess whether they could afford this payment based on their income. If the mortgage company approves the mortgage application, it provides the prospective homeowners with a mortgage loan so that they can purchase the home.

## How a Mortgage Company Earns Profits

The mortgage company can earn a profit from its business, because it charges an interest rate on the mortgage that is above its cost of funds. For example, consider a mortgage company that obtains $100,000 from deposits at 5 percent and provides the funds to a homeowner in the form of a mortgage loan at 8 percent. The interest earned on the loan exceeds its interest paid on deposits. It also charges homeowners upfront fees when it creates (originates) the mortgage. In general, its revenue is the interest received on its loans and the fees earned from creating mortgages. Its expenses are the interest payments to depositors and operating expenses such as wages paid to employees and renting an office. The difference between the revenue and expenses is the earnings (profits). Many entrepreneurs established mortgage companies, because they expected to generate sufficient earnings to satisfy their lifestyle.

In some cases, a mortgage company does not provide the funding for the mortgage that it creates, but it allows another financial institution to provide the funding. In this case, it earned the upfront fees for assessing whether the prospective homeowners qualify to own a home. It did not need to use its funds to provide the mortgage, because the mortgage funds are provided by another financial institution that will receive the interest payments from the homeowners.

## Lessons in Responsibilities to Stakeholders (related to Chapter 2)

Like any business, a mortgage company has responsibilities to customers, employees, owners, and creditors. It should attempt to provide its customers (prospective homeowners) with a fair assessment of their ability to afford a home. It should not grant a mortgage unless it really believes that the prospective homeowners will be able to make payments on the mortgage. However, mortgage companies sometimes approve mortgage loans that should not be approved so that they can create more mortgages in their attempt to earn higher profits. However, in this case, the mortgage companies adversely affect the customers who purchased a home that they could not afford and ultimately lost. Those homeowners not only lose their down payment, but they also may be unable to obtain credit because they defaulted on the mortgage loan.

The surge in defaults on mortgages led to the 2008 credit crisis. There was an excess supply of homes in the market, and the need for new mortgages declined. Mortgage companies had to lay off many of their employees. Furthermore, many of the mortgage companies went bankrupt. They took excessive risks in their attempt to make very large profits, and they lost much or all of the funds that were invested in the company by creditors or owners. Consequently, some investors who invested equity in the companies lost all of their investment. In addition, some creditors who provided loans to support the establishment of the mortgage company were never repaid. Overall, the mortgage company's greed reflected a lack of responsibility to its customers, its employees, its stockholders (or owners), and its creditors. If the mortgage companies had their focus on serving all of their stakeholders, they would not have made some of their bad decisions.

## Lessons in Assessing Economic Growth (related to Chapter 3)

Economic conditions had a major influence on housing market conditions. In the 2004–2006 period, economic conditions in the United States were strong, and many homeowners had good incomes. The demand for new homes was high, and most of the homeowners who were given mortgage loans were making their mortgage payments on a timely basis. Mortgage companies were creating many new mortgages, so their profits were high. Home prices continued to rise because of the strong demand for homes. In the 2007–2008 period, the managers and owners of some mortgage companies became overly confident that homeowners could afford homes.

If the homeowners defaulted on their mortgage payments, the mortgage company could seize the home as collateral. As long as home prices continued to rise, the mortgage company could take over the home, and it would be worth as much or more than the existing mortgage. Based on this logic, mortgage companies were not concerned about possible mortgage defaults and were using very liberal standards to provide some mortgages. They granted so-called *subprime mortgages* to applicants whose financial condition was below the typical standard. Many mortgage companies aggressively pursued these types of mortgages, because they charged a higher interest rate on them and also charged additional fees.

During the 2007–2008 period, the economy weakened and the demand for housing declined. Consequently, home prices declined. Some homeowners could not afford to make their mortgage payments. When the mortgage company seized the home as collateral, the collateral was often worth less than the amount owed on the mortgage. For example, the mortgage company may have provided a loan of $150,000 on a home that was valued at $160,000. Within the first year, homeowners defaulted on their payments. Though the mortgage loan amount was still close to $150,000, the home could be sold in the market for only $120,000 after considering the transactions costs. Thus, the mortgage company lost about $30,000 on this mortgage.

In some cases, the mortgage company did not provide the financing on the mortgage, but allowed another financial institution to provide the financing. The financial institution that provided the mortgage loan would suffer the loss. These financial institutions relied on the mortgage companies to determine whether the homeowners qualified for the home. During 2007–2008, there were many mortgage defaults, which meant that the lenders (mortgage companies or other financial institutions) were stuck with homes that had market values far below the mortgage amount. This led to the credit crisis. Suddenly, the number of homes available for sale was greater than the demand for homes, and this caused home prices to decline even further.

One reason why some mortgage companies were overly aggressive in granting mortgage loans is that they did a poor job of assessing economic growth. They presumed that the very strong economic conditions that occurred in 2004–2006 would continue. Thus, assuming that home prices would just keep rising, they continued to grant mortgages to homeowners who should not have qualified for loans. However, it should have been obvious that housing prices could not rise substantially every year into the

When the demand for homes declined in 2008, the supply of homes in the market was much larger than the demand. Thus, sellers of homes were forced to reduce their price in order to find buyers of their homes.

future. Other economic factors such as income levels were not rising as fast as housing, so it was only a matter of time before the housing prices would make housing unaffordable, and the demand for homes would decline.

## Lessons in Entrepreneurship (related to Chapter 6)

Entrepreneurs of a business must recognize the risk of the business and manage that risk. Entrepreneurs of a mortgage company should recognize that the risk of granting a mortgage to prospective homeowners is the possibility that the homeowners will default on the mortgage. Some mortgage companies did not seem to realize that homeowners might have trouble making mortgage payments if the economy weakened, or did not realize that home prices (and, therefore, the value of the collateral backing the loan) might decline. The entrepreneurs of mortgage companies who carefully assessed and managed their risk did not aggressively pursue subprime mortgages and were in a better position to survive when the economy weakened.

## Lessons in Management (related to Chapter 7)

Some mortgage companies might have avoided problems if their employees had performed their functions better. The companies could have benefited from employees who performed the leading function by taking the initiative to question the mortgage assessment process that was being used. Some mortgage companies lacked control, which allowed employees to approve mortgages that should have been rejected. Employees at some mortgage companies apparently lacked the conceptual skills to recognize that mortgage applicants would not be capable of making the mortgage payments. Some employees also lacked proper decision-making skills, because they did not recognize the potential adverse effects of the decision to grant mortgage loans to homeowners who could not afford homes.

## Lessons in Organizational Structure (related to Chapter 8)

Some mortgage companies might have avoided problems if they had had a better organizational structure. In some cases, the people making decisions about whether a mortgage application should be approved were not monitored by managers. In other cases, they were monitored by managers, but the managers encouraged them to use liberal rules when assessing the applicants.

## Lessons in Productivity (related to Chapter 9)

Mortgage companies produce mortgages. Their production process should be subject to a quality control system. If the process allows almost anyone who applies to qualify for a mortgage, there is no quality control. A lack of quality control normally leads to defective products or services. In the case of the 2008 credit crisis, the mortgages became defective, because many of the customers who received mortgages ultimately defaulted on them. Had the mortgage companies used a better quality control system, it would have reduced the number of defective mortgages.

## Lessons in Motivating Employees (related to Chapter 10)

Employees who assess mortgage applications can be motivated in different ways by a mortgage company. If they are rewarded for detecting problems within applications, they are more likely to screen applications carefully and approve only applications that deserve to be approved. However, if they are rewarded only by how many mortgages they extend each day, then they are encouraged to rush the screening process and use liberal rules when approving the mortgage.

## Lessons in Human Resource Evaluation (related to Chapter 11)

The work behavior of employees of a mortgage company is influenced by how they are evaluated. If they are evaluated based on quality control, they will likely impose quality control when they assess mortgage applications. Conversely, if they are evaluated based on how many mortgages they create, they will create as many as possible and will ignore proper screening criteria. Those mortgage companies whose employees were rewarded based on the number of mortgages created regardless of quality experienced major losses during the credit crisis.

## Lessons in the Creation of New Products (related to Chapter 12)

Many businesses increase their market share by revising their product to be unique. When mortgage companies create mortgages, they realize that they are competing against other mortgage companies. To attract more mortgage applications, they may use a more liberal assessment of the mortgage application and allow a lower down payment. When they did this in 2007–2008, they increased their market share because they reached a target market of customers that would be rejected by other mortgage companies. However, this strategy ultimately failed because many of these customers defaulted on their mortgages. The creation of a new product or service requires an understanding of its possible defects. Some mortgage companies did not recognize the defects in their strategy of liberal lending standards.

## Lessons in Promotion (related to Chapter 14)

When the housing market was strong, many new mortgage companies entered the market in order to capitalize on the strong business conditions.

Promotions were used by many mortgage companies to attract more mortgage applications. Some of the promotions were misleading, because they hid fees that were going to be charged for the mortgage. Some promotions also gave the customers a false impression of what they could afford. The misleading promotions ultimately backfired on the mortgage companies when their customers defaulted on the mortgages.

## Lessons in Financial Reporting (related to Chapter 15)

When financial institutions provide mortgage loans, these loans are assets on their balance sheets. They expect to receive interest income from these assets. However, when mortgages experience late payments, financial institutions can reduce the book value of the mortgages on their balance sheets to reflect some likely defaults. As the economy deteriorated in 2008, financial institutions could have revised their balance sheets to reflect the likelihood that customers would default on their mortgages. However, some financial institutions were unwilling to acknowledge this information. Consequently, their condition was worse than what they were reporting. Some financial institutions failed, because their financial problems were hidden and by the time these problems were realized, it was too late to correct them.

## Lessons in Financing (related to Chapter 16)

The process for mortgage financing in the United States involves many participants, as illustrated in Exhibit D.1. In many cases, a financial institution will purchase mortgages created by mortgage companies and will combine them into a package. The financial institution then sells packages of mortgages (called *mortgage-backed securities*) and earns a fee for this service. Before the packages of mortgages are sold, they are rated by rating agencies such as Moody's or Standard and Poor's for a fee. Some investors are more willing to purchase packages of mortgages that are rated high by rating agencies. For this reason, a financial institution can more easily sell packages of mortgages when the packages are rated high. Other businesses (typically financial institutions) are buyers of these packages of mortgages. When these businesses purchase the packages of mortgages, they provide the financing for the mortgages. If the payments on these mortgages are made in a timely manner, these businesses normally earn a good return on

**Exhibit D.1**

How Financial Institutions Finance Mortgages

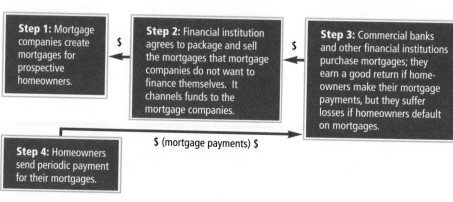

**Step 1:** Mortgage companies create mortgages for prospective homeowners.

**Step 2:** Financial institution agrees to package and sell the mortgages that mortgage companies do not want to finance themselves. It channels funds to the mortgage companies.

**Step 3:** Commercial banks and other financial institutions purchase mortgages; they earn a good return if homeowners make their mortgage payments, but they suffer losses if homeowners default on mortgages.

**Step 4:** Homeowners send periodic payment for their mortgages.

$ (mortgage payments) $

During the credit crisis, much media attention was focused on foreclosures of homes. Financial institutions holding the mortgages were forced to repossess the homes.

© SHUTTERSTOCK/TERRANCE EMERSON

their investment in mortgages. However, if some mortgages default, the businesses receive less periodic cash flows than expected.

Businesses such as commercial banks, securities firms, and insurance companies purchased large amounts of these mortgages and suffered severe losses on their investments because of defaults or late payments on mortgages. This led to the credit crisis. Many businesses (mostly financial institutions) experienced losses in the billions of dollars, because they had to repossess the homes when homeowners defaulted on the mortgages. Some financial institutions holding large amounts of mortgages failed because of this crisis.

## Reasons for the Credit Crisis

The underlying cause of the crisis was that many different businesses ignored the risk of the mortgages that they purchased. Consequently, they invested in many mortgages that defaulted or had late payments. Since there were many types of businesses involved in the transactions, they have all received a portion of the blame.

✦ **Mortgage Companies**   First, the mortgage companies that created the mortgages did not properly screen mortgage applicants. They approved mortgage applications of some prospective homeowners that should not have been approved. They also reduced required down payments in order to allow more applicants to meet their standards, which reduced the value of collateral in the event of default. Mortgage company managers were commonly motivated to create as many mortgages as possible, and so they approved mortgages even if prospective homeowners might have difficulty affording the mortgage payments.

✦ **Credit Rating Agencies**   Second, credit rating agencies receive fees for rating mortgage-backed securities. When the rating agencies rated the securities high, financial institutions could more easily sell the securities. The higher the ratings of the securities, the more easily they could be sold, and then financial institutions selling these securities would package additional batches of mortgages and start the process all over. If the credit rating agencies had applied higher standards by assigning lower ratings to these securities, some institutional investors might have been less willing to purchase these securities and would not have suffered such large losses.

✦ **Financial Institutions That Packaged and Sold Mortgages** Third, the financial institutions that packaged mortgages relied on the credit ratings assigned by credit rating agencies. If they had assessed the quality of the mortgages on their own, they might have realized that the ratings assigned by rating agencies were higher than they should have been. However, the financial institutions selling the mortgages were motivated to sell as many as possible because they were earning more fees from selling more mortgages. They were more concerned about selling many packages of mortgages than about the quality of the mortgages that they were selling.

✦ **Financial Institutions That Purchased Mortgages** Fourth, many of the businesses that purchased mortgages relied on the credit ratings assigned by the credit rating agencies. If they had assessed the quality of the mortgages on their own, they might have realized that the ratings assigned by rating agencies were higher than they should have been. If they had conducted their own assessment, they would have realized that some of the mortgages had a high risk of default, and they would not have invested in as many mortgages.

## Lessons in Business Investment (related to Chapter 17)

When businesses make investment decisions, they purchase assets that generate income for them. If a business makes proper investment decisions, its assets should generate sufficient income that represents a good return on its investment. Proper investment decisions are made by carefully assessing the alternative investments available. This includes an assessment of the risk involved. Businesses should consider how a proposed investment will perform under different economic scenarios. The lesson of the credit crisis is that many businesses did not properly assess the investments that were available. Many businesses purchased mortgages without a careful assessment of the risk that these mortgages might default, especially if economic conditions weakened. Because of their bad investments in mortgages, many businesses (financial institutions) that financed mortgages suffered large losses, and some of them failed.

## Example

As an illlustration of the points made above, consider this simplified example:

MM Mortgage Company performed well during 2005 when it processed mortgage applications. In 2005, many new mortgage companies were established to pursue this business. MM wanted to increase its market share. It reduced its requirements to make it easier for homeowners to qualify for a mortgage. It justified its strategy with the belief that as long as

During the credit crisis, commercial banks and other financial institutions that provided mortgage loans were forced to repossess (repo) homes due to mortgage defaults and attempted to resell the homes. This resulted in even more homes for sale in the housing market, which reduced home prices further.

© SHUTTERSTOCK/KEN BROWN

the economy remained strong, the applicants whose mortgages were approved would probably be able to afford the mortgage payments. Even if a homeowner defaulted, the mortgage would be backed by the home as collateral, and home prices should continue to rise.

MM Mortgage Company created more mortgages than it could afford to support with its own money. It earned a fee on each mortgage created, and arranged a deal with SS Securities Company in which SS would take all the mortgages that MM did not want to keep. SS packaged the mortgages and had them rated by RR Rating Agency. The agency rated them high, which allowed SS to easily find willing institutional investors to buy the packages. One of the buyers was BB, a large commercial bank. Each month, MM would create mortgages, and SS would have them rated by RR, package them, and sell them to BB. MM earned a fee on each mortgage it created. RR earned a fee for assigning ratings to the packages of mortgages that SS wanted to sell. The higher the ratings, the easier it was for SS to sell the packages, and SS would continue to hire RR to rate additional packages. SS earned a fee for selling the packages of mortgages. BB purchased packages of mortgages and in 2005–2006, the return on its investment was good because homeowners were making their mortgage payments. Overall, all four businesses—MM, SS, RR, and BB—were performing well.

In the 2007–2008 period, the economy weakened and demand for housing declined. Some homeowners earned less income or were laid off and could not afford to make their mortgage payment. The number of mortgage applications declined, which adversely affected MM's business. In addition, MM was holding some mortgages that it created, and had to take ownership of the homes when the homeowners defaulted on the payments. Since the economy was weak, MM could resell the homes to buyers only if it discounted the home prices substantially (much lower than the amounts it was owed on the mortgage loans it had provided). In addition, the packages of mortgages that were sold to institutional investors such as BB were performing poorly, because of mortgage defaults. Therefore, BB and all other institutional investors that had invested in a large amount of mortgages suffered major losses. Consequently, the shareholders of BB lost considerable money. They blamed the management of BB, but BB's managers said that the company that sold it packages of mortgages (SS) had lied about the quality of the mortgages. The management of SS stated that it relied on the rating agency (RR) for the ratings and that this agency deserved the blame. RR explained that it based its rating on the information provided by MM when the mortgage was created and that the financial information about the homeowners was inaccurate.

## Impact of the Credit Crisis on Other Businesses

Managers of businesses need to understand how their businesses can be affected by changes in economic or industry conditions. The credit crisis is a great example of how businesses rely heavily on each other and therefore are affected by each other. For those financial institutions that invested heavily in mortgages, their owners, creditors, and employees typically lost income in some form.

But the impact of the credit crisis stretches far beyond the financial institutions. While the credit crisis had a direct impact on many financial institutions, it had an indirect effect on all types of businesses. First, there are many businesses that are involved in the housing industry. Home builders built fewer homes during the credit crisis. Some of them had already built homes that they could no longer sell because the demand for housing declined. Thus, they had to sell homes at discounted prices, and some home builders went bankrupt. Other businesses that serve home builders such as cement companies, electrical wiring companies, plumbing companies, and landscaping companies lost business when the demand for new homes declined. Many employees of these types of companies had less work, and therefore less income. Some of the employees lost their jobs.

The decline in the income to employees resulted in less spending by these employees. When employees have lower wages, and spend less money, some businesses receive less revenue. For example, employees may reduce their spending at restaurants, which results in less revenue to restaurants. They may reduce their spending on groceries, which results in less revenue to grocery stores. Consequently, restaurants and grocery stores may reduce the work schedules of their employees or may even lay them off. Now those people have less income and will reduce their spending, which affects the revenue of the businesses where they normally spend their money.

## Discussion Questions About the Cause and Effects of the Credit Crisis

1. In your opinion, who was at fault for the credit crisis? Explain your opinion.

2. Do you think the business where you work or most recently worked was adversely affected by the credit crisis? If so, how were its revenue and its expenses affected by the credit crisis?

3. Do you think your income or financial position was affected by the credit crisis? If so, explain.

# Glossary

## A

**accounting** summary and analysis of a firm's financial condition

**accounts payable** money owed by a firm for the purchase of materials

**accounts receivable management** sets the limits on credit available to customers and the length of the period in which payment is due

**across-the-board system** a compensation system that allocates similar raises to all employees

**advertising** a nonpersonal sales presentation communicated through media or nonmedia forms to influence a large number of consumers

**affirmative action** a set of activities intended to increase opportunities for minorities and women

**agency problem** when managers do not act as responsible agents for the shareholders who own the business

**agents** marketing intermediaries that match buyers and sellers of products without becoming owners

**aggregate expenditures** the total amount of expenditures in the economy

**American depository receipts (ADRs)** certificates representing ownership of a stock issued by a non-U.S. firm

**appreciates** strengthens in value

**assembly line** a sequence of work stations in which each work station is designed to cover specific phases of the production process

**asset** anything owned by a firm

**auditing** an assessment of the records that were used to prepare a firm's financial statements

**autocratic** a leadership style in which the leader retains full authority for decision making

**automated** tasks are completed by machines without the use of employees

**autonomy** divisions can make their own decisions and act independently

## B

**balance of trade** the level of exports minus the level of imports

**balance sheet** reports the book value of all assets, liabilities, and owner's equity of a firm at a given point in time

**basic accounting equation** Assets = Liabilities + Owner's Equity

**bearish** periods in which investors are selling their stocks because of unfavorable expectations about the performance of firms

**benchmarking** a method of evaluating performance by comparison to some specified (benchmark) level, typically a level achieved by another company

**best-efforts basis** the investment bank does not guarantee a price to the firm issuing securities

**board of directors** a set of executives who are responsible for monitoring the activities of the firm's president and other high-level managers

**bond mutual funds** investment companies that invest the funds received from investors in bonds

**bonds** long-term debt securities (IOUs) purchased by investors

**bonus** an extra onetime payment at the end of a period in which performance was measured

**bookkeeping** the recording of a firm's financial transactions

**boycott** refusing to purchase products and services

**brand advertising** a nonpersonal sales presentation about a specific brand

**brand loyalty** the loyalty of consumers to a specific brand over time

**branding** a method of identifying products and differentiating them from competing products

**break-even point** the quantity of units sold at which total revenue equals total cost

**bullish** periods in which there is considerable demand for stocks because investors have favorable expectations about the performance of firms

**business plan** a detailed description of the proposed business, including a description of the product or service, the types of customers it would attract, the competition, and the facilities needed for production

**business responsibilities** a set of obligations and duties regarding product quality and treatment of customers, employees, and owners that a firm should fulfill when conducting business

**business risk** the possibility that a firm's performance will be lower than expected because of its exposure to specific conditions

**bylaws** general guidelines for managing a firm

## C

**call feature** provides the issuing firm with the right to repurchase its bonds before maturity

**capital** machinery, equipment, tools, and physical facilities used by a business; long term funds

**capital budget** a targeted amount of funds to be used for purchasing assets such as buildings, machinery, and equipment that are needed for long-term projects

**capital budgeting** a comparison of the costs and benefits of a proposed project to determine whether it is feasible

**capital gain** the price received from the sale of stock minus the price paid for the stock

**capital structure** the amount of debt versus equity financing

**capitalism** an economic system that allows for private ownership of businesses

**carrying costs** costs of maintaining (carrying) inventories

**centralized** most authority is held by the high-level managers

**certified public accountants (CPAs)** accountants who meet specific educational requirements and pass a national examination

**chain** a retailer that has more than one outlet

**chain of command** identifies the job position to which each type of employee must report

**chain-style business** a type of franchise in which a firm is allowed to use the trade name of a company and follows guidelines related to the pricing and sale of the product

**charter** a document used to incorporate a business. The charter describes important aspects of the corporation.

**closed-end funds** funds that are sold on stock exchanges

**co-branding** firms agree to offer a combination of two noncompeting products at a discounted price

**collateral** assets of the borrower that are transferred to the lender if the borrower defaults on the loan

**commercial banks** financial institutions that obtain deposits from individuals and use the funds primarily to provide business loans

**commercial paper** a short-term debt security normally issued by firms in good financial condition

**commission** sales fee

**commissions** compensation for meeting specific sales objectives

**common stock** a security that represents partial ownership of a particular firm

**communism** an economic system that involves public ownership of businesses

**comparative advertising** intended to persuade customers to purchase a specific product by demonstrating a brand's superiority by comparison with other competing brands

**compensation package** the total monetary compensation and benefits offered to employees

**composition** specifies that a firm will provide its creditors with a portion of what they are owed

**compressed workweek** compresses the workload into fewer days per week

**conceptual skills** the ability to understand the relationships among the various tasks of a firm

**conglomerate merger** the combination of two firms in unrelated businesses

**consumer markets** markets for various consumer products and services (such as cameras, clothes, and household items)

**consumerism** the collective demand by consumers that businesses satisfy their needs

**contingency planning** alternative plans developed for various possible business conditions

**contribution margin** the difference between price and variable cost per unit

**controlling** the monitoring and evaluation of tasks

**convenience products** products that are widely available to consumers, are purchased frequently, and are easily accessible

**corporate anorexia** the problem that occurs when firms become so obsessed with eliminating their inefficient components that they downsize too much.

**corporation** a state-chartered entity that pays taxes and is legally distinct from its owners

**cost of goods sold** the cost of materials used to produce the goods that were sold

**cost-based pricing** estimating the per-unit cost of producing a product and then adding a markup

**cost-push inflation** the situation when higher prices charged by firms are caused by higher costs

**coupons** a promotional device used in newspapers, magazines, and ads to encourage the purchase of a product

**craft unions** unions organized according to a specific craft (or trade), such as plumbing

**creditors** financial institutions or individuals who provide loans

**critical path** the path that takes the longest time to complete

**current assets** assets that will be converted into cash within one year

**cyclical unemployment** people who are unemployed because of poor economic conditions

# D

**debt financing** the act of borrowing funds

**debt-to-equity ratio** a measure of the amount of long-term financing provided by debt relative to equity

**decentralized** authority is spread among several divisions or managers

**decision-making skills** skills for using existing information to determine how the firm's resources should be allocated

**decline phase** the period in which sales of a product decline, either because of reduced consumer demand for that type of product or because competitors are gaining market share

**defensive pricing** the strategy of reducing a product's price to defend (retain) market share

**deintegration** the strategy of delegating some production tasks to suppliers

**demand schedule** a schedule that indicates the quantity of a product that would be demanded at each possible price

**demand-pull inflation** the situation when prices of products and services are pulled up because of strong consumer demand

**demographics** characteristics of the human population or specific segments of the population

**departmentalize** assign tasks and responsibilities to different departments

**depreciates** weakens in value

**depreciation** a reduction in the value of fixed assets to reflect deterioration in the assets over time

**design** the size and structure of a plant or office

**direct channel** the situation when a producer of a product deals directly with customers

**direct foreign investment (DFI)** a means of acquiring or building subsidiaries in one or more foreign countries

**discount brokers** brokers who ensure that a transaction desired by an investor is executed but do not offer advice

**distributorship** a type of franchise in which a dealer is allowed to sell a product produced by a manufacturer

**divestiture** the sale of an existing business by a firm

**dividend policy** the decision regarding how much of the firm's quarterly earnings should be retained (reinvested in the firm) versus distributed as dividends to owners

**dividends** income that the firm provides to its owners

**downsizing** an attempt by a firm to cut expenses by eliminating job positions

**dumping** selling products in a foreign country at a price below the cost of producing the products

## E

**earnings before interest and taxes (EBIT)** gross profit minus operating expenses

**earnings before taxes** earnings before interest and taxes minus interest expenses

**economic growth** the change in the general level of economic activity

**economies of scale** as the quantity produced increases, the cost per unit decreases

**electronic business (e-business) or electronic commerce (e-commerce)** use of electronic communications, such as the Internet, to produce or sell products and services

**e-marketing** the electronic interaction with consumers in order to develop, improve, or promote products

**employee benefits** additional privileges beyond compensation payments, such as

paid vacation time; health, life, or dental insurance; and pension programs

**employment test** a test of a job candidate's abilities

**empowerment** allowing employees the power to make more decisions

**entrepreneurs** people who organize, manage, and assume the risk of starting a business

**entrepreneurship** the creation of business ideas and the willingness to take risk; the act of creating, organizing and managing a business

**equilibrium interest rate** the interest rate at which the quantity of loanable funds supplied is equal to the quantity of loanable funds demanded

**equilibrium price** the price at which the quantity of a product supplied by firms equals the quantity of the product demanded by customers

**equity** the total investment by the firm's stockholders

**equity financing** the act of receiving investment from owners (by issuing stock or retaining earnings)

**equity theory** suggests that compensation should be equitable, or in proportion to each employee's contribution

**esteem needs** respect, prestige, and recognition

**excise taxes** taxes imposed by the federal government on particular products

**exclusive distribution** the distribution of a product through only one or a few outlets

**expectancy theory** holds that an employee's efforts are influenced by the expected outcome (reward) for those efforts

**expense ratio** for a mutual fund, expenses divided by assets

**exporting** the sale of products or services (called exports) to purchasers residing in other countries

**extension** provides additional time for a firm to generate the necessary cash to cover its payments to its creditors

**external recruiting** an effort to fill positions with applicants from outside the firm

## F

**family branding** branding of all or most products produced by a company

**fashion obsolescence** no longer being in fashion

**federal budget deficit** the situation when the amount of federal government spending exceeds the amount of federal taxes and other revenue received by the federal government

**Federal Reserve System** the central bank of the United States

**finance companies** financial institutions that typically obtain funds by issuing debt securities (IOUs) and lend most of their funds to firms

**finance** means by which firms obtain and use funds for their business operations

**financial accounting** accounting performed for reporting purposes

**fiscal policy** decisions on how the federal government should set tax rates and spend money

**fixed assets** assets that will be used by a firm for more than one year

**fixed costs** operating expenses that do not change in response to the number of products produced

**fixed-position layout** a layout in which employees go to the position of the product, rather than waiting for the product to come to them

**flexible manufacturing** a production process that can be easily adjusted to accommodate future revisions

**flextime programs** programs that allow for a more flexible work schedule

**floor traders** people on the trading floor of a stock exchange who execute transactions

**flotation costs** costs of issuing securities; include fees paid to investment banks for their advice and efforts to sell the securities, printing expenses, and registration fees

**forward contract** provides that an exchange of currencies will occur at a specified exchange rate at a future point in time

**forward rate** the exchange rate that a bank will be willing to offer at a future point in time

**franchise** an arrangement whereby a business owner allows others to use its trademark, trade name, or copyright, under specific conditions

**franchisee** a firm that is allowed to use the trade name or copyright of a franchise

**franchisor** a firm that allows others to use its trade name or copyright, under specified conditions

**free-rein** a leadership style in which the leader delegates much authority to employees

**frictional unemployment** people who are between jobs

**full-service brokers** brokers who provide advice to investors on stocks to purchase or sell and also ensure that transactions desired by investors are executed

**full-service retail store** a retailer that generally offers much sales assistance to customers and provides servicing if needed

## G

**Gantt chart** a chart illustrating the expected timing for each task in the production process

**general partners** partners who manage the business, receive a salary, share the profits or losses of the business, and have unlimited liability

**general partnership** a partnership in which all partners have unlimited liability

**generic brands** products that are not branded by the producer or the store

**going public** the act of initially issuing stock to the public

**gross domestic product (GDP)** the total market value of all final products and services produced in the United States

**gross profit** net sales minus the cost of goods sold

**growth funds** mutual funds that invest in stocks of firms with high potential for growth

**growth phase** the period in which sales of a product increase rapidly

## H

**hedge** action taken to protect a firm against exchange rate movements

**hierarchy of needs** needs are ranked in five general categories. Once a given category of needs is achieved, people become motivated to reach the next category.

**horizontal merger** the combination of firms that engage in the same types of business

**hotelling (just-in-time office)** providing an office with a desk, a computer, and a telephone for any employee who normally works at home but needs to use work space at the firm

**human resource manager** helps each specific department recruit candidates for its open positions

**human resource planning** planning to satisfy a firm's needs for employees

**human resources** people who are able to perform work for a business

**hygiene factors** work-related factors that can fulfill basic needs and prevent job dissatisfaction

## I

**importing** the purchase of foreign products or services

**incentive plans** provide employees with various forms of compensation if they meet specific performance goals

**income funds** mutual funds that invest in stocks that pay large dividends or in bonds that provide coupon payments

**income statement** indicates the revenue, costs, and earnings of a firm over a period of time

**indenture** a legal document that explains the firm's obligations to bondholders

**independent project** a project whose feasibility can be assessed without consideration of any others

**independent retail store** a retailer that has only one outlet

**individual branding** the assignment of a unique brand name to different products or groups of products

**industrial markets** markets for industrial products that are purchased by firms (such as plastic and steel)

**industrial unions** unions organized for a specific industry

**industry advertising** a nonpersonal sales presentation about a specific industry's product

**inflation** the increase in the general level of prices of products and services over a specified period of time

**infomercials** commercials that are televised separately rather than within a show

**informal organizational structure** an informal communications network among a firm's employees

**information systems** represent information technology, people, and procedures that work together to provide appropriate information to the firm's employees so they can make business decisions

**information technology** technology that enables information to be used to produce products and services

**initial public offering (IPO)** the first issue of stock to the public

**initiative** the willingness to take action

**injunction** a court order to prevent a union from a particular activity such as picketing

**inside board members** board members who are also managers of the same firm

**insider information** information about a firm that has not been disclosed to the public

**insider trading** transactions initiated by people (such as employees) who have information about a firm that has not been disclosed to the public

**institutional advertising** a nonpersonal sales presentation about a specific institution's product

**institutional investors** financial institutions that purchase large amounts of stock

**insurance companies** receive insurance premiums from selling insurance to customers and invest the proceeds until the funds are needed to pay insurance claims

**intensive distribution** the distribution of a product across most or all possible outlets

**internal auditor** responsible for ensuring that all departments follow the firm's guidelines and procedures

**internal auditors** specialize in evaluating various divisions of a business to ensure that they are operating efficiently

**internal recruiting** an effort to fill open positions with persons already employed by the firm

**international licensing agreement** a type of alliance in which a firm allows a foreign company (called the "licensee") to produce its products according to specific instructions

**international stock funds** mutual funds that invest in stocks of foreign firms

**international unions** unions that have members in several countries

**interpersonal skills** the skills necessary to communicate with customers and employees

**intrapreneurship** the assignment of particular employees of a firm to generate ideas, as if they were entrepreneurs running their own firms

**introduction phase** the initial period in which consumers are informed about a product

**inventory control** the process of managing inventory at a level that minimizes costs

**inventory management** determines the amount of inventory that is held

# J

**job analysis** the analysis used to determine the tasks and the necessary credentials for a particular position

**job description** states the tasks and responsibilities of a job position

**job enlargement** a program to expand (enlarge) the jobs assigned to employees

**job enrichment programs** programs designed to increase the job satisfaction of employees

**job rotation** a program that allows a set of employees to periodically rotate their job assignments

**job satisfaction** the degree to which employees are satisfied with their jobs

**job sharing** two or more persons share a particular work schedule

**job specification** states the credentials necessary to qualify for a job position

**joint venture** an agreement between two firms about a specific project

**just-in-time (JIT)** a system that attempts to reduce materials inventories to a bare minimum by frequently ordering small amounts of materials

# L

**labor union** an association established to represent the views, needs, and concerns of labor

**Landrum-Griffin Act** required labor unions to specify in their bylaws the membership eligibility requirements, dues, and collective bargaining procedures

**layout** the arrangement of machinery and equipment within a factory or office

**leading** the process of influencing the habits of others to achieve a common goal

**leasing** renting assets for a specified period of time

**leveraged buyout (LBO)** the purchase of a company by a firm or group of investors with borrowed funds

**liability** anything owed by a firm

**limit order** an investor's order that places a limit on the price at which the investor is willing to purchase or sell a stock

**limited liability company (LLC)** a firm that has all the favorable features of a typical general partnership but also offers limited liability for the partners

**limited partners** partners whose liability is limited to the cash or property they contributed to the partnership

**limited partnership** a firm that has some limited partners

**line of credit** an agreement with a bank that allows a firm access to borrowed funds upon demand over some specified period

**line organization** an organizational structure that contains only line positions and no staff positions

**line positions** job positions established to make decisions that achieve specific business goals

**line-and-staff organization** an organizational structure that includes both line and staff positions and assigns authority from higher-level management to employees

**liquid** having access to funds to pay bills when they come due

**liquidation value** the amount of funds that would be received as a result of the liquidation of a firm.

**liquidity** a firm's ability to meet short-term obligations

**liquidity management** the management of short-term assets and liabilities to ensure adequate liquidity

**load mutual funds** open-end mutual funds that can be purchased only by calling a broker

**local unions** unions composed of members in a specified local area

**lockout** prevents employees from working until an agreement between management and labor is reached

# M

**management** the means by which employees and other resources (such as machinery) are used by the firm

**management by objectives (MBO)** allows employees to participate in setting their goals and determining the manner in which they complete their tasks

**managerial accounting** accounting performed to provide information to help managers of the firm make decisions

**managers** employees who are responsible for managing job assignments of other employees and making key business decisions

**manufacturing arrangement** a type of franchise in which a firm is allowed to manufacture a product using the formula provided by another company

**market coverage** the degree of product distribution among outlets

**market order** an investor's order requesting a transaction at the best possible price

**market share** a firm's sales as a proportion of the total market

**marketing** means by which products (or services) are developed, priced, distributed, and promoted to customers

**marketing intermediaries** firms that participate in moving the product from the producer toward the customer

**marketing research** the accumulation and analysis of data in order to make a particular marketing decision

**materials requirements planning (MRP)** a process for ensuring that materials are available when needed

**matrix organization** an organizational structure that enables various parts of the firm to interact to focus on specific projects

**maturity phase** the period in which additional competing products have entered the market, and sales of a product level off because of competition

**merchants** marketing intermediaries that become owners of products and then resell them

**merger** two firms are merged (or combined) to become a single firm owned by the same owners (shareholders)

**merit system** a compensation system that allocates raises according to performance (merit)

**middle management** managers who are often responsible for the firm's short-term decisions

**mission statement** a description of a firm's primary goal

**monetary policy** decisions on the money supply level in the United States

**money supply** demand deposits (checking accounts), currency held by the public, and traveler's checks

**monopoly** a firm that is the sole provider of goods or services

**motivational factors** work-related factors that can lead to job satisfaction and motivate employees

**mutual funds** investment companies that receive funds from individual investors and then pool and invest those funds in securities

**mutually exclusive** the situation in which only one of two projects designed for the same purpose can be accepted

# N

**National Association of Security Dealers Automated Quotation (Nasdaq)** a computerized network within the OTC market for firms that meet specific size and capital requirements

**national unions** unions composed of members throughout the country

**natural resources** any resources that can be used in their natural form

**negative reinforcement** motivates employees by encouraging them to behave in a manner that avoids unfavorable consequences

**net asset value (NAV)** the market value of a mutual fund's securities after subtracting any expenses incurred

**net income (earnings after taxes)** earnings before taxes minus taxes

**net profit margin** a measure of net income as a percentage of sales

**net sales** total sales adjusted for any discounts

**news release** a brief written announcement about a firm provided by that firm to the media

**no-load funds** open-end mutual funds that can be purchased without the services of a broker

**nonprofit organizations** an organization that serves a specific cause and is not intended to make profits

**nonstore retailer** retailer that does not use a store to offer its products or services

**Norris-LaGuardia Act** restricted the use of injunctions against unions and allowed unions to publicize a labor dispute

**notes payable** short-term loans to a firm made by creditors such as banks

# O

**obsolete** less useful than in the past

**odd lots** less than 100 shares

**on margin** purchasing a stock by providing cash for only a portion of the funds needed and borrowing the remainder from the brokerage firm

**one-level channel** one marketing intermediary is between the producer and the customer

**open-book management** a form of employee involvement that educates employees on their contribution to the firm and enables them to periodically assess their own performance levels

**open-end mutual funds** funds that stand ready to repurchase their shares at the prevailing NAV if investors decide to sell the shares

**operating expenses** composed of selling expenses and general and administrative expenses

**operational planning** establishes the methods to be used in the near future (such as the next year) to achieve the tactical plans

**order costs** costs involved in placing orders for materials

**organizational structure** identifies responsibilities for each job position and the relationships among those positions

**organizing** the organization of employees and other resources in a manner that is consistent with the firm's goals

**outside board members** board members who are not managers of the firm

**outsourcing** purchasing parts from a supplier rather than producing the parts

**owner's equity** includes the par (or stated) value of all common stock issued, additional paid-in capital, and retained earnings

# P

**par value** the amount that bondholders receive at maturity

**participative** a leadership style in which the leaders accept some employee input but usually use their authority to make decisions

**participative management** employees are allowed to participate in various decisions made by their supervisors or others

**partners** co-owners of a business

**partnership** a business that is co-owned by two or more people

**patents** allow exclusive rights to the production and sale of a specific product

**penetration pricing** the strategy of setting a lower price than those of competing products to penetrate a market

**pension funds** receive employee and firm contributions toward pensions and invest the proceeds for the employees until the funds are needed

**perquisites** additional privileges beyond compensation payments and employee benefits

**personal selling** a personal sales presentation used to influence one or more consumers

**physiological needs** the basic requirements for survival

**picketing** walking around near the employer's building with signs complaining of poor working conditions

**planning** the preparation of a firm for future business conditions

**policies** guidelines for how tasks should be completed

**political risk** the risk that a country's political actions can adversely affect a business

**positive reinforcement** motivates employees by providing rewards for high performance

**predatory pricing** the strategy of lowering a product's price to drive out new competitors

**preferred stock** a security that represents partial ownership of a particular firm and offers specific priorities over common stock

**premium** a gift or prize provided free to consumers who purchase a specific product

**press conference** an oral announcement about a firm provided by that firm to the media

**prestige pricing** the strategy of using a higher price for a product that is intended to have a top-of-the-line image

**price skimming** the strategy of initially setting a high price for a product if no other competing products are in the market yet

**price-elastic** the demand for a product is highly responsive to price changes

**price-inelastic** the demand for a product is not very responsive to price changes

**prime rate** the rate of interest typically charged on loans to the most creditworthy firms that borrow

**private liquidation** creditors may informally request that a failing firm liquidate (sell) its assets and distribute the funds received from liquidation to them

**private placement** the selling of securities to one or a few investors

**privately held** ownership is restricted to a small group of investors

**privatization** the sale of government-owned businesses to private investors

**procedures** steps necessary to implement a policy

**producer brands** brands that reflect the manufacturer of the products

**product** a physical good or service that can satisfy consumer needs

**product differentiation** a firm's effort to distinguish its product from competitors' products in a manner that makes the product more desirable

**product layout** a layout in which tasks are positioned in the sequence that they are assigned

**product life cycle** the typical set of phases that a product experiences over its lifetime

**product line** a set of related products or services offered by a single firm

**product mix** the assortment of products offered by a firm

**production control** involves purchasing materials, inventory control, routing, scheduling, and quality control

**production efficiency** the ability to produce products at a low cost

**production management (operations management)** the management of a process in which resources (such as employees and machinery) are used to produce products and services

**production process (conversion process)** a series of tasks in which resources are used to produce a product or service

**production schedule** a plan for the timing and volume of production tasks

**profit sharing** a portion of the firm's profits is paid to employees

**program evaluation and review technique (PERT)** a method of scheduling tasks to minimize delays in the production process

**promotion** the assignment of an employee to a higher-level job with more responsibility and compensation; the act of informing or reminding consumers about a specific product or brand

**promotion budget** the amount of funds that have been set aside to pay for all promotion methods over a specified period

**promotion mix** the combination of promotion methods that a firm uses to increase acceptance of its products

**prospectus** a document that discloses relevant financial information about securities and about the firm issuing them

**protective covenants** restrictions imposed on specific financial policies of a firm that has issued bonds

**public accountants** accountants who provide accounting services for a variety of firms for a fee

**public offering** the selling of securities to the public

**public relations** actions taken with the goal of creating or maintaining a favorable public image

**publicly held** shares can be easily purchased or sold by investors

**pull strategy** firms direct their promotion directly at the target market, and consumers in turn request the product from wholesalers or producers

**push strategy** producers direct their promotion of a product at wholesalers or retailers, who in turn promote it to consumers

## Q

**quality** the degree to which a product or service satisfies a customer's requirements or expectations

**quality control** a process of determining whether the quality of a product meets the desired quality level

**quality control circle** a group of employees who assess the quality of a product and offer suggestions for improvement

**quota** a limit on the amounts of specific products that can be imported

## R

**ratio analysis** an evaluation of the relationships between financial statement variables

**rebate** a potential refund by the manufacturer to the consumer

**recession** two consecutive quarters of negative economic growth

**reengineering** the redesign of a firm's organizational structure and operations

**reinforcement theory** suggests that reinforcement can influence behavior

**reminder advertising** intended to remind consumers of a product's existence

**restructuring** the revision of the production process in an attempt to improve efficiency

**return on assets (ROA)** measures a firm's net income as a percentage of the total amount of assets utilized by the firm

**return on equity (ROE)** measures the return to the common stockholders (net income) as a percentage of their investment in the firm; earnings as a proportion of the firm's equity

**right-to-work** allows states to prohibit union shops

**risk** the degree of uncertainty about a firm's future earnings

**round lots** multiples of 100 shares

**routing** the sequence (or route) of tasks necessary to complete the production of a product

## S

**S-corporation** a firm that has 100 or fewer owners and satisfies other criteria. The earnings are distributed to the owners and taxed at the respective personal income tax rate of each owner.

**safety needs** job security and safe working conditions

**salary (or wages)** the dollars paid for a job over a specific period

**sales manager** an individual who manages a group of sales representatives

**sales promotion** the set of activities that is intended to influence consumers

**sampling** offering free samples to encourage consumers to try a new brand or product; randomly selecting some of the products produced and testing them to determine whether they satisfy the quality standards

**savings institutions** financial institutions that obtain deposits from individuals and use the deposited funds primarily to provide mortgage loans

**scheduling** the act of setting time periods for each task in the production process

**seasonal unemployment** people whose services are not needed during some seasons

**secondary market** a market where existing securities can be traded among investors

**secured bonds** bonds backed by collateral

**segments** subsets of a market that reflect a specific type of business and the perceived quality

**selective distribution** the distribution of a product through selected outlets

**self-actualization** the need to fully reach one's potential

**self-service retail store** a retailer that does not provide sales assistance or service and sells products that do not require much expertise

**sexual harassment** unwelcome comments or actions of a sexual nature

**shareholder activism** active efforts by stockholders to influence a firm's management policies

**shopping products** products that are not purchased frequently

**shortage** the situation when the quantity supplied by firms is less than the quantity demanded by customers

**social needs** the need to be part of a group

**social responsibility** a firm's recognition of how its business decisions can affect society

**socialism** an economic system that contains some features of both capitalism and communism

**sole proprietor** the owner of a sole proprietorship

**sole proprietorship** a business owned by a single owner

**span of control** the number of employees managed by each manager

**specialty products** products that specific consumers consider to be special and therefore make a special effort to purchase

**specialty retail store** a retailer that specializes in a particular type of product

**spot exchange rate** the exchange rate quoted for immediate transactions

**staff positions** job positions established to support the efforts of line positions

**stakeholders** people who have an interest in a business; the business's owners, creditors, employees, suppliers, and customers

**stock** certificates of ownership of a business

**stock market efficiency** a term used to suggest that stock prices reflect all publicly available information

**stock mutual funds** investment companies that invest funds received from individual investors in stocks

**stock options** a form of compensation that allows employees to purchase shares of their employer's stock at a specific price

**stockbroker** a person who facilitates desired stock transactions

**stockholders (shareholders)** investors who by purchasing the firm's stock become partial owners of firms

**store brands** brands that reflect the retail store where the products are sold

**strategic alliance** a business agreement between firms whereby resources are shared to pursue mutual interests

**strategic plan** identifies a firm's main business focus over a long-term period, perhaps three to five years

**stretch targets** production efficiency targets (or goals) that cannot be achieved under present conditions

**strike** a discontinuation of employee services

**structural unemployment** people who are unemployed because they do not have adequate skills

**supervisory (first-line) management** managers who are usually highly involved with the employees who engage in the day-to-day production process

**supply chain** the process from the beginning of the production process until the product reaches the customer

**supply schedule** a schedule that indicates the quantity of a product that would be supplied (produced) by firms at each possible price

**surplus** the situation when the quantity supplied by firms exceeds the quantity demanded by customers

**SWOT** method by which entrepreneurs develop a competitive advantage for their business

# T

**tactical planning** smaller-scale plans (over one or two years) that are consistent with the firm's strategic (long-term) plan

**Taft-Hartley Act** an amendment to the Wagner Act that prohibited unions from pressuring employees to join

**target market** a group of individuals or organizations with similar traits who may purchase a particular product

**tariff** a tax on imported products

**teamwork** a group of employees with varied job positions have the responsibility to achieve a specific goal

**technical skills** skills used to perform specific day-to-day tasks

**technological obsolescence** being inferior to new products

**technology** knowledge or tools used to produce products and services

**telemarketing** the use of the telephone for promoting and selling products

**tender offer** a direct bid by an acquiring firm for the shares of a target firm

**time management** the way managers allocate their time when managing tasks.

**times interest earned ratio** measures the ability of a firm to cover its interest payments

**top (high-level) management** managers in positions such as president, chief executive officer, chief financial officer, and vice-president who make decisions regarding the firm's long-run objectives

**total quality management (TQM)** the act of monitoring and improving the quality of products and services provided

**trade deficit** the amount by which imports exceed exports

**trademark** a brand's form of identification that is legally protected from use by other firms

**Treasury bills** short-term debt securities issued by the U.S. Treasury

**two-level channel** two marketing intermediaries are between the producer and the customer

# U

**underwriting syndicate** a group of investment banks that share the obligations of underwriting securities

**underwritten** the investment bank guarantees a price to the issuing firm, no matter what price the securities are sold for

**unlimited liability** no limit on the debts for which the owner is liable

**unsecured bonds** bonds that are not backed by collateral

**upward appraisals** used to measure the managerial abilities of supervisors

# V

**variable costs** operating expenses that vary directly with the number of products produced

**variety retail store** a retailer that offers numerous types of goods

**venture capital firm** a firm composed of individuals who invest in small businesses

**vertical channel integration** two or more levels of distribution are managed by a single firm

**vertical merger** the combination of a firm with a potential supplier or customer

# W

**Wagner Act** prohibited firms from interfering with workers' efforts to organize or join unions

**white knight** a more suitable company that is willing to acquire a firm and rescue it from the hostile takeover efforts of some other firm

**work station** an area in which one or more employees are assigned a specific task

**working capital management** the management of a firm's short-term assets and liabilities

**work-in-process inventories** inventories of partially completed products

# Y

**yellow-dog contract** a contract requiring employees to refrain from joining a union as a condition of employment

# Company Index

## A

Abbott Laboratories, 417
ABC television, 591
Abercrombie & Fitch, 582
Ace Hardware, 370, 371, 372, 455
Aetna Inc., 364
Albertson's, 301
Allstate Insurance, 425
Altria, 550
Amazon.com, 7, 8, 15, 67, 98, 99, 173,
    182, 183, 186, 291, 296, 306, 361,
    365, 366, 404, 406, 412, 418, 446,
    452, 476, 551
America Online (AOL) , 475, 483
American Airlines, 390, 418
American Express, 176, 364
Anheuser-Busch, 444, 473, 485, 487
Apex One, 582
Apple, 5, 403, 406, 418, 423
Arthur Andersen, 516
AT&T, 4, 99, 117, 221, 289, 306, 380,
    421, 474
Athlete's Foot, The, 457
Audi, 421
Autobytel, com, 451
Autozone, 98, 292
Avis, 336
Avon Products, 98, 476

## B

Bank of America, 14, 50
Barnes & Noble, 151, 407
Baskin-Robbins, 161
Bell Sports Corporation, 17
Best Buy, 442, 456, 474
Black & Decker Corporation, 252, 291,
    422, 442
Blockbuster Entertainment Group, 98,
    106, 286, 292, 423, 456, 515
Boeing Corporation, 98, 265, 291, 369,
    370, 392
Boys & Girls Clubs of America, 51
Bridgestone/Firestone, 392
Briggs & Stratton, 53
Bristol-Myers Squibb Company, 35, 220,
    228, 475
Buick, 269

## C

Cadillac, 269
Campbell's Soup Company, 336, 550
Capital Cities/ABC, 589
CarMax, 42
Carters, 408, 410
Cat Financial, 299
Caterpillar, 299, 372, 391, 392
CD Warehouse, 162
Center for Entrepreneurial Leadership,
    10
Checkers restaurants, 51
Cheesecake Factory, 50, 511
Chevrolet, 269
ChevronTexaco, 49, 553
Chrysler, 161, 490
Cisco Systems, 12, 364
Coca-Cola Company, 15, 40, 51, 75, 99,
    117, 118, 404, 414, 422, 423, 449,
    471, 473, 582, 583, 588, 595, 596
Company Corporation, The, 156
Compaq Computer, 453
ConAgra, 550
Continental Airlines, 263, 369, 390
Converse, 100, 582
Corning, 100

## D

Dairy Queen, 161
Darden Restaurants, 364
Dell, Inc., 4, 13, 15, 117, 120, 176, 271,
    296, 298, 330, 357, 406, 407, 426,
    442, 446, 443, 514
Delta Airlines, 390, 392
Denny's 373
Disney, see Walt Disney Company
Domino's, 145, 174
Donna Karan, 405
Dow Chemical Company, 14, 38, 51,
    100, 380, 406
Drugstore.com, 406
Dun and Bradstreet, 532
DuPont, 14, 49, 98, 104, 406, 582, 595
Duracell, 474

## E

Eastman Kodak, 49, 326, 336, 371, 418,
    421, 423, 594
eBay, 8, 98, 221, 257, 541
Eddie Bauer, 409

Enron, Inc., 13, 46, 48, 153, 256, 257,
    366, 367, 515, 516, 517
Enterprise Rent-A-Car, 151, 336
Ernst & Young, 370, 597
Ethics Resource Center, 52
ExxonMobil, 50, 51, 118, 406, 473, 583

## F

FedEx, 22, 51
Fisher Price, 422
Foot Locker, 444, 448
Ford Motor Company, 4, 48, 50, 67, 99,
    106, 108, 117, 151, 161, 290, 292,
    422, 477, 594
Frito-Lay, 112, 422, 473

## G

Gap, Inc., 4, 53, 98, 410, 446, 582
GapKids, 426
Garage.com, 176
General Dynamics, 306
General Electric, 98, 100, 103, 117, 255,
    336, 635
General Mills, 42, 422, 483, 550
General Motors, 13, 14, 16, 40, 67, 75,
    99, 100, 108, 117, 263, 269, 270,
    289, 292, 345, 391, 473, 589
General Nutrition Centers (GNC), 284,
    444, 473
Gillette, 445
Global Crossing, 13, 366
Glow Dog, Inc., 174
Goodyear Tire and Rubber Company,
    16, 340, 372
Google, 8, 151, 174, 185, 325, 344, 364,
    551

## H

Harley-Davidson, 65
Heinz, 117
Hertz, 98
Hewlett-Packard, 67, 117, 176, 413, 417,
    453
Hilton Hotels, 4
Holiday Inn, 162, 163, 477
Home Depot, 51, 301, 370, 410, 445,
    455, 485, 490, 634
Homestake Mining Company, 49
Honda, 107
Honeywell, 48

# I

IBM, 4, 13, 14, 40, 49, 50, 51, 53, 98, 99, 260, 263, 265, 298, 330, 336, 405, 417, 418, 422, 425, 473, 475, 582, 583, 634
Inland Steel, 48
Institutional Shareholder Services (ISS), Inc., 230
Intel, 104, 257, 258, 265, 422

# J

J.C. Penney, 258, 422, 456
J.M. Smuckers, 42
J.P. Morgan Chase, 369
Jaguar, 341
Jandy Industries, 458
Johnson & Johnson, 40, 50, 260, 306, 369

# K

KB Toys, 420
Kellogg Company, 106
Kenney's Shoes, 456
Kenya Airways, 98
KFC, 163
KMart, 456
Kodak, see Eastman Kodak
Kraft Foods, 108, 423, 490

# L

L.L. Bean, 151, 460
LA Fitness, 217
Land's End, 442, 457
Lear Seating, 290
Levi Strauss & Co., 38, 422
Little Caesars Pizza, 13, 14
Liz Claiborne, Inc., 404, 423, 442, 447

# M

Marriott International, 42, 364, 372, 476
Mastercard, 185
McDonald's, 98, 112, 161, 162, 163, 422, 474, 582
Mercedes, 422
Mesa Company, 109
Microsoft, 4, 51, 162, 364, 365, 422, 475
Miller Brewing, 487
Mitsubishi Materials, 107
Moody's Investor Service, 547
Motorola, 4, 16, 100, 234, 296, 306, 339, 369, 371, 373, 553, 634
MSN, 475
MTV network, 281

# N

Nabisco, 423
National Instruments, 53
National Semiconductor, 451
NepApp, 344
Netflix, 581

NFIB Research Foundation, 11, 19, 37, 100, 125, 178, 181, 184, 186, 285, 300, 360, 367, 405, 409, 414, 427, 478, 489, 513, 557, 584, 587, 597
Nike, 13, 97, 106, 117, 422, 448, 635
Nordstrom, 364
Northwest Airlines, 392
Nucor, 336

# O

Oracle, 291
OshKosh B' Gosh, 410

# P

Paperexchange.com, 451
Paychex, 336
PC Repair Company, 156
Pearle Vision, Inc., 161
PepsiCo, 98, 112, 255, 355, 368, 404, 583, 588, 422, 423, 447, 540
Pfizer, 286
Philip Morris International, 550
Pizza Hut, 162, 163
PPG Industries, 49
Procter & Gamble Company, 99, 117, 336, 404, 417, 422, 423, 472, 473, 475, 487, 490
Publix Super Markets, 42, 364, 456, 474

# Q

Quaker State, 404
Quicken, 176

# R

Radio Shack, 456
Ralston Purina, 442
Rand McNally & Co., 151
RCA, 126, 127
Reebok, 444, 487
Robert Morris Associates, 532

# S

Sara Lee Corporation, 14, 40
SAS Institute, 42
Saturn, 16, 452, 453
Schwinn, 249
Sears, 254, 263, 422, 431, 444, 456, 456, 457, 474
7-Eleven, 456
Small Business Administration, 176, 191, 209, 315, 395, 501, 613
Society for Human Resource Management, 39
Sony, 107
Southwest Airlines, 4, 282, 421, 423, 425
Standard & Poor's Corporation, 547
Starbucks Coffee Company, 33, 38, 67, 98, 286, 344, 364, 365, 406, 414, 420
Station Casinos, 42, 344

Stoner, 299
Subway, 162
SunTrust Bank, 14, 50
Super 8 Motels, Inc., 161
Symantec, 364

# T

Taco Bell, 404, 425, 425
Talbots, 477
Tata Motors, 341
TD Ameritrade, 425
Telecom, Inc., 327
Texas Instruments, 100, 364
Textron, 406, 582
TGI Fridays, 161
3M Company, 301, 417, 553, 582
Thrifty Rent-a-Car, 161
Timberland, 364
Time Warner, 444, 483
Toyota Motor Corporation, 107, 225, 284, 298, 370, 406, 450

# U

U.S. Steel, 284
United Auto Workers, 390
United Parcel Service (UPS), 151, 292, 372, 391
Urban Outfitters, 441
US Airways, 392
USA Today, 341

# V

Viacom, 281
Visa, 185

# W

Wachovia Corporation, 589
Wal-Mart, 15, 50, 51, 98, 103, 113, 330, 358, 365, 406, 420, 442, 444, 454, 455, 558, 582, 598
Walt Disney Company, 13, 53, 257, 358, 369, 372, 405, 422, 477, 589, 591
Wegmans Food Market, 42
Wells Fargo & Company, 589, 406
Whole Foods Market, 364
World Wildlife Fund, 49
WorldCom, 366, 515, 516

# X

Xerox Corporation, 40, 339, 371, 373
Xinjiang Airlines, 98

# Y

Yahoo!, 8, 176, 185, 340, 364, 475, 551, 634, 635
YouTube, 3, 8, 174

# Z

Zenith Electronics, 15, 104

# Subject Index

## A

accountability, 259
accounting, 21, 512-515
accounts payable, 521
accounts receivable management, 596, 598
across-the-board system, 335
advertising, 36, 473-478, 487
    forms of, 474-477
affirmative action, 43
Age Discrimination in Employment Act of 1967, 362
age, consumer, 410
agency costs, 227
agency problem, 153
agents, 444
aggregate expenditures, 68
air pollution, 48-49
air transportation, 449
American depository receipts (ADRs), 644
American Stock Exchange (AMEX), 553
Americans with Disabilities Act, (ADA) of 1990, 362
antitrust laws and acts, 37-38
annual dividend (DIV), 634
appreciates, 122
assembly line, 283
asset, 519
asset turnover, 525, 528
audit committee, 258
auditing, 515, 517
auditors, 515-516
autocratic, 226
autocratic leadership style, 226
automated, 301, 302
autonomy, 260

## B

B2B e-commerce, 9
balance of trade, 105
balance sheet, 518, 519
bankruptcy, 562
banks, 549
barriers, international business 109-112
    see also trade barriers
basic accounting equation, 519
bearish, 636
benchmarking, 301
benefits and bonuses, 367
best-efforts basis, 554

binding contracts, 38
board committees, 258
board members, 255
    conflicts of interest, 255-256
    resolving conflicts of interest, 257
board of directors, 254-258
    and proper reporting, 516
bond mutual funds, 549
bond ratings, 548
bonds, 546, 547
bonuses, 368
bookkeeping, 512
borrowing, 542
boycott, 391
brand advertising, 473
brand loyalty, 483
branding, 422-423
break-even point, 304, 428
bribery laws, 121
bribes, laws regarding, 112
budget deficit, revision of, 85
budget, 489-490
bullish, 637
business, 3-4
    creating new, 174
    international, see also international business
    motives, 4-6
    motives for starting small business, 5
    motives of nonprofit, 6
    new, 583
    resources, 6-9
        capital, 7-9
        entrepreneurship, 9
        human, 6
        natural, 6
    skill to succeed, 162
    stakeholders, see also stakeholders
business decisions, 20-23, 561
    affect earnings, 21
    affect performance, 20-21
    and promotion decisions, 491
    common, 20
    finance, 23
    key types, 22
    management, 22
    marketing, 22
    rely on information, 21
    revising, 18
business environment, 17-20
    assessment, 187
    economic, 19
    global, 19-20

    industry, 18-19
    social, 17
business ethics, 33, see also ethics
business functions
    economic effects across, 87
    industry effects, 196
business investment, 585
business loans, 544
business ownership
    changing, 156
    comparing, 155
    revising decisions, 160
business performance, economic growth, 66-69
business plan, 186-195
    assessing, 193
    benefits, 186
    contents, 194
    developing, 186, 192, 195
    feasibility, 192
    financial plan, 194
    for College Health Club, 607-611
    marketing plan, 194
    target marketing, 194
business responsibilities, 35, 37-38, 52
business revenue, 150
business risk, 195
business-to-business franchises, 164
business-to-business, 9
bylaws, 150

## C

call feature, 547
capital, 7, 542
capital budget, 583
capital budgeting, 582, 585, 588
capital expenditures, 583
capital gain, 155
capital structure, 558
capitalism, 113
    and socialism, 115
    conversion toward, 116
carrying cost, 291
cash flows, 586
Celler-Kefauver Act, 38
centralized authority, 260
certified public accountants (CPAs), 512
chain of command, 250
chain, 455
chain-style business, 161, 162
charitable organizations, 51
charter, 150

Civil Rights Act of 1964,  43, 362
Civil Rights Act of 1991,  43, 362, 379
Clayton Act, 38
closed-end mutual funds, 644
closing a sale, 480, 481
closing price of stock, 635
co-branding, 423
code of ethics, 41
code of responsibilities, 35, 41
collateral, 543
College Health Club, 24, 55, 87, 127,
        164, 200, 217, 240, 307, 345, 380,
        431, 461, 492, 533, 564, 598, 607-
        611
commercial banks, 549
commercial paper, 548
commission, 368, 642
common stock, 550
communication, 267
        nonverbal in different cultures, 114
communism, 114
community
        firm's responsibility to, 50-51
        versus stockholders, 51
comparative advertising, 473
compensation, 369
compensation committee, 258
compensation costs, by country, 101
compensation packages, 364, 365
compensation program, 335-338
competition, 37, 177-180, 490
        change, 179
        segments, 179
competitive advantage, 182-186, 489
        Internet183
        quality services, 184
competitive analysis, SWOT analysis,
        185
competitors, 183
        competing illegally or unethically, 37
        prices, 425
complaints, 36, 55, 298
composition agreement, 562
compressed workweek, 338
conflict of interest, 366
conglomerate merger, 589
consumer income, affect on market
        prices, 81
consumer markets, 408
consumer preferences, 81, 418
consumerism, 34
consumers, characteristics, 411
contingency planning, 223, 224
contribution margin, 429
control
        correct standards, 229
        correcting deficiencies, 228
        management process, 229-230
        reporting, 230
controlling function of management,
        228
convenience products, 404
conversion process, 282
co-owner, 11

corporate anorexia, 305
Corporate Citizenship Study, 51
corporation, 149-156
        advantages, 152
        board of directors, 150
        bylaws, 150
        charter, 150
        disadvantages, 152
        public versus private, 151
        tax effects on, 154
        taxes, 153
corrupt practices, 41
corruption, 120
corruption index, 120
cost of goods sold, 518
cost
        of complaints, 55
        of social responsibilities, 53-55
cost-based pricing, 424
cost-push inflation, 70
costs, fixed and variable, 302
coupon payments, 546
coupons, 482, 484
craft unions, 388
credit risk, 458
credit terms, 430
credit, 460, 597
creditors, 10, 13-14, 48, 190, 191, 514
creditworthiness, 542
critical path, 294, 295
culture, foreign, 112
current assets, 519
current ratio, 523, 528
customer feedback, 36
customer service skills, 372
customers, 10, 15, 198, 234, 479, 481
        responsibility to, 34-37
cyclical unemployment, 69

## D

debt, 562-564
debt financing level, 548
debt financing, 542, 553, 554
debt-to-equity ratio, 526, 528
decentralized authority, 260-261
decision-making stages, 237
decision-making skills, 371
decline phase of product life cycle, 407,
        408
defensive pricing, 425
deintegration, 290
delivery, 458
demand, 77-78, 176-177, 574
        effect on general price level, 81
demand and supply, determining
        equilibrium price, 77
demand schedule, 76-79, 574-575
demand-pull inflation, 71
Deming, W. Edwards, 296
democratic leadership style, 226
demographics, 17, 409
departmentalize, 268
departmentalizing tasks, 268

by customer, 271
by function, 268-269
by location, 270-271
by product, 268-269
depreciates, 122
depreciation, 521
design, 286-288
direct channel, 442, 443
direct foreign investment (DFI), 106-
        107, 111
direct mail advertising, 476, 477
discount brokers, 642
discounting, 430
discrimination, 388-389
displays, 483, 484
        product, 459
distribution, 190, 442-446, 554
        global, 461
        Internet, 451
        optimal, 446
        streamlining, 451
distribution decisions, 455
        revising, 459
distribution process, accelerating, 450-
        454
distribution systems, 445, 453
distributorship, 161
diversify, 405, 406
diversity, 39, 40
        benefits, 363
        firms recognized, 364
        international. 102
diversity incentives, 363
divestiture, 594
dividend policy, 550
dividend yield (YLD), 634
dividends, 17, 534
double taxation, 154
Dow Jones Industrial Average (DJIA),
        636
downsizing, 263, 305
dumping, 109

## E

earnings after taxes, 518
earnings before interest and taxes
        (EBIT), 518, 526
earnings before taxes, 518
earnings, 4, 21, 157, 192, 518, 549
        of sole proprietorship, 146
e-business (electronic business), 7, 9
e-commerce (electronic commerce), 7,
        9, 412-413
economic conditions, 346, 371, 431,
        490, 577
        government influence on, 82-86
        in foreign countries, 117
economic effects across business func-
        tions, 87
economic environment, 19, 187
economic factors, 411
        government influence on, 85

economic growth, 577, 66-69
   in foreign countries, 117
   indicators, 68-69
   on business performance, 65
   sensitivity, 69
   strong, 66
   weak, 66-68
economic systems, 113
economics conditions, assessing, 65
economies of scale, 188, 302, 424, 589, 590
economy
   free-market, 5
   impact of weak, 67
educational background of business owners, 12
EEOC, *see* Equal Employment Opportunity Commission
efficiency, 530
   measures, 524
electronic business (e-business), *see* e-business
electronic commerce (e-commerce), *see* e-commerce
e-mail advertising, 476, 477
e-marketing, 412-413, 415, 453
employees, 10, 14-15, 38, 235, 298, 360
   allocating their time, 372
   benefits, 367, 369
   best companies for, 344
   compensating, 368
   developing skills, 369
   disgruntled, 334
   dissatisfaction, 392
   ethical behavior, 52
   evaluation, of supervisors, 380
   firm's responsibilities to, 40-43
   goals, 337
   hiring, 371
   influence on business decisions, 342
   injuries, 199
   input, 264
      informal organizational structure, 266-268
      intrapreneurship, 266
      matrix organization, 264-265
   involvement programs, 339
   key, 198
   layoffs, 43
   loss from key employee's death, 199
   managing, 372
   motivating, 345, 346
   motivation, 335
   outsourcing, 107
   performance, evaluating, 373-380
   performance criteria, 374-377
   proper treatment, 39-40
   safety, 38
   training, 373
   unproductive workers, 393
employment tests, 359
employment, equal opportunity, 43
empowered employee, 343
empowerment, 339

enterprise resource planning (ERP) systems, 293
entrepreneur, 9, 10, 186, 200
   advantages/disadvantages, 175
   characteristics, 175
   risk management, 195-200
entrepreneurial plan, revising, 200
entrepreneurship, 9
environment, 49
   firm's responsibility to, 48-50
environmental expenses, 50
environmental responsibility, 49-50
environmental restrictions, international, 111
e-procurement, 289
equal employment opportunity, 43
Equal Employment Opportunity Commission (EEOC), 43, 379
equal opportunity, 362-364
Equal Pay Act of 1963, 362
equilibrium interest rate, 574
equilibrium price, 78, 82
   change in demand, 79
   change in supply, 80
   determined by demand and supply, 77
equity financing, 549, 553, 544
equity theory, 331, 332, 334
equity, 157, 558
e-risk, 200
ethical behavior of employees, 52
ethical responsibilities, 54
ethical standards, assessing, 44
ethical, situations, assessing, 45
ethics
   business, 33
   distorting performance, 46
   global, 41
   pledge of ethics and responsibilities, 35
euro, 118, 125
European Union, 110
exchange rate, 118
   effects on foreign competition, 126
   effects on U.S. importers, 122
exchange rate movements, 121, 125
   hedge against, 124
exchange rate on earnings, 530
excise taxes, 85
exclusive distribution, 448
existing business
   ownership, 160
   purchasing, 161
expansion, 73
expansion, interest rates impact on firm's, 73
expectancy theory, 331, 334
expense ratio, 645
expenses, 4, 192, 584
   environmental, 50
   interest rate impact on, 72
   production, 82
   social responsibilities, 54
   web-based business, 185

exporters,123-124
exporting, 104-106, 123
   Internet facilitates, 1-5
   trends, 105
extension, 562
external recruiting, 358

**F**

family branding, 422
family business ownership, 160
fashion obsolescence, 413
feasibility, 192
Federal Reserve System (Fed), 82, 576
   weak economy dilemma, 83
federal budget deficit, 85
Federal Open Market Committee (FOMC), 82
Federal Reserve System (the Fed), *see* Fed
Federal Trade Commission Act, 38
finance, 20
finance companies, 549
finance decisions, 23, 531
Financial Accounting Standards Board (FASB), 512
financial accounting, 512
financial analysis, 532
financial disclosure, 152
financial leverage, 525, 530
financial perspective, 196
financial plan, 190-192, 194
financial reporting, 513
financial statements, 514, 518
financing decisions, 561, 562
financing, 190, 553, 554, 560
   from suppliers, 555, 556
   global, 561
firm's responsibilities, *see* responsibility, firm's
firms, impact of weak economy, 67
firms, undervalued, 638
firm-specific characteristics, 196
first-line management, 218
fiscal policy, 84
fixed assets, 521
fixed costs, 302, 426
fixed-rate versus floating-rate loans, 544
flexible manufacturing, 287
flextime programs, 338
floating-rate versus fixed-rate loans, 544
floor traders, 641
flotation costs, 555
FOMC, *see* Federal Open Market Committee
forecasting, 356
foreign competition, affect of exchange rates on, 126
Foreign Corrupt Practices Act, 121
foreign countries, targeting markets, 412
foreign demand, attracting, 98
foreign operations, organizational structure, 262
foreign subsidiaries, 561

forward contract, 124
forward rate, 124
franchise, 161-164
  business to business, 164
franchisee, 161
franchising, 161-164
franchisor, 161
frazzle factory, 333
free-market economy, 5
free-rein management, 226
frictional, unemployment, 69
full-service retail store, 455
full-service brokers, 642
funds, obtaining, 555

## G

Gantt chart, 294
Gantt, Henry, 294
GDP, *see* gross domestic product
General Agreement on Tariffs and Trade
    (GATT), 110
general partners, 148
general partnership, 148
general price level, effect of demand and
    supply, 81
generally accepted accounting principles
    (GAAP), 512
generic brands, 422
geography, 410
global business, leadership styles, 229
global distribution, 461
global economic conditions, 75
global environment of business, 19-20,
    188
global ethics, 41
global financing, 561
global investing, 588
goals, of managers, 15
going public, 151, 551
government loans, 546
government policies, affect on business
    performance, 86
government regulations, 181
government, influence on economic
    growth, 86
government's responsibilities, see re-
    sponsibility, government's
grapevine, 266
grievance policy, 41
grievance procedures, 391
gross domestic product (GDP), 68
gross profit, 518
growth funds, 645
growth phase of product life cycle, 407,
    408

## H

Hawthorne Studies, 327, 334
hedge, 124
    against future payments in foreign
        countries, 124

future receivables in foreign
    countries, 125
  limitations, 126
Herzberg, Frederick, 328
Herzberg's Job Satisfaction Study, 328,
    329, 334
hierarchy of needs, 327
  esteem needs, 328
  physiological needs, 327
  safety needs, 327
  self-actualization, 328
  social needs, 327
high-level management, 218, 253
hiring, 233, 361
horizontal merger, 589
hotelling, 288
housing crisis, 75-76
human resource manager, 357
human resource planning, 356, 362
human resource skills, 373
human resources, 6, 189, 282, 355-362
hygiene factors, 328

## I

importers, 121-122
importing, 104, 122
    factors that influence, 104
    trends, 105
incentive plans, 335
income, 157
    consumer, 81
income funds, 645
income statement, 518
indenture, 547
independent project, 587
independent retail stores, 455
individual branding, 422
industrial markets, 408
industrial unions, 388
industry advertising, 473
industry environment, 187
industry environment of business, 18-19
inflation, 69-72
    expected, 577
    types, 70-71
    U.S. rates, 70
infomercials, 475
information, 21, 459, 460
information systems, 21
information technology, 7, 200, 252, 429
initial public offering (IPO), 551, 552
initiative, 225
injunction, 392
inside board members, 255
insider information, 644
insider trading, 644
institutional advertising, 473
institutional investors, 47
insurance companies, 549
insurance, 198
intensive distribution, 447, 448
interest expenses, 548

interest rate, 72, 87, 545, 573-578, 584-
    583
    effect on interest expenses and prof-
        its, 73
    Fed can increase/reduce, 82-83
    firm's expenses, 72
    impact among firms, 74
    rising affects on housing crisis, 75-76
interlocking directorates, 38
internal auditor, 258-259, 515
internal control process, 259
internal recruiting, 357
Internal Revenue Service (IRS), 512
international business, 98-100, 112
    barriers, 109-112
    conducting, 103
    corruption, 120
    economic conditions, 117-118
    economic systems, 113-116
    exchange rates, 118
    foreign culture, 112
    in weak economy, 125
    managing, 119
    motives, 103
    political risk and regulations, 118-121
international diversity, 102
international environment, 53
international licensing, Internet
    facilitates, 109
international licensing agreement, 108-
    109
international stock funds, 645
international trade, 109
international unions, 388
Internet, 302, 415
Internet advertising, 475, 477, 478
Internet business, 8
Internet orders, 446
interview, 359
intrapreneurship, 266
introduction phase of product life cycle,
    407, 408
inventory, 425
inventory control, 291-292
inventory management, 598
inventory turnover, 524, 528
investing, global, 588
investment, 582-585, 595, 597
    business, 585
    short-term, 595
investment decisions, 598
investors, 47, 514

## J

job analysis, 356
job description, 356
job enlargement, 339
job enrichment programs, 335
job positions, 260
job responsibilities, 375, 378
job rotation, 339
job satisfaction, 42, 326, 335, 344
job security, 335, 390

job sharing, 338
job specifications, 356
joint venture, 108
just-in-time (JIT), 291
just-in-time office, 288

# K

key employee, loss of, 199

# L

labor conditions, 180
labor laws, international, 111
labor strikes, 391
labor unions, 388-393
  and management, 389, 391
  employees' desire for, 393
  grievance procedures, 390-391
  history of, 388-389
  job security, 390
  management rights, 390
  management's criticism, 392
  membership, 389
  salaries, 389-390
labor,
  cheap, 107
  cost of, 284
  supply of, 284-285
Labor-Management Reporting and
    Disclosure Act of 1959, 389
laissez-faire management, 226
land pollution, 49
Landrum-Griffin Act, 389
Latin American trade agreement, 110
lawsuits,
  by fired employees, 379
  liability, 300
layout, 286-288
  fixed position, 287
leadership styles, 226-228
leading, of managers, 225-228
leasing, 556, 557
leverage buyouts, 593
liability, 519, 521, 522
limit order, 642
limited liability company (LLC), 149
limited partners, 148
limited partnership, 148
line of credit, 595
line organization, 252, 253
line positions, 252
line-and-staff organization, 252, 253
liquid, 595
liquidation value, 562
liquidation, 562-564
liquidity, 523, 529
liquidity management, 595
load mutual funds, 645
loan rate, 543
loanable funds, 573-576
loans, 544, 545
  government, 546
local unions, 388

location, competitive advantage, 285
  *see also* site
lockout, 392
loss, hedging against, 199

# M

magazine advertising, 474, 477
mail-order retailer, 457
Malcolm Baldrige National Quality
    Awards, 299
management, 20, 233
  levels of, 218-219
  time management 237-239
management by objectives (MBO), 339
management decisions, 22, 227, 531
management functions, 223, 231, 232
  applying, 233
  technology, 231
management plan, 188-189, 194
management rights, 390
management skills, 237
management style, centralized/
    decentralized, 262
managerial accounting, 514
managerial skills, 234-237
  conceptual skills, 234
  decision-making skills, 236-237
  interpersonal skills, 234-235
  management skills, 237
  technical skills, 235-236
managers, 15
  controlling function, 228-231
  expertise, 590
  functions of, 218-234
  goals of, 15
  leading function, 225-228
  organizing function, 225
  planning function, 218-224
  responsibilities, 219
managing employees, 194
managing production, 196
manufacturing arrangement, 162
market, global perspectives, 180
market conditions, 182
  assessing, 176
  competition, 176, 177
  demand, 176
  labor conditions, 176
  regulatory conditions, 176
market coverage, 447, 448
market order, 642
market prices, how determined, 76
market research, 414-416, 448
market segments, 179, 180
market share, 177
marketing, 20
marketing decisions, 22, 531
marketing employees, 337
marketing intermediaries, 442
marketing perspective, 196
marketing plan, 189-190, 194
Maslow, Abraham, 327

Maslow's Hierarchy of Needs, 327, 334
materials, purchasing, 288-290
materials requirement planning (MRP),
    291
matrix organization, 264, 265
maturity phase of product life cycle, 407,
    408
MBA Enterprise Corps, 116
McGregor's Theory X and Theory Y, 330,
    331, 334
mediator, 42
meetings, 239
merchants, 444
merger analysis, 591
mergers, 589-594
  corporate motives, 589-591
  financing, 593
  postmerger evaluation, 594
  procedures, 593
  tax benefits, 591
  types, 589
merit system, 335
middle management, 218, 219
Midwest Stock Exchange, 643
minorities, and women in various occu-
    pations, 39
minority, 363
mission statement, 220
monetary policy, 82, 85, 576
money supply, 82
monopoly, 37
motivation, 326
  across business functions, 337
  theories, 326-334
motivational factors, 328
motivational theories, 334
multinational corporations, 98, 286
  goal, 227
  organizational structure, 270
mutual funds, 549, 644
mutually exclusive, 586

# N

NAFTA, *see* North American Free Trade
    Agreement
name recognition, 163
National Association of Securities Dealers
    Automated Quotations (Nasdaq),
    553, 636, 643
National Labor Relations Act, 388
national unions, 388
natural resources, 6
natural unemployment, 69
needs, 327-328
negative reinforcement, 332
net asset value (NAV), 644
net income, 518
net profit margin, 527, 528
net sales, 518
New York Stock Exchange (NYSE), 553,
    643
news release, 485

newspaper advertising, 474, 477
no-load funds, 645
nominating committee, 258
nonprofit organization, 6
nonstore retailer, 457
nonverbal communication in different cultures, 114
Norris-LaGuardia Act, 388
North American Free Trade Agreement (NAFTA), 104, 110
notes payable, 521

## O

obsolete, 413
odd lots, 642
on margin, 642
one-level channel, 444
online reporting, 514
open-book management, 341
open-end mutual funds, 644
operating expenses, 518
operational planning, 222
operations management, 281
order costs, 291
organization, nonprofit, 6
organizational characteristics, 250-252
organizational height, 251
organizational structure, 188, 250, 272
    foreign operations, 262
    informal, 266
    multinational corporation, 270
    revising, 271
organizing, or managers, 225
outdoor advertising, 477
outlets, 455
outside board members, 255
outsourcing, 107, 289, 290
over-the-counter (OTC) stock market, 553, 643
owner's equity 519, 521, 522
owners, 10-13
    educational background, 12
    type of firm worked for, 11
    use of their time, 19
    worked for another firm, 11
    years of experience, 12
ownership
    hanging business type, 156
    comparing business types, 155
    of an existing business, 160
    of family business, 160
    revising business decisions, 160
    shared, 11

## P

Pacific Stock Exchange, 643
packaging, 421-422
par value, 546
participative leadership style, 226
participative management, 339
partners, 148
partnership, advantages/disadvantages, 148-149

patents, 417
penetration pricing, 425
pension funds, 549
performance, distorting, 46
performance evaluation, 375-380
perks, 369
perquisites, 369
personal selling, 478, 487
personnel evaluation, 233
personnel hiring, 233
personnel manager, 357
picketing, 391
pipeline transportation, 449
planning functions, 223, 224
planning, contingency, 223, 224
planning, operational, 222
planning, tactical, 221
policies, 222
political risk and regulation in foreign countries, 118
pollution, air, 48-49
    see also air pollution
pollution, land, 49
positive reinforcement, 332
predatory pricing, 426
preferred stock, 550
premium, 484
press conference, 485
prestige pricing, 426
price skimming, 407
price-earnings ratio, 635
price-elastic, 425
price-inelastic, 425
prices, competitor's, 425
pricing, 190, 424-431
    cost of production, 424
    decisions, 429-431
    strategies, 424
prime rate, 544
private accountants, 512
private liquidation, 562
private placement, 555
privately held corporations, 151
privatization, 116
procedures, 222
producer brands, 422
product, 404-408
    channels, 442-444
    characteristics, 190
    creating, 416-420
        design and test, 418
        distribute and promote, 419
        post-audit, 419
    demand and supply schedule, 76-77
    design, 420-421
    differentiated, 424
    differentiation, 420-424
    distribution, 445-448
    life cycle, 407, 408, 490
    market research, 414-416
    new, 414, 415
    packaging, 421-422
    price, 426-429
    variety, 456

product idea, 417
    feasibility, 418
product line, 287-288, 404
product mix, 404, 405
product plans, revising, 431
production, 188
    resources, 283
production capacity, 288
production control, 288
    inventory control, 291
    purchasing materials, 288-290
    quality control, 296
    routing, 292
    scheduling, 292-296
production costs and volume, 303
production decisions, 295
production efficiency, 301
production employees, 337
production expenses, 82
production management, 281, 282
production materials, 282
production practices, responsible, 34
production process, 282, 287, 306, 453
production schedule, 292, 293
production site, foreign, 286
production tasks, 295, 305
profit, 4
profit sharing, 369
profit, motive, 5
profitability, 304, 526, 530
program evaluation and review techniques (PERT), 294
projects
    feasible, 586
    new, 585
promoting products, 486
promotion, 190, 358, 459, 472, 490
promotion budget, 489
promotion decisions and business decisions, 491
    revising, 492
promotion mix, 472, 487
proprietorship, sole, 146-148, sole, see also sole proprietorship
prospectus, 554
protective covenants, 548
public accountants, 512
Public Company Accounting Reform and Investor Protection Act, 47
public offering, 554
public relations, 485-487
publicly held corporations, 151
pull strategy, 487, 488
push strategy, 488

## Q

quality control, 296
quality control circle, 298
quality of service, 455
quality standards, global, 299
quick ratio, 523, 528
quota, 104

# R

radio advertising, 474, 477
rail transportation, 449
ratio analysis, 522-532
rebate, 482, 484
recession, 67-68
recruiting, 360
reengineering, 305
references, 359
regulatory climate, among countries, 120
regulatory conditions, 181-182
reinforcement, theory, 332, 334
reminder advertising, 473
reorganization, 562
research and development, 416
resources, inexpensive, 99
responsibilities
    business, 35, 52
    business in international environment, 53
    code of, 35, 41
    environmental, 49-50
    ethical, 54
    firm's to creditors, 48
    firm's to employees, 38-43
    firm's to environment, 48-50
    firm's to the community, 50-51
    firm's violating, 48
    firm's, conflicts, 46
    firm's, ensuring, 44
    government's, ensuring, 47
    how firms ensure, code of responsibilities, 35
    how firms ensure, monitor complaints, 36
    how firms ensure, obtain customer feedback, 36
    how government ensures, regulate advertising, 36
    how government ensures, regulate competition, 37-38
    how government ensures, regulate product safety, 36
    pledge of ethics and, 35
    revising business, 52
    social, cost of, 53
    social, expenses, 54
    social, see social responsibility
    stockholders ensuring, 47
    to customers, 34-37
responsible production practices, 34
responsible sales practices, 34
restructuring, 304
résumés, 358
retailers, served by wholesalers, 459
retained earnings, 154
return and risk, business ownership affects, 157-160
return on assets (ROA), 527, 528
return on equity (ROE), 157, 158, 527, 528, 558, 559
return on investment, 151, 157

revenue, 4, 192
    interest rates' impact on firm's, 73
right-to-work, 389
risk, 158-159, 175, 547
risk and return, business ownership affects, 157-160
risk management, 195-200
risk of bonds, 547
Robinson-Patman Act, 38
round lots, 642
routing, 292

# S

safety
    employee, 38
    product, 36
safety skills, 372
salaries, 389-390, 365
sales, 197
    follow up, 481
    generating international, 100
    manager, 481
    measurement, 518
    practices, responsible, 34
    profitability outside U.S., 102
sales presentation, 479-48, 481
sales price, 430
sales promotion, 482-484, 487
sales promotion strategies, 484
sampling, 298, 483, 484
Sarbanes-Oxley Act (SOX), 47, 230, 259, 517
saving, 577
savings institutions, 549
scheduling, 292-295
S-corporation, 149
screening, 362
screening applicants, 358
search engines, 476
seasonal unemployment, 69
secondary market, 553
secured bonds, 547
securities, 554
Securities and Exchange Commission (SEC), 512, 517, 552, 554, 555
segments, 179
selective distribution, 447, 448
self-service retail store, 456
selling, personal, 478, 487
Service Corps of Retired Executives (SCORE), 155
service firms, 306, 421
sexual harassment, 40
shareholder, 514, 595
    see also stockholder
    equity, 519
shareholder activism, 47
shares, 595
Sherman Antitrust Act, 38
shopping products, 404
shortage, 78
short-term investment, 595

site
    characteristics, 287
    evaluation, 285
    foreign, 286
    location, 285
    selection, 284
small business, 285, 300, 478, 597
    concerns, 197
    websites, 176
Small Business Administration, 135, 155, 176, 191, 209, 315, 395, 501, 546, 613
social environment of business, 17
social responsibilities 33, 34
    cost of, 53-55
    expenses, 54
social values, 411
socialism, and capitalism, 115
Society for Human Resource Management, 359
software, 231
sole proprietor, 146
sole proprietorship, 146-148
    advantages/disadvantages, 146-147
    characteristics, 146
    earnings, 146
    tax effects on, 154
span of control, 251, 263
special events, 485
specialty advertising, 477
specialty products, 404
specialty retail store, 456
spot exchange rate, 124
staff positions, 252
stakeholders, 10-16
    interaction among, 16-17
    key, 16
stakeholders of business
    creditors, 13-14
    customers, 15
    employees, 14-15
    owners, 10-13
    suppliers, 15
Standard & Poor's (S&P), 636
standardization of products, 446
stock, 12, 514, 550, 551, 633-645
    52-week price range, 634
    dividend, 634
    foreign, 644
    listing, 552
    price, 633, 637, 638
    quotations, 633
    return on, 636
    return-risk tradeoff, 636
    symbol, 634
    transactions, 641
    valuing, 640
stock certificates, 152
stock exchanges, 643-644
stock market efficiency, 638
stock mutual funds, 551
stock options, 365, 366
stockbroker, 641

stockholder, 12, 43, 151
    responsibilities, 43-47
    versus community, 51
stockouts, 598
store brands, 422
strategic alliances, 108
strategic plan, 220, 249, 325
    achieving, 223
stretch targets, 301
strike, 392
    management response, 392
structural unemployment, 69
supervisors, evaluations of, 380
supervisory management, 218, 219
suppliers, 10, 15, 198, 289, 290
supplies, payments for, 290
supply, 77-78, 574
    effect on general price level, 81
supply and demand, determining equi-
    librium price, 77
supply chain, 305
supply schedule, 76, 79-81, 575-576
surplus, 77
SWOT analysis, 185, 186

**T**

tactical planning, 221
Taft-Hartley Act, 389
takeover attempts, 594
target market, 189, 406, 412, 478-479,
    481, 487-489
    economic factors, 411
    geography, 410
    size, 409
    social values, 411
target marketing, 194
target markets, foreign countries, 412
tariff, 104
tax benefits, of merger, 591
tax brackets, international, 112
tax effects, on corporations and sole pro-
    prietorships, 154
tax rates, revision of personal
    income, 84
taxes
    revision of corporate, 84
    revision of excise, 85

teamwork, 340
technical skills, 370
technological obsolescence, 413
technology, 7, 99, 186, 200, 231, 252,
    293, 296, 301, 338, 412
technology-based product pricing, 429
telemarketing, 477
television advertising, 474, 477
tender offer, 593
textbook, preview, 23
Theory X and Theory Y (McGregor's),
    330, 331
Theory Z, 330-331, 334
thrift institutions, 549
time management, 237-239
times interest earned ratio, 526, 528
top management, 218, 219
total assets management, 522
total quality management (TQM), 296,
    297
trade agreements, meetings to resolve,
    112
trade barriers, 104
    disagreements about, 111
    reducing, 110
    to international business, 111
    to protect local firms, 109
    to punish countries, 110
trade deficit, 105
trade, international, 109
trademark, 422
transfer of ownership, 152
Transparency International, 120
transportation, 284, 449-450
transportation advertising, 477
transporting products, 446
treasury bills, 595
truck transportation, 449
turnover, 524-525
two-level channel, 444, 445
tying agreement, 38

**U**

U.S. Foreign Corrupt Practices Act, 41
underwriting syndicate, 554
underwritten, 554

unemployment
    cyclical, 69
    frictional, 69
    natural, 69
    seasonal, 69
    structural, 69
unions, *see* labor unions
unsecured bonds, 547
upward appraisals, 380

**V**

variable costs, 302, 426
variety retail store, 456
vending machines, 457
venture capital firm, 551
vertical channel integration, 460
vertical merger, 589
volume discounts, 289
volume of shares, 635

**W**

wages, 365
Wagner Act, 388
warehousing, 458, 459
water transportation, 449
web-based business, expenses, 185
website retailing, 457
white knight, 595
wholesalers, 457-460
women, 363, 364
    and minorities in various occupa-
    tions, 39
work schedule, flexible, 338
work station, 283
working capital management, 595
work-in-process inventories, 291
workplace, 284
World Trade Organization, (WTO), 110

**Y**

yellow-dog contract, 388